ASIAN WOMEN AS TRANSNATIONAL DOMESTIC WORKERS

edited by
Shirlena Huang
Brenda S. A. Yeoh
Noor Abdul Rahman

Marshall Cavendish
Academic

© 2005 Marshall Cavendish International (Singapore) Private Limited

Published 2005 by Marshall Cavendish Academic
An imprint of Marshall Cavendish International (Singapore) Private Limited
A member of Times Publishing Limited

Times Centre, 1 New Industrial Road,
Singapore 536196
Tel: (65) 6213 9300
Fax: (65) 6284 9772
E-mail: mca@sg.marshallcavendish.com
Website: http://www.marshallcavendish.com/academic

ISBN-13: 987-981-210-386-4
ISBN-10: 981-210-386-4

Printed by Times Graphics Pte Ltd, Singapore
on non-acidic paper

London • New York • Beijing • Bangkok • Kuala Lumpur • Singapore

National Library Board Singapore Cataloguing-in-Publication Data

Asian women as transnational domestic workers/edited by Shirlena Huang, Brenda S. A. Yeoh, Noor Abdul Rahman.–Singapore: Marshall Cavendish Academic, c2005.
    p. cm.
    Includes bibliographical references and index.
    ISBN: 978-981-210-386-4
    ISBN: 981-210-386-4

1.   Women domestics. 2. Alien labour, Asian. 3. Asians – Employment – Foreign countries. 4. Women – Employment – Foreign countries.
I. Huang, Shirlena. II. Yeoh, Brenda S. A. III. Noorashikin Abdul Rahman.

HD6072
331.48164046—dc21   SLS2005036625

Contents

List of Tables

List of Figures

List of Appendices

Preface

Once an occupation traditionally associated with poor rural women who migrated to cities in search of work, paid domestic work is now a transnational occupational niche for millions of women from Asia's less well-off countries—including the Philippines, Indonesia, Burma, Sri Lanka and India—who embark on sojourns to the richer countries of the world—such as Singapore, Malaysia, Hong Kong, Taiwan, Canada, the Middle East and parts of Europe—in search of a more lucrative livelihood and promising futures for their families and themselves. Implicated in the rising tide of flows of Asian transnational domestic workers are international networks of gatekeepers that mediate the procedures involved in securing employment contracts and arranging migration passages for transnational domestic workers. These private and public institutions keep the process highly commoditised and, arguably, exploitative.

Transnational domestic workers are important contributors not only to the economies of the countries that receive them, but also to the volume of global migrant remittances sent home, estimated by the World Bank to exceed in volume, the official development assistance meted out by donor nations. Despite—or is it because of—their crucial role in the global economy, the growing numbers of transnational domestic workers, mostly female, continue to migrate and work in what is generally regarded as an unskilled or low-skilled job under unfavourable conditions in their host societies and remain highly vulnerable to exploitation. The attention of international organisations (such as the United Nations, the International Labour Organisation, the International Organization for Migration), various labour-sending and receiving governments, non-governmental organisations (NGOs), civil society and academics, does not appear to have changed the basic perception and reality of transnational domestic labour as dirty, demeaning and dangerous.

It is our hope that this book will enhance not only academic research on transnational domestic workers, but also the ability of governments, NGOs and civil society groups—especially in sending and receiving countries—to derive apposite policies for Asian transnational domestic workers, and to make appropriate recommendations to address the problems directly confronted by these migrant workers. The book arose out of a workshop that was specifically designed to bring together scholars who have long engaged with research on transnational domestic workers in their respective countries of focus. More fundamentally, the impetus for the workshop arose out of a desire to see the production of an academic volume that would allow for a broadly comparative perspective among sending and receiving countries of transnational domestic workers. We also wanted to attempt to understand why transnational domestic workers are largely absent in societies such as Australia, Japan and to a lesser extent, South Korea. By adopting a relatively consistent framework of analysis for all the papers, the collection in this volume provides a reasonably coherent platform to compare the contexts within which Asian transnational domestic workers live and work across a range of countries.

As suggested by the various chapter titles in this volume, many antithetical pairs of adjectives and qualifiers can be, and have been, used to describe the millions of transnational domestic workers traversing the world today—documented and undocumented workers; surrogate family or disposable labour; success stories versus tragic tales; women who are neither at work nor at home; domestic workers gone global. To some extent, these opposites reflect the extreme ends of the spectrum of sites and situations in which the women may find themselves. Thus, beyond offering a platform for comparative discussion, we hope that this book also manages to highlight the wide range of complex and often contradictory circumstances and conditions that characterise these women's lives.

Shirlena Huang
Brenda S. A. Yeoh
Noor Abdul Rahman
April 2005

Acknowledgements

The papers included in this volume were first presented and discussed at the International Workshop on Contemporary Perspectives on Asian Transnational Domestic Workers held in Singapore on 23–25 February 2004. We would like to thank the Asian MetaCentre for Population and Sustainable Development Analysis, headquartered at the Asia Research Institute of the National University of Singapore, for providing administrative support in organising the workshop. Particular thanks are due to Leong Wai Kit, Verene Koh and Theodora Lam of the Asian MetaCentre.

We are also grateful to the Wellcome Trust for their financial support, as well as the Commission on Gender and Geography of the International Geographical Union for working with us on the workshop. We would also like to thank Chng Nai Rui and Theodora Lam for their assistance in copy editing this volume.

Shirlena Huang and Brenda Yeoh would like to acknowledge the National University of Singapore for funding their first research project on transnational domestic workers some ten years ago, and which kick-started their ongoing research on the subject. Noor Abdul Rahman would like to extend her appreciation to the Institute of Southeast Asian Studies, Singapore for continuing to support her research in this area that she started six years ago as a doctoral candidate at Curtin University of Technology, Australia.

We also thank all the authors of the various chapters who turned each of their papers around quickly during the various rounds of reviews. Their cooperation ensured that this book could move from workshop to the printing press in just over a year.

Finally, as women who have, or have had, transnational domestic workers to shore up our homefronts, thus enabling us to pursue our own careers as academics, we would like to acknowledge the supportive role that these women have played in our own lives. We are grateful for the time they have spent with our families.

Contributors

Noor Abdul Rahman is a Research Fellow at the Institute of Southeast Asian Studies, Singapore. A recent graduate of Curtin University of Technology, Western Australia, she wrote her doctoral thesis on power and Indonesian foreign domestic workers in Singapore. Her research focuses on unskilled labour migration, development and social networks. She has been actively involved in advocacy work for foreign domestic workers in Singapore and as a volunteer English teacher to Indonesian domestic workers there.

Rita Afsar has been working in the areas of migration, urbanisation, urban poverty and issues related to labour market and gender roles for about two decades. Both her Ph.D. and Master's dissertations were based on rural-urban migration. She was honoured by Pi Gamma Mu honour society for her outstanding academic performance. She is an elected member of the International Union of Scientific Studies on Population (IUSSP). She has collaborative research experience with both developing and developed countries and publications in reputed journals and books. She is a Senior Research Fellow and Head of the Human Resources Division of the Bangladesh Institute of Development Studies (BIDS), Dhaka and is currently affiliated with the Institute of Regional Development (IRD) of the University of Western Australia.

Maruja M. B. Asis is Director of Research and Publications of the Scalabrini Migration Centre (SMC), based in Manila, Philippines. She is a sociologist who has long been involved in the study of migration in Asia. Her areas of interest are migration and social change, particularly the nexus of migration, gender and family relations, migration policies, and unauthorised migration. She recently directed a nationwide study on the impact of international labour migration on children and families left behind in the Philippines. She is Associate Editor of the *Asian and Pacific Migration Journal*, a refereed quarterly journal, and Co-editor of the *Asian Migration News*, a bi-weekly online news service. In line with the programs of SMC in the Asia-Pacific, she is also involved in working with working with NGOs and international organisations in promoting the rights of migrants.

Janeen Baxter is currently Professor and Head of the Sociology Program, School of Social Science, The University of Queensland. She has published extensively in a number of areas, including gender inequality in the household, the domestic division of labour, women's position in the labour market, the intersection of class and gender and comparative analyses of advanced societies. She is currently working on a project titled Negotiating the Lifecourse, a longitudinal study of the ways in which men and women negotiate paid and unpaid work over the lifecourse. She has also received funding, with colleagues at the University of Queensland and the University of

Tasmania, for a four-year study examining the impact of neoliberalism on inequality in Australian society.

Christine B. N. Chin is Associate Professor of International Relations at the School of International Service, American University, Washington DC. Her research and teaching interests are international communication, political economy of Southeast Asia, international migration and gender studies. She is the author of *In Service and Servitude: Foreign Female Domestic Workers and the Malaysian 'Modernity' Project* (Columbia University Press, 1998), and has published articles in various journals such as *International Migration Review, New Political Economy* and *Third World Quarterly*.

Michele Ruth Gamburd is Associate Professor of Anthropology at Portland State University. She received her Ph.D. in Anthropology from the University of Michigan in 1995. She has performed qualitative ethnographic fieldwork in a rural village on Sri Lanka's southwest coast since 1991. Her research focuses on the migration of labour from Sri Lanka to the Middle East, particularly women who go to work as housemaids in Saudi Arabia, Kuwait and the United Arab Emirates. She has written about this topic in numerous articles and in her book, *The Kitchen Spoon's Handle: Transnationalism and Sri Lanka's Migrant Housemaids* (Cornell University Press, 2000). Her interests include the study of violence, globalisation, social change, gender and ethnicity.

Shirlena Huang is Associate Professor and Head at the Department of Geography, National University of Singapore. One key area of her research is on gender issues in skilled and unskilled labour migration flows within the Asia-Pacific region; in particular, she has published widely on transnational domestic workers. Another strand of her research focuses on urbanisation and heritage conservation, and its impact on national identity and sense of place and belonging. She is co-editor (with Brenda S. A. Yeoh and Peggy Teo) of *Gender Politics in the Asia Pacific Region* (Routledge, 2002).

Graeme Hugo is Federation Fellow, Professor of the Department of Geographical and Environmental Studies and Director of the National Centre for Social Applications of Geographical Information Systems at the University of Adelaide. He is the author of over two hundred books, articles in scholarly journals and chapters in books, as well as a large number of conference papers and reports. His books include *Australia's Changing Population* (Oxford University Press), *The Demographic Dimension in Indonesian Development* (with T. H. Hull, V. J. Hull and G. W. Jones, Oxford University Press), *International Migration Statistics: Guidelines for Improving Data Collection Systems* (with A. S. Oberai, H. Zlotnik and R. Bilsborrow, International Labour Office), *Worlds in Motion: Understanding International Migration at Century's End* (with D. S. Massey, J. Arango, A Kouaouci, A. Pellegrino and J. E. Taylor, Oxford University Press), several of the 1986, 1991 and 1996 census based volumes of *Atlas of the Australian People Series* (AGPS) and *Australian Immigration: A Survey of the Issues* (with Mark Wooden,

Robert Holton and Judith Sloan, AGPS). In 2002 he was awarded an ARC Federation Fellowship over five years.

Pei-Chia Lan is an Assistant Professor of Sociology at National Taiwan University. She received her Ph.D. from Northwestern University and was a postdoctoral fellow at the University of California, Berkeley. She is completing a manuscript about the employment relations and identity politics of Filipina and Indonesian migrant domestic workers in Taiwan.

Hye-Kyung Lee is Professor at the Department of Sociology, Pai Chai University, South Korea. Since she finished her Ph.D. dissertation, Socioeconomic Attainment of Recent Korean and Filipino Immigrant Men and Women in the Los Angeles Metropolitan Area, 1980 at University of California, Los Angeles (UCLA) in 1987, she has published many papers on migration and transnational communities, gender and work. She was a coordinator of the Korea Migration Research Network (KMRN) from 2000 to 2002. There she co-authored two books, *Migrant Workers in Korea* (Center for Future Human Resource Studies, 1998) and *Works and Lives of Migrant Workers* (Center for Future Human Resource Studies, 2003), as well as a published article "A Comparative Study on the Labor Management Style in Domestic and Overseas Korean Companies" (*Korean Journal of Sociology*, 36(3):47–77). She is currently an editorial member of the *Korean Journal of Population Studies* and *Studies of Koreans Abroad*. She has also served as an advisory committee member for the Korean National Statistical Office, for the Korean Immigration Bureau and for Daejon City Council.

Deirdre McKay is a Research Fellow in the Department of Human Geography, Research School of Pacific and Asian Studies, The Australian National University. She completed her doctorate in Geography at the University of British Columbia in 1999. From 1999 to 2001, she carried out postdoctoral research, funded by the Social Sciences and Humanities Research Council, Canada, on Filipinas in Canada, in cooperation with the Philippine Women Centre, Vancouver. At ANU, her current work is on alternative economic development, transnational households and remittance landscapes in the Philippines.

Tomoko Nakamatsu is a lecturer in the Asian Studies Discipline of the University of Western Australia. She holds a Ph.D. in Asian Studies from Murdoch University, Perth. Her main research interests focus on social changes in gender and ethnic relations in contemporary Japan. Her latest publications include "International Marriage through Introduction Agencies: Social and Legal Realities of 'Asian' Wives of Japanese Men", in N. Piper and M. Roces (eds.), 2003, *Wife or Worker? Asian Women and Migration*, Boulder: Rowman and Littlefield.

Parvati Raghuram is Lecturer in Geography at the Open University. She co-authored *Gender and International Migration in Europe* (Routledge, 2000), *The Practice of Cultural Studies* (Sage, 2004) and co-edited *South Asian Women in the Diaspora* (Berg, 2003). She has published a number of articles on the experiences of migrants and minorities in the United Kingdom and on domestic work in India.

Amy Sim is a Ph.D. student in Anthropology in the Department of Sociology, University of Hong Kong. Her current research examines the impact of migration on issues of identity and cultural change among Indonesian domestic workers in Hong Kong. Her focus is on the "sensuous meaningfulness" of the lived experiences of migrants, not merely as workers or migrants but as persons in the construction of selfhood, making strategic decisions that alter life trajectories, relations with families and home communities. This research on processual change not only involves cross-cutting issues of class, ethnic and gender relations, but is necessarily multi-sited in Hong Kong and various sites in Java, Indonesia. Prior to her postgraduate studies, Amy worked in a regional NGO in Asia for five years, focusing on issues of sustainable development.

Mika Toyota is a Research Fellow at the Asia Research Institute, National University of Singapore. She is a social anthropologist, who works on transnational networks, gender and migration, tourism development, the geopolitics of borderlands, and the changing family in Asia. She obtained her PhD in Southeast Asian Studies at the University of Hull, UK in 1999 following long-term field research (1994–1997) with transnational ethnic minorities in the borderlands of Thailand, Burma and China. Subsequently she lectured at the University of Hull for three years before taking up a Postdoctoral fellowship at the Asian MetaCentre for Population and Sustainable Development Analysis, National University of Singapore (2002–2004). She has published 17 academic articles in English and Japanese, including "Contested Chinese identities among ethnic minorities in the China, Burma and Thai Borderlands" in *Ethnic and Racial Studies*, March 2003. She is currently engaged in various projects which examine the human security situation of border minorities, informal networks among female migrants in the Thai-Burma borderlands, delayed marriage in Thailand, and migration of Japanese retirees to Southeast Asia.

Vivienne Wee is Associate Professor in the Department of Applied Social Studies and Associate Director of the Southeast Asia Research Centre, City University of Hong Kong. Trained as an anthropologist, she has wide-ranging research interests in religion and ideology, nation-state evolution, ethnicity and ethno-nationalism, gender and development, as well as labour migration. She has done field research in almost every country in Southeast Asia. Her special expertise is in the remaking of the Malay world in Riau, Indonesia. She has done extensive field research in Southeast Asia and has worked on development issues with the United Nations, national governments, local communities and NGOs. She has published extensively in international journals and books. She is currently editing a volume titled *Political Fragmentation in Southeast Asia: Alternative Nations in the Making* (Routledge-City University of Hong Kong Southeast Asia Series).

Brenda S. A. Yeoh is Professor at the Department of Geography, National University of Singapore and Principal Investigator of the Asian Metacentre at the university's Asia Research Institute. Her research foci include the politics of space in colonial and post-colonial cities; and gender, migration and transnational communities. She has published over 60 scholarly journal papers and several books including *Contesting Space: Power Relations and the Urban Built Environment in Colonial Singapore* (Oxford University Press, 1996; reissued Singapore University Press, 2003), *Singapore: A Developmental City State* (John Wiley, 1997, with Martin Perry and Lily Kong), *Gender and Migration* (Edward Elgar, 2000, with Katie Willis), and *Gender Politics in the Asia-Pacific Region* (Routledge, 2002, with Peggy Teo and Shirlena Huang), *The Politics of Landscape in Singapore: Construction of "Nation"* (Syracuse University Press, 2003, with Lily Kong) and *State/Nation/Transnation: Perspectives on Transnationalism in the Asia-Pacific* (Routledge, 2004, with Katie Willis).

Asian Women as Transnational Domestic Workers

BRENDA S. A. YEOH, SHIRLENA HUANG AND
NOOR ABDUL RAHMAN

THE TRANSNATIONALISATION OF DOMESTIC WORK

While domestic work—the "labour activities that sustain the daily maintenance of a household"—is accomplished by "a variety of agents, with multiple formats, and in different settings" (Lan, 2003a:188) throughout periods and across places, it has in contemporary times come to be primarily, and sometimes solely, associated with "women's work". In the form of unpaid labour performed by female family members, domestic work is often considered to be a labour of love whose value is related to the ideological construction of women as "carers" and "nurturers" naturally suited to performing "emotional labour" (Palmer, 1989; Yeoh & Huang, 1999a; Parreñas, 2001). When performed by non-family workers (either for wages or returns in kind), domestic work continues to be delineated by gendered contours as women's work—although it also assumes other gridlines based on hierarchies of class, age, race, language, nationality, and immigration/citizenship status, all of which are rooted in asymmetrical webs of power. Indeed, as Lan (2003a:189) observes, unpaid household labour and waged domestic work should be treated as "structural continuities that characterize the feminization of domestic labour across the public and private spheres".

Gender norms governing the household division of labour rest in part on women's lack of collective economic and political power to persuade men and society in general to help bear the costs of caring for the home and the family (McKay, this volume). The durability of these norms across space and time, however, is also a product of the fact that they have been finely and firmly stitched into the ideological fabric of everyday life, and hence accepted as a taken-for-granted reality. Such ideology has been at work over long periods of time in a wide range of different societies. In Japan, for example, the ideal of *ryōsai kenbo* (a good wife and wise mother) advanced by the modern Japanese state from the Meiji period, promoted women's domestic responsibility and the family as the site of consumption and reproduction while advocating the gendered division of labour as a form of gender equality (Nakamatsu, this volume). In Canada, socially constructed notions of family altruism—where "an altruistic mother parents the ideal family"—inform the appropriate behaviour of men and women (McKay, this volume). Similarly in Australia, the "dominant model of a male breadwinner state" reinforced through various employment and welfare policies over the course of the 20th century "encouraged, if not forced, wives to remain at home as full-time mothers

1

and housewives" defining housework as "an integral component of women's proper role as mothers and wives" (Baxter, this volume). Indeed, the ideology of domesticity and the association of women with housework, childbearing and childrearing in the private sphere appears to be "endemic cross-culturally" and "remarkably resistant to macro-level economic circumstance" (Sanchez, 1993:454).

In situations where drafting other (usually non-familial, minority or migrant) women into the home to perform domestic work is sanctioned, socially and economically privileged women have the option of transferring selected reproductive tasks—usually the more physically demanding and most devalued labour—to other subordinate women, without diminishing (and often elevating) their status as mistresses, mothers or managers in the private domain (Glenn, 1992; Romero, 1992). In the process whereby women "use their class privilege to buy themselves out of their gender subordination" (Parreñas, 2000:562), reproductive labour is commodified, devalued and normalised as unskilled and lowly paid (but still women's) work. As Katz Rothman (quoted in Parreñas, 2000:562) puts it: "When performed by mothers, we call this mothering … when performed by hired hands, we call it unskilled". Indeed, it remains a highly stigmatised local occupation in many societies (such as Sri Lanka as noted by Gamburd, this volume) and there is often a failure on the part of governments to recognise domestic work as "work" even among locals (as in India, as highlighted by Raghuram, this volume).

The shift of reproductive work from the household to the market has intensified in recent decades as a result of global economic restructuring. On the one hand, in several countries in East and Southeast Asia such as Taiwan, Singapore, Malaysia and Thailand, state-led industrialisation from the 1970s drew more and more local women into the waged economy, resulting in a reproductive crisis on the domestic front in globalising cities and nation-states. From the mid-1980s, state adoption of neoliberal restructuring policies of economic privatisation, liberalisation and deregulation has further exacerbated the gap between the demand and supply of affordable institutional child and elderly care, worsening the "care deficit" (Hochschild, 1995) in countries where an extensive welfare system is not in place and where the provision of care is regarded as a family affair. All this has set in train strong market forces demanding transnational, flexibilised workers to fill the cracks and crevices in the domestic sphere, an arena often neglected by the state and treated as dispensable in terms of the globalising logic. The figure of the transnational domestic worker has also entered into the realm of social identity construction in many of these rapidly developing countries. Not only have state visions to build a modern knowledge-based society necessitated the continued participation of middle-class women in the economy and hence the need for reproductive labour substitutes in dual-career households, the construction of middle-class identity and status is "implicit in employers' ability to hire transnational domestic workers who facilitate their ability to meet the challenges of maintaining families and pursuing careers at the same time" (Chin, this volume). The need for transnational domestic workers seems to have also filtered down to the lower socio-economic classes: in Thailand, for example, Toyota (this volume) argues that with the economic crisis of the late 1990s, housemaids are no longer "luxury goods" in demand among Thai middle-class households but essential to less well-off families where the wife can no longer afford to remain a housewife but feels compelled to join the work force. At the same time, globalisation has aggravated economic disparities between countries experiencing rapid industrialisation and those with slower development, resulting not only in strong nodes of demand for domestic workers on the one hand, but also a ready supply of unemployed, unabsorbed female workers prepared to "defy [social] norms and geographic barriers" (Afsar, this volume) to find employment, on the other.

The shift of the domestic burden to low-status migrant "others" differentiated from "self" by dint of a range of cross-cutting social constructs from class to race/nationality has had the effect of further devaluing domestic work. Such devaluation often progresses in tandem with perceived social distance. In Canada, where immigrants have taken on domestic work since the mid-19th century, there has been a decline in rights accorded to migrant domestic workers with the shift away from European to Caribbean and then Asian sources of labour. Up to the 1950s, European women offered "assisted passage" would arrive in Canada as regular immigrants to join Canadian households as domestics. When the supply of European immigrant women dried up in the postwar era, the Caribbean Domestic Scheme was created in 1955 to import foreign domestics from Jamaica and Barbados and, for the first time, women were disqualified from migration under the scheme if they were married, living common-law, or supporting dependent children. The decline in rights proceeded even further in the 1980s as the source area shifted to Southeast Asia. The Foreign Domestic Movement Program initiated in 1981—later reworked as the Live-In Caregiver Program in 1992—admitted Caribbean and increasingly Asian women to only pre-immigrant status with even fewer rights (McKay, this volume).

In different parts of Asia, while domestic servants of the past—for example, the *amah* (single celibate Chinese female servants) and *mui tsai* (young girls "given" or "sold" into domestic service) in Singapore and Malaysia—were often members of the employers' larger ethnic communities, transnational domestic workers today are perceived as "aliens" or "foreigners" who transgress the integrity of the nation (Abdul Rahman et al., this volume; Chin, this volume). The presence of these "dangerous others"—foreign women who seduce male employers and teach undesirable social and moral values to employers' children—are seen to pollute the sanctity of the family, regarded as the very heart of the nation in many Asian societies. While employer-worker relationships in the past were informed by shared cultural norms and values (sometimes approximating patron-client or pseudo-kin relationships instead), such considerations are manifestly absent in the contemporary institution of live-in paid domestic work performed by transnational women. Today, the self/other divide is hence wider than before, and its location in a context of highly asymmetrical power relations in the employer's household as well as in the host nation has engendered

3

openly exploitative relationships between employer and worker unmitigated by culturally-based values and expectations (Chin, this volume).

Employer-worker relations undergirding the contemporary institution of transnational domestic work, however, may not be a completely radical break from past traditions of servanthood in some situations. In Thailand, while the domestic worker profile has shifted away from Thai women to migrant workers from minority groups across the border in Burma, Laos and Cambodia, the employer-worker relationship continues to hark back to patron-client patterns predicated on "a kind of reciprocity based on an exchange whereby the employer/master provides 'protection' in the form of food, clothes and board while the maid/servant provides service in return" (Toyota, this volume). In this context, Toyota (this volume) also notes that not all sexual relationships between employer and maid can be unambiguously defined as "abuse", for the line between becoming a housemaid or a wife is a blurred one, reflected in the Thai term *mae-baan* which can refer either to "housemaid" or "housewife". In other cases, the social distance between employer-self and worker-other is negotiated using a fine mesh to sort out difference from sameness. For example, in South Korea, live-in domestic work was for many centuries performed by male and female Korean servants called *nobi*. Today, however, it is dominated by middle-aged Korean-Chinese women who, despite having the advantage of sharing the same ethnicity and language as the locals, face discrimination as "unwelcome visitors" from a "poor" country. At the same time, they are also preferred to fill the domestic servant's role precisely because they are "foreigners" and hence not part of Korean society, therefore absolving Korean employers from feeling ill at ease in instructing an older person, an act that goes against the grain of Korean cultural norms of respecting the elders (Lee, this volume). The seeming contradictory dynamic of devaluing domestic work shifted onto the shoulders of transnational migrant workers and at the same preferring the same workers as more natural or suitable embodiments of domestic servanthood is also observed elsewhere. In Taiwan, employers' everyday practices of devaluation and discrimination in negotiating the boundary between "us" and "them" goes hand in hand with preferring Filipino, Indonesian and Vietnamese domestic workers as more "obedient" and "deferential", compared to the more rights-conscious *obasans* (local domestic workers) (Lan, this volume). Transnational domestic workers are, in Lan's (2003b:525) words, "the perfect example of the intimate Other—they are recruited by host countries as desired servants and yet rejected citizens".

Indeed, by embodying devalued domestic work and in performing such work away from the "natural" locus of the home (for women), those who become transnational domestic workers find that both their departure from home countries and insertion into host societies are comprehended in stereotypical terms. In making sense of their act of emigration, official state discourses in sending countries have tended to anoint migrant workers as modern-day heroines whose toil and remittances sustain and transform the national economy. In the Philippines, for example, all the presidents from Marcos to Macapagal-Arroyo have acknowledged the contributions of Filipino women working overseas and regarded them as the country's "new heroes" (Asis, this volume), while in countries such as Indonesia (see Robinson, 2000:275) and Sri Lanka (Gamburd, this volume), the state has couched its view of migrant domestic workers as an export commodity principally in terms of their rights to work. In contrast, popular discourses and debates in the media and non-governmental organisation (NGO) literature tend to portray these women as hapless victims of international politics and business, the "new 'slaves' of the global capitalist system" (Gibson et al., 2001:370–1), while at the same time decrying the care crisis created by the outflow of mothers, daughters and sisters. Gamburd (this volume), however, argues that "migrant mothers have broadened the spectrum of acceptable ways for women to love their children and care for their families" by using their new roles as breadwinners to counter charges of neglecting their nurturing role.

On insertion into host society, transnational domestic workers encounter a different range of intervening stereotypes constructed primary on the basis of nationality (conflated with race/ethnicity). Nationality- and/or race-based profiling which draws on visible physical difference is often utilised as a sorting mechanism in the complex process of fine-grained othering. For example, in order to protect its capital-rich territorial base by excluding mainland China's workers from migrating to and settling in Hong Kong, the Special Administrative Region "admits supposedly transient workers of different nationalities and physical appearances from South and Southeast Asia" (Wee & Sim, this volume).

To a large extent, similar stereotypical images of the Filipina vis-à-vis Indonesian domestic worker prevail in countries or cities such as Taiwan (Lan, this volume), Hong Kong (Wee & Sim, this volume), Singapore (Abdul Rahman et al., this volume) and Malaysia (Chin, this volume) where both nationalities are present in significant numbers. Filipinas are invariably characterised as streetwise, outgoing, well-educated and westernised but more aware of their rights and difficult to manage while, as a foil, Indonesians are described as traditional, obedient and loyal but slower and simple-minded. These stereotypes serve to segment the labour market according to nationality-race dimensions and as "product differentiation" for placement agencies anxious to promote the "domestic worth" of women of different nationalities in a lucrative but volatile industry (Abdul Rahman et al., this volume). They also constantly underlie the construction of the "self-other" boundary, between employers and transnational domestic workers in the everyday spaces of the home, as well as more generally between migrant contract workers and host society in public space. Lan (this volume), for example, contrasts the dynamic in Taiwanese *nouveau-riche* employers' transnational encounters with Filipina domestic workers vis-à-vis their Indonesian counterparts. While employing a well-educated English-speaking Filipina confers social status, it can also weaken employer authority as the Filipina domestic worker is able to deploy the English language as a means of symbolic resistance, "such as negotiating job terms to reduce their workload, or deliberately using advanced vocabulary and correcting the grammar or pronunciation of their employers" (Lan, this volume). In contrast, Taiwanese employers maintain the upper hand with Indonesian and Vietnamese domestic workers who do not speak English and have to learn Mandarin or Hokkien instead to win job orders in Taiwan. Racialised stereotypes are also drawn upon by the migrant workers themselves in advancing the superiority of their own group (for example, Filipinas may describe their Indonesian competitors as "stupid" and "uneducated" while Indonesians may counter these assertions by arguing that Filipinas are "arrogant" and that Indonesians "may be stupid but are good and courteous"), exacerbating the "us-them" divide and hindering the formation of cross-nationality alliances among transnational domestic workers in Taiwan (Lan, this volume). That these stereotypes are not fixed but contingent on the form of self-other dynamics at work is clearly indicated if attention is turned to other transnational contexts in which migrant domestic workers are inserted: in Canada, for example, the typical stereotypes of Filipina caregivers that emerge are of women who are "shy and submissive, with strong accents, but hardworking and easily intimidated by the children and parents", in counterpoint to "difficult" European nannies who expect "equal" relationships with their employers and "aggressive" West Indians who tend to insist on observance of the work contract (McKay, this volume).

STATE DISCOURSES AND POLICIES

As transnationalism draws attention to what it negates—that is, the continued significance of the national—it continues to remind us that we have far from reached a postnationalist state of affairs (Smith, 2001). Instead, the quickening of transnational flows in a globalising world has had the effect of re-igniting nationalisms in both sending and receiving states. Feminists have been particularly interested in how patriarchal norms of national belonging operate within transnational contexts, and the way sending states are increasingly institutionalising transnationalism through a range of state policies to manage and control transnational outflows and stake claims on transnational subjects. At the same time, precisely because the "transmigrant other" is a gendered subject and precisely because the state often articulates nationalism using "genderic" modes, receiving states have found it necessary to carefully manage the potentially disruptive presence of female "transmigrant others" through policies of inclusion and exclusion.

Sending Countries

Among the various "source" countries of female domestic workers in Asia, the state's involvement in transnational labour migration is present in a variety of ways. At one end of the spectrum, the Philippine state has been integrally involved since the 1970s with the formulation of an overseas employment programme crafted to take advantage of the employment opportunities created by the oil boom in the Middle East. Since then, the Philippines "has steered itself to become a major source country of workers, supplying workers of varying skill levels to over 100 countries" (Asis, this volume). Making up ten per cent of the country's 76 million-strong population, the 7.4 million Filipinos abroad at the turn of the millennium not only represent a far-flung social network facilitating flows of information and material goods but is also, through remittances, a significant and reliable source of revenue accounting for 8.9 per cent of the country's Gross Domestic Product, outweighing in magnitude the annual flow of foreign direct investment into the economy. State promotion of the deployment of Filipinos as overseas contract workers (OCWs) is wedded to a discourse of the OCW as "national hero", an appellation which arises "from a specifically economic calculus and an unquestioned belief in the national developmental potential of [remittances as an] income stream" (Gibson et al., 2001:369). It is accompanied by the development and elaboration of an institutional and legal framework governing all phases of migration, from pre-deployment to on-site services, to the return and reintegration of migrant workers. At the same time, and particularly with the increasing feminisation of labour migration flows, a discourse of "protection" also came into play alongside that of "promotion", made manifest from time to time in the form of bans or restrictions (e.g., minimum age requirements) in response to occasional heightened concerns over the vulnerability of (usually female) migrants to abuse, or the well-being of left-behind families (especially children). Recently, however, in the light of the Philippine state's globalising aspirations, there has been a shift to "a more aggressive marketing of the Filipino as a global worker" (in the words of Labour Secretary Sto. Tomas, cited in Asis, this volume) underscored by the target to send out a million overseas contract workers, a "development which might weaken the state's resolve to pay due attention to the protection of migrants' rights in the race to meet the target" (Asis, this volume).

While the discourses and policies promoting labour migration may be most explicitly articulated and institutionalised in the case of the Philippines, other Asian countries have also taken steps, if not to overtly encourage, then at least to facilitate the outflow of labour migrants. For example, as Hugo (this volume) notes, the Indonesian state—spurred by the onset of the economic crisis 1997 to aggressively explore new markets for migrant workers—moved "from being somewhat indifferent to international labour migration to recognising that it was a small but a significant contributor to national foreign exchange earnings" in the 1990s. In particular, the Indonesian state has employed a specific strategy of providing unskilled workers (including domestic workers) at relatively low cost to give it comparative advantage over the Philippines, an undertaking which has been aided by a "migration industry" that has been given liberty to proliferate and which has "worked assiduously to increase both the supply of women in Indonesia and in expanding the market of their labour overseas" (Hugo, this volume). Against a backdrop of a relatively liberal migration regime since independence—where currently three-quarters of the migrants are female—the Sri Lanka government has "taken productive steps" to set up structures such as the Sri Lanka Bureau of Foreign Employment (SLFBE) to facilitate the outflow of labour migrants through legal channels in order to minimise "corruption and exploitation in the recruiting process" (Gamburd, this volume). In India, the state perceives labour migration as a means of addressing the problem of chronic underemployment in the country while adopting a laissez faire approach to the question of protection. As Raghuram (this volume) notes, while the Emigration Act of India of 1983 governs and monitors the overseas migration of Indian workers, there has been little discussion of issues facing international migrant women as workers, and many clandestine recruitment firms continue to operate outside state channels and because no emigration clearance is required for many groups of émigrés, their movement goes unrecorded. Hence, while the state has set up systems of control over female transnational migration in order to protect them, these are managed, "from a paternalistic point of view, i.e., to protect the rights of *women*, rather than that of workers or of migrants" (Raghuram, this volume; emphasis added). For example, the practice of having the husband (if married) or parent of the domestic worker accompany her to the office of the Protector of Emigrants to obtain clearance for emigration as a domestic worker essentially removes the responsibility of the domestic worker from the state to the accompanying family member. This attitude of the government is ironic given that it is often the failure of patriarchal structures at home which drives Indian women—usually those who are divorced, separated or widowed and who find it difficult to earn a living within India—to migrate in the first place; as such, passing the welfare of these women to their families is problematic.

Among the South Asian countries, it is in Bangladesh that we find the strongest tensions between economic motivations to send women abroad as domestic workers and moral (generally paternalistic) imperatives to protect female migrants predicated on gendered discourses of vulnerability and/or sexualised discourses on the protection of virginity. While there were no specific policies on women's labour migration up to the 1970s, increased female migration, religious sentiments, and media reports of rape, sexual harassment and maltreatment of female migrants led to the imposition of restrictions since the 1980s, "ostensibly on the religious grounds that women's mobility presented a threat to decency and chastity" (Afsar, this volume). However, the presence of illegal channels has rendered state bans on unskilled women's migration ineffective, and may instead have contributed to women's vulnerability and the threat of trafficking.

Receiving Countries

As Nonini (2002:5) notes, "when labour migrates transnationally, this is not an incidental fact but signals crossing from one territorially and culturally specific regime of power and knowledge to another. … In moving across national boundaries labourers are moving in and out of range of regulation by these territorially based regimes". Transmigrant women drawn into labour-receiving societies are on the one hand needed to fill the reproductive labour gap, while often treated as transgressors of the nation on the other.

In what may be regarded as the "best case" foreign domestic worker programme in the context of the worldwide market for migrant domestic labour, Canada's Live-in Caregiver Program offers migrants under this programme a chance to apply for permanent residency in Canada (Stasiulis & Bakan, 1997 quoted in McKay, this volume).[1] Yet, even here, transmigrant women find that while they may have moved to a different country, they are permanently locked within a framework of domestic work: many first admitted under the Live-in Caregiver Program find that they are unable to re-skill or gain entry into their previous professions after spending several years as a domestic worker (sometimes including several years spent in a third country before coming to Canada in addition to the two or three years under the Program) (McKay, this volume).

In other receiving nations within Asia, transnational domestic workers brought in to perform what is perceived to be low-skilled work are admitted as contract workers embodying cheap labour, not as social or political subjects and, as such, are accorded few rights of participation in wider civil society. Their transience is carefully ensured by state regulatory mechanisms. In Hong Kong, for example, the occupational mobility of transnational domestic workers is highly restricted. Not only are they legally prohibited from employment in any sector other than domestic work, they are also legally required to live-in with their employers, hence decreasing their chances of seeking employment opportunities elsewhere. The introduction of the "two-week rule"[2] in 1987 compounds the vulnerability of foreign domestic workers as they are forbidden from changing jobs in the first two years of employment, are not allowed to work for multiple employers or outside of the field of domestic work, and can be fired by the employer for any reason at any time, without the option of then transferring to a new employer within Hong Kong, unless they can show proof of mistreatment or the employer's insolvency, emigration, transfer abroad or death. One unforeseen consequence of the "two-week rule" is the emergence of increasing numbers of illegal migrant workers who stay on in Hong Kong and disappear into the underground economy when they are unable to find new employers in two weeks (Wee & Sim, this volume).

In Singapore, more draconian policy measures have been put in place to ensure surveillance of migrant bodies and that they gain no permanent structural foothold in the geobody of the nation; these include framing migration conditions in such a way as to tie the validity of the work permit to employment under a specific employer at a specific address, and preventing family formation and settlement by disallowing accompanying dependents, prohibiting marriage to Singapore citizens and permanent residents, and immediately repatriating the worker if she is found to be pregnant (Abdul Rahman et al., this volume; Huang & Yeoh, 2003).

In Malaysia, as in Singapore, medical surveillance is used as a mechanism of the state to assert control over transnational domestic worker bodies, which are perceived to be dangerously associated with prostitution and related health issues such as unwanted pregnancies and the spread of sexually transmitted diseases. In addition, as Chin (this volume) notes, "left unsaid is that the prohibition of marriage between a transnational domestic worker and a Malaysian citizen is premised on preventing the contamination of national cultural identity". Managing contract workers using a strategy of transience is also part of the state's efforts to render labour more "flexible" for a new era of unprecedented levels of capital mobility and accumulation across geopolitical boundaries. As Chin (this volume) argues, given the increasingly competitive global environment, "states are compelled to facilitate labour flexibilisation via policies and legislation pertaining to the establishment (or not) of minimum wages, ... the rights of workers to collective action", a strategy which is easier to implement in the presence of a ready pool of transient contract workers as opposed to citizen-workers.

State strategies to construct migrant labour as transient and flexible are also evident in Taiwan. Here, migrant contract workers including domestic workers are treated as a form of "disposable labour", carefully regulated through quota control and point systems, while the temporary status of these workers is also ensured through a rotation system also aimed at "maximis[ing] economic benefits while keeping social costs to a minimum" (Tseng, 2004 quoted in Lan, this volume).

TRANSNATIONAL WOMEN'S ACTIVISMS AND CIVIL SOCIETY

Feminist scholars have been generally wary about overstating the emancipatory value of transnational migration and the opening up of "new" interconnected political spaces as a result (Pratt & Yeoh, 2003). In particular, for transnational domestic workers with limited material resources and who are accorded few civil rights in destination countries and trapped within patriarchal notions of "women's work" and "women's place", the task of building for themselves new roles and new political spaces quickly run up against state and society's rules of marginality and "otherness" (Yeoh & Huang, 1999b). Among the sending countries, the Philippines is clearly the most prominent example of a case where migrant NGOs and advocacy groups have had the greatest success in fostering transformative politics in the local arena. Asis (this volume), for example, argues that the advocacy work of migrant NGOs in the Philippines and their partners overseas has contributed to the higher level of protection of overseas Filipino workers compared to other Asian migrants. In addition, new developments such as the granting of absentee voting to overseas Filipinos and dual citizenship, both of which having passed into law in 2003, may signal the greater political participation of Filipinos abroad in domestic matters. More specifically, local NGOs that specifically cater to domestic workers such as the Visayan Forum have been at the forefront of pushing for a Magna Carta for household helpers and domestic workers.

In Indonesia, the fall of Suharto in 1998 and the more democratic environment that ensued, have given migrant NGOs more freedom "in lobbying the government to improve support and protection for female overseas contract workers" (Hugo, this volume). The first detailed report documenting the vulnerabilities of Indonesian migrant domestic workers and new initiatives introduced to protect them from exploitation was produced in 2003 with the co-operation and contribution of various NGO groups and relevant state agencies (*Komnas Perempuan* (Indonesian National Commission on Violence against Women) and *Solidaritas Perempuan*/CARAM Indonesia, 2003). In addition, NGO groups played an instrumental role in drafting and submitting a Bill on the "Protection of Migrant Workers and their Families" to the State (Hugo, this volume). The Bill was debated and passed in 2004 leading up to the presidential election as part of Megawati's campaign to win popular support.[3]

Among the South Asian sending countries, the pulse of civil concern for women who migrate transnationally as domestic workers is less distinct and more uneven. In Bangladesh, apart from a few locally-based groups (including at least one formed by return women migrants), there is no major NGO action focused on migrant workers and, in fact, Afsar (this volume) contends that migrants are often perceived to be relatively well-off individuals little deserving of public sympathy. Similarly, in Sri Lanka, while there are a few newly formed groups engaged in limited advocacy work on behalf of migrant women, civil society in general does not have the critical mass or strength to make an impact on state policies on labour migration in any significant way (Gamburd, this volume). In India, attempts at regulating the working conditions of Indian transnational domestic workers have tended to come from the outside, including international agencies such as UNIFEM (United Nations Development Fund for Women) as well as civil society initiatives based outside India such as Andolan based in New York and the Asian Migrant Center in Hong Kong (Raghuram, this volume).

The emerging spaces of transnational activism associated with domestic work are also unevenly developed across different labour-receiving countries. The domestic worker activist terrain is most developed in Hong Kong where a liberal, capitalist regime coupled with a relatively transparent legal infrastructure provides the civic space for foreign domestic workers to develop their capacity to assert their rights (Wee & Sim, this volume). For example, the Employment Ordinance enshrines the right of migrant workers to form and participate in trade unions. Hong Kong's vibrant civil society is populated by lively labour unions, NGOs, media, religious groups and other organisations, and abounds in public processions, meetings and protests. The city-state is host to migrant workers' unions such as the Asian Domestic Workers' Union and the Indonesian Migrant Workers' Union, as well as a number of NGOs that espouse migrant workers' issues as part of their cause (Sim, 2003, quoted in Wee & Sim, this volume).

Hong Kong also best exemplifies the potential and pitfalls of developing "a broader social space where new [transnational] alliances between migrant, feminist and workers' organizations" (Law, 2002:218). Drawing on several campaigns spearheaded by a coalition of NGOs in Hong Kong to address the protection of migrant workers' rights, Law (2002) shows how NGOs drew connections between the specificities of labour migration issues with government policies in both the Philippines (the sending country where the majority of female domestic workers in Hong Kong originate) and Hong Kong (the receiving country), as well as global discussions about human rights at the Beijing Conference. In this sense, NGOs operate as "transforming terrains" which connect up different fields of activist discourse including global discourses on human rights. At the same time, while these "terrains" allow for coalition-building—for example, when domestic worker groups of five different nationalities (Filipino, Thai, Indonesian, Sri Lankan and Nepali) came together to protest against minimum wage cuts—they also decentre other nationally-bound issues (such as differential wages among domestic workers) and may be themselves fraught with inequalities (Law, 2002).

The terrain of activism in Hong Kong is also crossed by other lines that divide, including that between local and transnational domestic workers. The fragile class solidarity between these two broad groups that apparently existed before was threatened by the introduction of a HK$400 (US$51.36) levy in February 2003, a poorly disguised means of reducing transnational domestic workers' minimum wage and transferring this amount as a levy from the employers to government coffers for the retraining of local employees. Whereas local and foreign domestic organisations had previously not viewed each other as competitors (given that they served the needs of different segments of the local market) and therefore worked together on almost all common issues, this was no longer the case with the introduction of the levy. As Wee and Sim (this volume) explain: "Because the levy taxes foreign workers to subsidise local workers, a conflict of sub-class interests has been generated with one sub-class of workers (the foreign domestic workers) positioned as the exploited, with another sub-class of workers (the local domestic workers-to-be) positioned as the beneficiaries of such exploitation. ... Furthermore, because the levy comes out of the wages of foreign domestic workers, their employers are not affected at all. This has led to a convergence of ethnocentric interests shared by local employers and local workers, leading to a deepened division between 'us' and 'them'".

No doubt ridden by criss-crossing lines that divide, the vibrancy of Hong Kong's activist terrain augurs well for transformative politics, especially when compared to far more muted civil society actions and concerns around domestic worker issues in less liberal regimes. While civil society in general has been effervescent in post-martial law Taiwan, "migrant-oriented NGOs, which provide service for non-citizens located at the bottom of social stratification, constitute a civil sector that is still marginal in terms of resources and influence" (Lan, this volume). Most NGOs are church-based and service- rather than advocacy-oriented, although in recent years NGOs have come together to form an advocacy network to campaign for policy changes to improve the working and living conditions of migrant workers. Three main discursive strategies to gain media attention are used: presenting migrant workers as victims of employer abuse to evoke public sympathy; portraying them as unsung heroes whose contribution to Taiwan deserve praise and recognition; and countering negative social stereotypes circulated through the media. However, migrant NGOs are also handicapped not only by resource deficits but difficulties mobilising live-in migrant domestic workers of different nationalities (some with no days off) in the face of state regulations discouraging migrant workers from participating in unionisation and other forms of collective action (Lan, this volume).

The Malaysian NGO landscape comprises a few prominent organisations engaged in service delivery and advocacy efforts on behalf of transnational domestic workers. While these NGOs have had some success in developing transnational alliances with non-Malaysian counterparts with the potential of exerting pressure on the state via collective lobbying of regional and international organisations, the state's capacity to draw the boundaries around legitimate space for civic activism is evident in the 2004 trial and sentencing of Irene Fernandez, head of activist group Tenaganita on a charge for publishing "false news" on the conditions of transnational worker deportation camps in Malaysia (Chin, this volume). The state's hegemonic control of the boundaries of civil action is also apparent in Singapore, where given the prevailing climate of political passivity and non-resistance, migrant-oriented NGOs have tended to focus on providing "ambulance" services than take on advocacy work (Abdul Rahman et al., this volume). More recently, the emergence of an ad hoc group specifically oriented towards foreign domestic worker issues has raised the level of public discourse and concern for the welfare of these workers in the city-state, albeit in non-confrontational ways and with a careful eye on not "politicising" these issues.

Following from van der Veer's (1995:15) observation that in any society, "the established" (e.g. citizens) and "the outsiders" (e.g. migrants) should be understood as "structurally interdependent" because they define each other, it can be argued that to understand the construction of the core of a nation, attention must be concentrated at the margins. The (non)-incorporation of the figure of a multiply marginalised "other" such as the transnational domestic worker into the civil strata of society provides an important barometer of the progress of democratisation at the very heart of society. Our survey of the way transnational domestic workers feature in the politics of inclusion and exclusion at the margins of several societies where their physical presence in homes and public places is already visible indicates that, as of the present, civil space for transnational domestic workers is, to different degrees, hegemonised by the state. In Chandhoke's (1995:179) words, the state defines civil space itself by "the construction of its exclusions and marginalisations; and the construction of the identities of its participants". In almost all receiving nations, NGO provision of social services such as social gatherings, educational classes, skills training workshops, shelters and halfway houses is a constant feature, testifying to the slippage between the level of state provision on the one hand and the needs and vulnerabilities of transmigrant women on the other. At a different level, however, NGO advocacy work to protect and advance the rights of transnational domestic workers is highly uneven across different societies, in part a result of the varying strength and hegemonising

13

effects of the state in its attempt to draw discursive and material boundaries between the "national self" and the "migrant other". At the same time, the development of interconnected linkages between migrant-oriented groups across national boundaries, while a fraught terrain, holds out the possibility not so much of transcending the nation-state but of creating new political spaces from which to act.

SUMMARY MAP

The historical and cultural antecedents (sometimes including deep tap roots tracing to slavery and colonialism) of paid domestic work in its contemporary transnational form have bequeathed a legacy of gendered subordination to those who perform such work. Today, in an intensely interconnected world, globalisation processes at the transnational scale have "strengthened the claims of powerful actors (such as global corporations, global financial markets, international institutions and treaties)", often at the expense of the vulnerable, including the poor, women and minorities who find themselves pushed into casualised and flexibilised work such as transnational domestic work (Nagar et al., 2002:7). As these women move across national borders, other axes of asymmetry—primarily race, nationality and class—have also come into play in intersection with gender. Different degrees of marginalisation and vulnerability of transnational domestic workers are produced by the complex dynamics between nation/transnation as well as between state/civil society. While these dynamics have to be interpreted within the context of specific societies (as is undertaken in the following country-specific chapters), it is clearly the case that, hitherto, the transnationalisation of domestic work has done little to trouble existing gender relations, or to question the fundamental underpinnings of what are still largely patriarchal worlds. It is hoped, however, that the continued resilience of transnational domestic workers—who have become a permanent feature of many societies despite state measures to render them transient—and the intense unpredictable energy of the changing ethnoscape will in time to come produce new modes of valorisation, incorporation and participation which will serve to enrich the social, economic and cultural lives of nations in an increasingly interconnected world.

This book aims to illuminate the complex factors, patterns and processes that underscore the persistent flow of Asian women as transnational domestic workers across the world's international borders. The book's 15 papers are divided into three sections: the major labour sending countries of the Philippines, Indonesia, Sri Lanka, Bangladesh and India; the key receiving nations of Hong Kong, Taiwan, Singapore, Malaysia, Thailand and Canada; and finally, for a comparative perspective, three case studies focusing on Korea, Japan and Australia as societies which have not yet turned to transnational domestic workers as an option to buttress the domestic front. Each of the country-specific papers is organised around a set of six common themes:

- the historical and cultural context of gendered mobility and paid domestic work in the countries concerned;
- the role of the state in facilitating and organising the migration, placement and employment of Asian transnational domestic workers;
- the migrant's experience such as the decision-making process and the relationship between Asian transnational domestic workers on the one hand, and their employers and the host society on the other;
- the various social, economic and health impacts of the phenomenon;
- NGO activities and civil society spaces and actions on the issue; and
- alternative pathways and recommendations to counter the negative aspects of the phenomenon, and improve the circumstances of migration for Asian transnational domestic workers.

These common threads tie the collection together and allow for direct comparison[4] of the convergences and divergences of the major issues associated with the steadily growing migration of transnational domestic workers not only in these various societies, but as a phenomenon that spans the globe.

NOTES

1   This "best case" scenario should be seen in the context of a country where immigration policy is tied to population policy (Ley & Hiebert, 2001). Fertility levels in Canada are below replacement rate, with no grounds for expecting a turnaround. Immigration is portrayed by the government as a means to stave off population decline and already accounts for more than half of Canada's population growth.

2   According to this rule, a foreign domestic worker whose contract has been terminated either by herself or by her employer, is not permitted to remain in Hong Kong to take up new employment. Instead she is required to leave before the expiry of two weeks after the date of termination (Wee & Sim, this volume).

3   The NGO community protested against this because the version that was passed was one put together by the labour ministry which the former claimed was more focused on recruitment procedures and not the rights of migrants (Nisha Varia, Researcher, Human Rights Watch, Women's Rights Division, personal communication with authors, 7 January 2004).

4   See Appendices 1 and 2 for tables of country-specific data comparing some key aspects of transnational domestic work among the various sending and receiving countries covered in this volume.

REFERENCES

Chandhoke, N. 1995. *State and Civil Society: Explorations in Political Theory*. New Delhi: Sage.

Gibson, K., L. Law, and D. McKay. 2001. Beyond heroes and victims: Filipina contract migrants, economic activism and class transformations. *International Feminist Journal of Politics*, 3(3), 365–386.

15

Glenn, E. N. 1992. From servitude to service work: Historical continuities in the racial division of labour. *Signs*, 18(1), 1–43.

Hochschild, A. 1995. The culture of politics: Traditional, postmodern, cold-modern and warm-modern ideals of care. *Social Politics*, 2(3), 331–47.

Huang, S. & B. S. A. Yeoh. 2003. The difference gender makes: State policy and contract migrant workers in Singapore. *Asian and Pacific Migration Journal*, 12(1–2), 75–98.

Komnas Perempuan (Indonesian National Commission on Violence against Women) and *Solidaritas Perempuan*/CARAM Indonesia. 2003. *Indonesian Migrant Domestic Workers: Their Vulnerabilities and New Initiatives for the Protection of their Rights*, Indonesian Country Report to the UN Special Rapporteur on the Human Rights of Migrants, Kuala Lumpur, 30 September–3 October, Jakarta: *Komnas Perempuan* and *Solidaritas Perempuan*/CARAM Indonesia.

Lan, P. C. 2003a. Maid or madam? Filipina migrant workers and the continuity of domestic labour. *Gender & Society*, 17(2), 187–208.

_____. 2003b. Negotiating social boundaries and private zones: The micropolitics of employing migrant domestic workers. *Social Problems*, 50(4), 525–49.

Law, L. 2002. Sites of transnational activism: Filipino NGOs in Hong Kong. In *Gender Politics in the Asia-Pacific Region*. B. S. A. Yeoh, P. Teo, & S. Huang. London and New York: Routledge, 181–204.

Ley, D. & D. Hiebert. 2001. Immigration policy as population policy. *The Canadian Geographer*, 45(1), 120–25.

Nagar, R., V. Lawson, L. McDowell, & S. Hanson. 2002. Locating globalization: Feminist (re)readings of the subjects and spaces of globalization. *Economic Geography*, 78(3), 257–84.

Nonini, D. M. 2002. Transnational migrants, globalisation processes, and regimes of power and knowledge. *Critical Asian Studies*, 34(1), 3–17.

Palmer, P. 1989 *Domesticity and Dirt: Housewives and Domestic Servants in the United States*, 1920–1945. Philadelphia: Temple University Press.

Parreñas, R. S. 2000 Migrant Filipina domestic workers and the international division of reproductive labor. *Gender & Society*, 14(4), 560–80.

_____. 2001. Mothering from a distance: Emotions, gender, and intergenerational relations in Filipino transnational families. *Feminist Studies*, 27(2), 361–90.

Pratt, G. & B. S. A. Yeoh. 2003 Transnational (counter) topographies. *Gender, Place and Culture*, 10(2), 156–66.

Robinson, K. 2000. Gender, Islam and nationality. In *Home and Hegemony: Domestic Service and Identity Politics in South and Southeast Asia*. Edited by K. M. Adams & S. Dickey. Ann Arbor: Michigan University Press, 249–82.

Romero, M. 1992. *Maid in the U.S.A.* London: Routledge.

Sanchez, L. 1993 Women's power and the gendered division of domestic labour in the third world. *Gender & Society*, 7(3), 434–59.

Smith, M. P. 2001. *Transnational Urbanism: Locating Globalization*. Malden, MA, Oxford: Blackwell.

van der Veer, P. 1995 Introduction: The diasporic imagination. In *Nation and Migration: The Politics of Space in the South Asian Diaspora*. Edited by P. van der Veer. Philadelphia, PA: University of Pennsylvania Press, 1–16.

Yeoh, B. S. A. & S. Huang. 1999a. Singapore women and foreign domestic workers: Negotiating domestic work and motherhood. In *Gender, Migration and Domestic Service*. Edited by J. Momsen. London: Routledge, 277–300.

————. 1999b. Spaces at the margin: Migrant domestic workers and the development of civil society in Singapore. *Environment and Planning A*, 31(7), 1149–67.

PART 1

Sending Countries

1

Caring for the World: Filipino Domestic Workers Gone Global

MARUJA M. B. ASIS

LIFE STORIES AND A NATION'S LIFE

Jenny is driven not just by her family's constant demands for support, but also by a self-appointed mission to redeem her family from the shame of her father's conviction for *estafa* [swindling], and then to redeem her own self-esteem.

Raised in a comfortable, middle-class home, her equanimity is shattered by the disaster that befalls her father, and the emotional devastation of her family. The task of getting her mother and brother back on their feet falls on Jenny, who is forced to trek the long and dangerous road of migrant work until she ends up in Milan.

But even from a distance, the family back home continues to hound Jenny, who must take on four jobs simultaneously while ever on the lookout for opportunities to make money, from peddling phone cards to renting out her apartment to transients (Jimenez-David, 2004).

... Abigail [is a] caregiver in Toronto who comes home after five years to marry her childhood sweetheart. She gets a hero's welcome. ... Abigail brings hope, but unknown to her and to many, she also brings home a dreaded virus [SARS—Severe Acute Respiratory Syndrome] that would disrupt life in the town of San Isidro (Doyo, 2003).

Jenny and Abigail are the protagonists in two recent films about overseas Filipino workers (OFWs). The films, *Milan* (2004) and *Homecoming* (2003), join the ranks of a number of films that have delved into the realities of overseas work and their multiple and multi-layered consequences on migrants, their families, their hometowns, and the country. A journalist reviewing *Homecoming* said that the reel version called to mind the magazine features and column pieces that she had written about OFWs in the past decade, and how, back then, she had thought they could be material for movie scripts: "Some of the stories were so raw, so real, so surreal, so dramatic, so cinematic" (Doyo, 2003). I am reminded of similar reactions evoked by the stories shared by women migrants that I have interviewed or come across. Indeed, some of their stories seemed like the stuff grand dramas and tragedies are made of, but many of the stories were also reminiscent of the struggles of ordinary Filipinos trying to carve a better life for themselves and for their families.

Since the 1970s, the search for a better life has driven flesh-and-blood Jennys and Abigails to work in the homes of better-off families in different parts of the world.[1] They join the hundreds of thousands of Filipino workers who leave the country each year to work in foreign lands (Table 1.1). Starting as a small proportion of legal overseas workers in the 1970s, the share of women consistently increased such that by the 1990s, they outnumbered their male counterparts among the *new hires* deployed each year (Table 1.2).[2] Of the ten major destinations of Filipino workers, women are the majority of migrants in seven countries: Saudi Arabia, Hong Kong, Japan, United Arab Emirates, Taiwan, Singapore, Kuwait, Italy and United Kingdom (Table 1.3). Although OFWs are

TABLE 1.1 Annual deployment of overseas Filipino workers (OFWs), 1984–2003

Year	Land-based	Sea-based	Total
1984	300,378	59,604	350,982
1985	320,494	52,290	372,784
1986	323,517	54,697	378,214
1987	382,229	67,042	449,271
1988	385,117	85,913	471,030
1989	355,346	103,280	458,626
1990	334,883	111,212	446,095
1991	489,260	125,759	615,019
1992	549,655	136,806	686,461
1993	550,872	145,758	696,630
1994	564,031	154,376	718,407
1995	488,173	165,401	653,574
1996	484,653	175,469	660,122
1997	559,227	188,469	747,696
1998	638,343	193,300	831,643
1999	640,331	196,689	837,020
2000	643,304	198,324	841,628
2001	662,648	204,951	867,599
2002	682,315	209,593	891,908
2003	651,938	216,031	867,969

SOURCE: www.poea.gov.ph/docs/Deployment%20Summary%20(LB_SB)%201984%to 202002.xls,accessed 22 November 2004.

distributed in a wide range of occupational categories, most migrants are recruited to work at less-skilled jobs; women migrants, in particular, are mostly in domestic work[3] (Tables 1.2 & 1.3). With the exception of Japan (where women migrants are largely in entertainment work, which is classified under the professional category) and the United Kingdom (where the majority are nurses), the remaining top ten destinations of Filipino workers are major markets for Filipino domestic workers. Other Asian women who venture into domestic work are concentrated in a number of countries: most Indonesian women go to Saudi Arabia and Malaysia and are a growing number in Singapore, Hong Kong and Taiwan; Sri Lankan women are mostly found in Middle East destinations (see Hugo, this volume; Gamburd, this volume).

In contrast, Filipino domestic workers are just about everywhere—in Asia, the Middle East, Europe and North America,[4] a ubiquity that has given rise to Filipino women being stereotyped as domestic workers. In at least two instances, the word "Filipino" has come to mean domestic worker,[5] a development which has been rued in the Philippines as one of the social costs of exporting poverty.

TABLE 1.2 Annual deployment of new hires: Per cent female by skill category, 1992–2002*

Skill Category	1992	1993	1994	1995	1996	1997
Professional &	75%	75%	78%	71%	67%	72%
Technical workers	72,230	64,830	73,705	43,629	36,055	51,381
Managerial workers	16%	18%	21%	23%	21%	20%
	289	326	335	346	305	572
Clerical workers	28%	30%	32%	37%	39%	42%
	5,442	4,226	3,785	3,435	3,169	3,632
Sales workers	38%	37%	36%	41%	37%	44%
	2,701	2,539	2,203	1,986	1,938	2,637
Service workers	82%	86%	88%	91%	91%	89%
	82,426	89,296	90,755	81,043	84,745	76,644
Agricultural workers	1%	2%	2%	1%	2%	7%
	2,020	1,753	1,268	981	822	546
Production workers	5%	12%	16%	22%	11%	17%
	95,415	93,149	86,798	82,537	75,683	85,829
For reclassification	15%	28%	4%	13%	9%	—
	71	78	137	200	3,074	—
Total	**50%**	**54%**	**59%**	**58%**	**54%**	**56%**
	260,594	**256,197**	**258,986**	**214,157**	**205,791**	**221,241**

(cont'd next page)

TABLE 1.2 Annual deployment of new hires: Per cent female by skill category, 1992–2002* (cont'd)

Skill category	1998	1999	2000	2001	2002
Professional &	75%	81%	86%	85%	85%
Technical workers	55,456	62,500	78,685	97,448	100,585
Managerial workers	21%	18%	27%	27%	34%
	385	333	284	385	376
Clerical workers	45%	49%	42%	59%	63%
	2,897	2,552	2,367	3,356	4,039
Sales workers	45%	35%	46%	57%	48%
	2,514	2,244	2,083	3,188	3,069
Service workers	91%	91%	92%	91%	90%
	80,675	84,138	91,206	92,351	98,007
Agricultural workers	3%	2%	1%	7%	3%
	388	452	526	550	617
Production workers	21%	26%	28%	24%	29%
	75,078	79,662	57,807	56,740	69,883
For reclassification	20%	27%	43%	31%	5%
	1,822	5,379	20,072	4,186	11,579
Total	**61%**	**64%**	**70%**	**72%**	**69%**
	219,215	**237,260**	**253,030**	**258,204**	**288,155**

SOURCE: www.poea.gov.ph/docs/Deployed%20New%20Hires%20by%20Skillby%0%20 and20 Sex.xls, accessed 17 February 2004.

* Highlighted figures refer to categories where women migrants are the majority of all migrantworkers in those occupational categories.

This chapter tries to explain how Filipino women have come to occupy a niche as domestic workers in so many countries. While recognising the importance of demand in generating female migration (Truong, 1996; Ehrenreich, 2003; Hochschild, 2003), this chapter focuses on factors internal to the Philippine context which have propelled and facilitated Filipino women's dominance in the global market for domestic and related workers.[6] The chapter examines the international migration of Filipino women in domestic work by tracing possible linkages to (as well as disjunctures from) the internal migration of women also engaged in domestic work. I begin with the macro level, highlighting the role of the state and the migration industry in capturing a large share of the global market for domestic workers. Next, I examine the role of the family and migrants' networks in the growth of female migration and the expansion of their presence in different destinations. This is followed by vignettes of what women migrants say about migration, domestic work and how they negotiate the constraints

TABLE 1.3 Top 10 destinations, 2002, and per cent female in OFW population

Country	Deployed workers[a] 2002	% Female, OFW population[b] 2002	Jobs commonly held by Filipino women migrants
1. Saudi Arabia	193,157	24	Domestic work, nursing, other health-related work
2. Hong Kong	105,036	**93**	Domestic work—Filipinos are the largest national group of foreign domestic workers in Hong Kong
3. Japan[c]	77,870	**53**	Entertainment work[c]
4. United Arab Emirates	50,796	**56**	Domestic work, other service work, sales
5. Taiwan	46,371	**53**	Domestic work, caregiving, factory work
6. Singapore	27,648	**72**	Domestic work—Filipinos are one of the two largest national groups of foreign domestic workers in Singapore
7. Kuwait	25,894	**74**	Domestic work
8. Italy	20,034	**63**	Domestic work
9. United Kingdom	13,655	**50**	Nursing, other health-related work—2002 was the first time that the UK figured in the top 10 destinations
10. Brunei	11,564	**33**	Domestic work

SOURCES: www.poea.gov.ph/docs/Depl;oyedOFWSByDestination1998-2003.xls;, accessed 17 February 2004; www.census.gov.ph/data/sectordat/2003/of0203.htm, accessed 17 February 2004.

NOTE: Data on deployment are flow data collected by the Philippine Overseas Employment Administration while data from the Survey of Overseas Filipinos 2002, an annual survey undertaken by the National Statistics Office, refer to OFWs working abroad for the period 1 April 2002 to 30 September 2002.

a Adapted from www.poea.gov.ph/docs/Depl;oyedOFWSByDestination1998-2003.xls, accessed 17 February 2004

b Adapted from Table 4: Survey of Overseas Filipinos 2002 (www.census.gov.ph/data / sectordat/2003/of0203.htm, accessed 17 February 2004).

c There are also Filipino domestic workers in Japan.

and opportunities confronting them as global domestic workers and as transnational mothers and family members. The last section of the paper discusses the dilemmas generated by the migration of domestic workers and how the larger Philippine society grapples with these issues.

This paper draws on data and insights from existing literature on Filipino overseas migration and the various research projects that I have worked on. In particular, two recently completed research projects were the main sources of the empirical material used in this chapter—the study of women migrants who have returned to the Philippines (henceforth the 2000 study) and the study of migrants who have ever worked in Singapore and members of their families (henceforth the 2001 study). The first study was conducted in 2000, involving interviews with 100 return migrants and further interviews with ten selected migrants for analysis of their life stories (see Asis, 2001 for details). Data from the second study came from in-depth interviews and observations of migrants who were working in Singapore (n=6), those who had returned home at the time of the study (n=9), and selected family members migrants (spouses, parents, siblings, children) left behind or who had rejoined in the Philippines (n=21). Altogether, the 2001 study provided the experiences of how 18 families with family members who had ever worked in Singapore negotiated family relationships (see Asis et al., 2004).

THE CONTEXT: THE STATE AND THE MIGRATION INDUSTRY

The State: Caught between Promotion and Protection

The beginnings of state involvement in labour migration date back to the enactment of the Labour Code of 1974 (also known as Presidential Decree or PD 442) which laid the foundations of the overseas employment programme. PD 442 created the Overseas Employment Development Board which, *inter alia*, was tasked to formulate and implement a system of promoting overseas employment with due regard for the workers' welfare and local human resource requirements. This was an opportune time as it coincided with the opening of the Middle East labour market to Asian workers in the 1970s. Pressed with domestic unemployment and balance of payments problems (which were exacerbated by the oil crisis), the Philippines was one of the Asian countries that swiftly responded to the labour needs of the oil-rich Gulf countries. The deployment of Filipino workers was intended to be temporary, in the hope that the economic situation would improve, at which time, labour migration was anticipated to end. Labour migration, instead, continued and expanded beyond the Middle East in response to the increasing demand for Filipino workers on the one hand, and the development of institutions and policies in the Philippines that enabled the state to seize opportunities in the global labour market on the other.

Some 30 years after it entered the arena of labour migration, several generalisations can be said about international labour migration from the Philippines. First, the Philippines has steered itself to become a major source country of workers, supplying workers of varying skill levels to over 100 countries. As Table 1.1 indicates, since the late 1990s, over 800,000 Filipinos are annually deployed to take up work in foreign countries. Data from the Survey of Overseas Filipinos 2002[7] provide information on where OFWs come from. Luzon, the largest regional grouping, accounts for 72 per cent of all OFWs; the Visayas, 15 per cent; and Mindanao, 13 per cent. Notably, the National Capital Region alone—which includes Manila, the nation's capital, and surrounding cities and municipalities (see boxed area in Figure 1.1)—accounts for 20 per cent of all OFWs. Comparing the distribution of OFWs by region and the distribution of the Philippine population, it can be seen that Luzon (particularly the National Capital Region) has a surplus of OFWs relative to their share in the total population (Table 1.4). Although some regions send more international migrants compared to the others, by now overseas migration has spread out to the rest of the Philippines.

Second, it can be argued that labour migration has played a structural role in the Philippine economy, of which remittances are the most telling indicator. Based on 2001 data, the volume of workers' remittances ploughed back to the Philippines by OFWs and overseas Filipinos is the third largest, after Mexico and India (International Monetary Fund, 2003, cited in Migration Policy Institute, 2003).[8] Accounting for 8.9 per cent of the GDP, remittances are a significant and reliable source of revenue for the Philippines. In a way, remittances have compensated for the small and fluctuating inflows of investments and development assistance to the country. All the presidents, from Marcos to Macapagal-Arroyo, have acknowledged the contributions of OFWs, for which they have been regarded as the country's "new heroes".[9] In President Macapagal-Arroyo's speeches when she meets with OFW communities in her state visits, she refers to the Philippines as "the home of the great worker". The OFWs' place in the national life has been enshrined in the commemoration of Migrant Workers Day every 7 June.[10] The homecoming of thousands of OFWs in December to celebrate Christmas with their families is not complete without the President showing up to welcome the arrivals. The Catholic Church has also set a special day to remember migrants and their families through the celebration of the first Sunday of Lent as National Migrants Sunday.

Third, sustained labour migration in the last 30 years has bred a culture of migration, characterised by a general acceptance of migration as part of Filipino life.[11] In the Philippines, this is evident in the prevalence of values and norms that are supportive of migration. Knitted into the survival or mobility strategies of many individuals and families in the Philippines, migration has become a common pathway to achieve the good life. Career aspirations, for example, are shaped by what would be "marketable" abroad (see also Tan, 2001).

Fourth, unabated migration has, over the years, built up a large and extensive overseas Filipino population, which has made migration easier and more accessible.

TABLE 1.4   Source regions of OFWs in relation to population size

Region	No. of OFWs 2002 (1,000s)	Per cent of total OFWs	Total population 2000	Per cent of total population
Philippines	1,056	100	76,498,735	100
Luzon	*765*	*72*	*42,810,872*	*56*
National Capital Region	216	20	9,932,560	13
Cordillera Administrative Region	18	2	1,365,220	2
Region I – Ilocos	90	9	4,200,478	5
Region II – Cagayan Valley	62	6	2,813,159	4
Region III – Central Luzon	143	13	8,030945	10
Region IV – S. Tagalog	203	19	11,793,655	15
Region V – Bicol	33	3	4,674,855	6
Visayas	*158*	*15*	*15,520,152*	*20*
Region VI – W. Visayas	96	9	6,208,733	8
Region VII – Central Visayas	38	4	5,701,064	7
Region VIII – E. Visayas	24	2	3,610,355	5
Mindanao	*135*	*13*	*18,133,864*	*24*
Region IX – W. Mindanao	28	3	3,091,208	4
Region X – N. Mindanao	26	2	2,747,585	4
Region XI – S. Mindanao	27	3	5,189,335	7
Region XII – C. Mindanao	28	3	2,598,210	3
Autonomous Region in Muslim Mindano	15	1	2,412,159	3
Caraga	11	1	2,095,367	3

SOURCES: Adapted from www.census.gov.ph/data/sectordat/2000/of0200.htm, accessed 17 February 2004; *2000 Census of Population and Housing*, 2000.

NOTE: Data on OFWs are from the Survey of Overseas Filipinos, 2000 (www.census.gov.ph/data/ sectordat/2000/of0200.htm); data on the Philippine population are from the 2000 Census of Population and Housing. Both datasets are collected by the National Statistics Office.

As of 2003, 7.8 million Filipinos (2.9 million permanent settlers, 3.4 million legal overseas workers, and some 1.5 million unauthorised migrants) were residing and working outside the country (www.poea.gov.ph/docs/ofwStock2003.doc, accessed 22 November 2004). The overseas population makes up close to ten per cent of the country's projected population of 82.7 million as of 2004 (www.nscb.gov.ph/secstat/ d_popn.asp, accessed 22 November 2004). These overseas Filipinos represent an invaluable social capital, serving as conduits of information, funds and assistance

FIGURE 1.1   The Philippines—Major island groupings

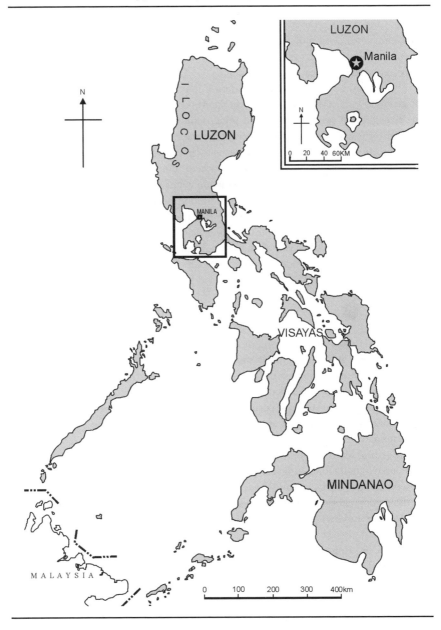

to aspiring migrants. These ties and exchanges are reinforced by greater access to communication and transportation facilities, resulting in more exchanges of people and ideas and the creation of transnational communities. As detailed in a later section, this openness to the idea of migration has raised concerns of breeding dependence on and vulnerability to external conditions, thereby crippling the initiative to promote a strong and sustainable path to development.

From an initial emphasis on marketing Filipino workers, the state had to address non-economic concerns, particularly the question of protecting Filipino workers, an issue that migrant non-governmental organisations (NGOs) have assiduously raised to the government. The attempt to combine marketing and protection can be seen in the creation of the Philippine Overseas Employment Administration (POEA) (from the Overseas Employment Development Board and the National Seamen Board), which was mandated to deal with the regulation of the migration industry and the deployment of workers, and the formation of the Overseas Workers Welfare Administration (OWWA) to take care of welfare-related issues of migrants abroad and their families in the Philippines.[12] The development of an institutional and legal framework governing all phases of migration, from pre-deployment to on-site services to the return and reintegration of migrant workers, is summarised in Table 1.5. These provisions have given rise to a number of good practices that have contributed to the higher level of protection of Filipino migrants compared to other Asian migrants (see also Villalba, 2002), including:

- the regulation and monitoring of recruitment agencies;
- information and training programmes to prepare migrant workers, in particular, the institutionalisation of the Pre-Departure Orientation Seminars (PDOS) in 1983, a requirement for departing OFWs to orientate them on the working and living conditions, laws and customs of their country of destination;
- the drawing up of model employment contracts to outline the basic minimum terms acceptable to the Philippine government;
- the setting up of Filipino Workers Resource Centres in countries where there are at least 20,000 Filipinos to serve as one-stop centres for the delivery of government services and assistance to OFWs; and
- the deployment of labour attaches and welfare officers in countries where there are large numbers of OFWs (Table 1.6).

A landmark in promoting the protection of OFWs was the enactment of the Migrant Workers and Overseas Filipinos Act of 1995 (Republic Act or RA 8042), "an act to institute policies of overseas employment and establish a higher standard of protection and promotion of the welfare of migrant workers, their families and overseas Filipinos in distress, and for other purposes" (POEA, 1997), which incorporated or instituted the good practices mentioned above. Despite the protective mechanisms established by

TABLE 1.5 Institutional landmarks—Philippine labour migration policy

Year	Development
1974	The Labour Code of the Philippines (also known as Presidential Decree or PD 442) created the Overseas Employment Development Board (OEDB) and the National Seamen Board (NSB) to carry out a more systematic deployment of workers.
1977	Creation of the Welfare Fund for Overseas Workers (Welfare Fund) through Presidential Letter of Instruction 537.
1978	PD 1412 amended the Labour Code—the private sector was allowed to participate in overseas employment due to demand for workers.
1980	PD 1691 further amended the Labour Code—OEDB was limited to recruit and place workers on a government-to-government basis.
1982	Executive Order 797 merged the OEDB, NSB and Bureau of Employment Services into the Philippine Overseas Employment Administration (POEA).
1987	Reorganisation of the POEA for the purpose of strengthening workers' protection and tighter regulation of recruitment agencies. The Welfare Fund was renamed Overseas Workers Welfare Administration; its mandate was broadened to promote the interests of OFWs and their families.
1995	Passage of the Migrant Workers and Overseas Filipinos (RA 8042) to institute a higher standard of protection and promotion of welfare of migrant workers and other overseas Filipinos and their families. On 5 July of the same year, the Philippine government ratified the UN Convention on the Protection of the Rights of All Migrant Workers and Members of their Families.
2003	Passage of the Overseas Absentee Voting Act of 2003 (RA 9189) allowing overseas Filipinos to vote in national elections. Two other migration-related laws were passed in 2003: Anti-Trafficking in Persons Act of 2003 (RA 9208) and Dual Citizenship Retention and Reacquisition Act of 2003 (RA 9225).

SOURCES: Adapted from Asis (1992) and Sto. Tomas (2002).

TABLE 1.6 Stock estimate of overseas Filipinos and the distribution of labour attachés and welfare officers

Region/Country	Stock estimate[a]	Labour attaché	Welfare officer
Asia (East & South)	**944,129 (1,532,872)**	**13**	**11**
Hong Kong SAR	185,500 (188,804)	2	2
Macau SAR	16,000 (17,056)	1	
Japan	197,268 (304,678)		
Tokyo		1	1
Osaka		1	1
South Korea	28,540 (42,116)	1	1
Taiwan	151,824 (158,116)		
Taipei		2	1
Kaohsiung		1	1
Taichung		1	1
Brunei	21,043 (22,569)	1	1
Singapore	58,194 (130,263)	1	1
Malaysia	59,599 (422,910)	1	1
Middle East	**1,361,409 (1,471,849)**	**18**	**12**
Bahrain	28,238 (33,301)	1	1
Kuwait	69,217 (79,310)	3[b]	1
Israel	9,186 (32,290)	1	1
Lebanon	21,521 (27,040)	1	1
Libya	n.a.	1	1
Oman	18,632 (20,150)	1	1
Qatar	44,279 (45,292)	1	1
Saudi Arabia	948,329 (966,572)		
Riyadh		4	1
Jeddah		2	1
Al Khobar			1
UAE	172,755 (193,144)		
Abu Dhabi		1	1
Dubai		2	1
Americas	**286,103 (3,381,815)**	**3**	**1**
Saipan, Commonwealth of the Northern Mariana Islands	15,399 (17,888)	1	1
USA	99,815 (2,589,223)	1	
Canada	30,027 (392,120)	1	

(cont'd next page)

TABLE 1.6 Stock estimate of overseas Filipinos and the distribution of labour attachés and welfare officers (cont'd)

Europe	165,030 (767,882)	7	4
Italy	69,998 (150,429)		
Rome		1	1
Milan		1	1
Greece	7,514 (25,098)	1	1
Spain	5,687 (43,330)	1	1
Switzerland	5,953 (15,858)	1	
UK	15,767 (70,000)	2	
Others (Africa, Oceania, unspecified and seafarers)	**118,287 (608,760)**		
Total	**3,385,001 (7,763,178)**	**41**	

SOURCE: www.poea.gov.ph/docs/ofwStock2003.doc, accessed 22 November 2004

NOTE: Estimates of the overseas Filipino population were prepared by the Commission on Filipinos Overseas, Department of Foreign Affairs; data on the distribution of welfare officers are from the Overseas Workers Welfare Administration (www.owwa.gov.ph.net, accessed 22 November 2004); data on the distribution of labour attaches are from the Department of Labour and Employment (www.polo.dole.gov.ph/directory.html, accessed 22 November 2004).

a As of December 2003, the figures represent the stock of legal or documented overseas Filipino workers, i.e., those whose work-related documents have been processed by the POEA. The figures in parentheses refer to the total stock estimate—these include permanent migrants and estimates of irregular migrants.

b Includes one labour attaché assigned to Iraq but based in Kuwait.

the Philippine government, these are not sufficient. The cooperation of the countries of destination is crucial. More importantly, the persistent view of domestic work as private and non-work has excluded it from national labour laws, leaving domestic workers unprotected.

In the early years of the overseas migration programme, the government probably did not anticipate that women would become an important component of labour flows.[13] The small numbers of women who sought overseas work in the 1970s were eclipsed by the hundreds of thousands of male workers who went to the Middle East. Also, the fact that women migrants were basically moving from their family household to that of their employer's added to the invisibility of women's migration. Particularly for the women who did not leave as contract workers (e.g., those who left the country using tourist visas, such as those who went to Europe), it can be said that their migration was more of an individual initiative than a state-driven phenomenon. The state assumed a greater role in women's migration when their numbers soared, accompanied by heightened concerns over their vulnerability to abuse and the well-being of the families (especially, children) left behind.[14] In the name of protecting migrants (frequently, women migrants), bans or restrictions (e.g., age requirement) were imposed from time to time when migrants' safety was at risk or conditions turned unfavourable. It can be argued, thus, that female migration, contributed to the discourse of migrants' rights and advocacy, and held the state to become more accountable for the protection of Filipino nationals abroad. The quick passage of RA 8042 in 1995 was, in part, hastened by the public clamour for more protection for OFWs, especially women migrants, in the wake of the Flor Contemplacion tragedy.[15]

In view of the large numbers of women in migration, Section 2(d) of RA 8042 provides that:

> The State affirms the fundamental equality before the law of women and men and the significant role of women in nation-building. Recognising the contribution of overseas women workers and their particular vulnerabilities, the State shall apply gender-sensitive criteria in the formulation and implementation of policies and programmes affecting migrant workers and the composition of bodies tasked for the welfare of migrant workers.[16]

To better ensure protection, Section 2(g) of RA 8042 is intended to pursue selective deployment:

> The State recognises that the ultimate protection is the possession of skills. Pursuant to this and as soon as practicable, the government shall deploy and/or allow the deployment only to [sic] skilled Filipino workers.

This would have affected women migrants as domestic workers are a large part of the less skilled. However, the resolve to carry this out has been undermined by the stable, if not increasing demand for domestic workers (including caregivers). Moreover, the economic crisis of 1997 interrupted the growth potential of the Philippine economy, and the state quickly reverted to the active pursuit of overseas employment.

Very recently, in the light of globalisation, Labour Secretary Sto. Tomas shared that there is a debate on "whether or not the government has to shift to a policy of 'managing' the flow of overseas migration, which is reactive, to 'promoting' labour migration as a growth strategy, which is proactive"; the shift would mean, "a more aggressive marketing of the Filipino as a global worker and the Philippines as a human resource centre for professionals and skilled workers" (Sto. Tomas, 2002:97). The target to send out a million OFWs every year is an indication of the return to a market orientation, a development which might weaken the state's resolve to pay due attention to the protection of migrants' rights in the race to meet the target.

The Migration Industry

As of 17 February 2004, there were 2,876 recruitment and manning agencies in the Philippines, of which about half were not in good standing (i.e., their licenses had been revoked, not renewed or cancelled). Of the 1,434 agencies in good standing, 1,029 catered to the recruitment and placement of land-based workers, while the remaining 405 were manning agencies, i.e., those in the business of recruiting and placing sea-based workers (www.poea.gov.ph/legi-binlaglist.asp?mode=alll, accessed 17 February 2004). Problems with recruitment agencies had surfaced in the early years of labour migration, prompting the government to prohibit their participation. However, the government could not cope with the huge demand for workers. After a brief hiatus, recruitment agencies re-entered the picture in 1978, and they have since specialised in recruiting and placing Filipino workers for overseas employment. Recruitment agencies also actively seek out markets for Filipino workers. The government, on the other hand, has since concentrated on its regulatory functions (see also Table 1.5).

On the downside, however, the irregularities committed by recruitment agencies have been a source of distress to migrants and their families. Recruitment agencies, both licensed and unlicensed ones, are notorious for charging excessive placement fees, thereby increasing the costs of migration. They can very well name their price because of the large numbers of aspiring migrants wanting to land jobs abroad. High transaction costs imply that migrants have to work abroad for a longer period in order to recover their expenses, or they are forced to suffer difficult working and living conditions to be able to pay off their debts. Illegal recruitment, non-deployment, contract substitution and facilitating unauthorised migration are the other problems that have long been associated with the Filipino migration industry, despite the regulatory mechanisms in place. While the regulation of recruitment agencies has been a central focus of pre-migration or pre-deployment programmes aimed at protecting migrants (Battistella & Asis, 2003), this function has become controversial of late.

A provision in RA 8042 on the deregulation of the migration industry and the phasing out of POEA's regulatory functions (Sections 29 and 30, respectively) has been the subject of lobbying by NGOs (who oppose deregulation) and the recruitment agencies (who are for deregulation).[17] In view of persisting irregularities committed by recruitment agencies, in 2002, the POEA introduced stringent rules to weed out "fly-by-night" recruitment agencies. The migration industry was up in arms over the new rules, which they considered too onerous, a factor, they argued, that would drive legal agencies underground. The new rules, which were upheld by a Supreme Court ruling, include allowing direct hiring (i.e., the worker can bypass the recruitment agency if he or she finds an employer on his or her own); reiteration of the placement fee pegged at one month's salary—with the added provision that one count of violation will entail the revocation of licence to operate; increasing capitalisation and other financial requirements; and setting a minimum of request of workers from 50 to 100 (Battistella

& Asis, 2003:44). This development has given the migration industry greater resolve to push for deregulation, and to lobby for the amendment of a provision in the same law which does not limit illegal recruitment as violations committed only by unlicensed agencies. NGOs, on the other hand, are waging a campaign to amend the provision in RA 8042 on deregulation and to retain the definition of illegal recruitment as acts that could also be committed by licensed agencies. The amendments have been passed at the House of Representatives and are now with the Senate.

Despite the dubious reputation of recruitment agencies (including licensed ones), they rank high as a source of migrants' information about jobs abroad, second only to relatives and friends who are part of migrants' networks. By comparison, government sources as well as NGOs rank low as sources of information (Scalabrini Migration Center, 1997; Battistella & Asis, 2003).

If migrants can find overseas jobs as direct hires, this would result in lower or minimal transaction costs. In the case of domestic workers, this possibility is not remote because of the role of migrants' networks in finding employers for prospective migrants back home.[18] The growth of the population of domestic workers from the Philippines in Hong Kong, Singapore and Taiwan, and most especially in Europe,[19] in part reflects the "multiplier effects" of migrants' networks in drawing in other kin or friends to the same destination and into the same occupational niche. Migrants' networks may have done away with the services of recruitment agencies in the Philippines, but not necessarily the brokers and employment agencies in the destination. For example, those going to Singapore as tourists with pre-arranged jobs have to rely on employment agencies to adjust their status to work permit holders. This is an area where the state in the receiving countries will have to intervene to protect migrant workers.

THE FACILITATORS: FAMILIES AND MIGRANTS' NETWORKS

The family has a far-reaching influence on migration in the Philippines, whether internally or internationally. The family's welfare plays a very important role in a migrant's decision to migrate, and the family's support is critical in making migration possible. The new economics of labour migration has highlighted migration as a survival or mobility strategy. As such, the family or household, rather than the individual, is the one involved in migration decisions.

Recent research in the Philippines and other countries in Asia indicates that while family support is important, the decision and initiative to migrate largely rests with the individual. Considering the history of overseas migration and the openness to the idea of migration in the Philippines, the primacy of individual initiative is not surprising. Based on what we know now, most Filipino women migrants consider that migration is done for the sake of the family, while pursuing their personal agendas in the migration project (see also, Tacoli, 1999; Asis, 2002). In not a few cases, women migrants go ahead with the migration project despite their family's objections. There are also notable variations to the motif of migration "for the sake of the family". Migration as a way out of abusive or troubled domestic situations, or to escape surveillance from patriarchal relationships, has surfaced in the narratives of some women migrants (e.g., Suzuki, 2002). Since there is no divorce in the Philippines, some women migrants have resorted to migration to achieve de facto divorce (see McKay, this volume). There are also indications that the experience of migration—specifically earning their own keep as migrant workers—has emboldened women to leave an unhappy marriage (Asis, 2001).

The impact of migration on the family has been a major source of unease in the Philippines. At the height of male migration to the Middle East in the 1970s, there was also concern about what would become of families in the absence of husbands and fathers. But since the mothers were present, it was assumed that the family would somehow pull together. With the migration of women who are the traditional caregivers (mothers are regarded as the "light of the home" in the Philippines), there is the question of who will take their place. My interviews with family members of women migrants indicate that if it was possible for other male family members to work abroad, family members would rather choose to have their mothers (or sisters) stay home. However, since the demand in the global labour market is for women workers, families realign the division of labour in the household to meet their needs.

Due to women's central role in the family and in the home, when women leave, families go through more adjustments than when it is the men who leave. Findings from studies suggest that while the women left behind assume multiple roles with the departure of their husbands (see Asis, 2001), husbands do not readily take on the role of caregivers when they are the ones left behind (e.g., Battistella & Conaco, 1998). Thus, female migration tends to rely on the extended family, usually other female relatives, to provide care-giving to the remaining family members, especially the care of young children. However, some studies are providing some insights that husbands are not completely averse to expanding their roles in the family (e.g., Asis et al., 2004).[20] Although women migrants are not freed from the guilt of leaving their families (particularly children) behind, the fact that other family members are pitching in helps in easing their anxieties.

Given the extensive migration of Filipinos, most migrants are networked with other family members or friends at the destination. In many instances, migrants' success in finding a job in the destination is facilitated by recommendations provided by kin or friends who have preceded them (Asis, 2001). As mentioned earlier, these circles of family and friends provide important support to migrants, and they have become family to migrants, too, in the sense that they support each other. For those who are truly pioneer migrants, one way to get connected with other Filipinos is to go to the Catholic Church, the gathering place of Filipinos abroad. In some destinations, Filipinos have appropriated some public spaces which have become Filipino enclaves on weekends, e.g., Lucky Plaza in Singapore, Chongshan North Road in Taipei, or Central in Hong Kong, much to the consternation of locals. These pockets of Filipino communities provide critical social support to Filipino migrants, particularly for domestic workers who otherwise work in isolation. Although domestic work is fraught with many vulnerabilities and difficulties, women migrants manage to overcome many obstacles. A major conclusion from one of the few studies that have looked into mental health issues found that Filipino women migrants in Hong Kong have adapted well to their situation: "The Sunday gatherings are an informal source of group counselling for these women for whom group relationships are of crucial importance in mental health adaptation" (Bagley et al., 2001:313). Some of the groups or networks that migrants form evolve into more formal organisations which promote the welfare of migrants in the destinations while others sponsor projects in their hometowns, such as contributions to the construction of community infrastructures (chapels or churches, basketball courts), scholarship programmes, or financial contributions in times of disasters. In many a migrant's narrative, their experience of being part of organisations abroad counts among the valuable things that they have learned from their sojourn.

THE ACTORS: MIGRATION AND DOMESTIC WORK AS OPTIONS

Internal Migration and Local Domestic Work

> I think if you are a woman, is it not true that for Filipinos, if you are a woman, you really need to go out, even if you only go to Manila, ... it's like looking for what's in store for you (Emma, 32 years old, return migrant from Singapore, 2001 study).[21]

In reply to a question on the kinds of adjustments her family had gone through on account of her ten-year absence, this former migrant to Singapore said that life went on for her family because as her statement above suggests, Filipino women are typically expected to engage in migration, "even if you only go to Manila".

Indeed, long before Filipinos became global workers, Filipino women were observed to be migratory within the Philippines and, as discussed below, it is a mobility that is not necessarily tied to marriage or family migration. Filipino women's participation in migration, traditionally a male preserve in some Southeast Asian cultures, is part of the latitude granted to women in Philippine society. Although the Philippines ranked only 77th in terms of the human development index (0.754), it ranked 35th in terms of the gender empowerment measure (0.523) in 2000 (UN, 2002:154 & 227). There are no marked gender differentials in literacy and educational measures or, if there are any, they show women to be more advantaged. Filipino women also have one of the highest singulate mean ages at marriage in Asia—23.8 years as of 1995 (www.census.gov.ph/data/quickstat/qsgender.html, accessed 3 March 2004). With a higher age at marriage, Filipino women continue on to acquire higher education and have the possibility to engage in economic activities, including migration, with fewer constraints than if they had married earlier and bore children.

It is in the realm of economic activity where gender differentials are pronounced. Data from the most recent labour force survey (January 2003) revealed a labour force participation rate of 65.7 per cent, but it was 80.6 per cent for males compared with

50.9 per cent for females (www.census.gov.ph/data/quickstat/gsgender/html, accessed 3 March 2004). This does not take into account the unpaid work done by women or the other economic activities that they engage in which are not captured by official statistics. The migration of women in search of work says much about the economic role of women in the Filipino family and in larger society.

Data on internal migration reveal that the mobility of Filipino women has been higher compared to other Asian women and is more comparable with that of Latin American women (Eviota & Smith, 1984; Lauby & Stark, 1987).[22] In the Philippines, women were the majority of migrants in rural-urban migration. In particular, women in the ages of 15–34 years old were predominant among those moving into metropolitan areas (Ibarra, 1979:77). Manila was the target destination of those who sought greener pastures, with other regional centres playing a secondary role. The celebratory implications of women's mobility, however, have been tempered by the observation that women migrants were relegated to service and tertiary jobs. Concepcion and Smith (1977 as cited in Ibarra, 1979:77–8) found that male migrants to metropolitan areas had more job choices while female migrants were confined to three sectors: services, professional/sales and craft.[23] As domestic workers, hawkers and vendors, hostesses, massage attendants and related workers, women migrants are concentrated at low-end, lowly regarded and lowly paid jobs. From another perspective, others see women's migration and relatively easy entry into jobs in the service sector (particularly in domestic work) in less negative terms. The income may be low, but it is a relatively stable source of income, enabling women to remit to their households in the rural areas (e.g., Lauby & Stark, 1987).[24]

Apart from economic reasons, the internal migration of Filipino women also had other dimensions. A study on domestic workers to Metro Manila revealed the primacy of adventure–the desire to see Manila—as the most frequently cited reason (32 per cent) for coming to Manila, outranking the search for job (22 per cent) or the motivation to help the family (13 per cent). Women's migration was mostly from the rural areas directly to Metro Manila. Recruitment into the job was either by relatives or friends who also worked in the same occupation or by the employers themselves.[25] The role of the family in the migration of these young, single women is palpable in the parents' involvement in agreeing to their daughter's migration, the role of relatives in providing information about employment, accompanying women as they travel to Manila, or in providing shelter to newly arrived migrants who have yet to find jobs (Ibarra, 1979:80–1).

In the Philippines, thus, domestic work has been a traditional source of employment for women, and has served as a ticket to women's movement from the rural to urban areas. Involving mostly young and single women, the migration literature would later acknowledge the migration of women as autonomous migrants, not just as associational migrants. The idea of going out extended beyond Manila when opportunities for domestic work in foreign countries came up.

As this section has demonstrated, migration and domestic work in the Philippines are closely associated with each other. The next section shows how the international migration of women domestic workers is an extension of what has been observed in internal migration.

International Migration: Being a Foreign Domestic Worker

As mentioned earlier, in the 1970s, the typical migrant was a male 20–39 years old bound for the oil-rich Gulf countries. In contrast to the very visible and large-scale migration of male workers taking up work in the Middle East, an invisible, incipient but growing migration was taking place involving women migrating as domestic workers. Hong Kong was one of the nascent destinations of Filipino women in the 1970s. Initially, Filipino women went there to work for expatriate families, those in the diplomatic community and upper class Chinese families. As more Hong Kong women joined the labour market, more families resorted to the hiring of domestic workers. Today, Filipino women comprise the largest group of foreign domestic workers in Hong Kong.

The 1970s was also the period when Filipino women started arriving in Italy, Spain and Greece in small numbers (Barsotti & Lecchini, 1995; Lazaridis, 2000; Ribas-Mateos, 2000). Since they did not have working papers, their migration did not register as labour migration. It was years later, when Filipino communities had grown, that this migration became more visible. The trend in other countries is similar—Filipino women arriving in trickles, but growing consistently over the years, indicating the high demand for domestic workers. These trends suggest that the labour shortage in households in the more developed economies—or care deficit or care crisis as some would put it—has also become structural like the labour shortage in the public and formal sectors of the economy.[26]

In terms of internal migration in the Philippines, the rural women who work in domestic service in the urban areas generally have lower levels of education, which partly explains their entry in this kind of work. In international migration, Filipino domestic workers tend to have relatively more years of education not only vis-à-vis local migrants but also compared to other Asian women in similar jobs. This has puzzled observers who have wondered why these relatively educated women enter domestic work. Women's consideration of entering domestic work overseas sheds light on this issue:

... If you do not have much education, it is difficult to get a job [in the Philippines] and the pay is low. Over there, even if you are just a DH [domestic helper],[27] you will earn a bit more, and you can save because you only have one day off each month. You won't spend much, so you will save (Loida, returnee from Singapore, 2001 study).

Asked about the advantages of working as a domestic worker, Loida added, "It is easy in the sense that you can find work easily as a DH [domestic helper]; you can leave the Philippines in a short time".

Thus, even if women have the educational or work background for other jobs, domestic work is where the demand lies. The higher wages of domestic work abroad compared to non-domestic work in the local labour market compensates for the loss in status. Lita (2000 study), a former migrant who worked in Hong Kong for 16 years, said that since the available jobs in Hong Kong are mostly for domestic work, their background in the Philippines has become immaterial:[28]

> It's very rare to find [Filipino] women there who work in the banks or financial institutions. Almost everyone, even principals or whatever, everyone was a DH there. You have a nurse cleaning the toilet, a secretary cleaning the toilet. Why would you be ashamed? It is not a bad job. Except that, when you are there, you will have to swallow your pride. Even if you are a professional, there is only one job there. If here [Philippines] you are called madam, when you are there, you will have to address your employer as ma'am.

The disadvantages of domestic work are largely seen in terms of the employer's treatment. A respondent painted the grim prospect of ending up with a bad employer:[29]

> Yes, there are disadvantages. When you land a bad employer, especially the men, there is a disadvantage because they could take advantage of you. You can be maltreated, as what happens to the others. Those things happen. The others are even raped. Also, the Chinese, some women can get jealous. If your male employer shows some goodness, this can be misinterpreted (Ester, 32 years old, returnee from Singapore, 2001 study).

Thus many are aware of the dangers of domestic work but, armed with resolve and prayers, they push through with their plans in the hope of finding a good employer. Migrants, men and women alike, have come to view overseas employment as a challenge and as a test of their resolve and will. They have to meet many requirements before they can go abroad (they not only have to provide documentary evidence as part of the application process, they also have to pass tests and interviews; they have to put up placement fees or money to pay to the agencies for finding them jobs). Not even encounters with unscrupulous agencies or difficult employers can stop migrants—if one does not succeed with one recruitment agency, or with an employer, there is the hope that perhaps next time, they would have better luck. The belief in *suwerte* (luck) and/or faith in God sustains migrants' hopes. Linda, a 12-year Hong Kong veteran (2000 study), said that she had prepared for her migration to Hong Kong by expecting the worst and hoping for the best. Many use praying as a form of preparation. In addition, although the agencies also provide some orientation, they emphasise unquestioning obedience:

> That you obey, whatever work they ask you to do. You cannot say no, you have to obey what the employer and the agency say (Ester, 32 years old, returnee from Singapore, 2001 study).

> For example, if your employer forbids you to use the telephone, don't use it. Whatever your employer says, as long as you know that it is right, you obey, you follow, that's what we were told. When you are told, don't touch this, don't ... (Loida, returnee from Singapore, 2001 study).

Despite their determination to surmount whatever obstacles come their way, domestic work is far from easy, even for those who have a very good relationship with their employers:

> It's difficult ... because you have to do everything. From morning till night, from cooking, washing, ironing, cleaning, taking care of the children, that one, that was the most important (Clara, 33 years old, returnee from Singapore, 2001 study).

Ester said that the work was "mind-numbing", a description that echoes the comments of other domestic workers. The low status accorded to domestic workers was something that Linda battled by instilling in herself the idea that the employer was paying for just her labour, not her humanity (*"trabaho ko lang ang binabayaran nila, hindi ang aking pagkatao"*). Cultivating inner strength and the support of family, friends and migrants' groups in the destination help women migrants cope with domestic work and the separation from their families.

Employers as Family

In such an intimate setting as the household, those with good employers often come to have a family-like relationship with them:

> They do not tell me what to do. It's up to you whether you work or not, it depends on you. I have to do my job. [Interviewer: They don't check on you?] ... yes, it was up to me because I know that I was an employee ... I was still an employee. ... But they give me encouragement. And what's OK, if I want to go to mass, it was OK. I can go to mass everyday because the church is close, just one crossing away (Clara, 33 years old, returnee from Singapore, 2001 study).

> ... they did not treat me like a helper. In all things, my employer was open with me. We talk. They treated me like that. [Interviewer: And the children?] And the children, with one word, they obey me. When they introduce me, they don't introduce me as their helper, they say, "This is my friend." The others (i.e. other employers), they will say, "This is my maid" (Ester, 32, returnee from Singapore).

Ester added that being part of the family, she and her employer reached a comfort zone, such that she could answer back or argue with her employer (a "no-no", according to the orientation they received from the agencies). Like Clara, however, Ester was keenly aware of her "place": "I still knew my limitation ... that I was an employee, that I was a helper. Even if we were friends, I was a paid worker".

For the women, the relationship with employers becomes "family" when the latter show concern for them as persons, not just as workers. Some of the indicators that they are more than just workers are when they eat with their employers (or eat the same food), when they communicate, when trust has been established, and when the employer shows an interest in their families' welfare. This contrast with the detailed rules, regulations and schedule imposed on domestic workers in non-family-like relationships (e.g., Constable, 1997; 2003).

For observers, the slip into family-like status could be tricky as this could camouflage abuse or exploitation (e.g., see Constable, 2003).[30] The following account suggests that because the women regarded their employers as family, the women considered the likely impact of their decisions on their employers. Clara, for example, had planned on working for just one contract in Singapore before moving to Hong Kong. However, because her employer (and her employer's family members) treated her well, she stayed on with the family for eight years:

> ... I told myself, I might have a higher salary but if I will not be treated well, what good is that? It will not serve any purpose. They treated me well ... on my birthdays, they gave me gold, gestures like that ... on my birthdays, without fail, I have a cake to blow and ... outings.
> Because the kids were very close ... It seemed that God wanted me to take care of them, something like that... [Interviewer: You felt that way?] Because ... yeah ... those kids only had me. Their mother, their father, they were not around. I was the only one.

The sense of family responsibility prevented Clara from pursuing better wages in Hong Kong, but on the other hand, she also factored in the certainty of the good treatment accorded her by her employer. Her decision to stay was a combination of what was good for her "family" (employer) and what was good for her, similar to the integration of family and personal agendas in women's decision to migrate.

Even as migrants find new families in the destination, the family context of their employment also calls to mind painful realisations—that while they minister to their employer's children or elderly parents, these are responsibilities that they have relegated to other people in their own families.[31] For mothers, in particular, their absence in the day-to-day life of their children is a major source of pain that hits them in the course of doing care work for other people's children.

Options beyond Domestic Work and the Balance Sheet

In my studies of women migrants, it is remarkable how many of them have stayed for a long time with one employer.[32] In such cases, it would seem that the transition to family-like relationship is a factor in this development. For example, in a study of 100 female returnees (not limited to domestic workers, although they were the largest group), about 54 per cent had worked abroad for five years or less, and the remaining ones had worked abroad for five years or more (Asis, 2001).[33] In this sense, domestic work has become a "career". In Asian countries, this is largely a forced situation because migrant workers are not allowed to transfer to another occupation. In other countries, even if there is no policy to this effect, migrants of different ethnic groups have somehow become trapped in certain occupations.[34]

At least among the women that I have interviewed, almost everyone has not been able to move out of domestic work while they are abroad. The prospects for mobility are limited to moving to better employers or to engage in "cross-country" moves, i.e., to move from Singapore or Hong Kong to Canada or the United States of America. Hong Kong ranks high in Filipino women migrants' consideration of better prospects in Asia.

Overall, when the balance sheet is drawn, the consensus among women migrants is that all things considered, their sacrifice has been worth it both in terms of what their family has gained out of their labour abroad (including houses built, children or siblings who have completed an education, savings, and capital for small businesses), and for themselves, a wealth of experience gained in overcoming many obstacles and realising their self-worth.

PROMOTING THE RIGHTS OF WOMEN MIGRANTS: THE ROLE OF NGOS

Despite the efforts of the Philippine government to promote the rights of women migrants in the domestic sector and despite the efforts of migrants to help themselves, these have not been sufficient to ensure their protection. The persisting view of domestic work as non-work has effectively blocked discussions to set minimum standards and to increase workers' access to support and assistance.[35] The reluctance of receiving countries to sign bilateral agreements with countries of origin, and the lack of international instruments to protect the rights of migrants, particularly those in domestic work, are telling signs of the apathy of the international community to the concerns of migrants.[36] In Asia, the challenge is even greater because regional or government-to-government discussion on migration issues has been slow and limited.

The discussion of migrants' rights has been taken up by NGOs and civil society, whose involvement has been uneven in the region. Based on data collected in 1997, the number (38) of migrant NGOs operating in the Philippines at the time was the largest among the countries of origin, several of which specifically address the concerns of women in migration (Asis, 1998). NGOs providing services and/or promoting the rights of Filipino migrants have developed in various receiving countries, complementing the efforts of and/or cooperating with migrant NGOs operating in the Philippines. One of the important reference points showing the vitality of NGOs to mobilise migrants was the successful campaign initiated by the Filipino community in Hong Kong to protest the governments forced remittance policy in 1984–1985. A state directive (Executive Order 857) requiring migrant workers to remit 50–80 per cent of their salary to Philippine banks every month (otherwise their travel papers will not be processed by the Philippine Consulate) was repealed on 1 May 1985 (Kanlungan Centre Foundation, 1992:31). If this was the first landmark event, the most recent was the passage of the Overseas Absentee Voting Law (RA 9189) in February 2003, providing OFWs and overseas Filipinos the right to vote in national elections. Although many migrant NGOs in the Philippines continue to provide direct services and assistance, several NGOs have started to shift to other areas, notably programmes to prepare migrants and their families for the return and reintegration of migrants to Philippine society.

The emergence of NGOs and more collective efforts to promote the rights of Filipino workers in the destination countries has been offered as one of the reasons for the better protection of Filipino migrants compared to other Asian migrants. The problems Filipino migrants experience assume a public face because they tend to approach institutions or groups for assistance, more than other migrant groups.[37] The presence of the Catholic Church in many countries—a place that Filipinos seek out—has facilitated the discussion of common concerns and the identification of possible solutions. The experience of "People Power" in the Philippines has also contributed to Filipino migrants' ability to organise and mobilise actions to address their problems (O'Neill, 2001:47).

The empowerment of Filipino migrants, however, comes with a "price". Because they are more assertive of their rights, employers are turning to other Asian workers who are perceived to be more "docile" and "cheaper". In recent years, there has been a notable decline in the number of domestic workers from the Philippines and an increase in the number of women from Indonesia going to work in Hong Kong, Taiwan and Singapore, or women from Vietnam going to Taiwan. This suggests that NGOs have a long way to go in promoting solidarity among migrant workers and in advancing the rights of *all* migrants, a task that will require NGOs to strengthen transnational linkages.

DISCUSSION AND CONCLUSION

... part of what makes this country hopeless is the attitude that we can always leave the country by becoming overseas Filipino workers in Saudi or caregivers in the United States or Canada when it begins to look hopeless. Other Southeast Asians do not think that way (de Quiros, 2004).

In a country where 7.8 million of its people are based abroad, the idea of leaving the country has become commonplace. The growing pessimism in the country's future is fuelling the desire to make a life elsewhere. In 2002, a survey conducted by Pulse Asia revealed that one in five Filipinos has lost confidence in the country and would live abroad if given the chance (*Asian Migration News*, 30 June 2002). Those who live in Metro Manila and those in the upper socio-economic status were most likely to express the desire to go abroad. The survey also showed that those who had ever worked abroad and those who had some family members based abroad seemed more willing to migrate than the others (*Asian Migration News*, 30 June 2002).

The country's experience with large-scale migration in the last 30 years, the expansion of the migration tradition to different regions, the participation of men and women of different skills in seeking greener pastures, the networks that have been established in different parts of the world, and the birth of overseas Filipino communities living out their versions of remembered Philippines—all of these have somehow contributed to the ease and inclination to leave (or to consider leaving) at the sign of impending trouble. Observers attribute this weakening sense of nation and identity as one of the negative impacts of migration, part and parcel of the inestimable (but damaging) social costs of massive migration.

The alarm over growing materialism, the dependence on remittances from abroad, and the affront to national dignity when Filipino nationals are abused and exploited are some of the issues that have received attention. In the case of OFWs, particularly women migrants, the discussion on the social costs of migration is even more intense because of women's roles in the family. Concerns have also been raised about the protection and well-being of women migrants, considering that majority are working in unprotected sectors, and the impact of women's absence on the families left behind (particularly, the rearing of children). If Filipino women have proven that they can do well in the absence of men, there are doubts as to whether Filipino men can rise to the occasion in the absence of women. Limitations in research design and methodology (including the lack of men's voices in many of the existing studies) and the complexity of mapping out the social consequences of migration have kept us from making definitive conclusions. Research findings, however, point to the resilience of families in adjusting to the distribution of family members in different locales and in finding new ways of relating as family members in this age of migration (e.g., Asis et al., 2004). Communication has been the key in sustaining family relations and, in recent years, this has been facilitated by cheaper long-distance calls and the popularisation of cell phones. There are indications that gender roles are being reconfigured, as women assume the role of breadwinners. Even so, it appears that among Filipino families, the husband's role as head of the family has not been diminished. On the whole, children too seem to have adjusted to the absence of mothers, largely because of the extended family (e.g., Asis, 1995; Battistella & Conaco, 1998; Parreñas, 2003).

The impact of international migration in fostering transformative politics in the local front is one area that is worth looking into. The advocacy of migrant NGOs in the Philippines and their partners overseas in advancing the protection of the rights of Filipino workers in general, and women migrant workers in particular, has contributed to the higher level of protection of OFWs compared to other Asian migrants. There is networking among migrant NGOs in the Philippines and their counterparts abroad in this regard. Whether this cooperation and solidarity also extends to local issues calls for further study, particularly the question of whether migrant advocacy has had some influence on advocacy for the rights of local workers.[38] One local NGO that specifically caters to domestic workers, Visayan Forum (VF), has been at the forefront of pushing for the Magna Carta for Household Helpers/Domestic Workers (also known as *Batas Kasambahay*). According to VF president Ma. Cecilia Flores-Oebanda, the overseas migration of domestic workers has resulted in the involvement of younger women entering domestic work, a development which makes the Magna Carta timely because of its special provisions for minor domestic workers[39] (www.visayanforum. org/misc/magna_carta.html, accessed 1 March 2004).[40] Other initiatives to promote the basic protection and security for workers in the informal sector (which includes household workers) are also underway. The links (or their absence) in the advocacy for migrants' rights in the international front and the advocacy for the rights of local workers presents the possibility for migration to have a more positive impact on the country of origin. New developments such as the granting of absentee voting to OFWs and other overseas Filipinos and dual citizenship, both passed into law in 2003, may signal the greater political participation of Filipinos abroad in domestic matters. If migration could bring about improvements in the working and living conditions of local workers, this would be a much welcome change and proof that migration could also be a source of positive transformation.

NOTES

1   The large numbers of Filipino women working in private households the world over, including the rich and famous, have prompted one writer to quip that Filipino domestic workers are the Philippines' secret plan for "world domination".

2   Data on the gender distribution of *all* deployed OFWs—new hires and rehires, and both land-based and sea-based—are not readily available. Most likely, the gender distribution is less skewed when the total number of deployed OFWs is considered. Note that in the Survey of Overseas Filipinos of 2002, the gender distribution was 52 per cent males and 48 per cent females.

3   In POEA data, the category domestic workers included caregivers up until 2000; thereafter caregivers came under a separate category.

4   In Canada, Filipinos are the largest group who come under the Live-In Caregiver Program (see McKay, this volume).

5   Several years ago, the Philippine government protested the definition of "Filipineza" as domestic worker in a Greek dictionary. Earlier, the government also objected to the definition of "Filipino" as domestic worker in the Oxford dictionary.

6   Oishi (2001) provides an integrative and multi-level approach in explaining high female migration from the Philippines, Indonesia and Sri Lanka.

7   The Survey on Overseas Filipinos is a yearly survey undertaken by the National Statistics Office. The 2002 survey obtained data on OFWs working abroad for the period 1 April to 30 September 2002. More details are available at www.census.gov.ph/data/sectordata/2003/of0201.htm.

8   See http://www.migrationinformation.org/Feature/display.cfm?ID=137.

9   OFWs and overseas Filipinos have also been targeted to serve as the country's agents for promoting tourism. The Macapagal government has invented another term for OFWs, "overseas Filipino investors", owing to the investments in housing, education, etc. that OFWs' remittances go into.

10 On 7 June 1995, the Philippine government enacted the Migrant Workers and Overseas Filipinos Act (RA 8042), which seeks to protect and promote the welfare of migrant workers and their families. This has been commemorated since 1996. Recently, the commemoration includes the citation of individual OFWs or migrants' groups who have contributed to the betterment of overseas Filipinos.

11 I thank Vivienne Wee for her observation of this phenomenon as "migrantisation".

12 A separate government agency, the Commission on Filipinos Overseas (CFO), handles the concerns of emigrants or permanent settlers.

13 In the case of Indonesia and Sri Lanka, their late entry into the Middle East labour market is one reason why they concentrated on sending domestic workers.

14 According to Oishi (2001), policies on male labour migration were mostly economically driven whereas policies concerning female labour migration were value-driven, i.e., the latter had to consider protection issues.

15 Flor Contemplacion was a domestic worker who was hanged in Singapore for the death of another Filipino domestic worker and the child under the latter's care. Many Filipinos believed that Contemplacion was unjustly punished. For more details about the impact of this incident on migration policies in the Philippines, see Gonzales (1998).

16 Prior to RA 8042, some of the gender-specific measures aimed at protecting women migrants are: requiring a minimum age (which is revised from time to time) and requiring household workers, most of whom are women, to attend PDOS provided by NGOs rather than the recruitment agencies. Some NGOs have also prepared educational materials for women migrants, e.g., Kanlungan Centre Foundation, Inc.'s (1997) *Destination Middle East: A Handbook for Filipino Women Domestic Helpers*.

17 These two sections are among the most inconsistent (or at least contentious) provisions of RA 8042, and have been the subject of calls for amendments since soon after the law was passed.

18 In an interview with an officer of an association of recruitment agencies, he said that he was gearing his agency for the placement of highly skilled workers, such as IT workers and

nurses, because of the many problems that could arise with domestic workers. The joint and solitary liability provision of Section 10 in RA 8042 (i.e., the recruitment agency has joint accountability with the principal or employer in complaints relating to money claims) has prompted him to turn more towards less problematic workers. As he acknowledged, securing a good employer for domestic workers cannot be guaranteed.

19   Research on unauthorised migration from the Philippines indicates that migrants would have to engage the migration industry due to requirements to present at least travel papers to gain admission to foreign countries. For example, those who went to Italy on a tourist visa had had some dealings with the migration industry (Battistella & Asis, 2003).

20   An ongoing study by the Scalabrini Migration Center also gathered similar findings in focus group discussions conducted with husbands left behind.

21   I have changed the names of the respondents.

22   If the more liberal concept of circulation were used, female mobility in the Philippines would register higher levels. Aside from work, school-related movements are quite common—females and males are equally likely to live apart from their families when they attend school in town centres, cities or metropolitan areas. In our studies of female migration, we found many cases of women having migrated to other parts of the Philippines either as students, as workers or as visitors prior to overseas migration.

23   In the Philippines, the occupational distribution of women is marked by a large concentration in the services and a notable proportion in the professional category.

24   Trager (1988) found that women migrants in a secondary city like Dagupan (Pangasinan) had greater average earnings compared to women migrants in metropolitan areas. In secondary cities, women migrants could go into self-employment, a less stable but higher yield economic activity; in metropolitan areas, women migrants may be limited to paid jobs, such as domestic work, which are low paid but stable.

25   A study on local recruitment agencies in Metro Manila found that most of these agencies cater to the demand for domestic workers. Majority of the applicants in these agencies are women who are single and in the ages 15–50 years old (Institute of Labor and Manpower Studies, 1982:5–6).

26   The migration of entertainers (officially referred to as "Overseas Performing Artists" in the Philippines) to Japan is another female-dominated occupational category. They are classified as professionals. This migration is a controversial issue in the Philippines because of concerns that women are being channelled into prostitution. Also, the large numbers of children of Japanese-Filipino children who have been abandoned or not recognised by their Japanese fathers are among the unsettling consequences of this migration.

27   Given the Filipinos' penchant for abbreviations, DH has long been one of the common abbreviations to refer to a domestic helper.

28   Filipino men have also gone into domestic work in situations where it is the only option, e.g., in Italy (Barsotti & Lecchini, 1995).

29   Some of the cases that have come to the attention of NGOs and the media speak of horrific situations that some women migrants have experienced. Interestingly, stories such as these have also figured in migrants' decision-making, but not to the extent that they would be discouraged from leaving.

30   Constable (2003:135) relates an exchange among Filipino women comparing their work situations in Hong Kong: "One woman complained of overwork, and the other grumbled about her early curfew. A third woman suddenly cut in, and said in a serious tone, 'So you're a member of the family too, eh?' The crowd burst out laughing".

31   The work of Parreñas (2001) discusses in detail the many forms of displacement experienced by women migrants.

32   I recently had an opportunity to sit next to a migrant who was returning to Italy. She related that after 13 years of working in Italy, she still had a hard time saying goodbye to her family. As her children are already grown up and have families of their own, I asked her why she continues to work in Italy. She said that she could not just leave her elderly employer. Her employer has been good to her and allows her to call her family in the Philippines whenever she wants to.

33   In countries, such as the US and Italy, which allow long-term residence, women can stay for an extended of time (see Parreñas, 2001).

34   Fe Caces (1986) called this the double-edged effect of migrants' networks—on the one hand, they facilitate entry into the labour market, but on the other hand, they limit migrants into occupations familiar or known to the networks. Domestic work is one occupation that capitalises on networks and in the process becomes associated with a particular ethnic group.

35   Interestingly, the state in receiving countries has found ways to exercise surveillance over foreign domestic workers, but not enough efforts have been given to monitoring the working and living conditions of workers.

36   Although the International Convention on the Rights of Migrant Workers and All Members of Their Families went into force on 1 July 2003, all the ratifying countries are countries of origin. In Asia, only the Philippines and Sri Lanka have ratified the Convention.

37   I would speculate that educational attainment, access to networks, and having information on where to go are part of the reasons why they seek assistance more readily.

38   I thank Nicola Piper and Ronald Skeldon for raising this point.

39   The Magna Carta for Household Helpers or *Batas Kasambahay* (literally, Law on Companions at Home) prohibits the employment of children below 15 years of age into domestic work as well as the employment of minors, 15–17 years old, in hazardous working conditions (p.7). As part of child protection, RA 7658 (which amends RA 7610) prohibits the employment of children below 15 years of age and enforces requirements for child workers in the ages 16–18 years old (p.5) (www.visayanforum.org/misc/acrobat/kasambahayjournal.pdf, accessed 7 June 2004).

40   The bill was filed at the House of Representatives on 7 December 1999. Among others, the Magna Carta provides for increased minimum wage, a 13th month pay, social security, health insurance and assured days off. Aside from domestic workers, the bill also covers other household personnel, such as gardeners, babysitters and caregivers. Based on 1995 data from the National Statistics Office, which provide the first ever listing of household members which included domestic workers, there were 766,200 domestic workers nationwide. More updated figures reveal higher estimates. The Bureau of Women and Young Workers 2001 Regional Labor Force Statistics reported that there are about 1.1

million private households with employed persons. The Visayan Forum estimates that child domestic workers alone number about 1.1 million, a sector that is mostly invisible (www. visayanforum.org/misc/acrobat/ handbook_cdw.pdf, accessed 7 June 2004). As of 7 June 2004, the records in the House of Representatives show that the bill (previously recorded as HB00608 and substituted by HB05904) was approved in the House of Representatives on 2 June 2003 and had been transmitted to and received by the Senate on 4 June and 5 June 2003, respectively (www.congress.gov.ph/search/bills/qry_showbasic.php, accessed 7 June 2004). For other details and updates, see www.visayanforum.org/misc/acrobat/ kasambahayjournal.pdf, accessed 7 June 2004.

REFERENCES

Asian Migration News. 2002. 30 June. www.smc.org.ph/amnews/amn020630/amn020630. htm. Accessed 17 February 2004.

Asis, M. M. B. 1992. The overseas employment program policy. In *Philippine Labor Migration: Impact and Policy.* Edited by G. Battistella & A. Paganoni. Quezon City: Scalabrini Migration Center, 68–112.

_____. 1995. Overseas employment and social transformation in source communities: Findings from the Philippines. *Asian and Pacific Migration Journal,* 4(2–3), 327–46.

_____. 1998. Working with and for migrants: Migrant NGOs in Asia. Paper prepared for the International Migration and Policy Program, November 1999 in Bangkok, Thailand,.

_____. 2001. The return migration of Filipino women migrants: Home, but not for good. In *Female Labour Migration in South-East Asia: Change and Continuity.* Edited by C. Wille & B. Passl. Bangkok: Asian Research Centre for Migration, 23–93.

_____. 2002. From the life stories of Filipino women: Personal and family agendas in migration. *Asian and Pacific Migration Journal,* 11(1), 67–94.

Asis, M. M. B., S. Huang, & B. S. A. Yeoh. 2004. When the light of the home is abroad: Unskilled female migration and the Filipino family. *Singapore Journal of Tropical Geography,* 25(2), 198–215.

Bagley, C., S. Madrid, & F. Bolitho. 2001. Stress factors and mental health adjustment of Filipino domestic workers in Hong Kong. In *Filipinos in Global Migrations: At Home in the World?* Edited by F. V. Aguilar, Jr. Quezon City: Philippine Migration Research Network, 305–15.

Barsotti, O. & L. Lecchini. 1995. The experience of Filipino female migrants in Italy. In *International Migration Policies and the Status of Female Migrants.* Edited by United Nations. New York: United Nations, 153–64.

Battistella, G. & M. M. B. Asis. 2003. Irregular migration from the Philippines: The underside of the global migrations of Filipinos. In *Unauthorized Migration in Southeast Asia.* Edited by G. Battistella & M. M. B. Asis. Quezon City: Scalabrini Migration Center, 35–127.

Battistella, G. & M. C. Conaco. 1998. The impact of labour migration on the children left behind: A study of elementary school children in the Philippines. *Sojourn,* 13(3), 220–41.

Caces, F. 1986. Immigrant recruitment into the labor force: Social networks among Filipinos in Hawaii. *Amerasia,* 13(1): 23–38.

Constable, N. 1997. *Maid to Order in Hong Kong: Stories of Filipina Workers.* Ithaca: Cornell University Press.

————. 2003. Filipina workers in Hong Kong homes: Household rules and relations. In *Global Woman: Nannies, Maids and Sex Workers in the New Economy.* Edited by B. Ehrenreich & A. R. Hochschild. New York: Henry Holt and Company, 115–41.

de Quiros, C. 2004. Staying put. *Philippine Daily Inquirer,* 1 January, http://www.inq7.net/opi/2004/jan/01/txt/opi_csdequiros-1-p.htm. Accessed 21 February 2004.

Doyo, M. C. P. 2003. Homecoming. *Philippine Daily Inquirer,* 18 December, www.inq7.net/opi/2003/ dec18/opi_mdoyo-1.htm. Accessed 14 February 2004.

Ehrenreich, B. 2003. Maid to order. In *Global Woman: Nannies, Maids and Sex Workers in the New Economy.* Edited by B. Ehrenreich & A. R. Hochschild. New York: Henry Holt and Company, 85–103.

Eviota, E. & P. C. Smith. 1984 The migration of women in the Philippines. In *Women in the Cities of Asia: Migration and Urban Adaptation.* Edited by J. T. Fawcett, Siew-Ean Khoo & P. C. Smith. Boulder: Westview Press, 165–90.

Gonzales, J. III. 1998. *Philippine Labour Migration: Critical Dimensions of Public Policy.* Singapore: Institute of Southeast Asian Studies.

Hochschild, A. 2003. Love and gold. In *Global Woman: Nannies, Maids and Sex Workers in the New Economy.* Edited by B. Ehrenreich & A. R. Hochschild. New York: Henry Holt and Company, 15–30.

Ibarra, T. E. 1979. Women migrants: focus on domestic helpers. *Philippine Sociological Review,* 27(2), 77–92.

Institute of Labor and Manpower Studies. 1982. The private local recruitment agencies: Their modes of operation. 1980. *Studies on Philippine Labor,* Philippines: Institute of Labor and Manpower Studies, Ministry of Labor and Employment.

Jimenez-David, R. 2004. Subtext to a love story. *Philippine Daily Inquirer,* 14 February, www.inq7. net/opi/2004/feb14/opi_rjdavid-1.htm. Accessed 14 February 2004.

Kanlungan Centre Foundation. 1992. Overseas Filipina domestic helpers: Issues and problems. In *Filipino Women Overseas Contract Workers... At What Cost?* Edited by R. P. Beltran & A. J. de Dios. Manila: Women in Development Foundation, Inc. and Goodwill Trading Co. Inc., 29–36.

Lauby, J. & O. Stark. 1987. *Individual Migration as a Family Strategy: Young Women in the Philippines,* Discussion Paper No. 35, Migration and Development Program, Harvard University.

Lazaridis, G. 2000. Filipino and Albanian women migrant workers in Greece: Multiple layers of oppression. In *Gender and Migration in Southern Europe.* Edited by F. Anthias & G. Lazaridis. Oxford and New York: Berg, 49–80.

Migration Policy Institute. 2003. www.migrationinformation.org/USfocus/display.cfm?ID=137. Accessed 3 March 2004.

O'Neill, P. 2001. Caring for all migrants. *Asian Migrant,* 14(2), 45–53.

Oishi, N. 2001. *Women in motion: Globalization, state policies and labor migration in Asia.* Unpublished Ph.D. dissertation, Department of Sociology, Harvard University.

Parreñas, R. 2001. *Servants of Globalization: Women, Migration and Domestic Work.* Stanford: Stanford University Press.

_____. 2003. The care crisis in the Philippines: Children and transnational families in the new global economy. In *Global Woman: Nannies, Maids and Sex Workers in the New Economy.* Edited by B. Ehrenreich & A. R. Hochschild. New York: Henry Holt and Company, 39–54.

Philippine Overseas Employment Administration (POEA). 1997. *Migrant Workers and Overseas Filipinos Act of 1995 (Republic Act No. 8042 and its Implementing Rules and Regulations),* 3rd printing, Mandaluyong City: POEA.

Ribas-Mateos, N. 2000. Female birds of passage: Leaving and settling in Spain. In *Gender and Migration in Southern Europe.* Edited by F. Anthias and G. Lazaridis. Oxford and New York: Berg, 173–98.

Scalabrini Migration Center (SMC). 1997. *Pre-departure Information Programs for Migrant Workers.* A research project commissioned by the International Organization for Migration, Philippines: Scalabrini Migration Center.

Sto. Tomas, P. 2002. Managing the overseas migration program: Lessons learned and new directives. *Asian Migrant,* 15(4), 94–8.

Suzuki, N. 2002. Gendered surveillance and sexual violence in Filipina pre-migration experiences to Japan. In *Gender Politics in the Asia-Pacific Region.* Edited by B. S. A. Yeoh, P. Teo & S. Huang. London and New York: Routledge, 99–119.

Tacoli, C. 1999. International migration and the restructuring of gender asymmetries: continuity and change among Filipino migrants in Rome. *International Migration Review,* 33(3), 658–82.

Tan, E. 2001. Labor market adjustments to large scale emigration: The Philippine case. *Asian and Pacific Migration Journal,* 10(3), 379–400.

Trager, L. 1988. *The City Connection: Migration and Family Interdependence in the Philippines,* Ann Arbor: University of Michigan Press.

Truong, T-D. 1996. Gender, international migration and social reproduction: Implications for theory, policy, research and networking. *Asian and Pacific Migration Journal,* 5(1), 27–52.

United Nations. 2002. *Human Development Report 2002.* New York and Oxford: Oxford University Press.

Villalba, M. A. M. 2002. *Good Practices for the Protection of Filipino Women Migrants in Vulnerable Jobs.* Geneva: ILO.

CHAPTER 2

Indonesian International Domestic Workers: Contemporary Developments and Issues

GRAEME HUGO

INTRODUCTION

In the transformation which has occurred in global international population mobility in the last two decades, four trends stand out. First, there has been an exponential increase in circulation as opposed to permanent migration from one country to another such that some have called for the concept of international migration being replaced by that of transmigration or transnationalism which involves frequent movement between origin and destination areas (Glick Schiller et al., 1995). Second, international *labour* migration has increased exponentially but it has "bifurcated" between highly skilled groups for whom transfer between nations has become easier and unskilled groups for whom such movement has been made more difficult. Third, women have become more significant in global mobility such that they now dominate many important international migration flows. Fourth, the scale of undocumented movement has greatly increased, as has the involvement of people smugglers and traffickers in international migration. One global international flow which has greatly increased in scale and significance during this period and in many ways encapsulates these four elements, is the transnational flow of domestic workers. As one of the world's poorest and largest labour surplus nations, Indonesia has become one of the largest suppliers of unskilled labour to wealthier nations and one of the major elements in this has been the outflow of Indonesians, overwhelmingly women, to work as domestics.

This paper outlines first of all, the growth in the flow of female domestic workers out of Indonesia over the last two decades as well as the changing origins and destinations of those workers. The flow of Indonesian overseas contract workers (OCWs) as domestics (henceforth referred to in this paper as domestic OCWs) has a number of distinctive characteristics: the bulk of women moving are from rural Indonesia and from relatively poor areas, and they have a high rate of non-fulfilment of contracts and premature return. The paper then examines a number of issues relating

54

to Indonesian domestic OCWs. The first set of issues relates to their recruitment, training and preparation of overseas work. The second revolve around their experience in destination countries and the failure to develop adequate protection mechanisms for them when in destination countries. The third set of issues examined relate to the return of female domestic workers to Indonesia and the impact that their migration has on their role and status as well as on the economic and social well-being of their families and communities of origin. The final part of the paper addresses policy issues relating to Indonesian domestic OCWs and some future issues in this movement. There has been a failure to develop adequate policies and protection for this group despite several decades of experience. Yet the outflow will undoubtedly continue for several decades and will continue to grow in scale. There is a need for a parametric shift in the development of policy and programmes in this area in Indonesia. The perspective taken in the paper is predominantly from the perspective of the sending country.

In assessing the situation with respect to Indonesian international domestic worker migrants, there are a number of obstacles. First, it is difficult to establish the number of women involved in the movement since data are only collected on those migrant workers who go through official channels and a substantial number either leave the country clandestinely or use non-working visas. Second, there is little research conducted on Indonesian workers in destination areas and much of this is in a narrow range of destinations like Singapore. In several destination areas, it is very difficult to gain access to the women for research purposes. The high degree of their exploitation in Indonesia also makes it difficult to carry out research with a representative group of these women.

TRENDS IN THE OUTFLOW OF INDONESIAN DOMESTIC WORKERS

Indonesian labour migration can be differentiated between that which passes through official channels and that which does not. Table 2.1 shows the annual changes in the number of *official* Indonesian OCWs, which have occurred over the last quarter century. Two features of the table stand out: there is a general pattern of growth in the numbers deployed overseas over the last two decades; and the movement has been consistently dominated by women. There also have been some apparent fluctuations in numbers.

The apparent downturn in movement in 1995–96 was due to the exclusion of some workers from the data while the exceptional numbers in 1996–97 includes a large number of workers already in Malaysia who received an amnesty (Hugo, 2000a). The downturn in recent years is also partly due to the expulsion of Indonesia workers in Malaysia following efforts by the then Prime Minister of Malaysia to replace Indonesians with other international workers (Inglis, 2002). However, following the devolution of power after the fall of President Suharto in 1998, it is apparent that provincial reporting of statistics to Jakarta became less complete than it had

TABLE 2.1   Number of Indonesian overseas workers processed by the Ministry of Manpower, 1969–2003

Year (Single year)	Middle East		Malaysia/ Singapore		Other		Total	Per cent change over previous Year	Sex ratio (Males/ 100 Females)
	No.	%	No.	%	No.	%	No.		
2003[a]	116,018	65	51,022	29	11,832	7	178,872	n.a.	35
2002	241,961	50	168,751	35	69,681	14	480,393	+42	32
2001[b]	121,180	36	144,785	43	73,027	21	338,992	−22	80
2000[c]	129,165	30	217,407	50	88,647	20	435,219	+2	46
1999	154,636	36	204,006	48	68,977	16	427,619	n.a.	41
1999–2000[c]	153,890	38	187,643	46	62,990	16	404,523	−2	44
1998–99	179,521	44	173,995	42	58,153	14	411,609	+75	28
1997–98	131,734	56	71,735	30	31,806	14	235,275	−55	20
1996–97	135,336	26	328,991	64	52,942	10	517,269[d]	328	79
1995–96	48,298	40	46,891	39	25,707	21	120,896	−31	48
1994–95	99,661	57	57,390	33	19,136	11	176,187	10	32
1993–94	102,357	64	38,453	24	19,185	12	159,995	−7	36
1992–93	96,772	56	62,535	36	12,850	7	172,157	15	54
1991–92	88,726	59	51,631	34	9,420	6	149,777	74	48
1990–91	41,810	48	38,688	45	5,766	7	86,264	3	73
1989–90	60,456	72	18,488	22	5,130	6	84,074	37	35
1988–89	50,123	82	6,614	11	4,682	8	61,419	1	29
1987–88	49,723	81	7,916	13	3,453	6	61,092	11	35
1986–87	45,405	66	20,349	30	2,606	4	68,360	23	61
1985–86	45,024	81	6,546	12	4,094	7	54,297	21	44
1984–85	35,577	77	6,034	13	4,403	10	46,014	57	79
1983–84	18,691	64	5,597	19	5,003	17	29,291	38	141
1982–83	9,595	45	7,801	37	3,756	18	21,152	18	n.a.
1981–82	11,484	65	1,550	9	4,570	26	17,604	11	n.a.
1980–81	11,231	70	564	4	4,391	27	16,186	56	n.a.
1979–80	7,651	74	720	7	2,007	19	10,378	n.a.	n.a.
1977	n.a.	n.a.	n.a.	n.a.	n.a.	n.a.	3,675	n.a.	n.a.

(cont'd next page)

TABLE 2.1 Number of Indonesian overseas workers processed by the Ministry of Manpower, 1969–2003 (cont'd)

Five Year planning periods:		Target	Total deployed
Repelita VII	1999–2004	2,800,000	1,201,830[e]
Repelita VI	1994–99	1,250,000	1,461,236
Repelita V	1989–94	500,000	652,272
Repelita IV	1984–89	225,000	292,262
Repelita III	1979–84	100,000	96,410
Repelita II	1974–79	none set	17,042
Repelita I	1969–74	none set	5,624

SOURCES: Suyono, 1981; Singhanetra-Renard, 1986:52; Pusat Penelitian Kependudukan, Universitas Gadjah Mada, 1986:2; Indonesia, Department of Labour, unpublished data; Departemen Tengara Kerja, Republic of Indonesia, 1998:14; Soeprobo, 2003; 2004.

NOTES:

a   To September 2003.

b   From 2001 the Ministry of Manpower was decentralised and there was less compulsion for regional offices to report the numbers of OCWs deployed to the central office.

c   In 2000, the Indonesian government transferred to a calendar year system of accounting (they previously used 1 April–31 March).

d   Year in which more than 300,000 Malaysian labour migrants were regularised (194,343 males and 127,413 females).

e   1 January 1999 to 30 September 2003.

been previously (Personal communication, officials from the Department of Labour, February 2000).

While there is a long tradition of women in Indonesia migrating to cities to work as domestics within the nation, there is not as long a history of them moving internationally. Most of the pre-independence international labour migration of Indonesians was of male "contract coolies" (Hugo, 1980). There was migration to Saudi Arabia of people going on the *haj* (pilgrimage) and staying on to work there but they also were predominantly men (Harun, 1984). Harun (1984) notes that the flow of substantial numbers of Indonesians to work in Saudi Arabia as domestics began in 1977 when a businessman in Jakarta, Saleh Alwaini sought permission from the Manpower Department to send 20 women to work as domestics in Saudi Arabia. He had, the previous year, sent 240 men to work there. While he readily got permission to send the men to Saudi Arabia, he was refused permission to send the women so he sent them on a *haj* visa. This is a practice which has continued over the subsequent half century, especially during periods when the sending of women domestic workers to the Middle East has been banned in Indonesia.

The dominance of women in the official outflow of labour migrants has been a consistent feature of the movement over the last two decades. Table 2.2 shows that in the 1994–99 period, three quarters of Indonesian official labour migrants went to two nations—Malaysia (38.1 per cent) and Saudi Arabia (37.7 per cent). In both nations women migrants outnumbered males, although in Malaysia they only slightly outnumbered males, whereas in Saudi Arabia there were 12 females for every male. Females were overwhelmingly dominant in flows to Singapore and Hong Kong while those to South Korea and Taiwan were male dominant. Among the OCWs deployed from Indonesia during the Sixth Five-Year Plan (1994–99), 2,042,206 were women compared with 880,266 men.

Table 2.3 demonstrates that the outflow of Indonesian domestic workers has increased but Table 2.4 indicates that there has been significant shifts in the balance of destination countries. The Middle East is an important destination and is dominated by

TABLE 2.2 Indonesia: Destinations of overseas workers in the Sixth Five Year Plan Period, 1994–1999

Destination	No.	%	Sex ratio[a]
Asia Pacific	848,543	58.1	79.9
Malaysia	556,575	38.1	96.1
Singapore	146,427	10.0	22.9
Taiwan	44,851	3.1	152.9
South Korea	37,288	2.6	524.7
Hong Kong	35,140	2.4	1.7
Brunei	14,040	1.0	28.3
Japan	12,274	0.8	4620.7
Other Asia	1,943	0.1	16,091.7
America	12,833	0.9	40,003.1
Europe	5,204	0.4	7,667.1
Middle East/Africa	594,656	40.6	8.3
Saudi Arabia	550,218	37.7	8.5
United Arab Emirates	41,768	2.9	2.6
Other Middle East/Africa	2,670	0.2	74.2
Total	1,461,236	100.0	43.1

SOURCE: *Depnaker*, unpublished data.
NOTE:
a Males per 100 females.

TABLE 2.3   Sector of employment of official workers deployed overseas, Pelita IV, V and VI

Sector	Pelita IV 1984–99		Pelita V 1989–94		Pelita VI 1994–99		1999–2000 (Oct.)	
	No.	%	No.	%	No.	%	No.	%
Plantations	34,398	11.8	144,403	22.1	158,994	10.9	189,397	22.0
Transport	41,438	14.2	92,882	14.2	103,097	7.1	41,424	4.8
Construction	4,409	1.5	624	0.1	102,920	7.0	7,995	0.9
Energy and Water	760	0.3	6,151	0.9	1	-	57	-
Hotel/Catering	958	0.3	124	-	1,808	0.1	198	-
Commerce/Finance	5,189	1.8	349	-	305,286	20.9	105,433	12.2
Mining/Oil	19	-	3,385	5.2	4	-	-	-
Manufacturing	12	-	13,863	2.1	199,390	13.6	189,945	22.0
Domestic Service	205,079	70.2	389,706	59.7	589,736	40.4	358,439	41.5
Other	-	-	785	0.1	-	-	-	-
Total	292,262	100.0	652,272	100.0	1,461,236	100.0	862,838	100.0

SOURCE: *Depnaker*, unpublished data.

Saudi Arabia. Table 2.4 also shows that over the 1984–2000 period, the flow continued to increase and more than a million Indonesian women were sent to Saudi Arabia; and the Indonesian Embassy in Riyadh reported that 92 per cent of Indonesian workers in the country were domestics (Anon, 1997). Although Saudi Arabia dominates the Middle Eastern flow, the movement to the United Arab Emirates has increased from zero in the early 1980s to 40,710 in 1994–99 and 26,573 in 1999–2000. In 1999–2000 there were 7,778 women sent to Kuwait (and only 215 men) and 1,228 (and 282 men) were sent to Qatar. Hence, the Middle Eastern flow has become slightly more diversified in recent years.

Table 2.4 indicates that the migration of Indonesian women to work as domestics in Asia is more recent. In 1984–89, there were only 11,031 Indonesian women who moved as labour migrants to the five major Asian destinations compared to 186,052 going to Saudi Arabia. By 1999–2000, however, they numbered 339,912 compared to 220,003 going to Saudi Arabia. The largest outflow to Asia is currently to neighbouring Malaysia where the legal movement of labour migrants until the 1990s was very male dominated. The second half of the 1990s saw a massive increase in the number of women moving to Malaysia to work as domestics and in this period there was a more or less equal number of males and females in the flow. Singapore has been the second major destination but Indonesian labour migration to the island has been dominated by women since the late 1980s and currently, nine out of ten Indonesian labour migrants

TABLE 2.4 Major destinations of official Indonesian female labour migrants, 1984–2000

Destination		Number of female migrant workers	Sex ratio[a] of total movement
Malaysia	1999–2000	174094	107.3
	1994–99	283822	96.1
	1989–94	52754	196.3
	1984–89	6606	422.0
Singapore	1999–2000	54608	10.9
	1994–99	119143	22.9
	1989–94	28951	68.9
	1984–89	3602	192.5
Brunei	1999–2000	8119	33.6
	1994–99	10943	28.3
	1989–94	9009	13.2
	1984–89	783	17.5
Hong Kong	1999–2000	34423	0.1
	1994–99	34553	1.7
	1989–94	3615	46.7
	1984–89	40	423.8
Taiwan	1999–2000	68668	16.3
	1994–99	17735	152.9
	1989–94	981	704.1
	1984–89	0	—
Saudi Arabia	1999–2000	220003	11.5
	1994–99	507113	8.5
	1989–94	342028	12.5
	1984–89	186052	20.2
United Arab Emirates	1999–2000	26573	2.1
	1994–99	40710	2.6
	1989–94	2080	11.7
	1984–89	0	—

SOURCE: Indonesian Manpower Department, unpublished data.
NOTE:
a   Males per 100 females.

to Singapore are female domestic workers. The oil rich small country of Brunei has had a significant inflow of Indonesian domestic workers for more than two decades.

A feature of the last decade has been the extension of the countries to which substantial numbers of female Indonesian domestic workers have gone to—Hong Kong and then Taiwan. This has occurred to such an extent that in 1999–2000, Taiwan was the third largest single destination of Indonesian female migrant workers. Table 2.4 indicates that in Hong Kong virtually all of the Indonesian migrant workers were female domestic workers. In Taiwan, the initial movement of Indonesian workers was overwhelmingly male until the late 1990s when the flow of domestic workers increased greatly.

The increasing diversity of Asian destinations for Indonesian domestic workers reflects the increasing differentiation of the economic and labour market gradients between Asian countries, which has seen several nations with rapidly growing economies and slow population growth, seek overseas workers in selected areas of the labour market including domestic service. Filipinos were the main group initially recruited as domestics in countries like Singapore, Malaysia, Hong Kong and Taiwan. However, Indonesians have increasingly replaced them. This is due to several factors. One is the higher wages paid to Filipino domestic workers but also Indonesian labour agents and recruiters have extended their activities within the Asian region. Moreover, the Indonesian government has become more active in Asia seeking out more markets for Indonesian workers. It would seem that now the numbers of Indonesian women working as domestics in foreign Asian nations is larger than the number of Filipinos. In the 1990s, Indonesia has emerged as one of the world's major origin countries of foreign domestic workers and now rivals the Philippines in this respect.

It is difficult to establish the impact on domestic worker migration of the massive changes in Indonesia following the 1997 financial crisis and the replacement of President Suharto in 1998. This is partly due to the deterioration in Department of Labour data on overseas workers since then. Field evidence (e.g., see Romdiati et al., 1998; Hugo, 2002a), however, would suggest that the pressures on women to work as domestics overseas have increased and it is likely that the numbers involved have increased. It is apparent, for example, in West Java that many households adapted to the financial crisis by raising funds to send women overseas to work as domestics (Romdiati et al., 1998). There appears to be an association between the increases in unemployment and underemployment following the crisis and the increasing outflow of Indonesian women to work as domestics in recent years (Hugo, 2002a).

It is important to note that women labour migrants from Indonesia are not drawn randomly from across Indonesia nor are they all drawn from the same areas as male labour migrants. This is evident from Table 2.5, which shows that Java supplied 59.2 per cent of male migrant workers in 1989–94, which is in approximate proportion to its share of the national population. However, Java supplied 88.6 per cent of female migrant workers. Indeed more than one in three official labour migrants leaving Java to work in foreign countries are female, whereas in the rest of Indonesia males outnumber females—85,561 to 50,381. Outside of Java, the sex ratio among labour migrants is

TABLE 2.5 Indonesia: Provinces of origin of official labour migrants by gender, 1989–1994

Destination	Male	Female	Total	Sex ratio[a]
Sumatra				
Aceh	3,033	28	3,061	10832.1
North Sumatra*	1,203	1,369	2,572	87.9
West Sumatra	77	50	127	154.0
South Sumatra	343	158	501	217.1
Riau*	10,114	15,765	25,879	64.2
Jambi	13	-	13	-
Lampung*	360	855	1,215	42.1
Benkulu*	5	7	12	71.4
Total Sumatra*	15,104	18,276	33,380	82.6
Java				
Jakarta	21,714	7,804	29,518	278.2
Yogyakata*	665	2,981	3,646	22.3
West Java*	67,362	228,669	296,031	29.5
Central Java*	15,870	88,112	103,982	18.0
East Java*	19,336	63,816	83,152	30.3
Total Java*	124,407	391,922	516,329	31.7
Kalimantan				
West Kalimantan	1,844	112	1,956	1646.4
East Kalimantan	42,654	11,711	54,365	364.2
South Kalimantan*	42	150	192	28.0
Central Kalimantan			-	-
Total Kalimantan	44,540	11,973	56,513	372.0
Sulawesi				
North Sulawesi	108	8	116	1350.0
South Sulawesi	11,086	2,476	13,562	447.7
Central Sulawesi	1,014	284	1,298	357.0
Southeast Sulawesi*	-	6	6	-
Total Sulawesi	12,208	2,774	14,982	440.1

(cont'd next page)

TABLE 2.5 Indonesia: Provinces of origin of official labour migrants by gender, 1989–1994 (cont'd)

Other Islands				
West Nusatenggera*	10,018	14,791	24,809	67.7
East Nusatenggera	3,164	2,515	5,679	125.8
Bali	491	52	543	944.2
Maluku	24	-	24	-
Irian Jaya	12	-	12	-
Total Other Islands*	13,709	17,358	31,067	79.0
Total	**209,968**	**442,303**	**652271**	**47.5**

SOURCE: Indonesian Department of Labour, unpublished data.
NOTES: a Males per 100 females.
    * Females outnumber males.

169.8 males per 100 females compared to 31.7 in Java. Moreover, it is clear that the outer island areas with substantial numbers of female OCWs include women originally from Java. Within Java, the province of West Java is by far the most important source of migrant labour, accounting for 51.6 per cent of all female labour migrants and 32.1 per cent of male labour migrants.

Why is West Java the dominant origin of female domestic workers? The dominant ethnic group in the province are Sundanese and traditionally, Sundanese women have had a much lower rate of female labour force participation than the national average and below that of the rest of Java. This has been attributed to cultural differences and a longstanding pattern of Sundanese women of West Java being subject to greater cultural constraints when working outside the home than their Javanese counterparts (Hugo, 1992). Clearly, there are other factors involved, including:

- the proximity of West Java to Jakarta, the main point from which labour migrants are sent overseas;
- the long history of activity of recruiters working in West Java to recruit workers for Jakarta but also for plantations which historically were concentrated in West Java in the nineteenth century (Hugo, 1975); and
- the operation of migrant networks and cumulative causation (Massey et al., 1993), which has seen overseas labour migration becoming "normal" in some regions of West Java.

One important feature of the origins of female domestic worker migrants is that they are overwhelmingly recruited from rural areas and, in general, from poorer rural areas. This is apparent in a range of surveys of these workers in Indonesia (Mantra et al., 1986; Pusat Penelitian Kependudukan, 1986; Adi, 1996; Dorall & Paramasivam, 1992; Yayasan Pengembangan Pedesaan, 1992; Graham, 1997; Nasution, 1997; Spaan, 1999; Hugo, 2000a; Mujiyani, 2000; Pujiastuti, 2000). In this context, it is interesting that in Jakarta, Indonesia's largest metropolitan centre, males dominate among labour migrants (Table 2.5).

In the Outer Islands, the largest numbers of female labour migrants are from the two "gateway" provinces of Riau and East Kalimantan. Riau is a major place from which migrants enter West Malaysia and Singapore to which they are very close while Nunukan in East Kalimantan is the main point of entry into the important destination of Sabah in East Malaysia (Hugo, 2000a). The third origin of significance is West Nusa Tenggara to the east of Java where international labour migration has become an important part of the economy (Mujiyani, 2000).

The official OCW movements briefly discussed above, however, are only part of Indonesia's international labour emigration. Indeed, documented labour migration is almost certainly greater in scale than the documented movement. Overwhelmingly, the main destination of undocumented workers is the neighbouring country of Malaysia although there are important flows to other nations as well. This movement has a long history which predates the formation of independent nations, or even colonies of European countries (Hugo, 1993; Wong and Teuku Anwar, 2003). Moreover, there is a great deal of ethnic, religious and linguistic similarity between Indonesians and the Malay majority in Malaysia. The numbers involved, of course, are not known. However, at the 1997 Indonesian elections, 1.4 million Indonesian citizens resident in Malaysia voted and the Malaysian government Immigration Department put the number of Indonesian workers resident in Malaysia at 1.9 million (Kassim, 1997). Much of the Indonesian undocumented migration involves the OCWs taking up low paid, low status jobs eschewed by Malaysians. There are two overlapping systems of undocumented migration from Indonesia to Malaysia shown in Figure 2.1. The first system focuses on Peninsular Malaysia and involves Indonesians largely from Sumatra, Java and Lombok while the second involves movement from Eastern Indonesia to Sabah and, to a lesser extent, Sarawak.

While undocumented migration out of Indonesia takes a myriad of forms, it can be broadly divided into three types:

- Migrant workers who enter the destination countries clandestinely and do not pass through any official border checkpoints. The main example in Indonesia is the large numbers who enter Malaysia across the Malacca Straits from the Indonesian province of Riau to the coasts of Johore in Malaysia.
- Those who enter a country legally but overstay their visa. An example of this is the large numbers who enter Sabah in East Malaysia through the Indonesian province of East Kalimantan.

FIGURE 2.1 Major routes of undocumented migration from Indonesia to Malaysia

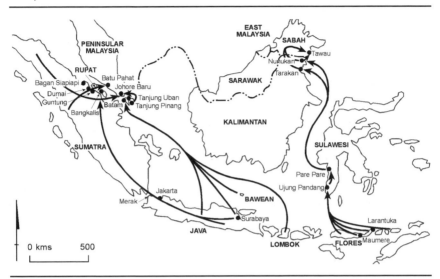

- Another important group enters the destination country under a non-working visa but proceeds to seek and obtain work there. Two important examples from Indonesia are first, those (mainly women) who enter Saudi Arabia on an *umroh*[1] visa but once they are in, seek and obtain work (personal communication, Department of Labour). In fact, in most cases the work is already arranged in advance. One estimate of the number of Indonesians living and working illegally in Saudi Arabia after entering under an *umroh* visa is 150,000, with 80 per cent being women (*Jakarta Post*, 11 November 1997). A second example relates to Indonesians at Malaysian border posts like Nunukan in East Kalimantan obtaining a visiting pass but instead working inside Malaysia.

It is, of course, difficult to establish with certainty the characteristics of undocumented Indonesian migrant workers and involvement of women. Some undocumented flows are dominated by women, such as the movement of undocumented workers to Saudi Arabia. It would seem that, unlike the documented flows, men probably outnumber women among undocumented migrant workers leaving Indonesia; however, there are indications that the proportion of the latter is increasing. The trend of increasing female participation over time is also evident in the outflow of migrant workers from East Flores to Sabah. Whereas the movement was previously dominated by males, women now make up a significant part of the migration as is evident in a village surveyed in East Flores. Table 2.6 shows that women made up a quarter of the migrants detected in the survey.

The fact that the involvement of women in the migration out of East Flores is predominantly a recent phenomenon is evident in Figure 2.2, which depicts the years

TABLE 2.6   East Flores survey village: Numbers of migrants surveyed

	Males		Females		Total
Migrants	**No.**	**%**	**No.**	**%**	
Returned	91	73	34	27	125
Still away	92	79	24	21	116
Total	183	76	58	24	241

FIGURE 2.2   Survey village: Number of migrants by sex, 1976–1996

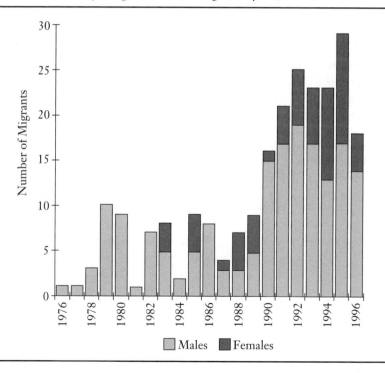

in which each of the migrants included in the survey first went to Malaysia. Overall, while just over half of men had left since 1990 (53 per cent), this was the case for almost three-quarters of the women (72 per cent).

Table 2.7 shows the gender breakdown of deportees. It indicates that women made up a third of those deported who had entered Malaysia with a passport and entry pass, and less than a quarter of those who entered Malaysia without documentation were women. It is noticeable that women were strongly represented among the deportees who had originally come from East Nusa Tenggara, East Java, East Kalimantan and South Sulawesi.

The evidence is clear then that women now make up a significant proportion of migrant workers travelling from Eastern Indonesia into Sabah. In a study of a village in East Flores carried out in the late 1980s, Graham (1997) was able to trace migration by village men back to the 1940s, but the movement of single women did not begin until the late 1970s. According to Graham (1997), the first female migrants from the survey village travelled to Malaysia accompanying husbands or in some cases to look for their husbands who had been absent for long periods.

Establishing which parts of Indonesia undocumented migrants come from is difficult but the deportation data for Sabah shows a concentration from the provinces of South Sulawesi, Nusa Tenggara and East Java (Table 2.7). Table 2.8 shows results of two surveys

TABLE 2.7   Undocumented Indonesian workers deported from Tawau (Sabah) to East Kalimantan, January 1994 to June 1996

Province of origin	Males No.	Females No.	Per cent females	Total
Entered Malaysia with documentation				
South Sulawesi	8,604	4,798	35.8	13,402
East Nusa Tenggara	6,871	3,923	36.3	10,794
East Java	2,428	1,512	38.4	3,940
West Nusa Tenggara	4,180	808	13.3	4,988
Southeast Sulawesi	1,029	244	19.0	1,283
Central Sulawesi	152	52	25.4	204
East Kalimantan	343	279	53.4	522
Other	594	275	31.6	869
Total	24,111	11,891	33.0	36,002
Entered Malaysia without any documentation				
All Indonesia	14,033	3,897	22.4	17,430

SOURCE: Provincial Development Office of East Kalimantan, Samarinda, unpublished data.

TABLE 2.8 Origin of female overseas migrant workers in various studies

	Kuala Lumpur[a]	Registered workers in Indonesian Embassy, Kuala Lumpur[b]	Return arrivals in Jakarta[c]
Java	50.3	70.0	87.5
Sumatra	43.2	13.1	–
Flores	0.7	–	–
Lombok	1.4	14.4	12.5
Other	–	2.5	–
Total	141	397	40

SOURCES: [a]Dorall and Paramasivam, 1992; [b]Nasution, 1997; [c]Pujiastuti, 2000.

of undocumented migrants in Kuala Lumpur and indicates that most came from Java and Sumatra. It is apparent from the surveys too that as is the case with documented migration, the movement of female undocumented OCWs is absolutely dominated by women working in the domestic sector, although the movement of women involved in the so called entertainment sector is also of significance (Hugo, 2002a).

There are also reports of undocumented migration of Indonesian women to work as domestics in other nations. For example, it was reported that "the illegal impact of domestic workers from Indonesia is a big business responding to the rising demand for baby sitters and cleaners by Dutch families and elderly people in the Netherlands" (*Jakarta Post*, 7 April 2001).

It is very difficult to estimate the stock of female Indonesian domestic workers in foreign nations. Table 2.9 presents some estimates. At any single time, a minimum of 600,000 and perhaps in excess of one million Indonesian women are working as domestics in foreign nations. Of course since the movement is circular, the number of households in Indonesia who have been affected by the migration of female domestic workers is substantially greater.

DRIVERS OF MIGRATION OF DOMESTIC WORKERS

Indonesia has become one of the world's major sources of domestic workers although the history of this type of movement extends over only a quarter of a century. What are the drivers which have seen Indonesia become one of the world's pre-eminent sources of domestic workers? Undoubtedly, one element has been the increasing global demand for such workers in the Middle East and the fast growing economies of Asia matched with the continuing labour surplus in Indonesia, a factor exacerbated by

TABLE 2.9   Estimates of stock of Indonesian female domestic overseas contract workers, 2001–2003

Country	Number	Source(s)
Saudi Arabia	200–330,000	*Kompas*, 17 March 2001; *Migration News*, 2 April 2003.
Malaysia	200–260,000	*Kompas*, 17 March 2001; *Asian Migration News*, 1–15 March 2003.
Hong Kong	80,000	*Asian Migration News*, 1–15 February 2003.
Singapore	55,000	*Asian Migration News*, 16–31 October 2002.
United Arab Emirates	33,000	*Kompas*, 17 March 2001.
Taiwan	85,677	Loveband, 2003:2.

SOURCES: *Kompas*, 17 March 2001; *Asian Migration News*, 16–31 October 2002; 1–15 February 2003; 1–15 March 2003; *Migration News*, 2 April 2003; Loveband, 2003.

the onset of the financial crisis in 1997. However, it is not simply a neo-classical economics situation of an increasing economic/demographic gradient between sending and receiving countries which have seen Indonesian migration of domestic workers increase from being of little significance two decades ago to being of major global significance. There are three elements which have been important in this process—the role of the state, the activities of the migration industry and the influence of social networks.

First, it is apparent that in the 1990s the Indonesian state moved from being somewhat indifferent to international labour migration to recognising that it was a small but significant contributor to national foreign exchange earnings. This recognition was especially sharpened after the onset of the crisis in 1997 when the decline in exports and the plummeting value of the Indonesian *rupiah* increased the profile of remittances. Hitherto the state had somewhat unrealistic expectations of transforming labour export to be almost totally skilled (Hugo, 1995a) to maximise remittances but there has been a realisation that Indonesia has a comparative advantage over countries like the Philippines in providing unskilled workers (including domestics) at relatively low cost. This has led to increased government activity in exploring new markets for Indonesian workers abroad. Unfortunately, it has not been matched by a substantially increased commitment to protect Indonesian workers in foreign nations. In addition, there has been some indication of a substantial degree of corruption in this area with underpaid officers of the Department of Labour in Indonesia receiving money from intending migrant workers and recruiters. Hence, increased involvement of the government has undoubtedly contributed to increased labour migration of Indonesian women to work overseas.

A second factor in the increased movement of Indonesian women to work as domestics in foreign countries has been the enhanced activity of Indonesia's "migration industry". This comprises an array of labour recruiters, agents, travel providers, training providers, etc., who have worked assiduously to increase both the supply of women in Indonesia and in expanding the market of their labour overseas. The influence of this group in international migration is often substantially underestimated. Their role in Indonesia is not just to facilitate the migration of women who have decided to move but also to plant the idea of moving in the first place. They are a crucial source of information for Indonesian women in deciding whether or not to work overseas (Hugo, 2003). They are of significance in both documented and undocumented migration and involve both large organisations and very small entrepreneurs who have a small role as a sub-agent or travel provider. This "industry"—which is highly organised and embedded in communities across the archipelago—is a substantial structural feature of Indonesian labour migration.

A third element in the increased flow of women overseas to work as domestic workers is the role of social networks. For each woman who moves to work in foreign countries as a domestic worker, there are many more who are related to her or who know her well. These other women gain social capital in that the migrant potentially can provide them with information and connections which will facilitate their migration overseas. This is apparent among both documented and undocumented female migrant workers. It is apparent that women migrants working as domestics overseas tend to come from particular regions and within those areas, particular villages. This reflects the fact that pioneer migrants will facilitate the movement of later migrants. Moreover, the onset of the financial crisis has reduced the opportunities for rural women to migrate to jobs in Indonesian urban centres so that overseas job opportunities assume greater significance than in the past.

CHARACTERISTICS OF INDONESIAN DOMESTIC OVERSEAS CONTRACT WORKERS

Surveys of female labour migrants, both documented and undocumented, from Indonesia have shown that they are quite young and have relatively low levels of education. In the early years of the migration, a minimum age of 30 years was placed on women being sent overseas to work, although this was clearly got around fairly readily. Hence, while studies in the early 1980s (e.g., Mantra et al., 1986) found that the average age of female migrant workers was the late 30s, in more recent times, younger women have been dominant although there are still many in their 30s and older (Figure 2.3).

FIGURE 2.3   Age-sex structure of migrants working in Sabah, field survey, 1998

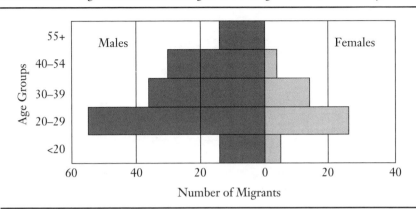

In terms of education, Table 2.10 indicates a dominance of primary education among female migrants in several samples of the last decade. It is probably the case that although the education levels are low, they are higher than the average in their home villages. Nevertheless, while they tend to have low education and are largely unskilled, surveys indicate that almost all are literate.

Female labour migration from Indonesia in the early years was restricted to married women although more recently single women could move (if given permission by a male relative!). Field studies, however, show some different patterns. It is apparent from studies in Java that the bulk of women moving are married. Adi (1996:231) found in West Java that 83 per cent of returned migrants, and the majority of those still away, were still married. In her study, Pujiastuti (2000:39) found that 68 per cent of returnees in Jakarta were married. Studies in East Flores, however, show a quite different pattern. Hugo's (1998) results, shown in Table 2.11, indicate that most women who were still away were unmarried while more than half of those already returned were married. It was found in several studies that single parents and divorced women are over-represented among migrant women workers.

THE MIGRATION PROCESS

The processes by which Indonesian women contract workers migrate overseas differ between those who move illegally and those who move outside the official system. The Indonesian Department of Labour (*Depnaker*), through its Overseas Worker Placement Agency, regulates the recruitment, placement, training, deployment and return of officially registered overseas workers from Indonesia. A typical pattern is for a female to be recruited by a registered recruiting company PJTKI (*Perusahaan Jasa*

TABLE 2.10 Indonesian female overseas contract workers in various studies: Educational background

	Kuala Lumpur[a]	East Flores[b]	Returnees to Jakarta Airport[c]	East Java Rural Development Foundation, 1992	East Kalimantan Deported Migrant Workers, 1995
No Education or did not complete Primary	13.4	32.4	20.0	-	26.8
Primary	57.4	64.7	42.5	64.8	46.1
Lower Secondary	19.9	2.9	18.5	27.5	11.3
Upper Secondary	9.2	-	20.0	13.7	9.9
Total	141	34	40	71	17,312

SOURCES: [a]Dorall & Paramasivam, 1992; [b]Hugo, 1998; [c]Pujiastuti, 2000.

TABLE 2.11 East Flores survey village: Relationships to head of household in origin community of migrant workers

Relationship to household head	Migrants still away		Returned migrants	
	Male	Females	Males	Females
	(%)	(%)	(%)	(%)
Household Head	23.9	-	87.9	8.8
Wife/Husband	3.3	-	2.2	55.9
Child (Not yet married)	58.7	91.7	8.8	8.8
Child (Married)	4.3	4.2	1.1	5.9
Parents (in law)	1.1	4.2	-	5.9
Other Family	8.7	-	-	14.7
Total	92	24	91	34

SOURCE: Hugo, 1998.

Tenaga Kerja Indonesia, or Indonesian Overseas and Domestic Employment Agency) or one of its agents. The PJTKI then arranges placement, training and deployment and registers the potential migrant with *Depnaker* for a fee. The process often takes several months and there are many stories of women being overcharged, receiving limited training and information about what awaits them and is required of them at the destination, and having to work for the PJTKI while they await deployment. For some undocumented migrants, a *calo* (middleman) arranges the entire process of movement but, in other cases, groups from a particular region migrate together and utilise the network of travel providers, recruiters, immigration officials, etc. They get work through the *calo* or through a friend or family member already working for an employer. In effect, an "industry" has developed to facilitate each stage of the migration process. To fund their initial migration the migrants borrow money from family members or friends or their *calo*. They then repay it during their first year of work. Often *calo* have a relationship with the employer in the destination so that loan repayments are deducted from the salary of the worker.

Only very few of first time migrant workers are able to fund their migration from their own resources. The proportion is higher among repeat migrant workers who often earn enough to fund their own re-migration. The bulk of migrant workers rely on their families for the money. This may involve the family taking out a loan and incurring a debt. In one study, Hugo (2003) found that around a fifth borrowed the money from *calo* or friends. Most (94.7 per cent) respondents took between six months and a year to pay back the money borrowed to make their migration.

Jones (2000:39) makes the important point that in Indonesia, "exploitation and abuse of migrants [begins] ... before the migrant ever sets foot abroad". Potential documented migrant workers are obliged to progress through a number of stages involving agents, travel providers, government officials, trainers etc., most of whom will charge a fee, which in some cases is much larger than warranted by the service provided. There is also evidence of migrant workers not being provided with the training they have paid for, being compelled to work for agents while working for deployment and being exposed to dangers of many kinds (Jones, 2000).

There is a great deal of evidence of Indonesian domestic OCWs experiencing exploitation and abuse while overseas. In fact, many are not covered by labour laws at the destination (see the relevant chapters on Hong Kong, Taiwan, Singapore and Malaysia, this volume). If they are undocumented as well, this often places them in a particularly vulnerable situation. They are often not free to leave the house of their employer or seek alternative work. They often have their documents held by their employers. The power relationship in their working situation can mean that they are overworked or exploited in other ways, including sexually (Anderson, 2000). One indicator of the bad experiences of many Indonesian female migrant workers while overseas is the high rate of premature return among some groups, especially among

TABLE 2.12   Studies of returned overseas contract workers: Per cent returning to Indonesia within one year

Origin	Destination	Year	Reference	Away less than one year %	No.
Central Java	Middle East	1986	Mantra et al., 1986	18.1	167
Yogyakarta	Middle East	1986	Mantra et al., 1986	63.4	93
West Java	Middle East	1986	Mantra et al., 1986	21.0	100
West Java	Middle East	1992	Adi, 1996	12.2	90
Java	Middle East	1999	Pujiastuti, 2000	60.0	40
Java	Middle East/Malaysia	1991	Spaan, 1999	31.0	18

SOURCES: Mantra et al., 1986; Adi, 1996; Spaan, 1999; Pujiastuti, 2000.

women going to Saudi Arabia to work. Table 2.12 shows that in several surveys of returned Indonesian OCWs from the Middle East, substantial proportions return within one year although most contracts are for at least two years. This high rate of premature return is undesirable from a number of perspectives. Most importantly, from the viewpoint of the migrant workers themselves, they not only suffer negative experiences at the destination but are likely to have also sustained substantial financial losses. In a majority of cases, first time migrant workers borrow large sums of money to finance their travel overseas. Given the high interest rates charged and the fact that they have worked for only short periods they are likely to retain large debts which will take a long period to pay off. From the perspective of Indonesia's reputation as a reliable supplier of labour and the recruiting agencies' credibility with their employer clients, it also is negative.

A West Java study (Hugo, 2000b) found that only 53 per cent of all respondents returned home because they had completed their contract. Further evidence of the high rate of premature return of OCWs in Indonesia is provided by government data collected at the Jakarta airport upon the return of migrant workers. In 1998 the government established a special terminal at Jakarta airport purely for OCWs (Terminal 3). All returning OCWs are required by the Department of Labour to answer a questionnaire which asks their name, home location, passport number, work, the PJTKI which sent them overseas, their dates of leaving and returning, country of destination and employer. They are also requested to indicate any problems which they experienced. There are also a number of other formalities to complete and costs to pay in Terminal 3. Data collected for the months September–October 1999 and December 1998 are presented in Table 2.13. These indicate that most OCWs processed in Terminal 3 in Jakarta are women from Java who had worked in the Middle East. Of these, more than one-third were returning prematurely. Indeed, more than one-quarter returned in less than a

TABLE 2.13   Reports of returning OCWs at Jakarta Airport, December 1998 and September–October 1999

	December 1998	September–October 1999
Total number	8,690	32,483
% Female	99.2	96.7
% Middle East	93.4	70.2
Period of working (%)		
<3 months	15.6	11.4
4–11 months	12.3	14.2
12–23 months	12.7	19.9
24+ months	59.4	54.5
Reasons for returning (%)		
End of contract	59.4	55.5
Holiday	2.9	4.7
Sick	4.8	2.4
Problems experienced	15.6	12.9
Other	17.3	24.5
Area of origin (%)		
West Java	–	49.2
Central Java	–	23.6
East Java	–	18.1
Outside Java	–	9.1

year and more than one-tenth within three months. This represents a very high rate of premature return.

The experience of many Indonesian domestics who move to Malaysia as undocumented migrants as part of an informal network linking their home areas with an employer in Malaysia can be quite different from those who move through a *calo*. In a study of women from East Flores moving to Sabah in East Malaysia, Hugo (1998) found that there was little exploitation reported. The process of obtaining work at the destination is very much one that utilises family and friendship linkages. Some 62 per cent of female migrant workers got their first job through a family member and 21 per cent through friends. Moreover, female migrants have a significantly greater chance of travelling to Sabah with other family members than is the case for males. It is indicative that of the 58 female migrants studied in the village, only four reported travelling to Sabah alone. This pattern was also reported by Graham (1997) in her village study where she found that women migrants were not subject to exploitation at the destination in Sabah because of the differential sequencing of males and female migration. This is similar to the findings of Robinson (1991) who compared the experiences of domestic workers in the Middle East with those coming to Jakarta as migrants. The latter, she argues, have much lower levels of exploitation because they move to Jakarta with friends and relatives who they can readily call upon for assistance should they need it. On the other hand, in the Middle East, they are generally isolated from such support systems.

INDONESIAN DOMESTIC LABOUR MIGRANTS AND HEALTH ISSUES

There are a number of health issues which are related to Indonesian domestic worker migration. Most destination numbers insist on potential migrant workers having (and passing) health tests before departing and some such as Singapore insist on a HIV test although compulsory HIV testing in Indonesia is not permitted. One study of returnees in several parts of Indonesia indicated that while such testing was usual among legal migrants leaving Java, it was not the case in the Outer Islands (Hugo, 2001:121). Moreover, it was found that even among those who had a medical examination, it was often limited and perfunctory. It is clear, however, that Indonesian women migrants often experience health problems when overseas, although it is not known the extent to which this is due to pre-existing conditions and how much this is caused by conditions in the destination.

One indication of the significance of health problems among Indonesian domestic workers is the high level of premature return, especially of those going to Saudi Arabia. As noted in one study (Hugo, 2003), nine per cent of those returning did so because they were sick and these included several who failed the medical test at the destination.

There is considerable discussion of the risk of HIV infection that domestic workers face while overseas. Data from one survey of returning Indonesian OCWs showed that less than half of the OCWs interviewed had any knowledge of the disease (Table 2.14). In many cases, respondents who indicated that they had heard of HIV/AIDS had no knowledge of what it actually was and how it was transmitted.

TABLE 2.14 Indonesian overseas contract worker information survey: Respondents' knowledge of HIV/AIDS, 1999

	Yes		No		No answer	
	No.	%	No.	%	No.	%
West Java	16	11.0	130	89.9	–	–
East Kalimantan	21	46.6	31	53.4	–	–
Riau	35	46.1	38	50.0	3	3.9

SOURCE: Hugo, 2001a:125.

There was little or no effort on the part of PJTKI and *calo* to provide any information about HIV/AIDS.

Migrant workers in the West Java study were asked about the sources of health information that were accessed to gain information about health (Table 2.15). The most striking feature here is the fact that more than half had not obtained health information from anywhere and less than one-tenth obtained it in the course of their training to go overseas. Clearly there is little or no health information being given to OCWs before they leave. There is a substantial and urgent need to provide OCWs leaving Indonesia with comprehensive information on health issues generally and especially on HIV/AIDS and sexually transmitted infections (STIs).

Among the large Indonesian migrant worker population in Malaysia there has long been a concern that they may be associated with the spread of infectious disease. Often this is part of a general "scapegoating" of migrant workers which sees them as the cause of a range of social, health and economic problems in Malaysia. Indeed, in 1992, it was reported in the Malaysian press (*Nation*, 31 July 1992) that 30 per cent of those who registered for work permits in Malaysia "were carrying the AIDS virus". The great majority of people applying for such permits are Indonesians. However, another newspaper (*Straits Times*, 6 August 1992) reported the Malaysian Minister of Health as saying that a random sample of 5,000 foreign workers (most of whom were Indonesian) who were tested for HIV found only 12 HIV positive cases.

In 2000 it was reported that some Indonesian women were among nine foreign spouses of Singaporean men who were deported because they were found to be infected with HIV (*Asian Migration News*, 31 May 2000). The Singaporean government decreed that non-citizens with HIV/AIDS were classified as prohibited immigrants which attracted opposition from non-governmental organisations (NGOs) (*Straits Times*, 14 May 2000). They were eventually permitted to return (*Borneo Bulletin*, 24 July 2000). In Brunei there were reports that of the 252 HIV cases detected in 1995,

TABLE 2.15 Indonesia: West Java overseas contract worker information study: Respondents' source of health information

Source	No.	%
Printed media	9	6.2
Electronic media	8	5.5
Training location	10	6.8
NGOs	1	0.7
Friends/family	8	5.5
Other	27	18.5
None accessed	83	56.8

SOURCE: Hugo, 2001:126.

only six were Brunei citizens and the rest drawn from the substantial expatriate worker population among which Indonesians are a major element (*Indonesian Observer*, 9 September 1995).

Increasingly, a number of employers of Indonesian OCWs require the recruited workers to undertake an HIV test before they leave Indonesia. Indeed, a requirement of all foreign workers entering Brunei (Parida, 2000) and Singapore (see Abdul Rahman et al., this volume) is that they have a test for HIV. Accordingly, some PJTKI in Indonesia (usually Jakarta) are required to have their candidate OCWs tested for HIV before they move overseas and provide certification to the employer at the destination that the workers being sent are not HIV positive. One report of such HIV testing in early 2001 from a clinic (Insani, located in East Jakarta) indicated that 22 candidate OCWs (13 women and 9 men) had tested positive for HIV. Unfortunately, no information was available on the total number tested.

Sabah is one of the main destinations of Indonesian OCWs, especially those who do not go through the official system. There have been reports of OCWs in Sabah being responsible for the spread of a range of diseases. It was reported that between April 1998 and March 2000, medical examinations had found 12,093 foreign workers in Sabah (the majority of whom are Indonesians) (Hugo, 2000c) were infected with HIV or suffering from Hepatitis B, leprosy and cancer (*Asian Migration News*, 15 April 2000). This led to the Malaysian Federal Task Force on Foreign Workers announcing that it wanted employers in Sabah to deport foreign workers infected with HIV or suffering from Hepatitis B or leprosy because it is "difficult to contain the spread of the disease because some of the workers absconded and [had] gone to work with other employers".

Indonesians, especially domestic workers, are one of the largest migrant workers' groups to Brunei Darussalam. Some 33,865 of the 156,614 migrant workers going to Brunei between 1996 and 1998 originated from Indonesia. Females outnumbered males (e.g., in 1998 there were 3,770 males and 6,355 females), with most going to work as domestic workers (Parida, 2000:28). Brunei began an HIV screening programme on all migrant workers on arrival, six months after arrival and on departure with 393,132 being tested between 1993 and 1999. Of the 33,865 Indonesians tested between 1996 and 1998, only one was found to be HIV positive whereas 449 males and 16 females were found to be HIV positive in the total of 149,875 migrant workers tested. Hence the prevalence among the Indonesian OCWs was very low. This may be indicative of low HIV prevalence among Indonesian women travelling overseas to work as domestics. Certainly, this is the case in Brunei.

It is necessary to caution against immediately making an assumption that all OCWs will, by definition, have a higher incidence of HIV/AIDS infection than the non-migrant population at either origin or destination. There is, as Skeldon (2000:9–10) correctly points out, little information available to substantiate or reject such contention. It is clear that some sub-groups of migrant workers are more vulnerable than other groups in this respect and one has to be careful of unwarranted stigmatisation and "scapegoating" of migrants. The fact remains that little testing data are available for migrants, both international and intra-national, in Indonesia. Indeed, the pre-testing which is being insisted upon by some employers of official OCWs from Indonesia may mean that among this group HIV infection may be low, especially too when there is also regular testing at the destination. Less is known, however, about the substantial numbers of OCWs who leave Indonesia through the undocumented systems.

A crucial question relates to the vulnerability of women Indonesian OCWs to infection from HIV. It has already been shown that women substantially outnumber men among official OCWs leaving the country. There is a great deal of debate about the degree to which Indonesian female OCWs experience abuse. Clearly, there is considerable difficulty in collecting such information with many women not wishing to divulge cases of abuse. Bandyopadhyay and Thomas (2000:60) found that 2.4 per cent of a sample of Indonesian housemaids in Hong Kong reported being victims of sexual violence.

Most host countries (of OCWs) in the Far East, Middle East and Southeast Asia require that potential migrant workers undergo mandatory testing for HIV and other infectious diseases. The manner in which the HIV screening has been applied to OCWs in the countries of destination of Indonesian migrant workers has been strongly criticised on a number of grounds (Verghis, 2000:92–93):

- Mandatory HIV testing of migrant workers is discriminatory, as HIV status does not preclude the capability to function at various levels. Such tests restrict the right to travel and, when used in conjunction with deportation, deny the right to work.

- Selection of migrant workers as a category for mandatory testing appears to arise from their marginalised status as other expatriate workers are excluded from testing. With the exception of Singapore, most host countries require only migrant workers to undergo mandatory HIV testing.

- Conduct of mandatory HIV testing of migrant workers without their knowledge and not providing pre- and post-test counselling violates the right to information, privacy and confidentiality.

- When a migrant is deported following an HIV test in the host country based on a false positive result, discrimination can become more severe.

- Testing is also unfair as it places the responsibility for handling the HIV epidemic on the migrant worker. Research and actions undertaken with migrant workers indicate that migration places them at risk of acquiring HIV. A false sense of security also occurs in the local population of the host country who consider that they are free of HIV when mandatory testing and deportation of migrant workers are undertaken.

- The social responsibility of governments, companies and other such institutions that test migrant workers for HIV and deport them is questionable. Many migrant workers enter the host country with a clean bill of health but subsequently become HIV positive.

IMPACTS OF MIGRATION OF DOMESTIC WORKERS

The impact of the migration of domestic workers to foreign countries can be considered at a number of levels—individual, family, community, regional and national. As it is not possible to consider all scales here, the analysis will concentrate only on the individual and family levels. In examining these impacts, there has been an emphasis on economic dimensions which is somewhat understandable given the fact that the overwhelming motivation of the women is to earn money for themselves and their families. A typical pattern is reflected in an East Flores case study (Hugo, 1998). Most respondents indicated that it was the perception of restricted opportunities that was the main factor pushing migrant workers out of the East Flores village. It is interesting that women migrants were more likely to cite family related reasons for leaving the village than men. The family factors involved in out-migration of women from the village were two-fold. First, it is clear that many women migrate as part of a strategy of the family spreading its labour resources in order to earn sufficient income. Such women saw their migration as being a response to the income needs of the family. This is in line with the findings in other research (Hugo, 1995b) that women migrants are often considered more reliable remitters to the village based family than men who are less inclined to honour their family obligations. Second, an equal number of women saw their migration as an escape from the constraints of the family in the village. Again, this has been found in other research in Indonesia to be an important motivation for young women leaving rural sector areas (Wolf, 1990; Sunaryanto, 1998).

The effects of female labour migration on families and communities of origin involve not only adjusting to the absence of mothers, wives and daughters but also to the influences of the newly acquired money, goods, ideas, behaviour and innovations sent back and brought back by the migrant workers. The impact of remittances transmitted by the women is of major significance. Official remittance figures are only the tip of the iceberg with much money flowing back with friends and when the migrants themselves return at the conclusion of their contracts. Many women also bring back high cost goods when they return. For example, 68 per cent of a sample of returned OCWs in Yogyakarta, West and Central Java had brought back goods like radios, television sets, motorcycles and furniture (Mantra et al., 1986). Adi (1996:266) found in the study of a village in West Java that households with a migrant domestic worker overseas had an income of Rp 495,000 (US$147) a month, more than twice that of households without workers overseas. Some two-thirds of income in the former households was due to remittances. He also found that 80 per cent of the remittances was spent on consumption such as house building/improvement, paying off debts, schooling of children and meeting the daily needs of the family. The remainder was used in investments in land and setting up small businesses.

This pattern of level of remittances and their use is repeated in a large number of studies (e.g., Mantra et al., 1986; Heyzer & Wee, 1994; Pujiastuti, 2000). The impact of remittances on family and village economies is immediately apparent when one enters rural communities with large numbers of OCWs in Nusa Tenggara Timur. Houses tend to be made of brick or stone rather than wood or *atap* and have glass windows, televisions and other modern appliances and there is an air of prosperity despite the often relatively poor agricultural potential of the areas of origin. A case reported in the *Kupang Post* (30 October 1997) involved a female migrant gaining employment as a household servant in Hong Kong where she is able to earn Rp1.2 million (US$126) per month and send back around Rp1 million (US$105) to her parents every few months. She was part of a group of 108 women sent from East Nusa Tenggara to Hong Kong to work as household assistants. The money was mainly used to provide the necessities of life for her parents but also to greatly improve their house.

There is less attention focused on the social effects of female labour migration in Indonesia. There has been some examination of the effects on families (Hugo, 1995b; 2002b). It is clear that Indonesian female labour migration is selective of unmarried women and divorcees (Adi, 1996; Pujiastuti, 2000; Hugo, 2002b), although married women predominate in the movement to Saudi Arabia (Heyzer & Wee, 1994). It would appear that mobility-induced separations of family members for the often extended periods involved in international labour migration can lead to marital instability and the consequent permanent break-up of the family unit. In fieldwork in East Flores, one of the most frequently voiced comments about the impact of migration to Sabah (East Malaysia) was marriage break-up. Indeed, in some cases, men and women absentees had taken another spouse at the destination. Studies have generally found a higher incidence of divorce among migrant households than among non-migrant households although this has not always been the case as in Adi's (1996) study of female domestic workers migrating from West Java, Indonesia to the Middle East.

A major question relates to the relationship between labour migration and changes in the role and status of Indonesian women. One study of returning female overseas workers (Yayasan Pengembangan Pedesaan, 1992) found that the women increased their involvement in the family's affairs after returning from employment overseas. Other relevant findings of the study included:

- Evidence that many husbands' respect for their OCW wives increased.
- Men took on more childrearing roles during the absence of their wives and there was a breaking down of the traditional division of family labour along gender lines.
- There was little evidence of negative effects on children due to the mother's absence.
- The extended family covered many of the tasks usually undertaken by the absent women OCW.
- Most women returning considered their main role to be a homemaker.

A more recent study by Sukamdi et al. (2001) also supports these findings.

Clearly, in some cases Indonesian women improve their status as a result of labour migration but not all women are empowered. The latter is due to the fact that many women leave one patriarchal structure (in their home village) for another in the destination. Many women are employed in situations at the destination where they are in unequal power situations in relation to their employers (Abdul Rahman et al., this volume). This is especially the case among domestic workers and those working in the sex industry.

In some contexts, women migrants may have enhanced the economic status of their families by contributing income earned at their destination but not experienced any increase in their own overall status as a result. This would appear to be the case among some Indonesian women going to work as domestics in the Middle East (Adi, 1996). In some cases there would appear to be a distinction made between the effects of migration on the overall status of women and that upon their economic situation. There may also be certain threshold effects operating so that one two-year stint in the Middle East by a West Java woman may not be enough to produce a change in her status whereas two such periods may be sufficient to produce a change.

There can be no doubt that while migration often results in women gaining a range of new freedoms, in some cases the opposite can occur. While there is emphasis placed upon how migration can result in a loosening of traditional restrictions upon women, there is another side to this change. For some, women migration can mean the loss of important and valued support systems based in the village which served to protect them and help in a range of household-based activities. Hence migration can result in disempowerment. Jones (1996:16) has reported that Indonesian (and other) international migrant domestic workers have high levels of vulnerability to exploitation because:

- They usually live with employers in their homes.
- They are separated from fellow workers and support networks.
- They do not have witnesses to observe mistreatment.
- In some destinations (e.g. Saudi Arabia) they are not protected by local labour laws.

In relation to Indonesians working as domestics in Saudi Arabia, Robinson (1991:50) points out that:

> The conditions of work—often in isolation in the employer's home—have great potential for exploitation. Within Indonesia the women have access to some resources, in particular their families and their social networks, giving them a limited degree of power in negotiating work relations and work conditions—something which is lacking in international migration.

It is interesting in the study of East Flores, that there is little evidence of abuse and exploitation of the females moving to Sabah, although many were employed as domestic workers. This appears to be due to the fact that most of the women moving did so as part of a group, usually involving male family members. This pattern was also reported by Graham (1997) in her village study where she found that women migrants were less subject to exploitation at the destination in Sabah because of the differential sequencing of male and female migration described above.

ISSUES CONCERNING FEMALE OCW DOMESTIC WORKERS IN INDONESIA

The migration of Indonesian women to work in foreign countries as domestics has long been a controversial issue in Indonesia. Indeed there have been times when their type of movement was banned in Indonesia, for example, for two years in the early 1980s, three months in 1998 (*Asian Migration News*, 21 October 1998) and also in the 2001, when migration to Saudi Arabia was stopped for two months in protest of the treatment of Indonesian domestic workers (*Jakarta Post*, 12 July 2001). However, the response in these cases has been to drive more domestic workers to go to the Middle East on *umroh* visas and their undocumented status exposes them to even greater exploitation. NGOs such as Muslim groups like Muhammadiyah have been speaking out against the abuse of domestic workers, especially in Saudi Arabia for more than two decades (Anon., 1984). However, the exploitation has continued and while there are many instances where domestic workers have positive experiences at the destination, the rate of exploitation has not diminished.

The files of NGOs are bulging with horror stories of women who worked in the Middle East where they are not protected by local labour laws because they work in homes. One NGO (*Solidaritas Perempuan*–Female Solidarity) published a dossier of complaints made by 172 returning migrants between 1995 and 1998. Similarly, Jones (2000) has documented a large number of cases of abuse and exploitation among Indonesian migrant women in Malaysia.

The horror of the experience of many Indonesian domestics in foreign countries is reflected in their high rate of premature return but especially in the significant death toll among them. For example, there was a report that 15 Indonesian domestic workers fell to their deaths from their employer's high rise apartment in Singapore in the first half of 2003 (*Asian Migration News*, 16–30 July 2003). In 1999–2001, 38 foreign domestic workers committed suicide in Singapore. It was noted that "new housemaids who know nothing about western culture and the English language making it difficult for them to communicate with their employers. Mentally, they are not ready to work in other countries. ... Many of them have problems before coming to Singapore" (*Indonesian Observer*, 25 May 2001). The Association of Indonesian Migrant Workers (*Kopbumi*) reported 176 cases of workers killed during their employment between January and September 2003, while another agency (Pancakarsa Foundation) put it at 135 (*Asian Migration News*, 16–31 December 2003).

However, it is not just in destinations that domestic OCWs are exploited. Indeed, in the pre-departure context they "become victims of deceit, incomplete information and forgery as they prepare their way to find employment abroad. Those responsible for this are recruiting agencies and their brokers as well as local government officials who are taking advantage of the high demand for official documents for these eager workers" (CARAM Indonesia et al., 2002:8). This exploitation takes a number of forms including the charging of exorbitant fees, providing misleading information about work at the destination, failure to provide the designated training, and keeping the women in barracks before the departure and making them work for the recruiter while awaiting departure. Exploitation is also rife on return to Indonesia where they are compelled to go through a special terminal (Terminal 3) at Jakarta airport, and required to pay a number of fees, charged exorbitant travel costs to their home area, and accosted by a range of people seeking to extort money from them.

There can be no doubt that Indonesian women experience more exploitation than most domestic workers who seek to work in foreign countries. This appears to be a function of the following:

- A lack of political will in Indonesia to support these workers at home and abroad. This is undoubtedly partly due to collusion at various levels between Indonesian government officials and those exploiting the domestic worker.
- A lack of adequate information being provided to potential workers to allow them to make a fully informed decision about whether to migrate (Hugo, 2003).
- A lack of adequate training to give women, not only appropriate work skills but also self protection strategies.
- A lack of support systems at the destination.

Destination countries vary in the extent of protection they provide with more being available in Asian destinations than the Middle East although there is variation between countries. Hong Kong, in particular, has taken significant steps to protect domestics (Chiu, 2004). Indonesia, until recently, has not shown as much commitment as countries like the Philippines to developing mechanisms to protect workers overseas. However, in the post-1998 context, there have been a number of steps taken (ministerial decrees, bilateral memoranda of understanding with destination countries like Saudi Arabia) to better protect Indonesian migrant domestic workers (KOMNAS *Perempuan*, *Solidaritas Perempuan* and CARAM 2003). There certainly has been an increase in government activity in migrant worker protection although it is too early to assess how effective it has been.

The involvement of Indonesian women in labour migration, especially those who work as domestics at the destination, has attracted considerable controversy in Indonesia, especially among religious and women's groups. Cases of mistreatment, excessively heavy workloads, abuse, rape and sexual harassment are given prominent coverage in the media. This, however, has had little apparent impact in depressing the level of demand among Indonesian women to work overseas. As Robinson (2000:251) pointed out:

> The situation of these women has given rise to a highly contested public debate in which the government's policies have been subjected to trenchant criticism. The public debate, which engages the ethical, moral, economic and political issues involved in labour export, has been widely reported in the Indonesian press. The rhetoric of the debate indicates these women have become pawns in the economic strategies of the Indonesian government and in its political relations with Saudi Arabia.

A growing number of NGOs in Indonesia are becoming involved in providing support services to Indonesian female international labour migrants and in lobbying the government to improve support and protection for female OCWs. Prior to 1998, NGOs working with migrant domestic workers were substantially constrained in their attempts to improve the conditions of the workers and to protect them from exploitation. However, the NGOs working in this area have been able to increase their advocacy for the rights of migrant workers and in improving protection for workers. They have been instrumental in drafting and submitting a Bill on "Protection of Migrant Workers and Their Families" to the State. Pudjiastuti (2003) has discussed the activities of NGOs in Indonesia such as *Solidaritas Perempuan*, Centre for Migrant Workers and KOPBUMI.

Despite the increased involvement in and commitment to the protection of female domestic workers in Indonesia by both government and NGOs since 1998, there still needs to be a greater commitment to their protection of each stage of the movement. In particular, the following needs to be addressed:

- Field surveys indicate that Indonesian potential female OCWs make their decisions to move and depart from Indonesia with limited and often incorrect information which influences whether or not they move and their experience at the destination. It is argued here that the timely provision of comprehensive, relevant and accurate information can empower migrants because if they are armed with knowledge about the costs and conditions involved in migration, and in areas like remuneration and conditions at the destination and the rights and responsibilities of migrants and employers, they can better resist exploitation. Moreover, such information can assist potential migrants to make decisions about whether or not to migrate and, if so, where to, and which destinations are more likely to be beneficial to them than would otherwise be the case.
- The protection of the rights of migrant workers demands the establishment of effective complaints procedures, effective regulation of the myriad of agencies involved in the process and development of a range of protective structures. This will assist in the empowerment of OCWs and the protection of their rights.

- Training and preparation is required for official OCWs but as Robinson (2000:274) has pointed out, "workers felt the training to be of a limited utility, having little relation to the jobs they had to perform. Much of the training was in the form of lectures and didactic instruction, and little of it was hands-on training ... some of the violence to the women comes after they have misused modern household appliances (like washing machines and vacuum cleaners)". The training and preparation given to potential OCWs thus needs to be made much more relevant and also arm them with strategies to protect themselves when confronted by problems.

- The issue of protection of OCWs in the destination countries is of crucial importance. Too often this issue is sidestepped by Indonesian officials who claim they cannot interfere in foreign country affairs. However, there are a number of options available. For example, while the Philippines has labour attaches in a large number of countries to protect and support their OCWs, Indonesia has only two (Riyadh and Kuala Lumpur) and there is little evidence of the attaches being highly active in supporting Indonesian women working overseas. There is a range of ways in which support can be provided through bilateral and multilateral efforts and ensuring OCWs are protected by labour legislation in destination countries (Chin, 1997). Similarly, it is apparent that NGOs can and do play a significant role in the protection of OCWs in destination countries and they need to be supported by governments. In short, the rights of female OCWs must be protected in destination countries and a range of strategies needs to be employed to achieve this.

- It is apparent that many of the problems faced by Indonesian OCWs in destinations relate to their undocumented status. Every effort needs to be made to regularise their movement. In doing this, however, care must be exercised not to penalise the OCWs themselves since regularisation can result in greater costs to the women themselves.

- The answer to improving the situation for OCWs does not lie in the banning of their migration. Such bans usually only result in women OCWs being forced to move as undocumented migrants and increase their vulnerability.

- There is also scope for greater protection of OCWs on their return to Indonesia. This is in view of evidence that women arriving home, often to the specially dedicated Terminal 3 at Jakarta airport, are prey to exploitation and in need of protection. Similarly, assistance in their adjustment to life back in Indonesia may be needed.

- There is a difficulty in the debate on Indonesian female OCWs that they are not seen as the victims they often are, but are blamed for their problems. Hence, their unskilled and low education status is given as a reason by officials for their problems in destination areas.

- Women moving overseas are often exposed to greater health risks than would be the case if they remained at home. They need the knowledge and means to protect themselves against diseases, especially HIV/AIDS and STIs.

CONCLUSION

Indonesia is already one of the world's major suppliers of female OCWs and especially those working as domestics and the numbers it sends overseas will increase over the next few years. Indeed, the onset of the financial crisis in the country led to an upturn in the outflow. The government has set targets for the numbers sent overseas since its Third Five-Year Plan (1979–84). The Sixth Five-Year Plan (1994–99) had a target of 1.25 million but 1,461,236 were deployed. The target for 1999–2004 has more than doubled to 2,800,000 (*Departemen Tenaga Kerja*, Republic of Indonesia, 1998:14). This recognises the increasing contribution that OCWs are making to the nation's well-being through foreign exchange earnings, reducing unemployment and underemployment and in assisting regional development. However, these benefits are coming at considerable human cost, especially to women migrant workers and there is a need for the government of Indonesia to demonstrate the political will and commitment to make a number of initiatives which will effectively protect and support the rights of its OCWs. The opportunity was provided for this with the introduction of a new set of labour laws to the Indonesian parliament in 2000 but little appears to have resulted from these. These include a number of provisions relating to international labour migration including the control and regulation of recruiting agencies and middlemen, protection of workers and providing information to intending OCWs.

The operationalisation of these innovations will require a transformation in government which will see it commit itself to these ends in a similar way to which it has embraced selected areas in the past like family planning. To improve the situation will certainly take more than the introduction of an information programme. It must be accompanied by other steps—the development of effective complaint procedures within Indonesia and at the destination, effective control of recruiting intermediaries and proper punishment of their exploitation of intending workers, ensuring that there is relevant and quality training of OCWs, providing support systems as well as health and other insurance at the destination, and empowering the women who are involved to stand up for their rights and protect themselves.

NOTE

1   An *umroh* visa is a visa issued to Muslims visiting and praying in the holy cities of Mecca and Medina outside the *haj* season.

REFERENCES

Adi, R. 1996. *The Impact of International Labour Migration in Indonesia*. Unpublished Ph.D. dissertation, Department of Geography, The University of Adelaide.

Anderson, B. 2000. *Doing the Dirty Work? The Global Politics of Domestic Labour*. New York: Zed Books.

Anon. 1984. *Desa desa yang kehilangan pria* (Villages which have lost their young men). *Tempo*, 7 April, 37–41.

Anon. 1997. Indonesia's overseas workers: Problems and solution. *Review Indonesia*, 17, 6–10.

Asian Migration News. Various issues.

Bandyopadhay, M & J. Thomas. 2000. Social context of women migrant workers' vulnerability to HIV infection in Hong Kong, China. In UNDP Southeast Asia HIV and Development Project, *Population Mobility in Asia: Implications for HIV/AIDs Action Programmes*. Bangkok: UNDP, Southeast Asia HIV and Development Project, 49–65.

Borneo Bulletin. 2000. 24 July.

CARAM Indonesia, KOPBUMI & National Commission on Violence Against Women (Komnas Perempuan). 2002. *Indonesian Migrant Workers: Systematic Abuse at Home and Abroad.* Indonesian Country Report to the UN Special Rapporteur on the Human Rights of Migrants, Kuala Lumpur, 2 June 2002.

Chin, C. B. N. 1997. Walls of silence and late twentieth century representations of the foreign female domestic worker: The case of Filipino and Indonesian female servants in Malaysia. *International Migration Review*, 31(2), 353–85.

Chiu, S. W. K. 2004. Recent Trends in Migration Movement and Policies in Asia: Hong Kong Region Report. Paper prepared for The Workshop on International Migration and Labour Markets in Asia, Japan Institute of Labour, 5–6 February, in Tokyo, Japan.

Departemen Tenaga Kerja, Republic of Indonesia. 1998. *Strategi Penempatan Tenaga Kerja Indonesia Ke Luar Negeri.* Jakarta: Departemen Tenaga Kerja.

Dorall, R. F. & S. R. Paramasivam. 1992. Gender perspectives on Indonesian labour migration to Peninsular Malaysia: A case study. Paper presented at The Population Studies Unit's International Colloquium entitled 'Migration Development and Gender in the ASEAN Region', 28–31 October in Kuantan, Pahang, Malaysia.

Glick Schiller, N., L. Basch, & C. Szanton Blanc. 1995. From immigrant to transmigrant: Theorising transnational migration. *Anthropological Quarterly*, 68, 48–63.

Graham, P. 1997. 'Widows' at Home, Workers Abroad: Florenese Women and Labour Migration. Unpublished manuscript.

Harun, L. 1984. *Mencari Tuan Di Negali Minyak* (Seeking a boss in oil countries). *Tempo*, 2 June, 12–17.

Heyzer, N. & V. Wee. 1994. Domestic workers in transient overseas employment: Who benefit, who profits? In *The Trade in Domestic Workers: Casues, Mechanism and Consequences of International Migration*. Edited by N. Heyzer, G. Lycklama & N. Weerakon. Kuala Lumpur: Zed Books, 31–102.

Hugo, G. J. 1975. *Population Mobility in West Java, Indonesia.* Unpublished Ph.D. dissertation, Department of Demography, Australian National University, Canberra.

————. 1980. Population movements in Indonesia during the colonial period. In *Indonesia: Australian Perspectives*. Edited by J. J. Fox, R. G. Garnaut, P. T. McCawley & J. A. C. Mackie. Canberra: Research School of Pacific Studies, Australian National University, 95–135.

————. 1992. Women on the move: Changing patterns of population movement of women in Indonesia. In *Gender and Migration in Developing Countries*, Edited by S. Chant. London: Belhaven Press, 174–96.

_____. 1993. Indonesian labour migration to Malaysia: Trends and policy implications. *Southeast Asian Journal of Social Science*, 21(1), 36–70.

_____. 1995a. Labour export from Indonesia: An overview. *Asean Economic Bulletin*, (special issue on Labour Migration in Asia), 12(2), 275–98.

_____. 1995b. International labour migration and the family: Some observations from Indonesia. *Asian and Pacific Migration Journal*, 4(2–3), 273–301.

_____. 1998. International Migration in Eastern Indonesia. Paper prepared for East Indonesia Project, The University of Adelaide.

_____. 2000a. Labour migration from East Indonesia to East Malaysia. *Revue Européene des Migrations Internationales*, 16(1), 97–124.

_____. 2000b. Establishing the information needs of Indonesian international labour migrants: Background and methodology. Paper prepared for Workshop on Information Needs and Indonesian Migrant Workers, Centre for Population and Manpower Studies, Indonesian Institute of Sciences (PPT-LIPI) and the International Labour Organisation, Jakarta, Indonesia.

_____. 2000c. *Indonesian Overseas Contract Workers HIV Knowledge: A Gap in Information.* Bangkok: UNDP.

_____. 2001. *Population Mobility and HIV/AIDS in Indonesia.* Jakarta: ILO, Indonesia, UNAIDS, Indonesia, UNDP South East Asia HIV And Development Office Aus AID.

_____. 2002a. Women's international labour migration. In *Women in Indonesia; Gender, Equity and Development*. Edited by K. Robinson & S. Bessell. Singapore: Institute of Southeast Asian Studies, 158–178.

_____. 2002b. Effects of international migration on the family in Indonesia. *Asian and Pacific Migration Journal*, 11 (1), 13–46.

_____. 2003. Information, exploitation and empowerment: The case of Indonesian overseas contract workers overseas. *Asian Migration Journal*, 12(4), 439–66.

Indonesian Observer. Various issues.

Inglis, C. 2002. Malaysia wavers on labor crackdown. *Migration Information Source*, http://www.migrationinformation.org/feature/print.cfm?ID=63. Accessed 28 May 2004.

Jakarta Post. Various issues.

Jones, S. 1996. Women feed Malaysian boom. *Inside Indonesia*, No. 47, July–September, 16-8.

_____. 2000. *Making Money off Migrants: The Indonesian Exodus to Malaysia.* New South Wales: ASIA 2000, Hong Kong and Centre for Asia Pacific Social Transformation Studies, University of Wollongong.

Kassim, A. 1997. International migration and its impact on Malaysia. Paper presented at 11th Asia-Pacific Roundtable, Labour Migration in Southeast Asia: The Impact (Political, Economic, Social, Security), 5–8 June in Kuala Lumpur, Malaysia.

KOMNAS Perempuan & Solidaritas Perempuan/CARAM Indonesia. 2003. *Indonesian Migrant Domestic Workers: Their Vulnerabilities and New Initiatives For The Protection of Their Rights, Indonesian Country Report to the UN Special Rapporteur—On the Human Rights of Migrants.* Jakarta: KOMNAS Perempuan and Solidaritas Perempuan/CARAM Indonesia.

Kompas. 2001. 17 March.

Kupang Post. 1997. 30 October.

Loveband, A. 2003. *Positioning the Product: Indonesian Migrant Women Workers in Contemporary Taiwan.* Working Paper Series No. 43, Southeast Asia Research Centre, City University of Hong Kong.

Mantra, I. B., T. M. Kasnawi, & Sukamardi. 1986. *Mobilitas Angkatan Kerja Indonesia Ke Timor Tengah* (Movement of Indonesian Workers to the Middle East), Final Report Book 1. Yogyakarta, Indonesia: Population Studies Centre, Gadjah Mada University.

Massey, D. S., J. Arango, G. Hugo, A. Kouaouci, A. Pellegrino, & J. E. Taylor. 1993. Theories of international migration: A review and appraisal. *Population and Development Review,* 19(3), 431–66.

Migration News. 2003. 2 April.

Mujiyani. 2000. *Gender and Forest Degradation: A Case Study in Two Villages in East Lombok, West Nusa Tenggara, Indonesia.* Unpublished Ph.D. dissertation, Population and Human Resources, The University of Adelaide.

Nasution, M. A. 1997. *Aliran Pekerja Indonesia Ke Malaysia: Kes Tentang Pekerja Indonesia Dalam Sektor Pembinaan Di Kuala Lumpur.* Malaysia. Tesis Yang Dekemukakan Untuk Memperolehi Ijazah Doktor Falsafah, Fakulti Sains Kemasyarakatan dan kemanusiaan, Universiti Kebangsaan Malaysia, Bangi.

Nation. 1992. 31 July 1992.

Parida, S. K. 2000. Sexually-transmitted infections and risk exposure among HIV positive migrant workers in Brunei Darussalam. In UNDP South East Asia HIV and Development Project, *Population Mobility in Asia: Implications for HIV/AIDS Action Programmes,* Bangkok: UNDP, South East Asia HIV and Development Project, 26–32.

Pudjiastuti, T. N. 2003. The changing roles of NGOs in relation to female Indonesian Labor migration. *Asian Pacific Migration Journal,* Vol. 12, No. 1–2, 189–207.

_____. 2000. *The Experience of Female Overseas Contract Workers from Indonesia.* Unpublished M. A. dissertation, Department of Geographical and Environmental Studies, The University of Adelaide.

Pusat Penelitian Kependudukan, Universitas Gadjah Mada. 1986. *Mobilitas Angkalan Kerja ke Timur Tengah.* Yogyakarta, Indonesia: Gadjah Mada University.

Robinson, K. M. 1991. Housemaids: The effects of gender and culture on the internal and international migration of Indonesian women. In *Intersexions: Gender/Cass/Ethnicity.* Edited by G. Bottomley, M. de Lepervanche & J. Martin. Sydney: Allen and Unwin, 33–51.

_____. 2000. Gender, Islam and nationality: Indonesian domestic servants in the Middle East. In *Home and Hegemony: Domestic Service and Identity in South and Southeast Asia.* Edited by K. Adams & S. Dickey. Ann Arbor: Michigan University Press, 249–82.

Romdiati, H., T. Handayah, & S. Rahayu. 1998. *Aplikasi Jaring Pengaman Sosial Bidang Ketenagakerjaan: Beberapa Isu Penting dari Hasil Kajian Cepat Di Propinsi Jawa Barat.* Jakarta: PPT-LIPI.

Singhanetra-Renard, A. 1986. *The Middle East and Beyond: Dynamics of International Labour Circulation Among Southeast Asian Workers.* Mimeo.

Skeldon, R. 2000. *Population Mobility and HIV Vulnerability in South East Asia: An Assessment and Analysis*. Bangkok: UNDP, South East Asia HIV and Development Project.

Soeprobo, T. B. 2003. Recent trends of international migration in Indonesia. Paper presented at The Workshop on International Migration and Labour Markets in Asia, Japan Institute of Labour, 6–7 February in Tokyo, Japan.

_____. 2004. Recent trends of international migration in Indonesia. Paper presented at The Workshop on International Migration and Labour Markets in Asia, Japan Institute of Labour, 5–6 February in Tokyo, Japan.

Spaan, E. 1999. *Labour Circulation and Socioeconomic Transformation: The Case of East Java, Indonesia*. Report No. 56, NIDI, The Hague.

Straits Times. Various issues.

Sukamdi et al. 2001. Country Study 2: Indonesia. In *Female Labour Migration in Southeast Asia: Change and Continuity*. Edited by C. Wille and B. Passl. Bangkok: Asia Research Centre for Migration, Chulalongkorn University.

Sunaryanto, H. 1998. *Female Labour Migration to Bekasi, Indonesia: Determinants and Consequences*. Unpublished Ph.D. dissertation, Population and Human Resources, The University of Adelaide.

Suyono, M. 1981. Tenaga Kerja Indonesia di Timur Tengah Makin Mantap. *Suara Karya*, 2–6.

Verghis, S. 2000. Promoting and protecting human rights to reduce the HIV vulnerability of migrant workers. In UNDP South East Asia HIV and Development Project, *Population Mobility in Asia: Implications for HIV/AIDS Action Programmes*. Bangkok: UNDP, South East Asia HIV and Development Project, 87–103.

Wolf, D. L. 1990. Factory daughters, the family and nuptiality in Java. *Genus*, XLVI(3–4), 45–54.

Wong, D. T. and T. A. Teuku Anwar. 2003. Migran Gelap: Indonesian Migrants in Malaysia's irregular labor economy. In *Unauthorised Migration in Southeast Asia*. Edited by G. Battistella and M. B. Asis. Quezon City: Scalabrini Migration Center.

Yayasan Pengembangan Pedesaan. 1992. *Trade in Domestic Helpers, Indonesia (with a Micro Study from East Javanese Domestic Helpers)*, final report. Indonesia: Yayasan Pengembangan Pedesaan.

CHAPTER 3

"Lentils There, Lentils Here!" Sri Lankan Domestic Labour in the Middle East

MICHELE RUTH GAMBURD

INTRODUCTION

Grumbling over shoddy treatment at the international airport, one returning Sri Lankan migrant reportedly remarked, "Lentils there, lentils here!" suggesting that after working hard at a low-status job abroad, she deserved more respect upon arriving in her homeland. Like the humble but nutritious lentil in Sri Lankan cuisine, housemaids are essential household features in many Middle Eastern countries, and their remitted wages form a major portion of Sri Lanka's foreign currency income. Despite their central contributions to both the host and sending countries, however, many transnational domestic workers find little recognition or validation in either place.

Since local poverty and the nation's unfavourable position in the global economy create a situation where 15 per cent of this island country's labour force works outside the country, this essay begins with an examination of the historical and economic context of Sri Lanka's transnational migration. A profile of the current transnational domestic worker community and a discussion of the migration process reveal gender- and class-based inequalities. The chapter then examines the practicalities of the state's administrative efforts to serve migrants at home and abroad, and analyses the rhetoric of patriotic paternalist voices that urge the government to ban female migration. Although economic and social developments have occurred in Sri Lankan society, including modifications of gender roles and the growth of middle-class non-governmental organisations (NGOs) dealing with migration, only by addressing international economic inequality can policy makers ameliorate the disadvantageous employment situation of transnational domestic workers. The essay concludes with some suggestions for future policy alternatives.

The analysis draws on statistical information, published sources, interviews and ethnographic fieldwork. Over a decade of anthropological research done in the village of Naeaegama on Sri Lanka's southwest coast provides qualitative data on labour migration.[1] Although some villagers hold significant acreage, most people rent or own small plots of land that cannot support a family's agricultural needs. Local employment opportunities for men include work in the armed services or the tourism industry, civil service jobs, daily manual labour jobs as well as self-employment as cinnamon peelers or makers and peddlers of coconut fibre brooms. Work opportunities for women include making coconut fibre rope, teaching, and working in local garment factories. Most significantly, since the early 1980s, a large and ever-growing number of women from Naeaegama have gone to work abroad as housemaids in the Middle East (Gamburd, 2000). In February 2004, 88 people out of a total population of roughly 1,100 had been or were then abroad. Current and returned migrants thus represented eight per cent of the village population and 16 per cent of the people of working age. Of the 174 village households, 73 (42 per cent) had or had had at least one person abroad. Three-quarters of these migrants were female. Thus, not only was information regarding migration readily available, but women had strong social networks abroad, and families who had not yet constructed new cement houses were highly aware of their neighbours' success in this endeavour.

HISTORICAL AND ECONOMIC CONTEXT OF SRI LANKAN LABOUR MIGRATION

Sri Lanka has a history of international trade dating back to the pre-Christian era. Strategically situated at an ocean crossroads, the island hosted traders from the Middle East, the Indian subcontinent, and South East Asia (McGilvray, 1998). Successively colonised by the Portuguese, the Dutch and the British, Sri Lanka achieved independence in 1948.

Since Independence, Sri Lanka's policies regarding the international movement of people have been relatively liberal (INSTRAW, 2000:110). The migration of male labour to the Middle East began in 1976, with female migration beginning about half a decade later. Initially men went to work as construction workers in the boom that accompanied the increase in oil wealth in the Gulf States. Thereafter, proportionally fewer men went abroad, but the demand for housemaids increased. By 1988, over half of the Sri Lankan migrants were female, with the percentage reaching a high of 79 per cent in 1994 (SLBFE, 1997:table 32). Since then, both male and female migration have increased, with male migration increasing more quickly. It has been estimated that in 2003, 1,003,600 Sri Lankans worked abroad (SLBFE, 2004:24), and migrant labourers (male and female of all skill levels) made up 14.5 per cent of the total number of employed Sri Lankans (SLBFE, 2004:42). Currently 93 per cent of Sri Lanka's migrants and 96 per cent of its transnational domestic workers depart for jobs in the Middle East (including the Kingdom of Saudi Arabia, the United Arab Emirates, Kuwait, Jordan, Lebanon, Oman, Bahrain, and Qatar) (SLBFE, 2004:8, 22). Along with Indonesian and Filipina women (see respectively Hugo, this volume; Asis, this volume). Sri Lankans have cornered a section of this competitive labour market).

Like many former colonies, Sri Lanka carries a high debt burden. The International Monetary Fund (IMF) reviews government fiscal policies and has advocated Structural

Adjustment Programmes that have adversely affected the poorer portions of the population (Ruwanpura et al., 2000:3). Despite market expansion after the February 2002 ceasefire in Sri Lanka's 20-year-old civil war, "[m]ajor economic problems such as widespread poverty, a low per capita income, high structural unemployment, high inflation, a rising public debt burden, continued exchange rate depreciation and vulnerability to external shocks have continued" (Central Bank, 2003:3). Persistent political instability has shaken investor confidence (Cassim, 2004:1; *Financial Times*, 2004:1), and the peace process has moved forward only haltingly. The tsunami on 26 December 2004 provided a drastic shock to the fishing and tourism industries on the coast and produced a drag effect on other aspects of the economy.

The Central Bank (2003:9) reports that 25–39 per cent of Sri Lanka's population can be classified as poor. Unemployment and underemployment remain high (Institute of Policy Studies, 2003:63–5), especially among women (Ruwanpura et al., 2000:60). In the third quarter of 2002, women's unemployment (13.2 per cent) stood roughly twice as high as men's (7.1 per cent) (Central Bank, 2003:164). Sri Lanka's transnational domestic workers come disproportionately from the poorer segment of society. Several studies suggest that each migrant woman supports an average of five members of her family (Weerakoon, 1998:109; Jayaweera et al., 2002:1). These figures suggest that the 693,000 women working abroad support roughly 3,465,000 people (18 per cent of Sri Lanka's estimated 19 million) through their migration (Central Bank, 2003:160; SLBFE 2004:24).

Foreign Exchange and Female Labour

The government finds labour migration useful in two ways. First, it relieves unemployment. Second, it brings in large and much-needed quantities of foreign exchange (Weerakoon, 1998:102). Sri Lanka has three main sources of foreign exchange: export of tea and manufactured garments, and the migration of labour. In 2002, migrant workers remitted roughly US$1.2 billion, (61 per cent of which came from workers in the Middle East). The total sum represents 27.4 per cent of the total value of exports. The export of garments represents 51.6 per cent of foreign exchange earnings, and the export of tea represents 14.0 per cent (SLBFE, 2003:39–40, Central Bank, 2003:208). Scholars interested in the international division of labour will note that all three of the major foreign exchange earning industries hinge on female labour. Tea gardens require plucking twice a week, labour-intensive work done mainly by female estate workers. Similarly, the garment industry depends on the labour of young women (mostly unmarried) who run the sewing machines in the factories (Lynch, 1999). Sri Lanka's foreign exchange earnings reflect the feminisation of the international working class.

Some critics feel that the Sri Lankan government relies too heavily on migration and suggest diversification of the labour force (Central Bank, 2003:165; William Conklin[2], personal interview, 5 February 2004). There are reports that Bangladesh will soon lift its ban on female migration to the Middle East, thus increasing competition in the region (Central Bank, 2003:165; see also Afsar, this volume). Another point of concern is the future of the garment industry after the expiration at the end of 2004 of the quota system set up under the Multi-Fibre Agreement (Central Bank, 2003:224; Institute of Policy Studies, 2003:45). Sri Lanka's economic well-being is intimately tied to the global economy.

Administrative Structure

Government structures have arisen to regulate the flow of migrants. The most significant organisation administering to labour migrants, the Sri Lanka Bureau of Foreign Employment (SLBFE), was established by the SLBFE Act #21 of 1985 and has grown larger and more sophisticated over the past 25 years as progressive government acts enlarge the Bureau's purview. The SLBFE licenses recruiting agencies, supervises training programmes, registers migrants, and administers a compulsory insurance scheme. Abroad, foreign missions provide shelter to housemaids who leave their employers' houses, give legal support in interactions with the police, and aid in repatriation. To address the needs of returnees and families left in Sri Lanka, the SLBFE has recently started a welfare scheme for migrants' families, including a scholarship fund and childcare programmes for migrants' children, and plans to initiate low-interest housing loans (Weerakoon, 1998:113–4). National banks offer savings and loan services and facilitate the flow of foreign currency.

The government's new initiatives are not necessarily well-known or effective (Conklin, personal interview, 5 February 2004). People's awareness of and confidence in the SLBFE's schemes are rather low (Jayaweera et al., 2002:5, 112–3, 120). For example, workers in the village of Naeaegama where I did my fieldwork noted that the pension scheme initiative that the government is planning (Nakkavita & Jayamanne, 2004) would be wonderful in principle; however, one particularly articulate returned migrant rhetorically asked how the SLBFE thought it could collect pension funds from overseas employers, many of whom failed to pay the housemaids' salaries on time, if at all. Migrants generally approved of the insurance scheme, but several individuals interviewed in 2004 noted that recently this system had not delivered as well as it had in the past. Instead of devising new schemes, housemaids wished that the government could better enforce basic aspects of the labour migration process, including policing bogus agencies, ensuring the timely and full payment of wages, and offering fuller support to housemaids at embassies in times of crisis.

Like government initiatives, international regulations have not aided migrants greatly. In 1996, Sri Lanka ratified the United Nation's International Convention on the Protection of Rights of All Migrants and Their Families (1990). This came into force in July 2003, when the 20th nation ratified the convention. No country receiving significant numbers of Sri Lankan transnational domestic workers, however, has ratified this convention. "You can't clap with one hand!" commented David Soysa[3] (personal interview, 5 February 2004), a migrant advocate, implying that for the convention to have a noticeable effect, both sending and receiving countries must adhere to its standards. Labour advocate William Conklin suggests that most receiving countries will never ratify the wordy and unwieldy convention because they object to a few sections; he feels that a more basic convention would have wider appeal and more chance of adoption (personal interview, 5 February 2004).

WHO ARE THE MIGRANTS?

Of the 208,803 Sri Lankans who departed for contract work abroad in 2003, 65 per cent were female (SLBFE, 2004:1). Of these women, 75 per cent went to work as housemaids (SLBFE, 2004:10). This means that transnational domestic workers made up 49 per cent of Sri Lanka's departing migrant workers in 2003 (SLBFE, 2004:23). Housemaids have consistently made up between a half and two-thirds of the departures for foreign employment for over a decade (SLBFE, 2004:23). Of the 101,414 housemaids departing for work abroad in 2003, over 96 per cent left for destinations in the Middle East (Table 3.1). Less than four per cent departed for other countries, including Cyprus, Singapore, Malaysia, Hong Kong and the Maldives (SLBFE, 2004:22).

Most departing Sri Lankan housemaids are in the age range of 20–45 years old (Table 3.2). Various surveys have found that roughly 75 per cent of Sri Lanka's migrant housemaids are married, and that roughly 90 per cent of the married migrants leave children behind (Eelens et al., 1992:6; Jayaweera et al., 2002:11; Gunatillake & Perera, 1995:160). Strong cultural norms stigmatise divorce in Sri Lankan society, therefore the few women who are de facto separated from their husbands still continue to maintain their official marital status (Gunatillake & Perera, 1995:131). Many families in Naeaegama report that access to reliable childcare is a major limiting factor on a husband or wife's ability to go abroad. In the recent past, more men and unmarried women have started going abroad. This could result in the postponement of marriage and childbearing as individuals and families defer these undertakings until at least one of the spouses has spent some time abroad.

Sri Lanka has an impressively high literacy rate, with 90.1 per cent of the surveyed population (excluding people in the war-torn areas of the north and east having basic reading and writing skills in 1994) (Central Bank, 2003). Nevertheless, the female migrant population falls on the lower end of educational standards (Jayaweera et al., 2002:24, 55). A survey of women returning from the Gulf War in 1990 found that only nine per cent had passed their "O" and "A" levels (Table 3.3). Despite high unemployment levels among all women, especially those with higher education levels, the women with more education are not migrating in great numbers. This reflects educated women's unwillingness to work in the low-status job of housemaid (Gunatillake & Perera, 1995:43).

TABLE 3.1 Departures for housemaid jobs from Sri Lanka to major labour receiving countries in 2003

Country	Year 2003	Percentage
Saudi Arabia	40,728	40.2
Kuwait	26,178	25.8
Lebanon	12,787	12.6
UAE	8,762	8.6
Qatar	3,280	3.2
Jordan	2,720	2.7
Cyprus	2,283	2.3
Bahrain	1,729	1.7
Oman	1,572	1.5
Singapore	7,91	0.8
Malaysia	203	0.2
Hong Kong	181	0.2
Maldives	99	0.1
Other	101	0.1
Total	101,414	100

SOURCE: SLBFE, 2004:22.

TABLE 3.2 Departures of housemaids by age groups, 2000–2003

Age	2000	2001	2002	2003
<19	21	47	795	1,786
20–24	6,391	10,065	16,777	13,640
25–29	14,909	17,456	21,794	20,324
30–34	17,234	18,643	21,380	18,828
35–39	19,356	19,471	22,125	21,053
40–44	17,460	16,243	15,119	15,383
45–49	9,411	7,529	5,429	6,061
>50	3,335	2,575	1,585	1,543
Not Reported	11,296	8,820	3,521	2,796
Total	99,413	102,850	108,535	101,414

SOURCES: SLBFE, 2003:38; SLBFE, 2004:40.

TABLE 3.3   Education at time of migration of female migrant returnees from the Gulf War

Level of education	%
No schooling	2.6
Passed Years 1–5	22.4
Passed Years 6–9	45.6
Failed GCE "O" Level	19.9
Passed GCE "O" Level	6.7
Passed GCE "A" Level	2.7
Total	99.9

SOURCE: Gunatillake & Perera, 1995:43.

While Muslims make up only seven per cent of the Sri Lankan population in general (Herath, 1993), Muslim women make up about 22 per cent of the housemaids (Dias & Weerakoon-Gunawardene, 1991) and Muslims make up as high as 27.8 per cent of the total migrant population (SLBFE, 1997). This reflects in part the preference of many households in the Middle East to hire Muslim housemaids (Gamburd, 1999).

Migrants come from all over the island, particularly from the densely populated areas of the southwest coast (SLBFE, 2004:59–76); significantly fewer come from the war-torn areas in the north and east.[4] The proportion of female migrants is relatively lower in urban areas and higher in rural areas. Presumably this is a sign of the higher levels of education in the urban areas, as well as the higher percentage of men sent to professional and skilled jobs. Sixty-five per cent of the country's job agencies are located in the capital district (SLBFE, 2004:36). This distribution reflects the small scale of the country and the relative ease of travelling between the capital and the rural areas.

In general, the "average" Sri Lankan woman who migrates to the Middle East comes from the 20–45 years age range, has six to nine years of schooling, is married and has two or more children, and has not otherwise worked outside the home (Weerakoon, 1998:102). This profile has remained stable over the years. Migrants who travel to Cyprus, Greece and Italy generally have smaller families than migrants going to the Middle East. They also have more experience in formal employment and more privileged backgrounds in Sri Lanka (Wanasundera, 2001:57–58). On average, migrant women departing for Cyprus, Greece and Italy have a higher educational level than women leaving for Singapore and Hong Kong, who in turn have higher qualifications than women departing for work in the Middle East (Weerakoon, 1998:103; Wanasundera, 2001:47–8).

Migrants' Decision-Making Process and Passage Abroad

In the village of Naeaegama, as in much of the rest of Sri Lanka, high unemployment and underemployment limit job opportunities. Existing opportunities are mostly poorly paid and temporary (Jayaweera et al., 2002:24). Although transnational domestic workers earn only an average of SLR10,000 (US$100) a month while abroad,[5] this is between two and five times what women can earn working in Sri Lanka, and equals or exceeds the wages earned by most village men.

Naeaegama women consistently assert that families cannot make ends meet on their husbands' salaries, and that migration to the Middle East is the only available economic alternative (Gamburd, 1995). Family motives for migration usually include getting out of debt, buying land and building a house. Women also state that they would like to support their family's daily consumption needs, educate their children, and provide dowries for themselves (in the case of unmarried migrants) and their daughters (in the case of married migrants) (Gunatillake & Perera, 1995:48, 55; Gamburd, 2003). Participants in the decision-making process (undergone repeatedly for migrants who return several times to the Gulf) weigh financial necessity and household improvements against separation, incursion of loans, and alternate arrangements for childcare (Gamburd, 1998).

Once they decide to migrate, women go abroad either through recruiting agencies or through personal contacts. Women using agencies can contact a local sub-agent or travel directly to a recruiting centre in Colombo, the capital city. Women who travel through private contracts receive a "ticket" from a friend or relative working in the Middle East, who puts them in touch with her employer's connections. Naeaegama women prefer this method because it is inexpensive and they can find out in advance about the households they will enter. These migrants register with the SLBFE and purchase insurance.

All first-time migrants must obtain passports and training certificates. Through a number of affiliated organisations, the SLBFE runs free training programmes for prospective migrants. The training course covers topics including housework, Arabic language and culture, banking, negotiating the airport, and dealing with crisis situations. Critics of the training programmes suggest that they make no special arrangements for illiterate migrants (Dudley Wijesiri[6], personal interview, 3 February 2004), and have no evaluative element to discover how much information trainees retain or whether they are suitable for employment (Conklin, personal interview, 5 February 2004).

All migrants are required to undergo a medical examination to acquire a medical certificate. Doctors are held responsible by sending agencies for the accuracy of their reports (which are verified with medical examinations in some receiving countries), therefore these certificates do not present opportunities for corruption. The agent takes the relevant paperwork and a model contract to the embassy of the foreign country and obtains a visa. The migrant pays the agency fees, and the agent registers the migrant with the SLBFE, obtaining mandatory insurance in the process. The agent then gives the migrant her airline ticket and passport, and the migrant proceeds to the airport.

Officially, migrants only pay SLR7,700 (about US$77) for insurance and agency fees, plus SLR500 (US$5) for their medical certificate, but most Naeaegama migrants report paying agency fees of SLR10,000 to 20,000 (US$100–200). Many women obtain this money from moneylenders at high rates of interest, often repaying twice the amount that they borrow. Although these rates may seem exploitative, moneylenders often fail to collect even the principle on their loans, thus making their business a high-risk one (Gamburd, 2000). The lack of easily accessible low-interest loans presents a major hurdle for migrant women.

Agents, sub-agents, and moneylenders can most easily exploit the poorest and least educated members of the population. Women in the plantation sector, from the rural hinterlands, and from dysfunctional families are especially vulnerable (Wijesiri, personal interview 3 February 2004; see also Dissanayake, 2002:72; Jayaweera et al., 2002:53). In the Naeaegama area, male migrants, whose jobs cost roughly three to four times as much as female migrants' jobs and who have fewer experienced male relatives and friends to rely upon, are more susceptible to exploitation by unscrupulous agents. In contrast, most women know the routine, refuse to pay exorbitant prices for their jobs, and usually arrive safely at their destinations. The long history of migration, compounded with the large numbers of women travelling, makes information readily available.

BAN FEMALE MIGRATION? PRACTICALITIES AND PROTECTIONIST VOICES

Unlike other South Asian countries, Sri Lanka has not restricted women in their quests to find jobs abroad (Jayaweera et al., 2002:4; see also Raghuram, this volume and Afsar, this volume). Instead, the government provides various welfare programmes and incentives for migrants. Female migration from Sri Lanka has always been legal and is likely to remain so in the future for three reasons. First, laws restricting women's migration would be challenged in the courts as violations of women's fundamental rights. Second, the sheer volume of female migration and the government's dependence on the money these migrants remit make such a ban impractical. Third, policy makers recognise that such a ban would funnel these women into undocumented and illegal migration, creating even greater problems of the same type (Conklin, personal interview, 5 February 2004). The result of Nepal's recent ban on female labour migration, with an increase of illegal networks that place women at greater risks, illustrates this point (O'Neill, 2001).

Strong patriotic protectionist voices against female labour migration ring out in the media. From reading journalists' reports, one would think that migration inevitably results in disaster. The stories circulate in numbers disproportionate to actual occurrences of unfortunate events. Two key themes are highlighted here: sexual harassment and the neglect of children.

Sexual Harassment

One theme in media stories is women's vulnerability to sexual assault. A journalist who emphasises the "cruelty and wickedness" of recruiting agents and "the lust of men" feels that it would be "a disaster" to remove the ban on female migration from Nepal to the Middle East (Bose, 2003:868). As emblems of the culture's purity, women are often "protected" in ways that can undermine their basic human rights.

Estimates vary widely on the numbers of negative experiences Sri Lankan transnational domestic workers have while abroad. The SLBFE received complaints from 6,474 women in 2003 (SLBFE, 2004:27). This number represents one claim in a hundred from the total estimated stock of 693,000 female migrants working overseas. Over half of the complaints received by the SLBFE concerned the non-payment of agreed wages, breach of contract, and the lack of communication with home; claims of harassment made up 21 per cent (SLBFE, 2004:28). A researcher in Kuwait reports that most returned domestic workers say that they are satisfied with their migration experience: "The numbers in Kuwait who have fled to embassy shelters for repatriation constitute 0.4 per cent of the total number of domestic workers" (Shah, cited in O'Neill, 2001:161). One study found that a small number of women (14 out of 1,000) had to satisfy sexual needs of employers, while seven per cent reported physical or mental harassment (Dissanayake, 2002:71). Another study found that 20 per cent of returned women reported sexual harassment (INSTRAW, 2000:126). These statistics suggest the range of reported information on harassment.

Migrant advocate Dudley Wijesiri (personal interview, 3 February 2004) thinks that the incidence of sexual abuse is much higher than generally documented. Based on his experience with migrant workers associations (MWAs), he estimates that 20 per cent of the women have suffered rape. He feels that 90 per cent of these women come from vulnerable groups in the population. Wijesiri argues that these women will report problems about salary and food, but not abuse or rape because of the social stigma attached (personal interview, 3 February 2004). My research in the village of Naeaegama reveals that a number of women have left employers' households because "the man there wasn't good". These women presented the clear and definite steps they took to defend themselves and get out of the untenable situation, including buying their own tickets home using jewellery or saved wages, and soliciting help from family in Sri Lanka, friends in the local country, job agencies, and Sri Lankan embassies. This sort of theme highlighting the women's agency is lacking in almost all media presentations of transnational domestic workers.

Vulnerability of Children

Protectionist voices fret not only about the sexual vulnerability of women but also about the effects that transnational domestic workers' absences have on their children. In a parliamentary discussion reported in the newspaper, a politician suggested that "[i]n a *large percentage* of [migration] cases, the children get neglected" (Nakkavita & Jayamanne, 2004:10, emphasis added). A high-ranking Sri Lankan politician reported:

> The girls in *most* of these families are harassed and abused whilst the husbands and boys go astray. *Most* of them become addicted to alcohol and drugs. We have to think of practical measures to arrest this situation and the best is to direct and encourage women to participate in self-employment projects (*Daily Mirror*, 30 October 2003:4, emphasis added).

These statements exaggerate the difficulties of families left behind, and suggest that keeping women at home will ameliorate these eventualities. Both are dangerous and unfounded assumptions.

Nonetheless female labour migration does indeed generate social costs. One study reports that migrant women's children tended to drop out of school to join the labour force or look after the household domestic work (Jayaweera et al., 2002:44). Another study compared the well-being of children ages one through five years whose mothers were in the Middle East, whose mothers worked locally, and whose mothers stayed at home. This study found that although over 90 per cent of the migrant mothers' children did not suffer behavioural abnormalities, they were roughly three times more likely to develop problems than children whose mothers were at home (Athauda et al., 2000:19). Potential problems included "bed wetting, night walking, clinging to the caretaker, temper tantrums and bad relationship with siblings" (Athauda et al., 2000:14).

The aforementioned study carefully notes that due to pre-existing conditions of poverty (indexed by low birth weight of infants), "these children could be at a disadvantage even before the mothers left them" (Athauda et al., 2000:20). Another author suggests that "the incidence of malnutrition among school children is increasing and about 25 per cent of school children are estimated to be chronically malnourished" (Economist,[7] 2004:13). Structural adjustment policies are in part to blame for this situation (Ruwanpura, 2000:10). Discussions of the social costs of female labour migration must carefully control for extensive poverty within this segment of the population, and must balance basic needs for food and shelter (which women strive to provide through migration) against the nurturing offered by a mother to her children.

Sri Lanka has an alarmingly high rate of male alcoholism. The study on children noted that their risk was increased with the presence of a father who was an alcoholic, drug addict, delinquent, or who did not visit the children frequently (Athauda et al., 2000:19). A complex cultural logic surrounds the use of alcohol. Local men suggest that if a man's wife goes abroad, he will either pursue other women or take to drink. In a symbolic sense, therefore, through alcohol dependency, a man shows the community that he has not been adulterous. Local women, however, are quite sceptical of this logic, noting that many men drink before their wives leave the village and continue to do so after their return. Further research is needed on this topic, but the available data suggest that there is no simple causal arrow leading from female migration to male alcohol abuse as commonly portrayed in the media.

While any breach of contract, violation of personal integrity, or harm to children is to be deplored, the exaggeration of these incidents also has a negative impact. The stories deprive the women in question of agency, portraying them as victims instead of active participants in the events of their own lives. Speaking of the migration of female domestic workers from Nepal to the Middle East, O'Neill (2001:153) notes:

> Efforts to protect young female migrants are articulated through discourses that are aimed, intentionally or not, to keep culturally subordinate people in their place by limiting their access to global labour markets. State protection thus conflicts with the interests of households where migration decisions are made.

One policy analyst suggests that "a dearth of balanced and objective research and analysis and an over-preoccupation with the aspect of female distress could have clouded the clarity regarding the critical policy issues which policy makers need to address regarding female migration" (Perera, 1997:1). More realistic stories could instead demonstrate women's cleverness and push toward government policies that enhance women's resources in times of trouble (Gamburd, 2000). That Sri Lanka has not fallen into this patriotic protectionist trap is a favourable aspect of its administration of migration.

LACK OF STATE ACTION

Countries of origin, often in a weak economic and political position, find it difficult to exert diplomatic pressure for the respect of the rights of their citizens (Sebastian & Raghwan, 2000:4). One Sri Lankan publication suggests that the SLBFE needs to protect the rights of the "unsung heroes" and minimise the harassment of migrant workers, but that it must also "take utmost care not to lose job opportunities... as labour receiving countries have been reluctant to enter into bilateral agreements with the Sri Lankan government on these matters" (Central Bank, 2003:165). In particular, the government hesitates to press for bilateral agreements on labour regulations or the ratification of International Labour Organisation (ILO) conventions for fear that employers in the Middle East will turn to labour from other countries. Labour organisers see this as an excuse for inaction, and feel that the government finds it easier to deal with individual cases than to effect systemic changes (Conklin, personal interview, 5 February 2004).

Embassies and consular offices overseas suffer from a number of weaknesses. Most offices are too understaffed to face the demands placed upon them (Conklin, personal interview, 5 February 2004), and embassy higher-ups are sometimes untrained and under-qualified political appointees. Host countries restrict the number of Sri Lankan diplomatic visas they issue. When embassy and consular officials do become involved with a case, they have only limited authority in the host country to inspect conditions, enforce contracts and intercede with the police (L.K. Ruhunage[8], personal interview, 13 November 2004). In addition, the system lacks informational coordination among the various ministries in Sri Lanka and between the SLBFE and the embassies (K.O.D.D. Fernando[9], personal interview, 14 January 2004). It has also been argued that if the Sri Lankan embassies in the Middle East networked with the embassies of other labour sending countries to share information, they could more effectively blacklist abusive employers and bad job agencies (Conklin, personal interview, 5 February 2004).

Some medical and counselling facilities are available for returnees. Treatment for physical ailments is readily obtainable through the free public health care system as well as through private doctors. The mandatory insurance scheme provides compensation for physical injuries to migrant workers. But, "as for migrants who have had major problems or had been exploited while overseas, for example ... survivors of physical, mental or sexual abuse, there are few services available for counselling, medical treatment or economic assistance" (Weerakoon, 1998:108). The SLBFE provides shelter at a centre near the airport for traumatised returnees, but the services there are limited to tracing the person's relatives and sending her home (Wijesiri, personal interview, 3 February 2004). There are only 32 psychiatrists in Sri Lanka, meaning one trained specialist for every 594,000 people (*Island*, 29 January 2004:11). The state does not recognise migrant mental health care as a high priority.

GENDER ISSUES

In South Asian families, mothers are charged with the well-being of the household. Although many women work at some sort of occupation, almost all assume the "second shift" of domestic chores as well. Unmarried women are not free to wander about unsupervised for fear that their reputations, and hence their eligibility for marriage, could suffer. Many unmarried women in the village of Naeaegama work in nearby garment factories, and their fathers or brothers escort them to and from the factory. Married women have more freedom to move, but they too must carefully guard their reputations. Some women have office jobs in the city of Colombo and commute daily by train. Reputations are most secure when women travel with friends and relatives and spend the night at home or in the company of their husbands. If a family can afford to keep its female members at home, they will generally do so (Kiribamune, 1992:xxxi).

Villagers in Naeaegama report that servant work is a highly stigmatised local occupation. When interviewed, women whom other villagers say have engaged in this work will minimise their stated involvement. Women perceive domestic service in Sri Lanka as dangerous and report that women working in Sri Lankan households are harassed and abused at a much higher rate than are women working in Middle Eastern homes. One interviewee estimated that only 20 per cent of Arabic men harass their servants, while "nearly all" Sri Lankan men do so. Whatever the truth of these figures, this interview suggests the prevailing assumptions of the local female population.

Over the past 25 years, as more women have gone to work in the Middle East, fewer women have been available to work as domestic workers locally. The current wages of food and lodging plus SLR1,000–2,000 (US$10–20) a month for a local worker compares unfavourably to the SLR10,000 (US$100) earned by housemaids abroad. Healthy women with the required skills much prefer to work overseas and earn the higher salaries. This has resulted in the inflation of workers' wages; currently, in the capital city of Colombo, domestic workers earn as much as SLR4,000 or 5,000 (US$40–50) a month in wealthy families. Middle class families often cannot afford domestic workers anymore. Due to the higher salaries and the greater distances, domestic service abroad carries less social stigma than working locally.

Although transnational domestic workers have entered the formal job market, their employment has not unequivocally empowered them to the extent that some early theorists predicted (Korale, 1983). Women have gained some authority and independence, but other forces work against a radical transformation of village gender norms. In their study of Sri Lankan female migrants to Singapore and Hong Kong, Dias and Weerakoon-Gunawardene (1991) suggested that returnees stepped relatively easily back into their household roles of wife and mother. At the same time, Sri Lankan transnational domestic workers have ready access to lucrative employment abroad, while the men in their households do not. When women go overseas, many men step in to do domestic duties. This shift in the breadwinner and caregiver roles challenges older patterns of male dominance in the village. Through the decision-making regarding the use of remittances, men and women continually negotiate these changing power hierarchies (Gamburd, 2000).

Since the inception of female labour migration in the early 1980s, images of ideal mothers and wives have undergone subtle changes. As transnational domestic workers leave home to work in the Middle East, families redistribute their responsibilities to other members, both male and female. In particular, the image of the ideal mother has stretched to include the component of paid labour. Through years of justifying their migration by pointing out that they have gone abroad to better their family's economic situation, migrant mothers have broadened the spectrum of acceptable ways for women to love their children and care for their families. Having become breadwinners to secure a good life for their offspring, they pragmatically dismiss charges of greed and heartlessness for failing simultaneously to fulfil a more traditionally nurturing role.

Women do not perceive their reintegration into the family and community as a problem (see also Jayaweera et al., 2002:22). Nevertheless, they often become fiercely protective of the material benefits (such as houses and jewellery) that they have earned for their families since these are what they have to show in exchange for spending years away from their children (Gamburd, 1998; 2000).

LACK OF LOCAL DEVELOPMENT ALTERNATIVES

Sri Lankan economists often complain that transnational domestic workers spend their money on daily consumption and housing rather than investing in entrepreneurial enterprises that would support the family with a modest income, precluding the need for the migrant to return to the Middle East. Due to returnee unemployment, savings are often lost to consumption. Self-employment schemes could halt this movement and give families a means of earning a living (de Silva et al., 1995:50).

Unfortunately, the majority of transnational domestic workers do not acquire marketable skills while working abroad. Upon their return, they find it difficult to set up viable self-employment schemes in the country (Woost, 1997; Williams, 1999). A number of large- and small-scale government poverty alleviation programmes aimed at the country's poorest citizens have attempted to stimulate small industries by providing start-up capital and business training, with limited success (Gunatilaka & Salih, 1999:32–3). Many people in the target population lack the education, skills, experience and capital to run a business, and often begin production in fields that are over-competitive, leading to greater risks and lower returns (Dias & Sanmugam, 1993; de Silva et al., 1995:41). The majority of self-employment endeavours end in bankruptcy.

It should be noted that families lose their social welfare support if a member goes abroad (Jayaweera et al., 2002:91). Similarly, many governmental and NGO development programmes hesitate to include migrant returnees for fear that they will suddenly leave again for the Middle East (Jayaweera et al., 2002:95). Thus returned migrants lack both financial and informational support for local development activities.

Naeaegama residents who realise the risks of entering into business will not embark on such endeavours unless they already own their own house and land and have taken care of other family obligations such as providing dowries for their daughters (Gamburd, 2003). Even if they have already addressed these earlier priorities, villagers find it difficult to start a business. In the Naeaegama area on the southwest coast of the island, the three main local industries display significant seasonal variations. Cinnamon peelers can only work during the eight months of the year when the bark of the cinnamon bushes separates easily from the sticks. Due to the use of rope in the cinnamon gardens, women involved in the coconut fibre industry find prices for their rope very low during the period when the local cinnamon industry is also in decline. Fishermen can only go to sea during the inter-monsoon period. Thus, the industries with which these local villagers are familiar do not present ideal venues for enlarged economic endeavours.

Nevertheless, migrants' remittances do spur development, channelling money from foreign sources to needy households. Many transnational domestic workers spend their earnings on housing and education, which can be considered investments for the future. Construction of housing redistributes money from migrants to local labourers, while education increases the capacity of the future workforce. Though it does not arrive in great quantities, the remitted money reaches the poor people directly, and they are in charge of deciding what to do with it. These are two of the main priorities of participatory development (Eversole, forthcoming). In many developing countries, funds received from remittances exceed official development assistance and direct foreign investment: "Worldwide, the estimated flow of remittances may exceed US$100 billion per year, with more than 60 per cent going to developing countries—more than official development assistance" (Migration Policy Issues, 2003:3). Easing travel and work restrictions and increasing migrants' wages would greatly enhance development in many labour-supplying countries, including Sri Lanka.

NGO ACTIVITIES AND CIVIL SOCIETY

In many countries the private sector initiates development activities, challenges state actions, and suggests alternative practices, but civil society in Sri Lanka does not have critical mass to affect government policies on labour migration. I now turn from the public sector to a discussion of NGO and union activities. Although the past ten years has seen the inception of a number of local NGOs, these groups are newly formed and still relatively small. A strong class barrier prevents Colombo-based civil society groups from getting involved in migration issues most pertinent to unskilled rural women (Conklin, personal interview, 5 February 2004). Rural women themselves hesitate to form organisations, feeling that these groups would quickly succumb to political factionalism, and only the government has the ability to protect migrants overseas.

One union, the American Federation of Labor and Congress of Industrial Organisations (AFL-CIO), has had an international branch, the American Center for International Labour Solidarity (ACILS) in Sri Lanka for roughly twenty years. Given that 15 per cent of Sri Lanka's labour force works abroad, migration forms a primary focus of the ACILS programmes. The organisation does not deal directly with migrants or provide them with services. Instead, it works with partner organisations and government bodies (Conklin, personal interview, 5 February 2004).

ACILS was instrumental in funding and establishing Migrant Services Centre (MSC) in 1994. Headed by David Soysa, a former chairperson of the SLBFE, MSC maintains a large office in Colombo. MSC does advocacy work, lobbying and campaigning. Soysa (personal interview, 5 February 2004) calls the migration situation "an unfinished symphony", with the protection and welfare of workers as the missing parts. Dudley Wijesiri, a central figure at MSC, suggests that the government eagerly sends labourers abroad, but offers little support while they are overseas and has no plan or policy for looking after workers once they return (personal interview, 3 February 2004). Other scholars agree that the government has not adequately addressed issues facing migrant returnees (Jayaweera et al., 2002:4).

MSC is affiliated with two local unions, the National Workers' Congress (NWC) and the All Ceylon Federation of Free Trade Unions (ACFFTU) (M. Witharana[10], personal interview, 5 February 2004). Locally, the Ceylon Workers Congress (CWC), the plantation workers' trade union, does some organising on behalf of their constituents who have migrated abroad (Wijesiri, personal interview, 3 February 2004). Activists report that other unions, although paying lip service to migrant issues, have not followed through or participated in any initiatives (Conklin, personal interview, 5 February 2004). Like other parts of society, the unions in Sri Lanka are quite fragmented.

MSC has 26 affiliated MWAs scattered around the country, with a total membership of 1,000 people (Wijesiri, personal interview, 3 February 2004). The MWAs build leadership potential and disperse information. They focus on a number of activities, including reintegration and self-employment projects for returnees; savings, micro-credit and welfare schemes; the channelling of complaints from overseas workers to the SLBFE; and advocating for voting rights for citizens overseas.

Action Network for Migrant Workers (ACT FORM), another organisation partially funded by ACILS, acts as an umbrella organisation for other NGOs working on migration issues as well as a liaison with international organisations such as Migrant Forum in Asia (MFA). Many of their constituents are the MWAs affiliated with MSC. The organisation was formed in 1999. ACT FORM channels complaints from migrants and their families to the SLBFE, and has put together a migrant worker handbook with practical information. It also publishes a quarterly newsletter, *Tharani*, which is distributed to MWAs, overseas embassies and current migrants. Vernacular newsletters such as *Tharani* raise awareness of issues surrounding migration. ACT FORM has organised a press and electronic media campaign concerning the UN 1990 Convention on the Protection of All Migrants and their Families. They have engaged in live televised debates, and two ACT FORM representatives now consult with the Foreign Ministry and the SLBFE (Violet Perera[11], personal interview, 1 December 2004).

The International Organisation for Migration (IOM) has been active in Sri Lanka since 1990, when it assisted the repatriation of refugees during the Kuwait War. Since May 2002, IOM has had an office in Sri Lanka, and has increased the scope of its programmes, which focus mostly on capacity building with the Department of Immigration and Emigration and the SLBFE (K. Yapa[12], personal interview, 3 February 2004). In April 2003, IOM organised a conference bringing together labour ministers from ten Asian countries to discuss mutual problems and come up with policy initiatives (Iredale, 2003; Nonnenmacher et al., 2003). This sort of initiative brings pressure from international organisations and local civil society to bear on policy makers in Sri Lanka and encourages multilateral consideration of migration issues.

Other local NGO groups are also tangentially involved in migrant worker issues. A number of scholarly institutions do research on migrant issues, and various activist and community groups, particularly human rights organisations and women's organisations, sometimes take up causes. Overseas, only a limited number of Sri Lankan groups, particularly churches, cultural organisations and professional societies, operate to assist migrant workers (Witharana, personal interview, 5 February 2004). The governments in many Middle Eastern countries prohibit the formation by foreigners of political and labour organisations. The Bahrain Centre for Human Rights lent help to migrants until its director was arrested in September 2004 for criticising the government (Malik, 2004). Volunteers reorganised, and the Society for the Protection of Migrant Workers' Rights received a licence to operate in December 2004 (Financial Times Information, 2004). In Cyprus, local churches and a Sri Lankan Welfare Association assist workers in distress and mediate with the officials (Wanasundera, 2001:123–4). In Greece and Italy, only informal migrant organisations function. In Greece, the Sri Lankan Consulate handles some matters, while in Italy most migrants avoid government organs due to their undocumented status (Wanasundera, 2001:126–7).

Despite the coordinating activities of ACT FORM, the NGO movement lacks cooperation and unity. It does not share information adequately and has not undertaken any large agitations, although associations in 2004 were campaigning for the government to provide a way for the approximately one million Sri Lankan citizens now working abroad to vote in local elections. This issue, covered in the United Nation's International Convention on the Protection of Rights of All Migrants and their Families (1990), may not be of high priority for the migrants themselves, but drawing attention to it is a good way to raise the topic of citizens' equal rights (Conklin, personal interview, 5 February 2004).

Naeaegama villagers whom I interviewed in 2004 were unaware of any formal civil society associations. Instead, they reported a sense of unity and cooperation among Sri Lankans working abroad. These migrants shared financial resources and more importantly, information among themselves, aiding fellow Sri Lankans in times of trouble.

ALTERNATIVES AND POLICY IMPLICATIONS

Sri Lanka has not forbidden any category of the population from working abroad and thus most Sri Lankan transnational domestic workers go overseas through legal channels. Jobs for women, in particular, are relatively cheap and easy to come by, with a minimum of opportunity for corruption and exploitation in the recruiting process. In these matters, the Sri Lankan government has taken productive steps to aid its migrant population.

Nevertheless, Sri Lankans do travel in extra-legal ways to countries that do not offer them legal admission. For example, the SLBFE estimated that 25,000 Sri Lankans were working in Italy in 1999 (Wanasundera, 4001:41); by 2003, the estimate had risen to 60,000 people, three quarters of them women (SLBFE 2004:24). Most of these migrants were smuggled into the country or sponsored by relatives who had entered Italy illegally and obtained regular residence status during one of the amnesties the government periodically offers (Wanasundera, 2001:38–41). A recent Sri Lankan newspaper article discusses the plight of 269 local men apprehended by the Sri Lankan Navy on their way to Italy (Nan, 2004:6). The men's wives argued that their husbands, most in their mid-twenties, were not hard-core criminals, and that they should not be thrown in jail. The article's author noted: "The root cause of this seemingly adventurous illicit ride on sea or land to Italy and other countries is because employment is so difficult to obtain in this country of ours, and even when employed, wages are so low" (Nan, 2004:9). Enhancing local job opportunities and regularising and monitoring these labour streams would greatly benefit the poorer population.

The Sri Lankan government does not need to adopt radical new policies. Instead, female migrant labourers in the village of Naeaegama suggest that the government should live up to its current promise to protect them abroad. They would like to see firmer controls over dishonest job agents locally, more efficient operation of the embassies and consular offices abroad, and greater protections for labourers who do not receive their salaries or who have been abused by their employers.

Labour advocates suggest that a freer flow of information among NGOs, among government ministries, and to migrant workers abroad would greatly enhance the efficiency with which various government and civil society organisations deal with issues of migration. Cooperation between NGOs would minimise the duplication of efforts and maximise the effectiveness of lobbying. Information sharing between government ministries would reduce bureaucratic red tape and increase efficiency in migrants' dealings with various government organs. And spreading information to workers abroad, for example through greater circulation of ACT FORM's migrant newsletter *Tharani*, would make transnational domestic workers aware of their rights and better enable them to protect themselves in cases of emergency.

While recognising the dangers that transnational domestic workers face, none of the women I spoke with thought that banning female migration would be plausible, let alone beneficial, unless alternative employment opportunities were available for men abroad or for men and women locally. The economic situation of returned migrants is intimately tied with the economic well-being of all rural Sri Lankans. A number of poverty alleviation programmes have been in place for over a decade, with limited success in stimulating self-employment ventures. Given the skills of returned migrants and the limitations of local industries, the best situation for these workers and their families would be ready access to wage labour that pays a living salary.

Transnational domestic worker welfare is tied up with larger macro-economic processes involving Sri Lanka's place in the global economy and the international division of labour. Sri Lankan workers are low down on the status and pay scale in many host countries (see also Abdul Rahman et al., this volume; Wee & Sim, this volume). Their geographical and social mobility lags far behind that of other countries' women, especially the Filipinas (see Asis, this volume; McKay, this volume). Even if the rhetoric of migrants' human rights does not stir the Sri Lankan government, officials must consider whether the protection of workers makes pragmatic sense. Can Sri Lanka sustain a situation where 15 per cent of its labour force works abroad? How should economists calculate the social costs incurred by migrant families, and what steps can the state take to encourage local development? These questions remain open for discussion.

NOTES

1   "Naeaegama" or "the village of relatives", is a pseudonym.

2   At the time of the interview, William Conklin was Field Representative, American Center for International Labor Solidarity, 9 Kinross Ave, Colombo 4, Sri Lanka.

3   David Soysa was interviewed as Director, Migrant Services Centre, 10, Council Lane, Dehiwela, Sri Lanka.

4   One must of course question whether migration from the war zone occurs at higher-than-recorded levels, but through unreported streams.

5   In February 2004, the exchange rate between the Sri Lankan Rupee (SLR) and the United States Dollar (US$) hovered near SLR98=US$1.

6   Dudley Wijesiri was interviewed as Co-ordinator, Migrant Services Centre, 10, Council Lane, Dehiwela, Sri Lanka.

7   "Economist" is the pseudonym of the person(s) writing a weekly column in one of Sri Lanka's Sunday newspapers.

8   L. K. Ruhunage was interviewed as Counsellor (Employment and Welfare) at the Consulate General of the Democratic Socialist Republic of Sri Lanka, Dubai, United Arab Emirates.

9   K. O. D. D. Fernando was interviewed as Deputy General Manager Information Technology, Sri Lankan Bureau of Foreign Employment, 61 Isipathana Mawatha, Colombo 5, Sri Lanka.

10   M. Witharana was interviewed as Project Officer, American Center for International Labor Solidarity, 9 Kinross Ave, Col 4, Sri Lanka.

11   Violet Perera was interviewed as Coordinator, Action Network for Migrant Workers (ACT FORM), 20/1 8th Lane, Nawala, Sri Lanka.

12   K. Yapa was interviewed as Project Officer, IOM (International Organization for Migration), 31 Police Park Ave, Colombo 5, Sri Lanka.

REFERENCES

Athauda, T., D. Fernando, & A. Nikapotha. 2000. Behavioral problems among the pre-school children of migrant mothers in Sri Lanka. *Journal of the College of Community Physicians of Sri Lanka*, 5, 14–20.

Bose, A. 2003. Migrant women workers: Victims of cross-border sex 'terrorism' in Asia. *Economic and Political Weekly*, 1 March 2003, 868–9.

Cassim, N. 2004. Forex market panics over politics. *Financial Times* (issued with Daily Mirror), 23 January 2004, 1.

Central Bank. 2003. *Central Bank of Sri Lanka Annual Report 2002*. Colombo: Central Bank of Sri Lanka, http://www.lanka.net/centralbank/Annual_index-2002.html. Accessed 3 March 2004.

Daily Mirror. 2003. 30 October.

de Silva, A., W. D. Lakhman, & M. D. A. L. Ranasinghe. 1995. *Migrant Remittances as a Source of Development Funding: A Study of Sri Lanka*. Working paper #GE9502, Colombo: University of Colombo Faculty of Graduate Studies.

Dias, M. & N. Weerakoon-Gunawardene. 1991. *Female Labour Migration to Singapore and Hong Kong: A Profile of the Sri Lankan Housemaids*. Manuscript. Colombo: Centre for Women's Research (CENWOR).

Dias, M. & T. Sanmugam. 1993. *An Evaluation Report: A Credit Programme for Kuwaiti Returnees*. Colombo, Sri Lanka: Centre for Women's Research (CENWOR).

Dissanayake, D. M. A. 2002. Working conditions of Sri Lankan housemaids employed abroad. *Sri Lankan Journal of Population Studies*, 5, 65–77.

Economist. 2004. 56 years after Independence: Economy at the crossroads. *Sunday Times*, 8 February 2004, 13.

Eelens F., T. Mook, & T. Schampers. 1992. Introduction. In *Labor Migration to the Middle East: From Sri Lanka to the Gulf*. Edited by F. Eelens, T. Schampers, & J. D. Speckmann. London: Kegan Paul International, 1–25.

Eversole, R. (forthcoming) "Direct to the poor" revisited: Migrant remittances and development assistance. In *Migration and Economy: Global and Local Dynamics*. Edited by L. Trager. Walnut Creek, CA: Altamira Press.

Financial Times. 2004. 20 January.

Financial Times Information 2004. Migrant Worker Rights Group Gets Licence (sic) in Bahrain, Financial Times Information. http://web.lexis-nexis.com/universe/document?_m= 38e988085ba38a4b127a5b6e11774822&_docnum=7&wchp=dGLbVtz-zSkVA&_md5=3 42df4a4cb939afd936cd733496c1157. Posted 31 December 2004. Accessed 27 February 2005.

Gamburd, M. R. 1995. Sri Lanka's "army of housemaids": Control of remittances and gender transformations. *Anthropologica*, 37, 49–88.

————. 1998. Absent women and their extended families: Sri Lanka's migrant housemaids. In *Negotiation and Social Space: A Gendered Analysis of Changing Kin and Security Networks in South Asia and Sub-Saharan Africa*. Edited by C. Risseeuw & K. Ganesh. New Delhi: Sage, 276–91.

————. 1999. Class identity and the international division of labor: Sri Lanka's migrant housemaids. *Anthropology of Work Review*, 19(3), 4–8.

————. 2000. *The Kitchen Spoon's Handle: Transnationalism and Sri Lanka's Migrant Housemaids.* Ithaca, NY: Cornell University Press.

————. 2003. In the wake of the Gulf War: Assessing family spending of compensation money in Sri Lanka. *International Journal of Population Geography*, 9(6), 503–15.

Gunatilaka, R. & R. Salih. 1999. *How Successful is Samurdhi's Savings and Credit Programme in Reaching the Poor in Sri Lanka?* Colombo: Institute of Policy Studies.

Gunatillake, G. & M. Perera, eds. 1995. *Study of Female Migrant Worker (sic).* Colombo: Marga Institute (Sri Lanka Centre for Development Studies), World Bank, and Ministry of Policy Planning and Implementation.

Herath, K. M. K. P. 1993. *Monthly Statistics on Labour Migration: October 1993.* manuscript. Colombo: Sri Lankan Bureau of Foreign Employment.

Institute of Policy Studies (IPS). 2003. *Sri Lanka: State of the Economy.* Colombo: Institute of Policy Studies.

INSTRAW. 2000. *Temporary Labour Migration of Women: Case Studies of Bangladesh and Sri Lanka.* Dominican Republic: Amigo del Hogar.

Iredale, R. 2003. *Asian Labour Ministerial Consultations, Sri Lanka, 1–3 April 2003: International Labour Migration in Asia: Trends, Characteristics, Policy and Interstate Cooperation.* Colombo: International Organization for Migration.

Island. 2004. 29 January.

Jayaweera, S., M. Dias, & L. Wanasundera. 2002. *Returnee Migrant Women in Two Locations in Sri Lanka.* Colombo: CENWOR.

Kiribamune, S. 1992. Introduction. In *Reconciliation of Roles: Women, Work and Family in Sri Lanka.* Edited by S. Kiribamune. International Centre for Ethnic Studies Series: 3, New Delhi: Navrang, xi–lix.

Korale, R. B. M. 1983. *Migration for Employment to the Middle East: Its Demographic and Socio-economic Effects in Sri Lanka.* Colombo: Ministry of Plan Implementation.

Lynch, C. 1999. The "good girls" of Sri Lankan modernity: Moral orders of nationalism and capitalism. *Identities: Global Studies in Culture and Power,* 6, 55–89.

Malik, A. 2004. Bahrain Human Rights Group Dissolved. Associated Press. http:// web. lexis-nexis.com/ universe/document? _m=4025f9a98e2483581f3870d28c6032b8&_ docnum=2&wchp=dGLbVtz-zSkVA&_md5=d8ea084d65e9ad0d4cc0f85dc8d10e68. Posted 29 September 2004, accessed 27 February 2005.

McGilvray, D. B. 1998. Arabs, moors and Muslims: Sri Lankan Muslim ethnicity in regional perspective. *Contributions to Indian Sociology, ns,* 32, 433–83.

Migration Policy Issues. 2003. *Facts and Figures on International Migration.* Migration Policy Issues (2), March 2003, Geneva: International Organization for Migration.

Nakkavita and Jayamanne. 2004. A pension scheme would be useful to migrant workers. *Island,* 10 January.

Nan. 2004. Youthful hope reverts to hopelessness. *Sunday Island*, 18 January 2004, 6.

Nonnenmacher, S. et.al. 2003. *Asian Labour Migration Ministerial Consultations, Sri Lanka, 1–3 April 2003: Compendium on Labour Migration Policies and Practices in Major Asian Labour Sending Countries*. Colombo: International Organization for Migration.

O'Neill, T. 2001. "Selling girls in Kuwait": Domestic labour migration and trafficking discourse in Nepal. *Anthropologica*, 43, 153–64.

Perera, M. 1997. *A Profile of Female Migrants: Analysis of Data from an AAFLI Survey of Polgahawela and the Estate Sector in Deniyaya*. Colombo: Marga Institute.

Ruwanpura, K. N. 2000. *Structural Adjustment, Gender and Employment: The Sri Lankan Experience*. Geneva: ILO.

Sebastian, M. & Raghwan. 2000. *Asia Pacific Regional Trade Union Symposium on Migrant Workers, 6–9 December 1999, Kuala Lumpur, Malaysia*. Geneva: ILO.

SLBFE. 1997. *Statistical Handbook on Foreign Employment*. Colombo: Sri Lankan Bureau of Foreign Employment (SLBFE).

———. 2003. *Statistical Handbook on Migration, 2002*. Colombo, Sri Lanka: Research Division, SLBFE.

———. 2004. *Statistical Handbook on Migration, 2003*. Colombo, Sri Lanka: Research Division, SLBFE.

Tharani: Newsletter of the Action Network for Migrant Workers (ACT FORM). Ratmalana, Sri Lanka: Navamaga Printers.

Wanasundera, L. 2001. *Migrant Women Domestic Workers: Cyprus, Greece and Italy*. Colombo: CENWOR.

Weerakoon, N. 1998. Sri Lanka: A case study of international female labour migration. In *Legal Protection for Asian Women Migrant Workers: Strategies for Action*. Edited by S. Sta. M. Amparita, J. J. Balisnono, R. Plaetevoet & R. Selwyn. Makati City, Philippines: Ateneo Human Rights Center, 97–118.

Williams, T. 1999. *The Impact of Credit on Small & Medium-scale Industries (SMIs) in Sri Lanka*. Colombo: Institute of Policy Studies.

Woost, M. D. 1997. Alternative vocabularies of development? "Community" and "participation" in development discourse in Sri Lanka. In *Discourses of Development: Anthropological Perspectives*. Edited by R. D. Grillo & R. L. Stirrat. Oxford: Berg, 229–54.

4

Conditional Mobility: The Migration of Bangladeshi Female Domestic Workers[1]

RITA AFSAR

INTRODUCTION

Migration is an age-old phenomenon which has received renewed attention in the context of its growing volume and increasing globalisation. International migrants worldwide, whether forced or voluntary, have reached a figure of 175 million (United Nations, 2002). Globalisation, characterised by the deregulation of trade, investment and financial transactions and accompanied by a technological revolution in transport and communication, has dramatically reduced geographical barriers between nation states. At the same time, the process of globalisation is arguably uneven, and flows of people in particular are seldom free. Border controls and public policies such as work authorisation or penalties on illegal entries, increasingly tough attitudes circumscribing the intake of refugees or asylum seekers, and an ideological paradigm shift to limit migration and population growth, pose severe restrictions to the free flow of migration. Subsequently, migration patterns are diversifying. Temporary migration—in the form of contractual international migration, circular and seasonal migration, and commuting—is gaining ascendancy within and across national borders.

As a transitional economy, Bangladesh generates immense interest among academics studying the transnational migration of domestic workers. On the one hand, the country is increasingly dependent on the remittances of its overseas workers, who are predominantly semi-skilled and unskilled, to support its economy. On the other hand, it has a conditional ban on unskilled female workers' emigration as a measure to ensure "safe migration" in the context of the growing volume of trafficking in women and children. This chapter will highlight the complex factors that underscore the persistent flows of women as migrant domestic workers from Bangladesh as a sending country, their major characteristics as well as the associated social, economic and health issues. The chapter is based on an extensive review of the literature on migrant domestic workers and a database generated by the Bangladesh Institute of Development Studies (BIDS).[2] This particular chapter also uses a data set generated from a survey of 25 return migrant domestic workers in 2000 with the help of a list procured from the Bureau of Manpower, Employment and Training (BMET) that is involved in the implementation of labour migration policies, particularly overseas migration. This list included women and men migrants from Kuwait and other Middle Eastern countries who were entitled to partial repatriation coverage as many of them were forced to return to Bangladesh mainly due to Iraq's aggression on Kuwait. The sample size was small because of difficulties in contacting the women migrants as they used to shuttle between the BMET office and their house or between their house and the local government functionary's office to obtain certificates and other relevant documents authenticated by a recognised authority in support of their claims. Moreover, as a large majority of these women lived in cities and towns in rental accommodation which they often changed, it was difficult to keep track of them. The difficulty of contacting them could be easily grasped from the fact that we spent more than a month drawing a sample of 25 return migrants spread across 25 wards of ten *thanas* of three districts. However, to redress this drawback we provide a broader picture from the other categories of migrants, employing surveys of female garment factory workers and male workers from both the formal and informal sectors to serve as a major basis for comparison.[3]

Taking into account both macro and micro level perspectives, the paper is organised into six sections: the migrant's experience; the role of the state; the historical and cultural contexts of gendered mobility and paid domestic work; social, economic and health impacts; non-governmental organisations' (NGOs) activities and civil society space; and alternative pathways and policy implications arising out of the migration of domestic workers from Bangladesh.

THE MIGRANT'S EXPERIENCE

Profile of Individual Migrants

The bulk (80 per cent) of the domestic workers in our survey were still youths and young adults (based on the United Nation's standard definition of youths as those aged 15–24 years old) at the time of migration and their average age was 28.5 years (Table 4.1). In comparison, youths constituted 70 per cent among emigrant male workers but were on average two years younger than the domestic workers. The high prevalence of a youthful labour force indicates age selectivity in the labour market as a measure to ensure loyalty and the belief that younger workers are more easily "tamed" into not bargaining or protesting.

Our survey also revealed that migration as domestic workers was the highest among married women (70 per cent), followed by widows, divorced and separated women (20 per cent) (Table 4.2). Working as domestic help has little appeal for unmarried women as compared to working in the readymade garment (RMG) sector. The

TABLE 4.1 Profile of individual migrants at the time of migration in 2000

Type of migrant labour surveyed	Age <30 (%)	Mean age	Duration of migration (in years)	Average level of education (in years)	Currently married (%)	Never married (%)	Divorced/ Separated (%)
Female domestic workers (N=25)	80	28.52	6.36	2.0	80.0	-	20.0
RMGª female factory workers (N=41)	80	24.72	1.8	5.3	51.1	29.8	19.1
Male workers (N=78)	70	26.92	6.2	6.9	69.2	28.2	2.5

SOURCE: Afsar, 2003.
NOTE:
a   Ready-made garment sector workers (female).

TABLE 4.2 Economic background of migrant labour and their families prior to migration

Type of migrant labour surveyed	Previous employment status		Size of landholding			Mean household income (US$ per month)	% Below poverty level
	Unemployed	Employed	<0.2 hectares	0.2–1.01 hectares	1.02+ hectares		
Female domestic workers (N=25)	4.0	28.0ª	81.3	12.5	6.3	61.00	72.0
RMG female factory workers (N=41)	-	85.7ᵇ	54.5	27.3	18.2	79.55	26.8
Male workers (N=78)	15.4	70.5ᶜ	54.3	31.4	14.3	87.70	39.7

SOURCES: Adapted from BIDS data sets, 2000; Economic Relation Division, 2003.
NOTES:
a   The remaining 68% were housewives.
b   The remaining 14% were housewives.
c   The remaining 14% were students.

predominance of married domestic workers migrating from South Asian countries (see also Gamburd, this volume) may be associated with the protection of virginity and the fear of pollution (as argued by Raghuram, this volume). Among the women workforce migrating overseas, one out of every three of the RMG workers was unmarried, the proportion squeezes to one-tenth in the case of domestic workers (Afsar, 2002a). What induces currently married women to opt for work as domestic workers needs to be examined. Women emigrating as domestic workers had two years of formal schooling on average and the level of illiteracy was almost three to four times higher among them (64 per cent) than either their female or male compatriots; little wonder then that more than two-thirds were housewives having no skills prior to migration. Nearly a quarter had prior exposure as domestic workers either at home or abroad, largely within the Middle Eastern region. An increase in illiteracy can be observed among older migrant domestic workers, and one may argue that the propensity to migrate as domestic workers is increasing among primary school dropouts in recent years.[4]

Based on existing evidence we may describe the overseas migration of female workers, whether domestic workers or RMG workers, as step migration (Afsar, 2002a), unlike male workers who migrated directly from their areas of origins (Afsar et al., 2000). Three out of four domestic workers had already migrated to Dhaka city during the 1980s and the remainder hailed from adjacent districts or cities.[5] Agriculture contributed only 12 per cent of their families' income prior to migration, and they were among the lowest income earners with nearly three-quarters from below poverty level (Table 4.3). The female domestic workers' monthly income was estimated at Taka 3,111 (approximately US$61) compared to more than Taka 4,000 (US$88) for the male and female migrant workers at the time of the survey (Afsar et al., 2000; Afsar, 2002a).[6]

Therefore, notwithstanding the prevailing patriarchal values and norms, globalisation is generating demand for low paid jobs for women. Women from landless and poor families having little or no skills avail themselves of those opportunities, defying norms of *purdah* and geographic barriers with the help of kinship networks and institutions of private recruiters and agents as discussed below.

Decision-Making Process

The rise of temporary labour migration in Asia may be mainly attributed to the development in oil-rich countries of the Middle East and rapid economic development of East Asia and Southeast Asia prior to the Asian crisis (Martin & Straubhaar, 2002). Not surprisingly, then, Kuwait was the top destination selected by 60 per cent of the migrant domestic workers surveyed, followed by Bahrain (24 per cent) and the United Arab Emirates (UAE) (16 per cent).[7] Existing literature reveals that economic factors trigger most population movements (Massey et al., 1998; Abella, 1999; Skeldon, 1999). Indeed, 84 per cent of the domestic workers surveyed indicated that they migrated

TABLE 4.3 Sources of finance for migrant domestic workers and migrant male workers, 2000

Sources	Female domestic workers (N=25)				Male workers (N=78)			
	No.	%[a]	Amount (US$)	% of the total fund	No.	%[a]	Amount (US$)	% of the total fund
Own savings	14	56.0	164.00	18.9	41	52.6	207.90	13.0
Loan from relative/friend	11	44.0	169.60	19.5	28	35.9	304.60	19.2
Loan from money lender	17	68.0	363.00	41.8	10	12.8	55.00	3.5
Sale/mortgage of property	7	28.0	108.90	12.4	27	34.6	320.90	20.31
Loan form Bank/NGOs	-	-	-	-	3	3.8	16.40	1.0
Deduction form salary	1	4.0	3.70	0.4	15	19.2	294.20	18.6
Gift	2	8.0	59.30	6.8	9	11.5	384.10	24.3
Total fund	25	100.0	868.50	100.0	78	100.0	1583.00	100.0

SOURCES: Adapted from Afsar et al., 2000; Afsar, 2002a.
NOTE:
a   Due to a multiplicity of sources, the totals do not add up to 100%.

because of better income-earning opportunities and the desire to attain economic solvency. Impelled by poverty, limited opportunities for paid work, and escalating levels of underemployment, and simultaneously pulled by remarkably high wage differentials between the home country and the Middle East, more and more Bangladeshi women are migrating as domestic workers abroad.

Equally important are the sociological factors[8] such as the kinship support umbrella which includes family members, relatives, friends and neighbours and the emergence of private and informal institutions of recruiters and their agents. These networks help sustain the transnational flow of domestic workers despite the imposition of a ban on their migration from time to time, by furnishing information on job opportunities abroad and helping out with the processes involved in applying for work permits and visas. Such informal channels are likely to exert considerable influence in the decision for migration. Migration decision-making is a complex process that depends, *inter alia*, on the material resources female domestic workers have (such as land, home, savings and loans), as well as the opportunity costs and types of social capital of these women both in the home country and at the destination. At the core of social capital, i.e., the institutions, mechanisms and norms and attitudes that help individuals relate to and interact with one another for mutually beneficial activities and to maximise their gains in the case of crisis (Coleman, 1999; see also Krishna & Uphoff, 1999), lies trust and informal norms that bind individuals in cooperation through networks.

By and large, the survey revealed that both the husband and wife jointly took the decision for overseas migration, although 60 per cent of the domestic workers claimed that they themselves played the major role in that process. Nonetheless, given that around two-fifths of the domestic workers surveyed were from nuclear households, it is likely that their decisions depended on their husband's willingness to play both the productive and reproductive roles.[9] From the husbands' perspective, perhaps it was the opportunity costs that influenced their decision-making. As the average monthly income of the domestic workers in nuclear families (Taka 2,273 or US$44.57) was about half that of those who came from joint or extended families (Taka 4,171.8 or US$81.80), it is quite logical for husbands of the former group to take an interest in their wives' migration to maximise material gains for the family. We can safely assume that under low-skill and low-income conditions, no better employment alternative was forthcoming at the time of migration. As such, the nucleation of families in the case of migrant domestic workers is arguably also contributing to the impetus for them to avail themselves of global job opportunities.

In order to finance their overseas migration, 68 per cent of the domestic workers or their families borrowed money from moneylenders who charged exorbitant interests rates. This source alone funded 42 per cent of their migration cost (Table 4.3). A little over two-fifths borrowed from relatives and friends who bore around a fifth of their migration cost. In contrast, only 13 per cent of male migrants and their families borrowed from moneylenders; instead, nearly 40 per cent did so from their relatives who shared nearly a fifth of their migration cost while savings and family's assets[10] financed more than half of their migration cost. This suggests that because of their poorer background compared with male migrants, female migrant domestic workers depend more on non-family sources for their passage to the Middle East. However, social capital plays an important role in both cases. Thus, poverty mediated by social capital induces women's mobility by weakening *purdah* in the face of global demand for female labour.

Passage

The existing literature suggests an ongoing international migration debate centred round the role of private recruitment agencies. On the one hand, there is strong evidence that these agencies make huge profits by transferring employers' liabilities of airfares and visa fees to migrants; these can comprise up to 95 per cent of the migrant's total migration cost and may take the initial two to three years to repay (Afsar et al., 2000). Workers from Bangladesh are also victims of bribery, forgery and cheating by recruitment agencies and employers. Private recruiters are also guilty of corruption with regard to job contracts; and there is a pervasive problem of discrepancies between the promised wages and entitlements and actual benefits received by emigrant labour. On the other hand, recruitment agencies have been hailed for extending opportunities of overseas employment to the poorer segments of the population, particularly women.

For example, three out of five domestic workers in our study (as opposed to a little over a quarter of the male workers) made their passage to the Middle East with the help of private recruitment agencies. In contrast, Bangladesh Overseas Employment Services Ltd., the formal organisation created as a public limited company, specifically for labour recruitment, channelled only a fraction of the flow of emigrant labour.

Domestic workers who used recruitment agencies waited for more than five months on average for their departure after paying all the necessary costs for migration (Table 4.4). The waiting period halved for those who managed work permits through relatives or friends. Interestingly however, the cost of migration does not vary much. Migrant male labour paid almost twice for their passage than female workers and the cost doubled for those who procured visas through their family members or relatives.[11]

None of the migrant domestic workers had training or a written contract prior to migration. All were simply verbally told about their wages and working conditions. After migration, they found a big difference—averaging over Taka 7,650 (US$150)—between the promised and actual wage levels. The working conditions were even worse: as migrant domestic workers are not covered by the labour laws of their host countries, all of the women in the study reported that they had long working hours, little or no rest, no weekly holidays and no freedom of movement outside the house. More than

TABLE 4.4 Average waiting period and passage cost by channels of recruitment

Channels	Female domestic workers (N=25)		Male workers (N=78)	
	Average waiting period in months	Passage cost in US$	Average waiting period in months	Passage cost in US$
Family members/Relatives	2.30	827.10	1.22	3344.60
	(10)[a]	(8)	(44)	(44)
Friends/Neighbours	2.45	1250.00	2.0	1395.00
		(2)	(12)	(12)
Recruiting agencies	5.20	829.63	2.77	3053.20
	(15)	(15)	(22)	(22)
Average	4.04	862.4	1.91	1680.42

SOURCE: BIDS data set, 2000.

NOTE:

a   Figures in parentheses are the number of respondents.

two-thirds also complained of verbal abuse, beatings and physical and mental torture by their employers. Irregular wages and salary cuts were also a big problem for nearly a third of the migrant domestic workers. In recent years, attending a pre-departure briefing session has been made compulsory; additionally, the Migrant Welfare Desk at the international airport in Dhaka ensures that each labour emigrant has a work permit/visa, clearance from BMET, a written contract and a briefing booklet (Afsar, 2003). However, focus group discussion with "would be migrants" revealed that the briefing session emphasised the importance of maintaining discipline and prohibited strikes/work stoppages abroad. "Would be migrants" were not given any orientation on the labour laws of the host country or the terms and conditions enjoyed by workers of other countries such as Sri Lanka or the Philippines. Thus Bangladeshi migrants remain largely unaware of their legal rights and entitlements.

Despite all their vulnerabilities and exploitation, the flow of domestic workers to overseas has remained uninterrupted and even increased due to demand for such workers in countries like Saudi Arabia. In fact, the recent move to grant conditional mobility to domestic workers by the government was largely due to such a "demand pull". We must also bear in mind that from almost no income of their own, Bangladeshi migrant domestic workers earned on average Taka 3,876 (US$76) per month while abroad; this was almost eight to ten times higher than what they would have earned had they been in the same job at home. Neither did they remain passive: four out of every five of the migrant domestic workers surveyed demanded more wages and a third also claimed bonuses and overtime for working long hours and on holidays. Although nine out of ten cases were unsuccessful in realising their demands, their courage to confront even the most unfavourable working conditions reflects their agency. More importantly, in order to escape poverty, a quarter of the migrant domestic workers wanted to migrate again to the same country as they were now familiar with it. In addition, nearly three-fifths wanted to send their sons there to earn more income due to the high gender inequality in wages in the Middle East.[12].

THE ROLE OF THE STATE

Contextual Factors Influencing the Outflow of Female Domestic Workers

With exhausted land frontiers, Bangladesh faces the daunting challenge of absorbing a rapidly growing labour force. With the onset of the fertility transition, a gradual shift is visible in the population structure of the country. From a predominantly youthful structure, the population is tilting towards the productive age group. Thus the civilian labour force (aged 15–64 years) expanded from 18.2 million to 40.7 million between 1974 and 2000, registering an annual (exponential) growth rate of 3.3 per cent (Afsar, 2002b). During the same period, the size of the population grew from 76 million to 130 million. The spectacular growth of the female labour force—from 0.6 million to

8.6 million—outstripped the population growth rate (2.2 per cent per year). Despite achieving considerable success in the field of social development and a respectable growth rate of the gross domestic product (GDP) of approximately five per cent during the 1990s, economists cautioned that the expected 5.5 per cent growth for 2004 would result in only a little over 3.5 per cent per capita income growth; this is unlikely to lift the more than 40 per cent of the country's population from below the poverty line (Centre for Policy Dialogue, 2004). What is worse is that the rising inequality and uneven distribution of economic gains tend to benefit the more developed regions, better-off households and men more than the poorer places, lower-income households and women (Afsar, 2004; Mujeri, 2002). Notwithstanding state policies to reduce poverty since independence, inequality in income distribution has worsened over time and gender inequality persists despite national and international recognition of the need for mainstreaming women in the development process.[13] The inefficiency of the labour market is reflected in the staggeringly high underemployment rate of 35 per cent, more than doubling (from three million to 6.5 million) within a span of 26 years (1983/84 to 1999/00). Underemployment among women is remarkably higher than men (seven per cent), suggesting the gender segmentation and gender imbalances of the labour market that leave extremely limited options for female labour (Bangladesh Bureau of Statistics, 2002b) in both rural and urban areas. Indeed, between 1983/84 and 1999/00, the only positive gain for women was an increase in self-employment opportunities.

Such opportunities were generated by about 1,200 Micro Finance Institutions (MFIs) with Grameen Bank, and leading NGOs[14] channelling around US$400 million as micro-credit to 11 million poor borrowers (mainly women). Despite the MFI's acclaimed success in poverty alleviation, there is a broad consensus that the majority of women borrowers of MFIs are not directly involved in income generating activities. Additionally, even when women are involved, they have not moved beyond paddy/rice husking and livestock/poultry rearing. Hence, not much change in women's occupational patterns can be observed as a result of the operation of MFIs (Mayoux, 1995; Afsar, 2002c). Whilst some of the NGOs also run market-oriented skill development programmes for youth, they only reach a fraction of the youth population. From the government's perspective, skill development programmes are "small in scale, deficient in quality and are hardly responsive to emerging trends in the job market" (Masum, 2000). Hence, globalisation has created the export of short-term overseas migrants as a profit maximisation strategy (Afsar, 2002b).

Labour Export as a Development Strategy

The government of Bangladesh, like other governments of developing countries, has facilitated labour emigration by creating in 1976, the BMET under the Ministry of Labour, and in 2001, the new Ministry of Expatriate Welfare and Overseas Employment (MEWOE), to generate overseas employment and resolve problems of balance of payments. Between 1975 and 2003, 3.5 million Bangladeshi nationals migrated overseas for employment and women represented three per cent of this stock (Table 4.5). The flow of remittances increased by 69 per cent from US$1.8 million to $3.1 million between FY 2000 and FY2003, equivalent to around 85 per cent of the country's net export earnings. The flow of remittances has been described as the "rare saving grace" of the Bangladesh economy as it has played a critical role in backstopping the balance of payment situation (Centre for Policy Dialogue, 2004). As a share of the GDP, remittances accounted for more than four per cent in the year 2000 compared to only 1.4 per cent in 1980 (Mujeri, 2002). Despite fiscal sector reforms and steps to improve the efficiency of the banking sector to boost the flow of remittances, the government failed to attract foreign direct investment (FDI), and FDI flow to Bangladesh averaged only two per cent of GDP in the 1990s, much lower than that to South Asia and other developing countries (Mujeri, 2002).

State Legislations and Policies Concerning Migrant Domestic Workers

International migration falls largely under the jurisdiction of the newly created MEWOE. Together with BMET, it implements regulatory activities and supervises a few welfare measures that were taken during 1990s. The Ministry is guided by its anchor Immigration Ordinance of 1982 that specifies the rules and regulations for Bangladesh's migrant workers; the Ordinance also regulates emigration, promotes immigration, oversees recruitment agencies and sets recruitment fees. Under the

TABLE 4.5 Trends in flows of migrants and remittances, and ratio of remittances to current balance of payment

Flow of migrants	1977/78	1986/87	Year 1996/97	2000	2003
Cumulative ('000)	44.60	548.14	2368.30	3258.81	3560
Annual flows ('000)	22.81	74.02	381.08	222.67	232[a]
Flow of remittances (US$ million)	56	565	1615	1807	3062
Remittances: current balance of payment ratio	12.3	52.5	302.4	221.4	–

SOURCES: Adapted from Afsar et al., 2000; Murshid et al., 2001; Bangladesh Bureau of Statistics, 2002a; Centre for Policy Dialogue, 2004.
NOTE:
a   Drawn from BMET records of overseas employees who migrated between January and November, 2003.

Ordinance, MEWOE has formulated Emigration Rules, Rules for Conduct and Licensing for Recruiting Agencies, and Rules for Wage Earners' Welfare Fund. There was no specific policy with regard to the emigration of female labour up to the 1970s. However, as the number of women migrants increased and religious sentiments within the ruling political party grew alongside media reports of the rape, sexual harassment and maltreatment of women migrants, restrictions were imposed on women's mobility in the 1980s, ostensibly on the religious grounds that women's mobility presented a threat to decency and chastity. Initially, there was a complete ban on women's *international* migration but this was lifted in 1991. The government re-imposed a ban on *unskilled* women's migration in 1998 believing it to be the best approach against the growing trafficking of women and children. In reality, however, the ban on unskilled women labour could neither stop their migration, through legal or illegal channels, nor did it help reduce their vulnerability and the threat of trafficking. Due to the heavy demand of female migrant domestic workers, the government reconsidered its decision and now permit selected recruitment agencies to send women to Saudi Arabia as domestic workers under certain terms and conditions (Afsar, 2003). These include:

- Migrants must be 35 years or more, married and accompanied by husbands.
- Employers must pay 400 Saudi Riyals (US$106) to the migrant domestic worker as a minimum wage, and offer free food and accommodation to the migrant, as well as give US$500 to recruitment agencies to cover migration cost.
- Recruitment agencies must show a receipt to BMET and charge no more than Taka 10,000 (approximately US$70) as well as have a permanent training centre in Dhaka and a round-the-clock office in Saudi Arabia.

Existing studies, however, show that women are still managing to obtain work visas with the help of private recruitment agencies and social networks consisting of family members, friends and neighbours (Afsar et al., 2000; Afsar, 2003; Siddiqui, 2003).[15]

Participation in International Conventions

Bangladesh has signed but not yet ratified the International Convention on the Protection of All Migrant Workers and Members of the Families. This convention ensures various rights of migrant workers (including irregular workers), their liberty and security, and the procedures to be followed in the event of arrest, detention or imprisonment (Matilla, 2001). It empowers migrant workers and entitles them to seek legal protection against harassment and exploitation. This is particularly important for migrant domestic workers whose mobility is restricted and who are often subjected to maltreatment, delayed payment and non-payment of wages and unhealthy living conditions. Bangladesh has also not ratified the International Labour Organisation

125

(ILO) Migration for Employment Convention (Revised) (No. 96) and the ILO Migrant Workers (Supplementary Provisions) Convention (No. 143). However, as a party to the Convention of the Elimination of All Forms of Discrimination against Women (CEDAW) and more recently the South Asian Association for Regional Cooperation (SAARC) as well as the Convention on Preventing and Combating Trafficking in Women and Children for Prostitution (2002), it is imperative for the government to ensure human rights for women migrants and reduce their vulnerabilities. Unfortunately, the huge volume of undocumented workers has not been brought under the protective coverage of the government. The Director General of the International Organization for Migration (IOM) also expressed regret over the fact that the protection of women migrants has seldom featured in bilateral agreements between the governments of Bangladesh and labour importing countries (Afsar, 2003). However, bilateral agreements may become only part of a "wish list" for engaging in regular dialogues on migration-related issues because host countries are reluctant to sign any labour-related bilateral agreements and memoranda of understanding that are legally binding.

Loopholes in the State's Legislations and Policies

The 1982 Ordinance and subsequent legislation have some important loopholes. First, the Ordinance is primarily regulatory in nature and does not effectively incorporate a human rights perspective of migrant labour. For example, under the Ordinance, migrant workers are not entitled to seek legal redress directly. Rather, they have to approach a government functionary to lodge complaints against any violation of the Ordinance (Siddiqui, 2003). Second, while the current conditions governing the mobility of migrant domestic workers have imposed stricter regulations of recruitment and training, and are hence likely to contribute towards safe migration, the provision of an accompanying husband as a necessary pre-condition for the migration of domestic workers not only undermines their capability as independent persons and their human rights, but also fails to ensure protection from abuse and exploitation. In the Gulf Coordination Council (GCC) states, nationals generally enjoy more legal protection than migrants. Many of these states do not have laws protecting domestic workers (Abella, 1997).[16] Hence, it is not binding on the employer to employ the couple together in the same household. Even if they work in the same household, there is no law under which the husband can seek protection for his wife against exploitative or abusive working conditions. Moreover this type of arrangement is likely to make room for false marriages and fake husbands. Third, since the country has experienced a sharp rise in the volume of male and female migration in a short span of time, job seekers often have unrealistic expectations. This often leads to exploitative practices in the job market—such as offers of employment and wages that do not exist in practice, false documentation, and overcharging—because a situation where supply exceeds demand often works against the interests of migrant workers, particularly in a situation of low educational levels and a lack of strict monitoring of policies by the government.

Most of the recruitment agencies operate through agents and sub-agents (*dalals*), who recruit workers from the villages and connect them with the main recruitment agency, as was the case for half of the domestic workers surveyed. However, as the *dalals* are not formally registered with the recruitment agencies they serve, dangers of cheating, fake passports and visas, and trafficking loom large, particularly for women who are often illiterate. Thus despite legislation, these informal channels have not been streamlined or institutionalised and continue to pose a formidable challenge to the process of safe migration.

Underlying Factors Underpinning the Lack of State Action

Low Budget, Low Capacity and Low Priority of MEWOE

The widely acclaimed Interim Poverty Reduction Strategy Paper (IPRSP) of the government and the 2003–04 budget failed to envisage the linkage between migration and trade policies and their impact on poverty alleviation. Subsequently, alternative employment opportunities and safety net programmes do not cover the interest of migrant labour. The new Ministry also has a miniscule budget: Taka 280 million (US$4.8 million) or 0.1 per cent of the total budget in 2003–04. Although the Ministry, as part of the welfare budget, gives about one-tenth of its budget to IOM for the welfare of migrants through research and advocacy, and more than a quarter goes to Bangladesh's diplomatic missions abroad (Afsar, 2003), these missions abroad have high administration and maintenance costs and there is no separate allocation for women migrants. Low budgets, the inefficient use of budgets, and low allocation for emigrants' welfare with no provision for emigrant women labour, suggest that greater efforts and commitment on the part of the government are needed to transform safe migration from rhetoric to reality.

Gaps in the Bangladeshi Diplomatic Missions' Role

So far there are only 13 labour attachés in the major host countries that recruit a large number of migrants mainly to facilitate recruitment and look after the welfare of emigrant labour. Although MEWOE claims to have strengthened its monitoring mechanism by requiring an official to make two visits to migrant dormitories[17] once a week, existing studies (Afsar et al., 2000; 2002a) reveal that more than 80 per cent of current emigrant labour are not aware of Bangladesh's diplomatic missions abroad, let alone its labour attachés. Doubts have also been raised about mission staff members' alleged involvement in malpractices along with recruitment agencies and employers (Afsar et al., 2000; 2002a; RMMRU, 2002). Moreover, the lack of adequate service motivation, staff, and infrastructure facilities are major barriers which stand in the way of rendering services to expatriate labour. Additionally, legal services rendered are often inadequate, ineffective and untimely because of the huge volume of litigations involved, and currently around 13,000 Bangladeshi workers are in the jails of UAE and Oman. The government has been unwilling to take responsibility for unauthorised migrant workers despite the availability of a repatriation service from IOM (Afsar, 2003).

Gaps in Service and Attitude of Service Providers

Stakeholders like the Bangladesh Association of International Recruiting Agencies (BAIRA) have shown overtly sympathetic attitudes towards migrants and expressed eagerness to reform the existing malpractices and protect the interest of women migrants. In contrast, officials of BMET have been more guarded about their reactions on policy reforms; this is understandable given their location in a bureaucratic set up (Afsar, 2003). The behaviour and attitudes of service providers to migrant women have varied according to their position and the nature of the job. In my survey, migrant domestic workers were most vocal against airport authorities and many recounted how badly they were treated at the airport in their own country. Airport authorities subject those returning from the Middle East, Dubai or Abu Dhabi to a whole range of activities including extra vigilance in baggage checking and tax collection, to demanding *bakshish* (tips for clearing baggage) and even theft and snatching.[18] The experience of Neherun, a return migrant from Kuwait, is a case in point. Upon Neherun's arrival, she needed to pay US$28 as tax to the airport authority. Unfortunately, neither she nor her relatives who came to pick her up was prepared for it. To her surprise, she found an intermediary on the spot notwithstanding the high restriction against public entry. This person lent her money on hourly interest. As it took a long time to release her baggage, the interest multiplied and she ended up paying US$13 and a *jainamaz* (small carpet) as interest.

Lack of Concern for Poor Emigrants in Existing Financial Reforms

Of the total remittances received by the country, transfers through informal channels are at 20–40 per cent, which is high by any standard (Afsar et al., 2000; Murshid et al., 2001; Siddiqui, 2003). The government has recently introduced some important financial and banking sector reforms to attract foreign direct investments (FDIs) and channel remittances through formal banks. Money laundering has been made a cognisable offence through the passing of a new law "Money Laundering Prevention Activity 2002". The Central Bank's monitoring and supervisory role over dealer banks has been intensified and special inspection teams are deployed to identify loopholes and inefficiencies in the foreign exchange management system. The government has also introduced, *inter alia*, a preferential exchange scheme for foreign exchange from reparable foreign-currency accounts (RCFA), the Wage Earners' Scheme (WES) which enables migrants to sell their foreign exchange to importers at daily auctions at a premium over the official exchange rate (Waddington, 2003), and two new bonds exclusively for Bangladeshi expatriates with the specific aim of drawing increased remittances through official channels. However, existing research shows that between two-thirds to three-quarters of expatriate workers are from landless and marginal landholding families and they not only save small amounts, but also cannot keep their savings for long in the bank

128

if they are to meet consumption and subsistence needs (Afsar, 2003). Hence, such financial reforms have little meaning for poor migrant workers, who constitute the bulk of those overseas. Moreover, women domestic workers are mainly dependent on their employers for remitting money due to restricted mobility and hence, they have little say in how the money is remitted.

Barriers to the State's Commitment in Ratifying International Treaties

The state faces some political and economic barriers to ratifying international standards of migrants' rights. None of the international instruments specifically cover the plight of female migrant workers. Moreover, neither the ILO nor the United Nations (UN) has an enforcement mechanism beyond collective political pressure. Given the political sensitivity surrounding labour export, it is difficult to forge cooperation among labour sending countries, for fear of losing their market share to others. The recent World Trade Organisation (WTO) forum in Cancun demonstrated how interests are divided among regions and how negotiations are increasingly becoming tougher. In its report regarding the implementation of CEDAW, the government recognised the severe constraints faced in enforcing existing legislation and regulations to combat all forms of gender-based violence and exploitation.[19] The speedy and humane repatriation of exploited women is not often forthcoming due to poor record keeping (ESCAP, 1999). Moreover, the effective implementation of the law becomes a formidable challenge for the government amidst the presence of vested interests, overarching multinational corporations and contending lobby groups both at home and abroad.

CULTURAL AND HISTORICAL CONTEXTS OF GENDERED MOBILITY AND PAID DOMESTIC WORK

In Bangladesh, rural-urban migration (both permanent and temporary) and overseas contract labour migration are predominant. Internal migration has been a livelihood strategy ever since the passage of the Permanent Settlement Act of Bengal in 1793. Under this arrangement, land was transformed from common property to a commodity, and its acquisition was based on the ability to pay. Increasingly, land became a major source of social stratification and with increasing population, the size of the landless population grew immensely. Over time, competing demand for land for other uses and the Muslim Family Law of Inheritance in 1961 also resulted in further squeezing of land frontiers. As a result, large-scale seasonal movements over long distances for harvests were common. The large majority of agricultural workers received payments in kind, and the monetisation of wages and incomes was common only for a small minority of industrial and service workers up to the 1970s when the country attained independence (Abdullah 1991). Under the "patron-client relationship" that largely prevailed as feature of the society in the absence of any other institutional social security system, poor women often rendered services to the rich and landed gentry in lieu of food, clothes and assurance of help in the time of crisis. This is particularly true for women domestic workers for whom it was—and still is— said that "a full stomach is all that a woman gets out of a day's hard work" (Arens & Beurden, 1977); sometimes "take home" food was provided (McCarthy, 1978).

Under the strict gender segregation of labour between home and outside, and patriarchal notions that considered home and kitchen as women's space and strictly controlled their mobility outside the home, poor women had limited options in the labour market. Impelled by poverty and in the absence of any social security benefits, a large number of women turned to the domestic sector as helpers. Hence, the Labour Force Surveys of the country have always shown a disproportionate share of women as paid or unpaid family labour and/or a persistence of female workers in the personal and community services.

By the 1980s, cash payment had assumed prominence both in rural and urban areas and for both agricultural and non-agricultural work (Abdullah, 1991). This may be related to the penetration of a market-oriented economy. Indeed, during the 1980s, selling labour to other households for food processing and menial work was the most common form of women's work. Such work was done on a daily or weekly basis or at regular intervals (Abdullah & Zeidenstien, 1982); a less common arrangement was year-round work and residence within the same village. Throughout this period, women also migrated to towns and cities in search of livelihood and worked as domestic help. With the advent of the RMG sector mainly in Dhaka City, the migration of young women experienced a manifold increase, leading to some notable changes in women's mobility and occupations due to their entry into the formal sector. However, the demand for female domestic workers in urban households remained and despite occasional shortages in supply, the flow of domestic workers from rural to urban areas was steady. In the face of the breakdown of joint and extended families and the lack of institutional support for childcare, upper- and middle- class women in urban areas have solicited domestic help in order to participate in the labour market. Women have also migrated in large numbers across borders to escape rape and torture by the Pakistani army and as a survival strategy. Since 1971, there has been a slow and steady movement of women across the border to work as domestic workers in India's major cities.[20]

ECONOMIC, SOCIAL AND HEALTH ISSUES

Remittances and Its Contribution

The contribution of remittances to the economy and the debate around its productive versus non-productive use has been a matter of interest to academics and policy makers of the country for long (Quibria, 1986; Mahmood, 1991; Murshid et al., 2001). From a paltry sum of US$56 million in 1976, the flow of remittances crossed US$1 billion in 1993/94 and reached more than US$3 billion in mid-2003. In 1977/78, remittances accounted for 1.1 per cent of the GDP and, the ratio of remittances to the GDP fluctuated at around four per cent. Despite a drastic fall due to the Gulf crisis in the 1990s that forced the return of some 56,000 workers and led to a sudden decline in remittances inflows from Kuwait and Iraq, the annual growth of remittances over the last two decades was around ten per cent. Remittances now contribute around two-thirds of the country's trade balance and are one of the major factors behind generating surplus in the country's current account balance, a great change from its chronic history of trade deficits (Afsar et al., 2000). In the late 1970s, remittances met less than 20 per cent of the deficits; from the 1990s, however, it has exceeded the current account balance and currently the overall balance showed a surplus of US$163 million (Afsar et al., 2000; Centre for Policy Dialogue, 2004). Major initiatives taken by the government to attract remittances through formal sources by streamlining the banking sector and introducing some incentives have helped to boost the flow of remittances not only from developing countries but also some developed countries in the West such as the United States of America, the United Kingdom and Canada.

It is difficult to determine the multiplier effects of migrant domestic workers' remittances in specific localities given that they constitute only a tiny fraction of the total population in areas of origin. Inferences, however, have been made from the existing macro-level data that might have direct or indirect bearing on remittances and regional economics. Using the 1999–2000 National Labour Force Survey's household level data, Rahman (2004) found a significant inverse relationship between remittances and poverty, suggesting that an inflow of remittances reduces the probability of household poverty. Clearly, it shows the poverty-alleviating role of remittances, which is particularly important given that women domestic workers belong to the poorest strata compared to other categories of male or female migrant workers. The spatial distribution of poverty also reveals that Dhaka City and Dhaka district were among the top achievers in the level of the Human Poverty Index (HPI). Given that many migrant domestic workers hail from this region (Afsar, 2004; Sen & Ali 2003), this reflects the level of social progress at migrants' areas of origin.

At the household level, migrants' direct remittances constitute the main economic benefits their households receive. Migrant domestic workers remitted a total of US$2.6 million at the time of the survey (Table 4.6). In absolute terms, the size of the remittances they sent was equivalent to a little over half of that sent by male migrants. The repayment of loans and recurrent consumption of the family were the two major items that took away the lion's share (nearly 60 per cent) of the total remittances sent back home, reflecting that unlike men, borrowing was the major source of finance for women's migration. Nearly 27 per cent of the remittances was used for productive purposes including the purchase of agricultural land, building houses, generating savings and investing in businesses. However, the productive use of remittances was found to be much lower in migrant domestic workers' households compared with their male counterparts who spent 40 per cent on this account. The big gap found in the pattern of use of remittances is partly the result of the duration of migration and

TABLE 4.6 Patterns of remittances used by families of migrant female domestic workers and male workers

Use of Remittances	Female domestic workers (N=25)		Male workers (N=78)	
	% of total remittances	% of total families	% of total remittances	% of total families
Recurrent household consumption	31.56	84.00	36.50	100.00
Buying land	13.64	24.00	20.05	26.66
Construction of house/ repairing room	9.28	16.00	17.11	39.05
Repayment of loan	30.41	84.00	9.18	47.62
Savings/fixed deposit	0.77	4.00	2.57	9.52
Jewellery/furniture/ electronic appliances	4.36	88.00	4.73	110.47[a]
Investments in business	3.38	20.00	0.46	1.90
Financed migration of other family members	0.98	8.00	2.29	6.67
Daughter's marriage	3.66	20.00	4.24	17.14
Treatment/litigation/ court case	0.84	12.00	1.35	11.42
Others	1.10	-	1.54	16.19
Total amount of remittances	100.0	100.00	100.00	100.00
(in US$)	2632.89		4934.24	

SOURCES: Adapted and computed from Afsar et al., 2000; Afsar, 2002a.
NOTE:
a   As families often spent on one or more of the three items (respondents were asked about expenditure on jewellery, furniture and electronic appliances as separate categories and the results merged), totals may exceed 100% (each row represents the percentage of total households).

the size of remittances, and partly reflects the household's ability to generate savings after meeting subsistence, the extent of liability of repayment and the prudence of fund managers (Afsar, 2002a).

Women migrants remitted mostly to male members of the household (husband, father or brother). While the wives of male migrants played a vital role in making productive use of remittances, the male recipients of female migrants' remittances were not very keen on thrift savings and some of the domestic workers complained of the misuse of remittances by their husbands. Upon their return, nearly a third of the domestic workers surveyed received about US$300 of savings on average, set aside from the remittances they sent home. Most of those who received money did so from their parents or siblings. The unlucky ones were those who had sent money to husbands, as many of them did not receive any savings. Ironically, husbands were the single largest recipients of remittances (48 per cent), whilst parent and sibling together constituted 40 per cent of the recipients.

However, compared to their pre-migration situations, the income of the domestic workers' households increased by 34 per cent or an average of US$15 per month (Table 4.7). It suggests that without any observable change in the composition of household income and despite limited productive use of remittances, remittances can make a difference in the level of income. However, as opposed to male migrants' households where the level of income increased by 55 per cent and remittances alone contributed two-thirds to the household income, remittances for domestic workers have had a relatively modest impact in determining the income of women migrant's households.

TABLE 4.7 Contribution of different sources of income to the families of female domestic workers and male workers before and after migration

Sources of income	Families of migrant domestic workers (N=25)			Families of emigrant male labour (N=78)		
	Before	After	% Change	Before	After	% Change
Agriculture	4.15	4.77	54.36	26.75	15.22	−11.63
Non-agricultural wage and salary	31.72	32.25	36.55	41.14	8.03	−69.70
Business	41.29	37.82	23.02	23.51	11.36	−24.91
Remittances	10.94	8.79	8.00	7.11	64.39	1305.98
Others sources	11.90	16.37	84.83	1.49	1.00	4.53
Total income	100.0	100.0	–	100.0	100.0	–
US$	677.17	909.6	34.32	994.15	1544.28	55.34
Families below poverty level (%)	72.0	44.0	−38.9	39.7	–	–

SOURCES: Adapted and computed from Afsar et al., 2000; Afsar, 2002a.

For domestic workers who had no paid job prior to migration, their overseas stint was an important source of income and livelihood (Afsar, 2002a). Our survey revealed that economic conditions improved for more than half of the domestic workers surveyed. This was mainly due to a change in the nature of their husband's job which ranged from non-agricultural labour to petty businesses such as the opening of a small shop, processing and selling mustard oil and vegetables, and running a poultry firm. While foreign domestic work does not generate new skills or employment opportunities for women themselves, it does open up some avenues for their family members to earn a greater income. Only four women were directly involved in petty businesses, mainly from the savings generated from their remittances. Nonetheless, using the poverty line income drawn from the existing estimates (Economic Relation Division, 2003), we found that the proportion of households earning above the poverty level doubled after migration (from 28 per cent to 56 per cent) compared with pre-migration situation. Moreover, around 40 per cent of the domestic workers managed to buy land and build their own huts in their hometowns or villages with their remittances. Thus, overseas employment empowers the women by strengthening their asset base and improving their family's economic situation.

An analysis of well-being remains incomplete unless the household expenditure interface is brought into consideration. Data on expenditure patterns partly corroborates with Engel's law, which in essence presumes a decline in food expenditure and an increase in non-food expenditure (particularly luxurious and other supernumerary items are important indicators of the level of family welfare). In comparison to the expenditure patterns of poor households in general (Bangladesh Bureau of Statistics, 2003), expenditure on food in the households of migrant domestic workers—estimated at around 64 per cent—was lower than both that of the urban and rural poor. With regard to expenditure on education, the net enrolment rate estimated for children (6–10 years old) of the domestic workers' households at primary level was 75 per cent, which is consistent with the national pattern (Economic Relation Division, 2003). At the secondary level, however, it is lower than the national level (56 per cent vis-à-vis 65 per cent) although much higher than for both rural and urban poor age cohorts (at 53 per cent and 47 per cent respectively) (Bangladesh Bureau of Statistics, 2003).[21]

Impacts on Family Politics

From the existing literature, it is difficult to ascertain changes in spousal relations due to lack of before-and-after data and longitudinal studies. Anecdotal evidence from post-migration experiences, however, suggests that there are both positive and negative aspects. On the positive side, the domestic workers we spoke to gained confidence and played a more active role in the family's decision-making process. More than two-thirds took decisions on family's vital matters related to purchasing and selling of land, the construction of a house or additional rooms, buying livestock and furniture, borrowing money, and their children's education. The proportion of women who took decisions was particularly high for those in nuclear families or in a de facto situation where they were heads of households. Likewise almost 70 per cent of current women migrants who made decisions were unmarried and lived in nuclear family with parents. Their parents often consulted them for borrowing money and or repairing house. Married women, who predominantly had joint and extended family types at origin, were only consulted about the education of their children. Overseas migration also helped increase their mobility and strengthened their social capital beyond the family. For example, a quarter of the migrant domestic workers went outside the home at night and another quarter went to the market whenever they needed, without having to ask for permission from or inform their husband or guardian beforehand. In a sex-segregated patriarchal society, this signifies a "big leap forward". More than three-quarters of them were also in a position to mobilise funds from relatives and friends, which suggests improvements in social capital, compared to pre-migration situation when they had to rely mostly on moneylenders.

On the negative side, we found ample evidence of money squandering by husbands and male relatives (Afsar, 2002a). The case of Hamida Begum is presented here as an example. Hamida returned from Kuwait in 1996 after two years of work as a domestic helper in a Kuwaiti family. Before leaving for Kuwait, she had married a man who already had a wife, but his parents did not recognise their marriage. Although he had pledged to remain faithful to her, he went back to his parents and first wife during her absence. As soon as he started receiving remittances regularly from her, he left his job. Within a year, Hamida had remitted about Taka 100,000 (US$1,961) to her husband for investment in a profitable venture. Fortunately, fear of interest and pressure from relatives compelled him to repay the Taka 65,000, which they had borrowed from moneylenders and relatives to finance Hamida's overseas trip; the remaining Taka 40,000, however, was squandered away without saving anything for Hamida. Thus after her return, Hamida had to start from scratch again. Although her husband left his first wife to rejoin her, the job he got as a night guard in a private textile mill did not pay enough (just Taka 1,500 per month) even for bare sustenance. Hamida was forced to borrow from her own relatives almost every month to make ends meet. Unfortunately, she also failed to get a job because of a leg injury that left her legs weak and painful. As a result she could not get enough strength and confidence to work in a factory. As she noted:

My unconditional trust in my husband put me in adverse situations both before and after migration. During all these years of sweat and drudgery, I saved such a huge sum of money, and remitted it to my husband with a dream of living a life free of want and uncertainty. But my dreams have faded away due to my husband's overindulgent behaviour and prodigality. I wonder how long I have to struggle against this ill-fate, ill-health and the crunch of poverty.

Family breakups that occurred during the domestic worker's absence were also quite common. About a quarter of the migrant domestic workers reported the remarriages of their husbands. For these men, their wives' overseas migration provided them with both an opportunity and excuse for remarriage. Husbands were the major custodians of children while their wives were working abroad as domestic workers. However, in terms of household chores, parents and siblings assumed greater responsibility. In cases where husbands managed domestic work, they did so with the help of older children. Some of the husbands complained about the problems they faced with regard to the supervision of children and their studies during their wives' absence, a few migrant domestic workers faced truancy among their school-going children and there was a solitary case of drug abuse. How women compromised their reproductive role can be seen from the following excerpt from an interview with Amin, a child of a current migrant domestic worker at the time of the interview (Afsar 2002a):

> I feel sad and miss my mother during sickness. My *khala* (maternal aunt) looks after me when I am sick. She is the most approachable person in the case of problems. Yet there is none with whom I can share the most intimate information. I feel neglected and jealous when I see my friends accompanied by their mothers to school. I will not allow my mother to leave me again.

Surprisingly, there is sharp divide between those children who want their mothers to be housewives upon their return and others who would like them to continue their job. Whilst some of them look forward to their mothers' love upon return, others are concerned about their loss of their freedom, and/or capital. Similar concerns are also found among male migrants' children who otherwise do not miss their father much since they are taken care of by their mother.

Access to Health Facilities for Returned Migrant Domestic Workers

Due to their heavy work loads and long working hours, a quarter of the migrant domestic workers we spoke to reported spending an average of approximately US$24 for medicine and pathological tests while abroad and many complained of recurrent sickness and even disability after their return. Unfortunately, they do not enjoy any free medical services or health check up facilities after return. There is no life and medical insurance policy. None of the existing safety-net programmes of the government cover migrant workers, and future pension plans for return migrants do not exist. During interviews, BMET officials claimed that workers are covered by insurance schemes of the employers. However, it has been found that workers are often prevented from claiming redress because of lack of awareness and unfamiliarity with rules/procedures (Rodrigo, 1992; Afsar et al., 2000).

A Wage Earner's Welfare Fund was created in November 1990. So far, its use has been limited to a one-time contribution to the families of deceased workers who are not covered by employers' insurance.[22] However, between 1996 and 2000, only three per cent of the total money under this fund had been spent for this purpose. It clearly shows that life and health insurance of workers remain grossly neglected by both the government and non government entities (private recruiting bodies and NGOs), despite high mortality and morbidity problems in the Middle East among migrant labour.

NGO ACTIVITIES AND CIVIL SOCIETY SPACE

The Work of Active NGOs and Civil Society in the Country

Although Bangladesh is well known for the massive involvement of NGOs in development activities, none of the major NGOs cover migrant labour in a big way (Siddiqui, 2003). Migrants are often perceived as better-off groups and hence, sympathetic public opinion is not always forthcoming within the country, particularly in terms of regular media campaigns and a strong voice in civil society. Nonetheless, it is encouraging that several NGOs—Bangladesh National Women's Legal Agency (BNWLA), Bangladesh Society of Human Rights (BSEHR), Bangladesh Legal and Services Trust (BLAST) and Ain-o-Shalish Kendro (ASK)—are active in providing legal assistance and protecting the interest of migrant workers both at home and abroad. They have lobbied for the signing of UN conventions and against the ban on migrant domestic workers. However, compared to the need and the volume of overseas migration, the services they render cover only a small proportion of the 20,000 workers who migrate annually.

In recent years, some human rights based organisations have introduced services for migrant workers. For example, the Christian Commission for Development of Bangladesh (CCDB) started HIV/AIDS-related services jointly with the Kuala Lumpur-based CARAM Asia. It also funded an education and health development programme, SHISUK (Shikka Shasta Unnayan Karzakram). Currently SHISUK provides pre-departure orientation to migrant workers going to Malaysia.

A few return women migrants also formed the Bangladesh Women Migrants Association (BWMA) with the active support of IOM. BWMA strongly feels that staff members of diplomatic missions abroad must treat migrant workers well and render effective services for their protection. They have demanded that the government supervise the activities of these missions and take an active interest in the repatriation of migrant workers detained in large numbers in the jails of host countries (Afsar, 2003). They run skill-training programmes in garment manufacture to help reintegrate return women migrants into the economy. They also run consciousness-raising programmes for migrant workers and their families to make them aware about the existing loopholes and fraudulent practices in the process of recruitment.

Following the UN Convention of Protection of All Migrant Workers and Members of Their Families, a section of return migrants formed the Welfare Association of

Return Bangladeshi Employees (WARBE) in 1997 mainly to protect the interests and rights of migrant workers and their families. More specifically, its objectives are to:

- empower migrant workers so that they can act as an advocacy group to influence the government in the formulation of appropriate policies on migrant workers and undertake welfare oriented programmes;
- take necessary measures against the spread of HIV/AIDS among migrant workers; and
- work as an information centre for migrant workers to make them aware of different forms of exploitation.

So far it has concentrated on organising branch offices in those districts that are marked by high overseas migration in order to maintain effective connections with migrants. They have also penalised a few private recruitment agents for exploiting migrant workers with the help of legal aid from BLAST. However, it is increasingly agitating to have migrants' representation in pre-departure briefing sessions and in the management of the Wage Earners' Welfare Fund to protect the interest of migrants. Notwithstanding their laudable objectives, they are still very much donor-dependent and, except for organising a few ceremonial activities, they do not have much visibility or many activities on a regular basis.

Research institutions like the Bangladesh Institute of Development Studies (BIDS) have been researching on international migration since 1980 (Mahmood, 1988; 1989; 1996; 1998; Afsar et al., 2000; Murshid et al., 2001; Afsar, 2002a; 2003) and have presented their findings in many policy forums for the protection of migrant workers. The Bangladesh Unnayan Parishad (Ahmad & Zohra, 1997) and the Refugee and Migratory Movements Research Unit (RMMRU) have also studied different aspects of international migration (Siddiqui, 2001; 2003; Siddiqui & Abrar, 2001). RMMRU, which is also registered as an NGO, is advocating the lifting of the ban against unskilled women labour. However, women migrants of all categories interviewed for this study (e.g., return, current and would-be migrants) were neither aware of such welfare associations nor of the other civil society institutions mentioned above. Media coverage on migrants' issues is sporadic and inadequate compared to the magnitude of the issues involved. Members of civil society, as well as migrants themselves and their family members, continue to voice the need to withdraw the ban on unskilled women migrants, as it puts women migrants in greater jeopardy instead of protecting them.

THE WAY FORWARD

The Bangladeshi government's recent move to permit women domestic workers to migrate with conditions that make the employer and private recruitment agencies transparent and accountable is a good one but it is important to watch how the government monitors the activities of the employers and the private recruiters. As accompaniment of husbands as a precondition for migrant domestic workers' mobility contravenes the human rights of women and the constitution of the country and cannot effectively protect them from abuse and exploitation, migrant domestic workers should be allowed to migrate on their own. *Dalals* or sub-agents of recruitment agencies must be registered and must display photo identity and, with the help of local government bodies and the district offices of BMET and MWCA, the list of registered sub-agents should be published to establish a more transparent system at the grassroots level. Good recruitment practices need to be identified and their geographical coverage extended. Following the example of the Philippines Overseas Employment Administration (POEA), MEWOE should specify a model contract, launch country-wide information dissemination campaigns about existing services and service providers (including NGOs and private recruitment agencies and their registered agents) through the mass media. It should also publicise complaints of migrant workers and their success stories.

There should also be "a complaints cell" both at the Department of Women's Affairs and BMET, where any aggrieved man or woman can walk in and lodge their complaints both at the headquarters and district level offices. Regular meetings between MEWOE and other authorities such as the Ministry of Employment, the Foreign Ministry, BMET's management, MOWCA and the Civil Aviation Authority should be held to examine those complaints and take necessary measures to redress them. Women's legal aid agencies and advocacy groups should also be invited to be part of the monitoring team. Although presently MEWOE claims to receive complaints and act accordingly, there is no publicity and awareness about this mechanism. Hence, it is important to have inter-ministerial coordination to help monitor the performance of different service providers and identify both "good" and "bad" performers. Whilst bad performers should be penalised, the good ones deserve rewards to induce healthy competition among recruiters. In consonance with the ratification of the International Convention on the Protection of the Rights of All Migrant Workers and Members of Their Families, efforts should also be made to document the abuse of migrant's rights.

Moreover, the briefing session at BMET must be made more effective by involving researchers, and return migrants to share their findings and experiences. Lawyers dealing with international migrants, former labour attachés, and ambassadors should be invited as guest speakers to talk about labour laws of the host country. Considering the low level of literacy among unskilled migrants, tape-recorded instructions can be given to departing migrant workers following Pakistan's example.

Given the high morbidity rate among migrants and their manifold vulnerabilities, a certain portion of the Welfare Fund should be used for providing legal and medical services from the Diplomatic Mission. Similar services can be offered by MEWOE. The relationship between migration and health concerns must be assessed carefully and monitored regularly at international, national and local levels. Return migrants and their families must be able to access government services in terms of health, counselling and social insurance. The current safety-net programmes of the government must develop social insurance for return migrant domestic workers and their family members.

In the light of the blatant gender discrimination in wage and other entitlements, and problems of irregular wage and employer misbehaviour faced by female workers, the government should negotiate to bring migrant domestic workers under legal protection and entitlements, with specified working hours a day, overtime pay, a weekly off-day, medical insurance and protection against physical and sexual abuses. In an era of interdependence among nations, enforcing the Convention on Migrant Worker's rights is dependent on international cooperation, coordination and advocacy. Since Bangladesh is one of the major labour sending countries, it must regularly present reports of violation of human rights at the UN Commission on Human Rights. Apart from such international advocacy, it is urgent for the government to network with both developing and developed countries to adopt free flows of human labour, under WTO agreements. This is important given the ever-increasing volume of migration and its potential for development and poverty reduction, and the reduction of the economic vulnerability of developing countries. If migration policy could be linked to economic and trade policies within the region such as SAARC and wider forums like the Organisation of Islamic Conference (OIC), the dangers associated with irregular migration can be reduced. It could facilitate regional and bilateral agreements on migrant protection, and foreign exchange or currency transfer (which would impact remittances).

Bangladeshi overseas labour migrants, both men and women, play an important role in contributing to the economic growth and development of the country. They deserve some facilities in return, such as easier access to loans for pursuing productive activities once they return home. As an incentive to remit through formal channels, migrants should be issued a receipt from the bank and, upon production of those receipts, they should be eligible for entrepreneurship loans. Similarly, nationalised banks through which migrants remit their cash could introduce compulsory savings schemes to safeguard against future uncertainty. Furthermore, following the example of the Sri Lankan practice of insurance, poor women's banks or credible NGOs can launch insurance programmes for migrants and their families.

There is also a need for a better system of data collection on migrants and remittances flows. The government's recent move to collect data at the airport is a welcome step in this direction. However, as noted earlier, the database still lacks gender disaggregation, an issue which demands immediate attention. It is also important for Bangladesh to monitor changes in labour and financial flows and remittances. All these will better enable foreign employment policy planning and administration, and facilitate appropriate policies for the re-integration of return migrants.

NOTES

1. Parts of the chapter on the existing services and stakeholders are heavily borrowed from Afsar's (2003) recent study on "Rapid Social Investigation on Policies, Mechanisms and Services and Issues of Migrant Women Workers of Bangladesh", which was sponsored and funded by UNIFEM under its Asia-Pacific Programme for Empowerment of Migrant Women Workers.

2. Interviews with key representatives of government, national and international organisations involved in international migration, private recruiting agencies and its apex body, NGOs working on emigrant workers, and focus group discussion with different categories of female migrants and their families in 2003 gave us an opportunity to get the "other side of the story" from the stakeholders.

3. In order to minimise recall bias, only women who returned from the United Arab Emirates (UAE) within the last two years were selected. To ensure compatibility with other groups, the women were initially chosen using a random number table. However, during fieldwork, because of the difficulty of accessing the women due to their frequent changes of address, women from Kuwait, Bahrain and Oman were also selected as a result. However, Saudi Arabia was avoided because of its different working conditions.

4. Migrant male and female RMG factory workers had seven and five years of schooling respectively. While migrant male labour had a wide range of options to be employed in other formal and informal sectors, women had only two frontiers of overseas employment: manufacturing and domestic service.

5. There are 64 districts in Bangladesh. The entire country is divided into six Divisions, with districts being the highest administrative tier under the Divisions.

6. The survey was conducted in June–August 2000 when US$1 was the equivalent of Taka 54.

7. This is also consistent with the macro-level pattern that shows Kuwait alone absorbing around 45 per cent of the domestic workers and 85 per cent of the cleaners from Bangladesh during 1991–1999 (Afsar, 2002a).

8. More than a tenth (12 per cent) of the women migrant domestic workers cited sociological factors such as marital discord, greater freedom, and the desire to get rid of family conflict as the main reason for migration.

9. Maximising the family's income was also a major motivation for migrant domestic workers who migrated from joint and extended families, but they had greater flexibility due to the presence of more than one adult member.

10. Family assets include land, houses or any other property, which they sold or mortgaged to manage their passage to the Middle East.

11. Male migrant workers who procured visas from their family members paid more than those whose visa providers were recruitment agents. This could partly be due to difficulty on the part of their relatives to get visas or work permit and negotiate for airfare. Increasingly, buying and selling of visas has become a lucrative business for a group of people, making it extremely difficult to procure them from regular channels.

12. For example, the gender wage ratio in UAE is one of the worst where a female factory worker in the RMG sector receives only 44 per cent of what is earned by her male

counterpart in the same sector and around half the wage of her male compatriot in other sectors. Migrant domestic workers were worse off, earning only 53 per cent of female RMG sector workers' gross incomes (Afsar, 2002a).

13 This has been highlighted in various declarations and documents such as the Beijing Declaration and Platform for Action (PFA), Convention on the Elimination of All Forms of Discrimination Against Women (CEDAW), Constitution of the People's Republic of Bangladesh, National Policy for the Advancement of Women, National Action Plan for the Advancement of Women (NAP) and the Fifth Five Year Plan (1997–2002).

14 The NGOs operate micro-credit programmes for landless and land-poor women. They cover around two-thirds of all villages.

15 Currently, there are 713 private recruiting agencies operating under the aegis of the Bangladesh Association of International Recruiting Agencies (BAIRA). Existing laws cover recruitment processes, licensing, ensuring minimum standards in working conditions and minimum wages of expatriate workers and penalties in the case of breach of rules or fraudulent practices.

16 The Dubai Workmen's Compensation Ordinance of 1965 does not apply to "persons engaged in domestic services including cooks, drivers, nurses, gardeners and similar workers". Similarly under *Shariah* Law practices of Saudi Arabia and Abu Dhabi, women are entitled to only half the compensation a man is entitled to (Waddington, 2003).

17 The dormitories or barracks for migrant labour in the UAE are referred to as "labour camps".

18 Sometimes migrants find their suitcases cut open from the bottom and the valuables removed. Others find that once they come out of the terminal, they often fall prey to privately-run transport services whose owners snatch valuables from their passengers.

19 Bangladesh CEDAW Report, 1 April 1997 (www.sdnpbd.org/sdi/international_day/women's_day/2004/women_trafficking.htm).

20 This movement has remained largely undocumented for political reason (see also Raghuram, this volume). Official documentation of women's emigration started only in the mid-1970s.

21 Enrolment rate for their age cohorts in rural and urban poor households were estimated at 52.7 per cent and 46.7 per cent respectively (Bangladesh Bureau of Statistics, 2003).

22 The Wage Earner's Welfare Fund was created by the government with the subscriptions from expatriate workers, interests earned from the security money deposited by private recruitment agencies, the ten per cent surcharge collected by Bangladeshi diplomatic missions abroad and personal as well as institutional contributions.

REFERENCES

Abdullah, A. A., ed. 1991. *Modernisation at Bay: Structure and Change in Bangladesh*. Dhaka: University Press Limited.

Abdullah, T. A. & S. A. Zeidenstein. 1982. *Village Women of Bangladesh: Prospects for Change*. Oxford: Pergamon Press.

Abella, M. 1997 *Sending Workers Abroad*. Geneva: ILO.

_____. 1999. Protecting temporary migrant workers: The challenges for modernising states in Asia. In OECD, *Labour Migration and the Recent Financial Crisis in Asia*. Paris: OECD Proceedings.

Afsar, R. 2002a. *International Labour Migration of Women: A Case Study of Bangladesh*. Dhaka: Ministry of Women and Children Affairs, Government of the People's Republic of Bangladesh.

_____. 2002b. Labour and employment sector and gender. Unpublished paper under RPM funded project, Mainstreaming Gender Perspective in the Planning and Development Process of the Economy with Special Emphasis on the 6th Five Year Plan. Dhaka: Bangladesh Institute of Development Studies.

_____. 2002c. *Micro Finance and Women's Empowerment: Insights from a Micro-level Sociological Study*. A report prepared for the Bangladesh Institute of Development Studies (BIDS) and World Bank Study on Impact of Micro Credit Program (MCP), Dhaka.

_____. 2003. *Rapid Social Investigation on Policies, Mechanisms and Services and Issues of Migrant Women Workers of Bangladesh*. Dhaka: Bangladesh Institute of Development Studies, Mimeo.

_____. 2004. Dynamics of poverty, development and population mobility: The Bangladesh case. *Asia-Pacific Population Journal*, 19(2), 69–91.

Afsar, R., Y. Mohammad, & A. B. M. Shamsul Islam. 2000. *Are Migrants Chasing After the Perilous Illusion? A Study on Cost-Benefit Analysis of Overseas Migration by the Bangladeshi Labour*. A report prepared for the International Organization for Migration (IOM), Bangladesh Institute of Development Studies, Dhaka, Mimeo.

Ahmad, Q. K. & F. Zohra. 1997. *Utilisation of Remittances from Abroad for Local Employment Promotion: A Case of Sylhet Division*. Geneva, Dhaka: ILO and Unnayan Prarishad, Mimeo.

Arens, J. & V. Beurden. 1977. *Jhagrapur: Poor Peasants and Women in a Village in Bangladesh*. Amsterdam: Third World Publication.

Bangladesh Bureau of Statistics. 2002a. *Statistical Yearbook of Bangladesh 2000*. Dhaka: Ministry of Planning, Government of the People's Republic of Bangladesh.

_____. 2002b. *Labour Force Survey 1999/2000*. Dhaka: Ministry of Planning, Government of the People's Republic of Bangladesh.

_____. 2003. *Report of the Household Expenditure Survey 2002*. Dhaka: Ministry of Planning, Government of the People's Republic of Bangladesh.

Centre for Policy Dialogue. 2004. *Independent Review of Bangladesh's Development on State of the Bangladesh Economy in the Fiscal year 2003–04*. Dhaka: Centre for Policy Dialogue.

Coleman, J. S. 1999. Social capital in the creation of human capital. In *Social Capital—A Multifacted Perspective*. Edited by P. Dasgupta, & I. Serageldin. Washington, D.C.: World Bank, 13–39.

Economic Relation Division. 2003. *Bangladesh: A National Strategy for Economic Growth, Poverty Reduction and Social Development*. Dhaka: Ministry of Finance, Government of the People's Republic of Bangladesh.

Economic and Social Commission for Asia and the Pacific (ESCAP). 1999. *High Level Intergovernmental Meeting to Review Regional Implementation of the Beijing Platform for Action*,

Panel IV: Monitoring and Evaluation Strategies for the Empowerment of Women. Bangkok: ESCAP, United Nations.

Krishna, A. & N. Uphoff. 1999. *Mapping and Measuring Social Capital: A Conceptual and Empirical Study of Collective Action for Conserving and Developing Watersheds in Rajasthan, India*. Social Capital Initiative Working Paper No. 13, Washington D. C.: The World Bank

Mahmood, R. A. 1988. *Post Migration Adjustment Problems and Policy Option: A Case study of Bangladesh*. Bangladesh Institute of Development Studies, Dhaka, Mimeo.

———. 1989. *Post Migration Adjustment of Returning Migrants: Problems and Policy Options: A Case study of Bangladesh*. Working Paper, Dhaka: UNU/ILO.

———. 1991. International migration, remittances and development: Untapped potentials for Bangladesh. *BIISS Journal*, 12, 527–57.

———. 1996. Immigration dynamics in Bangladesh: Level pattern and implication. Unpublished paper prepared for the Asiatic Society of Bangladesh, Dhaka.

———. 1998. Globalization, international migration and human development: Linkage and implications. Unpublished paper prepared for UNDP, New York.

Martin, P. & T. Straubhaar. 2002. Best practices to reduce migration pressures. *International Migration Quarterly Review*, 40(3), 139–42.

Massey, D. S., A. Joaquin, G. Hugo, K. Ali, A. Pellegrino, & J. E. Taylor. 1998. *World in Motion: Understanding International Migration at the End of the Millennium*. Oxford: Clarendon Press.

Masum, M. 2000. Youth Employment in Bangladesh. Paper presented at The XIII Biennial Conference of the Bangladesh Economic Association, 10–12 August in Dhaka, Bangladesh,.

Matilla, H. 2001. Migrant's human rights: Principles and practice. *International Migration*, 38(6), 53–72.

Mayoux, L. 1995. Beyond naivity: Women, gender, inequality and participatory development. *Development and Change*, 25(3), 497–526.

McCarthy, F. 1978. *The Status and Conditions of Women in Bangladesh*. Dhaka: Women's Section, Planning and Development Division, Ministry of Agriculture and Forest.

Mujeri, K. M. 2002. Bangladesh: External Sector Performance and Recent Issues. Paper presented at The Seminar on Performance of the Bangladesh Economy: Selected Issues, 2 April in Dhaka, Bangladesh.

Murshid, K. A. S., I. Kazi, & A. Meherun. 2001. *A Study on Remittance Inflows and Utilisation*. Research Report No. 170, Dhaka: Bangladesh Institute of Development Studies.

Quibria, M. G. 1986. Migrants workers and remittances: Issues for Asian developing countries. *Asian Development Review*, 4, 78–99.

Rahman, R. I. 2004. Unemployment and labour market situation in Bangladesh: Linkages with poverty. Paper presented at The Seminar on Employment Growth, Unemployment and Labour Market: Linkages with Poverty Alleviation, 12 June in Dhaka, Bangladesh,.

RMMRU. 2002. *A Review of Recruitment and Registration of Bangladeshi Emigrant Worker*. Dhaka: IOM South Asian Regional Office (in Bengali).

Rodrigo, C. 1992. Overseas migration from Sri Lanka: Magnitude, patterns and trends. *Asian Exchange*, 8(3–4), 41–74.

Sen, B. & Z. Ali. 2003. Spatial inequality in social progress in Bangladesh. Revised draft report prepared under Chronic Poverty Study, Dhaka: Bangladesh Institute of Development Studies.

Siddiqui, T. 2001. *Transcending Boundaries: Labour Migration of Women from Bangladesh*. Dhaka: University Press Limited.

————. 2003. Migration as a livelihood strategy of the poor: The Bangladesh case. Paper presented at *The Regional Conference on Migration and Pro-Poor Policy Choices in Asia*, 22–24 June in Dhaka, Bangladesh.

Siddiqui, T. & C. R. Abrar. 2001. *Migrant Workers' Remittances and Micro-Finance Institutions*. Geneva: ILO, Mimeo.

Skeldon, R. 1999. *Migration of Women in the Context of Globalization in the Asian and Pacific Region*, Discussion Paper Series No. 2. Bangkok: Women in Development, ESCAP.

United Nations. 2002. *International Migration Report*. Population Division, Sales No. E 03.XIII.4, New York.

Waddington, C. 2003. International migration policies in Asia: A synthesis of ILO and other literature on polices seeking to manage the recruitment and protection of migrants and facilitate remittances and their investment. Paper presented at The Regional Conference on Migration and Pro-Poor Policy Choices in Asia, 22–24 June in Dhaka, Bangladesh.

CHAPTER 5

Global Maid Trade: Indian Domestic Workers in the Global Market[1]

PARVATI RAGHURAM

GLOBAL MAID TRADE: INDIAN DOMESTIC WORKERS IN THE GLOBAL MARKET

During the last decade, skilled migrant workers from India "stole" the narrative on migration as the macroeconomic effects of such migration came to be recognised (Aneesh, 2000; Xiang, 2001; Gayathri, 2002). Although the period also saw an increase in domestic workers migrating from India to take up jobs in other countries, notably in the Middle East, the small proportion of such migrants to the total numbers of domestic workers employed in India, and their more marginal impact on Indian macroeconomics, has meant that interest in migrant domestic workers has been limited. As a result, there have so far been few sustained studies on the issues facing Indian domestic workers who migrate to work in other countries.

The neglect of foreign domestic workers is part of a larger lack of concern on the part of post-Independence governments in the fate of Indians who migrate to work abroad (Nair, 1999; Lall, 2001). From 1947, the nation state project and internal integration dominated the national agenda and its foreign policy priorities were "based on the ideology of economic self-sufficiency, anti-imperialism and non-alignment" (Lall, 2001:6). With few exceptions, this attitude to definitions of the nation and to foreign investment set the framework for dealing with those in the Indian diaspora. Economic liberalisation policies adopted by the Finance Minister Dr. Manmohan Singh in 1991 marked the beginning of a shift in this attitude with an increasing number of concessions made available to non-resident Indians (NRIs). These policies were designed to accelerate economic development and to increase foreign reserves and, as such, the incentives offered were primarily of relevance to investors and business people. The declaration of 9 January as Pravasi Bharatiya Diwas (Non-Resident Indian day), an annual celebration of the diasporic population, marked the further opening up of India to its diaspora and another step in the effort to better understand the demands and the requirements of the Indian diaspora and their expectations from the mother country (Ministry of External Affairs, 2001). The dominant narratives of the Indian government on the Indian diaspora are therefore either of cultural connections (especially within the context of older histories of migration) or of economic success and global connections. The role of Indian migrants in the information technology (IT) boom, particularly until 2001, and the continuing importance and dominance of outsourcing as a source of jobs in India have further determined the narrative about the diaspora. It is in this context that there has been little recognition of the importance of service workers migrating from India, particularly service workers who are at the lowest paid informal end of the sector—domestic workers.

Much of the existing literature on domestic work has highlighted the ways in which the undervaluing of care work within capitalism has meant that women in some parts of the world who can afford to do so are turning their back on this work and subcontracting it to migrant women (Anderson, 2000; Sassen, 2000; Hondagneu-Sotelo, 2001; Parreñas, 2001; Ehrenreich & Hochschild, 2003). Gender and generational inequalities in the division of care work in both sending and in receiving households also play a large part in shaping the causes and consequences of female labour migration. When men refuse to take part in childcare and the care of the elderly, women who are left with prime responsibilities for such tasks relegate them to other women rather than contend with these inequalities (Hochschild, 1997; 2000). Similarly intergenerational conflicts over care work between mothers-in-law and daughters-in-law, or mothers and children, too may be resolved through employing domestic workers (Lan, 2003). On the other hand, women often seek employment as domestic workers because they face marital difficulties that they find impossible to resolve at home (see McKay, this volume). In other cases, as I suggest below, migration is a response to economic hardships engendered by marital breakdown.

The state too plays an important role in the dynamics of the organisation of migrant domestic labour (Chang & Ling, 2000; Huang & Yeoh, 2003). In the receiving state, the casualisation of care work, the transfer of much of this work into the private sector and the deregulation of care has meant that people in First World countries have increasingly had to resort to private provision of care (Anderson, 2001). This has encouraged the employment of migrant labour. In sending countries, migrant women have been seen as key contributors to the national purse, as providers of foreign exchange so that some states are relying on migrant women's remittances to fund development and growth (see Asis, this volume). As such, they have facilitated the migration of women who take up domestic work in the receiving countries (Gamburd, 2000; Kottegoda, 2003) and are complicit in regimes of labour that provide "sexualized, racialised service for certain sectors and members of the world political economy" (Chang & Ling, 2000:36). But as Parreñas (2003) has forcefully argued, such women are also cast as deserting their caring responsibilities at home. Migrant women are both lauded for their contribution to the nation and decried for creating a care crisis at home.

The role of the Indian state in shaping migrant domestic work has been rather different. In India there has been little attempt to analyse the gendered nature of emigration (Shah, 1994; Premi & Mathur, 1995; Sasikumar, 2001) and little discussion of issues facing transnational migrant women, or about those who move to engage in paid domestic work. Within India itself there is also little recognition of domestic work as "work" and hence a refusal to bring domestic work under the remit of labour laws. The failure to recognise this sector within the country conditions the way in which these workers are seen (and see themselves) abroad. It is important and necessary to institutionalise rights for workers at home, for them to have a sense of their rights abroad. The Indian government has set up systems of control over domestic worker migration, which are deployed to protect migrants, but they are provided from a paternalistic point of view, i.e. to protect the rights of women, rather than that of workers or of migrants. This paternalistic attitude of the government is particularly problematic given the extent to which patriarchal relations at home condition the migration of Indian domestic workers. It is often divorced, separated or widowed women who find it difficult to earn a living within India, and hence migrate. As such, passing the welfare of migrant women to families at home can be inappropriate and inadequate. Finally, while current forms of control over domestic worker migration provides protection for some workers, by embedding the rights of domestic workers in their status (documented/undocumented), these regulations deny rights to most workers in this sector. As such current regulations play a limited role in addressing the needs of migrant domestic workers from India.

In this chapter, I outline some characteristics of transnational migrant domestic workers from India and provide an overview of some issues facing such workers. The chapter primarily draws on my research (Raghuram, 1993; 1999; 2001) on domestic workers in India as part of my doctoral fieldwork, a review of this work and interviews with key officials and recruitment agents in November 2003, as well as secondary data collection on transmigrant migrant domestic work conducted in November and December 2003.[2] It also draws on primary research data collected by Anderson (2000) in research on migrant domestic workers in the United Kingdom (UK) (IOM, 2003) between 1998 and 2001. This research involved in-depth interviews and focus group discussions with migrant domestic workers from India, the Philippines, Sri Lanka, Nigeria, Zimbabwe and Indonesia, and analysis of 1,200 workers applying for the regularisation of their immigration status. Interviews were conducted before and after their immigration status was regularised under a UK regularisation programme and focused on the impact of legal status on household strategies.

The paper begins with an exploration of the cultures of domestic work in India, the patterns of organisation of work, and the ways in which domestic work has been addressed by researchers in order to understand how aspects of these cultures have influenced Indian domestic workers abroad. This is followed by an attempt to trace the emigration data on migrant Indian domestic workers. The two sections that follow outline some characteristics of these workers and the migration process. The chapter then explores linkages with the homeland and the transmigrant characteristics of domestic workers, before offering a conclusion in the last section.

THE CULTURES AND PATTERNS OF DOMESTIC WORK IN INDIA

The service sector is less important as a source of employment in India than in some other parts of the world. In 1999–2000, it only accounted for about 25.8 per cent of total employment (Ministry of Finance, Government of India, 2003). However, the sector is an important source of employment for women: the distribution of women employees across industries shows that 55.6 per cent of women are employed in community, personal and social services. The sector has also been particularly important in urban areas. In a study conducted by the Town and Country Planning Organisation, 98 per cent of female workers in one squatter settlement in Delhi were employed in the service sector (Singh, 1984), mostly as casual wage labourers (Shram Shakti, 1988).[3] The representation of women in certain occupations is particularly large. Domestic work is one of the few occupational categories where more women than men are employed—nationally, there are more than half a million female workers in the category "maids and housekeepers" but only 0.28 million men. However, as shown in Table 5.1, these proportions also vary across the Indian states.

While the figure cited above clearly show the importance of women in domestic work, it must be treated with some caution. It is difficult to assess the validity of these figures, as statistical data on domestic work is rarely accurate. Naming an occupational category "maids", a feminised term, will itself lead to under-enumeration of men working in the sector. Second, the categories that are used to identify various categories of workers are not mutually exclusive. For example, occupation category 51 (of the National Occupational Classification used by the Census) includes housekeepers, matrons and stewards, while category 53 includes maids and housekeeping. Third, some categories such as 52—cooks, waiters, bartenders—do not entirely distinguish between work done in private household and that done for commercial enterprises. Domestic work is also notorious for under-enumeration for a range of other reasons: the privatised nature of work, the "informal" nature of the work which arises from the lack of a tradition of employment contracts and of enumeration for tax purposes, and the poor status of the sector which means that concealment rates are high. In India, the last is particularly important as the complex relationship between caste, class and domestic work has made it an occupation that few want to admit to taking up. As a result domestic work is generally undercounted. Moreover, the description of paid domestic work is itself complex. For this chapter, I take it to have some identifying characteristics including the relations under which the work is done (whether it produces use value or exchange value), the degree to which it is commoditised and mechanised, the site of its production (private or public), and by the characteristics of the worker (whereby certain tasks are inherently deemed to be domestic because of the gender of the doer and the differential ascription of men and women to the sphere of the

149

TABLE 5.1 Occupational classification of main workers in non-households industry, trade business, profession or service by class of worker and sex—Maids and housekeeping, India, 2001

Division, Group (NCO)[a]	Total Main Workers[b]		Class of Worker			
			Employees		Single Workers[c]	
	Males	Females	Males	Females	Males	Females
Bihar	26,809	13,603	22,901	11,643	3,908	1,960
Goa	1,185	5,977	1,132	5,577	53	400
Gujarat	7,310	25,581	6,140	20,270	1,170	5,311
Haryana	3,020	3,862	2,620	3,052	400	810
Himachal Pradesh	2,424	1,382	2,245	1,265	179	117
Karnataka	13,030	53,491	11,050	46,302	1,980	7,189
Kerala	11,830	48,526	10,880	44,286	950	4,240
Madhya Pradesh	10,358	24,390	8,418	15,110	1,940	9,280
Maharashtra	37,580	119,800	35,060	100,110	2,520	19,690
Manipur	132	194	115	185	17	9
Meghalaya	1,106	2,898	1,053	2,658	53	240
Mizoram	160	270	153	245	7	25
Nagaland	723	562	700	551	23	11
Orissa	14,584	11,114	12,534	8,707	2,050	2,407
Punjab	4,940	4,169	4,010	2,990	930	1,179
Rajasthan	8,440	2,830	7,210	2,010	12,30	820
Sikkim	995	737	984	737	11	0
Tamil Nadu	11,410	56,115	10,840	55,255	570	860
Tripura	525	4,753	423	4,066	102	687
Uttar Pradesh	33,621	14,893	28,731	11,913	4,890	2,980
West Bengal	52,300	121,579	46,710	102,259	5,590	19,320
Delhi	27,070	23,498	25,492	18,099	1,578	5,399

SOURCE: Census of India, 2001.

a   National Classification of Occupations (NCO): This classification involves a three-digit coding of 349 occupational categories. The coding is adopted from the International Standard Classification of Occupations (as submitted to the Eleventh International Conference of Labour Statisticians in 1966). The data provided here is for NCO category 53.

b   Main workers are defined in Census 2001 as those who had been employed for at least six of the preceding 12 months (i.e. were employed for 183 days or more) (in contrast to marginal workers who had worked less than six months within the last 12 months).

c   Single workers are self-employed workers.

domestic). With these caveats, one can make some generalisations about the nature of domestic work in India.[4]

The Catholic Bishops Conference of India (CBCI) conducted a survey in 1979 of eight Indian regions which revealed a predominance of women in domestic work, with 77.6 per cent of the interviewees being female (Roshni, n.d.) while the 32nd round of the National Sample Survey (NSS 1977–78) counted 1.68 million female domestic workers as against 0.62 million male domestic workers. Domestic work is thus a female-dominated profession and existing research suggests that this pattern of feminisation is becoming more marked. For instance, between 1971 and 1981, there was actual growth in the number of domestic workers employed in urban areas, but a decline in the number of men who were employed in this sector suggesting a marked increase in the number of female domestic workers (Mehta, 1960; Raghuram, 1993; Ray, 2000). Regional variations in the sex ratio among people employed in domestic work are marked (Table 5.1; Figure 5.1). For example, there are almost five times as many women employed as domestic workers (maids, housekeepers—category 53 of the Census) in Tamil Nadu as there are men (11,410 men to 56,115 women), while in Uttar Pradesh, only half as many women as men are engaged in this occupation (33,621 men to 14,893 women). However, in the CBCI survey, the only area employing more male than female domestic workers was Delhi (54.8 per cent of interviewees were male). Although dated, this data helps identify some patterns: the relative importance of men in domestic work particularly in rural areas, and the feminisation of domestic work particularly in urban areas.[5]

It is useful to highlight some other characteristics of domestic work in India. First, domestic work in India was regulated through feudal relations and such relations continue to be important in structuring the expectations of employers (Ray, 2000). Contractualisation of domestic work is incomplete and where attempted has primarily been about formalising the employer's demands. Illegal bonded labour also operates to secure domestic labour for some employers. Second, male workers still dominate the more formalised parts of the sector and domestic workers employed by the government to serve government officials are almost always men. Hence it is not the task that is feminised but the conditions under which they are performed (informal, poorly paid, insecure) that mark women's participation in this sector in India (Raghuram, 1993). Men also dominate the more "public" tasks such as gardening, car cleaning and driving. Third, notions of pollution and purity play a significant part in structuring domestic work so that certain tasks such as cleaning toilets and removing garbage are cast as highly specialised caste work performed by Balmikis, both men and women (Karlekar, 1983; Kasturi, 1990). Although existing research suggests that scheduled and lower caste[6] men and women are more likely to take up domestic work (see for instance, Pandey, 1998; Bhattacharyya, 2004), the particular tasks done are differentiated by caste, and Balmiki women are rarely permitted to perform anything other than their caste-specific tasks (Balakrishnan, 2004)[7].

FIGURE 5.1 India—States and Union Territories

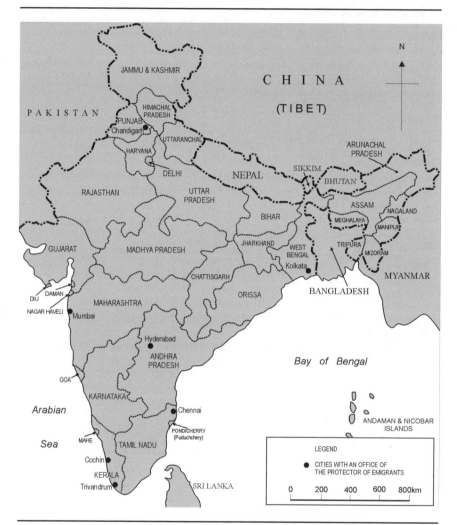

But even here, there is a nesting of opportunities as men dominate the more secure formal parts of the street-cleaning and garbage removal sector (Raghuram, 2001) while women are employed in the lower paid, more insecure private housework. Contact with women who are menstruating is also usually considered polluting and this has contributed to the employment of male cooks in many households. This, along with concerns over (the control of) women's sexuality, has led to a greater representation of

152

men in the (smaller) live-in full-time part of the sector, in comparison with the much more common female dominated part-time live-out sector. Many of the women who are employed as live-out part-time workers are married. In India as a whole, early marriage and multiple child-bearing depress work force participation in the 15–24 age group and employment rates rise for women from age 30 onwards (Ministry of Finance, 2003) and existing research suggests that this pattern is replicated in this sector too (Rao, 2002). This is not to deny the importance of child domestic workers. Families with young children will employ child labourers for domestic chores and to be playmates for the employer's children. Research conducted in Chennai found that 25 per cent of child domestic workers had started work before their ninth birthday, and a further 65 per cent between the ages of nine and 12 years old (UNHCR, 2000). Almost 70 per cent of them belonged to scheduled castes. One quarter of the children interviewed said that their parents had received advances on their salaries, effectively tying them to their employers. A significant number of children had experienced physical and sexual abuse.

A different pattern is seen among migrant women from tribal areas of central India entering domestic work; they are usually younger and unmarried (Indian Social Institute, 1993). For instance, young Christian women from the Oraon, Munda and Kharia tribes from the Chotanagpur and Chattisgarh areas of Bihar and Central India have moved to Delhi to work as live-in domestic workers. Their displacement is often connected to the development of mega-projects such as mining and dam-building (Labour File, 1997). Their employment is facilitated through Christian organisations and by non-governmental organisations (NGOs) working in tribal areas, overcoming parents' resistance to sending young daughters into domestic work as well as hesitations of employers in employing them. Involvement with the Church helps to allay anxieties over the control of these young women's sexuality (Tellis-Nayak & Tellis-Nayak, 1984). Finally, the dominance of migrant labour, which is recruited through networks, has meant that migrants from particular communities, areas and groups dominate domestic work in different parts of India. As a result, Pallan and Devanga women from Tamil Nadu have played a dominant part in domestic work in some parts of Delhi since drought in the home state triggered emigration in 1966 (Sundari & Rukmani, 1998; Raghuram, 1999; Rao, 2002). More recently, Bangladeshi immigrants have also become key players in this sector (Raghuram & Momsen, 1993).

There are two broad policy approaches to domestic work in India. The first demands a mixture of benevolence and state legislation as a route into improving the conditions under which domestic workers operate (see Singh, 2003 for an overview). Those working within this frame have sought to improve the conditions of work: lobbied for a six-day week, for formalisation of the payment of wages and assisted women who are abused by employers. However, they have largely sought to ameliorate the conditions of labour rather than change them. On the whole, they have not adequately questioned the class and gender distinctions that are embedded in this work but have delivered better working conditions for those whom they have assisted. Feminist activists, on the other hand, address domestic work as one sector in a broader politics around women's labour force participation. They criticise the class, caste and gender distinctions that are embedded in the organisation of domestic work (Karlekar, 1983; Kasturi, 1990). The two approaches enable and envisage very different forms of intervention into improving the conditions of domestic work in India but they have come together to make much more concerted attempts to organise domestic workers and demand legislation to protect their rights (Diwakar, 1996).

Currently, there are few means of regulating domestic work as it does not fall under the purview of labour laws, despite lobbying towards this. Repeated attempts to allow unionisation in the sector and to bring domestic workers under the purview of the Industrial Disputes Act have failed (Pathare, 2000). However, the National Domestic Workers Movement coordinated by Jeanne Devos has increased pressure to legislate on this issue. The movement has 100,000 members and has set up centres for protection of abused women, counselling centres and training centres. It has created awareness of the issues faced by domestic workers and has faced some limited success.

On the whole, however, the Indian government has so far resolutely prevented domestic workers from obtaining the rights accorded to other workers in India. "All this has led to regimes of labour at home which are characterised by the super-exploitation and immiseration of the working class. When, as a last resort, these workers turn to migration by legal and illegal means, their insertion into the international labour-market takes place with hardly any bargaining position" (Gardezi, 1997:116).

This is the culture underlying the organisation of domestic work in India. Some of these characteristics of domestic work travel abroad, particularly when the employers of migrant domestic workers are themselves Indians. Thus men are much more predominant among Indian domestic workers abroad than among those from any other country. They are often employed to serve in diplomatic households, the formal secure end of domestic work abroad, and this may be seen as transference of patterns seen in India. Similarly, the employment of male cooks by Indian households abroad, and the predominance of females in the 30–45 years old age group among migrant domestic workers, also mimic patterns found in domestic work in India. However, there are significant differences too between domestic workers in India and domestic workers abroad, as we will see below.

EMIGRATION DATA PATTERNS AND PROCESSES

The emigration of domestic workers from India is very difficult to trace. Some of this may be attributed to the way in which The Emigration Act of India 1983 governs and monitors the migration of Indian workers. Prior to 1983, labour outflows were regulated by the Emigration Act of 1922, which did not permit the emigration of unskilled workers and regulated the emigration of skilled workers by requiring them to obtain emigration clearance before leaving the country. As a result Indian workers were not able to benefit from the opening up of Middle East countries to expatriate labour which followed the oil boom in the Middle East in 1973–74. The Indian government therefore suspended the operative part of the Act in 1976 as it debated a new Act (Nair, 1993). The lack of a proper regulatory framework for emigration during a period of labour market opportunities abroad encouraged the growth of a large number of recruitment agencies who operated clandestinely to facilitate those who wanted to make their "Gulf dream" of remittances and wealth come true. Since the formulation of the 1983 Emigration Act, which came into effect on 31 December 1983, the operation of recruitment firms has continued, some registered but many clandestine. Domestic workers are sometimes recruited through such firms and, as such, the numbers of those emigrating go unrecorded in the Government of India statistics. The widespread prevalence of the use of informal networks in recruitment further complicates the picture and makes it hard to keep track of the numbers migrating to take up employment in domestic work.

Moreover, even official documentation does not allow any accurate assessment of the figures as many categories of people who want to emigrate are not required to obtain emigration clearance. For instance, no emigration clearance is required for large groups of people based on:

- the possession of skills (those holding graduate degrees, vocational qualifications);
- wealth (income-tax payers);
- the nature of employment (those working in skilled and semi-skilled sectors, in diplomatic service);
- the nature of the employer (those employed as gazetted government servants)
- destination countries (those migrating to Pakistan, Bangladesh, Japan, New Zealand, Australia, all countries in North America and in Europe excluding Commonwealth of Independent States countries). From 15 October 2003, those seeking to migrate to Singapore, South Korea, South Africa and Thailand were also exempted from requiring emigration clearance; and
- the reason for migration (spouses and families of those workers who fall in the above categories).

As a result, large numbers of workers, actual and potential, do not require emigration clearance and their movement therefore goes unrecorded. Lesser skilled workers do require emigration clearance if they are not travelling to the countries mentioned above. However, domestic workers—although moving to take up a job as an unskilled worker—may not require emigration clearance because of their country of destination. Moreover, those seeking employment as domestic workers in the destination country may have migrated as a spouse of those in one of the earlier categories and may therefore be exempt from seeking emigration clearance. Finally, as evidenced in the case studies below, those seeking employment as domestic workers may have graduate degrees and may also therefore be exempt from clearance requirements.

Overstayers and those who change status too are unaccounted for in the emigration clearance data.

Secondary data on domestic workers emigrating from India are also limited, as there have been few major studies of Indian domestic workers abroad (but see Asian Migrant Centre, 1998). A few broad estimates are provided by the Indian government's report on the Indian diaspora (Ministry of External Affairs, 2001). It suggests, for instance, that there are between 8,000 and 10,000 Indian domestic workers in Bahrain. Kuwait is another important receiving country for Indian migrant workers and Indians constitute the single largest expatriate community in Kuwait, accounting for almost 20 per cent of the resident population. The Indian government estimates that there are 113,000 domestic workers of Indian origin working in Kuwait, a large number of whom are working for Kuwaiti families and 49,000 are housemaids. The Indian consulate in Saudi Arabia estimates that about 100,000 domestic workers are employed there.

Another source of data on migrant Indian domestic workers is that maintained by countries to which domestic workers move. However, under-reporting (due to the nature of the job, of the contract and of the immigration status) shapes the available data. Moreover, the extent to which different countries acknowledge, record and regulate foreign domestic workers varies, so that there is no consistency in this data. The major receiving countries are the Middle Eastern states, particularly United Arab Emirates, Kuwait, Bahrain and Saudi Arabia; other major receivers are Singapore, Hong Kong, the United States of America (USA), UK and Italy (Asian Migrant Centre, 1998). One pattern that emerges from this data is that domestic workers from India have a different gender profile than that from other countries. Unlike domestic workers from other major sending countries such as Indonesia, Sri Lanka and the Philippines, a significant number of Indian workers are men: for example, in 1997, 5,254 were men compared to 3,693 women; in 2000 13,216 were men and 6,730 were women. In contrast, the next major sender Indonesia sent 21 men and 3,791 women in 2001 (Sabban, 2002).

WHO ARE THE MIGRANTS?

First, we must recognise that the migration of domestic workers from India is not a recent phenomenon. The movement of domestic workers often accompanied that of indentured workers. Where women were not indentured but were allowed to accompany men, some women must have entered domestic labour. Others migrated singly either as marriage migrants or in order to seek domestic work although these numbers were small. Thus, of the 74,454 Indian women in Mauritius, 868 were reported as domestic workers, 549 as gardeners and 244 as laundresses; domestic work was thus the largest single occupation for migrant women (Carter, 1995). Similarly, Indian domestic workers accompanied soldiers and assistants in 1819 when Thomas Stamford Raffles first went to Singapore to establish a base there (Ministry of External Affairs, 2001). The current movement of domestic workers could therefore be understood as an intensification of previous patterns of migration of domestic workers.

156

Currently, for many Indians, emigration has become the only way to adjust to and survive the failure of domestic employment generation in the 1990s. Neither the increased number of years spent in school (and the concomitant decrease in unemployment for that age group) nor the growth in private sector formal employment has been enough to overcome the effects of the slowdown in government and public sector job expansions (Ministry of Finance, 2003). At the same time, employment opportunities in other countries in Asia (especially Southeast Asia and the Middle East) have continued apace through much of the decade, acting as a magnet for Indian workers.

But the inability of the developmental state to improve people's welfare is not the only cause for the international migration of women (Gamburd, 2000). An equally important reason for migration has been the failure of the patriarchal household to provide for the welfare of women or children. Almost all the female Indian domestic workers who were interviewed in the London study stated that death, ill health or desertion of the husband had been the cause for migration. Take this example from a focus group discussion held with undocumented Indian domestic workers in London in 2000:

> A: Sometimes a wife just has to do it, just to save the marriage if you don't want the family to split. Because in India we cannot divorce. If you separate, then the family will leave you. You will not be helped by your own family. So we have to suffer...
>
> R: My husband left me. He was a very bad husband. He was beating me and treating me badly but then he left me for someone else. My four children were crying. I had to support them. I cannot divorce him.

In a country where marriage is nearly universal, the presence and support of a husband structures class mobility. It also affects the age at which migration occurs with few young women migrating. Thus Lakshmi Lingam (1990) found in her research that women who migrated abroad were either widowed or separated or having marital problems and usually over 35 years of age. However, later on in the interview the speakers recognised that these problems are not simply sited in their individual households, but it is the inter-relationship between the household and other sites of power—the state and the family—that makes migration the best or the only option.

Unlike domestic workers employed in India, it is likely that domestic workers who migrate abroad may have some education. Some women are highly educated. For example, a number of the women who were interviewed in the London study had completed secondary school education and a few even had graduate degrees (Anderson, 2000). On the other hand, Lingam (1990) found that few of the Andhra migrants she interviewed were educated. One possible explanation is that the education of migrant domestic workers entering domestic work may be largely influenced by the literacy levels of the states from which they originate. Thus migrant workers from Kerala, who dominate migration to the Middle East, are likely to be educated because literacy rates in Kerala are high. In comparison, literacy rates among domestic workers from Andhra Pradesh are lower, and reflect the literacy levels of the cohort from which domestic workers are drawn.[8] Another possible explanation could be based on differential skill and education levels by destination with those moving to the UK having higher levels of education than those to the Middle East. More research is required to confirm these patterns.

There is little work on the caste breakdown of migrant domestic workers. One exception is Chelpa's (1988) study. She found that lower caste women from Andhra Pradesh, i.e., those from the Mala Madhiga and Setti Balika castes were more likely to migrate as domestic workers as the upper castes find such work demeaning (Chelpa, 1988). However, her study also suggests the need to disaggregate caste figures and to examine the ecological factors that steer migration. She found that lower caste women from dry farming regions engage in seasonal migration to wet villages while women from lower castes in the wet region migrate to the Gulf countries as domestic workers.

Another important differential in emigration statistics is the religion professed by migrant women. Thus, Zachariah et al. (2001a) found that only 4.7 per cent of Muslim migrants from Kerala were women but this proportion increased to over 20 per cent among Christians and it is possible that this pattern is replicated amongst domestic workers too. Anderson's study (2000) also suggests the importance of Christian domestic workers from Goa in migrant flows.

The culture of emigration also influences migration so that it may be surmised that the number of women migrants entering domestic work is likely to be higher from states with high rates of emigration. In this context it is worth noting the importance of Kerala as the key sending state in India. Not only are the numbers highest from Kerala but the proportion of the population seeking to migrate is also very high, the highest of any Indian state (Nair, 1999; Zachariah et al., 2001a; 2001b).

To summarise, there is a long history of emigration of domestic workers from India but in recent times it appears that increasing economic pressures at home are leading more and more families to adopt such emigration as a survival or at least a sustenance strategy. There is little clear evidence of the socio-economic characteristics of such migrants, but migration undoubtedly reflects and reproduces existing hierarchies within contemporary Indian society, i.e., those of gender, class, caste and religion.

THE MIGRATION PROCESS

Domestic workers are recruited through a variety of channels, although documented domestic worker migration only occurs through official channels and is regulated by official controls.

Official "Controls" over Migration

As stated above, many of the domestic workers migrating abroad from India do not require emigration clearance. Domestic workers who do require emigration clearance may obtain it through the Office of the Protectorate of Emigrants based in Delhi, Mumbai, Chennai, Trivandrum, Cochin, Kolkata, Chandigarh and Hyderabad (see Figure 5.1).[9] The offices in Delhi and Mumbai deal with the bulk of applications and as such they are of higher status, being led by officials of the rank of Under Secretary (to the Indian government) rather than section officers. The Protector's office aims to determine whether there is a demand for the worker and whether the conditions under which the worker will operate will be adequate to meet the needs of the worker and equivalent to those that would have been given to local employees, particularly with respect to the period of placement, wages and conditions (personal communication with Protector of Emigrants, Delhi, 4 December 2003).

Recruitment firms are responsible for facilitating the migration of lesser skilled labour and the regulation of such firms is one of the key tasks of the Protector. Around 1,250 recruiting agents have valid registration certificates with the Protector of Emigrants (Ministry of Labour, 2003:111) and are required to meet a number of criteria with regard to "financial soundness, trustworthiness, adequacy of premises [and] experience in the field of handling manpower". They must also pay a registration fee which is dependent on the numbers of workers that they aim to place, ranging from Rs.300,000 (about US$6,670) for those aiming to place less than 300 workers, to Rs.1,000,000 (about US$22,220) for those who recruit over 1,000 workers per year. Recruitment agencies are required to produce a power of attorney letter and a demand for labour letter from the prospective employers, a specimen contract and a visa for the country in which the employee is to gain work. Recruiting firms are also responsible for the cost of repatriation of the employer and have to provide a guarantee that the details of the worker are being kept in a register. The only occupation where recruitment agents are not allowed to recruit employees is in domestic work (notice board, Protectorate of Emigrants, New Delhi). Raids are conducted against recruiting firms that are seen to be recruiting domestic workers. Despite this, advertisements by firms recruiting domestic workers to work overseas may be regularly seen in Indian national newspapers.

The rationale for not permitting domestic workers to seek employment through recruitment agents is that recruitment agents will not have adequate control over employers due to the privatised nature of the employment. The Ministry of Labour aims to "strictly control" the emigration of domestic workers and to protect the rights of domestic workers by checking that there is a direct relation between the employer and the employee and ensuring that the regulations of the Protector of Emigrants are all being met. Domestic workers seeking emigration have therefore to be recruited directly by the employer and have to give assurance that they will only work for the foreign employer who has recruited them and will only be engaged in the job for which they have been recruited. Those seeking emigration clearance must come personally to the office of the Protector to make their application to emigrate. A letter stating that the employer will receive them at the point of destination must accompany this application. Domestic workers are also required to produce a medical clearance certificate testifying that they are fit for the job and an employment contract that has been attested by the Indian mission in the country to which the worker is destined. The Emigration Act requires that the employee will be paid at least the minimum salary of the country in which they seek employment and that they will be governed by minimum standards of condition of employment. For domestic workers, the contract should stipulate that workers would only work for eight hours a day, six days a week and 11 months a year. The employees must provide medical insurance in the destination country (interview with the Undersecretary to the Government of India, November 2003; also see Ministry of Labour, 2003).

In order to obtain clearance, the husband (if married) or parent of the domestic worker must accompany them to the office of the Protector of Emigrants. This practice removes the responsibility of the domestic worker from the office of the Protector to the accompanying person. Officially applicants who seek emigration clearance to be employed as domestic workers must also be at least 30 years of age, although this may be relaxed where the employer is themselves an Indian citizen. However, in such circumstances, the office of the Protector seeks an affidavit from the employer to the effect that only they will employ this worker. Until 2002, this rule only pertained to women intending to migrate to the Middle Eastern countries but on the recommendation of the National Commission for Women, this regulation has since been extended to those bound for all countries.

The Protector is required to check that the intending emigrant has been appraised of any problems or issues that might arise in the country of employment. The prospective worker must deposit Rs.200 (about US$5) as an application fee, as well as a sum of money equivalent to a one-way fare from the country of destination. The last is deposited with the office of the Protector in the name of the employee by the employer in order to fund repatriation of the domestic worker in case any problems arise during the duration of the employment. The money is withdrawn on behalf of the domestic worker by the office and is sent to the Indian mission in the destination country under these circumstances. If no problems arise, this money is returned to the domestic worker once they return to India and is then reclaimed by the employer.[10] In order to keep track of all these issues, the office of the Protector maintains a separate register for those seeking employment abroad as domestic workers. However, the large number of exclusions for the requirement of emigration clearance means that there are no available official figures for domestic workers seeking emigration.

An analysis of the register of domestic workers applying for emigration clearance from the Delhi office of the Protector of Emigrants suggests some trends in the formal legal migration of domestic workers from India. Between 1 January and 1 December 2003, 235 domestic workers sought emigration clearance from the Delhi office of the

Protector. Of this, the bulk of applicants (156) were women who obtained clearance to go to Singapore.[11] Twenty women identified Hong Kong as their destination country. Other destination countries were Kuwait (two women), UAE (16 women, six men), Oman (ten women, one man), Beirut (two women), Bahrain (six women), Yemen (two men), Deira (one woman) and Riffa (one man). Three male cooks (one each destined for Israel, Kuwait and Bahrain) and two male domestic workers (one each for Nigeria and Russia) also obtained clearance during this period. Regional differences in destination countries is likely to be an important factor, with Mumbai and the two offices in Kerala more likely to deal with applicants destined for the Middle East as these centres have long histories of migration to the Middle East.[12] Most of those who emigrated went on either a one-year or the maximum permissible two-year contract.

Although the Delhi office channels only about one-sixth of the total applications for emigration clearance, it is useful to undertake such an analysis as some patterns are discernible. For instance, from April 2003, the numbers obtaining clearance to go to the Middle East increased. Second, it appears from this that domestic workers seeking emigration clearance are mostly women, but there are more men seeking to go to the Middle East as domestic workers than to other regions. Almost all the Singapore destined domestic workers on the register came from rural Punjab and were of the Sikh faith and their employers seemed to be Punjabi Sikhs too. These figures from the Delhi office reflect the regional catchment areas of individual offices, but it also highlights the presence of Sikh women in migrant domestic work. About seven per cent of Singapore's Indian population is Punjabi, usually people who originally moved to Singapore as members of the British Army and who have since remained there (Ministry of External Affairs, 2001). It is possible that they offer employment opportunities for Indian domestic workers. Finally, of the 235 domestic workers who obtained clearance between 1 January and December 2003, 27 or about 11 per cent returned early, before the end of their contract, suggesting that a number of domestic work contracts do "go wrong".

Channels of Migration—Undocumented Domestic Workers

Social networks play a key part in recruitment. A number of the interviewees in the London study said that they had come with the help of relatives—cousins, brothers, sisters—and through friends. Subsequent jobs were sometimes found through agencies but first placements were, in particular found through informal networks. Chelpa's study of return migrants to Andhra Pradesh too found that women had acquired passports and visas through their kinsmen in Bombay (Chelpa, 1988). Rich farmers had financed these applications at high interest rates because they knew that this was a good investment. Some domestic workers also find jobs through placement agencies although, as stated above, this is not legally allowed by the Indian government. Hence, the process of placement itself places domestic workers into the category of undocumented workers. Placement agencies may either specialise in recruiting people to a sector of work or, in states like Kerala with a large migrant population, may "specialise" in countries of destination. An interview with a placement agency in Delhi conducted in 2003, revealed that up to that point, six people (one each in USA, Holland and the UK, and three in Dubai) had been placed abroad while 700 people had been placed locally. Contacts with visa officials had made it possible for the agency to assist the domestic workers to obtain visas. However, of the six persons placed, three women had obtained visas as sisters of the employer. The salaries offered depended on the country in which they were placed. For the UK, Rs.15,000 (around US$330) was the recommended salary, to be paid either in India or abroad, depending on arrangements with the domestic workers. The recruitment company charges one and a half months' salary from the employer as commission if one of their employees is recruited.

TRANSMIGRANT PRACTICES

Domestic workers engage in a range of transnational practices, with the remittance of money being one of the key ones. In India, the value of remittances in non-resident Indian (NRI) deposits increased steadily through the 1990s and in 2002, were worth Rs.122,772 crores (US$25 billion) compared to just under Rs.28,258 crores (US$6 billion) for foreign investment inflows (Reserve Bank of India, 2002). However, accounting leakages, as well as leakages due to the undocumented form of many transactions—as money and goods brought back either personally or through friends and exchanged in the parallel economy— mean that official figures for remittances must always be considered as underestimates (Athukorala, 1993).

The importance of remittances varies by region but the only state which is heavily dependent on remittances is Kerala. By the end of the 1990s, remittances reached such levels that they were well above the total State Government expenditure and net inflow through NRI deposits increased 50 per cent to about Rs.10 crores (US$2.32 billion). Workers remittances to Kerala (about Rs.13–14,000 crores or US$2.9 billion by the turn of the century) constituted as much as 22 per cent of the Net State Domestic Product by 2000. Remittances in 2001 were larger than the annual budget of Kerala for the year 2001–02. In short, migration seems to have been the single most dynamic factor in the otherwise slow growth and dreary employment scenario of Kerala during the last 25 years (Kerala State Planning Board, 2003:27).

It is impossible to estimate the extent to which remittances from domestic workers contribute to these figures. Research from the London study, however, suggests some patterns in the nature and extent of remittances. For many domestic workers, the primary purpose of migration was the maintenance of the family left behind. Remittances were often used to educate children, to send them to "very expensive boarding schools", to build new homes and to engage in charitable work in the village. It is clear that women's earnings are not pin money but are essential to households that are dependent on this money. In particular, it appears that sending money home may enable class mobility through greater education of the next generation. In every case, it at least enables class stability, if not class mobility, in the context of male failure to provide for the household and very often to even care for the children left behind. However, depending on other women—sisters and mothers—to look after children in their absence must necessarily increase the circle within which the remittances must be distributed. As such, women's engagement in domestic work was often a consequence of and conditioned by the failure of patriarchal care at home. It also sometimes fostered dependence on migrant women's earnings. Thus one woman said that her sons spent her earnings on conspicuous consumption and on having an easy lifestyle.

It is not clear whether any of the gains that women made were long lasting. Repeat migration indicates that returning home did not provide women with a chance to enter the labour force at home in an enhanced position, necessitating further migration. Thus Nair's (1999) study of return women migrants reveals that once they returned, they remained in the lowest income bracket. All the female migrants surveyed by Nair (1999) earned less than Rs.1,000 (around US$22) per month both before and after migration, although their income went up during their stay abroad, only two per cent earned more than Rs.5,000 (around US$110) per month. Men, on the other hand, seemed to have been able to increase their earnings between the pre- and post-migration scenario.

The women in the London study all looked forward to their visits home. The frequency of visits was governed by the availability of savings. However, some women felt that they had few meaningful relations left at home. They had become accustomed to relative autonomy from familial relations or had sometimes replaced these emotional relations with that offered by friends. Contract workers who have been away for short periods may find this less of a problem but regularisation programmes that offer domestic workers rights to stay may ultimately lead to the weakening of their relations with those in the home country. This begs the question about who will care for these carers once they are no longer employable. For example, one worker who did not want to return to India permanently felt her sons there would not look after her. Countries that have become dependent on the emigration of domestic workers will in the future need to take account of the issues presented by ageing care workers who are distanced from their own families. Thus, while transmigrant practices may bind domestic workers to those whom they have to help, and to those who care for their children (this may act as a burden for them), the dissolution of transnational relations provides an even more frightening scenario, in which the welfare of the domestic workers themselves will not be assured through these relations.

PROBLEMS AND PROGRAMMES

Research conducted in London found that Indian domestic workers were particularly likely to be abused. Of the 203 Indian domestic workers going to one support organisation, 41 per cent reported being beaten, 85 per cent being psychologically abused, and 44 per cent being imprisoned; in addition, 74 per cent did not have their own room, and 66 per cent were not paid a regular salary. Domestic workers employed by diplomatic households have particular problems. Failure to keep the employers happy will influence not only their job but also their relationship with the consulate. For instance, a male domestic worker interviewed in the London study said that the employer, a high-ranking official in the Indian High Commission had instructed the consular service not to permit him to extend his passport.

Both the study in UAE (Sabban, 2002) and that undertaken by the Asian Migrant Centre in Hong Kong (Asian Migrant Centre, 1998) reveal that Indian domestic workers receive a lower salary than those from any other country. They appear to be at the bottom of the heap in an occupational sector that is already marked by disadvantage. This is an issue that should be of concern to the Indian government.

Another issue that emerges from the interviews undertaken in London is the extent to which it is difficult to change employers for live-in domestic workers as the loss of one's job also means the loss of accommodation. Workers who have been autonomous may then be required to depend on friends. As workers buy into concepts such as individualisation, through their prolonged separation from their families, this raises particular problems for migrant workers. Thus one domestic worker felt that "in the UK, I feel a different woman. In the UK, I can work and earn money. Women in India stay home and look after their children and gossip". Here, the locale of modernity is geographically specific and located in the receiving country where she leads a more autonomous life. It was therefore difficult for her to then adjust to seeking help from friends.

The government of India has seen migrant labour as a way of addressing chronic underemployment in India. It therefore adopted a laissez faire approach to problems faced by migrants with minimal attempts to address or redress discrimination that Indian employees might face from the employers or the policies of the receiving countries. As such, there has only so far been a piecemeal attempt at protecting the rights of domestic workers. For instance, in June 1999, the Indian government suspended the emigration of domestic workers to Kuwait in the face of widespread recognition of the problems faced by Indian domestic workers in that country but this was lifted in 2000. The Indian consulate in Kuwait also created a shelter for distressed women, where women are sheltered till they can obtain exit permits. The shelter has been built with the support of local Indians. However, the Indian government has come under pressure from the Kerala government to rescind this suspension as suspensions only drive such workers underground.

The Indian government is taking up some of the demands of contract labourers in the Gulf countries and it is this that is most likely to improve the lives of documented migrant domestic workers (Ministry of External Affairs, 2001). The demands include that employees should be allowed to hold on to their own passports, that the work permit fees should not be cut from their wages, that the Consular office should be more active in scrutinising employment contracts, and that the governments of the sending and receiving countries sign a Standard Labour Export Agreement in order to negotiate a better deal for Indian workers. If implemented these changes will improve the conditions of those who migrate legally.

Other changes that are likely to influence documented domestic workers include amendments to the Emigration Bill that are currently being discussed by the Indian government (Ministry of Labour, 2003). The amendments once passed will lead to the establishment of an insurance scheme for overseas workers, the Pravasi Bharatiya Bima Yojana. Identity cards will be issued to those who are registered with the scheme and this will provide them with security during their stay abroad. For instance, the insurance will offer cover of up to Rs.200,000 (around US$4,440) in the case of death or disability during the period of overseas employment. It will also offer maternity benefits to expatriate women workers. The establishment of an Overseas Workers Welfare Fund and a Manpower Export Promotion Council are also being debated (Ministry of Labour, 2003). The Kerala government also offers its women migrant workers insurance through the Pravasi Vanitha Suraksha Scheme. It covers issues that women are more likely to face such as workplace harassment (when certified by an Indian consulate abroad), snatching of jewellery worn by the NRI, and death due to female-specific medical problems.

However, these are changes that only affect documented workers. Undocumented workers are not protected by any laws, and this is a primary concern in a sector dominated by undocumented workers. Most domestic workers are more likely to be influenced by the blasé attitude adopted towards maltreatment of domestic workers as reflected in the report of the high level committee on the Indian diaspora. It states that there are "[o]ccasional cases of assault and maltreatment but this is not alarming either in numbers or in frequency". Similarly, the Indian consulate in Saudi Arabia defended the Saudi government's regulations around domestic work and said that only 163 complaints had been made by Indian domestic workers, "which was a minuscule 1.6 per cent of the 10,000 workers in the Kingdom" (Ministry of External Affairs, 2001:25). This suggests a denial of the importance of the issues facing domestic workers, or at least a disavowal of its significance.

Attempts at regulating the working conditions of Indian domestic workers more specifically have primarily come from other sources. For instance, the United Nations Development Fund for Women (UNIFEM) pressurised Jordan, a major receiving country for domestic workers, to regulate the employment conditions of domestic workers and some progress has been made towards this with the implementation of the "Special Working Contract for Non-Jordanian Domestic Workers". It augments co-ordination between the sending countries and Jordan, as a receiving country to increasing numbers of migrant workers from Asia, guarantees migrant workers' rights to life insurance, medical care, rest days, repatriation upon expiration of the contract, and reiterates migrant women's right to be treated in compliance with international human rights standards (see for instance, http://www.december18.net/web/docpapers/doc631. pdf, accessed 18 January 2004) This contract comes after signing the memorandum of understanding between UNIFEM and the Ministry of Labour in August 2001 marking the beginning of the project "Empowering Migrant Women Workers in Jordan". In the UK, regularisation programmes have benefited some Indian domestic workers in terms of immigration, although research suggests that workers whose visas were regularised found it even more difficult to find jobs in a sector. Seeking contracts and fairer working conditions often led them to unemployment. In Bahrain, the likelihood of the inclusion of domestic workers under Bahrain's Labour Laws will help to improve their working conditions. In Hong Kong, the Asian Migrant Centre has campaigned on behalf of domestic workers. In other countries such as Kuwait, little regulation exists. The demand for domestic labour, however, continues to expand and new theatres for exploitation are being opened up.

There have also been a number of civil society initiatives. Andolan is an NGO founded in 1998 by low-wage South Asian immigrant workers in New York City. It is a membership-based group that organises and advocates on behalf of immigrant South Asian workers. It is strongly committed to enabling domestic workers to realise their rights and to support and empower working-class communities that face obstacles including language barriers, discrimination, and immigration status. Andolan has three main programme areas: providing support and resources to workers through workshops, individual support, and facilitating the exchange of information among workers; bringing lawsuits against abusive employers; and organising, educating, and conducting outreach to new workers through campaigns (http://www.aafny.org/directory, accessed 21 January 2004). Another organisation that was founded in 1997 in New York is Awaaz. It aims to help South Asian domestic workers, campaigns "Against Workplace Servitude" as it influences immigrant workers and aims to persuade the Department of Justice and the United States Attorney's Office to prosecute a broader range of cases under the Victims of Trafficking and Violence Prevention Act of 2000. In Hong Kong, the Asian Migrant Centre has been very active in raising the profile of migrant domestic workers. They have published a number of books to assist domestic workers to settle in and to recognise their rights (Indian Domestic Workers Association and Asian Migrant Centre, 1999).

CONCLUSION

Domestic work in India is marked by inequalities of class, caste and gender. There is no legal protection for domestic workers and although there have been some attempts at unionisation, the lack of a legislative framework to protect domestic workers' rights has meant that migrant domestic workers have taken with them a culture in which this form of work is recognised as having little status or value.

The Indian government's laissez faire attitude to migration more generally is being replaced by one that emphasises narratives of success of emigrant Indians. This leaves little room for addressing the problems facing migrant domestic workers. The only way in which they can be incorporated is through paternalism, by restricting migration of young women for domestic work. The irony of this is that it is very often the lack of support of the patriarch at home, usually the husband, that has triggered such migration to begin with. The failure of male support in the context of a patriarchal society, and limited employment opportunities at home structures women's entry into domestic work abroad. Other men in other places, friends, placement agents and immigration officers "help" migrant domestic workers to move but this places them in an even more vulnerable position. There have been some initiatives to address this situation but their impact will be limited unless sending states recognise domestic work as legitimate work. Extending rights to migrants based on their affiliation to the home country rather than to their migratory status will provide protection to domestic workers, whether they are documented or undocumented. These are two essential steps that need to be taken if we are to rewrite the narrative of exploitation that currently marks Indian migrant domestic workers.

NOTES

1   I would like to thank Rajni Pisharody, Sanghita Bhattacharyya and Lakshmi Lingam for their assistance in different phases of the research.

2   I would particularly like to thank Bridget Anderson for allowing me to use this material and for her insights into the issues facing child domestic workers in India.

3   Data obtained during the 38th round of the National Sample Survey conducted in 1983.

4   Domestic work lies at the interface of productive work and reproductive work, producing use value (usually associated with reproductive labour) for exchange in the market (characteristic of productive work). It also lies at the junction between the private and public spheres, the employer's house representing private space for the employers but with a more public connotation for the employee. Finally, in domestic work, both employer and employee are usually women, and the exploitative work relations which are said to characterise domestic work are often cited as an illustration of the differences among women. Domestic work serves to reinforce and reproduce these distinctions.

5   This must also be placed in the context of higher urban areas where female labour force participation rates have gone up from 31.4 per cent in 1972–73 to 52.9 per cent in 1999 (Ministry of Finance, 2003: Section 10.17).

6   After Independence, castes that had traditionally been marginalised within the caste system were identified and placed on a schedule in order to target them for affirmative action. These castes are called "scheduled castes". There are local variations in the list of scheduled castes.

7   A joint study taken up by Women's Voice and the Bangalore Gruha Karmikara Sangha on domestic workers in Bangalore reveals that most Bangalore households discriminated against Scheduled Caste (SC) domestic help in various forms, be it paying them low wages or making them work long hours (Balakrishnan, 2004).

8   Female literacy rates in Andhra Pradesh were 51.2 per cent compared to Kerala's figure of 87.9 per cent (Census of India, 2001). Importantly, it appears that "educational levels are positively associated with proportion of females among the migrants; the higher the

educational attainment of a migrant group the higher its proportion of females" (Zachariah et al., 2001a:70).

9   The Protectorate of Emigrants does not involve itself with helping employees to obtain a visa or to meet regulations set by destination country.

10   However, in practice, many employers treat this as a loan to the employee and deduct the money from the domestic worker's wage. I would like to thank James Keezhangatte for pointing this out to me.

11   However, it must be remembered that as of 15 October 2003, domestic workers going to Singapore no longer needed clearance from the government.

12   Applicants from the three southern states of Kerala, Tamil Nadu and Andhra Pradesh accounted for more than half of the 367,663 people who received emigration clearance or Emigration Clearance Not Required (ECNR) endorsement during 2002 (Ministry of Labour, 2003). Almost 82,000 came from Kerala, followed closely by Tamil Nadu. However, only 0.5 per cent of all emigration clearances given by the office of the Protector go to domestic workers and there is no possibility of judging how many of those who obtained ECNR took up domestic work in the country of destination. It is therefore difficult to guess whether these figures reflect the state of origin of domestic workers.

REFERENCES

Anderson, B. 2000. *Doing the Dirty Work*, London: Zed Press.

————. 2001. Why madam has so many bathrobes: Demand for migrant domestic workers in the EU. *Tijdschrift voor Economisce en Sociale Geografie*, 92(1), 18–26.

Aneesh, A. 2000. *Rethinking Migration: High-skilled Labour Flows from India to the United States*, CCIS Working Paper No. 18, University of California, San Diego.

Asian Migrant Centre. 1998. *Asian Migrant Yearbook, Country Profile: India*. http://is7.pacific.net. hk/~amc/papers/AMY98IA.htm. Accessed 20 January 2004.

Athukorala, P. 1993. *Enhancing Developmental Impact of Migrant Remittances: A Review of Asian Experiences*. Bangkok: ILO-ARTEP.

Balakrishnan, D. 2004. Domestic workers face discrimination: Study. *Deccan Herald*, 16 January 2004.

Bhattacharyya, S. 2004. *Female Migration in India: A Case Study of Migrant Workers to Delhi*. Unpublished Ph.D. dissertation, Centre for the Study of Regional Development, School of Social Sciences, University of Delhi, India.

Carter, M. 1995. *Servants, Sirdars and Settlers: Indians in Mauritius*. Delhi: Oxford University Press.

Census of India. 2001. *Provisional Population Totals: India*. Paper 1 of 2001.

Chang, K. & L. H. M. Ling. 2000. Globalization and its intimate other: Filipina domestic workers in Hong Kong. In *Gender & Global Restructuring: Sightings, Sites & Resistances*. Edited by M. H. Marchand & A. S. Runyan. London, New York: Routledge, 27–43.

Chelpa, L. 1988. *Women's Role in the Reproduction and Production Spheres of Wet and Dry Villages in the East Godavari district, Andhra Pradesh*. Unpublished Ph.D. dissertation, Department of Humanities and Social Sciences, Indian Institute of Technology, Mumbai.

Diwakar, V. 1996. *Familiar Exploitation: An Analysis of Domestic Labour*. Pune: Women's Studies Centre, Department of Sociology, University of Pune.

Ehrenreich, B. & A. Hochschild, eds. 2003. *Global Woman: Nannies, Maids and Sex Workers in the New Economy*. London: Granta Books.

Gamburd, M. 2000. *The Kitchen Spoon's Handle: Transnationalism and Sri Lanka's Migrant Housemaids*. Ithaca: Cornell University Press.

Gardezi, H. 1997. Asian workers in the Gulf States of the Middle East. In *International Labour Migrations*. Edited by B. S. Bolaria & R. von Elling Bolaria. Delhi: Oxford University Press, 99–120.

Gayathri, V. 2002. Rethinking high-skilled international migration: Research and policy issues for India's information economy. In *International Mobility of the Highly Skilled*. Edited by OECD. OECD: Paris, 201–12.

Hochschild, A. 1997. *The Time Bind: When Work becomes Home and Home becomes Work*, New York: Metropolitan Books.

————. 2000. Global care chains and emotion surplus value. In *On the Edge. Living with Global Capitalism*. Edited by W. Hutton & A. Giddens. London: Jonathan Cape, 130–46.

Hondagneu-Sotelo, P. 2001. *Domestica: Immigrant Workers Cleaning and Caring in the Shadow of Affluence*. Berkeley: University of California Press.

Huang, S. & B. S. A. Yeoh. 2003. The difference gender makes: State policy and contract migrant workers in Singapore. *Asian and Pacific Migration Journal*, 12(1–2), 75–97.

Indian Domestic Workers Association and Asian Migrant Centre. 1999. *My Story, My Work*. Hong Kong: Home Affairs Bureau.

Indian Social Institute. 1993. *The Tribal Domestic Worker at the Crossroads: A Search for Alternatives, A Report on the Status of Tribal Delhi Domestic Working Women*. New Delhi: Indian Social Institute.

IOM. 2003. *Is Trafficking in Human Beings Demand Driven: A Multi-country Pilot Study*. Geneva: IOM Research Series.

Karlekar, M. 1983. *Poverty and Women's Work: A Study of Sweeper Women in Delhi*. Delhi: Vikas Publishing House.

Kasturi, L. 1990. Poverty migration and women's status. In *Women Workers in India: Studies in Employment and Status*. Edited by L. Kasturi & S. Brahme. New Delhi: Chanakya Publications, 3–173.

Kerala State Planning Board. 2003. *Kerala Economic Review*. Thiruvananthapuram: Government of Kerala.

Kottegoda, C. S. 2003. Bringing the money home: Poverty, migration and gender politics in Sri Lanka. Paper presented at the Women and Migration in Asia conference, 10–13 December 2003.

Labour File. 1997. *Recognizing Labour Rights of Domestic Workers*. Labour File 3, (7&8 July/August), 1–40.

Lall, M. C. 2001. *India's Missed Opportunity: India's Relationship with the Non-Resident Indians*. Aldershot: Ashgate.

Lan, P. C. 2003. Among women, migrant domestics and their Taiwaneese employers across generations. In *Global Woman: Nannies, Maids and Sex Workers in the New Economy*. Edited by B. Ehrenreich & A. Hochschild. London: Granta Books, 169–89.

Lingam, L. 1990. *Report of Interviews of the Andhra Pradesh Gulf Evacuees*. Mumbai: TISS report.

Mehta, A. 1960. *The Domestic Servant Class*. Bombay: Popular Book Depot.

Ministry of External Affairs. 2001. *Report of the High Level Committee on the Indian Diaspora*. New Delhi: Government of India.

Ministry of Finance. 2003. *Union Budget and Economic Survey*. New Delhi: Government of India.

Ministry of Labour. 2003. *Annual Report—2002-2003*. New Delhi: Government of India.

Nair, G. 1993. *International Labour Migration Statistics in India*. Bangkok: ILO-ARTEP.

————. 1999. Return of overseas contract workers and their rehabilitation and development in Kerala (India). *International Migration*, 37(1), 209–42.

Pandey, D. 1998. Migrant labour, employment and gender dimensions. *The Indian Journal of Social Work*, 59(3), 743–65.

Parreñas, R. 2001. *Servants of Globalization: Women, Migration and Domestic work*. Palo Alto: Stanford University Press.

————. 2003. The care crisis in the Philippines: Children and transnational families in the new global economy. In *Global Woman: Nannies, Maids and Sex Workers in the New Economy*. Edited by B. Ehrenreich and A. Hochschild. London: Granta Books, 39–54.

Pathare, S. 2000. Struggle for legislative protection: A case study of domestic workers. *Women's Link*, 6(4), 26–30.

Premi, M. & M. D. Mathur. 1995. Emigration dynamics: The Indian context. *International Migration*, 33(3/4), 627–667.

Raghuram, P. 1993. *Coping Strategies of Domestic Workers: A Study of Three Settlements in the Delhi Metropolitan Region, India*. Unpublished Ph.D. dissertation, Department of Geography, University of Newcastle-upon-Tyne, UK.

————. 1999. Interlinking trajectories: Migration and career paths among domestic workers in Delhi, India. In *Gender, Migration and Domestic Service*. Edited by J. Momsen. London: Routledge, 215–28.

————. 2001. Caste and gender in the organisation of paid domestic work in India. *Work, Employment and Society*, 15(3), 607–17.

Raghuram, P. & J. Momsen. 1993. Domestic service as a survival strategy in Delhi, India. *Geoforum*, 24(1), 55–63.

Rao, N. 2002. *Migration, Social Networking and Employment: A study of Domestic Workers in Delhi*. NOIDA: VVGiri National Labour Institute.

Ray, R. 2000. Masculinity, femininity, and servitude: Domestic workers in Calcutta in the late twentieth century. *Feminist Studies*, 26(3), 691–718.

Reserve Bank of India. 2002. *Handbook of Statistics on Indian Economy*. New Delhi: RBI.

Roshni, N. n.d. *A National Socio-Economic Survey of Domestic Workers*. Madras: CBCI.

Sabban, R. 2002. *United Arab Emirates: Migrant Women in the United Arab Emirates: The Case of female Domestic Workers.* Genprom Working Paper No. 10, ILO Geneva.

Sasikumar, S. K. 2001. *International Labour Migration from Independent India.* NOIDA: VVGiri National Labour Institute.

Sassen, S. 2000. Women's burden: Counter-geographies of globalization and the feminization of survival. *Journal of International Affairs,* 53(2), 503–24.

Shah, N. 1994. An overview of present and future emigration dynamics in South Asia. *International Migration,* 32(2), 217–69.

Shram Shakti. 1988. *Shram Shakti: Report of the National Commission on Self-Employed women and Women in the Informal Sector.* New Delhi: Government of India.

Singh, A. M. 1984. Rural-to-urban migration of women in India: Patterns and implications. In *Women in the Cities of Asia: Migration and Urban Adaptation.* Edited by J. T. Fawcett, S. Khoo & P. C. Smith. Boulder, Colorado: Westview, 81–107.

Singh, M. 2003. Tribal women and labour: Problems of tribal domestic help in Delhi. *Women's Link,* 9(2), 8–12.

Sundari, S. & M. K. Rukmani. 1998. Costs and benefits of female labour migration. *The Indian Journal of Social Work,* 59(3), 766–90.

Tellis-Nayak, V. & J. Tellis-Nayak. 1984. Women domestic workers in South India: The paradox of bonding and bondage. *Social Action,* 34(4), 340–53.

UNHCR. 2000 *Sub-commission on the Promotion and Protection of Human Rights.* Working group on Contemporary Forms of Slavery 25th Session, 14–23 June 2000.

Xiang, B. 2001. Structuration of Indian information technology professionals' migration to Australia: An ethnographic study. *International Migration,* 39(5), 73–90.

Zachariah, K. C., E. T. Matthew, & S. Irudaya Rajan. 2001a. Impact of migration on Kerala's economy and society. *International Migration,* 39(1), 63–87.

————. 2001b. Social, economic and demographic consequences of migration on Kerala. *International Migration,* 39(2), 43–71.

PART 2

Receiving Countries

6

Hong Kong as a Destination for Migrant Domestic Workers[1]

VIVIENNE WEE AND AMY SIM

THEORISING DESTINATIONS FOR MIGRANT LABOUR

Most analyses of labour migration focus on it as a movement of people caused by the inequalities that exist between different economies, and seek to explain the direction of labour migration from relatively less developed economies to relatively more developed ones. Such a focus extends beyond the line of debate that divides the neo-classical theorists from the world-system theorists. The former attributes the impetus for migration to the rational choice of individuals acting as free agents in a transnational labour market (see, for example, Todaro, 1969; Harris & Todaro, 1970; Harris, 1978), while the latter views core-semiperiphery-periphery relations as the structural forces that draw labour resources from the periphery to the core or the semiperiphery (see for example, Lomnitz, 1978; Rhoades, 1978; Kemper, 1979; Wiest, 1979). Nevertheless, both neo-classical theorists and world-system theorists share a concern with the direction of labour migration.

However, this theoretical concern with migratory flows does not adequately address how the destinations of labour migrants came to be such. Are these destinations merely passive recipient sites? Why does one destination come to have more labour migrants (in aggregate numbers) than another? And why does one destination have more labour migrants of a particular type than another? Does a destination change its character over time? Why and why not?

In this chapter, we argue that the destinations of migrant domestic workers are not passive recipient sites that just happen to be located in the path of labour migration flows. On the contrary, these destinations are actively shaped through the interactions of macro-politics at the policy level, meso-politics at the level of culture and society, and micro-politics in individual actions. In this process, the destination comes to be defined in terms of space, economy and polity, both as current realities, as well as future trajectories.

Of relevance to our argument is the "articulation theory" of Kearney (1986), Portes (1978) and Meillassoux (1972; 1981). "Articulation theory" derives from Marx's argument that the capitalist mode of production is subsidised by the imports of commodities from non-capitalist modes of production (see Marx, 1954–1959). Based on Marx's argument, Portes (1978:14) discusses labour power as a commodity that can be produced and reproduced outside the capitalist system, but that can nevertheless be incorporated into it through migration. Migrant labour thus becomes an important link that articulates spatially separated capitalist and non-capitalist modes of production.

In this chapter, we utilise "articulation theory" to analyse Hong Kong as the site of a particular process of capitalist development, where the labour power of migrant domestic workers that has been produced and reproduced outside Hong Kong's capitalist system, is nevertheless incorporated into it through migration. Moreover, such migration is routed not just to Hong Kong in general, but to Hong Kong's middle-class households in particular. The articulation of links between capitalist and non-capitalist modes of production is thus layered. It is simultaneously *local*—through the movement of Hong Kong middle-class women from home to workplace—and *transnational*—through the migration of women from less developed economies to work as domestic workers in Hong Kong, thereby relieving their middle-class women employers from the gendered labour of social reproduction.

We also argue that the development of this process is contextualised by the changing position of Hong Kong within the world-economy, especially its evolution from a manufacturing centre to a service-based economy. We pay particular attention to the role of the state as an active agent of the capitalist system. However, we do not take a deterministic view of the state's role in this context. Rather, we show how policy options exist even within the scope of supporting and steering the capitalist system. We further explore how different policy options can lead to different social, political and economic consequences, which are, in the long term, non-trivial. We end by discussing how the workers act, interact and negotiate in relation to the Hong Kong government's evolving policy framework, including in this context, their civic actions as organised labour.

AN OVERVIEW OF MIGRATION PATTERNS AND FEMALE LABOUR IN HONG KONG

Since its colonisation by Britain in 1841, Hong Kong has been a destination for migrants from mainland China, who have arrived in different chronological waves according to changing political conditions (see Skeldon, 1995; Sinn, 1995; Yue, 2000). Such migration intensified in the 1960s, accelerating from the mid-1970s to the early 1980s (see Athukorala & Manning, 1999; Chiu, 1999; Momsen, 1999; Stiell & England, 1999; Anderson, 2000). Significantly, this has developed into migration-as-transition, with Hong Kong serving as a stepping-stone for further migration to other destinations, such as Canada. Skeldon (1995:51) describes Hong Kong as "essentially a destination of human circulation", an observation corroborated by Sinn (1995:12):

> The emigration of Chinese from Hong Kong began as soon as the island became a British colony. By 1939, over six million Chinese had left to go to every part of the world.

Interestingly, such migration-as-transition via Hong Kong is relevant not only for migrants from mainland China, but also for migrant domestic workers, especially those from the Philippines, with intentions to work in a third country, such as Canada and European countries. Among Filipina migrant workers, "many of the young, single and educated ones ... think of Hong Kong as a stepping-stone to somewhere bigger and better" (Lowe, 2000:199).

While we have obtained anecdotal evidence of Filipina migration-as-transition via Hong Kong to third countries, it is difficult to obtain precise figures of the number of Filipina domestic workers who transit through Hong Kong. Nevertheless, the significance of this through-flow is indicated by the following:

- First, according to the Hong Kong Immigration Department, Filipinos (both males and females) are the second largest ethnic group in Hong Kong, next to the mainstream Hong Kong Chinese. Of the 202,900 foreign domestic workers in Hong Kong in May 2000, 147,400 or 72.7 per cent were Filipinas (Asian Migrant Centre et al., 2001).[2]
- Second, Hong Kong is the top destination in Asia for newly deployed Filipina domestic workers, accounting for 40–44 per cent of the new hires in Asia from 1998 to 2001 (Table 6.1).
- Third, it has been estimated that from 1981 to 2000, over 90,000 Filipino women arrived in Canada to work as domestic workers under the Foreign Domestic Movement Program, instituted in 1981, and its successor programme, the Live-in Caregiver Program, instituted in 1991 (Philippine Women Center of British Columbia, 2000; see also McKay, this volume). To qualify for the Live-in Caregiver Program, an intending applicant must have "twelve months of full-time paid employment, including at least six months of continuous employment with one employer in a field or occupation related to the job you are seeking as a live-in caregiver. ... This experience must have been obtained within the three years immediately prior to the day on which you submit an application for a work permit" (*Citizenship and Immigration Canada*, 2002). The significance of Hong Kong in this context is that Canadian employers regard it as a reliable source of potential caregivers. So-called "nanny placement agencies" or "nanny referral services" in Canada openly advertise "Filipino nannies/caregivers from Hong Kong" (see, for example, dmoz Open Directory Project, 2004; *ABC Nannies Canada*, 1999–2003; A-PRO Caregivers & Nannies: Helping Families across Canada, n.d.; also see

TABLE 6.1 Most popular destinations in Asia for newly deployed Filipina overseas contract workers

Country	1998		1999		2000		2001	
	No.	%	No.	%	No.	%	No.	%
Hong Kong	122,337	41.4	114,779	40.1	121,762	43.8	113,583	41.8
Japan	38,930	13.2	46,851	16.4	63,041	22.7	74,093	27.3
Taiwan	87,360	29.6	84,186	29.4	51,145	18.4	38,311	14.1
Singapore	23,175	7.9	21,812	7.6	22,873	8.2	26,305	9.7
Brunei	16,264	5.5	12,978	4.5	13,649	4.9	13,068	4.8
Malaysia	7,132	2.4	5,978	2.0	5,450	2.0	6,228	2.3
Total	295,198	100	286,584	100	277,920	100	271,588	100

SOURCE: Adapted and modified from POEA InfoCenter, 2002.

McKay, this volume). The articulation of links between economies at different levels of development thus extends to the link between Hong Kong as a transit point for Filipina caregivers bound for Canada.

This functional utility of Hong Kong for Filipina domestic workers who plan to go to Canada or other third country dovetails with Hong Kong's own developmental trajectory. In the early 1970s, there was a hardening of immigration policies towards Chinese mainlanders migrating into the colony, and the "racial" profiling of domestic workers was introduced as a permanent feature in Hong Kong's immigration and labour policies. "Foreign domestic helpers" (FDH)—the term used by the Hong Kong government—were preferred, as it was deemed possible to "tell them apart" from Hong Kong's Chinese majority so that the latter could not use this policy to recruit members of their own families from China as a way of enabling them to stay on in Hong Kong (Chiu, 1999). Thus, imported domestic labour became a cornerstone for the accelerated inclusion of middle-class women in the work force during the economic restructuring in the 1970s and 1980s that witnessed Hong Kong's transition from a manufacturing base to a commercial centre providing tertiary services for the operation of global capital (Chiu, 1999).

In terms of "articulation theory", Hong Kong's more developed capitalist mode of production became linked to less developed modes of production in two geographically bifurcated directions. While Hong Kong's capital in the manufacturing sector moved northwards to utilise the cheap labour of mainland China, supplied mostly by Chinese women,[3] Hong Kong's household-based social reproduction came to be linked to female labour supplied by less developed economies to the south—namely, the

Philippines, Indonesia, Thailand and Sri Lanka. As noted by Samers (1999:187) in the context of labour migration to Europe, "just when capital movements were allegedly '*flexibilised*'..., migration ...—that is the barriers to the movements of labour—became increasingly *rigid*". This inverse relationship is also discernible in Hong Kong.

Thus, while the scope of Hong Kong's capitalist system has expanded northwards through the movement of capital to mainland China, the system nevertheless protects its territorial base by excluding mainland China's workers from migrating to and settling in Hong Kong, and instead admits supposedly transient workers of different nationalities and physical appearances from South and Southeast Asia.[4] Nationality and visible physical difference are thus utilised as sorting mechanisms for the territorial protection of Hong Kong as a capital-rich base.

With the restructuring of the Hong Kong economy, paid domestic work became increasingly important as greater numbers of women received education and joined the formal sector (Leahy, 1990; Constable, 1997; Athukorala & Manning, 1999; Chiu, 1999; Lowe, 2000). By 1986, women's labour force participation had risen to 48.5 per cent (Kwitko, 1996:111). Concomitantly, the average age of marriage increased, fertility fell, and family size shrank.

However, the growing importance of fulltime paid domestic work within the household does not imply an absence of traditional child-fostering services provided on an ad hoc basis by female relatives, neighbours and friends, although these also came under pressure as these women too came to be incorporated into the formal workforce. Nor does the need for fulltime, paid domestic help imply the lack of governmental support in providing resources for childcare. Rather, it would seem that fulltime privatised domestic labour is preferred by the new middle class of professional women to relieve themselves not only of childcare duties but of housework in general, all of which has thus remained largely unchanged as women's work. Tam (1999:266) pointed out that despite the limited number of places in childcare centres—37,341 for 339,681 children under the age of four years—the average waiting period for these centres was only 1.6 months, which indicates either a lack of awareness of these services among the public in Hong Kong, or a concern about the quality of childcare services available.

As evidence of their importance to the Hong Kong economy, the number of foreign domestic workers in Hong Kong unexpectedly increased during the Asian Financial Crisis beginning in 1997, despite a local unemployment rate of 2.2 per cent in 1997 and 4.7 per cent in 1998 (Census and Statistics Department, 2004; n.p.).[5] However, the number of foreign domestic workers who faced unilateral premature contract terminations by employers in financial stress increased by 45 per cent during this period. Nevertheless, they were able to find re-employment without much delay (Chiu, 1999). This paradoxical situation can be explained by the number of returning Hong Kongers who had emigrated and satisfied requirements for residence status elsewhere prior to Hong Kong's handover to China in 1997. Emigration from Hong

Kong peaked in 1992 but by 1995, most émigrés had returned (Chiu, 1999) (Tables 6.2 and 6.3).

This allows us to develop new layers of understanding in "articulation theory". Hong Kongers emigrate to obtain alternative passports as commodities produced by relatively more developed capitalist economies, such as Canada, because they fear having their capital and labour trapped by China's relatively less developed economy. However, obtaining an alternative passport, as a ticket to geographical mobility, does not provide equivalent access to economic mobility. As a result, these middle-class émigrés return as newly mobile "foreigners" to Hong Kong to enjoy relatively higher incomes, as well as relatively affordable luxuries, such as the employment of a domestic worker. For example, the Canadian government openly boasts that among the developed countries, it has the second lowest wages next to Italy (Government of Ontario, n.d.: n.p.). Nevertheless, Canada had a relatively low Gini coefficient[6] of 0.341 in 1995 (Sharpe, 1998), as compared to Hong Kong's relatively high Gini coefficient of 0.518 in 1996 (Lui, 1997). This gap between rich and poor translates, in practical terms, to the wealth gap between employer and domestic worker. The wider the gap is, the more affordable it is for the employer to employ a domestic worker, as it means that the latter's wage would constitute a smaller proportion of the former's income. Furthermore, this wealth gap is widened by the migration of domestic workers from poorer economies with wages even lower than that of the poor in Hong Kong. Economic disparities within and between economies are thus articulated through the pricing of wages.

TABLE 6.2 Emigration by Hong Kongers

1987	1988	1989	1990	1992	1996	1997
30,000	45,800	42,000	62,000	66,000 (peaked)	40,300	30,900

SOURCE: Chiu, 1999:88.

TABLE 6.3 Percentage of returnees to Hong Kong among those who emigrated

1984–1993	1994	1995
12%	28%	60%

SOURCE: Chiu, 1999:89.

At the height of Hong Kongers' emigration in 1992, the demand for foreign domestic workers increased by 19 per cent (Table 6.4). This apparent contradiction occurred because the Hong Kong economy was then experiencing an accelerated economic expansion[7] (Chiu, 1999). Foreign domestic workers made redundant by émigré employers were quickly hired by local families who could now afford such services and by expatriate professionals hired to fill the newly-vacated jobs of émigrés.

After 1996, the employment of foreign domestic workers slowed, due to two reasons: first, a saturation effect whereby those who needed paid help had already hired a foreign domestic; and second, an increase in local unemployment among the middle class in 1995. However, demand for foreign domestic workers remained resilient after the Asian Financial Crisis when the number of foreign domestic workers hired expanded by 4.4 per cent for the first seven months of 1998, exceeding the growth in demand of 4.1 per cent for the entire 1997 (Chiu, 1999). By the 1990s, the presence of foreign domestic workers as a substitute for the working wife and mother had become

TABLE 6.4 Number of foreign domestic workers in Hong Kong, 1990 to 2000

Year	Number of Foreign Domestic Workers	Percentage increase /decrease
1990	70,300	na
1991	84,600	20.3
1992	101,200	19.6
1993	120,600	19.2
1994	141,400	17.2
1995	157,000	11.0
1996	164,300	4.6
1997	171,000	4.1
1998	178,500[a]	4.4
1999	202,900[b]	13.7
2000	216,790[c]	6.9
2001	235,280[c]	8.5
2002	237,110[c]	0.8
2003	216,860[c]	−8.5

SOURCE: Adapted and modified from Chiu, 1999:109; AMC, 2000:130.
NOTES:
a   Cited as 180,600 in AMC, 1999:111.
b   Cited in AMC, 2000:130.
c   Statistics from the Immigration Department of the Government of Hong Kong SAR, 2004.

a permanent feature for about 20 per cent of Hong Kong's households (Athukorala & Manning 1999).

A FLUCTUATING MINIMUM WAGE FOR MIGRANT DOMESTIC WORKERS

Hong Kong has the distinction of being one of two Asian countries to have a legislated minimum wage for migrant domestic workers.[8] This distinction becomes even more significant when we realise that Hong Kong has no minimum wage for its own workers. So why does Hong Kong have a minimum wage only for migrant domestic workers?

From 1982–1984, the British colonial government in Hong Kong set the minimum wage for migrant domestic workers at HK$1,150 (or US$147.66 at current exchange rates of US$1=HK$7.788) in 1982, raised it to HK$1,350 (US$173.34), and then to HK$1,650 (US$211.86), with the aim of protecting low-waged local workers from competition by foreign workers (French, 1986:19). At that time, this minimum wage was beyond what most Hong Kongers could afford for domestic help, yet was affordable for the few Hong Kong elite and expatriate families who wanted English-speaking domestic workers. This wage pricing thus served as a sorting mechanism, limiting the number of Filipina domestic workers by limiting the number of employers who could afford to hire them. This left jobs as domestic workers for less wealthy local employers open to local workers. As the minimum wage did not apply to local workers, many of them were paid at rates below the minimum wage legislated only for migrant domestic workers. Some even worked unpaid as members of extended families (French, 1986:19).

The rate of economic growth that took place in the 1980s and 1990s raised wages and was instrumental in the creation of a large middle class in Hong Kong (Suen, 1995). This resulted in two important consequences. First, there was a growing proportion of English-speaking families who could afford the minimum wage of foreign domestic workers and who came to see it as *sine qua non* for their lifestyle. Second, the general level of wages overtook the legislated minimum wage for foreign domestic workers, which came to be seen as highly affordable for many more local employers. However, at the same time, it became too low for most Hong Kong workers to consider as fair remuneration for any job, least of all a job that required live-in arrangements and 24-hour standby service for one's employers.

In view of this expanded demand for migrant domestic workers, the Hong Kong government continued to use wage-pricing to control their numbers and therefore raised their minimum wage in 1992 to HK$3,270 (US$419.88) a month and then in December 1996 to HK$3,860 (US$495.63) a month. In addition, employers were legally obliged to provide their employees with housing, worker's compensation insurance[9], travel allowances, and meals or a meal allowance. In the Hong Kong government's report to the United Nations Committee on Elimination of Discrimination Against Women, it was explicitly stated that the minimum wage for migrant domestic workers "was in place to protect foreign workers from exploitation and to protect the jobs of local workers" (United Nations, 1999). However, many Hong Kong Chinese view the minimum wage of the migrant domestic workers as indicative of the "generosity" of the Hong Kong government, which has caused them to be overpaid. Foreign domestic workers are said to be "extremely lucky" to be employed in Hong Kong (Lowe, 2000:118, 129). On the surface, it seems that the government is protecting foreign domestic workers rather than local employers, and this has caused much resentment. Locally, foreign domestic workers are considered as "abusers" of the "generosity" of the Hong Kong government (Lowe, 2000:118).

However, this perceived "generosity" becomes questionable when we realise that the minimum wage set for migrant domestic workers is actually lower than Hong Kong's poverty line, which has been set at HK$3,750 per person.[10] According to a Household Expenditure Survey conducted by the Census and Statistics Department in 1999/2000, 28 per cent of Hong Kong's 449,000 households were living below this poverty line. To this must be added the more than 200,000 migrant domestic workers in Hong Kong, whose minimum wage has been pegged below the poverty line.

The Hong Kong Confederation of Trade Unions (HKCTU) describes the migrant domestic workers' minimum wage as "extremely low". Nevertheless, the very existence of a minimum wage serves as a precedent for the HKCTU to press their demand for a minimum wage system in Hong Kong (The Hong Kong Confederation of Trade Unions, n.d.). In this context, it is not to the advantage of the HKCTU to ask for the abolition of the migrant domestic worker's minimum wage, given that it serves as a precedent and that it is the only minimum wage that has been legislated in Hong Kong. It is also not to the advantage of the HKCTU to have Hong Kong's only minimum wage pegged below the poverty line. In this context, we can see a convergence of workers' interests across national lines, between migrant workers and local workers in Hong Kong.

During the time that Hong Kong's economy was growing rapidly, there were few who doubted the economic contributions of foreign domestic workers. However, in the wake of the Asian Financial Crisis of 1997, the socially powerful Employers of Overseas Domestic Helpers' Association lobbied the government to reduce the foreign domestic workers' minimum wage by some 14–35 per cent, so that employers would be able to save by paying their workers less (AMC, 1999; *IHLO Solidarity Monthly New Bulletin*, 2002; Sim, 2003). Foreign domestic workers, their supporters and non-governmental organisations (NGOs) celebrated a "victory" when after numerous high-profile public processions, rallies, demonstrations, signature campaigns and protests, the government reduced the migrant workers' minimum wage by a "mere" five per cent in February 1999—that is, from HK$3,860 (US$495.63) to HK$3,670 (US$471.23) (AMC, 1999; *IHLO Solidarity Monthly New Bulletin*, 2002; Sim, 2003).

This reduction prompted NGOs in Hong Kong to warn that the "black market wages for domestic helpers" would fall even further below the reduced minimum wage (Sui, 1999). In its *Submission to the Pre-sessional Working Group of the United Nations*

Committee on Economic, Social and Cultural Rights, the Hong Kong Human Rights Monitor (2000:33–34) criticised the Hong Kong Government for reducing the minimum wage of migrant domestic workers:

> The failure of the Government to protect the right of foreign domestic helpers to a wage that is sufficient for a decent standard of living is contrary to Article 7(a) of the Convention [i.e., the ILO Convention on Minimum Wage Fixing (No. 131)]. [The Hong Kong] Human Rights Monitor requests the [UN] Committee to urge the Government to review the minimum wage for foreign domestic helpers and to ensure that they receive fair remuneration that will enable them to enjoy a decent standard of living. The Committee should also demand that the Government vigorously investigate and prosecute all violations of minimum wage laws.

In 2003, vociferous demands again emerged from certain sectors of Hong Kong's population, initially with the support of Employers of Overseas Domestic Helpers' Association, for the government to protect the unemployed, especially women, from the competition of foreign domestic workers. Such demands were spurred by Hong Kong's unemployment and bankruptcy rates, which had hit historically high levels in the sluggish economic conditions following the Asian Financial Crisis of 1997. Public dissatisfaction was further aggravated by the government's mishandling of the proposed national security law known as Article 23 under the Basic Law,[11] as well as its poor management of the SARS epidemic in 2003.[12]

In response, on 25 February 2003, the Hong Kong government decided to reduce the minimum wage of foreign domestic workers by HK$400 (US$51.36) per month from 1 April 2003 onwards and to impose a levy of HK$400 (US$51.36) per month on their employers from 1 October 2003 onwards (*Dole News*, 2 April 2003). The logic behind the two staggered dates was that the employers would save HK$400 (US$51.36) per month for six months, amounting to HK$2,400 (US$308.17), from the wages of the domestic worker (from April to September 2003), and would subsequently divert the HK$400 (US$51.36) per month to the Hong Kong government. The net effect is that the worker's minimum wage is reduced to only HK$3,270 (US$419.88), while the employer continues to expend HK$3,670 (US$471.23) for her service per month, but with the HK$400 difference going to the government.

For the foreign domestic worker, this wage reduction of HK$400—poorly disguised as a levy on the employers—is tantamount to a tax of 11 per cent on the minimum wage of HK$3,670. In protest against this wage cut, the Philippines government announced on 5 March 2003, a temporary suspension of processing of all contracts for domestic helpers in Hong Kong. Furthermore, the Philippines government's Department of Labor and Employment filed a case on 5 September 2003 before the International Labour Organisation (ILO), which agreed to send a team of investigators to Hong Kong to look into the complaint in connection with the minimum wage cut affecting Filipino domestic helpers there (*Philippine Headline News Online*, 6 September 2003).

The Philippines Senate subsequently adopted a Resolution which described the newly imposed tax burden on Filipino domestic workers in the following terms:

> This tax burden is cruel and unjust, as under Hong Kong's salary tax schedule, a Hong Kong resident must have a monthly income of HK$9,000 (US$1,155.62) (if single) or HK$18,000 (US$2,311.25) (if married) to be liable for salaries tax. A foreign domestic helper in Hong Kong earns only about HK$3,670 (US$471.23) a month and yet she would be required to pay the same amount of tax as a Hong Kong junior executive who earns more than 7 times her salary (Consulate General of the Philippines, n.d.).

PENALISING FOREIGN DOMESTIC WORKERS TO SUBSIDISE THE LOCAL UNEMPLOYED

The ostensible reason for the HK$400 levy is to raise revenue to pay for retraining local workers (Immigration Department of the Government of Hong Kong SAR, 2003a). The almost total relocation of Hong Kong's manufacturing industries to mainland China led to a concomitant loss of jobs in this sector, especially among women. A 2002 survey by the Hong Kong Federation of Trade Unions (FTU) showed that "women workers are more than twice as likely as men to be unemployed" (Chan, 2002:3). While Hong Kong's overall unemployment rate was a record high 6.7 per cent that year, the unemployment rate among women was possibly as high as 13.4 per cent, with women's unemployment highest in manufacturing (Chan, 2002: 3). In 1990, the manufacturing industry still employed about 27 per cent of all workers; this dropped to only ten per cent in 2000 (Census and Statistics Department, 2001).

To address this severe problem of unemployment, the Employees Retraining Ordinance was enacted in October 1992, with the aim of setting up and running an Employees Retraining Fund to finance the Employment Retraining Scheme (ERS) aimed at retraining "those unemployed aged 30 or above who are affected by economic restructuring", so as to enable them to find new employment (CAP 423 Employees Retraining Ordinance, 2004).

In the light of Hong Kong's budget deficit, which stood at HK$62 billion in 1998/99 and HK$32 billion in 1999/2000 (Lau, 2001), the government found it imperative to find alternative sources of revenue. This was the impetus for them to reduce the foreign domestic workers' minimum wage by HK$400 and transfer this amount as a levy from the employers to the government for the Employees Retraining Fund. Indeed, the government's website on the Employees Retraining Board states that "apart from capital injection from the General Revenue, the Employees Retraining Fund is financed by a levy charged on employers hiring imported workers" (Education and Manpower Bureau of the Government of Hong Kong SAR, 2004).

However, there is no mention that this levy is actually paid for by the workers, rather than the employers, since it comes from a reduction of the workers' minimum wage. The additional revenue that will be raised through this means is very substantial: HK$400 per month x 216,860 foreign domestic workers (in 2003) = HK$86,744,000 (US$11,138,161) per month or HK$1,040,928,000 (US$133,657,930) for the year 2003. This is more than double the amounts put in by the Hong Kong government into the Employees Retraining Fund previously: HK$300 million (US$38,520,801) in 1996, HK$500 million (US$64,201,335) in 1997, HK$500 million (US$64,201,335) in 1999, and HK$400 million (US$51,361,068) in 2001 (*Hong Kong Yearbook*, 2001).

After initially supporting the demand for reducing the minimum wage of foreign domestic workers, the employer class eventually fell silent when they realised that the HK$400 wage reduction was meant not to benefit them, as the wage reduction of 1999 did, but just to offset a levy of the same amount meant for the Employees Retraining Fund. The government's policy position is clear in that it does not want to reward or punish the employers, but it is very willing to penalise the foreign domestic workers to subsidise the retraining of the local unemployed. The way the levy has been structured to finance such retraining costs can thus be understood as an expedient means of extracting revenue from a disenfranchised group of foreign workers whose opinions are unimportant to the Tung Administration. Indeed, despite the storm of protests by domestic workers, their support groups and governments of sending countries, the Hong Kong government has remained unmoved. So at the time of writing this chapter, the minimum wage of the workers is still pegged at HK$3,270—i.e., HK$480 below the poverty line.

Significantly, a telephone interview conducted by the Hong Kong Institute of Asia-Pacific Studies of Chinese University of Hong Kong with 753 adult citizens in February 2003 showed that almost 60 per cent of the respondents agreed with the government's proposal to reduce the minimum wage of foreign domestic workers, while only 31.5 per cent opposed it—(Hong Kong Institute of Asia-Pacific Studies 2003:1). This indicates that the majority of Hong Kong people regard the earnings of foreign domestic workers as leakages from Hong Kong's economy. The opposing view, however, argues that the employment of foreign domestic workers primarily liberates Hong Kong women who contribute to economic growth, and secondarily boosts Hong Kong's economy through the many businesses generated in Hong Kong for these workers by their compatriots. These perceived leakages became one of the main sources of local criticisms during the lean years following the Asian Financial Crisis of 1997 when Hong Kong employers made comparisons with countries like Malaysia and Singapore, where employers paid even lower wages to their migrant domestic workers.

It is significant that the Employee Retraining Scheme (ERS) specifically mentions "domestic helpers training" and "personal care workers training" among the full-time courses provided (Education and Manpower Bureau of the Government of Hong Kong SAR, 2004). Indeed, there has been increasing demand by unemployed Hong Kong women for such jobs, even though they had previously disdained these during earlier periods of economic boom. However, the local domestic workers do not expect to provide the same standards of service that foreign domestic workers generally provide—i.e., a six-day live-in, 24-hour standby service, without being able to go home daily. Simply put, local domestics do not provide the same quality of service at the same rate, which means that any shift towards the use of local domestics on their terms, would effectively reduce the purchasing power of the employer's dollar.

So despite their sub-poverty-line minimum wage and their substantial contributions to the Hong Kong economy, the foreign domestic workers now have to work not just to support themselves and their families, but also the Hong Kong government's retraining programme, designed to enable local unemployed women to become domestic workers, supposedly to replace the foreign domestic workers themselves eventually. The subsidy provided by a non-capitalist mode of production for a capitalist mode is clearly articulated in this context. To ameliorate the job losses brought about by the capital flight of the manufacturing sector, subsidies are obtained not as compensation from the manufacturers who have pulled out their capital, but from the "primitive accumulation" of foreign domestic workers—obtained through their labour in the social reproduction of middle-class households.[13] Furthermore, to compound the irony of this process, the subsidies are used to re-channel a former industrial workforce into the work of non-industrial household reproduction, which is thereby made to fund its own change of personnel, from foreign domestic workers to local domestic workers. In this way, the capitalist class, which includes at least some of the employers of foreign domestic workers, is insulated from the negative social and political impact of its own economic actions.

As shown in Table 6.4 above, from 2002 to 2003, for the first time in 13 years since 1990, there was a decline in the number of foreign domestic workers in Hong Kong. In 2002, there were 237,110 workers—an increase of 0.8 per cent over the previous year—but in 2003, there were only 216,860 workers—a decrease of 8.5 per cent. It remains to be seen whether this trend continues or reverses in 2004. Why did such a decline occur? There are at least two possible reasons. First, as mentioned above, after 1996, there has been a "saturation effect" as most of those who needed paid domestic help had already hired workers. Second, the economic downturn has led to an increase in local unemployment since 1995, even among the middle class. However, despite the increasingly reduced minimum wage, Hong Kong remains the preferred destination of many migrant domestic workers. They are still willing to put up with the situation of increasing disadvantage, because even this reduced sub-poverty-line minimum wage is more than what they would get back home. The poverty of the sending countries, or more specifically, their relative lack of capital accumulation, thus allows the flexible appropriation of the "primitive accumulation" of their migrant workers who are servicing more developed capitalist systems. In short, capital once again triumphs over labour.

Before the levy was introduced, a fragile class solidarity had apparently existed between the foreign domestic workers and the local domestic workers. Demonstrations and protests by Filipino or Indonesian groups either against their own governments or jointly against the Hong Kong government, received the support of the Hong Kong

Domestic Workers General Union with its 10,000 members. According to a staff member of the Hong Kong Confederation of Trade Unions, these local workers did not view their foreign counterparts as competitors, as they serve the needs of different segments of the local market. There was thus no sense of rivalry. While the foreign domestic workers worked for families that required live-in services, the local domestic workers worked part-time for households that did not require live-in services.

However, the issue of the HK$400 levy has proven to be very divisive. Whereas local and foreign domestic organisations had previously worked together on almost all issues, this is now no longer the case. Class solidarity has been divided along the fault-line of capital flow. Because the levy taxes foreign workers to subsidise local workers, a conflict of sub-class interests has been generated with one sub-class of workers (the foreign domestic workers) positioned as the exploited, with another sub-class of workers (the local domestic workers-to-be) positioned as the beneficiaries of such exploitation. This division has emerged, notwithstanding the fact that an increase in the supply of trained local domestics would pose a more direct threat to the jobs of existing local domestic workers in the local employment market. Furthermore, because the levy comes out of the wages of foreign domestic workers, their employers are not affected at all. This has led to a convergence of ethnocentric interests shared by local employers and local workers, leading to a deepened division between the privileged local "us" and foreign "them". This new ethnic solidarity has thus come about at the expense of the previous class solidarity between foreign and local workers.

Meanwhile, divisions are being sharpened among the local domestic workers themselves. Because the legislated minimum allowable wage for foreign domestic workers legally does not apply to local domestic workers, there is wide variance in the wages received by local domestic workers. Asato (2004:8) provides the following information:

> Local domestic work part-timers' hourly wage is on the average between [HK] 50 [US$6.41] and 59 dollars [US$7.56]. Since the part-time workers go on duty for less than 10 hours per week, their overall monthly wage is about [HK] 1,680 dollars [US$215.38]. However, the most frequent range is from [HK] 501 [US$64.23] to 1,000 dollars [US$128.21] per month, in which 60 per cent of part-timers is included. … This shows the wage level of part-time LDWs [local domestic workers] is kept quite low. This becomes especially true when seen in the context of the fact that LDWs do not enjoy fringe benefits like food and shelter because of their stay-out living arrangement with their employers. … The employers' suggested monthly wage for full time LDWs is [HK]4,937 dollars [US$633.92], which is … more than the standard minimum wage set for FDWs [foreign domestic workers].

In this context, it is interesting that more is known about migrant domestic workers than local domestic workers. Our research indicates that local domestic workers who belong to the Hong Kong Domestic Workers General Union seem to receive higher wages than those who are not unionised. Unionised local workers suggest that even though the minimum wage for foreign domestics legally does not apply to them, they nevertheless find it useful as a baseline below which they are not willing to go. In other words, they use it as a "floor" and not a "ceiling" in wage negotiations with employers.

THE "NEW CONDITIONS OF STAY" AS A MEANS OF CONTROLLING MIGRANT LABOUR

In Hong Kong where the government has recently disallowed "rights of abode" to Hong Kong-born persons born to Chinese nationals and China-born persons of Hong Kong residents, it is clear that the right to reside in Hong Kong is fiercely guarded as an exclusive right that is protected through the stringent rules and policies of the Department of Immigration. One of the most significant of these that pertains specifically to foreign domestic workers is a policy issued by the Hong Kong Immigration Department in April 1987, known as the "new conditions of stay", also known as the "two-week rule". The scope of this policy is as follows:

> Whereas foreigners working in professional fields in HKSAR [Hong Kong Special Administrative Region] have the liberty to change jobs and are eligible for permanent residency after seven years of continuous work, MDWs [migrant domestic workers] under the Two-Week Rule are severely disadvantaged. They are forbidden from changing jobs in the first two years of employment, and if they break their initial contract they cannot apply for a new job from within Hong Kong. They cannot work for multiple employers or outside of the field of domestic work. MDWs do not qualify for permanent residency no matter how long they have been working in HKSAR and those who are terminated must leave within two weeks or at the expiration of their visas (whichever is earlier) (United Nations Economic and Social Council, 2003:1).

What this means is that a foreign domestic worker, whose contract has been terminated either by herself or by her employer, is not permitted to remain in Hong Kong to take up new employment. Instead she is required to leave before the expiry of two weeks after the date of termination. The only exceptions to this rule, where the workers are allowed to transfer directly to a new employer without going home first, are cases where a foreign domestic helper has been mistreated or where an employer is unable to continue with the contract because of financial difficulties, emigration, transfer abroad or death.[14] However, the burden of proof lies with the worker who has to show, for example, medical evidence of physical abuse or evidence of the employer's insolvency.[15] Without such proof, even if the worker were to find a new employer in the two weeks after the termination of her contract, she is still required to return to her country to await the processing of the necessary papers, instead of simply transferring to the new employer. This, however, would be a shorter wait—a matter of months—than if she were to go home without a new employer. If she does not find a new employer, she would have to re-commence the costly process of finding an employer through an employment agency in her home country, a process that will take much longer.

The "two-week rule" policy was instituted explicitly to stop foreign domestic workers from "job-hopping" (*Legco Paper* No. 3150/93–94, 30 May 1994, cited in Hong Kong Human Rights Monitor, 1996/97). The use of the term "job-hopping" is somewhat strange, as it implies that foreign domestic workers are at liberty to hop from job to job. In fact, apart from the "two-week rule", their occupational mobility is already highly restricted. First, they are legally prohibited from employment in any sector other than domestic work. Second, they are legally required to live-in with their employers, hence decreasing their chances of seeking employment opportunities elsewhere. Third, all potential employers of foreign domestic workers have to be vetted by the Labour Department to ensure that they can afford to hire such workers. So it would be very easy for the government to monitor and prevent any intended change of employers.[16]

The "two-week rule" thus compounds the vulnerability of foreign domestic workers as they can be fired by the employer for any reason at any time,[17] without the option of then transferring to a new employer within Hong Kong, unless they can show proof of mistreatment or the employer's insolvency, emigration, transfer abroad or death. As a result, an unjustly fired employee who cannot show such proof, is obliged to leave Hong Kong in two weeks' time, even if she manages to find a new employer before she leaves.

This forced departure after two weeks has been an issue over which there has been much labour organising and protest since 1987. Migrant workers demand[18] that they be given the same rights as foreign professionals, that they not be discriminated against on the basis of their occupational status, and that they be allowed to stay till the end of the visa-contracted period to find new jobs and to be allowed to start in their new jobs without having to go home first. But it does not appear that there will be any lifting of this policy for some time to come. A spokesperson from the Immigration Department confirmed this official view recently: "If a foreign domestic worker cannot find a new employer in two weeks, she will not find one if given more time!"[19] We cannot establish the basis upon which views of this kind are articulated with such confidence, and often doubly penalising workers whose terminations of contract may stem from no fault of theirs. Even worse, such early terminations of contract and the subsequent enforced departure within two weeks may befall indebted workers who have not worked long enough before termination to cover the initial costs of their migration and who thus fall ever deeper into debt. They return home with no money and no employment prospects, except to re-enter the costly and lengthy process of seeking overseas employment through exploitative labour agencies once again.

One unforeseen consequence of the "two-week rule" is the emergence of increasing numbers of illegal migrant workers, who stay on in Hong Kong when they are unable to find new employers in two weeks but are unwilling to return home in debt, without the prospect of returning to work in Hong Kong soon. According to the Hong Kong

Immigration Department, these overstayers have increased by 14 per cent in one year alone—from 15,554 to 17,681 between 1997 and 1998 (AMC, 1999:12). As a sending country, the Philippines estimates that there are more undocumented (5.3 million) than documented (4.7 million) Filipinos working overseas (AMC, 1999:112). The apprehension and treatment of illegal migrants fall outside the scope of this chapter, but it suffices to say that short-sighted policies may, in the end, result in compromising the welfare of a society where migrant workers who have lost their jobs and cannot find new employment in two weeks, simply disappear into the underground economy.

Underlying this issue and its ramifications is a clash of agendas between the government, migrant workers and local workers. The government obviously has segmented policies for a segmented labour market. While foreign professionals may be classified as "foreign talents" that Hong Kong wishes to attract, foreign domestic workers are seen as unskilled workers who are potential competitors with local workers for the decreasing number of low-waged jobs. Why such jobs are decreasing has to do again with capital flight from the manufacturing sector to mainland China. The timing of the legislation of the "two-week rule" policy in 1987 is thus not accidental.

As noted by To (n.d.:n.p.), with the relocation of manufacturing from Hong Kong to the mainland, "of the 178,532 workers displaced from their jobs between 1986 and 1991, 114,753 were women (64 per cent)". She further observes that at the time, the women who had lost their jobs in manufacturing were driven into the unskilled service sector. This would include domestic work and sex work. In this context, the "two-week rule" as a deliberate obstacle placed in the path of the foreign domestic worker when she seeks to move from one employer to another, thereby implicitly privileges the local worker in obtaining employment as a domestic worker, as she would be under no such constraints in her job quest.

It is, however, questionable whether local workers really seek such jobs. As noted above, up to 2003, only 10,000 local domestic workers had been registered with the Hong Kong Domestic Workers General Union. This figure by no means reflects the actual number of local domestic workers in Hong Kong, especially since there is historically a low rate of unionisation in this occupation. But even if we were to speculate that these unionised workers represent a ballpark figure of ten per cent of the total—an estimate which would be considered rather low—this would give us only a total of 100,000 local domestic workers, that is, less than half the number of foreign domestic workers.

Indeed, it is statistically unknown how many local domestic workers there actually are in Hong Kong, as it is not necessary for them to register as such. But this has not stopped the Hong Kong government from persisting in identifying domestic work as the future of unemployed workers who have lost their jobs in manufacturing. This policy focus can be unravelled as a continuous thread—from the "two-week rule" of 1987 to the HK$400 levy of 2003—which, at this late stage, is still trying to retrain the unemployed as domestic workers. Such policy persistence, without any indications of past, present or future success, attests to the bankruptcy of ideas about how to create new jobs for the majority once industrial manufacturing disappears as a mainstay of the economy. Hong Kong is thus caught in the unemployment crisis of late capitalism where low-waged jobs have migrated to zones of lower production costs.

MIGRANT DOMESTIC WORKERS IN A LIBERAL CAPITALIST SYSTEM GOVERNED BY THE RULE OF LAW

Despite the disadvantages discussed above, Hong Kong has nevertheless long been the Asian destination of choice for migrant domestic workers, as compared with other destinations in the region. Even though the number of foreign domestic workers declined by 8.5 per cent from 2002 to 2003 (Table 6.4), Hong Kong remains a preferred destination for many migrant workers from other countries in the region. Why is Hong Kong a preferred destination, despite its sub-poverty-line minimum wage and its "two-week rule"? Because these two conditions still offer migrant workers, by comparison, a better deal than what they would receive in other receiving countries in the region, including Brunei, Malaysia, Singapore and Taiwan.

As noted above, Taiwan is the only other Asian country that offers migrant domestic workers a minimum wage. However, while the minimum wage in Hong Kong is legislated, which means that employers who pay less than this wage are breaking the law, the minimum wage in Taiwan is merely a suggested guideline for contractual agreement between employer and employee. Thus, it is deemed legal for a migrant worker and her employer to agree contractually to a wage lower than the suggested minimum (Women Web, 2002). Thus, even though the Taiwanese "minimum wage" is nominally higher, at about NT15,840 a month (US$466),[20] than Hong Kong's current minimum wage at HK$3,270 (US$419), migrant workers' entitlement to the latter is protected by Hong Kong law.

Indeed, Hong Kong's justice system is praiseworthy for its protection of foreign domestic workers' rights. A number of legal instruments are used for this purpose:

- A standard employment contract: as stated in the Immigration Department's *Guidebook for Employment of Domestic Helpers from Abroad*, "The standard Employment Contract (ID407) is the only contract acceptable to the Immigration Department, the Government of the HKSAR. ... This contract is governed by Hong Kong laws, in particular, the Employment Ordinance (Chapter 57), the Immigration Ordinance (Chapter 115) and the Employees' Compensation Ordinance (Chapter 282)" (Immigration Department of the Government of Hong Kong SAR, 2003b: n.p.).
- The inclusion of foreign domestic workers in Hong Kong under the Employment Ordinance, which states specifically that all domestic helpers are entitled to wage protection, protection against anti-union discrimination, rest days, statutory holiday with pay, paid annual leave, sickness allowance, maternity leave, wages in lieu of notice (if any), payment in lieu of any untaken annual leave, and pro rata

annual leave pay for the current leave year (if applicable), long service payment or severance payment (where appropriate) (Labour Relation Promotion Resource Centre, 2002a).

- The inclusion of foreign domestic workers under the Employees' Compensation Ordinance, which compulsorily requires all employers to take out a valid insurance policy for the domestic helper to cover all their liabilities for compensation (Interactive Employment Service of the Labour Department of the Government of Hong Kong SAR, 2003).

- Enforcement action on breaches of the Employment Ordinance, including civil claims and criminal prosecution: while civil claims "are usually adjudicated by the Minor Employment Claims Adjudication Board or the Labour Tribunal, which will determine whether the defendant has to make compensation to the claimant ... in criminal proceedings, it is the Labour Department that would take out prosecution against the employer for contravening the employment provisions. Penalties would be imposed on the employer upon conviction. ... Criminal cases involving breaches of the Employment Ordinance would normally be heard at the Magistrates' Courts" (Labour Relation Promotion Resource Centre, 2003: n.p.).

The Labour Department states on its website that in cases of non-payment of wages:

> An employer is required to pay interest on the outstanding amount of wages to the domestic helper if he fails to pay wages within seven days after the end of the wage period, and is liable to prosecution and, upon conviction, to a fine of $200,000 [US$25,641.03] and to imprisonment for one year (Interactive Employment Service of the Labour Department of the Government of Hong Kong SAR, 2003: n.p.).

However, in practice, most of such cases are merely adjudicated as civil claims by the Labour Tribunal, which usually settles these in financial terms, and even so as partial compensation, rather than the full amounts owing, and hardly ever with interest added. The Labour Department hardly ever takes out criminal prosecution against deviant employers for having broken employment laws related to wage non-payment or underpayment. This seems to indicate reluctance on the part of the Hong Kong government to penalise a particular segment of society—namely, the employer class.

In 2000, the Labour Department handled 28,620 claims and in 2001, the figure rose 11 per cent to 31,698 cases, mostly related to wage arrears, holiday pay and wages in lieu of notice (Greenfield, 2003).[21] Labour disputes that are not resolved by the Labour Department are referred to the Labour Tribunal, a judicial branch of Government, which deals with financial claims arising from violations of the Employment Ordinance. In 2000, 9,611 cases were filed with the Labour Tribunal compared to nearly 10,500 cases, an increase of nine per cent in 2001 (Greenfield, 2003).[22] With only 13 presiding officers, the Labour Tribunal is heavily burdened, handling an average of 10,000 cases annually.

Compared with other receiving countries, Hong Kong has a relatively transparent legal infrastructure that governs employer-employee relations. It is no accident that Hong Kong is capitalist, liberal and governed by the rule of law. It is the historical outcome of British liberalism, explicitly implemented from the 1960s onwards, comprising three key elements:

- *laissez-faire* capitalism which coupled the expansion of the scope of the market with the reduction of the role of the state;
- the maintenance of the rule of law by the state as the legal backbone of open markets, including the labour market, "as one of the world's largest financial markets Hong Kong requires certainty and predictability of the law to maintain confidence in the operation and effectiveness of those markets" (Hills, 1994: n.p.); and
- freedom of speech and assembly in a pluralistic social order (Hills, 1994: n.p.).

Despite the handover of Hong Kong to China in 1997, this post-colonial legacy still continues under the formula of "one country, two systems". It is this blend of liberal capitalism with the rule of law that makes Hong Kong attractive to migrant domestic workers, especially when compared with relatively less liberal regimes in other receiving countries.

As mentioned above, even though the state plays an active role as an agent of the capitalist system, as illustrated above in the case of Hong Kong, this role is nevertheless not rigidly determined. There are indeed policy options to choose from within the scope of supporting and steering the capitalist system. The particular social, political and economic configuration that characterises Hong Kong as a destination for migrant labour is thus the result of specific policy options chosen by successive Hong Kong administrations, from colonial to post-colonial times. It is a buyers' market in that buyers can pick and choose the kind of labour they wish to purchase—for example, domestic workers from Southeast Asia and not from mainland China.

THE WORK OF MIDDLE-CLASS SOCIAL REPRODUCTION, WORKPLACE NEGOTIATIONS AND CIVIC ACTIONS

It is generally assumed that the term "domestic work" refers simply to housework, childcare, care of the elderly (and perhaps also the disabled). However, this interpretation is simplistic. The work of a paid domestic worker hired by a middle-class family involves the work of middle-class social reproduction. Middle-class status is indeed a prerequisite for employing a domestic worker: the Immigration Department of the Government of Hong Kong SAR (2003b) specifies that "for every helper to be employed, the employer must have a household income of no less than HK$15,000 (US$1,925.04) per month", which is 15 times Hong Kong's poverty line, and 1.5 times Hong Kong's lowest taxable income level of HK$9,000 (US$1,155.62).

The work of migrant domestic workers is thus not just "domestic work" in a generic sense but, more specifically, the work of reproducing the everyday life of middle class households. For example, it is not just the work of childcare, but more specifically, the work of caring and nurturing household heirs who are expected to succeed to or even raise their family's class status.

Obviously, there is variation in the competencies of different domestic workers in such class-specific work. In this context, the employer class has constructed a hierarchy of competencies for such work, based on perceived ethnic differences. The hierarchy constructed in Hong Kong resembles that described by Loveband (2003:5) for Taiwan: that is, Filipina domestic workers are valued as carers of children because of their English proficiency, which may even enable them to tutor the children in their schoolwork (see also Lan, this volume). Indonesian domestic workers, on the other hand, because of their greater proficiency in Chinese, are regarded as less suitable as carers of children but more suitable for general housework and as carers of the elderly. Thus, Filipina domestic workers are regarded as more competent in the middle-class reproduction of the next generation, while Indonesian domestic workers are regarded as more appropriate for the reproduction of everyday life, as well as for filial piety.

Perhaps because of this demand for their English-language skills, Filipina domestic workers in Hong Kong today are increasingly well educated with 62 per cent having received some form of tertiary education, as compared with only a third with such qualifications in 1986 (French, 1986; Asian Migrant Centre et al., 2001).[23] Indeed, Filipina workers' own awareness of their role in the middle-class social reproduction of their employers' families has motivated many of them to invest in their sisters', nieces' and daughters' education, with the expectation that the latter would follow their migratory footsteps. Lowe's research (2000) showed that there exists a phenomenon of chain migration where Filipina mothers working as foreign domestic workers are recruiting their daughters into domestic service overseas. This can be explained by the fact that the Philippine domestic economy is only able to absorb half its college graduates annually. In addition, one of the benefits of having had a college education is that it qualifies the person to apply for positions as care-givers and housekeepers in Canada which have college education as a pre-requisite. In addition to migrant workers' investments in the education of their children and other family members, the rise in the number of Filipina migrant domestic workers with tertiary education is also a consequence of structural unemployment in the Philippines, where there is a dearth of jobs for well-qualified, highly skilled Filipinos (Lowe, 2000).

The greater demand of the employer class in Hong Kong for Filipina domestic workers is reflected in the higher wages that they receive, as compared with Thai and Indonesian workers. Although it was established that 42 per cent of the Filipina domestic workforce was underpaid by at least ten per cent in 1986 (French, 1986),

99.56 per cent of Filipina domestic workers received at least the legislated minimum wage of HK$3,670 (approximately US$470) by 2001 (Asian Migrant Centre et al., 2001). This is all the more significant when compared with other groups such as Thai and Indonesian domestic workers of whom only 91 per cent and 52 per cent respectively, received the minimum wage in 2001.

If higher wages reflect higher status in a situation where job mobility into other sectors of formal employment is contractually not allowed, Filipina domestic workers evidently enjoy the highest status among foreign domestic workers. Indeed 0.65 per cent of Filipina respondents—in a survey of more than 2,500 workers in Hong Kong—reported earning more than HK$6,670 (US$856.45) per month, while 0.52 per cent reported earning between HK$5,670 (US$728.04) to HK$6,670 (US$856.45) (Asian Migrant Centre et al., 2001). These are substantially higher than the minimum wage by 50 per cent to 80 per cent and it is possible to infer that this small group of Filipina domestic workers are highly valued by their employers and enjoy some measure of status not available to other ethnic groups of domestic workers.[24]

The level of wages attainable is a prime factor for Filipinas when they select from between different destinations of overseas employment, given that the economic factor remains the most important push factor for labour migration from the Philippines (see, for example, Dizon-Añonuevo & Añonuevo, 2002:19). Aside from their relatively high wages, the benefits enjoyed by Filipina domestic workers, such as holidays and rest days, far exceed those of any other group.

The English-language skills of the Filipinas are particularly significant for the expatriate middle class in Hong Kong. In 1986, French (1986:18) found that only 66 per cent of Filipina domestic workers were working for Chinese employers. This is significant considering that 95 per cent of the population in Hong Kong is Chinese (Hong Kong Trade Development Council, 2000–2003). By 2001, the percentage of Filipinas working for Chinese employers had risen to 77 per cent (Asian Migrant Centre et al., 2001), as compared to 91 per cent of Indonesian and 94 per cent of Thai domestic workers who work for Chinese employers.

In an earlier paper (Wee & Sim, 2004), following French (1986:21), we found that foreign domestic workers generally prefer to work for non-Chinese employers, as they feel that these employers are less likely to exploit or abuse them. In that paper, we argued that the increasing trend of Filipinas working for such employers is an indication of their greater autonomy than that of either Indonesian or Thai domestic workers in Hong Kong. In this chapter, we want to complement this earlier argument by pointing out that the greater autonomy of the Filipinas in choosing non-Chinese employers is made possible by the latter's greater demand for their services in social reproduction that is, in this light, not just class-specific, but also ethnicity-specific (see Table 6.5).

This finding further deepens the "articulation" analysis of Hong Kong as a destination of migrant domestic workers. It is precisely because Hong Kong occupies the position of being a regional and indeed global hub in the global capitalist economy that middle-class expatriate professionals and their families have become a significant sub-class in Hong Kong society. As a result, one of the attractions of Hong Kong for these middle-class expatriate professionals is the availability of English-speaking domestic workers from the Philippines. So in an ironic twist of history, the earlier American colonisation of the Philippines has become a factor in the production of a particular type of domestic worker, whose labour migration to Hong Kong adds value to the territory's facilities for a globalising middle class.

At the same time, Hong Kong's tradition of liberalism, inherited from British colonial governance, enables the foreign domestic workers, especially the Filipinas, to organise themselves through NGOs and labour unions. Furthermore, it provides the civic space for foreign domestic workers to develop their capacity to assert their rights. Indeed, Hong Kong has a vibrant civil society populated by lively labour unions, NGOs, media, religious groups and other organisations. Between 1997 and 2000, 6,900 public processions, meetings and protests took place in Hong Kong (Tien, 2001). In the words of a Police Deputy Commissioner, "This is the price to pay for democracy".[25] Indeed, the Hong Kong Police Force prides itself for the "meticulous planning, disciplined organisation and accommodating stance taken by the officers concerned that the 490 public meetings and 194 public processions held during 2000 generally passed off peacefully with minimum inconvenience to the general public" (*Hong Kong Police Review*, 2000: n.p.).

Although it is debatable whether Hong Kong is truly democratic, it is nevertheless liberal enough to host the development of migrant workers' unions in Hong Kong, such as the Asian Domestic Workers' Union and the Indonesian Migrant Workers' Union, as well as a number of NGOs that have espoused migrant workers' issues as their cause (Sim, 2003). Indeed, the Employment Ordinance enshrines their right to form and participate in trade unions (Labour Relation Promotion Resource Centre 2002b).

Our research shows that a substantial number of foreign domestic workers acquire a greater degree of legal literacy concerning labour rights during their employment in Hong Kong. Many of them become extremely active as labour organisers, engaged in various civic actions, ranging from the formation of unions, advocacy of workers' rights, to public rallies and demonstrations. They also participate in public actions organised around wider social issues in Hong Kong (see for example, Law, 2002; Sim, 2003).

In her study of sixteen different NGOs working with migrant domestic workers in Hong Kong, Sim (2003) identified the dominance of those that focus on workers' rights, political organisation and agitation, both within Hong Kong and internationally, over those that merely provide welfare services. A key example of the former type is the Asian Migrant Centre (AMC), which has played an important role among the different ethnic worker groups in Hong Kong—for example, in catalysing domestic workers' labour unions, engaging in political campaigns, and pioneering reintegration and saving programmes.

In contrast to these rights-focused NGOs, there are others that focus on providing support for foreign domestic workers in Hong Kong. Prominent among these are church organisations that cater to the welfare and social needs of these workers. There are two main organisations—Domestic Helpers and Migrant Workers Programme (or DHMW, run by Christian Aid) and the Mission for Filipino Migrant Workers—that provide paralegal assistance to foreign domestic workers in preparing their documents and their clients for the ordeal of court proceedings, trials and financial negotiations, in the Labour Department and Labour Tribunal. They also assist with making police reports, helping domestic workers collect their belongings, passports and monies owed to them by employers and employment agencies. In the year 2002, DHMW alone counselled and assisted with more than 3,000 cases involving foreign domestic workers.[26]

What is notable about these NGOs is that ten out of the 16 are founded, staffed, catalysed or led by Filipinos:

> The presence of these Filipino-dominated NGOs in Hong Kong has significantly empowered Filipina domestic helpers. They have become much more aware of their rights and have been able to develop their capacity to organise and manage their own labour, not just as individuals but collectively (Wee & Sim 2003:23).

The result is an interaction between the greater demand of expatriate and other middle-class employers for Filipinas' perceived competence in social reproduction and the greater activism of Filipino-dominated NGOs. The consequence of such an interaction is evident in the gap between the working conditions of Filipina and Indonesian domestic workers in Hong Kong (Table 6.5).

In addition to these NGOs, a number of migrant workers' unions have also emerged in Hong Kong. The key difference between the NGOs and the unions is that the NGOs are "organisations *for*", whereas the unions are "organisations *of*". In other words, the members of the NGOs are not themselves domestic workers, whereas the members of the unions are. Two key unions that have emerged in Hong Kong are the Indonesian Migrant Workers Union (IMWU) and the Asian Domestic Workers Union (ADWU). The rise of such unions is a clear indication of the growing empowerment of the migrant domestic workers in Hong Kong.

Given that the Filipinas still comprise the majority of domestic workers in Hong Kong, despite the increase in the number of Indonesian workers in the last six years since the 1997 Asian Financial Crisis, it is clear that the demand for their perceived competence in middle-class social reproduction remains unabated. In relation to this class-specific demand, it is unlikely that the government's plan to replace migrant domestic workers with retrained, laid-off local workers from the manufacturing sector will succeed, as the latter would not be perceived as being competitive with the currently dominant Filipinas. Indeed, 78.3 per cent of local domestic workers declare that they are illiterate in English (Asato, 2004:3).[27]

TABLE 6.5 Comparison of benefits between Filipina and Indonesian domestic workers in Hong Kong

	Filipinas	Indonesians
Estimated numbers in 2000	142,556	46,000
Estimated numbers in 2003	148,000	78,000
Average age	33 years	27 years
Average employment with current employer	3.1 years	1.5 years
Average length of stay in Hong Kong	4.9 years	2.2 years
Wage:		
Less than HK$1,670	0.1%	0.5%
$1,671≤$2,670	0.1%	38%
$2,671≤$3,670	0.3%	9%
≥$3,671	99.6%	52%
Mean (average)	$3,847	$3,073
Median (50th percentile)	$3,670	$3,670
Mode (most common)	$3,670	$3,670
Days off per month:		
0 (none at all, or less than 1 day per month)	0%	6%
1 day	3%	14%
2 days	1%	39%
3 days	0.2%	1%
4 days	93%	39%
Mean (average)%	3.9 days	2.6 days
Median (50th percentile)	4 days	2 days
Mode (most common)	4 days	2 days
Statutory holidays per year:		
0–1 day (i.e. none at all, less than 1 day, up to 1 day per year)	3%	56.5%
2–3 days	0.5%	3%
4–5 days	0.6%	2%
6–7 days	0.5%	0%
8–9 days	1%	0.2%
10–11 days	5%	0.7%
≥12 days	89%	36%
Mean (average)	11.43 days	4.65 days
Median (50th percentile)	12 days	0 days
Mode (most common)	12 days	0 days
Nationality of employer:		
Chinese (least preferred)	77%	91%

SOURCE: AMC et al. 2001; Benitez, 2003; *South China Morning Post*, 23 February 2003.
NOTE: Shaded sections above show figures that are below the legal requirements.

On the other hand, Hong Kong has an ageing population:

At 76 years for men and 82 years for women, life expectancy is one of the highest in the world. The absolute number of those aged 85 years and over will rise from 30,000 in 1995 to 75,000 by 2005 (Woo et al., 1998).

As noted above, Indonesian domestic workers are preferred by Hong Kong employers for the care of the elderly members of their families. For this labour-intensive work of home-based geriatric care, it is unlikely that the part-time services of local domestic workers would suffice. Therefore, on both these fronts—in the care of the children and the elderly of middle-class families—it would seem that the services of the Filipina and Indonesian migrant domestic workers will continue to be in demand (although there is some emerging information that the care of the elderly is in the process of being relocated to mainland China).

ALTERNATIVE PERSPECTIVES AND POLICY TRAJECTORIES

The discussion above has illustrated how interactions of the macro and the micro are contextualised not only within a specific destination, such as Hong Kong, but more comprehensively, within a global employment opportunity structure that is located transnationally. In this paper, we have focused on Hong Kong as a destination for migrant labour and the role of the government as an agent of the capitalist system, particularly in the way it has shaped its policies on labour migration to fulfil its own political and economic agendas. At the same time, we have shown how a historically specific configuration of liberal capitalism, governed by the rule of law, can be conducive for the promotion and protection of migrant workers' rights. We have also discussed how relatively micro-level developments—such as the demand for perceived competence in a specific type of middle-class social reproduction—can interact with the capacity for social activism, resulting in an ethnic hierarchisation of domestic workers.

It is unlikely that the Hong Kong government can or will phase out paid domestic work in the foreseeable future in Hong Kong. As shown above, the government continues to promote the option of replacing migrant domestic workers with local domestic workers. However, this option does not seem to be favoured by middle-class employers with specific needs and job specifications. Therefore, our prognosis is that migrant domestic workers will continue to be in demand by middle-class employers in Hong Kong. So rather than try vainly to replace them with local domestic workers, it would be more fruitful for the Hong Kong government to reform its policies, so as to eliminate the unfair treatment, stigma and abuses of migrant domestic workers, and not increase their vulnerability by making their conditions of work and stay even more insecure. A step in the right direction would be to ensure that policies governing paid domestic work are brought in line with those extended to other workers, which specify working hours and the nature of the job. In this way, paid domestic work can and should command respect as a job, like any other job, with clear specifications, rights and obligations.

The migrant workers, on their part, are seeking employment in a global labour market that is, on the whole, unfavourable to them. In this context, the terms and conditions of employment as migrant domestic workers in Hong Kong may already be considered as superior to those found in other receiving countries in the region. Nevertheless, this situation can be improved upon and made more stable. This would enhance the productivity of the workers and hence the productivity of their employers. Therefore, the government should rescind the policy to cut the already sub-poverty-line wages of the workers, as well as the "two-week rule" which has enabled many employers to exercise arbitrary power in terminating their contracts with the workers and sending them home, often still in debt.

Finally, for Hong Kong to develop truly as a multicultural global city, it is necessary to implement social programmes to change the mindset of the public in their often prejudiced views of migrant workers, domestic workers and domestic work. Such programmes could include social education campaigns that address issues of discrimination in terms of more equitable values.

NOTES

1   This chapter is an outcome of a research project conducted by the authors in Hong Kong since 2002, funded by the Southeast Asia Research Centre (SEARC), City University of Hong Kong. The project involves a series of structured and semi-structured interviews, based on snowballing and random sampling techniques, as well as ethnographic field research utilising participant observation. The authors would like to acknowledge the assistance of Joanna Tam of SEARC in bibliographic editing.

2   This works out to a foreign domestic worker for every five families in the population.

3   By the end of April 2001, Hong Kong was the largest investor to mainland China, with an actual foreign capital of US$174.2 billion, accounting for 48.45 per cent of all foreign investments there (*People's Daily*, 24 May 2001).

4   We say "supposedly transient" because a certain (as yet unknown) number of these migrant workers do stay on, either legally (usually through marriage) or illegally (as overstayers who remain after the expiry of their visas).

5   Hong Kong still recorded a GDP growth of 5.3 per cent at the beginning of the Asian Financial Crisis (Chiu 1999:104). The unemployment rate for the third quarter of 1998 stood at 5.3 per cent (Chiu 1999:87) and at 4.8 per cent for the entire year of 1998 (OECD 1999:56).

6   The Gini coefficient is a measure of economic inequality: 0 = absolute equality; 1 = absolute inequality.

7   This is largely a consequence of the open-door policy in China and the exponential growth brought about by Hong Kong's economic integration with the Pearl Delta region of China.

8   Taiwan is the other Asian country that has a minimum wage for migrant domestic workers (see Lan, this volume).

9   The costs and coverage vary depending on the financial institutions providing the workers' insurance.

10   This poverty line was set in July 2002 through a landmark study of 3,086 low-income households in Hong Kong. Based on this research, they proposed a basic living wage system at a minimum monthly rate of $6,600, a daily rate of $250 or an hourly rate of $32 (Lau, 2002). The Hong Kong government does not provide an official figure for the poverty line (Hong Kong Human Rights Monitor, 2000:7.1).

11   The government's attempt to enact laws to give effect to Article 23 of the Basic Law was deemed by Hong Kongers to be a guise for increasing official power and scope in the interpretations of national security issues, and infringing on civil liberties.

12   Severe Acute Respiratory Syndrome (SARS), caused by what is thought to be a flu-like vector-borne virus, began in Southern China in late 2002 and spread via Hong Kong to other international destinations.

13   The term "primitive accumulation" is derived from Marx's (1867) *Capital*, Volume 1, Chapter 26, Part 8, where he describes this as a process of divorcing the producer from pre-capitalist means of production—hence "primitive". Rather than see this as a one-off historical process, we are applying this concept to an ongoing process of expropriating the accumulation obtained through the paid work of social reproduction done by domestic workers. This usage seems to be particularly apt in the context under discussion, as the foreign domestic workers are being asked to fund their eventual replacement by local domestic workers.

14   See "Reply of the Secretary for Education and Manpower in Legislative Council", 20 May 1992 (Question No. 10) (Hong Kong Human Rights Monitor, 1996/97).

15   Despite this rule, considerable discretion seems to be given to the immigration officer in charge. For example, in one case witnessed by Amy Sim, an Indonesian migrant worker whose termination of contact was due neither to abuse by the employer nor to the employer's financial difficulties, emigration, transfer abroad or death, was nevertheless told by the immigration officer that she could stay until the end of her visa. What may be significant in this case is that this worker was accompanied by a member of the Indonesian Migrant Workers' Union.

16   The Labour Department's requirements of employers are: 1) an annual income of more than HK$186,000 (US$23,846) or a monthly income of more than HK$15,500 (US$1,987) for the last six consecutive months, or a savings account in the last six consecutive months with a°term deposit balance of more than HK$200,000 (US$25,641); and 2) a home that is big enough to house a live-in domestic worker (the employer is required to declare the floor area of the rooms in the apartment or house).

17   The Labour Department allows the employment contract to be terminated immediately with good cause or with one month's notice for any reason and by either party.

18   For example, 11 migrants' organisations in Hong Kong issued a flyer in 2003, entitled *Protect the Rights of Migrants*, criticising the discriminatory practices embedded in an Immigration Department policy, called the Two-Week Rule. The organisations protested

that while foreign domestic workers are required to leave Hong Kong at the end of two weeks after the end or termination of their contracts, this particular clause did not apply to any other foreign worker groups, such as expatriate professionals. In addition, "[t]he Rule directly targets MDWs (migrant domestic workers) ... they are not accorded the same rights to freely change employers or apply for permanent residency, which are enjoyed by all other foreign 'professionals' working in HKSAR" (Asia Pacific Forum on Women, Law and Development et al., 2003; Asia Alliance of YMCAs, 1994).

19   We would like to thank Medelina Hendytio, a researcher with the Centre for Strategic and International Studies in Indonesia for sharing this information which stemmed from her interviews with officials of the Hong Kong Immigration Department in 2003.

20   The suggested "minimum wage" for live-in Taiwanese domestic workers is NT30,000-35,000 a month (US$1,000-$1,200).

21   These are gross figures and reflect neither the number of foreign domestic workers nor the nationality of the claimants.

22   The figure of 10,500 is annualised based on the number of cases for the first nine months of the year at 7,852.

23   Tertiary education is defined here as including those with a minimum of two years in a college or university-equivalent institution.

24   The highest figure cited by a respondent is a monthly wage of HK$12,000. These findings are derived from a research project conducted by the authors in Hong Kong in 2002, funded by the Southeast Asia Research Centre, City University of Hong Kong.

25   Deputy Commissioner of Wan Chai Police, Hong Kong, private communication with Amy Sim, 7 December 2003 at the "Protest March Against Manpower and Transmigration Ministerial Decree on Migration".

26   We would like to thank Kim Warren of Domestic Helpers and Migrant Workers Programme (DHMW), and Cynthia Ca Abdon-Tellez and Eliseo C. Tellez, Jr. of The Mission for Filipino Migrant Workers (HK) Society for this information.

27   Applicants' personal data disclosed on the Hong Kong government's webpage for cyber matching of employment (see Table 7.3, Asato, 2004:3).

REFERENCES

ABC Nannies Canada. 1999–2003. http://www.abcnannies.org. Accessed 28 April 2004.

Anderson, B. 2000. *Doing the Dirty Work? The Global Politics of Domestic Labour,* London, New York: Zed Books.

A-PRO Caregivers & Nannies: helping families across Canada (n.d.) http://www.a-procare.com/ApplicationforServices.html. Accessed 28 April 2004.

Asato, Wako. 2004. International commodification of reproductive labor: Creating a division between foreign and local workers—The Hong Kong experience. Paper presented at the International Workshop on Migrant Domestic/Care Workers & the Reconfiguration of Gender in Asia, 24–25 January in Tokyo, Japan.

Asia Alliance of YMCAs. 1994. Joint Statement by 22 Hong Kong-based organisations to the United Nations Committee on Economic, Social and Cultural Rights on the situation of migrant workers in Hong Kong. *A Report*, Hong Kong: Asia Alliance of YMCAs.

Asian Migrant Centre (AMC), 1999. *Asian Migrant Yearbook 1999*. Hong Kong: AMC.

————. 2000. *Asian Migrant Yearbook 2000*. Hong Kong: AMC.

Asian Migrant Centre (AMC), Asian Domestic Workers Union, Forum of Filipino Reintegration and Savings Groups, Indonesian Migrant Workers Union & Thai Women's Association. 2001. *Baseline Research on Gender and Racial Discrimination Towards Filipino, Indonesian and Thai Domestic Helpers in Hong Kong*. Hong Kong: Asian Migrant Centre, Asian Domestic Workers Union, Forum of Filipino Reintegration and Savings Groups, Indonesian Migrant Workers Union and Thai Women's Association.

Asia Pacific Forum on Women, Law and Development, Asia Pacific Mission for Migrants, Asian Migrants Coordinating Body, Asosiasi Tenaga Kerja Indonesia di Hong Kong, Association of Sri Lankans, Bethune House Migrant Women's Refugee, Far East Overseas Nepalese Association, Friends of Thai, Mission for Filipino Migrant Workers—Hong Kong, Thai Regional Association & United Filipinos—Hong Kong. 2003. *Protect the Rights of Migrants*. Hong Kong: Asia Pacific Forum on Women, Law and Development, Asia Pacific Mission for Migrants, Asian Migrants Coordinating Body, Asosiasi Tenaga Kerja Indonesia di Hong Kong, Association of Sri Lankans, Bethune House Migrant Women's Refugee, Far East Overseas Nepalese Association, Friends of Thai, Mission for Filipino Migrant Workers—Hong Kong, Thai Regional Association and United Filipinos—Hong Kong.

Athukorala, P. C. & C. Manning. 1999. Hong Kong and Singapore: City-states shaped by migrants. In *Structural Change and International Migration in East Asia: Adjust to Labour Scarcity*. Edited by A. Prema-Chandra & C. Manning. South Melbourne, Victoria: Oxford University Press, 112–148.

Benitez, M. A. 2003. 10,000 maids in protest against levy; Foreign domestic workers march to the government's headquarters, as Bishop Zen holds a mass for Filipinos. *South China Morning Post*, 24 February, 5.

CAP 423 Employees Retraining Ordinance (under Education and Manpower Bureau of the Government of Hong Kong Special Administration Region's website). 2004. http://www.emb.gov.hk/index.aspx?langno=1&nodeid=675. Accessed 25 May 2004.

Census and Statistics Department. 2001. *Women and Men in Hong Kong*, Hong Kong: Government of Hong Kong.

————. 2004. *Statistics on Labour Force, Unemployment and Underemployment*, Hong Kong: Government of Hong Kong, http://www.info.gov.hk censtatd/eng/hkstatfaslabour/ghs/labour1_index.html. Accessed 25 May 2004.

Chan, F. 2002. Surveys reveal plight of women: Unemployment at 13pc and domestic pressure taking its toll, prompting calls for new policies. *South China Morning Post*, 4 March, 3.

Chiu, S. W. K. 1999. Hong Kong (China): Economic changes and international labour migration. *OECD Proceedings: Labour Migration and the Recent Financial Crisis in Asia*. Paris: OECD.

Citizenship and Immigration Canada. 2002. http://www.cic.gc.ca/english/pub/caregiver/ caregiver-2.html#1. Accessed 28 April 2004.

Constable, N. 1997. *Maid to Order in Hong Kong: Stories of Filipina Workers.* Ithaca, New York, London: Cornell University Press.

Consulate General of the Philippines. n.d. *Resolution Expressing the Sense of the Senate to Denounce the Imposition of HK$400 Levy on Salaries of Domestic Helpers in Hong Kong.* Senate Resolution No. 558, introduced by Senator Franklin M. Drilon, http://www. philcongen-hk.com/ media/senate.resolution.htm. Accessed 28 April 2004.

E. Dizon-Añonuevo and A. T. Añunuevo, eds. 2002. *Coming Home: Women, Migration and Reintegration.* Philippines: Balikabayani Foundation and ATIKHA Overseas Workers and Communities Initiative.

dmoz Open Directory Project. 2004. http://dmoz.org/Home/Family/Childcare/Nannies/ North_America/Canada/. Accessed 28 April 2004.

Dole News. 2003. Foreign domestic helpers sue HK government on wage cut, levy. Department of Labor and Employment of Republic of the Philippines, 2 April 2003, http://www.dole. gov.ph /news/pressreleases2003/April/105.htm. Accessed 28 April 2004.

Education and Manpower Bureau of the Government of Hong Kong SAR. 2004. *Employee Retraining Board.* http://www.emb.gov.hk/index.aspx?langno=1&nodeid=675. Accessed 28 April 2004.

French, C. 1986. *Filipina Domestic Workers in Hong Kong: A Preliminary Survey.* Occasional Papers No. 11, Centre for Hong Kong Studies, Hong Kong: The Chinese University.

Government of Ontario. n.d. *Wages and Hourly Compensation Costs.* http://www.2ontario. com/ welcome/cosl_201.asp. Accessed 28 April 2004.

Greenfield, G. 2003. Workers' rights in the Hong Kong SAR. *Workers' Rights for the New Century,* Hong Kong: Asia Monitor Resource Center.

Harris, J. R. 1978. *Economic Causes and Consequences of Migrations within the Context of Underdevelopment in West Africa.* Working Paper No. 6, African Studies Center, Brookline, MA: Boston University,

Harris, J. R. & M. P. Todaro. 1970. Migration, unemployment, and development: A two-sector analysis. *American Economic Review,* 60(1), 126–42.

Hills, M. 1994. The rule of law and democracy in Hong Kong: Comparative analysis of British Liberalism and Chinese Socialism. *Murdoch University Electronic Journal of Law,* May 1(2), http://www.murdoch.edu.au/elaw/issues/v1n2/hills12.html. Accessed 28 April 2004.

Hong Kong Human Rights Monitor. 1996/97. *The Two-Week Rule,* http://www.hkhrm.org.hk/ english/reports/nw/ nw0796d.htm. Accessed 28 April 2004.

————. 2000. Paper submission to the *Pre-sessional Working Group of the United Nations Committee on Economic, Social and Cultural Rights Regarding the Report of the Hong Kong SAR of the People's Republic of China.* http://www.hkhrm.org.hk/english/reports/docs/ ICESCR2000. RTF. Accessed 28 April 2004.

Hong Kong Institute of Asia-Pacific Studies. 2003. 市民對2003/04 年度財政預算案態度意見調查結果摘要. February, press release, Hong Kong: The Chinese University of Hong Kong, http://www.cuhk.edu.hk/hkiaps/telpress/tung67press2.PDF. Accessed 27 May 2004.

Hong Kong Police Review. 2000. Hong Kong Island Region. http://www.info.gov.hk/ police/ review/2000/text_version/ch3_2_txt.htm. Accessed 28 April 2004.

Hong Kong Trade Development Council. 2000–2003. http://www.hktrader.net/200309/ hkoverview-index2003.htm. Accessed 28 April 2004.

Hong Kong Yearbook. 2001. Hong Kong: Hong Kong SAR Government. http://www.info.gov. hk/yearbook/2001/ehtml/index.htm. Accessed 29 April 2004.

IHLO Solidarity Monthly New Bulletin. 2002 Hong Kong: Hong Kong Liaison Office of the ICFTU/GUF. HKCTU/HKTUC, 1 February, http://www.ihlo.org/item1/item1e.htm. Accessed 28 April 2004.

———. 2003a. *FDH Employers to Pay Employees' Retraining Levy from October 1, 2003*, publications and press releases, 25 September, http://www.immd.gov.hk /ehtml/20030925.htm. Accessed 28 April 2004.

———. 2003b. *Guidebook for Employment of Domestic Helpers from Abroad*, http://www.immd.gov. hk/ehtml/hkvisas_5.5.htm. Accessed 28 April 2004.

Immigration Department of the Government of Hong Kong SAR. 2004. Foreign domestic helpers (FDH) populations in Hong Kong. *Statistics*, Hong Kong: Hong Kong Immigration Department.

Interactive Employment Service of the Labour Department of the Government of Hong Kong SAR. 2003. *Frequently Asked Questions*, http://www.jobs.gov.hk/eng/domestic/question/ question.asp. Accessed 28 April 2004.

Kearney, M. 1986. From the invisible hand to visible feet: Anthropological studies of migration and development. *Annual Review of Anthropology*, 15, 331-61.

Kemper, R. V. 1979. Frontiers in migration: From culturalism to historical structuralism in the study of Mexico-U.S. migration. In *Migration Across Frontiers: Mexico and the United States.* Edited by F. Camara and R. V. Kemper. Albany: SUNY Institute of Mesoamerican Studies, 9–24.

Kwitko, L. 1996. Filipina domestic workers in Hong Kong and the new international division of labour. In *Asia: Who Pays for Growth? Women, Environment and Popular Movements.* Edited by J. Lele & W. Tettey. Aldershot, Vermont: Dartmouth Publishing Company Limited, 107–23.

Labour Relation Promotion Resource Centre. 2002a. *A Concise Guide to the Employment Ordinance*, http://www.lrpu.labour.gov.hk /publicat/guide/index-e.htm. Accessed 28 April 2004.

———. 2002b. Protection against anti-union discrimination: Chapter 11. *A Concise Guide to the Employment Ordinance*, http://www.lrpu.labour.gov.hk/publicat/guide/11e.htm. Accessed 25 May 2004.

———. 2003. *A Guide on Civil and Criminal Proceedings Related to the Employment Ordinance*, http://www.lrpu.labour.gov.hk/ publicat/p7-e.htm. Accessed 28 April 2004.

Lau, P. 2001. Examining the Hong Kong government budget and fiscal reserves from a macroeconomic perspective. Reprinted from *The Hong Kong Centre for Economic Research (HKCER) Letters*, vol. 63, January/February 2001, Hong Kong: The Hong Kong Centre for Economic Research, http://www.hku.hk/hkcer/articles/v63/plau.htm. Accessed 25 May 2004.

Lau, R. 2002. Basic living wage urged. *CityU Today*, 12 July, http://www.cityu.edu.hk/cityutoday/news/category/research/general/n20020712_01.htm. Accessed 28 April 2004.

Law, L. 2002. Sites of transnational activism: Filipino non-governmental organisations in Hong Kong. In *Gender Politics in the Asia-Pacific Region*. Edited by B. S. A. Yeoh, P. Teo, & S. Huang. London, New York: Routledge, 205–22.

Leahy, P. 1990. *Female Migrant Labour in Asia: A Case Study of Filipina Domestic Workers in Hong Kong*. Unpublished M. A. dissertation, Comparative Asian Studies Programme, University of Hong Kong.

Lomnitz, L. 1978. Mechanisms of articulation between shantytown settlers and the urban system. *Urban Anthropology*, 7(2), 185–205.

Loveband, A. 2003. *Positioning the Product: Indonesian Migrant Women Workers in Contemporary Taiwan*. Working Paper Series No. 43, April, Hong Kong: Southeast Asia Research Centre, City University of Hong Kong.

Lowe, C. T. 2000. *The Outsider's Voice: Discourse and Identity among Filipino Domestic Workers (FDWs) in Hong Kong*. Unpublished Ph.D. dissertation, Department of English, City University of Hong Kong.

Lui, H. K. 1997. Poverty and income disparity in Hong Kong. *HKCER Letters*, January 42, http://www.hku.hk/hkcer/articles/v42/lui.htm. Accessed 28 April 2004.

Marx, K. 1867. *Capital*, volume 1. Moscow, USSR: Progress Publishers.

———. 1954–1959. *Capital*, volume 2. Moscow: Foreign Languages Press.

Meillassoux, C. 1972. From reproduction to production. *Economy and Society*, 1, 93–105.

———. 1981. *Maidens, Meal and Money*. London: Cambridge University Press.

Momsen, J. H., ed. 1999. *Gender, Migration and Domestic Service*. London, New York: Routledge.

OECD. 1999. *OECD Proceedings: Labour Migration and the Recent Financial Crisis in Asia*. Paris: OECD.

People's Daily. 2001. Hong Kong investments in China's Mainland come to over US$170 Billion. 24 May. http://fpeng.peopledaily.com.cn/200105/24/eng20010524_70925. html. Accessed 28 April 2004.

Philippine Headline News Online. 2003. Manila to protest HK levy on maids. 6 September. http://www.newsflash.org/2003/05/ht/ht003711.htm. Accessed 28 April 2004.

Philippine Women Center of British Columbia. 2000. *Canada: The New Frontier for Filipino Mail-Order Brides*. http://www.swc-cfc.gc.ca/pubs/0662653343/200011_0662653343_12_e.html. Accessed 28 April 2004.

POEA InfoCenter. 2002. *Stock Estimates on Overseas Filipinos*. http://www.poea.gov.ph/. Accessed 28 April 2004.

Portes, A. 1978. Migration and underdevelopment. *Politics Society*, 8(1), 1–48.

Rhoades, R. E. 1978. Foreign labor and German industrial capitalism 1871–1978: The evolution of a migrating nation. *American Ethnologist*, 5(3), 553–73.

Samers, M. 1999. "Globalisation", the geopolitical economy of migration and the "spatial vent". *Review of International Political Economy*, 6(2), 166–99.

Sharpe, A. 1998. Income distribution in Canada in the 1990s: The offsetting impact of government on growing market inequality. *Canada Watch*, June, 6(3), http://www.robarts.yorku.ca/canadawatch/vol_6_3/sharpe.htm. Accessed 28 April 2004.

Sim, A. 2003. Organising discontent: NGOs for Southeast Asian migrant workers in Hong Kong. *Asian Journal of Social Science*, 31(3), 478–510.

Sinn. E. 1995. Emigration from Hong Kong before 1941: General trends. In *Emigration from Hong Kong: Tendencies and Impacts*. Edited by R. Skeldon. Hong Kong: Chinese University Press, 11–34.

Skeldon, R. ed. 1995. *Emigration from Hong Kong: Tendencies and Impacts*. Hong Kong: Chinese University Press.

South China Morning Post. 2003. 23 February.

Stiell, B. & K. England. 1999. Jamaican domestics, Filipina housekeepers and English nannies: Representations of Toronto's foreign domestic workers. In *Gender, Migration and Domestic Service*. Edited by J. H. Momsen. London, New York: Routledge, 43–61.

Suen, W. C. 1995. Sectoral shifts: Impact on Hong Kong workers. *Journal of International Trade and Economic Development*, 4(2), 135–52.

Sui, C. 1999. Pay cut for maids on illegal rate. *South China Morning Post*, 5 February.

Tam, V. C. W. 1999. Foreign domestic helpers in Hong Kong and their role in childcare provision. In *Gender, Migration and Domestic Service*. Edited by J. H. Momsen. London, New York: Routledge, 263–76.

The Hong Kong Confederation of Trade Unions (HKCTU). n.d. *The Right to a Minimum Wage*. http://www.hkctu.org.hk/english/rights/wagerights.htm. Accessed 28 April 2004.

Tien, J. 2001. Legco addresses key issues of public concern. *Bulletin*, February, http://www.chamber.org.hk/info/the_bulletin/feb2001/legco.asp. Accessed 28 April 2004.

To, L. n.d. *Hong Kong Country Report*. http://www.itcilo.it/english/actrav/telearn/ global/ilo/frame/epzhong.htm. Accessed 19 January 2004.

Todaro, M. P. 1969. A model of labour migration and urban unemployment in less developed countries. *American Economic Review*, 59(1), 138–48.

United Nations. 1999. *Position And Status of Women in Hong Kong constantly improving, committee on Elimination of Discrimination against Women Told*. Press release WOM/1094, 2 February. http://www.un.org/News/Press/docs/1999/19990202.wom1094.html. Accessed 28 April 2004.

United Nations Economic and Social Council. 2003. Specific groups and individuals: Migrant workers. Written statement submitted by *Asia Pacific Forum on Women, Law and Development* (APWLD). 12 March. http://www.unhchr.ch/Huridocda/Huridoca.nsf/ (Symbol)/ E.CN.4.2003.NGO.122.En?Opendocument. Accessed 28 April 2004.

Wee, V. & A. Sim. 2004 *Transnational Labour Networks in Female Labour Migration: Mediating between Southeast Asian Women Workers and International Labour Markets*. Working Paper Series No. 49, Hong Kong: Southeast Asia Research Centre, City University of Hong Kong.

Wiest, R. E. 1979. Anthropological perspective on return migration: A critical commentary. *Anthropology*, 20, 167–87.

Women Web. 2002. *Women's Rights Issues in Taiwan*. 15 November. http://www.womenweb.org. tw/English/Issue_Show.asp?Issue_ID=6. Accessed 28 April 2004.

Woo, J., S. C. Ho, & E. Lau. 1998. Care of the older Hong Kong Chinese population. *Age and Ageing*, July, http://www.findarticles.com/cf_dls/m2459/n4_v27/21102353/p1/ article. jhtml?term=. Accessed 28 April 2004.

Yue, A. 2000. *Migration-as-Transition: Pre-Post-1997 Hong Kong Culture in Clara Law's Autumn Moon*, http://wwwsshe.murdoch.edu.au/intersections/issue4/yue.html. Accessed 28 April 2004.

CHAPTER 7

Surrogate Family, Disposable Labour and Stratified Others: Transnational Domestic Workers in Taiwan

PEI-CHIA LAN

INTRODUCTION

Taiwan has become one of the most popular destinations for transnational migrants in Asia since it opened its gates to foreign contract workers in the early 1990s. In 1989, Taiwan's government, for the first time, authorised a special order that allowed foreign contractors to work for a national construction project. Two years later, the recruitment of migrant labour was expanded to private sectors, mostly labour-intensive factories. In 1992, the Council of Labour Affairs (CLA) granted work permits to "domestic caretakers" employed to take care of the severely ill or disabled, and later released a limited quota for the employment of "domestic helpers" to households with children under the age of 12 years old or elderly members above the age of 70 years old.

Currently about 300,000 transnational contract workers reside in Taiwan; the number equals to approximately 2.5 per cent of the national workforce. More than one-third of them are employed in private households as domestic helpers or caretakers. Although migrant workers are categorised by Taiwan's government as temporary and supplementary labour, they have significantly transformed the ethnic and cultural landscapes of the island. Transnational domestic workers, in particular, play a critical role in the daily maintenance of 120,000 Taiwanese families.

The employment of transnational domestic workers has become prevalent in developed countries that suffer from a "care deficit" in both private and public life (Hochschild, 1995). Such a deficit is not any less significant in Taiwan, where an extensive welfare system is yet to be established and care is regarded as a familial duty. This paper describes a paradox in the policy on transnational domestic workers in Taiwan: transnational domestic workers are recruited as *surrogate family* to take care of children and elders; however, they are treated as *disposable labour* without adequate social recognition and legal protection. The tension between physical intimacy and

210

social distrust underlines transnational employment dynamics and everyday surveillance on migrant domestics. Transnational domestic workers, divided by nationality, are associated with distinct stereotypes and stratified labour conditions in Taiwan. Migrant-oriented non-governmental organisations (NGOs), still a marginal civil sector in Taiwan, are engaged in advocating policy reforms, raising public awareness, and uniting the segregated ethnic communities.[1]

THE CARE DEFICIT IN TAIWAN: RECRUITING SURROGATE FAMILY

Domestic service has long existed in Taiwan's history, even before the arrival of transnational domestic workers. The trade in women as domestic servants can be traced back to *chaboukan* (girl slaves) in the Ching Dynasty, a practice abolished by the Japanese colonial government in the early 1920s. Domestic service then shifted from a feudalist tradition of slavery to a modern occupation in which servants were free to sell their labour in exchange for wages, and often food and lodging. From 1920 to 1930, a period when Taiwan was incorporated into the industrialisation plan of the Japanese empire, the number of *shijonin* (Japanese for "servant") tripled according to the official statistics conducted by the Japanese colonial government (Bureau of Official Statistics 1924; 1934). Domestic employers included mainly colonial officials and some Taiwanese aristocracy.

After 1945, when the Nationalist regime took over Taiwan, the majority of domestic employers changed from Japanese governors to Chinese mainlander expatriates. The need for domestic help also came from double-income nuclear households, in which educated wives had been driven by urbanisation to seek employment in teaching, nursing and other white-collar occupations in cities (You, 1995). These employers, who were rural migrants themselves, recruited young single girls from their hometowns to reside and work in their urban households as a temporary passage before marriage.

After Taiwan's industrialisation took off in the 1960s and 1970s, a variety of waged jobs became available for women and domestic work was no longer the only option for young girls to start a new life away from their patriarchal families. The major source for domestic workers in the 1980s shifted from single girls to middle-waged *obasans*,[2] who were mostly married or widowed women with families living close by. Unlike live-in single girls, *obasans* preferred not to reside with their employers in order to take care of their own families at the same time.

By the 1990s, the employers found it more and more difficult to locate *obasans*, especially on a live-in basis. More importantly, the employers complained that *obasans* are difficult to deal with, calculating about working hours, selective about job assignments, and demanding on wages and raises. In comparison with rights-conscious local workers, migrant domestic workers are, in the words of an employer, "somewhat closer to the old time servants". Taiwanese employers seek foreign workers to approximate the nostalgic imagination of domestic servants—they are more obedient, deferential

211

and contract-bound; they are paid lower rates but offer live-in services that cover an unlimited variety of domestic tasks.

In fact, as early as the beginning of the 1980s, an increasing number of Southeast Asians entered Taiwan with tourist visas and overstayed to seek employment (Tsay, 1992). The flux of migrant domestic workers in the 1990s not only reflects the increasing shortage of local labour supply in domestic service. It is also a solution to the growing demand for commercial services of housework, childcare and eldercare, as a result of the recent transformations of household patterns and gender relations in contemporary Taiwan.

Dual-income households have become the dominant family model with the growth of women's waged employment during the last few decades. In 2003, about 47 per cent of Taiwanese women above the age of 15 years old were gainfully employed; the percentage of labour participation is more significant among women who are younger or college educated.[3] Dual-income families have become a social norm—an outcome of economic necessity due to rising housing prices and living expenses in urban areas. Concurrently, the nuclear household has become the primary residential pattern in contemporary Taiwan. Current generations of young married couples expect to live separately from their parents; this is especially the case among younger, well-educated wives, and among those who have arranged their own marriages (Thornton & Lin, 1994). However, despite the rising proportion of parents living alone, there remains a social expectation that sons, especially the eldest one, should take care of elderly parents.

Given changing family patterns and continuing filial traditions, labour to care for young children and elderly parents is in serious need. Nuclear households require assistance for childcare when cohabiting extended kin are no longer available. Adult children seek non-family caregivers for their ageing parents to either sustain separate residences or to outsource part of their filial duty in three-generation households (Lan, 2002). The recruitment of live-in migrants has become a convenient and affordable solution to the deficit of care services among many Taiwanese families.

And yet, the introduction of migrant domestic workers has created controversy and widespread concerns among the public. Media reports have raised worries about the impact of foreign workers on public health and social order (see later for details); in particular, they have raised alarms about the quality of childcare under the care of migrant women. Feminist organisations and scholars have also contested the policy on the grounds that it does not challenge but rather consolidates the gendered division of domestic labour and exacerbates inequalities among women across class and national divides (Hu, 1997; Lin, 1999). The government, on the one hand, celebrates this policy as facilitating the participation of Taiwanese women in waged employment but, on the other hand, is concerned about the presence of alien workers in an ethno-homogeneous society (Chao, 1992). In other words, transnational domestic workers are desired as surrogate family members only on the premise that their presence in Taiwan is temporary and their labour is disposable.

THE "STRONG/WEAK" STATE: MAKING LABOUR DISPOSABLE

In this section, I point out three major characteristics of Taiwan's policy on transnational domestic workers which have critical consequences on migrants' experiences. First, the supply and demand of transnational domestic workers are not regulated by market mechanisms but are under state intervention. State regulations on employer qualification, albeit strict, are loosely enforced, leading to possibilities of labour exploitation by placement agents and employers. Second, the selection of sending countries by Taiwan's government is subject to change under diplomatic concerns. Such policy shifts have shaped uneven experiences among migrants of different nationalities. Finally, a system of short-term contract employment has facilitated the dominance of private agencies in the recruitment process, while creating barriers for NGOs to organise guest workers.

Taiwan's government has carefully regulated the entry of migrant contract workers through quota control and point systems since it first opened its doors to them. In recent years, the government has imposed stricter restriction on the employer qualification for hiring "domestic helpers." Yet the employment of migrant "caretakers", categorised as "social welfare foreign workers" by the CLA, is approved on a "needs" basis (e.g. the frailty of elders and patients) without quota control. Many households I interviewed applied for caretakers in the name of elder family members but actually assigned them the tasks of housework or childcare. The number of "domestic helpers" has been decreasing because some employers have forfeited their quotas after their children grew older.[4] In contrast, the employment of "caretakers" (on paper) has continued to grow.

As CLA officials have repeatedly announced, one of the crucial principles in Taiwan's foreign labour policy is to strictly prohibit the permanent settlement of migrant workers. In the beginning, Taiwan's government mandated that the maximum duration of a migrant worker's contract was three years (two years plus a one-year extension) and each worker could work in Taiwan only once. Such a rotation system was also aimed at maximising economic benefits while keeping social costs to a minimum (Tseng, 2004). However, this stringent regulation increased training costs for Taiwanese employers and incentives for migrant workers to overstay their visas. To amend these problems, the recent version of the Employment and Service Law, promulgated on 21 January 2002, allows migrant workers "with good records" to re-enter and work in Taiwan for up to six years (including the first and second contracts).

Actually, such regulation of the resident status of foreign workers is selective on a class basis, which often intertwines with national hierarchies in the world system. Low-end migrant workers, mostly from Southeast Asian countries, are recruited on a contract basis and are not eligible for permanent residence or citizenship. By contrast, migrant professionals, technicians and managers, mostly citizens of North American and West European countries, are entitled to apply for permanent residence or naturalisation after residing in Taiwan with legal jobs for more than five years according to the current Law of Nationality.[5]

According to the Employment Service Act in Taiwan, migrant workers are entitled to rights and welfare stipulated in the Labour Standards Law, including a minimum wage, maximum working hours, and weekly and annual leave.[6] This policy is motivated less by concerns to safeguard the welfare of migrants and more by the desire to mitigate discontent among local workers. Business circles have long advocated the exclusion of migrant workers from the minimum wage regulation. Despite their failure to convince the parliament on this issue, the government tolerates covert forms of wage reduction. For example, employers are now allowed to deduct an amount up to NT$4,000 (US$121) from a migrant's monthly wage to cover food and boarding. This decision was made in the Economic and Development Congress in July 2001; it was endorsed not only by chambers of commerce but also by trade unions. Local workers, facing economic depression and rising unemployment in recent years, often blame migrant workers for "stealing" their jobs away.

After all, the legal protection of migrant workers is more a symbolic statement than a set of enforced measures. The government has failed to supervise actual working conditions or provide effective assistance for migrants. Although most local governments have founded a Foreign Workers' Consulting Centre as an official channel for redress and claims, only a few are equipped with sufficient numbers of staff with the linguistic capabilities to communicate with migrants of diverse nationalities. Many migrant workers receive only partial benefits, having no health insurance or paid vacations. The minimum wage required for local workers usually becomes the "maximum wage" paid to migrant workers.[7] More importantly, the Labour Standards Law in Taiwan does not cover the occupational categories of domestic helpers and caretakers, who are particularly vulnerable to exploitative working conditions.

As noted earlier, a primary concern in Taiwan's policy is to limit the number of migrant workers and ensure their transient status. The CLA attempts to conveniently oversee the whereabouts of transnational domestic workers by depriving their right to circulate in the local labour market. The government dictates that a migrant worker can work for only one particular employer during each stay in Taiwan. No transfer of employer is allowed except under the following conditions: if the original employer goes bankrupt, closes business, or cannot pay wages to the worker; if the care recipient of a migrant worker dies or migrates to another country; and if a worker is abused by the employer or illegally placed with an employer different from the one specified in the contract.[8] Taiwan's regulation on the transfer of employers is stricter than the equivalent policies in Singapore and Hong Kong (see Abdul Rahman et al., this volume; Wee & Sim, this volume). Under such conditions of personal subordination, migrant workers in Taiwan, when faced with unreasonable working conditions, have to either tolerate or escape from them. If they openly protest their working conditions, they risk being repatriated.

Taiwan's government also places migrant workers in the custody of employers as a way of externalising management costs. Each employer is requested to deposit a sum equivalent to the migrant worker's two-month salary as an assurance bond, as well as to pay a monthly "employment stabilisation fee" of NT$1,500 (US$45) for the employment of caretakers and NT$5,000 (US$152) for the employment of domestic helpers. This fee is designed to subsidise government expenses for managing migrant workers and retraining local workers. If a migrant worker "runs away", the employer is still obligated to pay an "employment stabilisation fee" every month until the worker is caught or the contract expires. A more serious punishment to the employer is that, if two of his/her migrant employees disappear from the custody, the quota associated with these workers is temporarily frozen so the employer is not able to hire a replacement until the workers leave Taiwan.

Another factor that underlines the formation of Taiwan's migration policy is the consideration of foreign affairs. Diplomacy has been a thorny mission for Taiwan, a country with limited recognition and formal ties as a sovereign nation. The selection of sending countries for migrant labour is actually based on the suggestions raised by the Department of Foreign Affairs. All these countries have signed bilateral agreements with Taiwan, initially including the Philippines, Thailand, Indonesia and Malaysia, and more recently, Vietnam and Mongolia. Taiwan's government continues to manoeuvre the recruitment of foreign workers as a bargaining chip to enhance diplomatic ties with the sending states. For example, in August 1999, Taiwan's government withdrew negotiation over a bilateral air agreement with the Philippines government, because the latter referred to Taiwan as a local province of the People's Republic of China. This diplomatic crisis led to a temporary suspension of labour migrants from the Philippines.

In August 2002, the CLA suspended recruitment of Indonesian migrant workers based on the allegation that Indonesians have the highest rates of "running away" from contract employers among all migrants.[9] This ban, meant to be a temporary warning, continued to be enforced over two years because of the trouble-fraught relations between Taiwan and Indonesia. In December 2002, Taiwan's president Chen Shui-Bien was scheduled to pay a private visit to Indonesia (so-called "vacation diplomacy"). This plan was cancelled after the media disclosed the information and the Indonesian government openly opposed the visit. Some Taiwanese parliament members urged the government to "take revenge against" the Indonesian government by replacing Indonesian workers with labour forces from more "friendly" countries (*China Evening News*, 18 December 2002). The ban was finally lifted in December 2004. Shortly after that, the CLA announced a freeze on the recruitment of Vietnamese workers due to rising cases of abscondment among these workers. To sum up, Taiwan's government has actively intervened in the recruitment of migrant workers (as the "strong" state), but these regulations, often poorly enforced (by the "weak" state), have led to unintended or even contradictory consequences. The CLA has set rigorous terms on employer qualifications, especially regarding the hiring of domestic helpers, but categorical abuse is commonly heard. Migrant caretakers are often assigned multiple tasks or even extra

215

work outside households (see next section). Although Taiwan's law has established some basic protection for migrant workers' benefits and wage, the government rarely supervises the enforcement and even tolerates certain covert violation of labour rights. The CLA prohibits migrant workers from transferring employers in order to control their whereabouts; however, such measures only exacerbate labour exploitation and personal subordination, thereby pushing workers toward "running away" from harsh working conditions. Finally, Taiwan's government sometimes manoeuvres the recruitment of foreign labour to serve diplomatic purposes; yet, sudden and arbitrary changes only bring about deeper costs for both migrant workers and the receiving society.[10]

THE STRATIFIED MIGRANTS: RACIALISED AND DIVIDED BY NATIONALITY

Filipina migrants used to be the largest group of transnational domestic workers in Taiwan until they were recently outnumbered by their Indonesian and Vietnamese competitors. A similar trend has also appeared in Singapore and Hong Kong (Abdul Rahman et al., Wee & Sim, this volume): an increasing number of employers, often on the advice of employment agencies, are replacing "smart but unruly" Filipina workers with "stupid but obedient" Indonesians. The proportion of Filipinas among all transnational domestic workers in Taiwan decreased from 83 per cent in 1998 to 18 per cent by the end of 2002, while the proportion of Indonesian workers rose from 15 per cent in 1998 to 70 per cent by the end of 2001 (Table 7.1). The number of Indonesian domestic workers in Taiwan has been decreasing since August 2002 when the CLA suspended labour import from Indonesia. In 2003, one-third of Taiwanese

TABLE 7.1   Migrant domestic workers in Taiwan by nationality, 1998–2003

End of Year	Philippines No.	%	Indonesia No.	%	Vietnam No.	%	Thailand No.	%	Malaysia No.	%	Total
1998	44,559	(83)	7,761	(15)	-	-	1,030	(2)	18	*	53,368
1999	42,893	(57)	27,948	(37)	33	*	3,912	(5)	7	*	74,793
2000	34,772	(33)	63,563	(60)	2,634	(2)	5,356	(5)	6	*	106,331
2001	24,875	(22)	78,678	(70)	5,221	(5)	4,158	(4)	2	*	112,934
2002	21,223	(18)	81,490	(68)	15,263	(13)	2,733	(2)	2	*	120,711
2003	29,347	(24)	47,891	(40)	40,397	(33)	2,901	(2)	2	*	120,598

SOURCES: Adapted from Council of Labour Affairs, 1998; 1999; 2000; 2001; 2002; 2003.
NOTE: * means <1%.

employers had turned to transnational domestic workers from Vietnam, a sending country that has been approved by the CLA only since November 1999.

In fact, both Indonesia and the Philippines are multi-ethnic countries that contain complex ethnic and cultural variations. However, the advertisements of labour brokers in Taiwan tend to objectify migrant workers from the same country as a social collective with homogeneous characteristics.[11] By essentialising and naturalising these "ethnic differences," labour brokers construct a popular discourse of "otherisation" that produces or reinforces a racialised classification to demarcate migrant workers by nationality. We[12] conducted a web search to systematically examine the discursive construction of migrant workers along the lines of nationality.

In these discourses, little mention is made about the historical or social contexts of national variations; some even bluntly use terms such as "in nature" and "born to be" to imply the essential nature of such ethnic characteristics. The racialised images that labour brokers project upon migration workers along national divides embody differential patterns of "otherisation". Filipinas are viewed as *the Westernised other*, portrayed as "optimistic, romantic, autonomous"[13] and "outgoing, individualistic, opinionated, and difficult to manage"[14]. In contrast to the Westernised Filipinas, the stereotype of Indonesians conjures up images of docile women trapped in rural villages with Muslim conventions. They are characterised as *the traditional other* who is "obedient, loyal, slow and living a simple life"[15], and therefore naturally suited to hard work and "no days off"[16].

The discursive construction of Vietnamese migrant workers is more ambiguous and complex. On the one hand, Vietnam is considered to have historically been influenced by Han-Chinese culture. Its nationals are therefore associated with some positive features related to Confucianism, such as diligence, frugality, and endurance. Racialised aesthetic standards also shape employers' evaluation of workers' appearances: the fair skin of Vietnamese women is considered better looking than the darker skin of Filipinas and Indonesians. Based on these assumed racial and cultural affinities, recruitment agencies market this new group of migrants as ideal servants suitable for Taiwanese families. On the other hand, the political background of Vietnam stimulates stereotypes about *the Communist other.* Vietnamese workers, previously locked behind the "iron curtain", are imagined to be politically narrow-minded and ignorant of the outside world. Living in a communist regime, they are suspected of being calculating and lacking a capitalist work ethic.

Abigail Bakan and Daiva Stasiulis (1995) have argued that the creation of racialised stereotypes about migrant domestic workers is endemic to the matching process that defines the parameters of placement agencies. In order to survive and thrive in this volatile industry, agencies must effectively project certain racialised images as a way of impressing upon their potential clients the need for professional screening. For a similar reason, Taiwanese agencies manoeuvre nationality-based racialised stereotypes to justify their promotion of Indonesian and Vietnamese domestic workers, especially by magnifying their differences from the social construction of Filipina maids.

In a system of contract employment and rotating migration, both employers and workers tend to rely on private agencies as intermediaries. The recruitment of migrant workers has therefore become a very lucrative business in Taiwan. The agency fee charged to a migrant worker going to Taiwan is reported to be higher than the amounts in other Asian host countries. Although the Taiwanese government has set the maximum amount of placement fees to be collected from a migrant worker,[17] employment agencies invent "service fees" to cover the actual charge of placement fees. And some agencies require workers to sign a receipt before their departure to Taiwan to disguise wage deductions as money the worker "borrowed".

Employment agencies usually charge Indonesian and Vietnamese migrants a higher amount in placement fees than their Filipina counterparts. Based on my investigations in 2003, the average amount paid by a Filipina domestic worker as a placement fee is about NT$90,000 to NT$110,000 (US$2,727 to US$3,333), about one third of which (45,000 pesos) (US$900 in 2003) would be paid to the Filipino agent with the remaining paid to the Taiwanese agent through wage deduction.[18] Yet an Indonesian or Vietnamese domestic worker pays a higher amount, about NT$140,000 to NT$160,000 (US$4,242 to US$4,848). The worker usually pays nothing at home, and the fee is collected in Taiwan through wage deductions of NT$10,000 (US$303) during the first 14 to 16 months.

By producing sharp lines to distinguish migrants of various nationalities, Taiwanese agencies suggest that employers assign them different tasks and adopt distinct methods of management. Indonesian workers, portrayed as dutiful, loyal, and accommodating, become ideal candidates for taking care of the elderly and the ill, while English-speaking Filipinas are considered better educated, more civilised, and thus more capable of caring for Taiwanese children. However, Indonesian workers are more likely to be assigned extra work outside the household, such as working in the factory or restaurant owned by their employers. The alleged stupidity and subservience of Indonesian women make them "suitable" candidates for such "double exploitation" (Loveband, 2004).

Ethnic divisions among transnational domestic workers not only demarcate their separate niches in the labour market, but also rationalise hierarchical differences in their status and rights. Employment agencies usually inform employers that it is feasible to ask Indonesians and Vietnamese to give up their day off, but the no-day-off rule is often not acceptable among Filipina workers, who are characterised as being calculating and militant about their labour rights. Most Indonesian and Vietnamese domestic workers, before their entry to Taiwan, sign an agreement to take no days off or only one day off each month.

On average, Filipina migrant workers in Taiwan have higher education than transnational domestic workers of other nationalities. This echoes previous research findings that a significant proportion of Filipino overseas workers are college educated and have held white-collar positions in the Philippines (Parreñas, 2001). This is related to the fact that the United States (US) widely established colleges during its colonisation of this archipelago. Filipina workers also hold a competitive advantage

218

in the global labour market with their English language proficiency, another legacy of the US colonisation. The cultural and linguistic heritage of their coloniser has thus ironically become the most valuable human resource for Filipinos to escape their stagnant economy and poverty in the post-independence era.

In a previous article (Lan, 2003a), I described the dynamics in transnational encounters between Taiwanese *nouveau-riche* employers and downwardly-mobile Filipina domestics. For Taiwanese employers who celebrate their recent financial achievements, hiring a well-educated English-speaking Filipina maid is a double-edged sword—it may facilitate "conspicuous consumption" (Veblen, 1994) but it can also weaken employers' authority. Some Taiwanese employers, especially those with a high school education or lower, have reported difficulties in communicating with and placing demands on their Filipina maids in English. These Filipina domestics are able to deploy the linguistic tool of English as a means of symbolic resistance, such as negotiating job terms to reduce their workload, or deliberately using advanced vocabulary and correcting the grammar or pronunciation of their employers.

In contrast, Indonesian and Vietnamese workers have to learn Mandarin Chinese or Hokkien to win job orders in Taiwan. After being recruited by sponsors, prospective migrants are sent to agencies for a month-long training programme. The subjects of training mainly include knowledge and skills of housekeeping and care taking, as well as basic language courses. Taiwanese employers frustrated at communicating with Filipina workers in English are now able to get the upper hand in their linguistic exchanges with Indonesian and Vietnamese domestic workers. The dominance of the Chinese language in these transnational encounters marks the employer's authority and silences the migrant workers.

The possession of linguistic skills also channels a migrant worker's venues to information and social support. English-speaking Filipino workers have access to a number of English newspapers and radio programmes, both of which serve a larger group of English-speakers in Taiwan. By contrast, migrant workers of other nationalities can only utilise a few radio programmes in their native languages. Only those who can speak local languages and have access to television at home are able to receive more information about the outside world.

Linguistic barriers also obstruct communication between English-speaking Filipinas and Chinese-speaking Indonesians and Vietnamese. A potential relationship of competition in the labour market further induces a sense of opposition among various ethnic groups. In some cases the migrant workers even reproduce racialised stereotypes to describe other migrants in order to mark the superiority of their own group. Oftentimes Filipina domestic workers feel hesitant about asserting their rights because their employers threaten to replace them with Indonesian women. Some Filipinas assert their superior capabilities over Indonesians by criticising the latter as uneducated, lacking in English skills, and too backward to handle modern housework. In turn, Indonesian workers expressed a feeling of unfairness about the uneven ways some employers treat their workers from different countries. And they discredit

Filipina competitors by portraying them as militant, ruthless, selfish and too lazy to accomplish hard labour.[19] All these factors—market competition, agency discourses, and shortage of interaction—have exacerbated the "we-they" divide even amongst transnational domestic workers and hindered the formation of a cross-ethnic alliance among transnational domestic workers in Taiwan.

THE "CONCERNED" EMPLOYER: PURIFYING THE ALIENS

The tension between "surrogate family" and "disposable labour" has impacted employers' attitudes toward their migrant domestics. Both the spatial proximity in the live-in condition and emotional involvement in care work create a sense of intimacy; however, the turnover of migrant workers often disrupts the accumulation of trust, and class and ethnic differences trigger fears and prejudices among employers. This section first describes the construction of transnational domestic workers as "the unclean other" in the media as well as the state's medical surveillance, and then demonstrates how Taiwanese employers conduct labour control to "purify" alien workers with whom they live together under one roof.

Taiwan's media reports about Southeast Asian migrants—especially during the 1990s when migrant workers had just arrived—are mostly associated with poverty, criminality, and backwardness. Local newspapers and magazines often cover stories of contagious diseases carried by migrant workers with sensational headlines such as "Parasites: The majority of the carriers are Filipina maids" (*United Evening News*, 21 July 1994) and "Two more AIDS infected migrant workers found" (*United Daily News*, 15 January 1994).[20] These diseases are allegedly related with the living conditions in Southeast Asia, which are negatively portrayed as "backward", "dirty" and "uncivilised" among the Taiwanese public. Under the media gaze, the poor hygiene of migrant workers is not only an indicator of underdevelopment but also an alleged consequence of "having low morals". Southeast Asian migrants are often suspected of promiscuity and thus carriers of dangerous sexually transmitted diseases, such as this headline implies, "Thai workers into prostitution: Be careful of spreading AIDS" (*China Times*, 13 May 1998).

Media reports on crimes committed by migrant workers have been filled with striking headlines like "A Filipina maid killed her employer" (*China Times*, 10 November 1995)[21] and "Low costs for employers, high costs for the Society: Don't wait until it is too late for the problems caused by foreign workers" (*United Daily News*, 7 September 1999).[22] A few cases of child and patient abuse by transnational domestic workers received enormous public attention. For example, on 3 November, 1999, a satellite television station aired a segment of video in which a Filipina domestic worker was shown kicking a three-month-old baby. This news triggered social panic about the potential harm done by migrant caretakers. Many articles followed in the newspapers and magazines to caution parents about the possibilities of negligence or underdevelopment of children under the care of foreign nannies. On 8 February 2003, Shia Liu, a well-known Taiwanese writer and an advocate of the rights of the disabled, died after being attacked by her Indonesian caregiver who suffered from a psychological disorder probably caused by emotional stress arising from having no off-days (*Taipei Times*, 8 February 2003) After this incident, public opinion urged the government to adopt more effective surveillance on the mental health of transnational domestic workers.

In fact, the average crime rate among migrant workers is significantly lower than the rate among Taiwanese citizens.[23] Similar cases of maltreatment have happened to those under the care of local workers as well, but disproportionate media attention has been given to migrant caregivers who are considered "intruders" not only in the family but also in society. These media reports project an imagined purity of the Taiwanese society, whose public health and safety are endangered by the presence of ethnic outsiders. Paralleling the media discourses of social pathology, the state requires that all migrant workers pass a medical examination before entering Taiwan and go through periodical medical checkups.[24] If a migrant worker fails any of these checks, he or she is repatriated immediately.

Only recently has medical surveillance upon migrant workers been relaxed, after local and international NGOs expressed concerns about the violation of human rights which has long resulted from this measure. The pregnancy test was lifted in November 2003 to comply with the Gender Equality in Employment Law, enforced since March 2002.[25] According to a new order released in January 2004, the number of medical checkups a migrant worker has to undergo during a contract is reduced to three times (after a stay in Taiwan of 6, 18 and 30 months). These examinations no longer include a urine test for marijuana, morphine, and amphetamines. In addition, all migrant workers are entitled to participate in Taiwan's national health insurance programme, but some employers, mostly those in private households, fail to apply for coverage for their migrant employees. The employer is responsible for 60 per cent of the insurance premium, the employee 30 per cent, and the government ten per cent.

Employment agencies usually offer manuals or guidelines written in English or the worker's native language about the instruction of "appropriate" behaviours and sanitary habits. Some employers adopt measures of segregation to prevent the "unhygienic" foreign domestic worker from "contaminating" the household. They ask their migrant workers to use a separate set of utensils, or do their laundry separately from the family clothes, or even ask their worker to drink water from a separate bottle and use a separate bathroom. Other employers attempt to discipline migrant workers by "civilising" their habits. For example, Taiwanese usually bathe in the evening, while most Filipinos take a shower in the morning. At least three employers I interviewed requested their domestic employees to change this habit that they consider "strange", "abnormal" or "unclean." A simple difference in living habits is interpreted as a sign of backwardness or an abnormality, which should be brought in line with the "normal" custom as defined by employers.

Domestic employers want migrant workers to be "clean" in the sense of personal hygiene as well as moral purity. Incidents of family property being stolen by migrant workers appeared frequently in my interviews with employers, regardless of whether this was the employer's personal experience or just hearsay. To safeguard family assets, employers keep valuables away from workers, avoid giving them house keys, and prohibit their visitors. It is very common for employers to "test" the worker's honesty by deliberately leaving money or jewellery around the house or in the laundry.

Some employers check the worker's room during the latter's day off to make sure no property has been stolen. They mistrust migrant employees based on the alleged association between poverty and criminal orientation. Migrant workers are also presumed to lack an appropriate work ethic, which "explains" their temptation to steal instead of to earn what they want. During interviews, several Taiwanese employers quoted their country's economic prosperity as living proof of the moral superiority of hardworking Confucians. In contrast, economic stagnation in Southeast Asia is seen as unavoidable because of the genetic nature of its people (e.g. "Filipinos are the descendents of pirates"), the tropical weather and, most commonly, a lack of a work ethic by the standards of modern capitalism.

A highly precious family asset that concerns employers is their children. The possibilities of child abuse and maltreatment especially worry parents if they both work outside during the day. Some employers alleviate their concern by minimising the amount of childcare assigned to migrant workers. Wealthier families hire a Taiwanese *obasan* to take care of children, leaving only household chores to the migrant worker. Less privileged employers seek assistance from the extended family: Some entrust grandparents who live together to supervise the performance of the migrant nanny; other parents drive their children along with the migrant nanny to the grandparent's house before work and pick them up after work.

Employers working outside try to monitor the situation at home when they are away; they make surprise visits or call home from time to time. More intrusive methods of surveillance are rare, but not unheard of. One employer secretly used an answering machine to record what happened at home during the day. Another employer set up a video camera in the house. As the worker was aware of the videotaping, it functioned more as a symbol of the absent employers than as a genuine surveillance tool. Some employers ask their homemaker neighbours to keep an eye on workers to prevent them from "running away" or kidnapping the children. Some entrust security guards in their building or housing community with the job of preventing workers from going out without permission, or they request grandparents who live nearby to pay periodic visits during the day. Some employers feel awkward about conducting surveillance in the intimate sphere and attempt to obscure their monitoring practices. They disguise their surprise visits as retrieving something forgotten at home or grandparents drop by to check on the worker with the excuse of missing their grandchildren.

The "running away" of the migrant worker is another primary concern of the labour control strategies of many Taiwanese employers. This results from the state regulation that the quota would be frozen if the associated workers disappear from their employer's custody. To avoid the loss of labour power and quota, many Taiwanese employers withhold migrant wages as "forced savings" or a "compulsory deposit". The deduction ranges from NT$2,000 to NT$5,000 (US$61 to US$152), the equivalent of between one-sixth to one-third of a worker's monthly wage. The money will not be returned to the worker until she completes the contract and leaves Taiwan. Some agents even suggest that the money be given to the worker when she reaches the airport gate on her return home. During my interviews, some employers attempted to legitimise forced savings as a benign act based on the patronising claim that "they [Southeast Asian migrants] don't know how to save money".

Although Taiwan's Labour Standards Law prohibits an employer from withholding a worker's wages for any purpose, a CLA regulation in 1998 once approved forced savings on the condition of mutual agreement. The measure was not outlawed until 2002. As NGOs have advocated, the so-called "agreement" obscured the unequal power dynamics between employers and workers. Despite being projected as a well-intentioned measure to assist workers, the practice of forced saving violates a worker's basic rights to freely dispose of her own property. In addition, the process of depositing forced savings is prone to abuse. Ideally, the money is deposited in a savings account under the name of the worker, but many employers, especially household employers, save the money in their own account or deposit no money at all. Some employers may even confiscate this money as indemnity for a worker's alleged negligence.

In addition to wage deductions, employers take upon themselves the supervision of the worker's physical stability and moral conduct. A worker's passport is usually withheld by her employer or agent during her stay in Taiwan, although the government outlaws such practice. Most agents suggest to employers that they not grant workers Sundays off, especially during the first three or six months of the contract. Some employers require that workers take a day other than Sunday off as a measure to distance individual workers from the larger community of migrant workers.

Many employers adopt covert measures to control a worker's whereabouts. Some check the worker's room or personal belongings during their days off to look for any unusual signs that suggest the worker might run away. Some request reports from the phone company detailing the telephone numbers of local calls in order to learn the workers' social networks. These employers looked embarrassed when describing these actions to me, but they rationalised the intrusion into the worker's privacy by viewing themselves as the worker's moral guardians. One employer noted, "We are not intruding, we are just concerned".

Some employers request their migrant employees to work on Sundays because of a special need, such as the care of a newborn baby or an invalid patient. However, others make this request for the reason of labour control. An employer explained to me, "We don't mind paying her [the worker] overtime[26] at all. We just don't want her to go out, messing around with too many friends. It's better to stay home. Doing no work is fine". It is common thinking among Taiwanese employers that granting rest days to migrant domestic workers will lead inevitably to negative consequences. "We are afraid she might go astray, once she goes to the church on Sunday and socialises with other Filipinas". "We have specified this in the contract—no day off. We don't want them to be polluted at church".[27]

Employers are also concerned that migrant domestic workers might "go astray" if they make boyfriends on their day off. Many transnational domestic workers receive messages such as, "my ma'am always asks me if I meet other men in the church". Employers consider dating a migrant boyfriend to be a sign of moral degradation leading to possible consequence of getting pregnant or running away. Mindful of the criminal acts committed by some migrant domestic workers and their boyfriends,[28] some employers worry about a connection between dating and kidnapping or burglary. The control of sexuality and socialisation of migrant domestic workers is similar to the gendered discipline within a family patriarchy—to protect the "purity" of daughters from seduction and pollution outside.

Another reason for employers to confine the workers is to distance them from the migrant community, which is considered a dangerous source of "pollution" by employers. The Catholic Church and church-based NGOs in Taiwan are major providers of legal information and assistance to migrant workers. During Sunday mass and the social gatherings that follow, migrant domestic workers compare notes on employers, express grievances, offer mutual advice, and swap tactics of resistance. When expressing concerns about the "pollution" of the migrant community, employers are concerned that workers might become more aware of their rights and more active in negotiating terms. The next section further discusses the roles of migrant communities and NGOs in Taiwan.

THE MARGINAL CIVIL SECTOR: NGOS' ACTIVITIES, DISCOURSES, AND DIFFICULTIES

In post-martial law Taiwan, civil society has become vibrant, giving birth to a growing number of NGOs championing a variety of issues. However, migrant-oriented NGOs, which provide services for non-citizens located at the bottom of social stratification, constitute a civil sector that is still marginal in terms of resources and influence. There are currently about 20 institutions that offer some services for migrant workers, but only a few are NGOs that provide systematic assistances to migrants, most of which affiliated with Catholic churches. The primary organisations include Catholic Hope Worker Centre (Chongli), Migrant Workers' Concern Desk (Taipei), Rerum Novarum Centre (Taipei), and Stella Maris International Service Centre (Kaoshiung). Taiwan International Workers' Association (TIWA) and the International Action and Cooperation Team (iACT) are the two migrant-oriented NGOs established by local activists without religious affiliation. The former focuses on labour issues and the latter health-related problems.

The church-based NGOs are mainly service-oriented, with the work of advocacy and lobbying on the side. Most of them are staffed with transnational missionaries and Taiwanese social workers (some are Southeast Asians married to Taiwanese). They provide migrant workers with emotional rapport, educational information, and case counselling. On Sundays, they hold social activities such as sports games, ethnic dances, and holiday celebrations. They also offer Chinese language courses, computer classes, and workshops on labour rights and taxation on an irregular basis. In cases of labour dispute, they assist migrant workers in negotiating with employers and monitor how labour bureaus in local governments handle the complaints of the workers.

These NGOs have also formed an advocacy network, which campaign for policy changes to improve the working and living conditions of migrant workers. They occasionally stage protests against policies or cases that violate the rights of migrants. A large-scale march demanding the protection of human rights for migrant workers successfully took place on 28 December, 2003, involving hundreds of migrant and local participants.[29] The NGOs with more Taiwanese staff are also engaged in raising public awareness through media representations, as they are more familiar with local languages and politics.

To make migrant workers "visible", these NGOs have deployed three major discursive strategies to gain media attentions. First, migrant workers are presented as victims of employer abuse in short of legal protection. NGOs have held press conferences to present cases of physical abuse or sex harassment, where the abused worker meets reporters with a pseudonym and facial features obscured. The pictures of bruises have pressed Taiwanese to face the brutality of their fellow citizens and stirred public sympathy towards the migrant victims. Second, migrant workers are presented as unsung heroes whose contributions to Taiwan deserve praise and recognition. For example, NGOs have pointed out the fact that, within three years, over 140 migrant workers have sacrificed their lives while working in Taiwan (Kung, 2003), including three Indonesian and two Vietnamese caretakers who died of Severe Acute Respiratory Syndrome (SARS) when the island was hit by an epidemic in 2003.

Finally, NGOs continually fight a discursive guerrilla war wherever social stigma is attached to migrant workers. A recent example concerns a newspaper advertisement of a cell phone company (KG Telecom) that included these sentences: "Daddy calls Mommy, Filipina Maid calls children" (China Times, 23 December 2003). The advertisement played with a homonym—the Chinese character for "call" can also be interpreted as "hit"—as black humour. TIWA and other groups staged a demonstration in front of the phone company, protesting against the advertisement's racist implication that migrant caretakers tend to be child abusers. The company then apologised and withdrew the advertisement.

Most migrant NGOs, however, struggle with deficiency in financial and human resource deficits. Only a few are staffed with certified social workers and legal professionals. The central and local governments in Taiwan have provided some support by subsidising some services for migrant workers. For example, the CLA sponsors some NGOs and religious institutions to establish shelters for migrant workers who are awaiting court litigation or transfers to new employers. The Taipei City Government has also sponsored the House of the Migrants Empowerment (HOME), a migrant community centre that offers space and facilities for cultural and educational activities on Sundays. The management of the centre is currently subcontracted to TIWA. The centre has become a home to several music bands, dancing groups, and poetry clubs of migrant workers; it has also facilitated the establishment of two burgeoning migrant organisations: KaSaPi (*Kapulungan ng Samahang Pilipino*, or Organisation of Filipinos) and TIMWA (Taiwan Indonesian Migrant Workers' Association).

It is worth noting that a successful cooperation between civil society and local state happened in Taipei City during 1999–2002. A long-time labour activist, Jeng Tsuen-Chyi, was appointed to the head of the Labour Bureau and he recruited Lorna Kung, who previously worked for a migrant NGO, to be the director of Taipei City Foreign Workers' Consultant Centre (FWCC). With the resources available in public sectors, FWCC held several innovative cultural activities to reconstruct the images of migrant workers in Taiwan. For example, it initiated an annual competition for "model foreign workers" as a way of praising migrants' contribution. It also started a migrant worker poetry competition and published prize-winning poems on city buses and subways. These poems, beautifully written about migrants' hardships in Taiwan, have impressed and touched many middle-class Taiwanese (Kung, 2002).

The NGOs face difficulties in mobilising migrant workers for several reasons. A major one is state regulations which discourage migrant workers from participating in unionisation and other collective actions. For a migrant worker who can only stay in Taiwan for a few years, participation in unions and other formal collective actions involves considerable risks but only temporary benefits. It is even harder to organise migrant domestic workers, who are isolated from other migrants under the live-in, and even no-days-off, condition.

Another challenge faced by migrant NGOs is reaching workers of different nationalities. As most NGOs are associated with Catholic churches, their clients are predominantly Filipino migrants. In order to extend their service to migrants of other nationalities, some church-based NGOs have been seeking cooperation with Buddhist and Muslim groups to reach Thai, Vietnamese, and Indonesian workers. In addition to religious diversity, community segregation is another factor that prevents the formation of trans-ethnic alliances among migrant workers. Migrant communities in Taiwan are intermittent, asleep during the week and only active on Sundays. And these "weekend enclaves" (Yeoh & Huang, 1998) are divided along ethnic lines: Filipino migrant workers mostly gather in the Chongshan area around St. Christopher church, while Indonesian migrants congregate at Taipei's Train Station, from which they expand their social networks and activities to nearby cities like Taoyun and Chongli.[30]

CONCLUSION: POLICY IMPLICATIONS

The recruitment of transnational domestic workers is a policy that exacerbates the privatisation of care in Taiwan. This policy, while excusing the absence of the state and husband, continues to define child and elder care as women's calling and family duty. Taiwanese women seek labour forces from overseas to outsource their domestic burden, but such a solution is only accessible to households with social privileges. To solve the care deficit in Taiwan, the government should provide affordable institutional care and establish universalistic welfare programmes such as pension programmes and child allowances, recognising care as an essential social right and public responsibility.

Although transnational domestic workers have become surrogate mothers of many Taiwanese children and fictive relatives of Taiwanese elders, ironically, they are treated as disposable labour by state policies. The current state regulations, too "strong" in some aspects yet too "weak" in others, have exacerbated personal subordination and economic exploitation of migrant workers. I advocate that some inadequate state interventions in the transnational labour market be abolished and the enforcement of legal protection for the rights of migrant workers be strengthened.

Migrant workers should not be treated as political bargaining tools for the Taiwanese government to fight the diplomatic battle. The CLA needs to deal with the root causes behind the "running away" of migrant domestic workers, such as abuse, unfair working conditions, and outrageous agency fees, rather than manoeuvring the suspension of labour import to negotiate bilateral relationships with sending governments. Another harmful state intervention is to deprive migrant workers of the right to circulate in the local labour market. As equals of local workers, transnational workers should be allowed to transfer employers on mutual consent and to extend their residency upon contract renewal.

In the meantime, the state should strengthen its protection of migrant rights and supervision on rule enforcement. So far the Labour Standards Law in Taiwan does not cover the protection of domestic workers. Such exclusion ignores the facts that private households have become a field of employment and management, and domestic workers are subject to the most intensive surveillance among all migrant workers. Currently, some NGOs are advocating the promulgation of a Household Service Act to protect domestic and care workers, who are not covered by the Labour Standards Law. It is also necessary to enforce the adoption of a standardised contract that stipulates reasonable working hours and days off.

Finally, receiving countries such as Taiwan needs to reconsider the transient status of migrant workers and the transformation of its model of citizenship (L. Cheng, 2003). As a matter of fact, the presence of "guest" workers in Taiwan has become permanent, and their active participation in the economic, social and cultural lives of the country has contested its foundational logic of citizenship. Taiwan is facing a changing ethnoscape comprising a growing number of marriage and labour migration. We need less ethnocentric immigration policies and reflexive cultural attitudes to break down the borders of nationalism and racial prejudice.

227

NOTES

1   The empirical data presented in this paper are based on a larger research project I have conducted over a period of several years (August 1998 to August 1999; and September 2002 to February 2004) including ethnographic observations of migrant communities in Taipei, in-depth interviews with 58 Filipina migrant domestic workers and 35 Indonesian ones, and in-depth interviews with 51 Taiwanese employers. For complete research findings and theoretical arguments, see Lan (forthcoming).

2   This Japanese term, which refers literally to "aunt" or "middle-aged women" in general, has become a common expression for middle-aged domestic workers in Taiwan.

3   In 2002, among Taiwanese women with a college or university degree, 62 per cent of them were gainfully employed; women aged between 25 and 29 had the highest rate of labour participation among all age groups (73 per cent), followed by women aged between 30–34 (67 per cent) (http://www.dgbas.gov.tw/census~n/four/yt3a.htm, accessed 12 May 2004).

4   Households with children under the age of 12 years and/or elderly members above the age of 70 were eligible to apply for quotas for the employment of "domestic helpers".

5   The Law of Nationality was first issued on 5 February 1929; it was never modified until the recent version promulgated on 9 February 2000.

6   In 2003, the minimum wage was NT$15,840 (US$480) per month; this amount is slightly higher than the minimum wage in Hong Kong and about twice that of the average transnational domestic worker's wage in Singapore. The maximum working hours were eight hours a day and 48 hours a week; workers were entitled to one weekly day-off plus seven days of annual leave.

7   According to a survey of 649 respondents conducted by a church-based NGO (Migrant Workers' Concern Desk) in November 1997, 24 per cent of the respondents were paid less than the minimum wage; nearly one half of respondents had neither rest days nor overtime pay; and over a quarter had no health insurance and most of these were domestic workers.

8   Article 59 in the Employment Service Act.

9   Chen Chu, chairwoman of the Council of Labor Affairs, announced the lifting of a long ban on Indonesian migrant workers on 19 December 2004. She also released the news that the CLA would not exclude the possibility of freezing the employment of Vietnamese workers due to increasing numbers running away from employers.

10 For instance, during the period when the legal venue of recruitment was closed to Indonesian migrants, some participated in forged marriages to come to work in Taiwan.

11 Chin-Ju Lin (1999), Ada Cheng (2003) and Anne Loveband (2004) have also looked at how labour brokers in Taiwan categorise migrant workers based on essentialised ethnic differences and mystified national characters.

12 I thank Lo Long's assistance on web searching and data coding. We browsed 93 employment agencies' websites found through the Google search engine. Among them, 29 websites offered nationality-based characterisations of migrant workers. See Lan (forthcoming: chapter 2) for a complete result of coding. Very similar stereotypes were found when we browsed the websites of employment agencies in Singapore and Hong Kong.

13 http//: www.beelief.idv.tw; accessed 15 July, 2002.

14 http//:www.885manpower.com.tw; accessed 15 July 2002.

15 http://www.phr.com.tw; accessed 13 October, 2003.

16 http://www.kc104.com.tw/main-3c.htm; accessed 13 October, 2003.

17 The CLA used to stipulate that the maximum amount of a placement fee should not exceed NT$7,000 (US$212). As this official amount was far below the amount collected in reality, the CLA approved a new regulation in October 2001. An agent can legally collect a placement fee up to the amount of a worker's monthly wage, plus a monthly service fee—NT$1,800 (US$55) during the first year, NT$1,700 (US$52) during the second, and NT$1,500 (US$45) during the third. Accordingly, the maximum amount of legal placement and service fees collected from a worker during three years totals NT$75,840 (US$2,298).

18 Some pay NT$10,000 (US$303) during the first six months, while others pay monthly service fees in amounts stipulated by the CLA. The money paid to Philippine brokers covers the airfare to Taiwan but workers have to pay for their medical checkups in both the Philippines and Taiwan.

19 I conducted all the interviews with Filipinas in English. With two-thirds of the Indonesian informants who spoke fluent Chinese (Mandarin or Hoklo), I conducted the interviews myself. With the rest who preferred to speak Bahasa Indonesian, a Malay-speaking assistant conducted the interviews and later translated the transcripts into Chinese.

20 These headlines were originally in Chinese and translated into English by the author.

21 A Filipina domestic worker, Angelina Canlas, killed her patient and then attempted suicide on 9 November 1995. She was diagnosed as clinically depressed and sentenced to 12 years for murder. Angelina told the judge that she was "out of control, out of mind" because she missed home and was worried about her debts (*United Daily News*, 11 November 1995).

22 The headline refers to a fight between Filipino migrant workers and Indonesia workers in a factory.

23 In 2002, the average crime rate among documented migrant workers was 0.06 per cent. The crime rate among undocumented migrants is higher (0.28 per cent), but it is significantly lower than the crime rate among Taiwanese citizens (0.83 per cent) (National Police Administration of the Interior Department, Republic of China, n.d.).

24 The examination originally included a chest X-ray, a blood test for syphilis, a Type-B hepatitis surface-antigen test, a blood test for malaria, a stool test for intestinal parasites, an HIV-antibody test, a urine test for illegal drugs, a pregnancy test, and a psychological evaluation.

25 However, the actual impact of this policy change is still ambivalent. Legally speaking, an employer cannot fire a migrant worker on the basis of pregnancy, and migrant workers covered by the Labour Standards Law (such as factory workers, but not domestic workers) are entitled to an eight-week maternity leave after giving birth (but the child would not be a Taiwanese citizen given the descent principle of citizenship). Yet, in practice, pregnant transnational domestic workers tend to go home voluntarily or under coercion by their employers.

26   The overtime pay for a migrant domestic working on Sundays is NT$528 (US$16) per day.

27   I conducted interviews with 51 Taiwanese employers, including 47 women, three married couples and four men. All of them are ethnic Chinese. These employers resided in metropolitan Taipei with the exception of four elderly care recipients in the provinces. Upon the time of interview, 25 employers had been hiring a transnational domestic worker for less than three years, 14 had been hiring for some time between four to six years, and six had hiring experiences for more than seven years. The average length of employment is four years. These interviews were conducted in Mandarin Chinese and later translated into English by me.

28   One such incident happened in a city in southern Taiwan on 13 October 1997. A Filipina domestic worker, along with her boyfriend, also a migrant worker, broke into the residence of her former employer, stole some cash and killed three family members.

29   Four main requests were petitioned to the CLA in this march: first, to include migrant workers under the protection of the Labour Standards Law; second, to replace the current employment agency system with a direct employment system; third, to set up a regulation that enforces time off for migrant workers; and fourth, to allow migrant workers to switch employers freely.

30   See Lan (2003b) for more details on the segregated communities and Sunday activities of Filipino and Indonesian migrant workers in Northern Taiwan.

REFERENCES

Bakan, A. & D. Stasiulis. 1995. Making the match: Domestic placement agencies and the racialization of women's household work. *Signs*, 20(2), 303–35.

Bureau of Official Statistics. 1924. *The First Taiwan Provincial Household Census (1920)*. Taiwan: Government-general of Taiwan.

————. 1934. *The 1930 Taiwan Provincial Household Census*. Taiwan: Government-general of Taiwan.

Chao, S. B. 1992. On the problem of foreign labour. In *Labour Policies and Labour Issues*. Edited by S. B. Chao. Taipei: Chinese Productive Centre, 143–72.

Cheng, A. S. J. 2003. Rethinking globalization of domestic service: Foreign domestics, state control, and the politics of identity in Taiwan. *Gender & Society*, 17(2), 166–86.

Cheng, L. 2003. Transnational labor, citizenship and the Taiwan State. In *East Asian Law: Universal Norms and Local Cultures*. Edited by A. Rosett, L. Cheng & M. Y. K. Woo. London: Routledge, 85–106.

China Evening News. 2002. 18 December.

China Times. (various issues).

Council of Labour Affairs. 1998. *Monthly Bulletin of Labour Statistics*, December 1998. Taipei, Taiwan, Republic of China: Executive Yuan.

————. 1999. *Monthly Bulletin of Labour Statistics*, December 1999. Taipei, Taiwan, Republic of China: Executive Yuan.

_____. 2000. *Monthly Bulletin of Labour Statistics*, December 2000. Taipei, Taiwan, Republic of China: Executive Yuan.

_____. 2001. *Monthly Bulletin of Labour Statistics*, December. Taipei, Taiwan, Republic of China: Executive Yuan.

_____. 2002. *Monthly Bulletin of Labour Statistics*, December. Taipei, Taiwan, Republic of China: Executive Yuan.

_____. 2003. *Monthly Bulletin of Labour Statistics*, December. Taipei, Taiwan, Republic of China: Executive Yuan.

Hochschild, A. 1995. The culture of politics: Traditional, postmodern, cold-modern and warm-modern ideals of care. *Social Politics*, 2(3), 331–47.

Hu, Yow-Hwey. 1997. A discussion on the policy of foreign domestic workers and the needs and constraints of working women. *Foreign Labor and State Development*. Taipei: National Taiwan University (in Chinese).

Kung, L. 2002. Migrant workers in Taipei: Biased central state policy and alternative administrative strategy of local state. *Taiwan: A Radical Quarterly in Social Studies*, 48, 235–86 (in Chinese).

_____. 2003. *After the death of a foreign caregiver (in Chinese)*, http://61.222.52.195/news/database/Interface/Detailstander.asp?ID=52681. Accessed 12 February 2004.

Lan, P. C. 2002. Among women: Filipina domestics and their Taiwanese employers across generations. In *Global Woman: Nannies, Maids, and Sex Workers in the New Economy*. Edited by B. Ehrenreich and A. Hochschild. New York: Metropolitan, 169–89.

_____. 2003a. They have more money but I speak better English: Transnational encounters between Filipina domestics and Taiwanese employers. *Identities: Global Studies in Culture and Power*, 10(2), 132–61.

_____. 2003b. Political and social geography of marginal insiders: migrant domestic workers in Taiwan. *Asian and Pacific Migration Journal*, 12(1–2), 99–126.

_____. Forthcoming. *Global Cinderella: Migrant Domestics and Newly Rich Employers in Taiwan*. Durham: Duke University Press.

Lin, C. J. 1999. *Filipina Domestic Workers in Taiwan: Structural Constraints and Personal Resistance*. Taipei: Taiwan Grassroots Women Workers' Centre.

Loveband, A. 2004. Positioning the product: Indonesian migrant women workers in contemporary Taiwan. *Journal of Contemporary Asia*, 34(3): 336–349.

National Police Administration of the Interior Department, Republic of China. n.d. http://www.npa.gov.tw/count/main.htm. Accessed 4 March 2004.

Parreñas, R. S. 2001. *Servants of Globalization: Women, Migration and Domestic Work*. Stanford: Stanford University Press.

Taipei Times. 2003. 8 February.

Thornton, A. and H. S. Lin. 1994. *Social Change and the Family in Taiwan*. Chicago: University of Chicago Press.

Tsay, C. L. 1992. Clandestine labor migration to Taiwan. *Asian and Pacific Migration Journal*, 1(3/4), 637–55.

Tseng, Y. F. 2004. Politics of importing foreigners: Foreign labor policy in Taiwan. In *Migration between States and Markets*. Edited by H. B. Entzinger, M. Martiniello & C. W. de Wenden. Aldershot: Ashgate, in press, 101-119

United Daily News. Various issues.

United Evening News. 1994. 21 July.

Veblen, T. 1994. *The Theory of Leisure Class: An Economic Study of Institutions.* New York: B. W. Huebsch.

Yeoh, B. & S. Huang. 1998. Negotiating public space: strategies and styles of migrant female domestic workers in Singapore. *Urban Studies*, 35(3), 583–602.

You, J. M. 1995. *Taiwanese Employed Women Under the Japanese Rule.* Unpublished Ph.D. dissertation, Department of History, National She-Fan University (in Chinese).

CHAPTER 8

"Dignity Overdue": Transnational Domestic Workers in Singapore

NOOR ABDUL RAHMAN, BRENDA S. A. YEOH AND
SHIRLENA HUANG

INTRODUCTION

Singapore is host to an estimated 140,000–150,000 transnational domestic workers hailing mainly from Indonesia and the Philippines, and to a lesser extent from Sri Lanka (*Straits Times*, 21 February 2005).[1] More popularly referred to as "foreign maids" by the local populace, these women currently constitute over one-fifth of Singapore's foreign workforce of 612,200 (Huang & Yeoh, 2003). Their entry into Singapore was facilitated under the Foreign Maid Scheme introduced in 1978 to encourage the continued participation of local women in the formal economic sphere (Purushotam, 1992).[2] Today, the transnational domestic worker has become an ubiquitous feature of the average double-income middle and upper-class Singaporean household. They are relied on to perform a multitude of tasks ranging from child-minding and general housekeeping to caring for the old and sick (*Straits Times*, 13 January 2002).

Over two decades after opening its doors to live-in transnational domestic workers, "the foreign maid" has also become periodically conspicuous in Singapore's public discourse, usually catalysed by flashpoints such as cases of brutal abuse of a transnational domestic worker by an employer, or the suicide of a transnational domestic worker. Such incidents often lead to "maids' issues" dominating everyday conversations, occupying the pages of print media, and being hotly debated in talk show programmes, ultimately resulting in public outcries and calls for Singaporeans to become more introspective and reflective about what such cases of abuse say of the deteriorating moral values in the community (*Straits Times*, 28 December 1999; 13 January 2002; 27 July 2002; 3 & 25 October 2003). In response, Singaporeans (usually the employers) are often quick to highlight the poor quality of transnational domestic workers available, the unsatisfactory services of employment agencies and the moral and sexual transgressions of transnational domestic workers (*New Paper*, 22 February 2003; *Streats*, 13 March 2003; *Straits Times*, 1 May 2003). More broadly, the host of issues unveiled by public discourse illuminates the complex interactions between the forces of demand and supply, the processes of recruitment and placement, the working conditions of the "foreign maid" and the tensions in the employer-domestic worker relationship.

This paper elucidates several key issues associated with the increasing presence of transnational domestic workers in Singapore, a major receiving country of such labour migrants in the Asia Pacific region. The paper first describes the historical evolution of the culture of live-in domestic help in Singapore and identifies the factors contributing to what has come to be known as the "maid dependency syndrome" in the country today. The paper then scrutinises the role of the state in regulating the demand for transnational domestic workers and the conditions of their employment, as well as the ideologies behind state policy. The third section of the paper moves into a discussion of the positioning and negotiations of the transnational domestic worker as the stereotyped "other" vis-à-vis employers on the one hand, and broader host society on the other.

Next, the paper discusses the debates within public discourse as well as private accounts surrounding the economic, social and health issues associated with transnational domestic workers in Singapore, before turning to an examination of the (un)availability of support services for this group of workers provided by either non-governmental organisations (NGOs) and foreign missions. The latter analysis gives particular focus to the advocacy work of The Working Committee 2 (TWC2), a civil society group in Singapore concerned with the welfare of transnational domestic workers, and highlights the barriers encountered by this group in championing the rights of these workers. Finally, the paper outlines various recommendations for both providing greater protection for transnational domestic workers and reducing the "maid dependency syndrome" in Singapore.

A CULTURE OF WAGED DOMESTIC HELP

For the many families that have come to depend on transnational domestic workers for household chores and as caregivers to members of their families who are too elderly, disabled or young to look after themselves, the transnational domestic worker has become an almost indispensable solution to their crisis in household reproduction. This crisis, in the local context, is often perceived to have arisen due to the absence of a full time mother/wife in the home (as many more women now stay employed after starting a family) and the inability to secure another female kin (often an elder member of the family such as a grandmother or the grandaunt) to take over the domestic duties. That one in seven households in Singapore employs a transnational domestic worker[3] (Singapore Department of Statistics, 2000) reflects not only a current (2003) female labour force participation rate of 53.9 per cent but also an ingrained patriarchal division of labour in Singaporean households. Research shows that Singapore society does view housework as "inextricably linked to/entwined with women's roles" and that women themselves

234

have accepted this notion (Purushotam, 1992:340; see also Huang & Yeoh, 1998:27 and Straughan et al., 2000). The bulk of domestic responsibilities and other tasks associated with domesticity such as childcaring, cooking and cleaning have traditionally been, and continue to be, shouldered by women both as unpaid and paid work.

Since the onset of economic modernisation in Singapore, it has been common for families able to afford it, to rely on live-in and/or live-out paid domestic help. During the colonial era, live-in help tended to be exclusive to the rich and elite European and Chinese households. While Hainanese cookboys were more popular among the Europeans, girl servants (*mui tsai*) were sought mainly by rich Chinese households who preferred the dedication of female servants under the system of obligation inherent in fictive kinship relations (Lai, 1986)[4]. The former were also more expensive and deemed as less subservient and flexible than their female counterparts. *Mui tsai* were eventually replaced by Cantonese women from the Pearl River Delta Region who started arriving in the colony in search of work in the early 1930s following the collapse of the silk industry in the region (Gaw, 1988). These women became the "black and white *amah*"[5] who were well respected for their loyalty to employers, dedication to their work and organisational skills in structuring both their work life and their personal welfare (Gaw, 1988). Following social and economic shifts and changes to immigration laws in China after the second World War, the stock of black and white *amah* started to dwindle and their era ended in the early 1970s (Gaw, 1988). Concurrently, the supply of young local girls (as live-in "servant girls") and older women (for tasks such as laundry and baby-sitting) from the rural areas of Singapore and Malaysia as a cheaper alternative to the *amah* for less well-off families, also began to decrease with the onset of industrialisation and the expansion of job opportunities in factories, offices, retail outlets and the like (Huang & Yeoh, 1996:483).

The industrialisation process that began in the late 1960s posed a significant influence on the demand and supply forces for waged domestic help in several ways. First, the attractiveness of a stable income and the prestige of employment in the formal sphere relegated the status of paid domestic work as an income source to that of second class. At the same time, the female labour force participation rate started to climb and, together with increasing household income and changes in lifestyle, the demand for waged domestic workers strengthened. However, with declining supplies of women willing to work as domestic help and few alternatives to turn to, employers found themselves at the mercy of a workforce that could be unpredictable and inconsistent in terms of their quality of work (Purushotam, 1992; Huang & Yeoh, 1996). In order to encourage continued participation of women in the formal economic sphere to further its goal of continued economic expansion, the state introduced the Foreign Maid Scheme in 1978 allowing women from the Philippines, Indonesia, Sri Lanka and Thailand to be employed as live-in domestic workers. While the demand for transnational domestic workers grew relatively slowly in the first ten years, the population of transnational domestic workers has since then climbed steadily to its current level.

While the state has cautioned against the development of a "maid dependency syndrome", Singaporean employers have been quick to point to the high costs of institutional facilities such as childcare centers and hospices, as well as the inconvenience, inflexibilities and perceived low quality of non-home-based help as compelling reasons for them to turn to a transnational domestic worker (*Straits Times*, 7 November 1997; 30 September 2003). The rigid work culture in the country has been cited as another causal factor, with Singaporean employers criticised for being slow to subscribe to pro-family work practices (such as flexible hours and work from home options) to allow families (read "women") to fulfil dual duties as both socially reproductive and economically productive units (*Straits Times*, 30 September 2003). The growing phenomenon of live-in transnational domestic workers can also be attributed to a certain degree of attaining and maintaining a middle-class quality of life that is synonymous with material trappings such as home and car ownership (which often requires both husband and wife to work), raising "quality children" and enjoying a quality of family life that excludes the menial tasks involved in running a household (Huang & Yeoh, 1998; Yeoh & Huang, 1999a). The ingrained perception of "the home as a site of physical, emotional and moral nurturing for the family, and as a safe haven for children" also makes the transnational domestic worker a more attractive option than non-home-based options such as childcare centres and babysitters (Yeoh & Huang, 1999a:284–5).

THE ROLE OF THE STATE

Estimated Stocks of Transnational Domestic Workers in Singapore

The consistent policy of the Ministry of Manpower (MOM) in Singapore has been not to release official figures of foreign nationals working in the country. MOM has only released, through statements issued via the media, ballpark estimates of the total population of transnational domestic workers in Singapore. Moreover, as not all transnational domestic workers report to their respective foreign missions upon arrival, the foreign embassies are also incapable of accurately quantifying the population of their nationals working as transnational domestic workers in Singapore. There is also a considerable flow of transnational domestic workers that takes place outside official channels of labour migration of their countries of origin, making it more difficult for these countries to ascertain the number of their workers in countries of destination.[6] Here, based on various secondary and primary sources–mainly academic publications, the local media (especially Singapore's most widely circulated daily newspaper, *The Straits Times*), and personal communications with representatives of foreign embassies and an employment agency association, we have identified two distinct trends with regards to the population of transnational domestic workers in Singapore and its composition by nationality. First, since the introduction of the Foreign Maid Scheme in 1978, the number of transnational domestic workers has continued to climb despite the state's effort of curbing the flow through periodic revisions to the levy and periods of economic slowdown (Table 8.1). Second, the estimates suggest that in the post-1995 period, there has been a huge jump in the population of Indonesian transnational domestic workers, whilst the estimated number of Filipina transnational domestic workers only registered a relatively slight increase. Currently, it is estimated that the population of Indonesian transnational domestic workers and Filipina transnational domestic workers in Singapore are more or less equal in making up the majority of the transnational domestic worker population in Singapore,[7] with Sri Lankan women comprising a noteworthy minority.

TABLE 8.1 Estimated stock of transnational domestic workers in Singapore, 1986–2004

Country of origin	1986	1988	1991	1993	1995	1999	2004
Philippines	28,000[a]	n.a.	30,000[a]	50,000[a]	55,000[e]	40,000–50,000[f]	60,000–70,000[h]
Sri Lanka	n.a.	n.a.	10,000[a]	17,000[a]	8,000[e]	n.a.	12,000[i]
Indonesia	n.a.	n.a.	5,000[a]	10,000[a]	15,000–18,000[e]	50,000–60,000[f]	50,000–60,000[j]
Other Countries	n.a.	n.a.	5,000[a]	4,000[a]	n.a.	n.a	n.a.
Total	n.a.	40,000[b]	50,000[c]	81,000[d]	80,000–85,000[e]	100,000[g]	140,000[k]

SOURCES: Adapted from Wong, 1996; *Strait Times*, 17 January 1999; Abdul Rahman, 2003; The Indonesian Embassy, 2004; The Philippines Embassy, 2004; The Sri Lanka High Commission, 2004.

NOTES:

a   Philippines Migration Review, April-June 1987 cited in Wong (1996: 99).

b   *Straits Times*, 4 December 1988, cited in Wong (1996:99).

c   *Straits Times*, 19 February 1992, cited in Wong (1996:99).

d   *Straits Times*, 2 June 1993, cited in Wong (1996:99).

e   Dr Chua Kim Seng, former President of Foreign Employment Agencies Association, cited in Wong (1996:99).

f   Woo, an owner of a recruitment agency, cited in Abdul Rahman (2003:104).

g   *Straits Times*, 17 January 1999.

h   The Philippines Embassy, personal communication with authors, 28 January 2004.

i   The Sri Lanka High Commission, personal communication with authors, 28 January 2004.

j   The Indonesian Embassy, personal communication with authors, 28 January 2004.

k   All three embassies, personal communication with authors, 28 January 2004.

Regulating and Managing the Flow of Transnational Domestic Workers

Despite the popular perception of the transnational domestic worker's indispensability in Singapore, the state has consistently maintained a tight policy of keeping the in-migration of transnational domestic workers in check and ensuring their transient status as contract migrant workers. The former is carried out through the enforcement of a monthly levy—currently standing at S$295 (US$179)—payable by the employer; and subjected to periodic adjustments to regulate the flow of transnational domestic workers. The transient status of the transnational domestic worker is enforced through a two-year work permit system.

In rationalising periodic increments to the levy,[8] the Ministry of Manpower (MOM) has contended that letting the number of transnational domestic workers go unchecked will potentially pose a high risk of affecting bilateral relations with sending states that may be triggered by cases of abuse of transnational domestic workers by employers (*Straits Times*, 2 September 2001). The ministry has also highlighted the state's concern over the amount of resources needed to mediate and solve the cases of runaway transnational domestic workers; disputes arising between employers and transnational domestic workers; and how uncontrolled entry of transnational domestic workers could lead to stunting the growth and quality of the institutional care industry in the country. Thus despite initiating the flow, the state views recruiting or admitting transnational domestic workers as a "necessary evil" that must be put under various controls and surveillance.

In most cases, transnational domestic workers are granted two-year work permits (renewable up to the age of 60 years) upon passing a medical examination in Singapore (over and above any which may have been conducted in their home country) to establish that the transnational domestic worker is not pregnant and is free from sexual diseases such as HIV/AIDS; a six-monthly medical check-up is required thereafter to ensure that she remains disease and procreation-free throughout her entire period of employment. Neither is a transnational domestic worker permitted to marry a Singaporean or a Permanent Resident of the country.[9] The decision to renew the transnational domestic worker's work permit depends largely on the employers' discretion, usually based on the perceived quality of her work and conduct vis-à-vis the employer's need for the transnational domestic worker. From the state's point of view, the work permit system ensures that transnational domestic workers only remain in the country for as long as their services are needed, and only under conditions that strictly bar them from marriage and procreation—all measures to ensure that they do not enter the folds of the Singaporean citizenry. Employers are made to shoulder the responsibility of ensuring that transnational domestic workers abide by these conditions through the imposition of a compulsory security bond policy worth S$5,000 (US$2,953) for each transnational domestic worker employed by them. Employers risk losing this bond if they fail to repatriate the transnational domestic worker should the latter be found to be pregnant, to have contracted a sexual disease or married a Singaporean. In addition, transnational domestic workers are not covered by the Workers' Compensation Act; instead, employers are required to purchase personal accident insurance policies (with a minimum value of S$10,000) (US$5,906) for their transnational domestic workers. This policy provides compensation to transnational domestic workers (or their families) in cases of their death or disablement from accidents (Ministry of Manpower, n.d.) but, ironically, not physical abuse for example bodily harm inflicted by employers.

Singapore's state policies not only ensure a relatively thorough mechanism of "controlling" transnational domestic workers in terms of keeping their numbers in check and limiting their potential of assimilation, they also arguably ignore their rights as workers and individuals on several counts.[10] First, transnational domestic workers fall outside Singapore's Employment Act.[11] In addition, Singapore is not a signatory of international conventions on protecting the rights of migrant workers; these include the International Labour Organisation's (ILO) Convention No. 97 (Migration for Employment, Revised) and Convention No.143 (Migrations in Abusive Conditions and the Promotion of Equality of Opportunity and Treatment of Migrant Workers), and the International Convention on The Protection of the Rights of All Migrant Workers and Members of their Families (MWC) adopted by the United Nations (Yeoh et al., 2004). In defending their evident lack of support for these conventions, the state has argued that while it supports the continued work of these international organisations in eliminating all forms of inequalities and discrimination against migrants, it is impossible to legislate standard employment terms for transnational domestic workers in Singapore due to the wide-ranging nature of domestic work; instead it leaves employment agencies and employers to draw up employment contracts for (rather than with) their transnational domestic workers (Yeoh et al., 2004), a process that certainly does not recognise the imbalance of power between the transnational domestic worker and the employer or the employment agent.

Until recently, the "domestic worker industry" was given the liberty to function without specific guidelines and standards for the processes of recruitment, training and placement of transnational domestic workers. The relative freedom to operate in the open and free market system in effect encouraged unethical business practices to thrive, allowing employment agencies to obtain a competitive edge while at the same time making transnational domestic workers open to exploitation. Over the years, some employment agents have been found guilty of inflicting physical abuse on transnational domestic workers and subjecting them to inhumane and undignified treatment (*Straits Times*, 7 July 2002; 15 October 2003). In response to increasing cases of complaints against employment agencies by employers, MOM has embarked on establishing a policy of compulsory accreditation for employment agencies that was made effective in mid-2004 (*Straits Times*, 19 May 2002). To date, two institutions, the Consumer Association of Singapore (CASE) and the Association of Employment

Agencies Singapore (AEAS) have been accorded the powers by MOM to certify and accredit employment agencies.

As we discuss in the following section, the lack of protection accorded to transnational domestic workers of all nationalities as workers and individuals, and the slowness of the state in disciplining the domestic worker industry in Singapore, has led to the perpetuation of an exploited market of transnational domestic workers.

A Ready Supply of Transnational Domestic Workers—Exploiting the Indonesian Market

In Singapore, approximately 80 per cent of transnational domestic workers are procured through formal channels whereby licensed employment agencies (and their counterparts in the countries of origin) play key roles in their recruitment, training and placement (*Straits Times*, 30 May 2002). The remaining transnational domestic workers are recruited through informal networks of families and friends. There are approximately 700 employment agencies in Singapore of various sizes specifically engaged in the business of recruiting and placing transnational domestic workers (*Straits Times*, 30 May 2002). Thus the business practices of these agencies have a considerable influence on the sources of supply of transnational domestic workers in Singapore, which in turn shapes the demography of this group of workers. A survey by Wong (1996:99–100) of 18 employment agencies to determine the effects of a ban of Filipina domestic workers into Singapore imposed by the Philippines government in 1995,[12] found that agencies either withdrew totally from promoting Filipina domestic workers or promoted Indonesian domestic workers more vigorously. Indeed, this probably helps to explain the huge increase in the population of Indonesian domestic workers starting in 1999.

More specifically, the interventionist nature of the Philippines embassy and the imposition of stricter rules to protect the rights of Filipina domestic worker when the ban on their flow was lifted in 1996 contributed to the increase in numbers of Indonesian domestic workers; additionally, employment agents also found it easier to market the latter as they are perceived to be more amenable to employers' preference for docile domestic workers (Abdul Rahman, 2003:107).[13] Then, employment agents who were willing to abide by Philippines' stricter regulations were required to agree to a "joint liability" clause in which they would be held jointly responsible with employers for unfair dismissal of transnational domestic worker. Many agents disagreed with these terms as it meant compromising their position in the market (Abdul Rahman, 2003). In contrast, due to the more lax attitude of the Indonesian government, there has never been an effective implementation of minimum standards of work for Indonesian domestic workers.[14] It has thus become the industry's norm to provide job placements for Indonesian domestic workers with less than satisfactory employment conditions, such as a denial of rest days (for at least the first two years of their employment) and lower starting wages.[15] It is evident that such market practices serve the interests of employers and employment agents at the expense of Indonesian domestic workers. By turning to Indonesian domestic workers, employment agents were able to take advantage of an alternative supply of transnational domestic workers thus countering institutional changes made by the Philippines authority aimed at protecting Filipina domestic workers from being exploited by employment agents (and employers). Arguably, this shift in market share was facilitated by the way Indonesian domestic workers were promoted to employers as an alternative who was not only more "compliant" but also cheaper to maintain, as wages of Indonesian domestic workers were, and continue to be, much lower than Filipina domestic workers.

The onset of the Asian financial crisis in 1997 also precipitated many agents to switch to marketing Indonesian domestic workers in order to remain competitive in a sluggish market. The crisis led to a ballooning supply of Indonesian domestic workers as many women left the country in search of work to counter the effects of inflation and spiralling unemployment and underemployment rates (Hugo, 2000; 2002). This reinforced employment agents' upper hand in dictating terms and conditions of placement. At the height of the crisis in 1998 and 1999, some agencies in Singapore offered to procure Indonesian domestic workers for a nominal agency fee of S$1(US$0.59) per transnational domestic worker, or even for "free", in an effort to undercut one another (*Straits Times*, 3 August 1998). This practice was clearly exploitative, as the domestic worker was obliged to pay a much higher recruitment fee to agencies to cover costs that would have been borne by employers.[16] The situation is aggravated by rampant corruption in Indonesia that allows employment agents there the liberty of slashing business costs further as required documentation such as passports and certificates from government approved training centres (Balai Latihan Kerja or BLK) can be bought at cheaper prices outside formal channels (Abdul Rahman, 2003:108–09). As a result, these agents and their counterparts in Singapore are able to offer Indonesian domestic workers at even more competitive "prices" to Singapore employers. The proximity of Indonesia and alternative entry points into Singapore via ferry from Batam and Tanjung Pinang (part of Indonesia's Riau Archipelago located just south of Singapore) also offer employment agents the flexibility of arranging cheaper passage for transnational domestic workers into Singapore and to respond more quickly to demand.

Thus, the ready supply of alternative sources of transnational domestic workers has led to the perpetuation of an exploitative market for transnational domestic workers in Singapore. The effort of the Philippines government in according better protection to its workers has inadvertently resulted in the substitution of "cheaper" and more "flexible" (i.e., subservient) Indonesian domestic workers for Filipina domestic workers. It would appear that the main beneficiaries of this shift are the Singapore employers, employment agents on both sides of the transaction, and the governments of Indonesia and the Philippines (in terms of remittances sent home) rather than the Filipino or Indonesian transnational domestic worker. This strongly suggests that any effort at addressing exploitative elements in the employment "industry" can only be made more effective if it encompasses standard recruitment and employment terms for all transnational domestic workers regardless of nationality.

THE STEREOTYPED SUBSERVIENT "OTHER": TRANSNATIONAL DOMESTIC WORKERS' EXPERIENCES IN DOMESTIC AND PUBLIC SPHERES

Stereotypes of Transnational Domestic Workers

The highly commodified nature of waged domestic help in contemporary Singapore is complicit in the production, propagation and institutionalisation of a range of stereotypes concerning transnational domestic workers. Defined primarily by "nationality" as the key marker, these stereotypes draw on various social relations of difference constructed around gender, race/ethnicity, religious affiliation, linguistic ability, class and educational qualifications (Huang & Yeoh, 1998:35). That these stereotypes serve as "product differentiation" for employment agencies advertising the "domestic worth" of women of different nationalities is evident in the way they are routinely drawn upon in employers' selection of transnational domestic workers from employment agencies. The selection process usually requires employers to make their choices mainly from viewing records of the prospective transnational domestic worker's biodata describing the nationality, physiological characteristics, work preferences and history, and five-minute videotaped introductions by the women of themselves. As these records are largely alike and hardly distinguishable from one another, nationalised stereotypes of who would make a "suitable" transnational domestic worker often weigh heavily in influencing the employer's decision (Huang & Yeoh, 1998). Table 8.2 shows prevailing negative and positive stereotypes of the three major groups of transnational domestic workers in Singapore as perceived and propagated by employers and employment agents.

These nationalised stereotypes serve to entrench the subservient "othering" of the transnational domestic worker in Singapore homes and society in general. As the next two sections demonstrate, these stereotypes constantly underlie the construction of the "self-other" boundary between transnational domestic workers and their Singapore employers—whether it is between "maid" and "ma'am" in the everyday spaces of the home, or more generally between migrant contract workers and host society in public space.

The Subservient "Other"—In the Private Sphere

As transnational domestic workers in Singapore are required to live-in with their employers (a condition attached to the work permit), the boundary between "home" and "work" for most of these migrant workers is non-existent or, at best, blurred. The physical co-presence provides employers with "personalistic idioms of power" which are used to control the transnational domestic workers' access to basic necessities such

TABLE 8.2   Prevailing stereotypes of Filipina, Indonesian and Sri Lankan transnational domestic workers in Singapore

Nationality	Positive stereotypes	Negative stereotypes
Filipina	Most naturally hardworking, quick ability to learn, competent, meticulous and possess more initiative, possess good command of English, honest and hygienic	Bold and streetwise, hence unreliable, dishonest and more assertive
Indonesian	Docile, compliant, simple and homely, submissive, poses no social problem	Slow learners, forgetful, poor command of English, naïve, not streetwise
Sri Lankan	Responsible, helpful/ pleasing, obedient and shy	Dark-skinned, too "blur", too slow, backwards, has poor hygiene, very poor command of English

SOURCES: Adapted from *Straits Times Classified*, 1997; Huang and Yeoh, 1998; Abdul Rahman, 2003.

as food, shelter, communication, medical facilities and the rights to private space and time (Anderson, 2000:6). The low wages actually received by transnational domestic workers in Singapore and their restricted movements outside the employer's home, often means that most are unable, or cannot afford, to purchase these necessities, further exacerbating the asymmetrical power relations between transnational domestic workers and employers. This leaves transnational domestic workers more vulnerable to various forms of mistreatment, infringing on their rights as both workers and individuals, to the minority of employers who go to extreme measures to control access to these necessities as a means of distinguishing the "self" from the "other" (Abdul Rahman, 2003). For example, food deprivation and inadequate rest (long hours of work) have been cited as amongst the most common complaints of mistreatment filed by transnational domestic workers at their respective embassies (*Straits Times*, 31 May 1995; 28 July 2002). Physical co-presence under conditions of unequal power also forces some transnational domestic workers to compromise expressions of religious and cultural identities as they are obliged to follow the rules and restrictions laid down by employers and employment agents. Some employment agents demand Indonesian domestic workers to be willing to forgo the five daily prayers and fasting on the ninth month of the Muslim calendar (two of the five pillars of practice that are incumbent upon a practising Muslim) to secure their marketability among non-Muslim employers

(Abdul Rahman, 2003). Similarly, there are also employers who express unwillingness to accommodate the religious particularities of Indonesian domestic workers (Abdul Rahman, 2003).

While the employer-transnational domestic worker relationship runs the gamut from those akin to master-slave relationships to businesslike relationships where the employer treats the transnational domestic worker as a worker while maintaining a comfortable distance, the transnational domestic worker's ambiguous position as neither "family" nor complete "outsider" may result in a tension-ridden relationship. In orientating the domestic worker to her work environment, employment agents often instruct domestic workers to observe a strict code of conduct and display complete deference—from being "always willing" to be reprimanded to not going to sleep before employers and their family members—should they wish to complete their employment contracts to the extent of compromising their rights as workers and as individuals (Table 8.3).

Controlling the bodies of transnational domestic worker by stipulating dress codes is another well-used means of distinguishing these women as the inferior "other". Some employers expect transnational domestic workers to observe strictly the standard "foreign maid" garb of oversized T-shirts, long shorts or bermudas and short and

TABLE 8.3 A set of rules for Indonesian transnational domestic workers issued by an employment agency*

- You are required to work in Singapore for two years with no rest days.
- You are not allowed to request a change in employer.
- You must be willing to be reprimanded by employers.
- You must always be humble.
- You must apologise to employers if you make a mistake.
- You must not talk back to your employers.
- You must not pull a long face in front of your employers.
- You must not meddle in your employers' family affairs.
- You must always be eager to learn.
- You must not be choosy about chores assigned to you.
- You must always follow your employers' instructions.
- You must never damage any property in your employers' house.
- You must never physically abuse your employers' children.
- You must not go to sleep before your employers and other family members unless it is exceptionally late.
- You must discuss any problems with your employers or your agent.

---

* Translated from a sample obtained from an employment agency specialising in Indonesian domestic workers.

simple (almost "tomboyish") hairstyles (Yeoh & Huang, 1998). Female employers are more likely to be irked if transnational domestic workers transgress this dress code as this potentially threatens their identity as "ma'am" as opposed to the identity of the transnational domestic worker as "maid" because both occupy the shared terrain of domesticity (Yeoh & Huang, 1998:597). Transnational domestic workers who dress attractively are not only deemed to be transgressing the "foreign maid" mould but they are often demonised as highly sexualised subjects intent on seducing Singaporean men, including their male employers, and hence posing a threat to the position of their female employers as wife/mother (*New Paper*, 28 December 2003).

The Inferior "Other"—In the Public Sphere

As a means to keep the balance of power in the employer-transnational domestic worker relationship tilted towards the employers' advantage, most employers view it necessary to curtail or at least exert some control over their transnational domestic workers' social networks and forays into public space (Yeoh & Huang, 1998). Employers are fearful that transnational domestic workers who socialise with others may start comparing notes and be more demanding of better terms and working conditions received by other transnational domestic workers, and ultimately challenge the employer's authority, thereby transgressing the subservient "other" ideal (Yeoh & Huang, 1998). In addition, prevailing notions of the transnational domestic worker as a "young girl forced by economic conditions to seek employment overseas" with rather "different" (and often, by inference, inferior) moral and cultural "standards" (*Straits Times*, 1984, cited in Yeoh & Huang, 1998:590) underscores employers' fear of these women succumbing to social and moral transgressions. Stories and rumours in circulation detailing the social ills that transnational domestic workers get up to given the freedom of off-days, also influence some employers to impose a "no day off" policy (Yeoh & Huang, 1998:591). These much feared social and moral transgressions include indulging in socially "deviant" acts such as prostitution, thefts and fights as well as socially harmless acts such as getting involved in romantic and/or sexual relationships and hanging out at malls and discotheques (Yeoh & Huang, 1998; Abdul Rahman, 2003). The risk of having to forfeit their security bonds (see above) in the event that the transnational domestic worker runs away or become pregnant also heightens employers' fears and hence the extent of surveillance. Apart from imposing a "no day off" policy, some employers resort to other measures of surveillance to control transnational domestic workers' freedom and liberty to their private time and life.[17]

In their limited forays into the public sphere, transnational domestic workers are again confronted with the "rapid reduction of 'self' to migrant (as well as ethnic, classed and gendered) 'other'" (Yeoh & Huang, 2000:424). It is not uncommon for transnational domestic workers to be subjected to verbal insults and comments that insinuate that they are morally loose or highly sexualised individuals who are often out to seduce other people's husbands or are prostituting themselves for money (Yeoh

& Huang, 2000; Abdul Rahman, 2003). Over the years, various public spaces such as shopping malls, public markets, parks and other places of interests have become popular meeting places for transnational domestic workers (i.e., those allowed off-days) and other foreign workers on Sundays.[18] These gatherings have evoked a range of reactions from Singaporeans from tolerance and ambivalence, to resentment (Yeoh & Huang, 1998:593). However, a common thread in these reactions suggests further entrenchment of the "self-other" boundary and the inferiorities associated with the latter. Reactions from Singaporeans transmitted through the media show that Singaporeans associate anti-social behavior like littering, fights and rowdiness with large congregations of foreign workers (Yeoh & Huang, 1998). Even those who view these "foreign worker weekend enclaves" more sympathetically hasten to take deliberate measures to stay away from these places on Sundays, indicative of strong discomfort in being amongst the "other" (Yeoh & Huang, 1998:594).

Sites of Power of Transnational Domestic Workers

Although largely marginalised, transnational domestic workers do display various strategies and styles and tap on sites of resistance. Some transnational domestic workers forge social networks by cleverly scheduling daily chores, stealing time to make telephone calls while running errands outside the house, and writing letters to enable them to reclaim some private space and time. The knowledge and contacts with other people gained by nurturing these networks also help some transnational domestic workers to escape abusive relationships and, for some, secure future employment contracts with preferable terms (Abdul Rahman, 2003).

Some transnational domestic workers who enjoy regular off-days choose to be involved actively in skills enhancement, as well as religious, social and recreational activities organised by their respective embassies, churches and mosques. For these transnational domestic workers, engaging in these activities enables them to free themselves of the drudgery and monotony of domestic work, live out other identities and recharge their souls (Yeoh & Huang, 1998; 1999b; Abdul Rahman, 2003). Although these activities have often been the initiatives of local religious organisations or the foreign missions, transnational domestic workers themselves have, over the years, taken over the running of many of these activities. One example is the Filipino Overseas Workers in Singapore (FOWS) Skills Training Programmes, which have been in existence for nearly 14 years and is presently headed and managed by Filipino transnational domestic workers themselves (Commission for Migrants & Itinerant People, n.d.). To some extent, either intentionally or unintentionally, participation in such activities provides a chance for transnational domestic workers to portray a moral, diligent and respectable image countering negative stereotypes and perceptions of their identities (Abdul Rahman, 2003).

Some transnational domestic workers also seek to capitalise on existing activities to advocate for their welfare, albeit covertly. Frustrated by the apathy displayed by the Indonesian Embassy on the welfare of transnational domestic workers, a group of Indonesian transnational domestic workers appropriated An-Nisa, the first social and skill enhancement group for Indonesian domestic workers established by a local mosque in Singapore, as a platform to make inroads into the agenda of the Consular Department of the embassy and win the empathy of some Indonesian expatriates to contribute to their cause. In seeking to publicise the work of An-Nisa by participating in activities organised by the Embassy—such as operating a stall during the embassy's open house on Indonesia's Independence Day and nurturing the networks with embassy officials—these women showcase a respectable and diligent image of Indonesian transnational domestic workers to their own community. In the process, this has helped embassy officials and other Indonesian professionals to not only regard them more respectably but also become aware of the benefits of skills upgrading courses like the ones hosted by the mosque. This in turn has helped to convince these groups of Indonesians to support the women's request of expanding such activities within the Indonesian embassy's compound, so as to attract even larger numbers of Indonesian transnational domestic workers to participate on their rest days (Abdul Rahman, 2003). To date, the Indonesian Embassy (with the support of some Indonesian expatriates) now organises skill courses such as English and Mandarin lessons and social activities such as informal gatherings and lunches for Indonesian transnational domestic workers on a regular basis; this can be regarded as a milestone as it was not until the efforts of that first proactive group of Indonesian transnational domestic workers in An-Nisa that such initiatives were taken up by the embassy (Abdul Rahman, 2003).

Habitual acts such as dressing up in style and gathering in large numbers in public places on their rest days to enjoy a picnic or celebrate a friend's birthday, eating local delicacies and speaking in their native languages may also present sites of empowerment for these women as they disrupt the image of the marginalised and inferior "other" (Yeoh & Huang, 1998). When subjected with insults by the host society (both in the private and public spheres), some transnational domestic workers seek to challenge them verbally by asserting their identity, "anchored precisely in those elements of nationality, gender and class that the dominant society degrades" (Yeoh & Huang, 2000:424). Verbal retorts to counter the stereotypical perceptions that Singaporeans (who also possess no qualms in articulating these patronising views) have of foreigners like them, enable transnational domestic workers to ride above the reduction of their identity as the alien "other" who is poor, promiscuous and stupid (Yeoh & Huang, 2000:425).

ECONOMIC, HEALTH AND SOCIAL IMPACTS

Economic Impacts

A study on dual career couples based on the 1990 census data suggests that the availability of transnational domestic workers has enabled more married women to continue with their careers after child-bearing and hence contribute to the economic productivity of

Singapore (Singapore Department of Statistics, 1994). According to the study, a high proportion (36 per cent) of working wives below the age of 35 years old who are not dependent on transnational domestic workers were childless compared to nine per cent of their non-working counterparts. As more Singaporean women are better educated and possess better skills, keeping them in the labour market could make a "significant contribution to the economy", according to the Minister for Manpower during the Parliamentary Budget Debate in 2000 (*Straits Times*, 11 March 2000). The Minister also pointed out that drawing just three per cent of unemployed housewives into the workforce would provide a boost of 40,000 workers in the labour market, further enhancing economic productivity (*Straits Times*, 11 March 2000).

The ability of married women to remain employed after childbearing also provides a substantial boost to household incomes. Statistics show that the average income of dual career households in 1990 at S$3,600 (US$2,124) was more than double that of sole career households (S$1,700 [US$1,003]) and that women accounted for 41 per cent of the dual career couple's income, an increase from 36 per cent in 1980 (Singapore Department of Statistics, 1994). It has been argued that sustaining the high standards of living and consumer lifestyles in Singapore demands a dual income within the household, therefore making the live-in transnational domestic worker indispensable in many cases (*Straits Times*, 13 May 1995).

Apart from contributing to Singapore's economic growth by way of enabling local women to be active in the formal work sphere and enabling Singaporeans to enjoy higher standards of living, the presence of large numbers of migrant workers (transnational domestic workers included) in the country has led to the proliferation of related businesses such as remittance and cargo agencies and specialty shops which conduct brisk business, especially on Sundays. Employment agencies also constitute a substantial proportion (63 per cent) (*Straits Times*, 30 May 2002) of licensed recruitment agencies in the country offering a wide range of services from consultancy to recruitment. In addition, the imposition of a hefty levy on the employment of transnational domestic workers generates substantial revenue for the state's coffers. With the current estimated population of 150,000 transnational domestic workers and a monthly levy of S$295 (US$179) charged for each worker, the state receives approximately S$531 (US$322) million annually from the "maid levy".[19]

Health Concerns

Beyond the personal accident insurance scheme worth S$10,000 (US$5,900) (see section above), transnational domestic workers do not automatically have access to basic medical cover such as free or subsidised consultation with general practitioners, medication, hospitalisation and treatment for illnesses and diseases (Iyer et al., 2004). Transnational domestic workers are largely dependent on employers' kindness and discretion to provide for health care needs as they are unlikely to be able to afford basic health cover on their low wages. While employers are generally willing to cover the occasional medical costs, there are some who expect their workers to pay for these expenses. Some employment agencies are also known to have advised employers against paying for transnational domestic workers' medical fees for common illnesses as a measure of not "pampering" or "treating them too well" (*Straits Times*, 14 March 2002). Recently, a free once-a-week clinic for foreign workers (transnational domestic workers included) run by a local voluntary welfare organisation was opened in Little India (a weekend gathering node for these workers) (*Straits Times*, 30 December 2003); its popularity attests to the urgent need to provide free or at least affordable health care for low-waged migrant workers.

An important but under-studied health concern among transnational domestic workers is mental health. Apart from one study on Filipino transnational domestic workers admitted to a local mental health hospital, there has not been any other study conducted in Singapore on the general state of transnational domestic workers' mental health such as stress levels and the likelihood of depression (Mahendran & Aw, 1993). Transnational domestic workers are vulnerable to mental health problems of different degrees given the long working hours, the isolation that many go through as a result of the nature of domestic work and strict controls exerted by employers to curtail communication and freedom to socialise, their marginalisation both within and outside the domestic sphere, and the extreme culture shock some of them experience. Between January 1999 and June 2003, 99 transnational domestic workers fell to their death in Singapore from high rise apartments, 90 of them from Indonesia (*Big O Weekly Reviewer*, 23 October 2003; *Straits Times*, 24 December 2003). According to Indonesian Embassy records, police investigation revealed that 39 per cent of these deaths were suicides, 39 per cent were caused by accidents (such as when hanging out clothes and cleaning windows) while the causes of deaths for the remaining cases were still undetermined and pending investigation at the time of writing this. The relatively high proportion of suicides amongst Indonesian domestic workers is alarming given that they are, as a group the most vulnerable to mistreatment and exploitation (see section above).

Social Impacts

The large (and almost inexhaustible) pool of foreign women from the region offers a convenient, low-cost solution to the Singapore state in addressing the crisis of household reproduction and in furthering its goal of economic expansion. This, however, does little to alter ingrained patriarchal notions of the gendered division of labour within the home, or disrupt gendered ideals of the roles of men and women in society. The freedom of Singapore women to pursue work in the formal sphere hinges on their ability to purchase the labour of another woman (more often than not, more than just labour is purchased) from relatively poor countries. This perpetuates the notion of domestic work as women's work and to a great extent further degrades its value given the extremely low wages accorded to gendered substitute labour. Research has also shown that employing a domestic worker does not totally free Singaporean women from shouldering domestic responsibilities as they are still primarily responsible for supervising, training and managing the transnational domestic worker, often leading to added stress (Huang & Yeoh 1998; Yeoh & Huang 1999a). The highly gendered contours of domesticity continues to be evident in research (based on reported cases of abuse) which found that female employers are more likely to physically abuse transnational domestic workers (while male employers are more culpable where it comes to sexual abuse) and that these abuses often take place in the kitchen, a traditional women's domain (Yeoh et al., 2004).

Indeed, the presence of the transnational domestic worker in the domestic sphere has also led to the emergence of various forms of tensions that may sometimes escalate into criminal abuse on the part of either employer or transnational domestic worker. While criminal abuse is not in any way rampant, several high profile cases whereby transnational domestic workers are subjected to various forms of brutalities such as scalding and burning with hot water or a hot iron, punching, kicking, biting as well as depriving the transnational domestic worker of food (*Straits Times*, 23 January 1996; 12 July 1997; 6 December 2000; 19 March 2002) are indicative of deep-seated fractures in the domestic sphere. Some errant employers (and employment agents) also resort to humiliating treatment such as forcing the transnational domestic worker to eat faeces, undressing her and making her do military style exercises as measures of discipline (*Straits Times*, 7 July 2002; 15 October 2003). In addition, the presence of a vulnerable "other" in the domestic sphere has also been exploited by some male employers (or other male members of the household) to gain free sexual favours (*Straits Times*, 7 October 2000; 26 April 2002; 5 February 2003). On the other hand, various types of crimes committed by transnational domestic workers against their employers and/or employer's family members have also surfaced, ranging from murder, intimidation and threat to kill the child under their charge, theft, robbery and assault (*Straits Times*, 14 July 2003; 7 August 2003; 4 & 5 September 2003). Often, it is the friction between the transnational domestic worker and her employer that triggers of the crime. For example, in a recent case involving an Indonesian transnational domestic worker who was found guilty of murdering her employer and burning her employer's office (the scene of crime) to cover her tracks and in the process killing her employer's three-month old child, the transnational domestic worker in question claimed during the trial that she had been abused and starved by her female employer (*Straits Times*, 9 & 25 September 2003). A witness account and the employer's history of having employed numerous transnational domestic workers over a short span of time suggest that the alleged abuses may not have been without foundation.

Apart from public concern over flashpoints such as abuse cases, anxiety has also been raised with respect to the impact of transnational domestic workers on the upbringing and care of children. Some children have exhibited patronising behaviour towards the transnational domestic workers who care for them; this has stirred up criticism among members of the public who feel that such behaviours, left unaddressed, will lead to a deterioration in the moral values of the future generation (*New Paper*, 10 November 2003). Similar concerns have also been raised about discipline problems among children—such as lying, conniving in order to get their way, and failing to listen to instruction—traits which are said to have been picked up from transnational domestic workers who care for them (*Straits Times*, 19 February 2003). Other concerns relate to the negative impact of leaving children in the hands of "strangers", some with little or no experience in looking after children. Apart from the fear of negligence on the part of the transnational domestic worker (*Straits Times*, 25 March 2003; 30 August 2003), anxieties have also centred on the strain on the mother-child bond where the mother has been substituted by the transnational domestic worker (*Straits Times*, 19 February 2003).

NGO MOVEMENTS AND CIVIL SOCIETY GROUPS

Religious institutions such as churches and mosques are active in providing social and welfare services to transnational domestic workers (Yeoh & Huang, 1999b; Abdul Rahman, 2003). These services include organising special religious classes, skills enhancement opportunities and social gatherings to mark various religious events, counselling services as well as the provision of shelter for abused transnational domestic workers. The Catholic Church is perhaps the largest provider of these services, especially after the establishment of the Commission for Migrants and Itinerants (CMI) in 1998. Apart from the provision of services, CMI has also been active in raising public awareness about the plight of migrant workers and in promoting better employer-transnational domestic worker relations through public education, seminars and May Day celebrations involving various other religious-based migrant groups under its umbrella. Typically, these celebrations feature cultural performances, a fun fair and an award ceremony to recognise the "Best Employer" and the "Best Domestic Worker" based on written nominations made by these two parties.

Religious institutions providing support for transnational domestic workers generally limit their work to the provision of "ambulance" services rather than engage in advocacy work. Partly a legacy of the arrest of 16 members of the Geylang Catholic Centre for Foreign Workers in 1987 under the Internal Security Act (Yeoh & Huang, 1999b), they have tended to be cautious about treading too closely to what may be deemed political boundaries and prefer to stay clear of human rights issues for fear that such advocacy work may be misconstrued as being "political". More recently, however, CMI has taken a step further by engaging MOM (and other stakeholders such as employment agencies and embassies) in regular dialogues on issues concerning foreign workers, including the possibility of putting in place a statute governing the employment of transnational domestic workers. Couched in terms of the spiritual discourse of love vis-à-vis the secular discourse of rights, CMI's approach in advocating better treatment for transnational domestic workers is non-confrontational, preferring to stay away from media limelight and do things on "the quiet" so as to avoid being viewed as an adversary of the state (Devasahayam, 2004).[20]

In early 2003, spurred by a more open climate for civil activism in Singapore, an ad hoc group consisting of individuals and organisations called The Working Committee Two (TWC2) was established to champion the rights and dignity due to transnational domestic workers. Led by a Nominated Member of Parliament, the group embarked on a nine-month long programme to act upon their concerns for the better treatment of transnational domestic workers in Singapore. The group was informally formed in mid-2002 after a group of friends were deeply disturbed by the remarks made by a neighbour of Ng Hua Chye, a tour guide who was convicted of abusing his Indonesian domestic worker, Muawanatul Chasanah, and who admitted to repeatedly beating and kicking her which eventually led to her death; the neighbour was quoted to have said that Ng's brutality was not his business and that he (Ng) could do whatever he wanted as "God can see" (*Straits Times*, 20 July 2002). This small nucleus of concerned individuals was appalled by the apathy displayed by the neighbour, which they also viewed as an embarrassing reflection of the shallowness of society and the lack of civil concern in the country.[21]

In its nine-month existence as an ad-hoc committee, TWC2 held various forums (both public and closed-door) involving all the key players such as transnational domestic workers, employers, employment agencies, officials of foreign missions and the Ministry of Manpower (The Working Committee 2, n.d.). It also held various closed-door meetings with relevant institutions such as the Consumer Association of Singapore (CASE), The Association of Employment Agencies Singapore (AEAS), MOM, the then Ministry of Community Development and Sports (MCDS, now the Ministry of Community Development, Youth and Sports), and the various foreign missions (the Indonesian, Sri Lankan and Philippines Embassy) with the objective of exploring possibilities of cooperation and exchanging information. Supported by volunteers from all walks of life, TWC2 also organised various public awareness-raising activities including advertisement campaigns, a photographic exhibition, an essay writing competition for primary school children, and a forum for college students. It also embarked on a campaign to encourage employers to grant their transnational domestic workers off-days by organising "Sunday Off" parties with local resident committees in public housing estates. Apart from these, TWC2 was also active in policy making by providing comments on accreditation schemes offered by the AEAS and CASE, and drafting a proposal for laws to protect transnational domestic workers' interests and to guide employer-transnational domestic worker relations. This has been submitted to MOM for comment in anticipation of tabling a bill in Parliament for a new "Foreign Domestic Worker Act" (*Today*, 4 December 2003). TWC2 was legally registered as a society in August 2004 and renamed Transient Workers Count Too while keeping the acronym "TWC2"; it intends to expand its scope to include the welfare of other transient workers in Singapore, such as foreign construction workers, other than domestic workers (*Straits Times*, 28 August 2004).

Supported by the media, TWC2's efforts catalysed considerable public discourse on the "maid issue" and feedback received at events and those transmitted to the media suggest that "more people [Singaporeans in general] supported the objectives of the committee than those who were against it".[22] That the chair of TWC2 and other more active members were sought by local and foreign media on numerous occasions to comment on the "maid issue" in Singapore is indicative of a degree of legitimacy in the eyes of the media as well as the topic's newsworthy nature. At the same time, heightened media publicity (especially foreign media) on the dignity due to transnational domestic workers raised eyebrows and some consternation in some quarters, as it was felt that TWC2's actions risk tarnishing the image of the state and Singapore as a society. More generally, the premise underlying the "Dignity Overdue" and "Sundays Off" campaigns was criticised as unsympathetic to issues of concern to employers including poorly trained transnational domestic workers, unethical business practices of employment agents, and the difficulty in having to police a stranger in the house. Of perhaps the greatest significance hitherto is the fact that TWC2's efforts have raised consciousness and debate on transnational domestic worker issues, as well as spurred key players such as MOM and employment agents to address the "maid issue" more seriously and to acknowledge the imbalance of power between the transnational domestic worker and the employers or their agents.[23] Recent moves by MOM to implement compulsory orientation for both first-time employers and transnational domestic workers, the setting up of a special unit to offer conciliatory services and swift action to stop employment agencies from parading transnational domestic workers at shopfronts and in window displays, perhaps, are at least in part pushed by civil concern channelled and ventilated by TWC2 (*Straits Times*, 15 October 2003; 6 February 2004; *Channel News Asia*, 18 October 2003).

ALTERNATIVE PATHWAYS AND IMPLICATIONS

Vulnerabilities and Loopholes

The factors underscoring transnational domestic workers' vulnerabilities to exploitation and mistreatment are complex and require not only better laws to govern the processes of recruitment, training, placement and employment, but also a mindset change in society to render the dignity due to this group of workers. Over the years, MOM has introduced various measures in response to calls to "clean up the maid market" and to address the mistreatment of transnational domestic workers by employers and employment agents (*Straits Times*, 30 October 2003). The Penal Code was amended in 1998 to impose heavier penalties for various forms of offences—such as causing hurt, wrongful confinement, and the outrage of modesty—against foreign domestic workers (Yeoh *et al.*, 2004). The number of substantiated cases of abuse against domestic workers declined sharply from 157 in 1997 to 41 in 2001; this reduction, according to state officials, is indicative of the effectiveness of the amendments (Yeoh et al., 2004).

MOM has also begun blacklisting employers and their family members convicted of abusing domestic workers and preventing them from employing transnational domestic workers (*Straits Times*, 30 October 2003). MOM's current moves requiring all employment agencies to gain accreditation (either under the CASE or the AEAS scheme) is a step in the right direction to professionalise the "domestic worker industry". These schemes lay down guidelines and basic standards of business practices for employment agencies to ensure that placement of transnational domestic workers are conducted ethically. On the employers' front, as noted above, MOM now requires all first-time employers and transnational domestic workers to attend a half-day orientation in which issues such as safety, welfare of domestic workers and duties and responsibilities of both parties will be emphasised. In October 2004, MOM has also started to crack down on employers who are found to be changing domestic workers too frequently (at least four domestic workers in a year). Such employers are now required to go through an interview process, repeat the orientation course and justify their need to hire subsequent domestic workers in writing. This is because MOM has identified through experience that such employers are more likely to encounter employment-related problems with their domestic workers (*New Paper*, 16 October 2004). In addition, MOM set up the Foreign Manpower Management Division in August 2003 to attend to various issues concerning foreign workers (including foreign domestic workers) such as the protection of their safety, the treatment received from employers, and the standard of professionalism of employment agencies (*Straits Times*, 10 June 2004).

Despite these initiatives, there are still major loopholes in rendering protection to transnational domestic workers. First, these measures fail to take into account the asymmetrical power relations between the transnational domestic worker vis-à-vis the employers and employment agents. For example, although the amended Penal Code to some extent led to a reduction in the number of substantiated cases of abuse against domestic workers, very often those who are subjected to abuse confront great difficulties in seeking help and are only able to do so after suffering prolonged abuses (Yeoh et al., 2004). The private nature of their employment and the control that employers have over them present major barriers to transnational domestic workers seeking recourse through the protective arm of the law. Moreover, as transnational domestic workers are constrained by the high loans they are forced to take up in securing their employment contract (see section above), their anxiety to complete their contract also incapacitates them from seeking justice against employers who turn abusers.

Second, whilst the amendments made to the Penal Code has sent a very strong signal of the state's intolerance of criminal abuses against transnational domestic workers, no law has been legislated to accord civil rights to these women. The current practice is for either embassy officials or officials from MOM and sometimes with the aid of employment agencies and civil society groups to mediate in cases involving civil disputes such as non-payment of salaries, deprivation of adequate rest and food. Employers who admit to withholding salaries are usually required to pay up but deprivation of adequate meals and rests are usually more difficult to prove and are more often than not addressed by finding alternative employment for the transnational domestic worker.

Recommended Solutions

It is imperative for the Singapore state to legislate standard employment terms for transnational domestic workers spelling out minimum wage, numbers of day off, meal provisions, medical cover, repatriation costs and maximum working hours. In addition, the state should also allocate resources to install a proper facility and procedure such as a labour tribunal to facilitate a swift mediation for cases of infringements. This will help prevent transnational domestic workers from losing out on salaries while waiting for their cases to be solved and will also ease the pressure on available shelters for transnational domestic workers who have to stop working while waiting for their complaints to be investigated. Stiffer penalties such as pecuniary fines should also be introduced for infringements to ensure effective implementation of these basic standards. Although the state has argued repeatedly that it is impossible to legislate standard terms of employment for transnational domestic workers due to the wide ranging nature of domestic work, regulations to ensure equal minimum rights for transnational domestic workers of all nationalities is a necessary and crucial first step forward in correcting the imbalance of power in the transnational domestic worker-employer relationship and reducing the exploitation of more vulnerable groups of transnational domestic workers (such as Indonesian domestic workers). A law requiring employers to grant a compulsory day off for transnational domestic workers can also pave the way for transnational domestic workers to break away from the confines of the private sphere and empower themselves through access to knowledge and networks of peers and friends.

A more radical proposition is to facilitate the option for live-out transnational domestic workers. As shown above, the physical co-presence with employers exacerbates unequal power relations, the root cause of the exploitation of transnational domestic workers. This proposition does not appear feasible in the short term as it requires the state to either shoulder the task of providing for the welfare of transnational domestic workers such as subsidised housing or to compromise on the amount of monthly levy contributed by employers for each transnational domestic worker so that wages may be increased (in order to allow transnational domestic workers to be able to afford to provide for their own welfare). As the levy has been adopted by the state as a tool to keep the population of transnational domestic workers in check and is also a lucrative contribution to state coffers, the possibility of it being revised is slim. Alternatively, the state may require employers to increase the wages of transnational domestic workers, again an unlikely proposition as the cheapness and convenience of this pool of labour are the main drawing points in the first place. Indeed, the state's economic objectives often supersede the importance of protecting the rights of migrant workers such as transnational domestic workers. It would not be surprising if the measures of protection that have so far been adopted are mainly motivated by the need to placate possible tensions in bilateral relations that might erupt from rising cases of abuse against transnational domestic workers or to quell the louder voices of civil activists and media protesting against the lack of rights accorded to transnational domestic workers.

Faced with these barriers, changes from the top may be slow to come. In the meantime, more concerted efforts from below by NGOs or civil society groups to exert pressure and crank up the volume in advocating policy change would help to ensure that transnational domestic workers remain firmly on the public agenda. Transnational domestic workers must also be empowered with knowledge of their rights through workshops and programmes and existing avenues available for recourse before and after their departure from countries of origin. These groups must also focus on stepping up welfare provisions such as shelters, mediation and counselling facilities, and provision of skill enhancement and other social activities for transnational domestic workers as these services are not only useful but present sites of empowerment for transnational domestic workers. NGOs and civil society groups campaigning for an end to the "quiet indignities" faced by transnational domestic workers would also be crucial in continuing the long-term process of social change.

CONCLUSION

Given the developmental goals of the Singapore state, its limited human resource and a deeply entrenched patriarchal view of gender roles, transnational domestic workers are likely to be a long-term phenomenon in the country. The "maid dependency syndrome" will continue to become even more pervasive as more women are drawn into, choose or are compelled to participate in, the formal economic sphere to keep up with the demands of a middle-class lifestyle, which has become part of the aspirations of the average Singaporean. As transnational domestic workers present a cheap and easy solution for the state to address the crisis in household reproduction, it will continue to open its doors to this group of workers for as long as the country needs them. However, discriminatory policies and strict controls imposed by the state to ensure the transient status of this group of foreign workers seek to marginalise transnational domestic workers, which further entrenches the "self/other" divide between this group of workers and the host society. Being the inferior alien "other", transnational domestic workers are vulnerable to exploitation and often treated with very little dignity by employment agents, employers and host society in general.

Despite being forced into a position of weakness, transnational domestic workers display their own strategies and styles which do challenge their place as the "other" in the host country. Moreover, informal social networks and social and skills upgrading groups present sites of power for transnational domestic workers (as well as members of host society) to advance their welfare and the rights due to them as workers and individuals.

However, in the context of a strong state and a weak civil society in Singapore, mindset changes and institutional reforms are undoubtedly crucial ingredients in advancing the dignity due to transnational domestic workers for some time to come.

NOTES

1   This figure is the official ballpark estimate released by the Ministry of Manpower, Singapore when making statements through the media.

2   Three-quarters of the economically active women who left the Singapore workforce between the mid-1970s and the late 1980s did so for reasons associated with housework, childcare and marriage (Ministry of Labour, cited in Huang & Yeoh, 1996:483).

3   This estimate is derived from dividing the estimated total population of transnational domestic workers by the total number of dwelling units in the year 2000. There were 964,138 dwelling units of all types in that year (Singapore Department of Statistics, 2000) against a total population of transnational domestic workers of 140,000.

4   *Mui tsai* as young as ten were sold away by poor families or single parent prostitutes. In return for a lifetime of servitude, *mui tsai* were provided with the basic necessities of life and are also sometimes married off by their employers. However, many fell victim to physical and sexual abuse and a life of extreme hardships. In response to numerous serious cases of ill-treatment, the colonial government legislated the *Mui Tsai* Act in 1933 which called for compulsory registration of *mui tsai* arriving in the colony to allow for greater monitoring (Lai, 1986). Later, a total ban on the practice of hiring *mui tsai* drove the *mui tsai* trade underground.

5   They were referred to as "black and white *amah*" because of the colour of the *samfoos* they wore: black trousers and white tops.

6   Wong (1996) notes that in 1984, when it was estimated that one in every ten working households in Singapore employed a transnational domestic worker, the official figures for worker arrivals in the country obtained from the Philippine Overseas Employment Administration (POEA) in the same year was only 5,886. As there was an overwhelming majority of Filipina domestic workers in that year, she concludes that it is fair to assume "that some of the 54,875 tourist arrivals from the Philippines recorded in that year joined the labour force" (Wong, 1996:96).

7   President of the Association of Employment Agencies Singapore, personal communication with authors, 28 January 2004.

8   Since its inception, the levy has been periodically raised as a means of controlling the number of transnational domestic workers in Singapore. In August 2004, however, the levy was reduced for the first time as part of a basket of incentives offered by the state to boost fertility rates in the country. Under this measure, the monthly levy payable by employers with children below 12 years of age or elderly parents/grandparents above the age of 65 living with them was reduced to S$250 (US$150) (*Straits Times*, 26 August 2004). Most recently, the government announced a blanket reduction of S$50 (US$30) for all employers of foreign domestic workers, effective from 1 April 2005 (*Straits Times*, 19 February 2005).

9   There are anecdotal cases of marital union between transnational domestic workers and

local men. In some of these cases, the transnational domestic workers concerned have also been granted permanent residency. However, this is more an exception than the norm. There are also transnational domestic workers who return to their home countries and re-enter Singapore under a different identity so as to be able to marry Singaporean men and seek permanent residency. Others resort to marrying their Singaporean partners in their countries of origin before seeking to re-enter Singapore and applying for permanent residency after several years.

10   In late 2004, MOM introduced several other regulations. With effect from 1 January 2005, first-time transnational domestic workers must be between 23 and 50 years old and must have completed at least eight years of schooling; if the foreign domestic worker has previously worked in Singapore, she must be between 18 and 50 years old. New domestic workers are also required to attend a compulsory safety awareness course in Singapore. In addition, first time employers are also required to attend Employer's Orientation Programme. Employers who change more than four domestic workers in one year will be put under closer scrutiny and will have to provide satisfactory reasons to employ another one. All these measures are targetted at improving the quality of transnational domestic workers and to clamp down on cases of domestic worker abuse.

11   The following occupations also fall outside the Employment Act: executive, managerial or confidential positions, seamen, civil servants and local domestic workers. Arguably though, these workers have alternative bargaining power by virtue of their higher-status occupations and/or through their rights as citizens.

12   In March 1995, succumbing to pressure from the Filipino public over the Flor Contemplacion case, the Philippines government temporarily suspended the flow of Filipina domestic worker into Singapore. Flor Contemplacion was a Filipino domestic worker who was found guilty by the Singapore High Court in 1995, and sentenced to death for murdering her friend (another domestic worker) and her eight-year-old charge. The case sparked loud protest and criticism in the Philippines, which led to the (temporary) suspension of diplomatic relations between the two countries and the flow of Filipina domestic workers into Singapore (Hilsdon, 2000).

13   Employment agents view the compulsory weekly day off, the ban on domestic worker performing non-domestic duties such as the washing of cars, and the minimum wage of S$350 (US$208) spelled out in the standard work contract endorsed by the Philippines Embassy as "problematic" as these terms do not serve employers' interests (Abdul Rahman, 2003:107).

14   The Indonesian Embassy (KBRI) requires all employers and domestic workers who plan to extend the validity of the latter's passport to sign an endorsed employment contract that stipulates standard terms of employment for transnational domestic workers. However, this protective measure lacks teeth because of the lack of monitoring. It also excludes new transnational domestic workers who are serving their first employment contract.

15   The average starting salary of an Indonesian domestic worker in Singapore is S$230 (US$136). This is approximately S$100 (US$59) lower than the average salary of a Filipina domestic worker (with no prior experience) which starts at S$330 (US$195). Sri Lankans command starting wages ranging from S$180–S$220 (US$106–US$130) (*New Paper*, 7 February 2005; *Straits Times*, 20 February 2005). In the absence of a minimum wage rule,

wages are determined by market forces that hinge on employers' perception and agents' promotion of varying skills and capabilities of domestic workers of differing nationalities (Huang & Yeoh, 1998:39).

16   Indonesian domestic workers pay recruitment fees through a system of salary deduction. Prior to the financial crisis, on average, Indonesian domestic workers were paying recruitment fees equivalent to three or four months salary (S$600–S$800 or US$354–US$473), but at the height of the crisis, Indonesian domestic workers were entering into agreements requiring salary deductions of up to eight months (*Straits Times*, 14 October 1998).

17   Employers resort to various measures of control such as not granting off days, monitoring telephone calls (via electronic devices that record incoming and outgoing calls); specifying "acceptable" activities for off days and imposing strict curfews; assigning a trustworthy domestic worker to act as chaperon; and eliciting information from their domestic workers by engaging them in conversations and going through their photo albums (Huang & Yeoh 1996; Yeoh & Huang 1998).

18   These places include Lucky Plaza in Orchard Road, also known as "Little Manila"; Zhujiao Market in Little India, identified with Indian and Bangladeshi workers; Joo Chiat Complex and City Plaza in Geylang, which is known to attract large numbers of Indonesians; and also Marina City and the Botanic Gardens that attract foreign workers of various nationalities.

19   This figure is obtained by multiplying the monthly levy charged per transnational domestic worker (S$295) by 12 months and then multiplying the total by the estimated population of transnational domestic workers (150,000).

20   Bridget Lew, the driving force of CMI recently left the organisation to form the Humanitarian Organisation of Home Economics (HOME). HOME offers, *inter alia*, counselling services, legal aid and shelter to foreign workers in need (*New Paper*, 7 June 2004).

21   The title of our paper gives due recognition to TWC2's tagline, "Dignity Overdue: Respecting the Rights of Maids". The tagline reflects the group's concerns with "the attitudes towards and treatment of domestic workers in Singapore" and its desire to educate Singaporeans that "all labour is dignified, and the contributions of domestic workers to the economic and social well-being of Singapore must be recognised and valued" (The Working Committee 2, n.d.). It plays on the double entendre that transnational domestic workers deserve their dignity as much as, if not more than, their due wages, on the one hand, and that respect and dignity for transnational domestic workers in Singapore are long overdue, on the other.

22   Chair of TWC2, personal communication with authors, 16 February 2004.

23   Chair of TWC2, personal communication with authors, 16 February 2004.

REFERENCES

Abdul Rahman, N. 2003. *Negotiating Power: A Case Study of Indonesian Foreign Domestic Workers in Singapore*. Unpublished Ph.D. dissertation, Department of Social Sciences, Curtin University of Technology, Perth Western Australia, http://adt.curtin.edu.au/theses/available /adt-WCU20040119.111646/. Accessed 1 June 2004.

Anderson, B. 2000. *Doing the Dirty Work: the Global Politics of Domestic Labour*. London: Zed Books.

Big O Weekly Reviewer. 2003. 23 October, No: 48.

Channel News Asia. 2003. 18 October.

Commission for Migrants and Itinerants (CMI). n.d. http://www.migrants.org.sg /milestone.htm, accessed 17 February 2003.

Devasahayam, T. 2004. Commissioned to care: The Catholic church in the lives of foreign domestic workers in Singapore. Paper presented at the In Search of a Humanised Globalisation: The Contribution of Spiritually Based Social Movements Conference, Institute for Religion and Culture, Nanzan University, 28–30 April in Nagoya, Japan.

Gaw, K. 1988. *Superior Servants: The Legendary Cantonese Amahs of the Far East*, Oxford: Oxford University Press.

Hilsdon, A. M. 2000. The Contemplacion fiasco: The hanging of a Filipino domestic worker in Singapore. In *Human Rights and Gender Politics*. Edited by A. M. Hilsdon, M. Mcintyre, V. Mackie & M. Stivens. London: Routledge, 172–92.

Huang, S. & B. S. A. Yeoh. 1996. Ties that bind: State policy and migrant female domestic helpers in Singapore. *Geoforum*, 27(4), 479–93.

––––––––. 1998, Maids and ma'ams in Singapore: Constructing gender and nationality in the transnationalisation of paid domestic work. *Geography Research Forum*, 18, 21–48.

––––––––. 2003. The difference gender makes: State policy and contract migrant workers in Singapore. *Asian and Pacific Migration Journal*, 12(1–2), 75–98.

Hugo, G. 2000. Indonesian overseas contract workers HIV knowledge: A gap in information. http://www.hiv-development.org/publications/CONTRACT%20WORKERS. asp. Accessed 14 July 2001.

––––––––. 2002. Women's international labour migration. In *Women in Indonesia: Gender, Equity and Development*. Edited by K. Robinson & S. Bessell. Singapore: Institute of Southeast Asian Studies, 158–78.

Iyer, A., T. W. Devasahayam & B. S. A. Yeoh. 2004. A clean bill of health? Filipinas as domestic workers in Singapore. *Asian and Pacific Migration Journal*, 13(1), 11–38.

Lai, A. E. 1986. *Peasants, Proletarians and Prostitutes: A Preliminary Investigation of Chinese Women in Colonial Malaya*. Singapore: Institute of Southeast Asian Studies.

Mahendran, R. & S. C. Aw. 1993. Psychiatric illness in Filipino maids admitted to Woodbridge Hospital. *Singapore Medical Journal*, 34, 38–40.

Ministry of Manpower (MOM). n.d. *Employing Foreign Domestic Workers: A Guide for Employers*, Singapore: Ministry of Manpower.

New Paper. Various issues.

Purushotam, N. 1992. Women and knowledge/power: Notes on the Singaporean dilemma. In *Imagining Singapore*. Edited by K. C. Ban, A. Pakir & C. K. Tong. Singapore: Times Academic Press, 320–61.

Singapore Department of Statistics. 1994. *Dual-career Couples in Singapore*. http://www.singstat. gov.sg/papers/op/op-s2.pdf. Accessed 17 February 2003.

_____. 2000. *Census of Population 2000*. http://www.singstat.gov.sg/keystats/c2000/topline5.pdf. Accessed 17 February 2003.

Straits Times. Various issues.

Straughan, P. T., S. Huang, & B. S. A. Yeoh. 2000. Family ideology and practice: Implications for marital satisfaction. Paper presented at The Australian Sociological Association Conference, Flinders University, 6–8 December in Adelaide, Australia.

Streats. 2003. 13 March.

The Working Committee 2. n.d. http://www.aware.org.sg/twc2/. Accessed 2 June 2004.

Today. 2003. 4 December.

Wong, D. 1996. 'Foreign women domestic workers in Singapore', in G. Battistella & A. Paganoni (eds.), *Asian Women in Migration*, Quezon City: Scalabrini Migration Center, 87–107.

Yeoh, B. S. A & S. Huang. 1998. Negotiating public space: strategies and styles of migrant female domestic workers in Singapore. *Urban Studies*, 35(3), 583–602.

_____. 1999a. Singapore women and foreign domestic workers: Negotiating domestic work and motherhood. In *Gender, Migration and Domestic Service*. Edited by J. H. Momsen. London and New York: Routledge, 277–300.

_____. 1999b. Spaces at the margins: Migrant domestic workers and the development of civil society in Singapore. *Environment and Planning A*, 31(7), 1149–67.

_____. 2000. Home and away: Foreign domestic workers and negotiations of diasporic identity in Singapore. *Women's Studies International Forum*, 23(4), 413–29.

Yeoh, B. S. A, S. Huang, & T. Devasahayam. 2004. Diasporic subjects in the nation: Foreign domestic workers, the reach of the law and civil society in Singapore. *Asian Studies Review*, 28(1), 7–23.

CHAPTER 9

Neither at Work nor at Home: Asian Transnational Domestic Workers in Malaysia[1]

CHRISTINE B. N. CHIN

INTRODUCTION

Malaysian household demands for temporary low wage Asian transnational women domestic workers began during the 1970s as a result of state-led industrialisation that provided alternative employment opportunities for local women. Since the mid-1980s, state adoption of economic privatisation, liberalisation and deregulation policies has increased rather than decreased Malaysian demands for transnational domestic workers. Presently, there are about 230,000 transnational domestic workers out of approximately 800,000 transnational workers in regular status. It is estimated that, on an annual basis, at least an additional 20,000 transnational domestic workers seek employment in Malaysia (*Star*, 12 October 2003). Significantly, the size of the regular and irregular transnational worker populations in Malaysia have grown in tandem with neoliberal restructuring processes designed to render labour more "flexible" in relation to capital (when the numbers of irregular transnationals are taken into consideration, the total population exceeds one million persons). Transnational domestic workers have come to constitute a significant percentage of the "flexibilised" worker population who do not have job/income security, opportunities for social advancement or the acquisition of additional economic skills.

Especially given efforts to sustain economic growth in the wake of the 1997–1998 financially induced economic crisis, state authorities are concerned with managing a large population of transnational labour. Even though transnational domestic workers have been exempt mostly from the more restrictive regulatory changes governing the entry and employment of workers in other sectors, their presence in the country has been paralleled by heightened public discourse linking them to a variety of topics, e.g., prostitution, sexual/physical abuse, and threats to public health and safety. In this kind of milieu, Malaysian demands for and the employment of transnational domestic workers effectively obscure important issues, notably the absence of labour and health protection, rights and benefits that long has characterised live-in domestic work.

The growing presence of transnational domestic workers in Malaysia raises important questions with regard to the relationship between domestic labour, transnational migration and neoliberal development in the receiving country. Why are Malaysian households increasingly dependent on the domestic labour of Asian transnational women as opposed to the services of childcare and/or elderly care centres as well as that of day-workers? What role does the state play in encouraging or mitigating Malaysian demands for the women? Under what conditions can and do transnational women enter the country to perform live-in paid domestic work? What are the key economic, social and health issues related to the women's presence in the country? What is the nature of advocacy efforts with regard to these issues and how are they advanced in a larger context that tends to privilege economic growth and social stability in its multiethnic society over that of protecting foreign or "alien maids"?

To facilitate answering these questions, this chapter will be divided into the following sections: the historical context of paid domestic work; transnational women's experiences; the role of the state; the major economic, social and health issues; the nature of civic activism; and policy recommendations. The analysis will reveal more fully the complexities and challenges of paid domestic labour performed by transnational women in Malaysian households today. It will be demonstrated that contradictions in state policies and regulations contribute to sustaining Malaysian demands for transnational domestic workers while affirming an overall perception that such workers must be managed and contained for their protection and the protection of the receiving household and society. The chapter concludes with policy recommendations to better address existing contradictions.

SERVICE, NOT WORK: HISTORY OF PAID DOMESTIC WORK IN MALAYSIA

The history of paid domestic work in Malaysia is mostly that of a silent record relative to occupations located in the public domain. Available literature on paid domestic work has tended primarily to be part of larger studies on the relationship between gender and urbanisation or industrialisation (see especially Fawcett et al., 1984; Hing, 1984; Khoo 1992). Of interest is that many of the studies were informed by the modernisation paradigm. Extrapolated from the historical experiences of advanced industrialised societies, the modernisation paradigm anticipated the ascendancy of capitalist market forces everywhere to replace the highly personalised, intimate and non-contractual relations between employers and their live-in domestic workers in the household (Coser, 1973; Chaplin, 1978).

Up until a certain point in Malaysian history, the case of paid domestic work appeared to follow this trajectory. Since the late 20th century, however, not only has the unregulated institution of live-in domestic work "survived" economic restructuring policies but it has been revitalised in Malaysia as well as several advanced industrialised countries such as Canada, the United States and Italy, with the employment of transnational women in receiving households (Hondagneu-Sotelo 1994; Milkman et al., 1998; Ehrenreich & Hochschild, 2003).

In the case of Malaysia, what can be known thus far is that personnel changes over time have occurred at the intersections of migratory and employment patterns, with cultural pre- and proscriptions governing the performance of domestic labour. Since the era of British colonial rule, paid domestic work in the multiethnic society has had a characteristically gendered-ethnicised dimension. It can best be summarised as the transition from Chinese and Indian transnational men servants in the late 19th century, to Malaysian women of Malay, Chinese and Indian descent and, finally, transnational women from neighbouring Southeast Asian countries in the late 20th century (Chin, 1998). Despite, or perhaps because of, such changes in personnel, live-in paid domestic work remains an unregulated occupation. At best, domestic workers are considered "informal" workers.

Chinese and Indian transnational men were the earliest recorded paid domestic workers during 19th century British Malaya. Pejoratively called "Hylam boys" (Chinese men from the Hylam clan) and "*klings*" respectively, the presence of transnational men in European households came about not because of European preference for men workers per se but because of the low numbers of transnational women in the country (Vaughan, 1879). The colonial preference was for Chinese women to participate in the more profitable profession of prostitution (that generated brothel-related revenues for the treasury) while Indian migrant women were expected to provide sexual services for their men workers and European managers on plantations (Ramasamy, 1997). Malay men and women, on the other hand, were segregated from the transnational populations in order to "protect" their status as the indigenous peoples of the country (Syed, 1977; Kratoska, 1982).

By the 1930s, employer dissatisfaction with the demands of transnational male domestic workers for higher wages and rest days led to their replacement by transnational women, particularly Chinese women who began to arrive in greater numbers as a result of economic depression and changing immigration rules. In British Malaya, Chinese women domestic workers could be categorised according to whether they worked as an *amah* or a *mui tsai*. An *amah* was typically a single celibate woman who belonged to a well-established anti-marriage movement in the Kwangtung region. These women reconstituted their social networks upon arrival in Malaya (Gaw, 1991) and the networks operated as informal employment agencies that referred each *amah* to potential European and Chinese employers, as well as mediate employer-employee disputes. A *mui tsai* on the other hand was usually a young girl who was "given" away by her parents, or "sold" by Chinese secret societies, to more wealthy Chinese employers who then provided board, lodging and informal education in return for the girls' domestic labour (Lai, 1986). In 1957, settled transnationals from China and India joined Malays in becoming citizens of a newly independent multiethnic country.

While Malaysian women of Chinese descent were known to perform live-in paid domestic work, and women of Indian descent were observed to prefer day-work, there are contending perspectives on the category of paid domestic work performed by women of Malay descent. One perspective argues that they favoured day-work because live-in work was tantamount to being considered "*hamba orang* (literally, someone else's slave), who in the traditional Malay society of social stratification occupies the lowest stratum" (Azizah, 1986:52). Another perspective asserts that women who eventually moved to the urban areas tended to favour live-in domestic work because it offered them independence from their families while protecting them "from the perceived risks of big city living" (Armstrong, 1990:156–57). In any case, the performance of live-in domestic work tended to be characterised along ethnic lines in the multiethnic society. This helped affirm the kin or pseudo-kin superior-subordinate relations between employer and employee in the household.

Newsprint reports indicated on numerous occasions that live-in women domestic workers had complained about and called for state intervention to regulate their work hours, to ensure rest days and holidays, to establish base salaries and to provide workers' insurance. Even as the Employment Act 1955 defined a domestic servant as "a person employed in connection with the work of a private dwelling house ... and includes a cook, house servants, butler, child's nurse ... gardener, driver or cleaner of any vehicle licensed for private use", it failed to consider servants as formal workers with rights and benefits. This similarly was the case with other important labour legislation such as the Employee Social Security Ordinance 1969 or the Employee Provident Fund 1951.

By the 1970s, domestic workers began to pursue employment opportunities beyond the homes. In the midst of state mandated restructuring policies (New Economic Policy 1971–1990 or the NEP) designed to elevate Malays' economic and social status in relation to non-Malays, Malaysian women from the three major ethnic groups were able to obtain alternative employment opportunities generated by new foreign investments especially in the manufacturing sector (Ong, 1987; Jamilah, 1992).

The gradual decline of live-in Malaysian domestic workers paralleled the expansion of the middle classes. Urbanisation in the context of rapid industrialisation could not but fuel the middle classes' demands for domestic workers to perform childcare and housework especially since many employers no longer lived within the vicinities of their parents or extended families. Unable to hire Malaysian women, employers began to look overseas for labour. In the mid-1980s, roughly 4,000 work permits were issued to Filipina and Indonesian women. By early 2003, it was reported that 233,000 work permits had been issued to women domestic workers mostly from Indonesia and the Philippines, and to a lesser extent, women from Sri Lanka, Thailand and Cambodia (*New Straits Times*, 1 June 2003).[2]

Given the experiences of their counterparts especially in advanced industrialised countries, a key question arises from the Malaysian middle classes' increasing dependence on live-in transnational domestic workers. Why are employers choosing to hire transnational women to care for their children instead of relying on the capitalist market for the provision of childcare and other household services? At the outset, childcare centres are a fledgling industry in Malaysia. State recognition of the need for alternative childcare services arose during the 1980s in the form of the Childcare Centres Act or the Creche Act in 1984 that offered tax breaks to firms for establishing on-site or near site crèches as well as designate childcare benefits as non-taxable items.[3] Yet, many firms have not taken advantage of the Act because of the potential costs (including designating space and ensuring adequately trained staff) incurred in establishing on-site care. Additionally, the administrative process involved in operating a crèche is considered too lengthy and complicated especially since three different sets of permits are required respectively from the Department of Health, the Department of Fire and Rescue, and Local Councils. In 2003, approximately 28,000 children below the age of four years were sent to 1,309 crèches, although only 23 per cent of the crèches had valid permits. Presently, not even one crèche has been cited for failure to register, while only 22 per cent of all registered childcare centres employ trained staff (*New Straits Times*, 10 Aug 2003). Despite the state's amendment of the Creche Act to standardise management and to improve the quality of care, many parents still consider it a hassle to drop off and pick up their children at centres (*New Straits Times*, 21 October 2002).

The middle classes' aversion to crèches is not due exclusively to the unregulated, and hence potentially dangerous, environments for their children. The need to ensure care for their children only represents one, albeit, important dimension for middle-class employment of transnational women domestic workers. Persistent patriarchal definitions and practices of gender roles in the midst of rapid industrialisation have meant that men are not expected—especially or even by the state—to participate in childcare and other household related responsibilities (*New Straits Times*, 29 May 1998). This is clearly discernible in the latest state effort—a new programme called SOHO ("small office, home office") proposed by the Women and Family Development Ministry in 2003 to reduce middle-class dependence on transnational domestic workers. SOHO was introduced in response to a study conducted by the National Population and Family Development Board in which 13.5 per cent of working women surveyed said that they had childcare problems and that 68 per cent of this sub-group would leave their jobs if they continued to experience the problems. SOHO encourages employers to allow women to telecommute and/or to participate in "flextime/flexitime" arrangements so that they can fulfil their household and work-related responsibilities (*New Straits Times*, 5 September 2003). This programme is seen as a less costly way to retain the labour force participation of the anticipated 330,000 women (out of 3.6 million working women) workers in the economy, rather than to extend maternity leave.

The proposed SOHO programme is premised on, or leaves intact, women as the gender responsible for childcare, elderly care if applicable, as well as other household tasks such as cooking meals and doing laundry (see especially Lee, 2000; Rohana,

2001). It is important to note that state authorities' vision and plan for building a modern knowledge-based society necessitates the continued participation of middle-class women in the economy (see the following section on the state). It should not come as a surprise then that many middle-class women have transferred housework to transnational domestic workers who can perform the tasks of nanny-housekeepers.

Of interest is that transnational domestic workers have become more than substitute homemakers. Their presence contributes to the construction and maintenance of middle-class status and identity in a context of sustained economic growth that visibly has stratified Malaysian society (see especially Chua, 2000). For dual career middle-class spouses, comprehensive "round-the-clock" household help is provided by live-in transnational domestic workers who also have come to signify a distinctive or higher social status for employers (Chin, 1998; Lee, 2000). As succinctly put by the *Business Times* (10 March 2003), the "maid for the Malaysian lifestyle" has become an "indispensable linchpin of the household" in both material and symbolic dimensions. Of significance is that middle-class demands for transnational domestic workers are not driven per se by the desire to construct class status and identity, but that the construction of status and identity is implicit in employers' ability to hire transnational domestic workers who facilitate their ability to meet the challenges of maintaining families and pursuing careers at the same time. However, as will be discussed later, the middle classes' employment of transnational domestic workers does come at certain costs, particularly to women employers.

The kind of culturally-based values and expectations that may have mitigated more severe acts of mistreatment and abuse by pseudo-kin employers in the past manifestly are absent in the contemporary institution of live-in paid domestic work performed increasingly by transnational women. Whereas the *amah*, *mui tsai* and other servants of the past, in many cases, were also members of employers' larger ethnic communities, transnational domestic workers today are "aliens" or "foreigners" living in Malaysian households.

"ALIEN MAIDS": THE DANGEROUS "OTHER"?

Even though transnational domestic workers have been employed in Malaysian households since the 1970s, it is "almost impossible to estimate accurately" the total numbers by year, by immigration status (regular and irregular), by nationality and so forth (Azizah, 2001:266). As one analyst asserted, "Malaysian data systems are not transparent" (Wickramasekara, 2002:13) since the presence of transnational women and men workers have become a highly politicised issue in the multiethnic country (see the following section on the role of the state). Culled from a variety of sources, the data presented in Table 9.1, at best, are a rough approximation of regular transnational domestic workers in the country since 1985.

Escalations in the number of work permits issued, especially during the first half of the 1990s, can be traced to state implementation and clarification of immigration

267

regulations governing the entry and employment of domestic workers, i.e., the introduction of employer eligibility rules in the late 1980s followed by an extended amnesty programme for irregular domestic workers in the early 1990s (Chin, 1998; 2002). These state measures were put in place to manage the middle classes' demands for household help as the economy grew at an average rate of 8 per cent per annum. Yet, such demands did not weaken considerably despite the 1997–1998 severe economic downturn. By 2003, state officials estimated that an additional 20,000 transnational domestic workers would enter annually to seek work in Malaysian households (*Star*, 13 October 2003).

The overall costs involved in employing domestic workers of different nationalities are key to understanding persistent growth in work permits. What the data in Table 9.1 do not reveal are the percentage breakdowns according to nationality. As will be discussed below, Indonesian women have come to constitute the overwhelming majority of transnational domestic workers in Malaysia. One possible and obvious explanation for their dominance lies in cultural and religious proximities: Indonesians and Malays have shared geo-cultural histories predating colonialism, and that the majority of Indonesian women domestic workers are Muslims. Yet, this does not explain why Indonesian women are also employed increasingly by non-Malays who mostly are non-Muslims. From this viewpoint, the cultural-religious explanation is superseded by a financial explanation: of all transnational domestic workers, it is the least expensive to employ Indonesian women. The ease with which regular and irregular Indonesian women can be hired with the cheapest upfront and monthly cost outlay (e.g., administrative and employment agency fees, and monthly wages) contributes to the ever increasing numbers of Indonesian transnational domestic workers in Malaysia today.

TABLE 9.1   Total number of transnational domestic workers (based on work permits) in Malaysia, 1985–2003

Year	1985	1990[a]	1995[b]	2000[c]	2003[d]
Domestic workers	3,935	5,838	81,000	176,000	233,204

SOURCES:

a   Based on Pillai (1992).

b   Migration News, 1 December 1995, http://migration.ucdavis.edu/mn, accessed 27 October 2003.

c   "Immigration Laws: December 2001 #16: Malaysia, Singapore, Thailand", http://www.migrationint.com.au/news/adelaide/dec_2001-16mn.asp, accessed 27 October 2003.

d   *Star On-Line*, 12 October 2003.

From the 1980s to the mid-1990s, only Filipina and Indonesian women were issued work permits by the Immigration Department to perform domestic labour in Malaysian households (Pillai, 1992). Since the late 1990s however, women from other Asian countries, i.e., Thailand, Cambodia and Sri Lanka have been permitted to enter for domestic work. Nonetheless in 2001, the Ministry of Human Resources estimated that Indonesian women constituted 70 per cent of the total 155,000 (*New Straits Times*, 31 January 2002) transnational domestic workers. One year later, Indonesian women constituted 95 per cent of all transnational domestic workers (*Bernama*, 26 March 2003). There exists no available estimates of women from the Philippines, Thailand, Sri Lanka or Cambodia.[4] It can be deduced from the services offered by employment agencies that Filipinas constitute the second largest group, followed by the rest. Indonesian domestic workers have surpassed that of Filipinas largely because their market determined monthly salaries (ranging from RM300–450 (US$79–118))[5] are considerably less than that of Filipinas whose salaries (the monthly base salary being RM750 (US$197)) were determined by an earlier bilateral agreement between the sending and receiving states).[6] The corresponding qualifying minimum annual income for employers of Indonesian women (i.e., RM36,000 (US$9,474)) is approximately half of those who employ Filipinas. Further, employment agency fees are lower for those who select Indonesian women over other nationalities largely because of less expensive recruitment and transportation costs.

Given the geographic locations of Peninsular Malaysia and East Malaysia, transnational women domestic workers can arrive via sea, land or air. The majority of women who enter without appropriate work permits come from neighbouring islands/ provinces of Indonesia. In the case of Peninsular Malaysia, women can contract *taikong* (informal labour brokers or agents) who smuggle them into the country via clandestine boat landings along the coastal areas (Spaan, 1994). Indonesian domestic workers tend to come from the more rural areas of the country, and they are relatively less educated but younger than Filipinas (Jones, 2000). The age difference is mandated by Malaysian immigration regulations: a minimum age of 30 years old for Filipinas and a minimum age of 18 years old for Indonesian women. This is the result of a prevailing belief that Filipinas tend to moonlight or run away to work as prostitutes. Although Filipinas may be considered more socially desirable by employers because of their command of the English language and their knowledge of modern utilities involved in housework, they also are considered more "uncontrollable" than Indonesian women.

Over the course of the past three decades, "immigration industries" (Hugo, 1992) such as transportation, employment, banking, medical and other services-related companies, have arisen to facilitate Malaysian demands for and the employment of transnational workers. Particularly in the case of women domestic workers, they are the only category of transnational workers whose recruitment, migratory and employment processes are allowed to be handled exclusively by private sector employment agencies as opposed to the "G2G" or government to government route. In 2002, there were 230 employment agencies registered with the Immigration Department, and 120 of them were members of the Malaysian Association of Foreign Housemaid Agencies or PAPA (*New Straits Times*, 10 February 2002). The agencies, licensed by the Immigration Department and the Ministry of Human Resources, act as brokers matching potential employers with transnational domestic workers, after which they collect and submit employers' applications to the Immigration Department for hiring the domestic workers.

Transnational domestic workers do not sign contracts with their employers. Instead, domestic workers and employers respectively sign contracts with the employment agencies. Agency fees range from RM3,000 (US$790) to RM5,000 (US$1,316) that cover services rendered in addition to the costs of paying annual levies, security bonds and medical examinations for the women. Certain fees such as the annual levy and medical examinations may be and are passed on to the domestic worker in the form of deductions from her monthly salary. These are in addition to agency placement fees incurred by the domestic worker (amounting to 3–4 months of wages). Employers pay this upfront on behalf of domestic workers, who then will work uncompensated for several months in order to pay off the debt.

Although employment agencies are allowed to form their own national association (e.g., PAPA) for lobby purposes, the law prohibits transnational domestic workers from organising for their interests. During the late 1990s, PAPA lobbied the state for a standardised work contract between employment agencies and employers. According to the head of PAPA, this was rejected because the Ministry of Human Resources "would like to inculcate the entrepreneurial spirit of competition amongst agencies" (*Malaysian Business*, 1 March 2003). The entrepreneurial spirit is affirmed also by the Immigration Department's licensing requirement that employment agencies must bring in a minimum of 60 transnational domestic workers annually (*Malaysian Business*, 1 March 2003).

It has only been in the past few years, with increased newsprint reports of employer related acts of mistreatment and abuse, that PAPA has identified "best practices" for employment agencies that are inclusive of post-arrival training programmes to facilitate the women's entry into employers' homes, as well as advice for employers on managing domestic workers. Such best practices appear to forestall or make irrelevant any public discourse on the need to consider establishing a nationally recognised accreditation process for all employment agencies. On the one hand, employment agencies have made progress in addressing employer-employee relations vis-à-vis their offer of advice to employers, in addition to the implementation of training programmes for workers. Given heightened competition for clients, however, the agencies have begun to establish internet websites offering a host of services from information on transnational domestic workers to application forms. This competitive milieu cannot but encourage the commodification of women. State regulation of employment agencies has yet to cover what Tyner (1999:200) calls on-line "catalogues" of products or women's biographical information packages (including physical attributes, marital status, family history and work experience) that are published on internet websites to facilitate employer selection of domestic workers. Potential employers are able to research and purchase their "on-line products" that come with retail prices, instruction manuals and specific warranty (return or exchange) periods.

One employment company's web-site simplified potential Malaysian employers' selection of women by organising information into four columns respectively titled "Photo" (of domestic worker), "Code" (cataloguing number of file), "Retail Price" which was filled in with "RM" (presented in this manner, conceivably, to encourage potential employers to enter the website) for single women and RM3,880 (US$1,021) for married women, and "Description" of the woman's name, age, height, weight and marital status (http:///www.rcamall.com/merchant/maid, accessed 10 April 2002). Another company disclosed an obscene sense of racialising transnational women: potential employers can select a domestic worker whose command of the English language is "fair", and whose complexion is rated "fair" as opposed to "tanned" or "dark" (www.aptg.com.my, accessed 15 June 2002). Transnational domestic workers have no control over the conditions in which their personal information is packaged and published on-line.

Already preconstituted and represented as "commodities" by employment agencies, and as "alien" or "other" by immigration regulations upon arrival in Malaysia, the lack of specificity in unregulated work environments for some transnational women has led to reports of women running away from the work place and/or allegations of employer mistreatment and abuse. Approximately 23,484 women ran away from their workplace in 1999. The numbers increased to 30,122 in 2000. In the first half of 2001, approximately 6,988 women were reported to have run away (*Xinhua*, 15 August 2001). In 2003, the Deputy Home Minister stated that the top three reasons for runaway transnational women were their reluctance to work as maids, mental/physical abuse and heavy workloads. In terms of reported abuse cases, there were 50 cases in 2000, 40 cases in 2001 and 32 cases in 2002 (*Bernama*, 26 March 2003). When juxtaposed, these two sets of data imply that transnational domestic workers tend to run away from their workplace because of non-abuse related reasons. The decline in abuse cases also may be attributed to the introduction of punitive legislation against employers and/or the effectiveness of employment agencies' training programmes for domestic workers. Nonetheless, it should be noted that mistreatment or abuse by employers, if and when it occurs, may often go unreported primarily because many domestic workers are prohibited by employers from leaving the workplace or interacting with strangers. From this perspective, the decline in reported abuse cases then does not necessarily reflect actual incidences.

The nature of more sensationalised abuse cases is revealing of the dangers inherent in maintaining the status quo of live-in paid domestic work as an unregulated occupation. Transnational domestic workers have been stoned to death (*New Straits Times*, 22 February 2000), abused sexually (*New Straits Times*, 31 October 1999), forced into prostitution (*Bernama*, 31 March 2003), beaten for stealing food and neglecting to turn off the lights (*Malay Mail*, 14 August 2003), and made to live in a cage in the backyard (*Asiaweek*, 16 June 2000). This should not imply that all employers are uncompassionate

271

and uncaring individuals. There are employers who treat their domestic workers well and some even have considered transnational women as members of the family (*New Straits Times*, 7 January 2002). Yet, as one employer asserted, that which constitutes a decent work environment can be ensured to some extent when the "'good' ones [transnational domestic workers] are the intelligent, but honest, servile, unquestioning sort whose rights to dignity and respect are meekly sacrificed for a steady monthly wage" (*New Straits Times*, 7 January 2002).

Unregulated work environments help rationalise and sustain employers' demands for longer work days, the performance of a range of tasks inside and outside of the home, charging domestic workers for food and utilities and so forth. Moreover, unregulated work environments embedded in the larger public discourse focusing on runaway transnational domestic workers cannot but associate all women potentially with prostitution and related health issues of unwanted pregnancies and/or the spread of sexually transmitted diseases. Hence, the Department of Immigration requires annual medical examinations and will demand immediate deportation if transnational women test positive for any of the stated conditions. Left unsaid is that the prohibition of marriage between a transnational domestic worker and a Malaysian citizen is premised on preventing the contamination of national cultural identity.

Given that labour and immigration legislation deny transnational women the right to organise and articulate their work-related issues, some women have attempted to renegotiate their work conditions on an individualised basis reminiscent of Scott's "infrapolitical" activities (Scott, 1990) of undeclared resistance, such as shaming employers in front of guests, feigning illness to limit the length of the work day, and so forth (Chin, 1998). Of late, some transnational women's resistance to their work conditions has been alarming in terms of the level of violence involved in such acts. Reported incidences range from an Indonesian woman who stabbed and killed her female employer for abusing her (*Agence France Presse*, 15 August 2001) to the Indonesian woman who served sandwiches sprinkled with glass to her employer's son (*New Straits Times*, 8 March 2002). In other incidences, the line between retaliation and psychological disorder may be harder to distinguish, e.g., a domestic worker who sexually abused her employer's three-year-old daughter (*New Straits Times*, 21 February 2002), and another who ran away from her employer claiming abuse only to find out that her employer had videotaped the domestic worker abusing herself and the employer's sons (*Bernama*, 5 December 2001).

An important underlying issue in all of these cases is the absence of any notion that paid domestic labour constitutes work in the formal sense. The official rationale in Malaysia has been that the state "will have problems defining, for instance, their [domestic workers'] hours of work and the value of their accommodation" (*New Straits Times*, 6 June 1982). As late as 2003, the Minister of Human Resources argued that there was no need to amend the Employment Act to cover the women as workers because "a household is generally not considered a workplace" and that there was no need for contracts between employer and employee because "present arrangements worked well and that employers were satisfied with them" (*New Straits Times*, 8 May 2003).

Although existing reports of mistreatment and abuse on the part of both employers and employees ought to elicit public discussion of the nature of paid domestic work in general, and live-in domestic work performed by transnational women in particular, these issues can be and are quickly obscured by a larger and more potent perception that all transnational workers are threats to society. They are seen as the major source of social and economic problems ranging from those who have encroached on squatter land and the informal economy, to transnational women who seduce their male employers and who teach "foreign values" to employers' children (see, for example, *New Straits Times*, 21 January 1998). Transnational domestic workers then become the dangerous alien or other to be controlled for the sake of employing families and society. Their public identity as "alien maids" is the outcome of simultaneous processes of infantilisation and sexualisation within and beyond the workplace.

The migratory and employment structures shaping transnational women domestic workers' experiences in Malaysia ensure that the women can stay and work as long as their employers want them to do so, that they are not expected to gain new skills outside of domestic labour, and that they will not be able to qualify for permanent residency under most circumstances. It is necessary then to examine the role of the state in constituting transnational domestic workers as one group of flexibilised but invisible workers of 21st century Malaysia.

OPENING BORDERS, CLOSING SOCIETY: ROLE OF THE RECEIVING STATE

As noted earlier, the inflow of transnational workers occurred in two successively distinct phases of the political economy of development in Malaysia. In the earlier phase from 1970s to mid-1980s, transnational workers entered the country to fill in occupations that were vacated as a result of the confluence of increasing foreign investments in the manufacturing sector, with the state's NEP that was designed to dismantle the colonial legacy of ethnic identification with economic function and geographic space. Agriplantations hired temporary low wage men workers from the Philippines and Indonesia, whereas households employed transnational women from the same countries as their Malaysian counterparts found work in newly established electronic and garment factories.

State regulation of transnational workers began in earnest during the late-1980s in response to criticisms from various ethnic-based political parties and labour organisations (Dorall, 1989; Pillai, 1992). The earlier segmentation of the labour market according to nationality-class-gender dimensions was expanded and clarified as the state elite began implementing neoliberal-based socioeconomic restructuring policies to facilitate the free flow of capital and goods. Since then the pursuit of former Prime Minister Dr. Mahathir Mohamad's "Vision 2020" of creating a knowledge-based or Information Technology society and economy by the year 2020 has entailed not only the in-migration of skilled or "expatriate" workers for knowledge transfer, but also low wage transnational workers for the manufacturing, construction, forestry, agriplantation and services industries. By 2002 and with a ratio of one low wage transnational worker per 11 Malaysian workers, the country had one of the largest low wage transnational labour pools in the region, second only to Singapore (Jayasankaran, 2002:24; IOM, 2003:308).

To manage the growing low wage transnational population, the state's policy has been to assign different nationals to different sectors e.g., Vietnamese and Indian men workers in agriplantations only, and Indonesian women workers in paid housework only (*Star On-line*, 6 February 2002). By 2003, Memoranda of Understanding (MOUs) were signed with several labour-sending countries such as the People's Republic of China, Vietnam, Bangladesh, Pakistan, Thailand and Sri Lanka that are anticipated to fill the economy's demands for at least one million transnational workers (*Bernama*, 3 December 2003).

An MOU with the largest sending state of Indonesia was delayed in early 2004 because of disagreements concerning a variety of issues. At the time of this writing, representatives from both states have agreed in principle to sign the memorandum (*Kompas*, 24 February 2004; *Berita Harian*, 27 February 2004). Nonetheless, non-governmental organisations (NGOs) from both countries continue to voice their objections because the MOU (that specifies recruitment procedures for workers, age range, required skills levels, language proficiencies and knowledge of Malaysian culture) has failed to address the need to protect workers while in the receiving country, e.g., the absence of minimum wage levels, the absence of explicit sanctions against exploitation by employment agencies and employers, and so forth. In fact, Indonesian workers are expected to be responsible for the payment of administrative fees while employers retain the right to determine wages, benefits and work hours (www. tenaganita.net, accessed 31 January 2003; *Jakarta Post*, 11 February 2004).

The overarching principle governing MOUs is one of managing the flow and "quality" of transnational workers rather than worker rights and benefits. For Indonesian domestic workers, the proposed MOU's failure to specify minimum wages and work conditions appear to represent, if not underscore, a continuation of market-based practices. For all other categories of potential transnational workers in the public domain, however, MOUs accord them the privilege of legally working in Malaysia while approximating the status and work conditions of transnational domestic workers in the private sphere of the home.

The secondary labour market now is characterised by transnational workers on temporary contracts who can be hired and fired at will, and who are not accorded similar legal rights and benefits as citizen-workers. Importantly, the employment of transnational workers in Malaysia and elsewhere is indicative of states' efforts to "socially reconstruct" labour for a new era of unprecedented levels of capital mobility and accumulation within and beyond geopolitical borders. "Labour flexibilisation" is the euphemistic neoliberal phrase that is frequently used in reference to the processes of rendering labour less demanding in relation to capital. Given the increasingly competitive global environment, states are compelled to facilitate labour flexibilisation via policies and legislation pertaining to the establishment (or not) of minimum wages, the ability of firms to parcel-out or subcontract work (and hence to shield themselves from accountability and responsibility to workers), the right of workers to collective action, and so forth that attempt to naturalise new meanings and conditions of work.[7] To be sure, the processes of socially reconstructing labour are no longer bound by clearly delineated geopolitical borders. They are enhanced greatly instead by transnational migration: at the labour-sending end, state promotion of overseas employment mitigates the political, economic and social costs of under- and unemployment, and at the labour-receiving end, state regulation of the entry and employment of migrant workers reduces the social and economic costs of labour as it furthers the bifurcation or segmentation of labour markets.

The question remains, however, as to paid domestic work's specific relation to labour flexibilisation processes in Malaysia: it is not manifestly linked to "productive labour" because "[the] daily maintenance, and generational replacement tasks are spatially, temporally and institutionally, isolated from the sphere of production" (Vogel, 2000:158). Phrased succinctly, domestic labour is situated in the private or domestic domain of the house, and since it is concerned exclusively with activities that allow formal workers to "go to work", then it cannot be treated as "work" because it does not produce "use value" that can be "exchanged" in the market. In Malaysia and elsewhere, the Employment Act's failure to designate domestic workers as formal workers only reaffirms the belief that the house is not a workplace subject to labour regulations.

What the above rationale ignores is that the performance of domestic labour (buying and cooking food, cleaning house, caring for children/elderly, and so forth) is necessary labour that frees formal workers "to live" in order "to work" for wages. As many peoples find themselves working more and earning less in this era of labour flexibilisation, the allocation of time and energy to performing domestic labour can be reduced significantly. Clearly, in some advanced industrialised countries, workers have come to rely on childcare centres and/or house-cleaning firms, while in other countries including Malaysia, household responsibilities are being transferred to transnational women who previously were caught in cycles of joblessness or underemployment in their home countries.

Given that the institution of live-in paid domestic work remains unregulated in Malaysia, then the expansion of neoliberal flexibilisation processes in the formal economy is predicated partly on the continued presence of transnational domestic workers in the household. Specifically, the employment of transnational domestic workers has been linked intimately to the state's pronatalist National Population Policy (NPP). Introduced in 1984, the NPP encouraged women to have between three and five children if they could afford to do so in order to increase the national population (a target of 70 million within 115 years) as a key way to sustain economic growth.

Hence, the NPP indicated an expansion of a specific gender-class intersection in the ideological basis of the state as legislation governing citizenship, income tax benefits and deductions, as well as employment, encouraged middle-class women primarily to be reproducers and nurturers of future generations of citizens.

Since then, the labour needs of the economy have helped ensure that the in-migration of domestic workers from neighbouring Asian countries facilitates middle-class women's ability to work outside the home without undermining state construction of its "caring family" as the social foundation for Vision 2020's modern society (Chin, 1998). Immigration regulations since the 1990s are premised on and seek to naturalise the dual career based middle-class nuclear family: potential employers of transnational domestic workers must furnish proof of specified minimal annual incomes, together with marriage and children's birth certificates. Single applicants can qualify only if they provide evidence of one or more elderly parents who require assistance in the household.

Only women can enter the country as paid domestic workers. They are subject to many immigration regulations that cover other categories of workers, e.g., authorisation to work only for a designated employer, and the prohibition against collective bargaining. Yet, women domestic workers are exempt from terminal contracts as their work permits are renewable every two years for an indefinite period of time. While transnational women may benefit from this specific regulation, nonetheless they are subject to state discipline of their physical bodies. They are required to undergo annual medical examinations to be conducted only by the state authorised medical consortium, FOMEMA (Foreign Workers' Medical Examination Monitoring Agency) that was established in 1997. Similar to other categories of transnational workers, they are tested for communicable diseases: HIV/AIDS, tuberculosis, sexually transmitted diseases, hepatitis A and B, urine cannabis, urine opiates, cancer and epilepsy. However, women must undergo an additional medical examination, i.e., the annual pregnancy test (costing an additional RM10 (US$3)). FOMEMA-authorised doctors must report the examination results to the authorities. Deportation within 24 hours is undertaken upon detection of pregnancy or failure of any other medical test. The emphasis is on immediate deportation as opposed to treatment of the medical condition.

Immigration regulations have had uneven, if not contradictory effects on transnational women's experiences in Malaysia. Women can be and have been rendered "illegal" under a variety of unanticipated conditions. For example, they are considered to have transgressed the conditions of entry and employment if, upon arrival, they are transferred by employment agencies to different employers; if their employers make them work in households of relatives, offices or restaurants; and if their passports are held by employers and they fail to furnish it at the request of Police or Immigration officials. The women become illegal also if their employers collect fees from them but then fail to apply for work permit renewals; if they become pregnant as a result of sexual assault by their men employers or strangers; and/or if they run away from abusive employers (Fernandez, 1997; Shamsulbahriah, 1998; Spaan et al., 2002).

Intensified newsprint reports of employer-related abuse in 2002–2003 have led to the introduction of two major state measures. The first measure tried to address abuse by regulating employer selection of domestic workers. In March 2003, the labour-sending state of Indonesia responded to reported abuse cases of women nationals in labour-receiving countries such as Saudi Arabia, Singapore and Malaysia, by implementing a temporary freeze on the out-migration of domestic workers. At the very same time in Malaysia, immigration officials publicly announced that the Department considered prohibiting non-Muslim employers from hiring Muslim domestic workers as some non-Muslim employers had contravened the terms of their contract by prohibiting Indonesian domestic workers from praying at specific times of the day, as well as forcing them to handle forbidden food items such as pork (*New Straits Times*, 12 March 2003). This proposed regulation was met with vehement complaints from PAPA and employers. Although framed partly in terms of resistance against state enforced discrimination, an underlying issue was the proposed regulation's financial cost to employment agencies and employers, especially since over 90 per cent of transnational domestic workers were Indonesian women. As asserted by the Vice-President of PAPA, "[m]any families no longer favoured maids from the Philippines, who have to be paid higher wages, while Sri Lankans and Thais preferred employment in countries with higher pay such as Saudi Arabia, Hong Kong and Taiwan". Not only would employers have to incur higher costs for purchasing the labour of domestic workers from other nationalities, the regulation potentially could cause the collapse of many employment agencies (*New Straits Times*, 22 April 2003). State authorities withdrew the proposed regulation two months later.

The second state measure, however, was introduced successfully and with public support. Employers who failed to pay monthly wages to their domestic workers would be subject to a one- to two-year ban on employing transnational women. Employers who were found guilty of emotional or verbal abuse would be subject to a two- to three-year ban. Employers who sexually/physically abused domestic workers would be banned for life from employing transnational women (*Agence France Presse*, 11 March 2003). While this kind of deterrence is necessary and timely, a recent change in immigration regulations potentially can undermine its relevance and effectiveness. In the past, transnational women who filed complaints against their employers could apply for a "special visa pass" that allowed them to remain in legal status as they awaited adjudication of their cases in the judicial system or by the Labour Department. In 2003, however, the Immigration Department changed its policy on the visa: transnational workers now must await their cases in detention camps and applications for new work permits will not be approved while their cases are pending (www.tenaganita.net, accessed 31 January 2003). As a consequence, transnational domestic workers are punished for filing complaints against abusive employers or employment agencies (www.wao.org, accessed 15 January 2003). Even though immigration regulations may be designed to clarify and ensure orderly entry and employment conditions, they can and do have the exact opposite effect when their implementation occurs without consideration for the many ways in which transnational women become illegal and/or are made to bear the burden of contradictory policies.

On the international arena, the primary focus has been on the need to stem irregular migration. As such there have been various regional fora designed to deal with the topic and related issues including the 1996 Manila Process, the 1996 Intergovernmental Asia-Pacific Consultation on Refugees and Displaced Persons, the 1999 Bangkok Declaration on Irregular Migration, and the 2000 Asian Regional Initiative against Trafficking (Lee, 2003). Discernibly missing is dialogue and consensus on managing regular migration. The Malaysian state assumes a similar stance to other labour-receiving states in their refusal to be signatories to existing international conventions governing the rights of regular transnational workers: the 1949 International Labour Organisation (ILO) Convention No. 97 concerning Migration for Employment; the 1974 ILO Convention No. 143 concerning Migration in Abusive Conditions and the Promotion of Equality and Opportunity and Treatment of Migrant Workers; and the 1990 (United Nations) UN International Convention on the Protection of the Rights of All Migrant Workers and Members of Their Families (in force since 1 July 2003). The UN convention is the most comprehensive convention that stipulates common standards for recognising the rights of transnational workers and their families including the ability to file complaints against the signatory country. The unspoken belief is that to accord citizen rights and benefits to transnationals in a multiethnic country like Malaysia not only will increase economic costs (thus undermining a key rationale for encouraging the employment of low wage transnationals) but potentially destabilise the social fabric of society. In the same vein, although the Malaysian state is a signatory—with reservations on specific articles—to the UN Convention for the Elimination of All Forms of Discrimination against Women (CEDAW) in 1995, women's rights as designated in the Convention are deemed inapplicable to transnational women domestic workers because of their status as aliens in the country.

THE CHALLENGES OF INTERRELATED LIVES: KEY ECONOMIC, SOCIAL AND HEALTH ISSUES

Transnational domestic workers' presence in Malaysia highlights a number of key economic, social and health related issues. It can be said that the Malaysian economy offers them opportunities to earn wages that can be remitted to sustain households in labour-sending countries. At the very same time that domestic workers facilitate middle-class women's participation in the building of a knowledge based society, they also benefit a wide cross-section of the economy. At ports of entry/exit, the women generate revenue for ground, sea and air transportation companies (e.g., in the states of Johor, Melaka, Negeri Sembilan, Penang and Selangor). Especially for Filipinas who are given rest days, their consumption of food and other goods and services contribute to the revenue of large, medium and small-scale consumer industries.

278

While it is extremely difficult to estimate the total economic value derived from transnational domestic workers, a review of administrative fees, at the very least, can illustrate baseline revenue generated from their entry and employment in the country (Table 9.2). Assuming a conservative estimate of 200,000 regular transnational domestic workers in 2003, the revenue from annual levy fees alone would have been RM72,000,000 (US$18,947,368).

It is also difficult to ascertain the relationship between revenue gained from annual levy and other fees, with that of transnational domestic workers' remittances to their families in home countries as there are no available data on remittances according to the category of transnational workers. State officials estimate that RM3 billion (US$790 million) are remitted annually (*Agence France Presse*, 19 February 2002). However, official estimates only account for transfers via financial institutions (Azizah, 2001:270). Unless available data are released and/or data collection methods are clarified and standardised, it is impossible to determine the relative percentages of remittances even according to the two major categories of the professional/"expatriate" and the low wage transnational worker.

During the 1997–1998 economic crisis, transnational remittances became an issue in the midst of public discourse on foreign exchange losses. One consequence was the

TABLE 9.2   Administrative fees per transnational domestic worker in Malaysia

	Administrative fees per transnational domestic worker	
A	Annual levy	RM360 (US$95)[a]
B	Visa fee	RM15 (US$4)[b] (RM36/US$9.50 for Filipinas)
C	Work permit fee	RM60 (US$16)[c]
D	Processing fee	RM10 (US$3)[d]
E	Annual medical exam	RM190 (US$50)[e] (charged by FOMEMA)

SOURCES:

a In October 2003, the Immigration Department announced that it would collect levies and other fees every two years instead of every year: levy + visa + work permit + processing fee = RM445 x 2 = RM890 (*Star On-Line*, 12 October 2003).

b Agency Pekerjaan Career Focus Sdn. Bhd., http://www.careerfocus.com.my/phcosts.html, accessed 23 September 2003.

c Agency Pekerjaan Career Focus, Sdn Bhd., http://www.careerfocus.com.my/indoncosts.html, accessed 23 September 2003.

d Magnificent Communications, Lawyermen Web Portal, 2001, http://www.lawyerment.com.my/library/doc/empl/hr/1000000-4.shtml 2001, accessed 23 September 2003.

e FOMEMA Sdn Bhd., 2000, http://www.fomema.com.my/faq.htm, accessed 23 September 2003.

introduction of mandatory employee contributions to the Employment Provident Fund as a way to mitigate the outflow of currency. Transnational domestic workers were exempted from this requirement. Still, the women were implicated in an overall fear of Malaysian children's growing ignorance of national cultural values, i.e., children were being socialised into the "foreign" values of transnational women.[8] Letters to newspaper editors called for employers to "learn to cope without foreign maids" (*New Straits Times*, 21 January 1998) and argued that "re-engineering our chores can reduce dependence on maids" (*New Straits Times*, 6 November 1997). Such advice proffered in public not only constructs transnational domestic workers as the overt source of contaminating the younger generations but significantly, public discourse indicts women employers for failing to better socialise their children. Given the sociocultural and economic pressures of pursuing consumption oriented middle-class lifestyles, it is not surprising that in a study conducted by the All-Women's Action Society of Malaysia (AWAM), 90 per cent of abuse cases could be traced to women employers (*Interpress Service*, 25 February 2003). Despite the fact that the majority of women employers are active in the economy, they still are expected to be responsible—directly or indirectly—for the performance of domestic labour. Indeed, one outcome is that "sometimes when there is conflict between husband and wife, or between parents and children, there is this aspect where you just want to let go, and you let go on the most vulnerable person in the house ... and usually it's the maid" (*New Straits Times*, 7 January 2002).

Another outcome of household managerial responsibilities has been surveillance or disciplinary strategies designed to control the activities and movements of transnational women within and beyond the home (e.g., retaining passports, monitoring visitors/ phone calls). Transnational women's presence in households is characterised by a lack of privacy and fear on the part of employers, e.g., fear of being financially penalised by the state for runaway domestic workers, and of domestic workers spreading contagious diseases contracted from beyond. As ascertained in Healey's (2000) analysis of letters to newsprint editors, Malaysian employers and the public-at-large find themselves in ambiguous positions of having to rely on transnational domestic workers but fearing them at the same time.

Lost in this larger context are understandings of, and responses to, the mental and physical health issues of transnational domestic workers. Since health insurance coverage is not required as a condition of work, the women are expected to pay double fees for medical consultation and/or hospitalisation because of their immigration status as temporary alien workers. NGOs report that because of the fear of deportation and/or to save money, transnational women tend to self-medicate which potentially worsens their medical conditions. Private medical practices in Penang have estimated that at least 30 abortion cases are performed every month on transnational women, the majority of whom are Indonesians. The abortion costs an average RM100–300 (US$26–79) per person (*Interpress Service*, 25 January 2002).

There are no specific medical examinations covering transnational women's mental health. The responsibility is assumed by PAPA and employment agencies that offer advice on dealing with the women's cultural adaptation to employing households and society. It is expected that somehow employers can and are able to differentiate between psychological symptoms arising from cultural adaptation and that of the more serious psychological disorders. Although several Malaysian NGOs offer counselling and referral services to transnational domestic workers, the women's access to NGOs depends on their knowledge of the services, their ability to leave the workplace and, to be sure, NGO-state relations.

CHALLENGING PLACE-BASED CITIZENSHIP RIGHTS IN AN ERA OF MIGRATION: NGOS AND CIVIC ACTIVISM

For the past three decades, the Malaysian state has applied existing repressive legislation that signals its intolerance of discourses and activities emanating from civil society which highlight irrationalities or inconsistencies in policies (Gurowitz, 2000; Chin & Tiwon, 2002; Weiss, 2003). Operating within this context, NGOs specialising in human rights, democracy and social justice (ALIRAN or National Consciousness Movement, and SUARAM or Voice of the Malaysian People), women's issues (WAO or Women's Aid Organisation, and AWAM), and workers' rights (Tenaganita, and MTUC or Malaysian Trade Unions Congress) have called for the establishment of economic, political, social and health rights for transnational domestic workers. Examples of the most prominent NGOs that engage in service delivery and advocacy efforts on behalf of transnational domestic workers are Tenaganita and WAO. In terms of service delivery, both organisations have offered shelter, legal representation and medical referrals for transnational women, and both have designed protocols that involve sheltering abuse transnational women and facilitating the processes involved in filing complaints and civil suits.

Oftentimes however, their ability to deliver services to transnational women is dependent on not appearing to politicise issues, as well as their ability to negotiate effectively among different state agencies such as the Immigration Department, Ministry of Human Resources, Labour Department and the Police, to resolve allegations of employer or agency-related mistreatment and abuse. The seven-year ordeal of the trial of Irene Fernandez, head of Tenaganita, is revealing of state authorities' response to what is perceived as direct confrontation. Fernandez released a report in 1996 on the conditions of transnational worker deportation camps in Malaysia: the report was read as a frontal assault on the state. Consequently, she was charged with publishing "false news" under the Printing Presses and Publications Act. In October 2003, the trial was resolved in favour of the state, and Fernandez was sentenced to a one-year prison term. The state's response thus clearly delimited the boundaries and nature of acceptable discourse with regard to the subject of transnational workers. The experiences of WAO, its ability and inability to render support to abused transnational domestic workers who seek shelter, also indicate that what can be considered acceptable discourse is evaluated on a case by case basis, as well as the extent to which contradictions in immigration regulations can be resolved among the different state agencies (www.wao.org.my, accessed 15 January 2003).

In the light of that which can be considered state enclosure on legitimate space for civic activism, both NGOs have developed regional and transnational alliances with their non-Malaysian counterparts to pursue policy, research, and educational advocacy on behalf of transnational domestic workers. An example is Tenaganita's success in establishing the CARAM Asia (Coordination of Action Research on AIDS and Mobility) network. Today, CARAM Asia has programmes designed to pursue initiatives and interventions in reducing HIV/AIDS within transnational populations in South and Southeast Asian countries. WAO also is part of a national and internationally based network of NGOs that monitor the Malaysian state's compliance with CEDAW. Overall, the regional and transnational alliances developed by Tenaganita, WAO and other Malaysian NGOs have the potential to exert pressure on the state via collective lobbying of regional (e.g., Association of Southeast Asian Nations, ASEAN) and international (e.g., UN and ILO) organisations to address the absence of transnational worker labour rights. Their ability to affect substantive change in policy and legislation will depend on a two-pronged strategy of negotiating among different state agencies, together with foregrounding issues at regional and transnational levels and organisations.

ROUTE TO A DIFFERENT BUT BETTER FUTURE?

Given the complex and interrelated issues that have come to characterise transnational domestic workers' entry and employment in Malaysia, efforts to address one dimension necessitate addressing related dimensions. For example, state efforts to reduce the middle classes' dependence on transnational domestic workers require more than enforcing legislation on childcare centres and/or the construction of homes for elderly care. It necessitates public discourse on norms governing gender relations and the division of labour within households. The creation of "caring families" also must target male employers and their relationship to housework. Until then, it can be expected that the middle classes will continue to demand the domestic labour of transnational women.

Many issues concerning employer-related mistreatment and abuse of transnational domestic workers can be addressed effectively if the Employment Act is amended to consider maids or servants as workers. The designation of domestic workers as workers per se with labour rights and benefits carries with it the potential of encouraging more local women to participate in live-in and day work. The state ought to implement a standardised contract of employment signed between transnational women and their employers specifying terms of work and so forth. Concomitantly, amending immigration regulations to prevent women falling out of legal status if and when they lodge complaints for work-related incidents can address an existing contradiction that has prevented some women from doing so. Enforcement of immigration regulations should be consistently applied not only to transnational women but also to employers and employment agencies. Oversight of employment agencies should be extended to clarify what may and may not be considered best practices in the cyberspatial marketing of transnational domestic workers.

The state's interests in managing an ever-growing transnational worker population can be better served by adopting a less aggressive and repressive stance toward NGOs involved in service delivery and advocacy efforts as the latter are frontline organisations most familiar with a range of issues related to transnational workers in the country. Particularly since Malaysian employment of transnational domestic workers continues to involve a variety of key stakeholders, the state can benefit from the establishment of a permanent taskforce. Taking into consideration the fact that transnational workers are not legal citizens of the country, such a permanent taskforce should comprise representatives from NGOs, PAPA, and state agencies such as the Immigration, Labour and Police Departments, the Ministry of Human Resources and the Ministry of Health. This kind of taskforce is better suited to highlighting linkages, identifying and coordinating issues, and recommending policy changes that can protect transnational workers and society at the same time.

Ultimately, the Malaysian state's ability to limit or decrease the regular and irregular transnational worker population and to ensure its welfare is dependent partly on the economic health and out-migration policies of labour-sending states. To this end, continued regional dialogue on regular and irregular migration is a pre-requisite to possible coordination and action. A necessary first step will be labour-receiving states'—including Malaysia's—accession to the UN Convention on the Protection of All Migrant Workers and Members of Their Families. To do so is to insist that labour flexibilisation processes in Malaysia and elsewhere will not be allowed to strip the region of its humanity.

NOTES

1   The author wishes to thank Brenda Yeoh, Shirlena Huang and other reviewers for their critical and constructive comments on earlier drafts of this chapter, as well as Caroline Low for her research assistance.

2   The numbers do not take into consideration irregular transnational domestic workers. Irregular migration from Indonesia to Malaysia constitutes the second largest flow of irregular migration in the world, after that of the Mexico-United States flow (see Liow, 2003).

3   The 1984 Act was implemented on the heels of a survey conducted in 1982 by the Ministry of Social Welfare (renamed as the Department of Social Welfare that currently is housed in the Ministry of National United and Social Development). The survey findings were a cause of alarm as the majority of the 537 crèches had no adequate basic facilities such as kitchens and toilets, few stimulating activities for children and no programmes for parental involvement. The Act stipulated mandatory registration, basic facilities and so forth (Sayed, 1993).

4   In 2003, 98 per cent of 3,000 Sri Lankan migrants were women domestic workers (*Business Times*, 13 March 2003).

5   At the currency exchange rate of RM3.8 to US$1.

6   In 1997, the Philippine state proposed raising the minimum monthly wage for women from RM500–RM750 (US$132–197). The Malaysian state responded by freezing the intake of Filipinas (*New Straits Times*, 11 September 1997). The freeze was lifted following complaints from employers and employment agencies.

7   For data on women and national-level labour flexibilisation processes in different regions of the world, see Standing (1999).

8   When placed within the context of varying versions of the "Asian values" debate since the 1990s, public discourse on the fear of future generations being "contaminated" by transnational domestic workers cannot but reveal a particularly nationalised, class-based and gendered response that continues to segregate the international from the national (and the household). While all women may be considered the guardians of cultural identity—of Asian cultural values—working class transnational women in labour-receiving countries do not qualify in this instance.

REFERENCES

Agence France Presse. Various issues.

Agency *Pekerjaan* Career Focus *Sdn. Bhd.* n.d.a. http://www.careerfocus.com.my/phcosts .html. Accessed 23 September 2003.

Agency *Pekerjaan* Career Focus *Sdn. Bhd.* n.d.b. http://www.careerfocus.com.my/indoncosts .html. Accessed 23 September 2003.

Armstrong, M. J. 1990. Female household workers in industrializing Malaysia. In *At Work in Homes: Household Workers in World Perspectives*. Edited by R. Sanjek & S. Cohen. Washington, D. C.: The American Anthropological Association, 146–63.

Asiaweek. 2000. 16 June.

Australia Immigration Visa Services. 2001. *Immigration Laws: December 2001 #16: Malaysia, Singapore, Thailand*. http://www.migrationint.com.au/news/adelaide/dec_2001-16mn.asp. Accessed 27 October 2003.

Azizah, K. 1986. The squatter women and the informal economy: A case study. In *Women and Work in Malaysia*. Edited by A. Y. Hing & R. Talib. Kuala Lumpur: Department of Anthropology and Sociology, University of Malaya; University of Malaya's Women's Association; Asian and Pacific Development Centre, 46–60.

————. 2001. Integration of foreign workers and illegal employment in Malaysia. In OECD Proceedings, *International Migration in Asia: Trends and Policies*. Paris, France: OECD, 113–35.

Berita Harian. 2004. 27 February.

Bernama. Various issues.

Business Times. Various issues.

Chaplin, D. 1978. Domestic service and industralization. *Comparative Studies in Sociology*, 1, 91–127.

Chin, C. B. N. 1998. *In Service and Servitude: Foreign Female Domestic Workers and the Malaysian 'Modernity' Project*. New York: Columbia University Press.

———. 2002. The 'host' state and the 'guest' workers in Malaysia: Public management of migrant labour in times of economic prosperity and crisis. *Asia Pacific Business Review*, 8 (4), 19–40.

Chin, C. B. N. & S. C. Tiwon. 2002. Capital, crises and chaos: Malaysia and Indonesia in an age of globalization. In C. N. Murphy. *Egalitarian Politics in the Age of Globalization*. Basingstoke: Palgrave, 145–73.

Chua, B. H., ed. 2000. *Consumption in Asia: Lifestyles and Identities*. London: Routledge.

Coser, L. A. 1973. Servants: The obsolescence of an occupational role. *Social Forces*, 52(1), 31–40.

Dorall, R. 1989. Foreign workers in Malaysia: Issues and implications of recent illegal economic migrants from the Malay world. In *The Trade in Domestic Helpers: Causes, Mechanisms and Consequences*. Edited by Asian Pacific and Development Centre. Kuala Lumpur: Asian Pacific and Development Centre, 287–313.

Ehrenreich, B. & A. R. Hochschild, eds. 2003. *Global Woman: Nannies, Maids, and Sex Workers in the New Economy*. New York: Henry Holt and Company.

Fawcett, J. T., S. E. Khoo, & P. C. Smith, eds. 1984. *Women in the Cities of Asia: Migration and Urban Adaptation*. Boulder: Westview Press.

Fernandez, I. 1997. Migrant workers and employers in Malaysia. *Asian Migrant*, 10(3), 94–7.

FOMEMA *Sdn Bhd*. 2000. http://www.fomema.com.my/faq.htm. Accessed 23 September 2003.

Gaw, K. 1991. *Superior Servants: The Legendary Cantonese Amahs of the Far East*. Singapore: Oxford University.

Gurowitz, A. 2000. Migrant rights and activism in Malaysia: Opportunities and constraints. *Journal of Asian Studies*, 59(4), 863–88.

Healey, L. 2000. Gender, 'aliens', and the national imaginary in contemporary Malaysia. *SOJOURN*, 15(2), 222–54.

Hing, A. Y. 1984. Women and work in West Malaysia. *Journal of Contemporary Asia*, 14(2), 204–18.

Hondagneu-Sotelo, P. 1994. Regulating the unregulated?: Domestic workers' social networks. *Social Problems*, 41(1), 50–64.

Hugo, G. 1992. Women on the move: Changing patterns of population movement of women in Indonesia. In *Gender and Migration in Developing Countries*. Edited by S. Chant. London: Belhaven, 174–96.

Interpress Service. Various issues.

IOM. 2003. *World Migration 2003: Managing Migration, Challenges and Responses For People On The Move*. Geneva: International Organisation for Migration.

Jakarta Post. 2004. 11 February.

Jamilah, A. 1992. *Women and Development in Malaysia*. Petaling Jaya: Pelanduk Publications.

Jayasankaran, S. 2002. Wanted: More workers. *Far Eastern Economic Review*, 12 (September), 24–5.

Jones, S. 2000. *Making Money off Migrants: The Indonesian Exodus to Malaysia*. Hong Kong: Asia.

Khoo, K. J. 1992. Grand vision: Mahathir and modernization. In *Fragmented Vision: Culture and Politics in Contemporary Malaysia*. Edited by J. S. Kahn & F. K. W. Loh. Sydney: Allen & Unwin, 44–76.

Kompas. 2004. 24 February.

Kratoska, P. H. 1982. Rice cultivation and the ethnic division of labour in British Malaysia. *Comparative Studies in Society and History*, 24(2), 280–314.

Lai, A. E. 1986. *Peasants, Proletarians and Prostitutes: A Preliminary Investigation into the Work of Chinese Women in Colonial Malaya*. Research Notes and Discussion Papers No. 59, Singapore: Institute for Southeast Asian Studies.

Lee, C. C. 2003. International labour migration and social development. Paper presented at the Expert Group Meeting on Assessing Regional Implementation of Commitments from the World Summit for Social Development, Bangkok: Economic and Social Commission for Asia and the Pacific, 16–18 September in Bangkok, Thailand.

Lee, M. W. Y. 2000. Gendered transmigration and extended motherhood. Paper presented at the Conference on International Migration: New Patterns, New Theories, Nottingham Trent University, 11–13 September in Nottingham, UK.

Liow, J. 2003. Malaysia's illegal Indonesian migrant labour problem: In search of solutions. *Contemporary Southeast Asia*, 25(2), 44–64.

Malay Mail. 2003. 14 August.

Malaysian Business. 2003. 1 March.

Magnificent Communications, Lawyermen Web Portal. 2001. http://www.lawyerment.com. my/library/doc/empl/hr/1000000-4.shtml 2001.

Migration News. 1995. 1 December, http://migration.ucdavis.edu/mm. Accessed 27 October 2003.

Milkman, R., E. Reese, & B. Roth. 1998. The macrosociology of paid domestic labor. *Work and Occupations*, 25(4), 483–510.

New Straits Times. Various issues.

Ong, A. H. 1987. *Spirits of Resistance: Capitalist Development in Malaysia*. Albany: State University of New York Press.

Pillai, P. 1992. *People on the Move: An Overview of Recent Immigration and Emigration in Malaysia*. Kuala Lumpur: Institute for Strategic and International Studies.

Ramasamy, P. 1997. *Plantation Labour, Unions, Capital and the State in Peninsular Malaysia*. Kuala Lumpur: Oxford University Press.

Rohana, A. 2001. *Domestic Work and Servitude in Malaysia*. Hawke Institute Working Paper Series No. 14, Hawke Institute, University of South Australia.

Sayed, A. R. M. 1993. Parental involvement in childcare centres: A Malaysian experience. *Jurnal Kebajikan*, 15(2), http://www.kempadu.gov.my/jkm/jurnal/dis%2093/dis_93_2.htm. Accessed 20 September 2003.

Scott, J. C. 1990. *Domination and the Arts of Resistance: Hidden Transcripts*. New Haven: Yale University Press.

Shamsulbahriah, K. A. 1998. The constant flux, the mobile reserve and the limits of control: Malaysia and the Legal Dimensions of International Migration. In *Migration and Citizenship in the Asia Pacific: Legal Issues*. Edited by P. Brownlee. Asia Pacific Migration Research Network Working Paper No. 5, Wollongong, Australia: APMRN Secretariat.

Spaan, E. 1994. Taikongs and calos: The role of middlemen and brokers in Javanese international migration. *International Migration Review*, 28(1), 93–113.

Spaan, E., T. van Naerssen, & G. Kohl. 2002. Re-imagining borders: Malay identity and Indonesian migrants in Malaysia. *Tijdschrift voor Economische en Sociale Geografie*, 93(2), 160–72.

Standing, G. 1999. Global feminization through flexible labour: A theme revisited. *World Development*, 27(3), 583–602.

Star. Various issues.

Star On-Line. Various issues. www.thestaronline.com.

Syed, H. A. 1977. *The Myth of the Lazy Native: A Study of the Image of the Malays, Filipinos and Javanese from the 16th to the 20th Century and its Function in the Ideology of Colonial Capitalism*. London: Frank Cass.

Tyner, J. A. 1999. The web-based recruitment of female foreign domestic workers in Asia. *Singapore Journal of Tropical Geography*, 20(2), 193–209.

Vaughan, J. D. 1879. *The Manners and Customs of the Straits Chinese*. London: Oxford University Press.

Vogel, L. 2000. Domestic labor revisited. *Science & Society*, 64(2), 151–71.

Weiss, M. 2003. Transnational activism by Malaysians: Foci, tradeoffs and implications. In *Transnational Activism in Asia: Problems of Power and Democracy*. Edited by N. Piper & A. Uhlin. London: Routledge, 129–48.

Wickramasekara, P. 2002. *Asian Labour Migration: Issues and Challenges in an Era of Globalisation*. International Migration Papers No. 57. Geneva: International Labour Office.

Xinhua. 2001. 15 August, www.xinhuanet.com.

10

"Burmese" Housemaids[1] as Undocumented Workers in Thailand

MIKA TOYOTA

THE SHIFT FROM THAI HOUSEMAIDS TO FOREIGN HOUSEMAIDS

Domestic service is the most common job for young single females like us. In fact, there are not many choices for us. I actually finished high school in Burma, but as I had not gone to school in Thailand, I have no certificate to prove my educational status, consequently a lot of job possibilities are closed to me. For example, to work at a department store requires a high school leaving certificate, but not having one means that I am not entitled to work in such formal occupations (a 20-year-old Lisu woman).[2]

Historically, domestic servants in Thai society were treated as a part of the "family"[3] and performed domestic work in return for room and board. Among the urban middle classes in Thailand, employing young unmarried Thai girls from rural areas such as the northeast part of Thailand as housemaids used to be common practice. For these girls, however, domestic service was not a preferred occupation and as soon as other opportunities became available, such as in the booming textile industry and commercial sector in the 1970s–90s, they left. As Mills (2002) notes, what often motivates Thai women from rural areas to leave their home villages is the desire for *thansamay* (meaning "modern" in Thai) status and a commodified urban lifestyle, and to be able to exercise a degree of personal autonomy (Hugo, 2000). Working in new modern industries—textile factories, service industries, departmental stores, and the like—is regarded as being in a "modern occupation" which satisfies these desires, unlike domestic service which, lacking money and status, does not.

By the end of the twentieth century, however, domestic service continued to persist as a common occupation in Thailand. It is estimated that approximately 158,000 housemaids were employed in 1997, increasing to 250,000 in 2000 (Paitoonpong et al., 2002:2). Estimates given by the Department of Labour Welfare and Protection within the Ministry of Labour and Social Welfare put the number of Thai housemaids employed each year during 1991–2000 at approximately 200,000,

288

but this figure only takes into account the numbers employed in Bangkok and some of the other large cities. According to a recent study (Department of Labour Welfare and Protection, 2001:43), most Thai housemaids in Bangkok continue to be women (89.3 per cent). The majority (71.2 per cent) are single, and originate from the Northeast region (40.2 per cent), the Central area (28.6 per cent) and the North (17.9 per cent). The same study also showed that 47 per cent of Thai housemaids considered domestic service a job of the last resort while about the same proportion said they would not choose to do such work at all (Department of Labour Welfare and Protection, 2001:83). This indicates the negative status attached to being a housemaid in Thai society in general. In fact, the term "housemaid" is considered a polite word for "servant" (Paitoonpong et al., 2002:3). While Thai housemaids today refuse to be called *khon-chai* (directly translated as "servant") or *dek-rap-chai* (directly translated as "child servant"), some employers continue to use these terms. More common among employers are the terms *khon-rap-chang-tamngan-baan* (paid houseworker), *luk-chang* (employee), *dek* (kid/girl) or *phi-liang* (nursemaid). In contrast, most housemaids use the term *mae-baan* (literally meaning a woman who takes care of a household and organises domestic chores, a term which may refer to either a housekeeper or a housewife) when asked to indicate their occupations. Most of the foreign housemaids interviewed use the term *chao-nai* (master/mistress) when referring to their employers.

Not only is household work seen to be unskilled and of no worth, it is regarded as demeaning and looked down upon as not "honourable"; hence women with social status are not supposed to perform such work. Domestic service is not seen as a proper or "formal occupation" either by employers, the state, or employees themselves. The negative status of household work is reflected in the attitude of housemaids towards their own work: "[they] are not proud of their work, they do not see worth in their work, most maids do not dare tell other people they are housemaids, so they do not speak of it and do not acknowledge the work they do as work" (Migrant Action Programme, 2001:210). It is not surprising therefore to find some housemaids referring to their "employers" as their "relatives" in order to disguise their real status. Furthermore, since being a housemaid is generally seen as a job for those of little account—something done only by people from the poorest families where parents cannot afford to send their children (daughters in particular) to school—it was observed that some parents will conceal the fact of having a daughter in domestic service.

Faced with a shortage of quality Thai housemaids, a programme called "Supply of Domestic Workers 1999" was conducted by the Department of Employment in Bangkok and a few provinces in 1999 with a budget of 1.5 million baht (about US$37,000); from the start, the programme had major problems attracting trainees and there were only 329 trainees in all (Paitoonpong et al., 2002:3). The failure of the programme reflects the pervasive perception, on the part of both employers and employees, that domestic service is not an occupation that requires any training. Indeed, people work as housemaids precisely because it requires no qualification whatsoever. The scheme was further complicated by other problems. On completing the programme, a number of trainees were not ready for work and some wanted to work only near their residences; at the same time, some employers were not prepared to pay a wage that recognised the value of training.

The reluctance of Thai women to enter domestic service created a lacuna in the domestic sphere which soon began to be filled by migrants. Since the 1970s, due to increasing political instabilities in neighbouring countries, there has been an influx of refugees and migrants, particularly from Burma[4], and this has provided the basis for the flow of foreign housemaids filling the gaps in the Thai domestic service sector. By the 1990s, there was a notable shift from the employment of Thai maids to foreign maids. Although there are no official statistics available tracing the shift in a systematic fashion, a survey in 2001 showed that the number of registered foreign housemaids had risen to 82,389 (Table 10.1), which is equivalent to approximately 40 per cent of all the housemaids in Thailand.

While the Thai state is anxious to manage and control the number of migrant workers, the demand for low-cost foreign housemaids has been steadily increasing. In particular, after the Asian economic crisis, demand escalated as both husband and wife in many Thai households found it necessary to seek paid work outside the home. Reflecting this, official statistics indicate that the number of foreign housemaids jumped from 34,283 in 1996 to 82,389 in 2001 (Table 10.1). If the number of "unregistered workers" had been included, doubtless the figure would have been even greater. Indeed, it is likely that the number of foreign housemaids might exceed that

TABLE 10.1 Registered migrant housemaids in Thailand, 1996 and 2001

Region	1996		2001		Change 1996–2001	
	Number	Percentage	Number	Percentage	Number	Percentage
Bangkok	12,929	37.7	45,130	54.8	32,201	249.1
Central	5,244	15.3	13,005	15.8	7,761	148.8
Eastern	1,984	5.8	4,313	5.2	2,329	117.4
Western	2,989	8.7	2,245	2.7	−744	−24.9
Northern	7,959	23.2	9,883	12.0	1,924	24.2
Northeastern	231	0.7	3,006	3.6	2,775	1,201.3
Southern	2,947	8.6	4,807	5.8	1,860	63.1
Total	34,283	100	82,389	100	48,106	140.3

SOURCE: Office of the Administrative Commission on Irregular Migrant Workers, 2002.

of Thai maids (see later). The high demand for non-Thai maids is also a consequence of the fact that their wages (ranging from 1,500 to 4,000 baht (US$38–US$101.30) per month according to informants interviewed in 2003) tend to be lower than those of Thai housemaids (between 2,000–5,000 baht (US$50.70–US$126.60) per month (Department of Labour Welfare and Protection, 2001)).

That "good Thai housemaids are very hard to find nowadays and even harder to keep" is the main complaint of Thai employers who find themselves turning to employing foreign housemaids instead. The difficulties in retaining a Thai housemaid vis-à-vis a foreign housemaid is also evident in the following account, given by an informant (a Lisu woman in her mid-30s) who had been working in Chiang Mai for two years at the time of the interview:

> My employer is a Chinese Thai working woman with a 10-year-old son. She used to employ two maids—one was Thai, the other foreign. I think the reason she kept one Thai maid instead of having two foreign maids was because she did not entirely trust maids from Burma. Within one year, I worked with seven different Thai maids. The longest spell was about three months and the shortest only three days. Thai maids do not have much patience. When they are not happy with their employer they quit straight away. So, again and again, the employer has to find another Thai maid. My employer is not a bad person but she likes everything to be clean and perfect. When the work is not done properly she gets angry and she can be short tempered. But after observing her for a long time I can now understand her well. So after I had worked for her for a year my employer changed her mind and asked me to find another foreign maid. Now she employs two foreign housemaids.

As a result of the economic crisis, housemaids are no longer "luxury goods" in demand only among Thai urban middle-class households; instead, less well-off families have also started employing foreign housemaids to shore up the domestic sphere as wives can no longer afford to stay at home as housewives. Household dependency on foreign housemaids now cuts across various socio-economic classes. And while the demand for housemaids has increased, the ready supply from neighbouring countries keeps the wages low and at the same time encourages further replacement of Thai maids by migrants. Attempts by the state to keep their number under control by repatriation or applying a quota system (see below) have been largely nullified by the pressure of high demand and the main effect has been to increase the number working in the "black economy". While there is a clear shift in the balance of housemaids from Thai to foreign maids, the basic profile of housemaids and the nature of the work have been relatively unchanging: those employed as housemaids in Thailand are still largely made up of young single females with low educational levels employed through informal recruitment networks.

MIGRATING ACROSS THE THAI-BURMA BORDERLANDS

Foreign housemaids in Thailand are drawn from neighbouring countries—approximately 71 per cent from Burma, 22 per cent from Laos and another seven per cent from Cambodia (Table 10.2).[5] While those from Burma are officially categorised as "Burmese migrants", many of them are not necessarily "Burman" but ethnically diverse. These non-Burmese for the most part belong to minorities concentrated along the border states (namely, Kayah, Karen, Mon, Shan, Chin, Kachi and Rakhine), often without any legal status.[6] Prior to the demarcation of national territory which accompanied the establishment of the modern nation-state, people not only crossed the border region freely but cross-border intermarriage was also not unusual. For instance, the majority of those living in Burma's Shan state are Tai-speaking people who have close historical and socio-cultural affinity with northern Thai people. Thus, it is common to find among northern Thai people that many have ancestors originally from the Shan state in Burma. Similarly, upland peoples whose kinship and trade networks spread transnationally across China, Burma, Laos and the Thai borderlands often have kin connections in Thailand (Toyota, 2000). In the context of a historically longstanding mix of diverse ethnic groups in Thailand, while officially designated as "foreign" housemaids, these notional outsiders become physically and culturally indistinguishable once they intermingle with the Thai population.

Even after national borders had been drawn, people continued to flow across the borderlands; that is, across the 2,500 kilometre-long Thai-Burma border stretching along nine Thai provinces. With only six official border-crossing points along it, it is impossible for the Thai border police to effectively control cross-border movement, particularly in the remote upland areas. During the decades from the 1970s to the

TABLE 10.2 Labour demand and quota for alien workers, and illegal workers granted work, under the Resolution of the Cabinet, 2004 (1 July–28 August 2004): The case of housemaids

	Labour demand	Quota	Who are granted
Employer	106,981	48,590	3,391
Burmese	109,525	52,298	2,872
Laotian	42,928	15,917	1,012
Cambodian	10,998	5,146	294
Total	163,451	73,361	4,178

SOURCE: Personal communication with author, Bureau of Migrant Worker Administration, Department of Employment, Ministry of Labour, Thailand.

1990s, people from Burma continued to flow into Thailand because of political unrest at home.[7] Initially, the Thai authorities took a relaxed attitude to the inflow of cheap labour, particularly during the years of booming economic development. Indeed, the "miracle" of economic development could not have been achieved without cheap foreign labour. However, as the scale of the influx started to become more visible, the state decided in 1994 to implement a regularisation policy in order to bring immigration under some form of control.

According to the official census, the estimated number of undocumented[8] non-Thai workers continued to increase with regularisation—nearly doubling in less than five years from 525,000 in 1994 to 987,000 in 1998.[9] After the economic crisis when the unemployment rate shot up from 1.5 per cent in 1997 to over four per cent in 1998, law enforcement against "illegal workers" became an issue. The estimated figure of undocumented workers in 1998 was equivalent to almost 70 per cent of Thailand's unemployment. It was therefore suggested that if the government could cut immigration, the employment situation among Thais would improve considerably (Chalamwong, 2001:306). Given this and their lack of legal recognition, "illegal migrants" became prime target for deportation. According to statistics provided by the National Security Council (NSC), 319,629 "illegal migrants" were arrested and deported in 1999, followed by another 444,636 in 2000. More than 1,000 employers who continued to hire undocumented workers after the period of grace expired were arrested and sentenced in 2000 (Chalamwong, 2001; 2002).

These strict measures aimed at controlling illegal migration created a strong sense of distrust towards the state on the part of both employers and employees. At the same time, repatriating migrant workers did not solve the problem of unemployment, as increasing numbers of local businesses and households continued trying to cut costs by hiring more low-wage illegal foreign workers from neighbouring countries. The control measures did not stop employers from hiring foreign housemaids, but simply rendered migration a more clandestine activity. In fact, tighter border control created openings for a lucrative migration industry to flourish, involving a range of individuals including, on the Thai side of the border, Buddhist monks, policemen and officials who became clandestine agents. Both sides of the border have seen the emergence of migration entrepreneurs who earn a good living facilitating border crossings and providing recruitment and placement services in the villages. For instance, an aunt of one of my informants—an Akha woman born in the Thai-Burma borderlands who became a restaurant owner after coming to Thailand and marrying a Thai national (and hence has possession of Thai identity papers)—has taken on such an entrepreneurial role.

In the early 1990s, agents used to charge a lump sum of 5,000–6,000 baht (US$125–US$150 at current rates), which included the brokerage fee, travel expenses and bribes for the Thai authorities. However, in 2003, one informant told me she had to pay altogether about 20,000 baht (US$510) to get from her village in Kachin state in Burma to Chiang Mai (Thailand) where she found a job. Another informant said,

"Thai people normally think that people from Burma are poor but, actually, really poor Burmese people can never make it to Thailand. People who get to Thailand are lucky or better-off or they borrow". For her trip she borrowed some money from her relatives but it was not enough; as a result, she also had to borrow informally from a moneylender in her village and had to start her first job saddled with debt repayments. It will take her at least a year to pay off the debt.

Among informants, the motivation in migrating often stems from a sense of family obligation (especially among daughters) in the context of impoverished family circumstances, as well as their own desire to improve life chances:

> One day, Thai officials came to stay at our village. Before they went back they asked my parents whether they were interested in sending me to Bangkok to work as a "domestic servant". That night my parents did not say much but I knew what they wanted me to do. We are poor and I felt that I should help the family. I was also a bit curious about Bangkok and wanted to go. I wanted to see what it was like to live there. I had never really liked working in the fields. It is so tiring and makes me dark[10] and dirty. But there is no alternative work in the village. There are no prospects of anything new in the future. So I decided to go (Akha woman, 16 years old at the time of migration, interviewed in August 1996).

> I started working as a domestic maid when I was ten years old. After the death of my father, we experienced real hardship. It was so difficult for my mother to look after all of us (five children). So when my older sister asked me whether I wanted to come along with her to work for a Chinese family in Thailand, I decided with little hesitation to follow her (Lahu woman, ten years old at the time of migration).

The combination of a family regime where "a desire to help the family" alongside the hope to gain personal independence and experience through migration as reflected in the above narratives has also been noted elsewhere (Yeoh et al., 2002). The importance of structural conditions in shaping migration decisions does not necessarily blunt informants' sense of their own agency in making the move; for example, when asked who made the decision to come to Thailand, almost every informant said that it was her own decision. While there is no doubt that young single females are vulnerable in a transnational labour market, it is clear that they are not simply victims of necessity but are also individuals seizing the opportunity to chart new life experiences. Some, indeed, have done well. In fact, my observations in the field reveal that some of those who used to work as domestic servants in 1997 had established their own families and by 2003, were themselves employing foreign housemaids.

On arrival in Thailand, migrant women seeking domestic service are matched with Thai employers primarily through informal clandestine market arrangements rather than formal employment agents. This means that these migrants have to rely mainly on their own networks to find a job. While not having a formal contract means that foreign housemaids have to depend solely on the generosity of their employers in negotiating wages, this is not always disadvantageous. Informal arrangements may translate into higher wages, especially where the migrant woman has a good network of friends and relatives who can help her find the right position (as in the first account below), or where an employer values particular skills such as being able to speak English or sing hymns (as in the second account below):

> I had relatives in Tacheleik. I can speak Lisu, Kachin, Burman, Tai Yai and English but when I came to Tacheleik my Thai (standard Thai) was not very good. My relatives helped me learn Thai; they also provided me with food, clothing and a place to stay. I learn about Thailand by watching Thai TV every day and helped out in their shop in Tacheleik for a while. Then I heard that a Korean Christian couple were looking for four maids. I heard that they are nice people and gave Saturdays and Sundays off. I contacted my friend who has a Thai Identification Card[11] in Mae Sai and he arranged the trip for me. I paid 5,000 baht (US$126.60), which was the fee to come to Chiang Mai. They paid us 6,000 baht (US$151.70) per month. I worked for them for two years (20-year-old Christian Kachin woman).

> When I was 12 years old, my aunt and uncle came to visit us in my home village in Burma. When they returned to Thailand they took me along with them back to their place in Chiang Mai. My family is all Christian since my grandparents' time. An American customer came to visit my aunt's shop where I helped. She needed some help to help her settle in. My English is much better than that of other Thai people and this American customer liked me. She asked me whether I was interested in working for her. She had two children, four and five years old, who needed to be looked after. Since she was a Christian missionary and seemed a good person I decided to work for her. She employed two of us, my friend and myself. I worked for her for three years until she left for the United States. Because she was a Christian she gave us a day off on Sunday. My wage at the beginning was 4,500 baht (US$113.80) a month but towards the end I was receiving 7,000 baht (US$177) a month. She liked me because I could read English and I could sing hymns to her children. I managed to send some money back home, too, through a friend who goes back and forth between Mai Sai and Tacheleik[12] (22-year-old Christian Lisu woman).

REGISTRATION OF FOREIGN HOUSEMAIDS

When Royal Decree (Revolution Order) 281 was issued on 24 November 1972 to reserve occupations for Thai people along with Article 12 of the Foreign Employment Act 1978 which specified the requirement of a work permit for aliens, housemaids were not specifically mentioned (Pantip, 1997; Paitoonpong et al., 2002:2). Based on Article 12, a Ministerial Order was issued by the Ministry of Interior to specify 27 types of occupation permits for foreigners. The occupations included "laundry work" and "labouring" (Pitsawat & Pattamaporn, 1997:54) and these categories were used to accommodate migrants who worked as "domestic servants", as had been the practice for registration purposes by some government employment service agents (Paitoonpong et al., 2002:2). While there was still no direct category to refer to "housemaids" in the law regulating the employment of foreign labour from 1978 to 1996, a Cabinet Resolution on 6 August 1996 specifically identified "housemaids" as an occupation open to migrants (Pantip, 1997:75). However, the following three registration exercises in 1998, 1999 and 2000 excluded the category of "housemaids" from those who could register to work legally (Migrant Action Programme, 2001:5). It was left to the Cabinet Resolution of 28 August 2001 to stipulate "housemaid" as a permissible occupation for migrant workers (Office of Administrative Commission on Irregular Migrant Workers, 2002).

In a recent "Registration of Irregular Immigrant Workers" exercise, the number of foreign housemaids who registered between 24 September and 25 October 2001 was 82,389, of which 73,006 (88.6 per cent) were female and 9,383 (11.4 per cent) male. Domestic service is the main type of work among registered female migrant workers in Thailand, accounting for 30 per cent of their total number. Registration rates for housemaids could arguably be one of the lowest compared to other occupations, as their workplace in the privacy of the home renders them less visible. According to the recent official statistics under the resolution of the Cabinet 2004, the total number of housemaids demanded was 163,451 but the quota was 73,361; as such, the undocumented workers who were allowed to work as housemaids from 1 July to 28 August was 4,178.

THAI EMPLOYER-FOREIGN HOUSEMAID RELATIONSHIPS

After one year of working as a domestic servant for a Thai family in Bangkok, I became fluent in Thai. I felt that there is nothing much more I could learn by staying there for any longer, so I decided to come back north to look for a job in Chiang Mai where my sister lives. I was seventeen then. When I told them I wanted to go back, my employer understood and let me go. But after a whole year of working for them they only gave me just about enough money to take a bus back to Chiang Mai. They were nice to me but they did not think that I was an employee to whom they had an obligation. They must have thought that providing food, bed and occasionally clothing was good enough for people like me from Burma. I was upset because I had no money to take back home. But what could I do? Everything was informally arranged. I was too innocent a year ago when the agent came to talk to my parents. I did not realise that I was accepting a job with no wages (Karen woman who was 17 years old at the time of entering domestic service).

I was the first-born in my family. My mother could not get pregnant for several years after me, so my father decided to take a second wife who could produce a son. The second wife soon had two sons and my father cherished them. But he treated my mother (his first wife) and me badly. My mother became ill and died when I was 14 years old. After her death, my father sometimes physically abused me and I was scared of him. Once when he got angry with me he grabbed my hands and chopped off a part of my third finger. Living with my father was like being in hell, but fortunately my brothers were very kind to me. They often brought food. Without their help I would not have survived. One day when I was 15 years old, my brother found out that my father had sold me to an agent. My brother told me not to go home but to secretly run away from the village. So I did. I decided to go to Chiang Mai. I met [my current employer,] a woman looking for a housemaid so I joined her. She bought me clothes and let me stay at her place. I do not receive a wage but she buys me occasional gifts. I feel that she saved my life and treats me like one of the family so I work hard for her. If I had not met her I could have been sold to a brothel (26-year-old Akha woman).

The two cases above show that the relationship between the Thai host family and the foreign housemaid does not necessarily follow the lines of a normative employer-employee relationship. As in the first case related above of the Karen woman who received no wages apart from board and lodging, there are also those who received as little as 500 baht (US$12.80) after a whole year's work. In these cases, since "employment" was "informal" or even "illegal", there was no legal contract which could force the employer to provide a minimum wage. In the second case of the Akha woman, while the informant was getting far less than the legal minimum wage of US$105.30 month in 1994[13] and was working seven days a week without a day off, she did not feel exploited and instead saw her "employment" as a housemaid as a major step forward. From her perspective, the warm and intimate relationship she enjoys with her employer more than made up for the lack of legal or contractual rights governing wages and working hours. It is hence not always appropriate to assess the level of exploitation on the sole basis of wages or working conditions.

Having an unpaid live-in servant is a long established practice in Thailand, and the particular nature of employer-maid relationship harks back to patron-client patterns operative in the traditional concept of the "bond servant" of the pre-colonial past (Watson, 1980; Aung Thwin, 1983; Reid, 1983a; 1983b; Terwiel, 1983; Kelly & Reid, 1998; Loos, 1999; Reynolds, 1999). Indeed, a multitude of factors and networks of relationships helped bind a very broad range of vaguely defined 'family' members together (Koizumi, 2000:255). As Reid (1983a:7) suggested:

> the imagery of bondage is most commonly that of the extended family (p.7) ... Society was held together by the vertical bonds of obligation between men. The wealth of the rich and the power of the strong, lay in the dependent man-(and woman-) power they could gather around them. For the poor and weak, on the other hand, security and opportunity depended upon being bonded to somebody strong enough to look after them (p.8).

Historically, "slavery was an integral part of the Siamese social system and it was embedded in a complex body of laws" (Terwiel, 1983:122). Servants in the household did not expect to receive monetary payment and accepted the restrictions placed upon them in return for material provisions and protection from the master. Similarly, in today's context, given the nature of a job that entails living in the home of the employer for 24 hours a day, the relationship often develops into a kind of reciprocity based on an exchange whereby the employer/master provides "protection" in the form of food, clothes and board while the maid/servant provides service in return. Dependency on the employer is particularly clear in the case of foreign maids for they normally have nowhere else to go. To leave domestic service and find other employment such as in a garment manufacturing factory or restaurant requires information networks and contacts which migrants are less likely to have compared to their Thai counterparts. As such, foreign housemaids are less likely to find other employment opportunities or move on to better paid jobs.

Given the relatively few alternative paths before them, foreign housemaids tend to accept restrictive working conditions and work hard at establishing the best possible relationship with their current employer. Living in the employer's home seriously limits the chance to meet fellow migrants or spend time with friends. Not always does the employer give a Sunday off. Nor is it usual for housemaids to be allowed to use house telephones (at best, they are restricted to receiving calls only). Days off may be limited to medical necessity or to allow for attendance to some emergency in the maid's family back home. Many foreign housemaids do not take leave at all for lack of a place to go, or because travelling back to Burma is too expensive or difficult. Foreign housemaids usually stay in their employer's house day and night, hardly daring to go out because of their "illegal" status, afraid that they may be arrested, detained or deported by the police. As a consequence, employers of foreign maids tend to perceive them positively as "attentive", "hardworking", "devoted", "diligent", "patient" and "obedient". This is echoed in Paitoonpong et al.'s (2002) finding that Thai employers prefer foreign housemaids to Thai maids as the latter are less committed, being quick to switch jobs, not only because of low wages and resentment at the low status of being "servants", but also because of the physical restrictions and lack of privacy attendant on having to live in the employer's home.

In contrast, foreign housemaids can be remarkably patient in the face of harsh working conditions, such as long hours, low wages (or sometimes no wages) and sexual abuse because they face even worse conditions back home. For them, the present is still an improvement on the past. Some employers take advantage of this:

> I worked for a northern Thai family who had two children. They used to employ one Thai maid but lately they decided to employ two foreign housemaids. As we are Tai Yai from Shan state they pitied us. They know that we suffered from the oppressive military regime in Burma. They also do not like the Burmese[14] and they think that Tai Yai people are like cousins to Thai people. I was skinny and shy, whereas my friend (the other maid) was talkative and prettier, so the employer liked her more. When the family went out they would take her with them and I got left behind to look after the house. One day when the wife and children were away, the male employer called my friend to his room. I knew what would happen and I worried about her, but she did not tell me anything and I did not dare ask her. About eight months later my friend got pregnant and then she told me that she had been having a relationship with the male employer. We did not know what to do. Then the wife

found out that my friend is pregnant. I told her that it was her husband who sexually abused her, but of course she did not believe me. Instead, she got angry and threw us out of the house (Tai Yai woman who was 17 years old at the time).

While there are very likely countless instances of sexual abuse against foreign housemaids which go unrecorded, it is important to note—as suggested in the case narrated above—that not all sexual relationships between employer and maid can be unambiguously defined as "abuse". Referring to the fact that currently there are more women than men crossing the borders as there are more informal job opportunities available for the former, an informant noted that, "if you are female, it is much easier to find a place to live, working as domestic servants or otherwise". What is obliquely implied and left unsaid is that "opportunities" are more forthcoming for women as there are many more cases of Thai men marrying migrant women from Burma than Thai women marrying poor migrant men.

Indeed, the boundary between becoming a housemaid and a wife is sometimes rather ambiguous, particularly when the employer is a single male. These men may select a potential wife from among the young, healthy and good-looking foreign maids in the household. For some (but not all) maids, a sexual relationship with the male employer may be perceived as a means to becoming a wife, a step up from being a maid as the former enjoys greater security that comes with recognised economic and socio-legal status. Indeed, whether the relationship is that of employer-employee or husband-wife is sometimes difficult to distinguish, particularly because the Thai term *mae-baan* can refer either to "housemaid" or "housewife". An informant who became the wife of her former employer said:

> I lost my father when I was only four years old and then lost my mother when I was 10 years old. I grew up at my aunt's house. When the Burmese military came to our village I ran away with my younger brother and came to Thailand in 1996. I first worked at the small factory making sweet cake. My employer liked me and introduced me to his friend, the current *chao-nai* (master). To me he is just like my father.[15] If I stayed on in Burma I might be dead by now. Here in Thailand I have a house to stay in and a child of my own to look after. I have never been to school but my child is entitled to go to school in Thailand and have a better life in the future and my daughter can look after me when I am old. Sometimes life is not easy but I can look for a better future (24-year-old Akha woman).

MIGRANT VULNERABILITIES AND LOOPHOLES OF THE REGISTRATION SYSTEM

While it is critical to reduce the vulnerability of foreign housemaids, the Thai government's main strategy of enforcing a registration system does little to help them. On the contrary, it has some negative effects. For each migrant, first-time registration costs 3,250 baht (US$82) while subsequent registration costs 1,200 baht (US$30.30).

Since foreign housemaids often do not have enough money to pay the registration fee, it is usually paid first by the employer and then deducted from the maid's wages. Coming on top of broker's fees paid first by the employer, this further increases the maid's indebtedness to her employer.

Also, even after being "registered," foreign housemaids are still technically "illegal"—their status simply shifts from "unregistered illegal" to "illegal workers who are granted work" but their "illegality" remains unchanged. There is no clear consensus about the rights of "registered-but-illegal" migrant workers. Registration confines their mobility to permitted areas only and exposes them to police harassment or fines if they travel beyond these areas. Those who have registered and then sought a work permit continue to fear repatriation when the permit expires after its validity period. If they are deported on the expiry of the work permit, they are faced with the same hazards all over again, having essentially no safe place to return to. In fact, in order to escape from an oppressive military regime in Burma the next time, they have to resort to clandestine routes requiring even higher brokerage fees as their name and face are more easily recognisable, having already been captured in the registration system.

Registration also does not necessarily provide the foreign housemaids with greater access to medical facilities or better medical protection.[16] While a medical examination is required of those wishing to apply for a work permit, often, neither employer nor employee is keen to comply. Many employees cannot afford to pay the 1,000 baht (US$25.40) deposit required while employers are generally unwilling to put up the sum. The requirement for migrant workers to purchase annual health insurance is likewise limited in its effectiveness. The decision whether to purchase health insurance is often entirely in the hands of employers who normally keep the maids' health insurance cards. As a result, most of my informants knew little about health insurance procedures and the benefits, did not know whether they had insurance coverage, and had no means of knowing how to apply.

In sum, the vulnerability of housemaids from Burma in Thailand is at least in part socially constructed by the larger institutional mechanisms at work. Loopholes in the system are compounded by the predominant perception in Thai society that rarely regards the relationship between the housemaid and her "master" as an employment contract, but as a patron-client relationship. People consider hiring a housemaid a purely "private" activity beyond the purview of the state. The policy stance adopted by the Thai government before 1996 which refused to list domestic service as an occupation subject to regulation reinforced this deeply ingrained perception and automatically rendered foreign housemaids "illegal". While the Thai government officially recognised domestic service as an occupation in 1996, policy implementation has been far from smooth. In 1998, 1999 and 2000, the government excluded the category of "domestic service" again from its migration registration scheme and once again created large numbers of "illegal" female migrants who were working as housemaids. The renewed attempt since 2001 to regulate domestic service has not been satisfactory because the gap between the state's goal and the pervasive perception of domestic service as a "private" matter has been so wide that resistance to policy regulation remains strong. Therefore, in order to address the vulnerability of housemaids in Thailand, formal policies imposed from above will not be sufficient. Instead, the larger social and historical context in which domestic service has developed needs to be taken into account and the government may consider working with grassroots agencies to address the issues from below, for example, by working to change people's perception of domestic service and by setting up a community-based monitoring system. Given the near complete paucity of non-governmental organisations in Thailand catering to housemaids' needs, encouraging the establishment of such organisations should be accorded immediate priority.

NOTES

1   I use the term "housemaid" instead of "domestic worker" to highlight the fact that domestic service in contemporary Thailand is not merely a descriptive occupational category, but a historical and socio-culturally embedded institution.

2   Long-term fieldwork was conducted by the author in North Thailand between 1994–97, supplemented by in-depth interviews in December 2003 and February 2004 in Mae Sai and Chiang Mai, Thailand. In 1996, a questionnaire survey of 1,647 (790 male, 857 female) was conducted among the border ethnic minorities from Burma and China studying or working in Chiang Mai. This was followed by ten in-depth case studies chosen to illustrate the situation of foreign domestic workers of various ethnic minorities from Burma in Thailand.

3   In pre-modern Southeast Asia, the realm of family used to be a great deal broader and more porous, with a high level of temporary and or permanent adoption. (Reid 1983a:8) These maids usually use fictive kinship terms such as *mae* (mother), *pho* (father) or *na* (aunt) when referring to their employers.

4   I use the term "Burma" instead of "Myanmar" in this paper as it is less politically loaded. In the Thai language (which is the language in which I conducted interviews with my informants), Burma/Myanmar is referred to as *Muang Pama* without distinction.

5   According to the most recent official statistics, the total quota for the domestic service sector was 73,361 (52,298 from Myanmar, 15,917 from Laos and 5,146 from Cambodia) (see Table 10.2) .

6   Myanmar has over 46 million people, half of which are ethnic Burman while the rest are ethnically non-Burman. Since 1962, due to fierce conflicts between successive military regimes and these ethnic minorities, the legal status of significant numbers of these minorities is not recognised and they are in effect without citizenship.

7   For example, large intensive forced relocation programmes were carried out in Shan state in 1996–97 by the Burmese military. Over 300,000 people from over 1,400 villages were forced to move from their home villages into relocation sites. It is estimated that over half have fled to Thailand (The Shan Human Rights Foundation, 2002).

8   The term "undocumented" is used here because the majority of foreign domestic workers are not formally recognised as workers either by the employer or by the state. The category of "domestic maid" did not exist in law and regulations on the employment of foreign

labour before 1996. The term "undocumented" instead of "illegal" is used throughout the chapter in order to indicate the unauthorised status of foreign domestic workers without criminalising them.

9   When Prime Minister Thaksin took office in early 2001, the government decided to start registering all "illegal" migrants in all areas and occupations throughout Thailand who had been in the country from 28 August 2000 or earlier. This change of policy seeks to register all who are already working in the country instead of indiscriminately "criminalising" foreign workers. Obviously, the Thaksin government is aware of the pressures from international organisations monitoring labour and human rights issues and the danger that hiring "illegal" workers for low wages and with low welfare standards could attract adverse attention and damage the country's reputation. "Illegal" migrant workers already residing and working in Thailand were told to report to the Royal Immigration Police and could apply for temporary work permits from the Ministry of Labour and Social Welfare (MOLSW) before the end of October 2001. In total, 562,527 illegal workers (79.8 per cent Burmese, 10.4 per cent Laotian and 9.8 per cent Cambodian) responded to this registration. From 1 July to 31 July 2004, the total number of registered illegal workers was 1,269,074 (71 per cent Burmese, 14 per cent Laotian and 14 per cent Cambodian).

10   In general, dark tanned skin is not considered desirable for women in Thailand

11   There are a whole range of different Minority Identification Cards issued by the Thai authority for people who fled Burma in the 1990s. For example, pink cards were issued to political refugees from Burma before 1976 and their descendants born between 1972–92; orange cards were issued in 1993–94 to "illegal" immigrants from Burma after 1976 who had their own residence in Thailand while purple cards were issued to a similar group who worked and stayed with employers; yellow cards with blue frames were issued in 1997 for displaced Thai people left behind in the Burmese territories after the new demarcation of the border; and orange cards were issued in 1994 to Tai Lue people mainly from Shan state. Orange cards were also issued in the years 1992, 1996, 1998, 1999 and 2000 as "illegal alien labour work permits".

12   Mai Sai is one of major border crossing towns in the north of Thailand, situated in the Chiang Rai province. Tacheleik is a border town across from Mai Sai in the Shan state of Burma.

13   It should be noted that the stated goal of providing low-paid workers with decent living conditions is not systematically reflected in the process of adjusting minimum wages. In practice, changes in minimum wages used to be based on changes in the Consumer Price Index but since 1990, minimum wage adjustments also depended on GDP growth in Thailand. As a result, the minimum wage has been growing faster than the average wage (International Labour Office, 2000). According to the Thailand Development Research Institute (2002), the minimum wage per day increased from 12 baht (or US$0.31) in 1973, 28 baht (US$0.73) in 1978, 66 baht (US$1.71) in 1983, 78 baht (US$2.02) in 1989, 125 baht (US$3.24) in 1993, to 162 baht (US$4.22) in 1998.

14   This view reflects the general negative perception of the Burmese in Thai society. The Burmese are considered the traditional enemy of Thai people. This popular perception was reinforced in the process of Thai nation-building.

15   The Thai employer was in his mid-fifties and the age difference between the informant and him approximates that of daughter and father.

16   While it may be claimed that government health services treat both Thai and non-Thai equally on the basis of humanitarian principles (Isarabhakdi, 2004:122), it has also been acknowledged that government health facilities have limited human and financial resources to cope with large numbers of migrants. Migrants from Burma face serious health problems, as has been documented by Caouette et al. (2000). The Thai health policy instrument tends to target the supposedly "high risk groups" such as sex workers, however; an "invisible group" such as housemaids has been largely ignored in existing health promotion programmes (Toyota, 2004).

REFERENCES

Aung Thwin, M. 1983. *Athi, Kyun-Taw, Hpayà-Kyun*: Varieties of commendation and dependence in pre-Colonial Burma. In *Slavery, Bondage and Dependency in Southeast Asia*. Edited by A. Reid. New York: St. Martin's Press, 64–89.

Caouette, T. M., K. Archavanitkul, & H. H. Pyne. 2000. *Sexuality, Reproductive Health and Violence: Experiences of Migrants from Burma in Thailand*. Nakhonprathom, Thailand: Institute for Population and Social Research, Mahidol University.

Chalamwong, Y. 2001. Recent trends in migration flows and policies in Thailand. *OECD Proceedings, International Migration in Asia: Trends and Policies*. Paris: OECD.

————. 2002. Thailand. *Migration and the Labour Market in Asia: Recent Trends and Policies*. Paris: OECD.

Department of Labour Welfare and Protection (DLWP). 2001. *A Study on Work Condition and Problems of Domestic Workers* (in Thai). Thailand: Ministry of Labour and Social Welfare.

Hugo, G. 2000. Migration and women's empowerment. In *Women's Empowerment and Demographic Processes: Moving Beyond Cairo*. Edited by H. B. Presser & G. Sen. Oxford: Oxford University Press, 287–317.

International Labour Office. 2000. *Country Employment Policy Review, Thailand*. Geneva: ILO.

Isarabhakdi, P. 2004. Meeting at the crossroads: Myanmar migrants and their use of Thai health care services. *Asian and Pacific Migration Journal*, 13(1):107–126

Kelly, D. & A. Reid, eds. 1998. *Asian Freedoms: The Idea of Freedom in East and Southeast Asia*. New York: Cambridge University Press.

Koizumi, J. 2000. From a water buffalo to a human being: Women and the family in Siamese history. In *Other Pasts: Women, Gender and History in Early Modern Southeast Asia*. Edited by B. W. Andaya. Honolulu, Hawaii: Centre for Southeast Asian Studies, University of Hawaii at Manoa, 254–68.

Loos, T. L. 1999. *Gender Adjudicated: Translating Modern Legal Subjects in Siam (Thailand)*. Unpublished Ph.D. dissertation, Department of History, Cornell University.

Migrant Action Programme. 2001. *Domestic Workers Consultation*. Coordinating Action Research on AIDS and Mobility in Asia (CARAM-ASIA), Bangkok, September 2001.

Mills, M. B. 2002. *Thai Women in the Global Labour Force: Consuming Desires, Contested Selves*. New Brunswick, New Jersey, London: Rutgers University Press.

Office of Administrative Commission on Irregular Migrant Workers (ACIRW). 2002. *Statistical Data of Irregular Migrant Workers Registration under the Resolution of the Cabinet, 1996–2001.* Thailand: Department of Employment.

Paitoonpong, S., J. Plywej, & W. Sirikul. 2002. Thailand: Improving migration policy management with special focus on irregular labour migration, case study of housemaids. submitted to International Organization for Migration (IOM)/International Labour Organization (ILO). Bangkok: Thailand Development Research Institute Foundation (TDRI) March 2002.

Pantip, K. S. 1997. *Immigrant Workers in Thailand: A Survey of Legistration, Problems and Policy Options.* Research Project on Policy Option for Thailand for Employment of Foreign Labour (in Thai), Institute of Population and Social Research, Mahidol University,

Pitsawat, S. & B. Pathamaporn. 1997. *An Analysis of Laws on Business and Employment of Foreigners,* Research Project on Policy Option for Thailand for Employment of Foreign Labour (in Thai), Institute of Population and Social Research, Mahidol University.

Reid, A. 1983a. Introduction: Slavery and bondage in Southeast Asian history. In *Slavery, Bondage and Dependency in Southeast Asia.* Edited by A. Reid. New York: St. Martin's Press, 1–43,

Reid, A. 1983b. "Closed" and "open" slave systems in pre-colonial Southeast Asia. In *Slavery, Bondage and Dependency in Southeast Asia.* Edited by A. Reid. New York: St. Martin's Press, 156–81.

Reynolds, C. J. 1999. On the gendering of nationalist and postnationalist selves in twentieth-century Thailand. In *Genders and Sexualities in Modern Thailand.* Edited by P. Jackson & N. Cook. Chiang Mai: Silkworm Books, 261–74.

Thai Development Research Institute. 2002. Thailand Economic Information Kit: 2002. www. info.tdri.or.th/kit_web/t20.pdf. Accessed 16 May 2004.

The Shan Human Rights Foundation. 2002. *License to Rape: The Burmese Military Regime's Use of Sexual Violence in the Ongoing War in Shan State.* Chiang Mai: Shan Human Rights Foundation.

Terwiel, B. 1983. Bondage and slavery in early nineteenth century Siam. In *Slavery, Bondage and Dependency in Southeast Asia.* Edited by A. Reid. New York: St. Martin's Press, 1–43,

Toyota, M. 2000, Cross-border mobility and social networks: Akha caravan traders, In *Where China meets Southeast Asia: Social and Cultural Change in the Border Regions.* Edited by G. Evans et. al.. Singapore: ISEAS, 204-221.

Toyota, M. 2004. Health concerns of "invisible" foreign housemaids in Thailand. *Asian MetaCentre Research Paper Series, No.19,* Singapore: Asian MetaCentre for Population and Sustainable Development.

Watson, J. L. 1980. Introduction: Slavery as an institution: Open and closed systems. In *Asian and African Systems of Slavery.* Edited by J. L. Watson. Oxford: Basil Blackwell, 1–15.

Wongboonsin, P. 2003. Labour Migration in Thailand. Paper presented at International Conference on Migrant Labour in Southeast Asia: Needed, Not Wanted, University of New England, 1-3 December in Armidale, Australia.

Yeoh, B. S. A., E. Graham, & P. J. Boyle. 2002. Migrations and family relations in the Asia Pacific region. *Asian and Pacific Migration Journal,* 11(1), 1–11.

11

Success Stories? Filipina Migrant Domestic Workers in Canada[1]

DEIRDRE MCKAY

INTRODUCTION

Domestic worker migrants arrive in Canada under a special immigration programme, the Live-in Caregiver Program (LCP) (see Fig. 11.1 for the numbers involved in this scheme). The government has designed the programme to provide live-in care for Canadian households, but the LCP offers migrants a chance to apply for permanent residency in Canada. This "landed status", in the Canadian vernacular, is what makes the programme unique; migrants can settle permanently and leave domestic work.[2] LCP migrants in Canada define "success" in terms of "regaining" their professions—leaving domestic work for other sectors of the labour market. By apparently offering this opportunity, Canada provides the "best case" foreign domestic worker programme in the context of the worldwide market for migrant domestic labour (Stasiulis & Bakan, 1997:33). The Canadian programme is officially a "caregiving" programme. This means that the worker is hired on the basis that she or he will be primarily engaged in providing care for a child, disabled or elderly person with household chores as a secondary concern. In practice, the programme is used to provide both care and housekeeping. Agents placing caregivers through the LCP market European migrants as "trained nannies" while women of colour, the majority being Filipinas, are directed towards employers looking for "maid/housekeeper" workers (Pratt, 1997). Thus, in Canada, LCP migrants are referred to as "nanny-caregivers" or "nannies" as well as "domestic workers".

IMMIGRATION FOR DOMESTIC WORK IN CANADA'S HISTORY

Canada has imported nationals from other countries as domestic workers since the mid-19th century. Until the 1950s, most of these women came from Europe and arrived in Canada as immigrants under the regular immigration scheme. Many were not specifically recruited as "housekeepers", but their presence in the Canadian labour market increased

FIGURE 11.1   Live-in caregivers and total other class

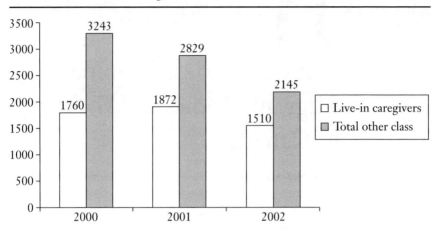

SOURCE: CIC, 2003a.

the demand for household services. Others, mostly from Britain and then from northern and western Europe, were offered "assisted passage" to join Canadian households as domestics (England & Stiell, 1997:199). In the post-World War Two period, the supply of immigrant women willing to take on this kind of work dried up. Canada looked to other source countries and, in 1955, signed a bilateral labour-importing agreement with Jamaica and Barbados, creating the Caribbean Domestic Scheme. Under this programme, foreign domestics were, for the first time, disqualified from migration if they were married, living in common-law arrangements, or supporting dependent children (Timmoll, 1989:57–8, cited in Stasiulis & Bakan, 1997:49).

By the early 1970s, paid employment outside the home was the norm for approximately 40 per cent of Canadian women (Status of Women Canada, 2000). Currently, 61.6 per cent of women aged 15 years and over are in the workforce and participation levels have been above 58 per cent for the last five years (http://www.statcan.ca/english/Pgdb/ labor05.htm, accessed 16 May 2003). The Canadian state did not follow the examples of Europe and Scandinavia and provide subsidised off-site childcare for the children of these working mothers. As the salaries of women in the workforce increased, so did the demand for paid, live-in workers (England & Stiell, 1997:198). The government attempted to meet the demand for these workers from overseas. In 1973, Canada introduced a temporary employment authorisation scheme to provide in-home workers, ending the open immigration of domestic workers and replacing it with short-term contracts. These contracts tied the migrant worker to a specific employer. Daenzer (1993, cited in Pratt, 1998:288) notes that the rights accorded to migrant domestic workers have declined since the 1940s, in concert with a shift in source countries for workers from Britain and Northern Europe to Southern Europe, then the Caribbean and, since the 1980s, Southeast Asia. Workers' rights have largely been determined by their immigration status and, since the shift to non-European sending countries, domestic worker migrants are no longer admitted as permanent residents.

In 1981, the government began to bring in migrant domestic workers under a unique and separate piece of immigration legislation. From 1981–91, this programme was known as the Foreign Domestic Movement (FDM) Program. Apart from living-in, this programme required migrants to undertake "upgrading" courses and volunteer time in the community to demonstrate potential for "self-sufficiency"—a requirement for permanent residency. The assessment for FDM applicants included marital status and family commitments that might preclude applicants from becoming "self-sufficient" in Canada. Many women thus concealed their marital status and children from immigration officials. For some time, misrepresentation of marital status constituted grounds for deportation, but this policy was enforced unevenly from province to province.

In 1992, the FDM was reworked and the name changed to the Live-In Caregiver Program. The government raised the qualifications required for entry, effectively transferring the training and upgrading aspects of the programme to sending countries. Under the LCP, immigration authorities assess applicants independently of their spouses and children. This means that misrepresentation of marital status is now only relevant at the time of application for landed status.

Successful applicants for the LCP require educational qualifications that are considered the equivalent of a Canadian high school diploma; six months of full-time training in a field or occupation related to the caregiving job, or a year of practical experience including six months of continuous work with one employer, all within the three years preceding the application; ability to speak, read and understand either English or French; and a written contract of employment with the future employer (Human Resources Development Canada, 2003). Before they can receive their temporary work authorisation, applicants for the LCP must be examined by a doctor approved by Citizenship and Immigration Canada (CIC). The applicant pays the cost of the examination. There is no further medical surveillance while they are working in Canada. Caregivers enter the country not as immigrants, but with pre-immigrant status. The success of their eventual application for landed immigrant status depends on their meeting the main requirements of the programme: they must work for 24 months as a live-in employee in a Canadian home. The 24 months of live-in work must be completed within 36 months of arrival. After the 24-month requirement is completed, the worker can apply for an open visa, allowing her to take up any form of employment and, subsequently, submit an application for landed immigrant status. After three years residency as a landed immigrant, she can apply for citizenship.

Changing Profile of LCP Workers

Under the FDM, 78 per cent of landings were visible minority women, with only 58 per cent Filipinas and the rest from the Caribbean, South America and the rest of Asia (Stasiulis & Bakan, 1997:35). Although 89 per cent of Filipinas were granted landed status under the FDM, only 50 per cent of British and 30 per cent of other European applicants were granted landed status, suggesting that fewer European women were using the FDM as an entry point for immigration to Canada (Stasiulis & Bakan, 1997:35). Over time, the proportion of European workers entering as temporary migrants under the programme has declined from 70 per cent or more in 1982 to under ten per cent in 1996 (Pratt, 1999a:26). Meanwhile, the programme has attracted new kinds of applicants—economic migrants looking for eventual immigration. In the 1980s, many Latin Americans entered the country through the LCP in Toronto after Canada refused their applications for refugee status. Toronto still has a larger number of domestic workers from the Caribbean (Pratt, 1999a:26) while Vancouver has predominantly Asian workers.

The Canadian government does not publish data on LCP migrants as they enter the country on temporary work permits.[3] Instead, statistics record information on migrants at the point of their successful application for permanent status or "landing", some two to four years after their initial arrival. Migrants who fail to meet the criteria of the programme or comply with immigration regulations are never recorded. There are also no official data on the total number of applications for the programmes. The government assesses the LCP immigration stream within Canada's "Other" immigration class. This separation distinguishes LCP landings from landings of skilled workers. "Other" includes refugees, caregivers and their spouses and dependents.

Data published in CIC annual reports often do not separate LCP applicants from the rest of the "Other" class, or the principal applicants (the women) from spouses and children. From what can be discerned, LCP migrants constituted the majority of the "Other" immigration class (Fig. 11.1). According to immigration officials I interviewed, applicants for the LCP in 1999/2000 were predominantly Filipino, with over 90 per cent of the applications coming from the Philippines. This has been the case since the early 1980s, when Filipinas replaced Caribbean women as the domestic worker migrants of choice. As women of colour and coming from a single ethnic group, Filipinas predominate in the LCP migration stream itself. Filipinas are thus more "visible" than the proportionately much smaller number of women from other ethnic backgrounds working as live-in nannies. This is also reflected in Figure 11.2. Government data indicates that since the LCP was introduced as a special immigration category, the vast majority of LCP entrants have been female (Fig. 11.3).[4] Women in the "Other" category (predominantly live-in caregiver migrants) are, on the whole, well educated (Fig. 11.4) and, at landing, the majority are single (Fig. 11.5). Most migrants landing through the LCP do so in urban areas that receive high numbers of immigrants—the

FIGURE 11.2   Other class by source area (Philippines and Europe and other developing countries) (Principal applicants and dependents)

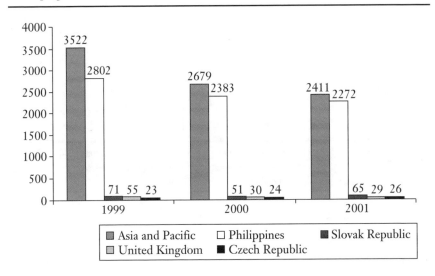

SOURCE: CIC, 2002a.

FIGURE 11.3   Immigrants landing as principal applicants in the Live-in Caregiver category, 1980–1994

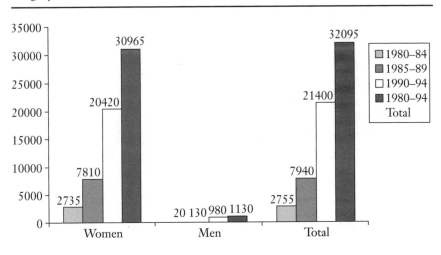

SOURCE: Statistics Canada, n.d.

309

FIGURE 11.4   Other class by gender and level of education—15 years of age or older, 2002 (Principal applicants)

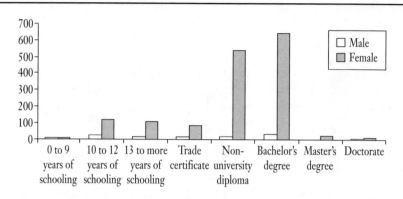

SOURCE: CIC, 2002b.

FIGURE 11.5   Other class by marital status—15 years of age or older, 2001 (Principal applicants and dependents)

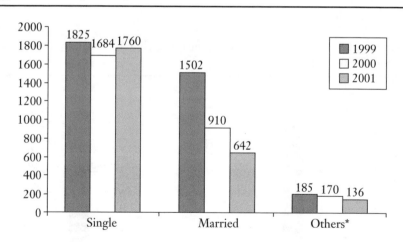

SOURCE: CIC, 2002c.

cities of Vancouver in British Columbia, Toronto in Ontario, Montreal in Quebec, and Calgary and Edmonton in the province of Alberta.

In the period 1990–1994 (the last period for which comprehensive longitudinal Immigration Database (IMDB) data breaking down all classes is available), of those landing in the LCP principal applicant group (a total of 21,400 people), 15,440 people (72.2 per cent) listed their country of origin as the Philippines. Almost all (98 per cent) of these Filipino LCP principal applicants were women (15,090 women in 15,440 Filipino caregiver migrants).[5] LCP landings only represent about 1.5 per cent of Canadian immigration with, on average, about 200,000 immigrants landing each year (CIC, 2000b). However, the over-representation of women of a single ethnic origin supports a stereotype of Filipinas as domestic workers.

Data on Live-in Caregiver principal applicants is infrequently isolated from the rest of the "Other" class or the LCP migration stream as a whole (where spouses and dependents are included). The figures I provide here draw on those published in CIC annual reports which do not separate principal applicants (the women) from spouses and children.

Most of the LCP migrants are between 25 and 44 years old at landing. In the period 1990–94, the IMDB records 13,770 Filipino women in this 25–44 years old age group as achieving landed immigrant status as principal applicants through the LCP. Only 3,805 women from other ethnic origins landed in that class and age group. Filipinas thus made up 78 per cent of the LCP principal applicants (aged 25–44 years old) achieving landed immigrant status, while women from other national origins represented 22 per cent of this group. In the early 1990s, then, at least 70 per cent of live-in caregivers were Filipinas. Given the under-representation of immigrants likely in the tax records that contribute to the IMDB and the fact that it only picks up landed immigrants rather than migrant arrivals working under the LCP, 70 per cent is an underestimate.

The IMDB data also ask women to indicate their future plans for work. Filipinas are significantly over-represented in that cohort of women who list live-in caregiving work as their intended occupation at landing. Figure 11.6 shows the occupation listed at landing for women who landed between 1990 and 1994. The number of Filipinas listing "caregiver" as their occupation at landing could reflect the women coming "cross-country"—as domestic worker migrants from third countries.

The number of women arriving after working in a third country is another salient feature of domestic worker migrant flows to Canada not tracked by Canadian immigration statistics. In 1999, I undertook a cooperative study of Filipinas in Canada with the Philippine Women's Centre of Vancouver (PWC).[6] With the PWC team, we interviewed 72 women in five cities across the country; 42 were LCP migrants. Our interviews indicated that most of them returned to the Philippines after working overseas and applied to Canada from there, though a few processed their papers in Hong Kong or Singapore. They listed their place of birth and country of origin as the Philippines and travelled on Philippine passports.

311

FIGURE 11.6   Intended occupations of women at landings, 1990–1994 LCP

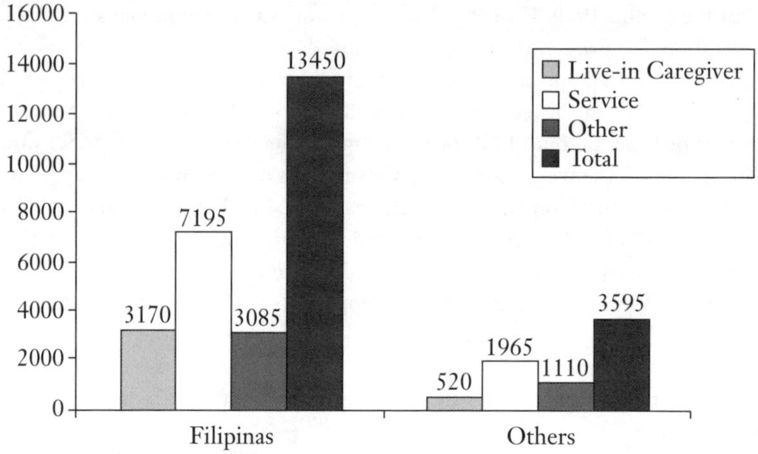

SOURCE: Statistics Canada, n.d.

Officials at the Canadian Embassy in Manila corroborated this assessment of cross-country deployment as "easier", explaining that verifiable records of employment experience from Hong Kong and Singapore would get women through the approval process much more quickly. In the experience of immigration assessors, documentation of employment and education in the Philippines was often very difficult to verify and frequently false. In contrast, work experience in Singapore and Hong Kong can be authenticated by independently verifiable references.

Women who applied from overseas explained that their choices to apply for Canada rather than return to the Philippines were made for a variety of personal and economic reasons. The rationale they gave usually entailed both personal factors and economic concerns that combined to make permanent residency outside the Philippines their preferred option. Some respondents cited relationship breakdown and social isolation due to their status as single mothers as a reason to remain abroad. Economic dependence on the part of their family in the Philippines was also a common concern for migrants already overseas—they worried that their family could no longer make ends meet without a foreign currency income stream. For others, their time in Hong Kong or Singapore meant that their professional skills would no longer be current in the Filipino labour market. Non-governmental organisation (NGO) representatives interviewed in Manila suggested that many returning domestic workers could only look forward to similar low-skilled, low-paid work at home.

Prevailing Stereotypes

The creation of a special immigration stream for foreign domestic workers in Canada coincided with the expansion of a global market for female contract domestic labour from the mid-1970s onwards. During this period, there was an intensification of the labour export industry in response to economic crisis in the Philippines. These two factors resulted in a large pool of "experienced" Filipina domestic workers who could meet the requirements of either six months training or a year of practical experience.

In Canada, agencies placing domestic workers market Filipina workers to employers as experienced, used to long hours and hard work, and motivated by the possibility of citizenship at the end of the programme, rather than money or "cultural experience". Partly through the advertising of such agencies, employers are aware of employment conditions in third countries. Pratt (1999a:34) found that the employers she interviewed were "curious about, and aware of, the highly exploitative conditions for domestic workers in Singapore and Hong Kong". Intermediaries representing placement agencies market specific nationalities of domestic workers in terms of ethnic stereotypes (Stasiulis & Bakan, 1997:39). These "nanny agencies" have not been characterised in terms of the immigration history and ethnic backgrounds of their owners, but it is quite likely that many have transnational ties to sending countries and recruiting agencies there. The owners may themselves be immigrants, part of the large wave of immigration Canada has absorbed since the 1980s.

Nanny agencies produce stereotypes of Filipinas as docile, passive, unskilled, unintellectual and hardworking, and these perceptions circulate widely in Canada. For instance:

> Your average Filipino girl is a quiet, shy personality. She does her job and that's the most important. The house has to be clean, spotless when God's coming home, sorry, the parents are coming home (Canadian nanny agent, quoted in Pratt, 1997:163).

Nanny agents contrast Filipinas who migrate as caregivers with European nannies in terms of their reliability:

> Europeans ... It's just a jumping board that they used because they have their own plan, their own career, their own training back there. They are not going to stay nannies. Filipinos will. That's the only thing they know how to do ... What they're trained for ... (Canadian nanny agent, quoted in Pratt, 1997:172).

These quotes show how the relative worth of domestic workers reflects the relative poverty or wealth of their sending country, rather than their personal education or experience (Pratt, 1997; England & Stiell, 1997). Canadian stereotypes for the different ethnic groups are summarised in England and Stiell (1997). Europeans tend to use the LCP as a work-abroad programme, rather than a stepping-stone to citizenship.

Employers of Europeans describe them as more difficult employees because they are accustomed to better working conditions and expect "equal" relationships with their employer. Many Europeans, particularly English women, will only work as childcare providers and will not take on housekeeping work. Nanny agencies market "Brits", in particular, as having better manners and professional "nanny training".[7] Nanny agencies market workers of less "worth"—women of colour such as Filipinas and West Indians—as cleaning staff, housekeepers and cooks as well as childcare workers. West Indians supposedly have good "discipline" with children, but are "aggressive" when it comes to working conditions and observance of the contract. Stereotypes of Filipinas include being shy and submissive, with strong accents, and characterised them as hard workers who are easily intimidated by children and parents.

DOMESTIC WORK AS EMPLOYMENT

Migrant workers experience a combination of class and racial discrimination in an "anti-third world attitude" that diminishes their qualifications and experience. The following exchange between a worker and her Canadian employer's adult daughter illustrates this:

> I was telling her, I never worked as a domestic back home. All of my family are educated, all the children and everything ... She said to me, even though you are educated, they don't acknowledge your education here and you still belong to a poor country (Filipina, quoted in England & Stiell, 1997:353).

Canadians understand that Canadian working conditions for migrant domestics are generally better than conditions in other receiving nations. Therefore, they feel migrant workers should be grateful. Advocates for migrant domestic workers continually have to point out that migrants are legally entitled to working conditions that meet Canadian standards, regardless of their nationality or previous experience and that anything less is exploitation.

Canadian employment relations reveal colonial notions of employing "others" who are used to or should expect conditions not tolerated by nationals. This begins with immigration where officials refer to the LCP as a "back door" for applicants whose skills, education, work experience or family situation would not have qualified them for acceptance as skilled workers. Immigration assessment grants "points" for education, training and work experience according to the anticipated demands of the Canadian labour market. Qualifications in nursing, teaching and midwifery (those required for the LCP) have not been awarded immigration points in the recent past on the basis that there is already a sufficient supply of skilled workers in the Canadian labour market already. The LCP thus opens a route for those without the skills or education assessed as desirable by Canadian government labour market analysis. On the part of the general Canadian population, this creates the impression that LCP migrants are "unskilled" and "uneducated". These "others" should be grateful to have a chance at immigration, rather than complain about working conditions.

LCP migrants, as unskilled "Other" class immigrants rather than skilled workers, offer a chance to create a "Canadian" identity through the construction and negation of an Other (Sartre, 1962). By constructing a group of visible minority women as "unskilled" migrants, the LCP allows Canadians, particularly Canadian women who are in the workforce, to identify themselves as "skilled" in a global context. In doing their caregiving work, migrant women are further isolated from mainstream Canadian society. Annie, an agency worker said:

> That isolates those women as well, as professionals. I mean as care givers—the racism and class issues around it. The nannies are in some of the wealthiest neighbourhoods in the city. ... They are all over now and more middle-income families are turning to the use of nannies. For the Filipinas then, they rely on each other all that much more as a community—which on one level is a good thing, but on another level the reason that they have to rely on each other is because they are not really welcome in our community as caregivers because the other parents have judgements about them and their employers are employers, they are not their friends. Layers and layers of racism are involved in the whole domestic work reality. One level of it is the actual employer-employee relationship and the fact that it is generally non-white women who are doing the care for low wages etc. But the other racism inherent in it is the parents who are also home, caring for children in the same community as the nannies. There's judgement ... and a lack of relationship between these people.

Responses to Stereotyping

LCP migrants in Canada tend to focus on activities within their ethnic community, looking to co-ethnics for support, particularly those who have already "graduated" from the programme. Migrants see self-presentation as a key to addressing negative stereotypes. Women trade advice about what television programmes to watch, how to learn a more "Canadian" accent, how to dress to avoid being mistaken for a "nanny" on their days off and how to respond to demeaning comments about their skills and education. Unfortunately, it is often co-ethnics who have the most difficult time in accepting that LCP workers are legitimate Canadian migrants (Pratt, 1999a; McKay, 2002). For Filipinos, "upgrading" one's profession—re-qualifying for the same kind of work one had at home—is seen as the ultimate indication of success in Canada. In re-attaining a professional status in Canada, migrant women show that they are "good enough" despite their "third world" backgrounds.

As work done in the "private" sphere, Canadians identify domestic work with a set of "traditional" or "family" values, as opposed to those values that underpin market relations (Aitken, 1987:410). According to these values, domestic work is "caring work", a form of labour specifically constructed as being "natural" to women (Badgett & Folbre, 1999; Pratt, 2003) and thus undervalued. In Canada, a good domestic worker is supposed to be motivated by caring and love and not "materialism"—a common charge thrown at foreign migrants (Pratt, 1999b).

Canadian society is ambivalent about the value of skills involved in caregiving work. Caregiving jobs are often, in comparison to paid work outside the home, described as more or less "recreation"—hanging out with the kids at the pool, playing games, etc. (Pratt, 2003). Canadian attitudes towards domestic work mean that the job is a "dead-end" career with no opportunities for pay raises or skills upgrading. "Nannying" is work usually performed by women waiting to move on to "something else", whether that is marriage and children of their own, or another career. Canadians assume that if someone is doing domestic work, they are of a lower status—a lower class background or of lower intellectual ability—and are somehow deserving of their work and permanently fixed in that position. Shona, a service agency worker and former LCP worker said:

> Most employers ... will not recognise this as a Canadian work experience, being a live-in domestic worker. It is not considered as a job. It is not considered as a profession. The problem is domestic work is considered something anybody can do. In the general public, if you are a domestic worker you would be considered probably as intellectually a little bit limited. You have limited education; so the job that is left over for you to do is maid work.

Relations with Canadian Employers

Jamieson (1999:11) describes employers as follows: "Canadians who employ nannies generally have no previous experience of having employees living in their home and, though they were generally kind and meant well, they were unsure about how much or what kind of work they should expect from domestic workers or how they should behave with employees". LCP workers report that their Canadian employers expected workers to be "on call" around the clock, adjust schedules at a moment's notice and not turn away requests for affective or domestic work when off-duty, all outside the contract provisions. These conditions may be common in domestic work abroad, but are unacceptable under law. Employers would not attempt to enforce such conditions in any other occupation in the Canadian labour market for fear of legal reprisals.

Pratt (1999a:28–33) lists nine tactics that employers use to extend hours and reduce the wages paid: 1) refusing to raise wages over time; 2) using minimum wage laws as a ceiling, rather than a minimum; 3) expecting low wages and long hours from relatives of former employees; 4) counting hours of work in terms of "only when the children are awake" or "not if you are home alone"; 5) accusing workers of "materialism" when they assert their rights to fair pay; 6) arguing that the $325 deduction for room and board undervalues employers' costs, based on local real-estate prices; 7) subcontracting the caregiver's time to another employer and pocketing the money; 8) demanding one to three month free "try-out" periods; and 9) insisting a worker begin work before her employment authorisation is processed. Tactics 1, 2, 3, 5 and 6 are exploitative and demeaning. Tactic 4 contravenes employment standards and is illegal. Tactics 7, 8 and 9 violate the terms of the LCP and thus place the worker in a position of vulnerability where immigration authorities could deport her if these activities come to their attention.

Many migrant workers and their employers are not familiar with Canadian labour standards as applied to domestic work or their contract provisions. The government does not regulate employers, except through follow up at the provincial level on employment standards complaints filed by their (former) employees. Employers have been known to threaten employees with "reporting them to immigration" for violations compelled by the employer in the past. Pratt's (1999b) respondents reported that some employers were actually making a profit in contracting out employee's services and no share of this profit went to the worker. Complaints about the sale of Filipina domestic and childcare workers over the internet have been tabled in the Canadian parliament (Hansard, 2003; National Alliance of Philippine Women in Canada, 2003).

The Federal government, through CIC and Human Resources Development Canada (HRDC), oversees the LCP programme and contract. Provincial governments set wages and hours of work. However, migrants often approach employment conditions from their experiences in third countries and the advice of friends, rather than consult provincial authorities. LCP migrants are frequently under misapprehensions about the programme and their rights. Interviews indicated that many workers perceive employers as able to report any contract irregularities to immigration officials and thus produce the worker's deportation. Employers are also seen as able to cancel a contract and send the employee away to fend for herself in a largely unknown environment. Lastly, employers are understood to have the power to delineate between the worker's usual rights and special privileges in the home/workplace. Workers report that employers have asked them to use separate plates and utensils as well as separate their bathing and laundry activities from those of their employers, as if the workers were vectors of disease. In this situation, the power a worker may perceive as held over her by the employer can be intimidating and thus preclude active negotiation of working relations.

Resisting Exploitation in Employment Relations
Since labour and employment standards are under provincial jurisdiction, workers unsure of the legality of their employers' practices can contact the provincial labour standards office for advice. Contact information for these offices is available over the web and through advocacy groups. However, the government does not enforce such advice on the employer. It is up to the worker to negotiate change or leave her job, citing the employment standards legislation as "leverage" with her employer. The contract is thus not binding on the employer. Immigration authorities monitor migrant workers over the course of their work authorisation. Workers must extend their temporary work authorisations at the end of their first year and every subsequent year of their LCP

work. Workers must notify immigration to change their authorisation each time they change employers. The government does not keep any records of employers' failure to comply with contracts. Employers who fail to abide by the terms of one contract and thus "lose" a domestic worker are granted requests for subsequent domestic workers.

Workers can report physical abuse to the police and have their employer charged with assault. In the event of an abusive employer or exploitative working situation, the worker can quit her job and apply for an authorisation to work for another employer. Approval for this can take several months and the migrant may not work in the interim.

SUBSEQUENT EMPLOYMENT

Subsequent employment is the key issue and definition of "success" for LCP migrants. Fely, one of the respondents in a 1999 focus group interview, could be considered the prototypical successful LCP migrant from the Philippines. Fely arrived in Canada in 1992, under the LCP. She had a university degree in commerce and had worked as an accountant in the Philippines. She is single and is the only daughter of a small, middle-class family from a town a few hours north of Manila. Her Canadian employer hired her through social networks, rather than an agency. Fely spent two years as a live-in nanny and housekeeper in the couple's central Ottawa home. There was only one child, a boy, aged two. After completing the requirements of the LCP, she applied for her open visa and, several months later, attained her landed immigrant status. She remained with her employer as a live-in caregiver for a third year, until the child was old enough to start school. During this last year, she enrolled for night classes at the local university to gain a Canadian accounting qualification. Her employer supported her in this endeavour with a pay raise and time off. After the child began school, Fely applied for a position with the Revenue Canada, the Canadian tax authority. In 1999, she was living in her own rental accommodation and earning C$55,000 per year (US$37,032)[8], more than the average Canadian wage.

What is interesting about this case is its singularity—of the 42 LCP migrants I interviewed in 1999, only Fely had found this kind of success—leaving domestic work and "upgrading her profession" through the programme. Fely does not owe her success to the design of the programme, the availability of government support or training, or even to her own exceptional skills or motivation but to a benevolent employer. Only by staying with her employer under special circumstances that gave her less than the full LCP work schedule was she able to attend university. Unfortunately, not all employers can afford or are willing to be so generous and supportive.

Filipinas, in particular, come to Canada under the programme precisely because they expect to be able to leave domestic work and re-enter their previous profession. Yet, for many Filipinas, having completed contracts as domestic workers in other countries as well as two to three years in Canada, caregiving dominates the employment history for the previous decade. Following the instructions on the landing form, they would be directed to list caregiver as their intended occupation. IMDB data indicates that the largest influx of women with intended occupation listed as caregiver is the cohort of Filipinas landing between 1990 and 1994. Their landing and entry into the (wider) Canadian labour market coincides with the CIC's assessment that new female immigrants are having more difficulty in finding work and working for low pay, below their skill levels. Spending two to seven years as a domestic worker in a third country before coming to Canada and then two to three years working under the LCP meant that many migrant women had lost their mastery over their original professional skills set. Once landed, they find themselves unable to re-skill or gain re-entry to their "old" professions. Instead, Filipino women in particular find themselves in low-skill, low-paying service jobs that are not dissimilar from live-in caregiver work—live-out nanny, childcare worker, housekeeper, home health-care worker, nurse's aide, sales clerk, cashier and food service worker (McKay, 2002).

> Deirdre: What about entering into the workforce after the caregiver contract ends?
>
> Shona: You probably know very few people who are in that other field that you may be looking at. Because you have been working in isolation, mostly you work with other domestic workers. And I see that even more in the Filipina community, where actually between the Filipino community which is already landed immigrant—or people who came directly as landed immigrants—they look down on the domestic workers. There's a very strong separation. "So you're only a nanny; we don't really communicate with you or we don't really deal with you". And so the Filipinas have a tendency to stick within their domestic workers group.

Filipina immigrants, as childcare and housekeeping workers have some of the lowest returns for educational qualifications in the labour market (Hiebert, 1997). CIC reports that 32 per cent of all Philippine immigrant women have post-secondary qualifications in health-related fields but only 20 per cent have employment in this area in Canada (CIC, 2000a). Problems of professional certification are likely to be significant in explaining the 12 per cent of potentially qualified women who are not working in health-related areas. In focus groups, women discussed their deskilling in terms of the economic hardship involved in reuniting their families while working multiple minimum-wage jobs. "Upgrading" one's profession remains out of reach for these women because they cannot afford the cost of upgrading courses or preparing for examinations.

PLACING THE LCP IN THE BROADER CANADIAN ECONOMY

A G8 country, Canada has estimated revenues of C$2.64 billion (US$1.78 billion) in 2000–01 (CIA, 2003). The contribution of the LCP to these revenues is minimal. A very generous estimate is that there are 16,000 workers saving 16,000 households each

C$12,000 (US$8,000) per year for a total of C$19,200,000 (US$ 12,928,000). No data is available on the fees collected by agencies and their clients. The cost of applying for a work permit is C$150 (US$100) and the number of applications unknown. The processing fee at the Canadian Embassy in Manila is PHP5,400 (C$225, US$150) and non-refundable. This fee varies from Embassy to Embassy.[9] With 16,000 workers under the LCP, and tax on salaries (with an average of C$900, [US$606] per month taxable income) at 14 per cent, 16,000 workers contributing C$126 (US$85) per month will amount to C$24,192,000 (US$16,289,000) per year. However, the tax office returns much of this revenue to the workers, depending on the level of tax offsets they can claim. The cost of changing employer on employment authorisation (EA) is C$150 (US$100), but the number of changes made is unknown. The cost of extending an EA is C$150 and each worker needs at least one extension, and possibly more. About 1,800 workers are granted landed status through the LCP each year. At a total cost of C$1,975 (US$1,330) each, this generates C$3,555,000 (US$2,394,000).[10]

While migration for live-in caregiving work represents a relatively insignificant contribution to the economy, immigration as a whole is seen as a significant contribution to the economy. Immigrants occupy most of the low-wage, low-skills jobs in a highly segmented labour market. The labour shortage for caregiving is only for live-in work, according to the government. The Live-in Caregiver Program exists only because there is a shortage of Canadians or permanent residents to fill the need for live-in care work. There is no shortage of Canadians or permanent residents available for caregiving positions where there is no live-in requirement (CIC, 2002f)—many of these live-out carers are also recent immigrants.

IMDB data show Filipinos arriving under the LCP tend to be located in particular segments of the urban labour market. This coincides with the findings of CIC (2000b) that very recent immigrant women—those who landed during the 1990s—are found in jobs that require a lower level of skill than Canadian-born and previous immigrants. In Hiebert's (1997) data on labour market segmentation based on the 1991 census, the occupations he identifies as featuring over-representation of Filipino women—housekeeping and childcare—are also dominated by immigrants who had landed in the preceding five years (1986–91). Statistics on labour market segmentation from the 1991 census show that women of Philippine ethnic origin are 8.6 times more likely to be found in the occupations of "housekeeper" and 6.9 times more likely to be "childcare worker" (Hiebert, 1997). Women from the Philippines exhibit the highest degree of occupational segmentation of any group of women (Hiebert, 1997:26). On the streets of upper middle-class Canadian suburbs, immigration statistics for Filipinas translate into a visible presence: "brown" women pushing the prams of "blonde" babies.

Hiebert (1997:2) argues that the location of a particular ethnic group within the labour market comes to define the intra-community relations and shared imagination of that ethnic group. As one community organiser commented, "The LCP filters and forms the Filipino community".[11] The LCP bisects the Filipino community into two groups: "independent" immigrants and LCP workers. The independent immigrants who were assessed as "appropriate" for immigration to Canada distinguish themselves from LCP migrants and their families—those who came to Canada under different, less stringent, regulations and are thus ascribed a "lower" status. This is reflected in data collected on labour market segmentation by ethnicity. Hiebert (1997) found that the Filipino community had the highest index of dissimilarity of any ethnic-origin group in the labour markets of Canada's major cities. Thus the Filipino community, in terms of the work done by its members, is not similar to any other ethnic-origin group. A significant section of the community, arriving through the LCP, is found in low-paying domestic work. Other community members, largely those who landed as independent immigrants, are employed in the professions.

Eighty per cent of Filipino immigrant women (aged 15–64 years old) participate in the workforce, a higher rate than other immigrant women and native-born Canadians (CIC, 2000a). This participation figure is virtually identical to that for Filipino immigrant men. Hiebert (1997) also shows that, across Canada, Filipino men and women do very different kinds of work, more so than the average Canadian man and woman. These findings can be explained because recently arrived Filipino women are over-represented in domestic and service occupations, even as compared to other recently landed immigrant women. Research to date indicates that when women leave the LCP, they become part of a labour surplus at the low-skilled end of the market (see Pratt, 2003 and above).

The LCP and "Women's Work"

Gender norms that govern the interpretation of appropriate behaviour of women and men are linked to socially constructed concepts of family altruism and individual self-interest (Badgett & Folbre, 1999). In Canada, government programmes and policies indicate that an altruistic mother parents the ideal family. She either stays at home or sacrifices her earnings to pay for childcare. Childcare services are privatised and do not attract subsidies by the state but formal daycares are regulated in terms of health, safety and standards of education. Most children are sent to informal "in home" childcare that is largely unregulated. Commenting on childcare, one nanny agency representative said, "The government think [sic] a nanny as just any female—you know, if you are a woman, you must be able to cook, clean and look after children" (agency worker, interviewed in England & Stiell, 1997:209). Folbre (1994, cited in Badgett & Folbre, 1999:317) argues that "women's collective economic and political power affects their ability to persuade men—and society in general—to help bear the costs of caring for dependants". In Canada, many of these costs are being deferred to migrant women, indicating once again women's low status.

Regulating the LCP

The official regulations that structure the LCP describe the employment relationships in terms of contract relations. A worker's contract stipulates that she will only work for one employer, limits her hours of work, and sets days off and minimum remuneration in cash and in kind, including a deduction for room and board (Pratt, 1998; 1999b). Wages are supposed to be scaled to family size and increase with the numbers of people in the household (Pratt, 1999b:28). Employers are required to provide the worker with a separate, lockable bedroom and access to a bathroom. The employer can subtract up to C$325 (US$219) from the monthly salary in compensation for room and board. Deductions for taxes, Canadian Pension Plan and Employment insurance are paid from the employee's salary. The employer is responsible for paying medical insurance until the employee is eligible for socialised insurance. LCP workers must track their own hours, negotiate the employer's agreement of the veracity of their calculations and then ask for overtime pay. Overtime should be paid at time-and-a-half the minimum hourly wage (determined by provincial regulations in province of employment) for any work beyond the stipulated work week (usually set at 40 hours, except in Quebec).

While the Federal government regulates the LCP, provincial governments regulate the employment conditions of domestic workers. Conditions, including minimum wage, work weeks and employment standards vary from province to province. Most provincial governments do not keep separate records on the LCP because they do not want to take responsibility for the problems this creates. In British Columbia, employers must register with the government; yet in 1997–8, while there were more than 3,000 LCP workers working in the province, only 72 registrations were recorded with the Employment Standards Branch (ESB).[12] The regulations have now been changed so that registration is mandatory for all employers before they make an offer of employment to a caregiver. The ESB also stipulates wages for live-in caregivers as follows: four or fewer people in a home, a minimum of C$8 (US$5.39) per hour; five people, C$8.38 (US$5.64); six people, C$8.76 (US$5.90); seven people, C$9.14 (US$6.15); eight, C$9.52 (US$6.41) and, for each additional person beyond eight, C$3.00 (US$2.00) per day. The job offer form now stipulates that a foreign live-in caregiver is considered to be working if required to be in an employer's home, and that caregivers cannot be on call 24 hours per day.

Migrants under the LCP can take part-time courses for credit if they succeed in their application for a Student Authorisation from CIC. The LCP worker must show that she has accommodation, demonstrate that the studies are part-time, and present a letter offering her a place from the educational institution. The authorisation costs C$125 (US$84) and is valid for only one educational institution.

The lack of implementation of policies on employment produces exploitation. In the case of live-in work where the state does not intervene to regulate working conditions and yet punishes workers who cede to employers' demands that they violate the terms of the LCP, it is understandable that workers cannot trust public institutions (Pratt, 1999b). Workers feel and are told by employers that "immigration" and the "government" are on the side of the employer. They may also infer this from their experience with government offices. In the absence of regulation, finding a good employer seems to be the LCP migrant's preferred option.

Canada, the LCP and International Conventions

In the totality of the Canadian labour market and immigration programme, the LCP is not considered to be a significant issue. In fact, the Canadian government considers it to be an immigration, rather than migrant worker programme. Thus, Canada is not a signatory to the United Nations (UN) International Convention on the Protection of Rights of All Migrants and their Families 1990. No western country has signed the convention thus far. Canada has ratified six ILO conventions, one more than the United States, and less than any other G8 country. It has not ratified c.29, c. 97, c.98, c. 138 or c.143 (International Labour Organization, 2004).[13] Canada is a member of the International Organisation on Migration (IOM).

In response to pressure to ratify the UN Convention, Canada has taken the position that there are no migrant worker issues in the country. Advocacy groups disagree. Internal government documents, obtained under the Freedom of Information Act make it clear that the government is anxious. A 1996 government memo explains: "Canada may also be forced to answer concerns raised before the committee by other States and by individuals. Under all these procedures, any deficiencies in Canada's performance may therefore become the subject of public discussion at an international level" (Lyons, 2000).

In the UN Economic and Social Council's, Commission on Human Rights, Canada was examined in the report of the Secretary-General on violence against women migrant workers (UNHCHR, 1999). Canada responded with information on benefits available to migrants, references to ongoing research, and explanations that the Convention does not reflect the Canadian situation. This is because persons covered by the Convention would generally enter as permanent residents (this would not apply to LCP migrants) and be eligible for provincial services. Moreover, the Canadian Charter of Rights and Freedoms is argued to give a broader range of coverage. Canada argues that migrants who have the right to permanent residence in the destination country are in a different situation from temporary migrants.

Protection for LCP Workers' Rights

The legislation and policies in place to protect migrants' rights as workers are highly ineffective, mainly because responsibility for the workers is split between the federal and provincial levels of government. Jurisdiction over the workers and their working conditions is "shared yet ambiguous" (Stasiulis & Bakan, 1997:32). Many provincial service agencies initially deny LCP migrants assistance because they are unfamiliar with the programme and think it is a "federal" matter. Advocates have handled cases where it has taken months for a migrant woman to access provincial medical insurance, employment insurance or training programmes funded by immigrant services. Until 2002, LCP migrants were not eligible for training programmes while under the LCP, so they were unable to participate in many existing immigrant support programmes. Since then, they can request permission to study.

Moreover, the LCP workplace is protected by norms of privacy that prevent the home from being constructed as part of the market economy. There is no government oversight on working conditions and workers can only activate their contractual rights by complaining against their employers. Research on LCP experiences has shown that, in many cases, contract conditions are ignored or met at a bare minimum by employers. This is a result of the lack of informed understanding on the part of employers combined with the absence of any state sanctions on employer's behaviour.

The discourse of privacy applied to the private home is used to defend inaction on LCP worker's rights. For example, in British Columbia, up until 1995, live-in domestic workers were excluded from the protection of the British Columbia Employment Standards Act. They were paid a flat daily rate of C$48 (US$32) per day and not entitled to overtime pay.[14] One provincial representative made the following comments in a legislative debate, arguing for the continued exclusion of domestics:

> Remember that a domestic has to be accepted into the family ... That is the reason that a domestic worker cannot keep time. You are accepted into the family as part of the family, and the principle that you have your time recorded doesn't work in the family scene.[15]

The LCP creates what is a technically non-existent category of visiting immigrant. When someone classified as a visiting immigrant presents himself or herself at provincial government offices in search of services, provincial bureaucrats are unsure how to proceed. Visitors are ineligible for assistance, while landed immigrants are eligible. In some cases, monies transferred to provincial governments to provide support for new immigrants are denied to LCP migrants by provincial agencies, on the basis that LCP migrants do not yet have "landed" status. Though the Federal government claims LCP migrants are eligible for immigrant settlement services—Immigrant Settlement and Adaptation Program (ISAP) services such as reception, orientation, translation and counselling (CIC, 2003b:7)[16]—in practice, women reported that the services are difficult to access not only because they are temporary workers and not yet landed immigrants but also because they cannot arrange for time off when settlement offices are open. Transfers of federal money support provincial programmes for immigrants that are not addressed to LCP migrants' needs. In British Columbia, for instance, government funded settlement services for immigrant women target stay-at-home mothers with small children who require basic language training (Lee, 1999) rather than working women who need specialist skills and access to retraining to help them in their careers.

Another source of inaction on the part of the government may be suspicions about the "deserving nature" of LCP applicants. It has become evident that the LCP also functions as a supplement for family sponsored immigration. When family members in the Philippines do not meet the requirements for assisted-relative sponsorship, their Canadian relatives may find them an "employer" in Canada to sponsor them through the LCP. Often this "employer" is non-existent or must be paid for their services as sponsor. This means that the woman arriving under the LCP comes to Canada without work, in violation of the programme and in debt but nonetheless obligated to her family network for "petitioning" her to the country.

Lobbying by a particular group, the Coalition for In-Home Care, representing licensed domestic placement agencies, has been the most influential non-governmental voice in determining the lack of reforms to the LCP programme (Stasiulis & Bakan, 1997:39). 0Immigrant advocacy groups have publicised the myriad problems with the LCP through the media since the early 1990s. No substantive changes were made in that decade, largely due to lobbying by a particular group, the Coalition for In-Home Care, representing licensed domestic placement agencies (Stasiulis and Bakan, 1997:39.) However, advocates' attempts to force the federal government to take action on the LCP appear to have been heeded. As of January 2005, Citzenship and Immigration Canada is undertaking a formal review of the programme and substantive changes are expected to be announced by the end of the year.

Successive governments have maintained the LCP's live-in requirement for migrant domestic workers, despite campaigns mounted by groups such as INTERCEDE in Toronto and the Philippine Women Center in Vancouver. Both have been vocal in calling for the live-in requirement to be scrapped. The initiation of a review suggests that their lobbying activities have successfully focused the government's attention on the exploitive aspects of LCP working conditions.

Available Alternatives for the Work of Caregiving

While the LCP provides caregiving labour, it does not necessarily enhance the quality of life for employers. Often, employers are not prepared personally and emotionally to deal with the management of live-in help, nor are their homes designed to provide privacy for both employer and employee (Pratt, 2003). Employers find conflict over working conditions and the turnover of caregivers taxing and distressing for their families. They may also resent becoming entangled in the personal lives and transnational households of migrant employees (see Pratt, 2003).

Out-of-home care for children, the elderly and the sick is available in the market, but more costly and less convenient than employing a live-in worker under the LCP. Placing one child at a professionally managed childcare centre costs C$600–C$900 (US$400–$600) per month, or from C$7,000 to C$11,000 (US$4,700–$7,400) per year (Jamieson, 1999:12). A live-in worker costs an average of C$1,200 (US$810) per month, making it cheaper to hire a live-in caregiver than send two children to childcare. Childcare workers have professional qualifications and childcare centres claim to provide a safe and stimulating environment. Yet, childcare workers are themselves seriously underpaid relative to jobs of similar skill and responsibility (Pratt, 2003). This is part of a wide undervaluing of caring labour in North American society. Hiring a live-in caregiver provides more freedom for parents than the childcare provided by the private sector. For instance, if a child shows signs of illness, the childcare centre must return the child to parental care. Childcare centres operate with restricted hours, compared to live-in workers and parents must drop off and pick up children at appointed times. Centres may only cater for one particular age group. Live-in nannies can care for sick children, supervise children of multiple ages and work to flexible schedules.

Similarly, home health-care or nursing attendants for the disabled and elderly cost around C$14 (US$9) per hour, rather than the approximately C$8 (US$5) paid to an LCP worker (based on figures for Vancouver, in Pratt, 2003). Again, nursing attendants are not required to work outside their contracted responsibilities and thus will not perform housekeeping or prepare meals for anyone other than their patient. Whether self-employed or working with a health service company, they have stipulated paid overtime. The other popular option for parents is non-professional in-home childcare or "babysitting", often available at C$4.50–C$6.50 (US$3.00–US$4.50) per hour, depending on the neighbourhood, facilities in the home, and number of children in care. Doherty (cited in Pratt, 2003) estimates that 69 per cent of Canadian children under six are in unregulated childcare situations.

SOCIAL AND HEALTH ISSUES

The LCP reinforces stereotypes about femininity and caring and continues to exclude men from responsibility for caregiving labour in the home. As in other migrant receiving nations, employing a migrant domestic worker may enable the wife to enter the labour market without renegotiating the gendered nature of domestic reproductive labour (Gregson & Lowe, 1994; Pratt, 1997; Yeoh & Huang, 1999; Westwood & Phizacklea, 2000; Parreñas, 2000; 2001). The migrant worker's labour may also replace services formerly provided by the state, such as care for the elderly or disabled. Such services, now devolved back to the household by the economic restructuring brought about under rhetoric of global competitiveness, are also "traditionally" the work of female household members. The LCP makes live-in care affordable not just for wealthy families, but also for working class households.

In most Canadian households where women work, they alone are responsible for paying for childcare. In Canada, domestic work is largely not a responsibility taken on by men, thus a woman's wage is expected to cover the costs of replacing her domestic labour. Even in dual-income households, Pratt (2003) found that women, who earn on average approximately 65 per cent (Canadian Council on Social Development, 1997), of that of men with similar skills and qualifications, were solely responsible for purchasing childcare. Childcare arrangements were part of a rhetoric of choice for Canadian women—women could choose to have a career or stay at home with their children. Their husbands' salaries would only be used to compensate wives and mothers who choose to remain at home. If a woman chose to work, her earnings were used to replace her labour. This marginalises the paid work of both female employers and caregivers in different ways (Pratt, 2003:585).

Public Debates on the LCP

The impact of migrant caregivers on Canadian values is a minor consideration in Canada. Pratt (1997; 1999a; 1999b) reports that employers express concerns about the food preferences and accents their children may develop from spending time with Filipina nannies. Filipinas are also seen as providing less intellectual stimulation but more affection, whereas British nannies provide better education and values. Canadian employers are not interested in having their children acquire Filipino language skills, although they do see French and German as improving children's cultural capital.

The anxiety expressed around the LCP is mostly about the implications of the programme for Canada's self-image as a benevolent, rights-oriented and responsible nation in the global community. Pratt (1997:167) observes: "If nannies are constructed as other than employees and their jobs as not quite jobs, wage levels and working conditions unacceptable to Canadian citizens are legitimated". Canadians are anxious about the implications for social cohesion and the rhetoric of equality when the LCP segregates a specific national group of visible minority women into low-paid service jobs. The UN Special Rapporteur on the Human Rights of Migrants visited Toronto in 2000 as a guest of CIC. During this visit migrant advocacy groups and the media were given only restricted access to her, apparently to prevent them from exposing abuses under the LCP (Lyons, 2000). As one advocate explained, "there's a real disconnect between the public perception of Canada and the practices of Canada" (Lyons, 2000).

Health and the Health Sector

The LCP is recognised as supporting inexpensive privatised health care, bringing in foreign-trained nurses who do not have Canadian accreditation and who then take jobs providing "assisted living" for disabled and elderly patients in a privatised care system.[17] CIC has recognised that "increasingly higher skilled primary health care workers use this category because of the independent skilled worker selection criteria".[18]

327

After retrieving the IMDB for LCP immigrant Filipinas whose employment history over the ten years before landing classified them as nurses and who then listed nursing as their intended occupation, the correlation between their industry of employment at their 1995 tax return and their experience/intention at landing was assessed. The data suggest a definite deskilling trend for nurses arriving under the LCP (Fig. 11.7). In the 1980–84 period, only five Filipina nurses arrived under the LCP (then the FDM) intending to return to nursing. In 1995, all five of these women were employed in nursing. Of those LCP women landing in the 1985–89 period, 80 Filipinas were nurses through experience and intended to nurse, but only 25 per cent or 20 of those women had nursing as industry of employment in 1995. For the 1990–94 landings, a smaller proportion of Filipinas again, 24 per cent (30 out of 125) were working as nurses, but with a relatively larger number of nurses intending to nurse at landing. Tax records indicate most of the nurses landing in this period were in caregiving or service sector jobs in 1995. The service sector work would include occupations such as nurse's aide, geriatric care worker, live-out nanny, sales clerk, food service worker etc. Reports from the Filipino community indicate, however, that many more women with nursing education and experience as nurses arrive under the LCP than the few who are classified as nurses on the basis of their employment history as given on the landing form.[19] This may be explained, in

FIGURE 11.7 Intended occupations in 1995 of landed Filipino female nurses under the LCP

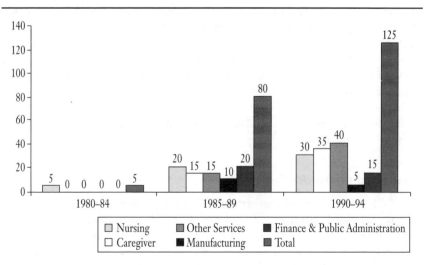

SOURCE: Statistics Canada, n.d.

part, by the confusion over the requirements that employment history and intended occupation match up on the landing form and the general anxiety that surrounds landing for LCP migrants.

Health Issues at Landing

Ironically, for a group of migrants who largely end up in the health care and health services sector, it is often the health status of their own families that disqualifies them from achieving landed status. While the principal LCP applicant has her health assessed before arriving in Canada, an LCP worker's immediate family members are examined only when the application for permanent residency is processed. All members of the immediate family are examined, regardless of whether the applicant has requested they be issued visas to join her in Canada under the LCP spouse and dependent stream. This can prove particularly difficult when couples are legally married but have separated and lost contact. The applicant must also pay for these medical examinations. A serious medical problem is grounds for rejection of the applicant's visa application as "medically inadmissible". It does not matter if the applicant is not planning to sponsor this spouse or dependent for residency.

Women working under the LCP also experience problems in accessing socialised healthcare through provincial medical insurance. Waiting periods for insurance apply and it is unclear who pays visitors' cover during this period, employer or employee. In British Columbia, LCP workers are not eligible for provincial concessions to support the cost of their insurance because they do not have landed status. While LCP workers are entitled to paid sick leave, few employers consider this and accessing it becomes a problem. If their employer replaces them with another worker, they lose their accommodation and board.

The government makes contact information for community groups and counselling available over the web and through community groups and advocates. Maintaining that LCP workers are eligible for ISAP services, the government has trained ISAP workers to recognise signs of mental health problems and refer new immigrants on to general practitioners who will then send them to local clinics. In practice, few of the workers interviewed had accessed ISAP services and service agencies reported ongoing debates about the eligibility of LCP migrants.

NGO ACTIVITIES AND CIVIL SOCIETY SPACE

In Canada, the LCP produces such a small and distinct group of migrants that the same organisations often combine advocacy and service provision. Advocacy groups provide a great deal of counselling and support for women, allowing them to learn about their rights in Canada and swap stories of how to coax employers into compliance. Federal and provincial governments both provide funding to support specific information programmes run by these agencies.

CIC (2002g) currently lists eight "Live-In Caregiver Associations" across Canada as resources for LCP migrants to contact. Seven of these agencies or NGOs are multi-ethnic in scope, while one is specifically for Filipinas. Three are specifically restricted to women. Five restrict their activities to working with domestic workers, while the other three deal with all members of the immigrant community.

Advocates perform the key tasks of tracking and informing domestic worker migrants of changes in the government policies affecting LCP migrants. This includes investigating the application of policies on a case-by-case basis, lobbying particular government offices and providing legal clinics and other support services for migrants under the programme.

Advocates will take specific cases of misrepresentation or abuse to the media and it is "media power" that seems to have had the most impact in terms of changing LCP conditions. Advocacy groups arrange access to media and publicise information on the situation of domestic worker migrants and specific cases of abuse. Government rhetoric that the LCP is a "small" programme, which provides a few "unskilled" migrants with a chance at a better life, also receives media coverage. Advocacy groups tend to push stories that undermine the government position and attempt to humiliate the government into taking action. This strategy has had some notable successes.

Advocacy groups usually offer advocacy and counselling as well as links to government-funded services. Some advocacy groups, such as the Philippine Women Centre, have set up programmes and hired community workers to reach out to LCP migrants. These initiatives are successful in attracting participation and assisting women under the programme, but it often takes some months for women to access these networks, if they are able to. For most women at the beginning of their LCP contract, the experience is one of deep isolation.

Barriers to Success

Through Human Resources Development, I was able to access the training that I need. Like the computer skills—with the help of some of the non-profit organisations—and also the training on business management (Marilyn, journalist, social worker and accountant, interviewed at the PWC in 1999).

In Marilyn's case, the Philippine Women Centre advocacy group had to argue with the local HRD office to accept her as a student. The local office attempted to deny her access because she was not yet a landed immigrant.

The barriers experienced by migrants are in the areas of recruitment, availability of places, eligibility criteria and time. Many LCP graduates are working at two or three jobs and sleeping four hours per night, to save money to reunite their families. Agencies and advocacy groups rely on word-of-mouth, internet references, media coverage and one-on-one recruiting (usually in shopping malls) to find the LCP community they serve. There is no list of LCP workers and their contact details available for agencies; they must rely on the workers hearing of the organisation and services and having the time and confidence to approach advocates directly. Some workers are referred to service agencies by considerate employers who hope that advocates can help the workers access skills and training. Other workers are discouraged by their employers or other community members from "making trouble"; instead they are told to "keep quiet" and finish the programme.

Much of the lobbying carried out by advocates has to be directed at those responsible for provincial employment standards. As single workers, LCP migrants cannot bargain collectively. Advocacy groups have lobbied for broad-based bargaining. They have also called for the creation of a central registry of employers that would provide an official avenue through which advocacy groups and service agencies could identify and contact workers, inform them of their rights and represent them in disputes (Stasiulis & Bakan, 1997:52).

Political and Discursive Strategies

Advocacy groups approach the LCP and its effects through two broad strands of discourse: slavery and professionalism. The Vancouver-based Philippine Women Centre and allied organisations across Canada often draw on a discourse of "slavery". In a 2003 press release, for example, in response to internet auctions of Filipina nannies reported in the Canadian parliament, the National Alliance of Philippine Women in Canada asserted that live-in conditions, "legislate our women into poverty and modern-day slavery". The slavery discourse creates embarrassment among government officials but can backfire, producing denial and accounts of the gratitude of "nannies" for their chance to remain in Canada.

Groups such as West Coast Domestic Workers Association, Vancouver, and Association des Aides Familiales du Quebec, Montreal, put forward an alternative discourse of professionalism. These groups link the poor working conditions of LCP migrants to the deprofessionalisation of caregiving work across society. For example, Denise Caron from Aides Familiales asserts that "the work of a home caregiver often amounts to managing a household, taking charge when the usual heads of household are absent. Given the responsibility involved in many present-day home caregivers' positions, it can in fact be considered as a profession which deserves recognition and respect".[20] The problem with this discursive strategy is that the particularly onerous conditions applied to migrant domestic workers can become lost in the broader feminist struggle to professionalise caregiving work.

Another strand of the professionalism discourse is put forward by the Canadian Association for In-Home Care, Toronto, which represents nanny agencies and a largely formally "trained" (NNEB) group of professional British nannies.[21] In the wider

331

Canadian context, focusing on the "professional" qualifications of British migrant workers puts Filipinas, who may have a tertiary degree and years of experience in fields such as pediatric nursing, in a poor position. In the context of Canadian attitudes to women's work and caring labour, professionalism is a discourse that wider society may find hard to take seriously.

Achievements by Advocates

Lobbying efforts have brought changes to the Federal programme and made much more specific information available to both workers and employers. Each revised version of the CIC handbook for employers and workers reflects the efforts of advocacy groups. Before 2002, regulations governing the LCP denied workers access to education. Now, study applications are considered.

At the provincial level, advocacy groups have challenged employment conditions across the country. In British Columbia, the government, in response to lobbying, brought LCP workers under the Employment Standards Act in 1995 (Pratt, 1999b). This set a workweek comparable to other workers and made LCP workers eligible for overtime pay. Again, in response to lobbying, the British Columbia's Employment Standards Act is now available in Tagalog. In an innovative pilot project, British Columbia has combined with Citizenship Immigration Canada and Human Resources Development Canada to introduce a mandatory registry of employers. For caregivers going to British Columbia, the hiring forms provided by CIC will become the employment contract. The results of the current government review of the LCP will likely reflect the lobbying efforts of advocacy groups, but it remains to be seen to what extent advocates' recommendations will influence the review outcomes.

RESHAPING THE LCP

Advocates have long argued against the temporary nature of the LCP and the live-in requirement. Providing workers with permanent residency on approval of their temporary employment authorisation would give them landed status. Landed status would ensure that they could access health insurance, immigrant settlement services and orientation programmes immediately after they had arrived in Canada. Moreover, if an application for residency was going to be denied on the grounds of medical or criminal inadmissibility, this assessment would be made before a migrant woman separated from her family.

Eliminating the live-in requirement would best minimise the exploitation and vulnerability of LCP migrants. If the live-in requirement cannot be removed, it could be reduced to one year. The standard contract, being piloted in British Columbia, may go some way in educating employers as to the rights of workers and should be extended to the rest of the country. The mandatory registry of employers has been created in one province, but should be extended to all. At the provincial level, legal penalties should be legislated to address employers who violate employment standards and LCP contract provisions. Periods of illness, covered by a doctor's certificate, should not be considered as falling within the time calculated as the 36 month eligibility period for the LCP. Currently, migrants are penalised by the LCP immigration requirements if they become ill after starting the programme. The fee attached to the change of employer should be removed. Nanny agencies operating in Canada should be monitored in terms of their representations of the programme, their treatment of migrant workers and their recruiting activities overseas. Each province should set out a schedule of minimum pay levels relative to household size and another schedule of pay rises for long service. LCP workers should be granted their requests to undertake part-time training courses and be eligible for provincial low-income subsidies on health insurance. Employers should be responsible for paying the costs of private insurance during any provincial waiting periods.

Improving LCP Workers' Abilities to Redress Exploitation

Mandatory meetings between employers, employees and an advocate/counsellor should be instituted within the first two months of contract and again at six months. Families employing live-in caregivers should receive orientation on the federal and provincial regulations that apply to the programme, the employment standards and salary schedules in force, and guidelines to follow in case of disputes with their employee. Provincial governments should fund advocacy groups to independently monitor the conditions of work for live-in caregivers. Provinces receiving immigrant settlement transfers from the Federal government should ensure that classes in advanced English as a second language are made available to LCP workers at appropriate times (such as Saturdays or in the evenings). The employer registry would offer a way to inform workers about free language classes and institute meetings with a counsellor/advocate.

Reducing Pressures to Exploit LCP Workers

Provincial governments should follow the example of Quebec and fund income-linked subsidised public daycare. Income tax regulations should be reassessed to provide support for households requiring in-home nursing for the elderly and disabled, allowing those households to pay market rates for nurses' aides and live-out caregivers.

CONCLUSION: RECONSIDERING SUCCESS

If the LCP is truly an immigration programme, workers should not be disadvantaged in comparison to other immigrants of similar education and skill in terms of their access to education and employment. The live-in requirement, however, combined with the other features of the programme, has effectively devolved the responsibility for offering "immigrant settlement services" to LCP employers. As Fely's story indicates, the LCP can provide a "successful" transition from domestic to professional work for migrant women, but only when an employer is in a position to act as patron for their worker and relations between the two are good. Hoping for this situation to eventuate is clearly insufficient as the basis for government policy. Meanwhile, Canada is accepting the cream of applicants for the LCP—foreign doctors, lawyers and PhDs who are all prepared to endure two years of domestic work for the chance to enter the broader Canadian labour market. Based on the data above, it appears that re-entry into the professions from the LCP is very difficult. As more educated and articulate LCP migrants arrive to find that they are "stuck" in the low-skill, low-paying service sector, there will be increasing pressure on the government to find better ways to help these immigrants develop their skills and careers. Otherwise, deskilling foreign health care workers through the LCP and then allowing them to support the roll-back of the socialised health care system as cheap labour will be seen as racialised exploitation. The Canadian public, long accustomed to the image of Canada as a conscientious and benevolent G8 global citizen, is now facing an uncomfortable confrontation with the ugly truth of contemporary immigration.

NOTES

1   I would like to thank the Philippine Women's Centre of Vancouver for collaborating with me in the research process. I acknowledge the support of the RIIM Project (Metropolis), Vancouver and Professor David Ley. The research was funded as part of a SSHRC post-doctoral Fellowship on the genealogies of Filipina identities. Colleagues at the University of the Philippines, Baguio, hosted my visits to the Philippines. Sandra Davenport from the Department of Human Geography, Australian National University, provided assistance with editing and formatting the paper and producing the graphs. As always, my deepest thanks go to my friends and respondents from the Philippines, whether there or in Canada.

2   Landed immigrants have the same rights as full citizens, except they cannot vote, hold political office, or take jobs involving national security. They can apply for citizenship after residing in Canada for three years.

3   There is a lack of data on not only the women entering the programme and the country, but where the women who do land eventually end up in the labour market (http://www.cic.gc.ca/english/irpa/gender-irpa.html. Accessed 20 January 2002).

4   Data from a Statistics Canada special data order from the Immigration Database (IMBD) which I use separate figures on LCP principal applicants from figures on their spouses and dependents.

5   A Filipina landing in the 1990–94 period had approximately a 45 per cent chance of being an LCP immigrant (McKay, 2002).

6   I also interviewed seven NGOs and service agencies as well as officials from Citizenship and Immigration Canada.

7   This refers to the NNEB qualification, a two-year childcare certificate.

8   The conversion rate in mid-October 1999 was C$1/US$0.67.

9   Conversion of Philippine pesos to Canadian dollars was at a rate of PHP24/$1, the prevailing

rate in the autumn of 1999.

10   This total cost is broken down as follows: cost of interview for landing—C$300; cost of open visa—C$150; processing fee —C$550 (C$300 in Quebec); and Canadian right of landing fee —C$975 (Canada Immigration, 2004).

11   M. Farrales, personal communication with author, 9 October 1998.

12   Annual report of BC Employment Standards Branch, 1997-98. See http://www.labour.gov. bc.ca/annrep/ar97-98/esb.htm.

13   C29 is the Forced Labour Convention, C97 Migration for Employment, C98 the Right to Organise and Collective Bargaining Convention, C138 is the Convention concerning Minimum Age for Admission to Employment, and C 143 Migrations in Abusive Conditions and the Promotion of Equality of Opportunity and Treatment of Migrant Workers. Canada had not signed these as of 1 November 2004.

14   Annual report of BC Employment Standards Branch, 1997–98. See http://www.labour. gov. bc.ca/annrep/ar97-98/esb.htm.

15   British Columbia Hansard, 22 August 1980: 4173 (cited in Stasiulis & Bakan, 1997:44, note 18).

16   Government Response to the Report of the Standing Committee on Citizenship, page 7. See http://www.cic.gc.ca/english/pub/response-settlement.html.

17   FNSG memo on http://www.tripod.com/what_is_new/press_releases_2002/may9.htm. Accessed 18 January 2003.

18   From Gender based Analysis Chart of the 2002 Immigration and Refugee Protection Act Regulations (see CIC, 2002d:9).

19   C. Diocson-Sayo, Philippine Women Center, Vancouver, British Columbia, Canada. Personal communication with author, 10 March 2000.

20   D. Caron, Aides Familiales, Montreal, Quebec, Canada. Personal communication with author, 11 October 1999.

21   NNEB refers to the National Nursery Examining Board qualification from the United Kingdom; see http://www.parklanenannies.com/Nannies/NNEB.asp for an example of how it is marketed as a "nanny" degree.

REFERENCES

Aitken, J. 1987. A stranger in the family: The legal status of domestic workers in Ontario. *The University of Toronto Faculty of Law Review*, 45(2), 394–415.

Badgett, M. V. L. & N. Folbre. 1999. Assigning care: Gender norms and economic outcomes. *International Labour Review*, 138(3), 311–27.

Canada Immigration. 2004. *Frequently Asked Questions: Government Fees and Application Costs*, http://canadavisa.com/documents/faq/fees.htm. Accessed 9 February 2004.

Canadian Council on Social Development. 1997. *Free Statistics*, http:www.ccsd.ca/facts. html. Accessed 24 January 2004.

CIA. 2003. *The World Factbook*, http://www.cia.gov/cia/publications/factbook/geos/ca.html.

Accessed 9 February 2004.

CIC. 2000a. *A Profile of Immigrants from the Philippines to Canada*, http://cicnet.ci.gc.ca/ english/ pub/profile/philippines-e.html. Accessed 18 January 2004.

——. 2000b. *Immigration Facts, 2000*, http://cic.gc.ca/pub/facts2000. Accessed 12 November 2001.

——. 2002a. *Facts and Figures 2001: Immigration Overview*. http://www.cic.gc.ca/english/ pub/facts2001/9other-05.html. Accessed 20 January 2004.

——. 2002b. *Facts and Figures 2002: Immigration Overview*. http://www.cic.gc.ca/english /pub/facts2002/others/others_7.html. Accessed 20 January 2004.

——. 2002c. *Facts and Figures 2001: Immigration Overview*. http://www.cic.gc.ca/english/ pub/facts2001/9other-10.html. Accessed 20 January 2004.

——. 2002d. *Gender-based Analysis Chart—Immigration and Refugee Protection Act Regulations*, http://www.cic.ca/english/irpa/gender-irpa.html. Accessed 20 January 2004.

——. 2002e. *The Live-in Caregiver Program for Employers and Caregivers Abroad—Employee*. http://www.cic.gc.ca/english/pub/caregiver/caregiver-2.html. Accessed 20 January 2004.

——. 2002f. *The Live-in Caregiver Program for Employers and Caregivers Abroad—Employee*. http://www.cic.gc.ca/english/pub/caregiver/caregiver-5.html. Accessed 20 January 2004.

——. 2003a. *Facts and Figures 2002: Immigration Overview*. http://www.cic.gc.ca /english/pub/ facts2002/others/others_1.html. Accessed 20 January 2004.

——. 2003b. *Government Response to the Report of the Standing Committee on Citizenship and Immigration*. http://www.cic.gc.ca/english/pub/response-settlement.html. Accessed 23 January 2004.

Clark, T. 1999. *Why it Makes Sense for Canada to Reconsider Ratifying the Migrant Workers Convention*, Toronto, http://www.december18.net/web/docpapers/doc207.htm. Accessed 20 January 2004.

England, K. & B. Stiell. 1997. "They think you're as stupid as your English is:" Constructing foreign domestic workers in Toronto. *Environment and Planning A*, 29(2), 195–215.

Gregson, N. & M. Lowe. 1994. Waged domestic labor and the renegotiation of the domestic division of labour within dual career households. *Sociology: the Journal of the British Sociological Association*, 28(1), 54–79.

Human Resources Development Canada. 2003. *The Role of the CIC*, http://www.on.hrdc-drhc. gc.ca/english/ps/fwp/lcp_cic_e.shtml. Accessed 23 January 2004.

Hansard, House of Commons of Canada. 2003. *Question Period/Questions Orales: Citizenship and Immigration*. Ms Madeleine Dalphond-Guiral (Laval Centre, BQ) and Hon. Denis Coderre (Minister of Citizenship and Immigration), excerpt, 2 April.

Hiebert, D. 1997. *The Colour of Work: Labor Market Segmentation in Montreal, Toronto and Vancouver*. 1991 RIIM Working Paper Series #97–02, Vancouver: RIIM, Simon Fraser University.

International Labour Organization (ILO). 2004. *Ratifications of the ILO Fundamental Conventions*. http://webfusion.ilo.org/public/db/standards/normes/appl/applratifconv.cfmLang N. Accessed 9 February 2004.

Jamieson, K. 1999. *Making New Canadians or Making Martyrs? Foreign-born Domestic Workers Views and Recommendations about Immigration Policy and Legislation.* A Report Prepared for the West Coast Domestic Workers' Association.

Lee, J. 1999. *Immigrant Settlement and Multiculturalism Programs for Immigrant, Refugee and Visible Minority Women: A Study of Outcomes, Best Practices and Issues.* A Report Submitted to the B.C. Ministry Responsible for Multiculturalism.

Lyons, T. 2000. 'Migrant headache: The complaints of Canada's migrant workers get short shrift during a UN special rapporteur's visit', *Eye Weekly*, http://www.eye.net eye/issue/issue_09.28.00/news/migrant.html. Accessed 20 January 2004.

McKay, D. (In collaboration with the Philippine Women Centre of British Columbia). 2002. *Filipina Identities: Geographies of Social Integration/Exclusion in the Canadian Metropolis*, Metropolis Working Paper Series, Vancouver Centre of Excellence. http://riim.metropolis. net.

National Alliance of Philippine Women in Canada (NAPWC). 2003. *Canada Immigration Perpetuating Abuse of Filipino Women, Says National Group; Asks for Support from Canadians.* Media Release, 5 April 2003.

Parreñas, R. S. 2000. Migrant Filipina domestic workers and the international division of reproductive labor. *Gender & Society*, 14(4), 560–80.

———. 2001. *Servants of Globalization: Women, Migration and Domestic Work.* Stanford, California: Stanford University Press.

Pratt, G. 1997. 'Stereotypes and ambivalence: The construction of domestic workers in Vancouver, B. C. *Gender, Place and Culture*, 4(2), 159–77.

———. (In Collaboration with the Philippine Women Centre, Vancouver). 1998. 'Inscribing domestic work on Filipina bodies. In *Places through the Body*. Edited by H. Nast & S. Pile. London, New York: Routledge, 283–304.

———. 1999a. From registered nurse to registered nanny: Discursive geographies of Filipina domestic workers in Vancouver, B. C. *Economic Geography*, 75(3), 215–36.

———. (In Collaboration with the Philippine Women Centre). 1999b. Is this Canada? Domestics Workers' Experiences in Vancouver, B. C. In *Gender, Migration and Domestic Service.* Edited by J. H. Momsen. London, New York: Routledge, 23–43.

———. 2003. Valuing childcare: Troubles in suburbia. *Antipode*, 35(3), 581–602.

Sartre, J. P. 1962. *Anti-Semite and Jew.* Trans. G Becker, New York: Schocken Books.

Stasiulis, D. K. & A. B. Bakan. 1997. Regulation and resistance: Strategies of migrant domestic workers in Canada and internationally. *Asian and Pacific Migration Journal*, 6(1), 31–57.

Statistics Canada. n.d. Special data order on the IMDB for the years 1990–1999.

Statistics Canada. 2004. *Latest Release from the Labour Force Survey.* http://www.statcan.ca/english/Subjects/Labour/LFS/lfs-en.htm. Accessed 16 May 2004.

Status of Women Canada. 2000. *Statistics on Women in Canada throughout the 20th Century.* http://www.swc-cfc.gc.ca/dates/whm/2000/stats_e.html. Accessed 18 May 2004.

UNHCHR. 1999. *Report of the Secretary-General on Violence Against Women Migrants.* http://www.unhchr.ch/Huridocda/Huridoca.nsf/0/0553f2c33246dd0b802568860052d710. Accessed 20 January 2004.

Westwood, S. & A. Phizacklea. 2000. *Transnationalism and the Politics of Belonging*. London: Routledge.

Yeoh, B. & S. Huang. 1999. Singapore women and foreign domestic workers: Negotiating domestic work and motherhood. In *Gender, Migration and Domestic Service*. Edited by J. H. Momsen. London, New York: Routledge, 277–301.

PART 3

Comparative Countries

12

Changing Trends in Paid Domestic Work in South Korea

HYE-KYUNG LEE

INTRODUCTION

In countries like Korea which for many centuries have had a strong reliance on live-in domestic workers—usually teenage girls or young women from rural areas—the onslaught of industrialisation in the 1970s significantly altered the trend. By the 1980s, domestic workers servicing middle-class families in Korean towns and cities were primarily those who had few employment opportunities in the Korean labour market, such as local, middle-aged women who worked part-time, offering their services to several households at any one time. Compared to rapidly industrialising economies in Asia such as Singapore, Malaysia, Taiwan and Hong Kong, the import of foreign workers to shore up the domestic front has been a much less commonly used option in South Korea.[1] To clarify these observations, this chapter will first review the cultural and historical context surrounding domestic work in Korea as well as current ideologies concerning the division of household labour. It will then examine the role of the state, women's position in the Korean labour market, and the changing lifestyles of middle-class Korean families in explaining why reliance on transnational domestic workers is an uncommon option in Korea before giving attention to clarifying the presence of these workers who service a very small minority of households.

DOMESTIC WORKERS IN THE CULTURAL AND HISTORICAL CONTEXT

While housework has long been women's responsibility from the pre-modern period in Korea, it was during the Chosun Dynasty (1492–1910) that the division of labour by gender became more rigidly defined than before, given the Dynasty's strong patriarchal social structure. Confucian ideology within this period distinguished two very separate, clear-cut roles for men and women. Men sought public work, whilst women were confined to the home (Cho, 1988). Furthermore, as traditional Chosun society was highly status-oriented and looked down on those who performed manual labour, most housework was performed by servants called *nobi*.[2] It has been estimated that from a high of about 30–50 per cent of the population during the early and mid-Chosun Dynasty belonging to the *nobi* class, numbers began to decline (Kim, 1999:151). Some *nobi* were able to run away during the series of invasions by Japan and China during the 16th–17th centuries, while others climbed in status by serving in the military or by bribing local officials to cancel their *nobi* status.

In general, most high-status or *Yangban* families had *nobi*. Some had several female servants each specialising in a particular household task such as cooking, needlework and so on. *Yangban* wives oversaw the managerial element of domestic work such as looking after the overall welfare of family members, kinship relations, as well as family or kin rituals such as ceremonies to show respect for dead ancestors. The actual execution of housework was done by their *nobi*. Apparently, some middle-status farmers (*Sangmin*) and even low-status families (*Chunmin*) could also afford *nobi*. For example, in 1630, it was found that 39 per cent of *Sangmin* and nine per cent of *Chunmin* had *nobi* in the Kyungsang area (Kim, 1999:154).

After the "*nobi*-system" was officially abolished in 1894, high and middle status families began to hire lower status women as domestic servants. According to a newspaper survey during the Colonial Period (1910–1945), 92 per cent of upper class families had at least one paid live-in domestic workers in 1932 (Shin Dong A, 1932:6, cited in Kim, 1996:54; *Chosun Newspaper*, 22 February 1996).

THE GENDER DIVISION OF LABOUR IN MODERN KOREAN HOUSEHOLDS

Cultural and social expectations of a strongly gendered division of household labour have persisted in modern Korean society. During the Japanese Colonial Period, the *ryōsai kenbo* or the good wife/wise mother ideology was introduced in which the view that "housework should be done with 'love' by the wife" was propagated (for the historical origin of this ideology in Japan, see Nakamatsu, this volume). In the 1960s and 1970s, a combination of state patriarchy and capitalism led to a strengthening of this ideology, which was also drawn upon in the mass media to discourage the employment of domestic workers (Cho, 1988:106, 111). Today, the ideology continues to be congruent with the relatively weak position of Korean women in the labour market, characterised by slow growth of female labour force participation rates (Tables 12.1 and 12.2), "M-shaped" career patterns, much irregular employment, and occupational gender segregation (such as much lower proportions of women in professional and managerial jobs compared to blue-collar work) (W. Y. Kim, 2003).[3] It has been noted that the level of education and the labour force participation rate among women are inversely related, even as change is beginning to happen among the younger generations. In particular, married women with a high educational background have fewer job opportunities compared to those with lower educational qualifications.

TABLE 12.1   Labour force participation rate by gender in Korea, 1963–2003

	Population age 15+		Non-farm population age 15+	
	Male	**Female**	**Male**	**Female**
1963	78.4	37.0	76.9	30.8
1970	77.9	39.3	78.0	30.4
1980	76.4	42.8	76.6	36.9
1990	74.0	47.0	73.9	44.1
2000	74.2	48.6	73.7	46.6
2003	74.6	48.9	74.0	47.2

SOURCE: Korea National Statistical Office, http://kosis.nso.go.kr/cgi-bin/sws_999.cgi, accessed 18 January 2004.

TABLE 12.2   Labour force participation rate by gender and marital status

	Married		Unmarried	
	Male	**Female**	**Male**	**Female**
1980	88.3	40.0	52.4	50.8
1990	88.4	47.2	43.7	46.5
1999	85.5	47.9	49.1	45.9

SOURCE: Korean Women's Development Institute, 2000:165.

In the context of the strong differentiation of male and female roles rooted in cultural ideology as well as women's relatively weak positions in the labour market, housework has remained the wife's responsibility while the husband's share of domestic work has not changed during the past three decades. For example, the average amount of time that a husband spends helping with domestic work was calculated to be 35 minutes per day in 1975; in 1999 the equivalent figure is still about 30 minutes per day (Yoon, 1975; Moon et al., 1997; B. S. Kim, 2003). While there may be some change among the younger generations, most husbands today still do not think of household work as their responsibility. In contrast, the amount of time that a wife spends doing domestic work is considerably higher, even as it varies with employment status (about nine hours per day for full-time housewives and about six hours a day for wives in employment in 1975) (Yoon, 1975). In 1999, comparable figures are considerably reduced[4] but still much higher than what husbands put in (6 hours and

343

33 minutes for full-time housewives, and 3 hours and 36 minutes for working wives) (B. S. Kim, 2003).

In sum, domestic work continues to remain the province of Korean women, many of whom become full-time housewives on marriage as seen in available data. For instance, drawing on data in the "1998 Korean Labor and Income Panel Study" by the Korea Labor Institute, Kim Woo Young (2003) showed that 58.2 per cent (62 per cent of salaried women and 55.2 per cent of self-employed women) of working women (among 3,225 women aged from 25 to 64 years old in 1998) gave up their jobs on marriage. Although the Korean government has tried to increase women's labour force participation rates by providing childcare facilities and maternity leave, most increases in job opportunities are in irregular work (that is, as "daily" workers and "temporary" workers).

The typical middle-class nuclear family comprising "a salary man husband and a full-time housewife" couple and one or two children living in an apartment does not usually wish to hire a "live-in" domestic worker. Instead, where work-family conflicts among working wives persist, part-time domestic workers has become a common solution for middle-class Korean households. This has become such a norm that it is even adopted by some middle-class, full-time housewives in Korea. In this case, housework is perceived to be divided into two parts: the "managerial element" and the "actual execution of housework" (Park & Kim, 1999). The Korean housewife takes care of the managerial aspects of housework such as maintaining social networks, managing home economics, and looking after the educational achievement of the children,[5] while the part-time domestic worker ensures the actual performance of housework.

In sum, while hiring a local part-time domestic worker has become the norm for some middle-class urban Korean families, reliance on live-in domestic workers is much less common given the ideological association of Korean women with housework, their changed lifestyle, and their weak labour market positions. The next section examines the changing trends associated with local domestic workers while the subsequent section turns attention to the two groups of transnational live-in domestic workers who service a minority of households, usually with young children or sick elderly relatives.

LOCAL PAID DOMESTIC WORKERS IN THE MODERN PERIOD

As an informal sector occupation, accurate official statistics on domestic workers in Korea—such as numbers, composition and changing trends over time—are hard to come by. For example, according to the 2000 Korean Census, there are about 70,000 local domestic workers, most believed to be working on a part-time basis (Korea National Statistical Office, 2000). However, given the low status that domestic service carries in Korean society, it is likely that this is an under-reported figure. In the absence of accurate data, a compilation of findings from a number of different studies as reflected in Table 12.3 may be used to suggest possible trends over the past four decades.

During the 1960s, about 40–60 per cent of urban households in Seoul and other cities hired live-in domestic workers: 90 per cent of the upper class, about 60 per cent of the middle class, and about 30 per cent of working class families had such help (Kim & Chang, 1968; *Joongang Newspaper*, 26 June 1969:5). Although the proportion of households with live-in domestic workers decreased thereafter, 40–46 per cent of urban families in Seoul and Kyunggi-do continued to hire domestic workers until the 1970s (Table 12.3). During the 1960s and 1970s, teenage girls (14–19 years old) from rural areas were the major source for live-in domestic workers (called *Sik-mo*) in urban households (*Joongang Newspaper*, 8 May 1972:5; 29 March 1973:5; Park, 1973; Kim, 1996:55). Many of these migrated to the cities in order to contribute to their parents' household economy as well as their brothers' education (Park, 1973). It was common for some urban households to take on teenage girls from poor relatives or neighbours. Often, these girls from poor families provided their services in return for food and shelter only. Since there were no clear specifications with regard to wages, rights and obligations, the girls working under such a system were prone to physical and sexual abuse (*Joongang Newspaper*, 18 February 1975:2).

Since the mid-1970s, however, structural changes of the Korean economy have led to an exhaustion of the rural labour surplus. In particular, young women were

TABLE 12.3   Urban households that hired domestic workers, 1967–2000

Year	Live-in DWs %	Part-time DWs %	Source	Survey area
1967	59	n.a	Kim and Chang (1968)	Seoul (n=150)
1967	40	n.a	Kang et al. (1968)	Taegu & nearby cities (n=1,796)
1970	41.5	n.a	Young (1970)	Seoul & Kyunggi-do (n=551)
1972	46	n.a	Lee (1972)	Seoul (n=100)
1975	40 (Emp: 100)	n.a	Yoon (1975)	Seoul (n=171) (Emp: 20.5%)
1979	16.5	7.8	You (1980)	Seoul (n=346) (Emp: 23.1%)
1983	27.4		Lee, 1983 quoted in Chung (1987:23)	Seoul
1984	15.4		Kang (1984)	Seoul (n=376) (Emp: 22.3%)

(cont'd next page)

TABLE 12.3 Urban households that hired domestic workers, 1967–2000 (cont'd)

Year	Live-in DWs %	Part-time DWs %	Source	Survey area
1984	11.1	23.3	Shin (1985)	Seoul (n=516)
	53.8(Emp)	22.7(HW)		Middle-class households
1986	4.8	17.4	Chung (1987)	Seoul (n=419) (Emp: 29.6%)
1986	5.1	17.6	Lee (1987)	Seoul & other 5 cities (n=982) (Emp: 26.6%)
1989	12.5		J.H. Lee (1989)	Pusan (n=240) (Emp: 48.1%)
1989	14.3		S.M. Lee (1989)	Seoul (n=374)
1990	21.9		Lee (1990)	Pusan (n=255) (Emp: 21.2%)
1990	36.4		Choe (1991)	Seoul (n=268) (Emp: 100%)
	15.6	20.8		
1992	13.1		Lee and Lee (1992)	Seoul (n=487)
1994	22.4		Lee and Lee (1997)	Seoul (n=596) (Emp: 100%)
1995	9.4		Seok and Lee (1999)	Seoul (n=159 couples) (Emp: 53.8%)
1996	6.6	14.8	Jin et al. (1996)	Seoul (n=255) High-school teachers
2000	1.9 (D) 3.0 (M)	14.5 (D) 15.8 (M)	Lee and Park (2000)	Seoul & Kyunggi-do (n=375 pairs of mothers and married daughters)

SOURCES: Adapted from Lee, 1983 quoted in Chung, 1987:23; Chung, 1987; Choe, 1991; Jin et al., 1996; Kang et al., 1968; Kang, 1984; Kim and Chang, 1968; Lee, 1972; Lee, 1987; J.H. Lee, 1989; S.M. Lee, 1989; Lee, 1990; Lee and Lee, 1992; Lee and Lee, 1997; Lee and Park, 2000; Seok and Lee, 1999; Shin, 1985; Yoon, 1975; You, 1980;Young, 1970.
NOTES:
Emp: married women employed outside the home.
HW: full-time housewives.
D: employers in the married daughters group surveyed by Lee and Park (2000).
M: employers who are mothers of the married daughters surveyed by Lee and Park (2000).

attracted to and absorbed within the expanding manufacturing and service sectors which offered better employment opportunities than domestic work. In addition, the labour force participation rate also declined among the youth population (15–19 years age group), including females in the same age group, as a result of increasing educational opportunities for these groups (Table 12.4).

As the supply of young, local domestic workers dried up after the mid-1970s, middle-aged married women began to fill the lacuna in the domestic sphere as part-time domestic workers. The term *Pachulbu*—to describe those who work as part-time domestic workers—was coined by the Young Women's Christian Association (YWCA) in 1966 in order to render domestic work a type of job with clear specifications, and to offer job opportunities for working class married women (*Joongang Newspaper*, 28 August 1975:5; 10 December 1983:11). Since then, several women's associations such as YWCA and the Korean Wives Association, have recruited and trained women to perform domestic tasks. Hiring such part-time domestic workers became increasingly popular after the 1980s. In fact, the available data (Table 12.3) suggests that the proportion of households with part-time domestic workers began to outnumber those with live-in domestic workers by the middle of the 1980s. Overall, it also indicates a decrease in the proportion of urban households relying on domestic workers: according to a

TABLE 12.4 Labour force and educational participation rates of females in their teens (15–19 years old), 1970–2000

	Population aged 15–19 (Thousand)	Economically active population (Thousand)	% of economically active population	% Entering junior high school (at about 13 years old)	% Entering high school (at about 16 years old)
1970[a]	1,850	716	38.7	46.5[b]	24.1[b]
1980	1,847	635	34.4	92.6[b]	62.2[b]
1990	2,091	389	18.6	98.2[b]	83.8[b]
2000	1,850	230	12.4	99.9[c]	99.5[c]

SOURCES: Adapted from Kim, 1996:56; Korean Statistical Association, 1970; 1980; 1990; 2000; Ministry of Education and Human Resources Development, and Korean Educational Development Institute, 2001:15.

NOTES:

a   Population aged 14–19 years old.

b   Kim, 1996:56.

c   Ministry of Education and Human Resources Development, and Korean Educational Development Institute, 2001:15.

2000 study, the proportion of households in Seoul and Kyunggi-do employing live-in domestic workers was only two to three per cent while the corresponding percentage for part-time domestic help was 15–16 per cent (Table 12.3).

CHANGING TRENDS IN MIGRANT WORKERS

Until the early 1990s, Korea's immigration law prohibited the entry of unskilled labour migrants. This was to change, with the main influx of migrant workers from neighbouring Asian countries. From about 20,000 in 1990, the total number of migrant workers—a large proportion undocumented—rose to 340,000 in 2002 (Table 12.5). Beginning with visiting Korean-Chinese (see later) who found work opportunities on

TABLE 12.5 Number of migrant workers by status, 1990–2002

Year	Industrial trainees				Undocumented		Total migrant workers	
	Trainees		Regular workers					
1990	0	-		-	18,402	-	18,402	-
1991	599	-		-	41,877	-	42,476	-
1992	4,945	-		-	65,528	-	70,473	-
1993	8,048[a]	(27.7)		-	54,508	(32.5)	62,556	(31.9)
1994	24,050[a]	(31.3)		-	48,231	(30.7)	72,281	(30.9)
1995	42,716[a]	(35.6)		-	83,103	(33.0)	125,819	(33.9)
1996	46,79[b]	(32.4)		-	129,054	(32.1)	175,845	(32.2)
1997	61,416[b]	(30.6)		-	148,048	(31.9)	209,464	(31.5)
1998	41,820[b]	(33.5)		-	99,537	(34.6)	141,357	(34.3)
1999	52,944[b]	(31.5)		-	135,338	(35.5)	196,433	(34.8)
2000	69,492[b]	(29.2)	2,068	(24.2)	188,995	(36.0)	260,550	(34.1)
2001	43,855[b]	(30.4)	8,065	(20.6)	255,206	(35.9)	307,126	(34.7)
2002	33,699[b]	(30.0)	12,191	(22.1)	289,239	(36.3)	335,129	(35.1)

SOURCES: Adapted from Lee, 1998:41; Ministry of Justice, Republic of Korea, 1993; 1994; 1995; 1996; 1997; 1998; 1999; 2000; 2001; 2002a.

NOTES:

Data for 1990–1991 are taken from Lee, 1998:41.

Data for 1993–2002 are recalculated from the Ministry of Justice, Republic of Korea, 1993; 1994; 1995; 1996; 1997; 1998; 1999; 2000; 2001; 2002a.

– Not classified.

[a] Registered trainees.

[b] Registered trainees, excluding those who ran away and therefore became undocumented.

construction sites in the late 1980s, labour shortages in the manufacturing sector began to attract migrant workers (some under the industrial trainee programme[6] but the majority undocumented) from a range of Asian countries from the early 1990s. Among both industrial trainees and undocumented migrant workers, the proportion of female migrants has remained stable at around 30–35 per cent during the past decade.

Up to the early 1990s, Korean-Chinese and Filipinos were the major migrant groups working in Korea. With the expansion of the trainee programme in November 1991,[7] the ethnic composition of migrant workers began to diversify (especially since 1994) as trainees were imported from some 14–15 different Asian countries (Table 12.6). As of 2002, Korean-Chinese still form the numerically dominant group, followed by the Chinese.[8]

Filipino Domestic Workers

While the influx of both male and female migrant workers from neighbouring Asian countries has featured prominently as part of the industrial landscape over the past decade, their presence in the domestic sphere has been far more muted and unsustained. In the early 1990s, Korean households attempted to turn to Filipino migrants as an alternative source of paid live-in domestic help.[9] Apart from performing household chores, Filipino women were particularly valued for their command of English as this was an asset in teaching the language to Korean children. At that time, Filipino domestic workers earned about 400,000 Korean won (about US$500) which was only slightly higher than the earnings of their counterparts working in factories (*Joongang Newspaper*, 7 May 1990:18; 23 May 1994:21).[10]

By the mid-1990s, the attraction of Filipino women as a source of domestic workers began to fade. First, their wages, like those of other migrant factory workers, have increased since 1995 (Lee, 1998; 2003a) and consequently, their merits as cheap labour and English teachers have decreased. Second, difficulties with Korean culture, especially the language and food, proved an important barrier that discouraged Filipinos from working in Korean households. Third, the fact that most Filipino migrant women were young (in their 20s and 30s) was soon perceived to be another shortcoming in assessing their suitability as domestic workers for compact private households. Since the 1980s, living in apartments has become a way of life for urban middle-class Korean families.[11] Middle-class Korean wives tended to feel uncomfortable living with young foreign women within the closed confines of apartments because of the potential for sexual scandals involving their family members. Instead, they began seeking out another option in the form of the large number of older Korean-Chinese women in the Korean labour market (see later). Finally, hiring migrant workers in service sectors including domestic work was not made legal until December 2002, and even then, only the Korean-Chinese have been given this right; other ethnic groups, including Filipinos, continue to be prohibited. As such, the hiring of Filipino domestic workers

TABLE 12.6 Countires of origin of migrant workers in Korea, 1993 and 2002

Country	1993					2002		
	Total number	Total %	Male %	Female %	Total number	Total %	Male %	Female %
China	26,970	43.1	35.6	59.3	168,519	50.3	43.2	63.5
(Korean-Chinese)	(23,272)	(37.2)	(29.6)	(53.5)	(83,989)	(25.1)	(20.3)	(33.9)
(Chinese)	(3,698)	(5.9)	(6.0)	(5.8)	(84,530)	(25.2)	(22.9)	(29.6)
Philippines	10,552	16.9	17.2	16.1	21,595	6.4	6.6	6.2
Vietnam	395	0.6	0.5	1.0	18,913	5.6	5.8	5.3
Indonesia	613	1.0	1.0	1.0	23,848	7.1	8.8	4.0
Thailand	1,242	2.0	2.4	1.0	22,107	6.6	6.2	7.2
Bangladesh	6,002	9.6	14.0	0.1	17,832	5.3	7.9	0.5
Pakistan	1,533	2.5	3.6	0.0	7,537	2.2	3.4	0.1
India	401	0.6	0.9	0.2	3,558	1.1	1.6	0.1
Nepal	2,914	4.7	6.6	0.6	2,812	0.8	1.1	0.3
Mongolia	4	0.0	0.0	0.0	13,895	4.1	3.5	5.3
Uzbekistan	58	0.1	0.1	0.0	9,317	2.8	3.4	1.6
Kazakhstan	18	0.0	0.0	0.0	1,931	0.6	0.6	0.5
Others	11,854	18.9	18.2	20.6	23,265	6.9	7.8	5.4
Total	62,556	100.0	100.0 (42,630)	100.0 (19,926)	335,129	100.0	100.0 (217,452)	100.0 (117,677)

SOURCES: Adapted from Ministry of Justice, Republic of Korea, 1993:238, 286; 2002a:272, 328, 468.

has dwindled and is now largely confined to foreign embassy staff and other foreign employees operating in Korea.

Korean-Chinese Domestic Workers

The category Korean-Chinese refers to those ethnic Koreans and their succeeding generations who have resided in China since migrating there from the 19th century. Today, the two million Korean-Chinese in China constitute one of the 55 minority ethnic groups[12] in China. Some voluntarily crossed the Duman River in response to famines and natural disasters after the mid-19th century while others, sometimes involuntarily, migrated to the Manju area during the 1920s and 1930s, after Japanese colonisation. After Korea was liberated in 1945, and when the Communist Party took over China in 1948, the Korean-Chinese community could not return to their home country as a result of the severance of diplomatic relations between South Korea and Communist China. Instead, they settled in three provinces in the northeastern part of China, predominantly in the Yanbin Korean self-governing autonomy area (Fig. 12.1), maintaining their own language and culture under China's favourable minority policy. However, since they are concentrated in a marginal area of China, they have not enjoyed the rapid economic development characteristic of other parts after China opened its doors to capitalist investments. Instead, during the late 1980s and early 1990s, it is in visiting their relatives back in Korea that they find economic opportunities in South Korea. As many of them overstayed and became undocumented workers and peddlers, the Korean government began to find ways to reduce their influx, primarily by setting a minimum age limit on those intending to visit their relatives.[13]

With the establishment of official relations between Korea and China in 1992, international marriages between Korean men and Korean-Chinese women began to increase. Farmers and lower-class Korean men, whom Korean women are reluctant to marry, try to import foreign "picture-brides". Korean-Chinese women are preferred to other Asian women, because of a common ethnicity and the emphasis on the purity of bloodlines. These international marriages were initially organised by the Korea Red Cross Organisation and some local governments. Later, private agencies and some Korean-Chinese who were already residing in Korea began to arrange such marriages (Lee, 2003b:143). In 1992, there were about 400 Korean men married to Chinese women (mostly Korean-Chinese women). This rose to about 2,000 in 1993 and 1994, peaked at 9,300 in 1996 before falling to 2,900 in 1999 (a consequence of the economic crisis of 1997 and 1998 and the change in the Nationality Law in 1998; see Lee, 2003b:143, 147), and then rising again to about 7,000 in 2001 and 2002.

Not only have international marriages become an important channel for Korean-Chinese women of marriageable age entering Korea, they also provide a route for older Korean-Chinese to return to Korea as Korean-Chinese wives may send two invitation letters to their parents to come to Korea (Hong, 2000). The numbers who have returned have also been inflated as a result of abuses such as "disguised marriages", the sale of

FIGURE 12.1   Major settlement areas in China of Korean-Chinese

"invitation letters", a rise in forged documents, while there has also been an increase in victims swindled by brokers and serious social problems in both South Korea and among the Korean-Chinese communities in China.[14] There were about 10,000 Korean-Chinese women in 1992 and 1993, rising to 18,000 in 1996, then falling to 14,000 in 1998 due to the economic crisis, before rising again to over 40,000 in 2001 and 2002 (Fig. 12.2). It would seem ironic that while the Korean government is anxious to limit the return of the Korean-Chinese, its promotion of international marriages between Korean farmers and Korean-Chinese has resulted in widening the doors for both young and older Korean-Chinese women to enter the country.

Exploitation of the "invitation of parents" visas (as well as the "visiting relatives" visas where an age limit of 45 years applies) has resulted in a distinctively older age profile for Korean-Chinese female migrants (Table 12.7). Compared to the stable proportion of Filipino women in Korea in their 20s or below (about 40 per cent in

FIGURE 12.2   Number of female migrants, 1992–2002

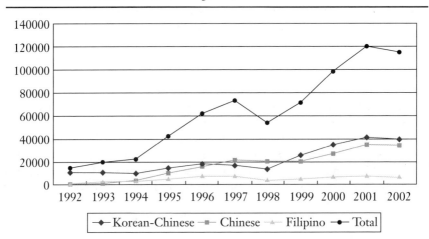

SOURCES: Adapted from the Ministry of Justice, Republic of Korea, 1992; 1993; 1994; 1995; 1996; 1997; 1998; 1999; 2000; 2001; 2002a.

TABLE 12.7   Age ranges of female undocumented migrant workers, 1993 and 2002

Age	1993			2002		
	Korean-Chinese	Chinese	Filipino	Korean-Chinese	Chinese	Filipino
20 & below	5.2	12.0	8.5	0.4	0.9	0.7
21–30	33.1	34.5	31.3	9.5	14.6	39.9
31–40	21.5	23.3	27.6	29.8	38.2	42.1
41–50	12.9	18.0	18.8	26.6	26.9	14.7
51 & over	27.4	12.3	13.7	33.6	19.4	2.6
Total	100.0	100.0	100.0	100.0	100.0	100.0
(N)	(4,707)	(5,434)	(7,871)	(30,552)	(22,693)	(3,703)

SOURCE: Adapted from Ministry of Justice, Republic of Korea, 1993; 2002a.
NOTES:
Data for 1993 are taken from Ministry of Justice, Republic of Korea, 1993, *Statistics for Arrivals*.
Data for 2002 are taken from Ministry of Justice, Republic of Korea, 2002a, *Statistics for Short-term Undocumented Foreigners*.

both 1993 and 2002), the equivalent figure for the Korean-Chinese dropped from nearly 40 per cent in 1993 to about ten per cent in 2002. Conversely, the proportion of middle-aged or older Korean-Chinese women in their 40s, 50s and above increased rapidly from 40 per cent in 1993 to 60 per cent in 2002. A recent study of 110 live-in Korean-Chinese domestic workers carried out during May and June 2002 confirmed the preponderance of older women—20 per cent were in their 40s, 61 per cent of them are in their 50s, and 19 per cent in their 60s (Ryu, 2002).

The availability of large numbers of older Korean-Chinese women in the labour market and the need for cheaper "live-in" domestic workers seemed to have coincided since the late 1990s. These women find it difficult to work in factories which usually have a preference for younger women. Instead, those in their 40s tend to work in the kitchens of Korean restaurants, while those in their 50s or over prefer domestic work. Ironically, as more Korean-Chinese daughters become "unpaid housewives" through international marriage with Korean men, their "mothers" (whether their biological mothers or those who have purchased "invitation letters") often become "paid domestic workers" in Korea.

The concentration of older Korean-Chinese in domestic work is indicated by data compiled from a recent 2002 amnesty where some 96 per cent of unauthorised migrants voluntarily registered with the local authorities between March and May 2002 (Ministry of Justice, 2002b; *Yonhap News*, 1 June 2002) so as to be allowed to stay in Korea until March 2003 (later postponed till 15 November 2003). Based on this registration data and other data from the Ministry of Justice (2002a), Table 12.8 categorises female migrant workers by industry. Ethnic concentration in certain industries is clearly indicated, for example, Korean-Chinese women in the service industry, and Filipino, Vietnamese and Indonesian women in manufacturing.

There are about 9,000 (or 8.9 per cent of 102,347 female migrant workers) unauthorised migrant domestic workers, the majority of which being Korean-Chinese (6,200), followed by Chinese (2,600), Mongolians (88) and Filipinos (57).[15] It should be noted, however, that some Korean-Chinese tend to report themselves as Chinese, and therefore the number of Korean-Chinese domestic workers is likely to be under-reported. Therefore, it is reasonable to say that while a relatively uncommon option for Korean households, hiring migrant workers as live-in domestic workers is largely confined to the employment of Korean-Chinese women.

The concentration of Korean-Chinese women in domestic work can be explained by several factors. First, while the employment of migrant workers in the service sector has been prohibited for a long time, a significant number of Korean-Chinese are able to bend the rules given their ability to speak Korean and similar physical appearance to Korean citizens. Second, modern Korean families living in apartments find it uncomfortable to employ young women as live-in domestic workers (as in the case of Filipino migrant women discussed above), and those with young children or elderly parents to care for prefer older women to provide such "live-in" service. However, where the live-in domestic worker is a local older woman, a younger employer may also

TABLE 12.8 Female migrant workers categorised by industry, 2002

Industry	Female migrants	Agri-culture/ Fishery %	Manu-facturing %	Con-struction %	All %	Service Domestic work % (n)	Unknown[c] %
Documented[a]	12,791	0.08	99.9	0.02	0	0	0
Undocumented[b]	89,556	0.7	25.2	6.8	47.9	10.2 (9,109)	19.5
Korean-Chinese	41,660	0.6	8.7	7.8	66.4	15.0 (6,244)	16.4
Chinese	30,855	0.4	33.7	7.7	44.3	8.6 (2,667)	13.9
Filipinos	6,648	0.2	81.0	0.4	2.7	0.9 (57)	15.7
Vietnamese	4,732	0.1	83.3	0.7	1.5	0.1 (7)	14.4
Indonesian	2,790	0.0	86.8	0.4	1.1	0.1 (3)	11.7
Thai	4,316	1.5	65.0	0.8	1.5	0.2 (8)	31.2
Mongolians	6,368	0.5	56.4	3.3	12.5	1.4 (88)	27.3
Uzbekistan	1,459	2.0	66.1	3.0	11.4	0.7 (10)	17.5
Others	3,519	1.2	62.7	3.4	6.7	0.7 (25)	26.0
Total	102,347	0.6	34.5	6.0	41.9	8.9 (9,109)	17.0

NOTES:
a   Adapted from Ministry of Justice, Republic of Korea, 2002a.
b   Adapted from Ministry of Justice, Republic of Korea, 2002b.
c   Unknown: Occupation was not declared to the authorities.

feel ill at ease directing or controlling her, as it runs counter to the Korean culture of respecting the elderly. Where older Korean-Chinese women are concerned, however, their employment as live-in domestic workers can be justified on the basis that they are foreigners and not part of Korean society, and as a means of offering employment opportunities to "disadvantaged, poor visitors". As a professional Korean woman whom I interviewed explains:

> I prefer Korean-Chinese domestic workers to local live-in [domestics], because a local older domestic worker pretends she knows better than I regarding the housework. Besides, a local domestic worker tends to compare her former employers with me and she talks frequently about the details of their lives. This means that she will gossip about my life. In contrast, Korean-Chinese women cannot discuss my private matters with other Koreans because, as a foreigner, she hardly knows any citizens.

The ability of the Korean-Chinese to speak Korean is also an added advantage in the eyes of Korean employers.

Finally, Korean-Chinese communities are able to access information about available jobs in domestic service through friends and relatives, as well as non-governmental organisations (NGOs) and private agencies[16] that post job-openings and job-seekers' memos on bulletin boards and internet "job-search" sites for the Korean-Chinese. For example, the Seoul Korean-Chinese Church website features job vacancies for which Korean-Chinese may apply, as well as detailed profiles of job searchers including photographs, age and expected income from which prospective employers may view and select.

According to Ryu's (2002) study, most employers of Korean-Chinese domestic workers are in professional occupations, including doctors, professors, instructors, pharmacists, lawyers and civil servants. In 29 per cent of the cases, the employers are older widowers or single fathers living in households with no women present. In 86 per cent of the cases where women are present, the female employer works outside the home. It was also found that 77 per cent of the Korean-Chinese domestic workers live with their employers in apartments while 22 per cent live in houses.

The study also found that 27 per cent of Korean-Chinese domestic workers perform housework, while 48 and 23 per cent take care of babies and the elderly respectively, in addition to housework duties. Another two per cent take care of all these three sets of duties at the same time. About half (52 per cent) earn about 1.0–1.1 million Korean won (about US$770–850) per month, 24 per cent earn 0.7–1.0 million Korean won (about US$540–770) while the other 24 per cent earn 1.1–1.4 million Korean won (about US$850–1,100). The small minority caring for both babies and the elderly in addition to housework earn about 1.2–1.5 million Korean won (about US$930–1,200). Compared to the average salary of about 1.2–1.4 million Korean won (about US$930–1,100) of local live-in domestic workers, Ryu (2002) concludes that Korean-Chinese domestic workers earn about 80–85 per cent of the wages of local domestic workers. In addition to what may be considered reasonable pay, most of these workers enjoy one day off every week or every fortnight. The strong NGO support networks provide Korean-Chinese domestic workers with updated information about job vacancies and prevailing wages, empowering them to switch employers if they are not satisfied with their working conditions or salary.

CURRENT ISSUES AND CONCERNS

While they enjoy reasonable working conditions in some respects, Korean-Chinese domestic workers have to confront a number of problematic issues. The first relates to the issue of citizenship. Allowing ethnic Korean-Chinese to work in the service sector, including the domestic work sector, from December 2002 was a major change in immigration and labour laws.[17] Another important forthcoming change in immigration law—already passed by the National Assembly in July 2003—is the conversion of the "trainee programme" to a "work permit programme" from August 2004. During the ensuring amnesty period to prepare for the change, 260,000 migrants registered (it is not known how many actually returned to their home countries by the deadline) and, just before the deadline, about 5,700 Korean-Chinese filed for Korean citizenship and then staged a sit-in demonstration to press their claims (*Chosun Newspaper*, 20 November 2003; 22 December 2003). The question of gaining Korean citizenship is hence an important issue for the Korean-Chinese migrant workers, including domestic workers. However, some Korean-Chinese who had worked in China and are expecting to get their pensions do not want Korean citizenship, although they would like the ability to come and go as they please. The citizenship issue also poses a delicate problem in terms of diplomatic relations with China.

Second, as the majority of Korean-Chinese domestic workers are in their 50s or 60s, health concerns loom large. Before December 2002, over 90 per cent of them had undocumented status and were not eligible for medical insurance (Ryu, 2002). Although their status has been legalised since then, they still cannot obtain national health insurance as they are working in private households.

The third and most important issue Korean-Chinese face is social discrimination by the locals. On the one hand, it has been noted that the community is the most advantageously placed in terms of wage earnings compared to other migrant groups in Korea (Lee, 1998). Given strong NGO support since 1995, the Korean-Chinese have also been able to organise protests against injustices and improve their working conditions (Lee, 2003b; Seol, 2003), as was the case with contributing to pushing for the passage of the bill converting the notorious trainee programme to the new work permit programme in the National Assembly on 31 July 2003.

On the other hand, several studies (Seol, 1996; Lee, 1998; 2003a; Lee et al., 2002) have reported that the Korean-Chinese are the least satisfied migrant group in Korea and outlined their relative deprivation. As ethnic Koreans, they expect equal treatment from citizens but are often treated as "unwelcome visitors" from a "poor" country. Their concentration in the domestic work sector and rumours of "disguised marriages" further lower their status in the eyes of the locals. Caught in the intricacies of identity politics, their "double-minority status" in both China and Korea has led to identity crisis and social discrimination given their status of being the-same-yet-different.

CONCLUSION

In recent years, given that there are over 14 million households in Korea, the presence of some 9,000 migrant live-in domestic workers (mainly Korean-Chinese) in the country suggests that reliance on this form of domestic help is not a common option in Korea. Unlike Singapore, Hong Kong, and Taiwan where the state has developed schemes to import migrant domestic workers in order to improve women's labour force participation rates, the Korean government did not allow migrant workers to participate in the domestic work sector until December 2002, and then only for the Korean-Chinese who already had managed to gain employment as live-in domestic workers for many years before that (as they are less easily distinguishable from the locals and can therefore "hide" their migrant status). The relatively weak position of Korean women in the labour market as well as prevailing gender ideologies that thrust the burden of housework on the Korean wife (in terms of the management of housework among the middle-class and the actual performance of housework for the lower classes) further render the live-in domestic worker an uncommonly sought after option. Instead, most middle-class households turn to local part-time domestic workers to complement the role played by Korean wives in maintaining a middle-class lifestyle. Among the small number of households which require live-in domestic help, Korean-Chinese women provide the main source of labour as they combine the advantages of sharing a similar ethnicity and language while, at the same time, being "outsiders".

In summary, it is expected that the number of Korean-Chinese domestic workers will increase in South Korea due to the recent change in the immigration policies. However, the size of future demand for such domestic workers will depend on Korean women's position in the labour market, as well as the quantity and quality of Korean family welfare programmes and facilities such as daycare and nursing homes.

NOTES

1   This is also reflected in the fact that while there have been many studies on migrant workers in Korea (see Lee et al., 1998; Seok et al., 2003), little is known about migrant women in general and migrant domestic workers in particular.

2   The *nobi* ("no" referring to male servants and "bi" to female servants) was an ascriptive status and as such, children of *nobi* automatically became *nobi* by birth.

3   The occupational distribution of married Korean women in 1999 was: professionals, managers and technicians (9.4 per cent), clerical workers (7.7 per cent), sales and service workers (37.4), farmers and related workers (14.6), operators and other blue-collar workers (30.9 per cent) (Korean Women's Development Institute, 2000). In other words, among the approximately 4.6 million employed married women in urban areas in 1999, only about 0.5 million worked as managers, professionals and technicians.

4   The reduction is likely to be a consequence of improved household technology and the development of convenience services such as ready-cooked foods and laundry services.

5   Organising their children's education to ensure entrance to a quality university and progression up the social-economic ladder is an important managerial role for the Korean mother. Success in this arena reaps status for the whole family.

6   As labour shortages worsened, the Korean government began to utilise the trainee programme as an avenue for importing unskilled migrant workers, beginning in November 1991. The government decided to expand it into the "industrial trainee programme" in November 1993 and later modified it into the "employment after trainee programme" in 1998 (Lee, 2003b:132).

7   The original trainee programme was intended for Korean firms with overseas operations or subsidiaries to bring their foreign employees back to Korea for training. As the labour shortages became extreme, beginning in November 1991, the government began to expand the programme. At first, the number of foreign trainees was expanded, followed by the number of firms allowed to utilise this programme. In 1992, there were ten (mainly "3D") industries in the manufacturing sector which were allowed to utilise this programme, regardless of whether the firm possessed overseas operations. In 1993, the number of industries expanded to 21. In November 1993, the government decided to expand the trainee programme (called the industrial trainee programme thereafter) further to include firms in almost all manufacturing industries, and to authorise the Korea Federation of Small Business to manage the programme. Under this industrial trainee programme, 142,000 Asian trainees entered Korea from 1994 to May 2000. In 1998, the government revised the "industrial trainee programme" to the "employment after trainee programme" to allow some unskilled foreigners to receive one-year work permits as long as they passed an examination after two years of training in Korea (enacted from April 2000). This new programme is similar to the "technical intern programme" in Japan.

8   In 2002, about half of the male migrant workers and two-thirds of the female migrant workers in Korea are from China. Since December 1993, many Chinese workers have entered Korea as industrial trainees. With the relocation of many Korean firms to China since the early 1990s, Chinese-based Korean companies have been able to send their Chinese workers to Korea.

9   There are no available figures of the number of Filipino domestic workers in the early 1990s.

10   Up to the middle of the 1990s, the earnings of migrant workers in factories were set very low at around 300,000 Korean won (about US$300) per month (Lee, 1998).

11   The first apartment block was built in Mapogu in Seoul in the early 1960s. Housing shortages soon led to the construction of more of such blocks in Seoul since the 1970s, and in other cities since the 1980s. Until the late 1970s, it was popular to have a small separate "maid's room" designated in blueprints for new apartments. Since the early 1980s, however, this has disappeared, reflecting changes in middle-class lifestyles in Korea (for more information, see http://arch.hannam.ac.kr/~kih/mr.htm; http://nwk.joins.com/newsweek/program/nwk_article_print/?aid=185553; and *Chosun Newspaper*, 9 February 1982) (all accessed 18 January 2004).

12   If Han Chinese are included, the number of minority groups would be 56.

13   The age limit was 55 years old in 1992, rose to 60 years, then decreased to 55 years in 1998 and 45 years in 2002 (Hong, 2000).

14   In a recent study (Ryu, 2002) of 110 Korean-Chinese domestic workers, 71 per cent came to Korea through "visiting relatives" visas, including 37 per cent who came through the "invitation of parents" visas facilitated by their daughters who married Korean men. Only 35 per cent had legitimate visas and did not have to pay commission to a broker; the other 65 per cent paid about 60,000–70,000 Chinese yuan (or 9,600,000–11,200,000 Korean won). More than half (55 per cent) came to Korea in order to save money for their children's education or marriages. Most of them wanted to raise funds to send their children to universities in China or even in Japan, but worry about the tuition and dormitory fees which have increased rapidly since China began to liberalise its educational system. Others are saving to prepare houses for their sons, as is the usual responsibility of the bridegroom's parents among Korean-Chinese communities in China (Hong, 2000; Ryu, 2002).

15   The fact that more Chinese and Mongolian women than Filipino women work as domestic workers in Korea confirms the importance of factors such as age and appearance in Korea.

16   Internet sites for job postings are provided by various organisations including the Seoul Korean-Chinese Church (http://211.172.225.111, accessed 18 January 2004; http://chosunjock.x-y.net, accessed 4 May 2004), the Korean-Chinese Shelter in the House for Migrant Workers (http://218.38.19.123:18599, accessed 18 January 2004), the Dongpo-Job-dot-com (http://www.dongpojob.com, accessed 18 January 2004), and the Korean-Chinese Village (http://moyiza.net, accessed 18 January 2004). The first two organisations are civic NGOs and the latter two private organisations.

17   This change, however, is mainly symbolic as it serves to legitimise an existing practice. A significant number of Korean-Chinese, especially Korean-Chinese women, have already found work in the service industry since the early 1990s. It should also be noted that, if the Immigration and Legal Status of Overseas Koreans Act which permits overseas Koreans to enter, work and engage in economic activities more easily than before includes Korean-Chinese from 2004, restrictions on their entrance to and employment in Korea will no longer apply. For more information, see Lee (2003b:135).

REFERENCES

Cho, H. J. 1988. *Women and Men in Korea*. Seoul: Moonhak Gua Jisung Sa (in Korean).

Choe, J. R. 1991. *A Study on the Role Management Strategies and the Level of Role Conflict in Working Wives*. Unpublished M. A. dissertation, Department of Home Management, Graduate School of Ewha Womans University (in Korean).

Chosun Newspaper. Various issues. http://www.chosun.com. Accessed 18 January 2004.

Chung, Y. J. 1987. *The Study on the Socialization of Household Work in Food Preparation*. Unpublished M. A. dissertation, Department of Home Management, Graduate School of Ewha Woman's University (in Korean).

Hong, K. H. 2000. *The Gender Politics of Migration Viewed through Marriages between Chosun-jock (Korean-Chinese) Women and Korean Men*. Unpublished M. A. dissertation, Department of Women's Studies, Graduate School of Ewha Woman's University (in Korean).

Jin, K., H. Song, & S. Kim. 1996. Multiple roles and stress of married female teachers. *Family and Culture*, 1(1), 83–102 (in Korean).

Joongang Newspaper. Various issues. http://news.joins.com. Accessed 18 January 2004.

Kang, J. O. 1984. *The Survey on The Socialization of Household Labor—in Meal Preparation*. Unpubl. M.A. dissertation, Department of Home Economics, Graduate School of Kon-Kuk University (in Korean).

Kang, S. J., S. S. Yung, & B. K. Choi. 1968. A status survey of time management in home life. *Journal of the Korean Home Economics Association*, 6, 973–81 (in Korean).

Kim, B. O. & M. Y. Chang. 1968. The rate of kitchen management of Korean housewives. *Journal of the Korean Home Economics Association*, 6, 959–72 (in Korean).

Kim, B. S. 2003. A life-style of Korean couples. Paper presented at the Workshop on Everyday Lives of Koreans, The Academy of Korean Studies. 25 November (in Korean).

Kim, S. H. 1996. *The Changes of Housework Following the Introduction of Household Technology*. Unpublished Ph.D. dissertation, Department of Consumer and Child Studies, Graduate School of Seoul National University (in Korean).

_____. 1999. The changes from the traditional society to the industrial society in housework. *Journal of Korean Home Management Association*, 17(4), 149–58 (in Korean).

Kim, W. Y. 2003. The dynamic analysis of women's labor force participation rates through marriage and child-birth. Paper presented at *A Conference on Korean Labor Panel Studies*, Korea Labor Institute, 21 February in Seoul, Korea (in Korean).

Korea National Statistical Office. 2000. *2000 Population and Housing Census*, Vol. 6, Korea: Korea National Statistical Office.

Korean Statistical Association. 1970. *Annual Report on the Economically Active Population Survey*, Korea: Korean Statistical Association.

_____. 1980. *Annual Report on the Economically Active Population Survey*, Korea: Korean Statistical Association.

_____. 1990. *Annual Report on the Economically Active Population Survey*, Korea: Korean Statistical Association.

_____. 2000. *Annual Report on the Economically Active Population Survey*, Korea: Korean Statistical Association.

Korean Women's Development Institute. 2000. *Statistical Yearbook on Women*, Korea: Korean Women's Development Institute.

Lee, H. K. 1997a. The employment of foreign workers in Korea: Issues and policy suggestions. *International Sociology*, 12(3), 353–371.

_____. 1997b. The employment of foreign domestic workers in Asia. *Journal of Social Sciences*, 15, 227–247 (in Korean).

_____. 1998. The socio-economic situation of migrant workers in Korea. In *Migrant Workers in Korea*. Edited by H. K. Lee, K. S. Jung, S. D. Kang, D. H. Seol & H. H. Seok. Seoul: Center for Future Human Resource Studies, 11–101 (in Korean).

_____. 2003a. The employment situations of migrant workers in Korea. In *Works and Lives of Migrant Workers*. Edited by H. H. Seok, K. S. Jung, J. W. Lee, H. K. Lee & S. D. Kang. Seoul: Center for Future Human Resource Studies, 167–202 (in Korean).

_____. 2003b. Gender, migration and civil activism in South Korea. *Asian and Pacific Migration Journal*, 12(1–2), 127–53.

Lee, H. K., K. S. Jung, S. D. Kang, D. H. Seol, & H. H. Seok, eds. 1998. *Migrant Workers in Korea*. Seoul: Center for Future Human Resource Studies (in Korean).

Lee, H. K., K. Jung, J. Lee, & D. Seol. 2002. Comparative study on the labour management style in domestic and overseas Korean companies. *Korean Journal of Sociology*, 36(3), 47–77 (in Korean).

Lee, J. H. 1989. A study on service purchasing behaviour related household work of the urban housewives (I). *Journal of Kosin University*, 17, 405–22 (in Korean).

_____. 1990. A study on service purchasing behaviour related household work of the urban housewives (II). *Journal of Kosin University*, 18, 163–90 (in Korean).

Lee, J. W. 1972 A study on the shares of household work. *Journal of the Korean Home Economics Association*, 10(2), 63–76 (in Korean).

Lee, J. W. & E. J. Lee. 1992. A study on the socialization of household work and related Factors. *Journal of the Korean Home Economics Association*, 30(1), 179–98 (in Korean).

Lee, K. Y. 1987. *A Study on the Commodity Substitution of Housework in Korea*. Unpublished Ph.D. dissertation, Department of Home Management, Seoul National University (in Korean).

Lee, M. S. & J. W. Lee. 1997. A study on the housework management strategies and the housework management satisfaction of career women. *Journal of the Korean Home Economics Association*, 35(2), 201–16 (in Korean).

Lee, S. M. 1989. *Time Pressure Perceived by Housewife and Housework Performance Strategy*. Unpublished M. A. dissertation, Department of Home Management, Graduate School of Seoul National University (in Korean).

Lee, Y. S. & K. E. Park. 2000. Generational transmission of household works from mothers to married daughters. *Journal of Korean Home Management Association*, 18(2), 29–44 (in Korean).

Ministry of Education and Human Resources Development, and Korean Educational Development Institute. 2001. *Educational Statistics*, Korea: Ministry of Education and Human Resources Development, and Korean Educational Development Institute.

Ministry of Justice, Republic of Korea. 1992. *Annual Report on Emigration and Immigration*, Korea: Ministry of Justice.

_____. 1993. *Annual Report on Emigration and Immigration*. Korea: Ministry of Justice.

_____. 1994. *Annual Report on Emigration and Immigration*. Korea: Ministry of Justice.

_____. 1995. *Annual Report on Emigration and Immigration*. Korea: Ministry of Justice.

_____. 1996. *Annual Report on Emigration and Immigration*. Korea: Ministry of Justice.

_____. 1997. *Annual Report on Emigration and Immigration.* Korea: Ministry of Justice.

_____. 1998. *Annual Report on Emigration and Immigration.* Korea: Ministry of Justice.

_____. 1999. *Annual Report on Emigration and Immigration.* Korea: Ministry of Justice.

_____. 2000. *Annual Report on Emigration and Immigration.* Korea: Ministry of Justice.

_____. 2001. *Annual Report on Emigration and Immigration.* Korea: Ministry of Justice.

_____. 2002a. *Annual Report on Emigration and Immigration.* Korea: Ministry of Justice.

_____. 2002b. *Inside Report.* Korea: Ministry of Justice.

Moon, S. J., O. H. Kyung, & J. H. Young. 1997. The effects of the division of household labour in couples and the sense of fairness on marital satisfaction. *Journal of the Korean Home Economics Association,* 35(2), 345–58 (in Korean).

Park, C. J. 1973. A study on the live-in domestic workers. *Journal of College of Education,* 4(1), 241–249 (in Korean).

Park, S. M., & K. U. Kim. 1999. Meaning of household work and identity of Korean women in 1980s and 1990s. *Korean Social Science,* 21(4), 33–74 (in Korean).

Ryu, K. S. 2002. *A Study on the Korean-Chinese Live-in Domestic Workers in Korea.* A report by the Study Group Supporting the Assembly woman, Kim Kyung Chun (in Korean).

Seok, D. & K. Y. Lee. 1999. The perception of housework self-responsibility and attitude to paid labour substitution of wife and husband. *Journal of Korean Home Management Association,* 17(3), 171–85.

Seok, H. H., K. S. Jung, J. W. Lee, H. K. Lee, & S. D. Kang, eds. 2003. *Works and Lives of Migrant Workers.* Seoul: Center for Future Human Resource Studies (in Korean).

Seol, D. H. 1996. The Earnings Attainments of Migrants: 1992–1996. Paper presented at the Conference by the Korean Sociologist Association, Ajou University, Soo Won, Kyunggi-do, 6 December in Korea (in Korean).

_____. 2003. Migrant movements in Korea, 1992–2002. In *Resist, Coalitional, and Memorial Politics 2: Trends of Social Movements in Korea.* Edited by J. K. Kim. Seoul: Culture and Science Press, 76–102 (in Korean).

Shin, K. J. 1985. A study on the rationality of household work—with special emphasis on electric appliances and measuring utensils. *The Journal of Korean Living Science Research,* 3(1), 385–424 (in Korean).

Yonhap News. 2002 1 June, http://www.yonhapnews.co.kr (accessed 18 January 2004).

Yoon, B. C. 1975. Time spent on household work. *Journal of the Korean Home Economics Association,* 13(2), 151–69 (in Korean).

You, Y. S. 1980. A study on the survey of the meal management. *Journal of the Korean Home Economics Association,* 18(1), 53–66 (in Korean).

Young, M. S. 1970. *A Study on the Kitchen Management of Korean Household.* Unpublished M. A. dissertation, Department of Home Economics, Graduate School of Sookmyung Women's University (in Korean).

13

Unpaid Domestic Work: Gender, State Policy and the Labour Market in Japan

TOMOKO NAKAMATSU

INTRODUCTION

"The woman's dream [in life]", says Chikako Ogura, in her book *Kekkon no Jōken* (The Terms of Marriage), "is to win either by marriage or by job" (Ogura, 2003:46). Unable to become winners in either of these ways are "the wives who have to work to supplement their husbands' earnings" (Ogura, 2003:46). The majority of married women in Japan fall into the category of the "working mother", who typically struggles in "harmonising a double burden" of unpaid domestic work and paid part-time work (Eccleston, 1989:190). They offer cheap and flexible labour, which partly contributed to Japan's non-reliance on foreign workers during its period of high economic growth (Kajita, 1994). Career opportunities for married women remain limited, and are worsened by the current economic recession. Data in 1996 show that mothers with paid work spend almost 13 times as much time on domestic work than their husbands. Indeed, fathers spend less time on domestic work when their wives are in employment than when they are not (Iwama, 2000b:39–42). Until very recently, state policies such as those of the tax system offered incentives for women to stay at home or in part-time employment. At the same time, discourses that value domestic work performed by the wife and mother were pervasive, establishing domesticity as a possible site for women's self-expression. While the "men at work, women at home" view of the sexual division of labour no longer has the overwhelming support it once enjoyed in the 1970s, the vast majority of women continue to bear domestic responsibilities.[1]

This paper explores the various cultural, social and political factors that underpin the above phenomenon. First, it traces the historical construction of the sexual division of labour in Japanese society elucidating the ideology of *ryōsai kenbo* (a good wife and wise mother) and the historical evolution of the performance of domestic work in Japan. Second, it describes state welfare policies as well as business and workplace practices, highlighting how these seek to marginalise women in the formal economic sphere and instead favour their remaining at home as full-time mothers. Next, it describes recent changes in Japan's demographic and economic characteristics and recent shifts in policies and incentives targeted at encouraging women to remain employed and to reproduce. Whilst the prospect of hiring foreigners for care work in hospitals in the future is currently being debated in the context of a rapidly ageing population, the possibility of hiring foreign women to perform domestic work within Japanese households still remains outside the imagination of a large majority of Japanese. It concludes that the ideology of *ryōsai kenbo*, which values women's work in the domestic sphere, underscores the closed mindset of the Japanese towards this option. Recent shifts in policy that are still rooted in privileging traditional family form based on heterosexual marriage, coupled with the current slump in the economy that makes it difficult for women (and men) to gain full-time employment, contribute to domestic work remaining largely as the unpaid work of women in contemporary Japan.

DOMESTIC WORK: HISTORICAL OVERVIEW AND DISCOURSES

The employment of domestic workers is not culturally foreign to Japanese households. Anecdotal evidence suggests that Japanese families of corporate employees living abroad often employ a domestic helper in cities such as Jakarta and Singapore where the service is readily available. Moreover the history of working women in Japan reveals that the *jochō* (live-in maid) was among the most common occupation after farming and factory work for women of low socio-economic background in the early twentieth century (Saitō, 2000:72–94).[2] The growth of paid domestic work in Japan is similar to trends observed elsewhere. Demand tends to increase with the process of industrialisation and modernisation (Momsen, 1999). During Meiji Japan (1868–1912), modernisation meant catching up with the West in terms of colonial and economic expansion as well as living standards. The state embarked on promoting the home and family as sites of consumption and reproduction, which it viewed as essential for economic progress. Women were identified as playing a pivotal role in reconstructing the private sphere. As such, the ideology of *ryōsai kenbo* was introduced and institutionalised through various state-led programmes such as girls' higher school education.[3] These programmes provided formal training on home management for women of relatively well-off families—at that time the only women able to afford to go to higher schools—to learn the ways of becoming "good wives and wise mothers". The ideology of *ryōsai kenbo* propagated the "modern woman" as one committed to bearing and raising quality children in addition to carrying out other tasks associated with domesticity responsibly. Essentially, women and men were identified as playing separate but equal roles in Japan's economic development. Women were groomed to become primary carers and nurturers of the family while men were trained to take the lead in the public sphere as productive economic units (Koyama, 1991). Thus the ideology of *ryōsai kenbo* advocated a gendered division of labour as a form of gender equality (Koyama, 1991).

Industrialisation and urbanisation in the early 1900s brought about the emergence of a new middle-class in large cities comprising company employees, government workers, doctors and lawyers which in turn led to an increase in demand for domestic helpers (Muta, 1996). Prior to this, the option of having a domestic helper had previously been affordable only for upper class but this luxury spread to the expanding urban middle class with their increasing affluence. Indicative of this phenomenon was the introduction of the management of domestic helpers in the *ryōsai kenbo* syllabus of women's private colleges established in the early 20th century that were attended mostly by the middle class (Saitō, 2000:87). The urban middle class households were able to attract helpers with post-elementary education. These helpers comprised rural women who had attended girls' higher schools and were seeking a job in domestic work to learn the practical knowledge of being a good wife and mother in the urban, middle (or upper) class environment (Hamana, 1998). At that time, employing a domestic helper came to be seen as a symbol of status and middle-class identity (Hamana, 1998:84). In 1920, it was estimated that about 580,000 women or 5.7 per cent of the women in the labour force were employed as domestic helpers (Hamana, 1998). By 1930, this proportion increased to 17 per cent, which meant that one in every 17 households employed a female domestic worker (Hamana, 1998). The numbers peaked by the mid-1930s and started to decrease gradually as manufacturing and service sectors started to absorb women's labour power (Hamana, 1998).

According to Hamana (1998), until around 1910, a young woman's main motivation for becoming a domestic worker was to learn the practical knowledge of sewing, cooking and the proper manners expected of a good wife and wise mother. It was considered not so much as paid work but as an education. These women were not necessarily of poor origin and some had more than elementary education. The situation started to change in the 1920s when job opportunities for young women began to diversify as noted above. As a consequence, live-in domestic work became predominantly a job for rural women who were lowly educated and were mainly in their late teens and early twenties (Hamana, 1998:84). At this point, the working conditions for domestic helpers also started deteriorating. These women were made to work long hours with very little free time. It was also quite common for employers and family members to mistreat them and treat them with little dignity (Saitō, 2000:85–7). In addition, their wages were comparably much lower than women factory workers (Hamana, 1998:66). As such, by the early 1930s, households below the new middle-class could afford live-in domestic helpers. Subsequently all these factors contributed to the low status of paid domestic work and its complete loss of significance and importance as an avenue for training to become a proper wife and mother (Hamana, 1998).

Until the 1960s, a large population remained in rural areas and was engaged in farming.[4] The rapid economic growth experienced by Japan in the 1960s brought about accelerated rates of urbanisation and an explosion of middle-class nuclear families headed by husbands who were white-collar employees. This new family form and burgeoning wealth led to an intensification of the sexual division of labour as the site of production and reproduction became separated and a majority of married women became *sengyō shufu* or "full-time" housewives. As the country's post-war reconstruction neared completion, companies began closing their doors to young women (Ueno, 1990:193). The notion that women's proper place was at home became reinforced. Thus, embracing the role of housewives that was once a privilege among middle- and upper middle-class women became widespread. However, unlike housewives in the early 20th century who had hired domestic help, those of the expanding middle class in the 1960s themselves shouldered household chores and child rearing without the assistance of hired help (Ueno, 1990:197). Further, as labour shortage became apparent, these housewives were soon encouraged to enter the workforce as part-time workers with their domestic role fully intact.

The narrative of Kayama is indicative of such social change.[5] Kayama, born as a daughter of a rural farming family in 1937, worked as a live-in domestic helper after graduating from middle-school in the 1950s until her marriage. She was referred to the job by her schoolteacher, like most of her classmates at that time in her home village. The family she worked for had a daughter who was of a similar age to her. The daughter was attending a dress-making school while learning the art of tea ceremony and flower arrangement. Kayama recalled that she often thought how extreme the class differences were between her life and the daughter's, saying that she still could not forget how sad she felt. Kayama then added with laughter, "but then the daughter, too, married a salaried man, and became a housewife, making lunch boxes. We still laugh about how different [our lives turned out to be] from those days" (Kayama, personal communication, 5 January 2003). The economic growth of Japan gave Kayama the chance to become a housewife as her husband was able to provide for the family. As an outcome, the overwhelming class division Kayama felt as a young working girl of rural origin ceased to exist. The fact that she did take up part-time work after her youngest child finished primary school, however, showed the difference in household wealth between her family and that of her former employer's daughter.

In the 1960s, discourses emphasising women's domestic responsibilities encouraging them to stay home during the early period of child-rearing started circulating, coinciding with the introduction of compulsory health checks for children as young as three. An example is the discourse of *sansai-ji shinwa* (myth of the three-year-old) that stressed the importance of the mother-child relationship for the healthy development of the child (Iwama, 2000c:185). In the 1980s, the notion that mothers with children under the age of three years should stay at home was once again vigorously promoted through campaigns organised by public health centres with the support of the media. The overemphasis of the mother's role in the upbringing of children drew criticisms from some feminists (Inoue, 1992:98). However, a survey conducted by a government agency in 1993 showed that 89 per cent of the respondents (6,083 married women) supported the notion that mothers with young children should not be working (Iwama, 2000c:185). This suggests that the "myth of the three-year-old" has been imbibed by a majority of the society (even women), reflecting an entrenched perception of women's rightful role as full-time mothers. Alternatively, these dominant discourses have the unintended impact of propagating negative perceptions of working mothers, provoking some of these women to develop a sense of guilt over their conscious choice to remain in employment.

The domestic services industry has shown some growth since the late 1990s with large-scale firms entering the business. Small-scale local based companies and Non-Profit Organisations (NPOs) offer a range of aged care and childcare services and other domestic services. The Ministry of Health, Labour and Welfare through various agencies also started offering similar subsidised homecare services by employing the elderly (those who are 60 years old and above) for such work. In 1995, the Statistics Bureau recorded that approximately 55,000 people were employed in the domestic services industry of which 30,000 are working as *kaseifu* (live-out care/domestic workers), 5,000 are employed as live-in domestic workers, and the remaining are categorised as employees of other related occupation (The Statistic Bureau et al., n.d.). Household spending on domestic services in the year 2000 grew by 1.51 times compared to 1980; however, expenditure on domestic services constituted a mere 0.18 per cent of total household spending (Suzuki & Kitada, 2001). In the 1990s, only 25 per cent of married women of reproductive age with preschool children used public day-care centres, reflecting the unpopularity of commercial domestic services (Ogawa, 2003). While there seems to be a demand for domestic services (which is likely to boost the industry in the near future), current prices are generally not competitive enough, and available services are not well known by the general public (Suzuki & Kitada, 2001).

Currently, only the diplomatic community and staff in multinational companies employ live-in foreign domestic helpers who are mainly Filipinos (Osteria, 1994; Tenegra, 2003b).[6] This is because this group of workers command high wages that are beyond the means of the majority of working mothers who are usually only employed in part-time employment.[7] Moreover, under law, foreign domestic workers can only be employed by foreign expatriates and not by local Japanese. Unlike countries such as Singapore, Taiwan, Hong Kong and Malaysia (see Abdul Rahman et al.; Lan; Wee & Sim; and Chin, this volume), paid domestic workers in Japan are almost exclusively locals. Until recently, Japanese immigration policy welcomed skilled foreigners and prohibited the entry of unskilled foreign workers (Mori, 1997). Policy makers have been cautious about the adverse effects of allowing a free flow of foreign workers into Japan, especially pertaining to social costs associated with the potentially permanent residence of foreigners. In addition, Japan's ongoing ambiguity with its long-term Korean residents whose origin stems from the colonial past, complicates the issue of social, labour and citizenship rights of foreigners (Kajita, 1994).

Recent changes to immigration policy to cater to rising demand for unskilled workers in Japan were careful to maintain the cultural homogeneity of Japan, which was institutionalised in the national identity discourse after the Second World

War (for a discussion on homogeneity, see Befu, 2001). As such, only unskilled migrants of *Nikkeijin* or Japanese descendants were allowed when the Immigration Act was amended in 1990 (Mori, 1997).[8] Despite the tight control on the flow of unskilled foreigners, foreigners performing unskilled jobs have nonetheless become a familiar sight in Japan. One example is the foreign women who work in bars and other associated entertainment industries. These women who are mainly from the Philippines, South Korea and other Asian countries enter Japan under the "entertainment" visa category (Nakamatsu, 2002). Over the years, foreign women entering Japan under other visa categories have also been employed illegally in the entertainment industry (Nakamatsu, 2002).

Recently, some female *Nikkeijin* who are well versed in Japanese have been employed in hospitals as orderlies (Shinozuka & Yokomura, 1994; Yamanaka, 1997). Faced with an ageing problem, the Liberal Democratic Party panel on free trade agreements is debating whether to allow more doctors and nurses from the Philippines and Thailand to work in Japan (*Japan Times Online*, 25 February 2004). Policy makers are also beginning to consider allowing more foreign workers in the near future to be employed in care work for the sick and elderly. However, the employment of foreigners in daily housework of cleaning or cooking in the domestic domain is currently not under public discussion.

In summary, married mothers currently perform most of the domestic work in Japan. Although there has been some growth in the domestic services industry, domestic work largely remains outside the realm of paid work. The ideology of the good wife and wise mother is deeply entrenched in Japanese society. The reproductive work of full-time mothers such as making healthy and elaborate lunches for the child and the husband are highly valued in Japanese culture as these acts live up to the *ryōsai kenbo* ideology (Hagiwara, 2003). Thus the performance of reproduction and domestic work provide a site for self-expression for women, especially in a climate where women find limited opportunities (and satisfaction) in full-time formal employment.

In recent years, many young women are known to aspire to lead the life of a *sengyō shufu*, that is, a professional housewife who is married to a communicative and cooperative partner who can also provide them with material comforts (3Cs) (Mukuno, 2000:184). For these women, their ideal marital life would be one in which they are full-time mothers when their children are young, re-entering the workforce only after their children are grown-up to fill time. However, they would only like to take up jobs that do not disrupt their duties as wives and mothers (Ogura, 2003).[9] This suggests a widespread perception among today's women that devoting oneself fully to reproductive and domestic work presents a better life option than shouldering the double burden of paid work and domestic work. This is because gender discrimination in the Japanese labour market makes it extremely difficult for women to seek satisfaction when juggling these two roles. This issue is taken up further in the next section.

GENDERED LABOUR MARKET AND DOMESTIC RESPONSIBILITY

The primary identification of women as wives and mothers means that their labour power in the formal sphere is perceived as having secondary significance. According to a 2001 labour force survey, the labour force participation rate for women was 49.2 per cent (approximately 10 million women were engaged in formal employment), accounting for 40.4 per cent of the total workforce (excluding the agriculture sector) (Nihon Fujin Dantai Rengōkai, 2002:257). However, 47.9 per cent of women who are working are engaged in part-time employment as opposed to only 12.5 per cent of working males (Nakashima, 2002:80–4). The proportion of women in part-time work rose from 56.1 per cent to 71.6 per cent between 1975 and 2000 (Nihon Fujin Dantai Rengōkai, 2002:264).[10] A significant proportion of women part-time workers are mothers re-entering the workforce after their child-rearing period.

The common labelling of pōto or shufu pōto (housewife part-time workers) for female non-full-time workers reflects the inferior position of married women in the workforce. Male part-time workers are often employed under a different job category with better employment conditions and financial benefits. As Broadbent (2003) rightly argues, the use of married women as a pool of low-cost flexible labour has benefited employers and secured the position of male workers as full-time employees. Until the recent slump in the economy, the high representation of married women in part-time employment shows that the Japanese labour market is highly gendered with married women having limited or no opportunity to pursue full-time employment upon re-entering the workforce after their child-rearing years. Moreover, highly educated married women have very little incentive to return to the work force after having children. First, they have no real economic need to do so as they tend to be married to highly educated men with high income earning capacity. Second, job options for women re-entering the workforce are more than often limited to unappealing part-time jobs. As such, the full potential earning capacity of these more highly educated women is not likely to be realised if they choose to re-enter the paid workforce (Iwama, 2000a:35–8).

There has been inconsistent progress on improving the working conditions of full-time female employees. In the year 2000, the average full-time female employee was still earning 65 per cent of the wages earned by their male counterpart (Nakashima, 2002:81). Since 1986, many large-scale companies have created two distinct career paths for women: sōgōshoku (managerial track) and ippan shoku (clerical track). This division is not applicable to men and serves to legitimise tough working conditions for women in the former track, while denying appropriate promotion for those in the latter. The Equal Employment Opportunity Act enacted in 1986 and revised in 1999 prohibits sexual discrimination in recruitment, training, promotion and other major areas. Generally, however, this is poorly enforced as no penalty is imposed on errant employers. Only very few women who claimed to have been discriminated against have succeeded when bringing their cases to court (Nakashima, 2002).

Conventional employment practice of awarding wages based on seniority discriminate women whose careers are interrupted when they have children. Recently, the decade-long recession forced some employers to adopt a system of wages and promotion based on merit in order to enhance competitiveness. The Labour Standard Act was also amended in 1999, removing the ban on overtime, night work, and work on public holidays for women. These changes gave some women more opportunity to reach management positions. However, as Nakashima (2002) argues, it made working conditions for women worse as a whole with over time and night work expected as a norm. Women now have to perform overtime work and night work, making it impossible for them to carry out paid work with household responsibilities, forcing more women to go part-time. The glass ceiling is prevalent and female managers are understandably often single or have no children (Broadbent, 2003:17).

In summary, current conditions of the Japanese labour market discourage married women from engaging in full-time work. Mothers who seek to re-enter the workforce can only find part-time work. In addition, the severe working conditions of full-time employment for women make it almost impossible for women to juggle domestic responsibilities and full-time work. Those women who go far in their careers are often single women or married women with no children. Gender-based discriminatory practices leave women in dead-end career paths with very limited job satisfaction. This perhaps explains why many young women aspire to become a full-time professional housewife, given the right partner (previous section). Women are perceived and constructed to play a secondary role in the Japanese labour market because of the primary identification of their roles as wives and mothers.

GENDERED SOCIAL POLICIES, DOMESTIC WORK, AND REPRODUCTION

In recent years, falling fertility rates and an ageing population gave rise to a change in state social policies concerning women's productive and reproductive roles. Between 1970 and 2000, the number of people aged 65 years old or older to the total population increased from 7.1 per cent to 17.4 per cent while the fertility rate fell from 2.13 to 1.36 (Nihon Fujin Dantai Rengōkai, 2002:234, 237). Compared to their counterparts 30 years ago, today's young women, especially those in their late twenties, are staying in the labour force, remaining single, and are not having children. They can now afford to postpone marriage and childbirth primarily because they are better educated and can choose from a wider range of jobs with better salaries. Given these emerging demographic trends, the state appears to be attempting to "restructure" gender relations. The model of the "salaried-man husband and housewife" that was once held as ideal is no longer deemed as feasible for Japan's continued development and survival.

371

In the 1970s, the state advocated *Nihongata fukushi shakai* (Japanese-style welfare society), which emphasised the responsibility of the family in providing child and aged care (Broadbent, 2003:93). As the family carer was a woman in the existing sexual division of labour, government rhetoric reinforced domestic burdens on the wife and mother in the name of culture and tradition. Reduction in welfare spending in the 1970s and 1980s resulted in the long-term shortage of pre-schools (Sakai, 2002) and aged-care facilities up until the 1990s. Tax, health and pension insurance policies also work to discourage married women from having full-time employment. Currently, those who are earning less than ¥1.03 million (approximately US$8,900) annually are exempted from paying income tax. Since 1961, a person (usually the husband) whose spouse's income is within the non-taxable threshold receives a dependent tax deduction. Companies that give their employees a dependent spouse allowance often base their assessment on this threshold.

Furthermore, a dependent spouse (usually the wife of a company employee or public servant) who earns less than ¥1.3 million a year (US$11,300) is entitled to the national pension scheme and national health insurance for free. It is estimated that 11 million people currently fall into this category. In 1985, a special dependent tax deduction was introduced, providing further tax benefits for a husband whose wife earns less than ¥1.41 million a year (US$12,200). Thus when a wife's income exceeds these thresholds, the actual household income may decrease as the family loses out on subsidies and tax incentives unless her earnings reach a certain amount (Kayano, 2000). The wife typically has to earn more than ¥1.53 million (US$13,300) to have a positive effect on the household income. Overall, these policies encourage the majority of married women to stay either in low-paying part-time employment or become full-time housewives upon having children.

The state is currently revising the dependent tax deduction and pension policies to reduce the benefits granted for dependent wives in order to encourage married women to re-enter or remain in full-time employment. The state is beginning to realise that the male-headed, nuclear family model can no longer be sustainable in the long-term, given changing family forms that encompass single-person households and female-headed households. At the same time, by encouraging women to remain in full-time employment and earning wages above the minimum threshold income level, the state could also increase the tax and pension premium paying population to support the rapidly ageing population. Some feminists have long argued for a social welfare system based on the individual, rather than the household. However, under the current severe working conditions, reforms might simply shift the welfare costs back to families and afflict the household economy, with little effect on advancing married women to full-time employment or improving pension schemes for women.

The state has also made some changes with regard to employment policies in its effort to alleviate the shrinking labour force. The main objective of the state is to encourage women and the elderly to remain engaged in full-time employment. The Basic Law on Measures for the Ageing Society introduced in 1995 that focused on promoting employment among the elderly was one such change. Paid parental and nursing leave for aged-care was also legislated and revised in the 1990s to encourage women to remain in full-time employment. Both forms of leave are now in principle accessible to men and women in full-time employment. Since 2001, employees are entitled to receive 40 per cent of their pre-leave wage from their employment insurance for the duration of up to one year for parental leave and three months for nursing leave (Muraki, 2000:55–8).[11] Plans to improve inadequate childcare facilities are also underway (Sakai, 2002; Ogawa, 2003). These changes may not provide much benefit to women currently working part-time but they are vital to encourage young mothers to stay in full-time employment.

In addition to rectifying the shrinking workforce, the state has also introduced various policies and incentives to address the low fertility problem. For example, the revised child allowance scheme was introduced in the year 2000 to provide incentives for families with children. However, the scheme is not as generous as that in Singapore.[12] Two Basic Laws, the 1999 Basic Law for a Gender-equal Society and the 2003 Basic Laws on Measures for the Low Birth Society, were also enacted. The former advocates equal and collaborative participation of men and women in all areas of society including domestic activities and the workplace. Its preamble states that a gender-equal society is a matter of urgent importance in responding to socio-economic changes such as fewer children, the ageing of the population, and the maturation of the domestic economy (Cabinet Office, 2003b). While the law's possible implications for gender equality should not be underestimated, it again emphasises the complementary roles men and women play in nation building (Muta, 2003). Similarly, Dales (2003) argues that the law reinforces the idea of heterosexual, reproductive, married couples as the core social unit, and hence privileges them over other forms of family or relationships.

The Basic Law on Measures for the Low Birth Society essentially promotes the idea of marital fertility. Calling the current state of the falling fertility rate and ageing population as "an unprecedented historical situation", the Law declares promotion of the parental leave system, childcare facilities and support for infertility treatment, among other recommendations (Prime Minister's Office, 2003). The first two areas have already been addressed in other policies, as discussed above, but the issue of infertility indicates a new development in state policy. The plan is to give financial support to married couples undergoing infertility treatment. As such, in addressing low birth rate, the Law privileges married couples. However, the measures highlighted above fall short of dealing with the issue of the growing number of singles in reproductive age. Delayed marriage, a trend that was first observed in 1975, is a major cause of fertility decline in Japan (Ogawa, 2003). For example, improvements in child-care facilities would have little direct impact on young women's decision to marry earlier. Moreover, to date, de facto couples and female-headed families have so far been excluded from benefiting from these policies which discriminate against these alternative family forms in increasing the nation's low birth rate.

If government measures in addressing low fertility achieve some success and women do reproduce and stay in full-time employment, the demand for domestic services will certainly surge. Suzuki and Kitada (2001) estimate that if dormant demand for the services is realised, it will create 830,000 jobs. However, the current trend of domestic work suggests that these jobs are likely to be intended for "housewives", and hence low paid, and casual. Alternatively, if Japan's fertility remains low or falls further, the need for aged-care work will greatly increase in the near future. A government opinion-survey on foreign workers carried out in the year 2000 specifically asked about the option of accepting them for aged-care work (Cabinet Office, 2003a). More women than men disagreed with the idea (50.4 per cent and 45.8 per cent of the respondents respectively), with housewives most opposed to it. The lack of knowledge of the Japanese language, social systems and customs are common reasons for this opposition. The result suggests that housewives value care-work more than men or single women. They may also be expressing the need for more recognition for the work they perform. It also suggests a lack of openness in Japanese society to engage foreigners in care-work.[13] More interestingly, the survey did not include any question on the possibility of introducing foreigners to supplement domestic work. This strongly suggests that employing a foreign domestic worker is still beyond the imagination of the majority of Japanese. However, if this question was posed, a stronger opposition to this idea among women is not hard to imagine, given that performing domestic duties is viewed as integral to being a good wife and wise mother in Japan.

CONCLUSION

Despite the increasing presence of foreign workers in Japan since the 1980s, the employment of foreign domestic workers is uncommon in contemporary Japanese households. Foreign domestic workers are mainly employed by foreign expatriates and the diplomatic community. Recent changes in easing the inflow of unskilled foreigners has so far only favoured Japanese descendants from Brazil and Peru, signalling the state's commitment in maintaining cultural homogeneity in the country. These workers are not employed in domestic services although a growing number who are well versed in the Japanese language have started to work in hospitals doing care work. The ideology of *ryōsai kenbo* or the good wife and wise mother introduced in the Meiji era to reconstruct the domestic sphere as a site of consumption and reproduction, deemed vital to Japan's development and process of modernisation, is entrenched in Japanese society.

The emerging middle-class in the late 19th and early 20th century had access to the services of paid domestic workers who were mainly young educated women eager to learn the proper ways of becoming a good wife and wise mother. However, expanding employment opportunities in the formal economic sphere in the 1930s lured these women into the formal workforce. Poor women from rural areas who were driven more by economic need then filled demand for paid domestic workers.

Eventually, this led to paid domestic work losing its cultural significance as a training platform for the propagation of the ideology of *ryōsai kenbo*. Nearing the completion of the post-war reconstruction, companies began closing their doors to women, reinforcing the value of home as the proper place of women. Other factors such as state welfare policies and the norms of business practices favoured married women to either remain at home as full-time housewives or to engage only in lowly paid part-time employment. In general, the nuclear family model consisting of a company-employed husband, a housewife and children became a norm and was hailed as ideal in Japanese society until the late 1980s.

Changes in Japan's demographic and economic characteristics led to various policy changes in the 1990s. Faced with an ageing population, low birth rate and a shrinking workforce, the Japanese state through the introduction of various incentives and policies is now making it more conducive for women to remain in the workforce as full-time employees after marrying and having children. Anecdotal evidence suggests that Japan might approve the employment of more foreign workers in aged care given its fast-ageing population. However, little public debate has taken place on bringing in more foreign workers for childcare and housework to supplement the responsibility of married women. Although household expenditure on domestic services has increased over the years, it still remains a very small proportion of household expenditure, suggesting the unpopularity of commercial domestic services such as childcare and cleaning services in contemporary Japan. The ideology of *ryōsai kenbo* assigns a high value to the contribution women make in the domestic sphere; thus, shifting this work to foreign women or contracting it out to commercial service providers remains outside the imagination of a large majority of Japanese. Moreover, currently the demand for such services is not high due to the slump in the economy, which has made it difficult for married women (and other workers) to gain or stay in full-time employment. New laws aimed at promoting Japanese to procreate and for women to remain engaged in formal employment after childbirth are still rooted in the traditional model of heterosexual marriage and family form and do not address the needs of female-headed households or de facto couples in reproduction. Given the complex interactions of all these factors, domestic work in contemporary Japan so far remains largely in the private sphere as the unpaid work of wives and mothers.

NOTES

1   In 1972, 83.2 per cent of female respondents and 83.8 per cent of males agreed with the notion. This decreased to 51.9 per cent and 64.9 per cent respectively in 1997 (Iwama, 2000b:42).

2   The term *jochū* was commonly used around the first half of the 20th century, but is not currently used, owing to its discriminatory connotation. Instead, *o-tetsudai-san* is used to refer to a domestic helper. Official document use the term *kaji tetsudai* to describe the occupation.

3   Girls attended higher schools after completing six years of compulsory elementary co-education. On the other hand, boys attended either middle school or technical schools.

4   Watanabe reports that some rural policy makers advocated the adaptation of a variation of the *ryōsai kenbo* model, which promoted an ideal of a hard working wife and healthy reproductive mother, to apply to the role expectations for rural women (Kumazawa, 1993).

5   Kayama is a pseudonym. This interview took place in Wakayama prefecture on 5 January 2003 as part of my research on women's views regarding the practice of the family-grave.

6   Approximately 2,000 foreign women, 65 per cent of whom were Filipinas, entered Japan as domestic workers under the residential status "designated activities" between 1990 and 2000 (Tenegra, 2003a; 2003b). Tenegra's interviews with 50 Filipino female domestic workers in 2000 and 2001 show that most of them (90 per cent) work for non-Japanese employees of multinational companies, the majority (63 per cent) had worked as domestic helpers before coming to Japan, and some (34 per cent) have been working in Japan for more than 10 years. These women commonly accompany their business elite employers on their transfer to Japan from overseas, but also find employment through their own personal network such as relatives or acquaintances working as domestic helpers in Japan. They tend to take up a live-out arrangement as their stay in Japan is prolonged (2003a; 2003b).

7   The average minimum monthly wage for a foreign domestic worker is ¥150,000 (US$1,300 based on the exchange rate of ¥115=US$1). One live-out worker interviewed by Tenegra (2000b) noted that she is paid an hourly wage of ¥1,200 (US$10). This is much higher than the average hourly wage of a Japanese woman engaged in part-time employment, which was approximately ¥890 in 2001.

8   The amended Immigration Act granted residential status for up to three years exclusively to descendants of Japanese emigrants up to and including the third generation. This visa category made no restrictions on the type of work an applicant was engaged in and allowed an applicant to bring his or her non-*Nikkei* spouse (Mori, 1997). These migrants came mainly from Brazil and Peru.

9   The unrealistic expectations in a marriage partner and marital life have been argued by some as contributing to the growing number of single women resulting in the nation's low fertility rate.

10   The official term used in labour force surveys is *tanjikan koyōsha* (short-time workers) and refers to those who work less than 35 hours a week.

11   Not surprisingly, women dominate among leave-takers. A 1996 survey shows that women occupied 99.2 per cent of the parental leave-takers and 81.3 per cent of the aged-care leave-takers (Muraki, 2000:55).

12   Japanese children are not eligible to qualify for this allowance once they enter primary school (Ogawa, 2003). In Singapore, the child allowance extends to children and young adults up to 16 years of age. Moreover, dependents above 16 years of age who are in full-time study also qualify for this allowance (Singapore Government et al., n.d.).

13   Currently, the only group of migrants who are engaged in care work are female *Nikkeijin* (Japanese descendants from Peru and Brazil who possess Japanese language skills). These women are employed as orderlies or care-workers of the elderly (Shinozuka & Yokomura, 1994; Yamanaka, 1997).

REFERENCES

Befu, H. 2001. *Hegemony of Homogeneity: An Anthropological Analysis of Nihonjinron.* Melbourne: Trans Pacific Press.

Broadbent, K. 2003. *Women's Employment in Japan: The Experience of Part-time Workers.* London: Routledge Curzon.

Cabinet Office. 2003a. *Gaikokujin rōdōsha ni kansuru seron chōsa* (An Opinion-survey on Foreign Workers). http://www8.cao.go.jp/survey/h12/gaikoku/1.html. Accessed 11 September 2003.

————. 2003b. *The Gender Equality Bureau. The Basic Law for a Gender-equal Society (Law No. 78 of 1999).* http://www.gender.go.jp/english/basic_law/. Accessed 18 September 2003.

Dales, L. 2003. Legislating for harmony: The law for a gender-equal society. Paper presented at 13th biennial conference of the Japanese Studies Association of Australia, Queensland University of Technology, 2–4 July in Australia.

Eccleston, B. 1989. *State and Society in Post-war Japan.* Oxford: Polity Press.

Hagiwara, N. 2003. *Professional Kyōiku Mama: Being a Good Mother Via the Practice of Ojuken Among Educated Women in Modern Tokyo.* Unpublished Ph.D. dissertation, School of Social and Cultural Studies, University of Western Australia, Perth.

Hamana, A. 1998. *Meiji makki kara shōwa ni okeru "jochū" no henyō* (Change in "maids" between the end of Meiji and the beginning of Showa period). *Journal of Social Science,* 49(6), 31–87.

Inoue, T. 1992. *Joseigaku e no shōtai: kawaru/kawaranai onna no isshō* (Invitation to Women's Studies: Have Women's Lives Changed or Not?). Tokyo: Yūhikaku Sensho.

Iwama, A. 2000a. *47.0% vs 39.6%: Tomobataraki setai to sengyō shufu setai no hikaku* (Comparison between dual and single income households). In *Joseigaku kī nambā* (Important Data in Women's Studies). Edited by Y. Inubushi, M. Mukuno & A. Muraki. Tokyo: Yūhikaku Sensho, 35–8.

————. 2000b. *4jikan 33pun vs 20 pun: Kon'nani chigau! Tomobataraki tsuma to otto no kaji jikan* (4 hours and 33 minutes versus 20 minutes: How different! Time spent on housework between working wives and husbands). In *Joseigaku kī nambā* (Important Data in Women's Studies). Edited by Y. Inubushi, M. Mukuno & A. Muraki. Tokyo: Yūhikaku Sensho, 39–42.

————. 2000c. *3saiji shinwa: 3sai made wa hahaoya no te de katei de kodomo o sodateru bekidato iwareteiru ga* (The myth of the three-year-old child: They say that a child should be cared by the mother at home until three, but...). In *Joseigaku kī nambā* (Important Data in Women's Studies). Edited by Y. Inubushi, M. Mukuno & A. Muraki. Tokyo: Yūhikaku Sensho, 185–88.

Japan Times Online. 2004. LDP against more Filipino, Thai M.D.s, nurses here. 25 February, http://www.japantimes.co.jp/cgi-bin/getarticle.pl5?nb20040225a4.htm. Accessed 26 February 2004.

Kajita, T. 1994. Gaikokujin rōdōsha to Nihon (Foreign Workers and Japan). Tokyo: Nihon Hōsō Shuppan Kyōkai.

Kayano, C. 2000. *103man-en, 130man-en, 141man-en: Tsuma ga zei shakaihoshō no "yūgū" o ukerareru shōnyo kingaku* (103 million yen, 130 million yen and 141 million yen: The income thresholds for a wife to receive tax and social security "favour"). In *Joseigaku kī nambā* (Important Data in Women's Studies). Edited by Y. Inubushi, M. Mukuno & A. Muraki. Tokyo: Yūhikaku Sensho, 119–24.

Koyama, S. 1991. *Ryōsai kenbo to yū kihan* (The Norm of a Good Wife and Wise Mother). Tokyo: Keisō Shobō.

Kumazawa, T. 1993. *Mohanyome hyōshō ni miru "kaigo" to "yome ishiki'* (The meaning of "care" and "wifely sensibility" in the commendation of "model wives"). *Ochanomizu joshi daigaku josei bunka kenkyō sentā nenpō*, 7, 119–43.

Momsen, J. H. 1999. Maids on the move: Victim or victor? In *Gender, Migration and Domestic Service*. Edited by J. H. Momsen. London: Routledge, 1–20.

Mori, H. 1997. *Immigration Policy and Foreign Workers in Japan*. London: Macmillan Press.

Mukuno, M. 2000. *3 kō kara 3c e: Josei ga kekkon aite ni motomeru jōken* (From 3-highs to 3Cs: Women's preferences for a marriage partner). In *Joseigaku kī nambā* (Important Data in Women's Studies). Edited by Y. Inubushi, M. Mukuno & A. Muraki. Tokyo: Yūhikaku Sensho, 181–84.

Muta, K. 1996. *Senryaku to shite no kazoku: Kindai nihon no kokumin kokka keisei to josei* (Family as Strategy: Women and the Formation of the Nation-State in Modern Japan). Tokyo: Shinyōsha.

———. 2003. *Danjo kyōdō sankaku jidai no "jotei"ron to feminisumu* (Feminism and the question of "empress" in the era of gender-equality). *Gendai Shisō*, 31(1), 115–129.

Muraki, A. 2000. *0.8%: Sukunai dansei no ikuji kyugyō shutokusha* (0.8 Percent?: Few men take parental leave). In *Joseigaku kī nambā* (Important Data in Women's Studies). Edited by Y. Inubushi, M. Mukuno & A. Muraki. Tokyo: Yūhikaku Sensho, 55–8.

Nakamatsu, T. 2002. *Marriage, Migration and the International Marriage Business in Japan*. Unpublished Ph.D. dissertation, Department of Asian Studies, Murdoch University.

Nakashima, H. 2002. *Henbōsuru josei rōdō* (Changing women's paid work). In *Fujin Hakusho 2002* (White Paper on Women 2002). Edited by Nihon Fujin Dantai Rengōkai. Tokyo: Horupu Shuppan, 80–84.

Nihon Fujin Dantai Rengōkai, ed. 2002. *Fujin Hakusho 2002* (White Paper on Women 2002). Tokyo: Horupu Shuppan.

Ogawa, N. 2003. Japan's changing fertility mechanisms and its policy responses. *Journal of Population Research*, 20(1), 89–106.

Ogura, C. 2003. *Kekkon no jōken* (The Terms of Marriage). Tokyo: Asahi Shimbunsha.

Osteria, T. S. 1994. *Filipino Female Labour Migration to Japan: Economic Causes and Consequences*. Manila: De La Salle University Press.

Prime Minister's Office. 2003. *Heisei 15nen 7gatsu 30nichi Kanpō* (Gazette, 30 July), http://www. kantei.go.jp/jp/kanpo/jul.5/g10730t0009.html. Accessed 18 September 2003.

Sakai, N. 2002. *Hoiku: Kisei kanwa to taiki jidō zero sakusen* (Childcare: Removal of restrictions and the policy of no-children-on-the-waiting-list). *In Fujin Hakusho 2002* (White Paper on Women 2002). Edited by Nihon Fujin Dantai Rengōkai. Tokyo: Horupu Shuppan, 118–23.

Saitō, M. 2000. *Modan gāru ron: On'na no ko ni wa shusse no michi ga futatsu aru* (Modern girls: Women have two ways of succeeding in life). Tokyo: Mazazin Hausu.

Shinozuka, E. & A. Yokomura. 1994. *Ibunka no naka no nikkeijin josei rōdōsha'* (Female *Nikkeijin* workers in the cross-cultural work environment). *Joseigaku Kenkyū* (Japanese Journal of Women's Studies), 3, 5–29.

Singapore Government, Family and Community Development @ eCitizen (n.d.), Marriage and Parenthood Schemes, http://fcd.ecitizen.gov.sg/family/htm. Accessed 23 November 2003.

Suzuki, N. & E. Kitada. 2001. *Kongo no seichō bunya toshite chūmokusareru kaji shien sābisu* (Domestic services: potential area of growth), *Makuro keizai repōto*, August issue, http://www.yokohama-ri.co.jp/report/economic/macro/report/ma200108.html. Accessed 29 February 2004.

Tenegra, B. 2003a. *Nihon ni okeru Firipin-jin josei kaji rōdōsha no koyō* (Employment of Filipino Women Domestic Workers in Japan). Paper presented at the 51st Kantō shakaigakkai taikai, Taishō University, 15 June in Japan.

————. 2003b. Transnational domestic workers: Are they transnational migrants? Paper presented at the International Conference on "Women and Migration in Asia", Developing Countries Research Centre, University of Delhi, 10–13 December in India.

The Statistic Bureau, The Public Management, Home Affairs, Posts and Telecommunications Ministry (n.d.) *Shokugyōbetsu shōbunruibetsu shōgyōshasū no sui'i* (Trend in the Number of Employees by Occupation and Minor Classification), http://www.jil.go.jp/statis/kako/sansyoku/2208.html. Accessed 12 September 2003.

Ueno, C. 1990. Kafuchōsei to shihonsei: Marukusushugi feminizumu no chihei (The System of Patriarchy and Capital: A Viewpoint of Marxist Feminism). Tokyo: Iwanami Shoten.

Yamanaka, K. 1997. *Return migration of Japanese Brazilian women: Household and search for the "homeland"*. In *Beyond Boundaries: Selected Papers on Refugees and Immigrants*. Edited by D. Baxter & R. Krulfeld. Arlington: American Anthropological Association, 11–34.

14

Male Breadwinners and White Australians: The Role of Employment and Immigration Policies in Shaping Domestic Labour Patterns in Australia[1]

JANEEN BAXTER

INTRODUCTION

Unlike other countries in the region, Australia has never relied on transnational domestic workers to perform routine household tasks. In order to understand why Australia has not followed a pattern similar to other countries in the region, such as Taiwan, Hong Kong, Singapore and Malaysia, we need to examine the broader question of why domestic service, particularly live-in domestic service, is not a feature of Australian households. In this chapter, I argue that the absence of live-in domestic workers in Australian households is due to a gender division of labour that defines housework and childcare as non-work, and women as the primary carers of husbands and children. Although the participation of married women in paid employment has risen dramatically in recent decades, this has not been accompanied by major changes in women's levels of responsibility for childcare and housework. The result is that domestic work is still largely women's work. Nakamatsu and Lee make similar arguments for Japan and Korea (see chapters in this volume). Policies ostensibly designed to address the problems faced by women with a dual burden of paid and unpaid work have primarily focused on strategies that help women to combine these competing responsibilities, rather than strategies that might alter the gender division of labour or encourage households to employ paid help for domestic work.

In addition, Australia's immigration policies have always been focused on addressing changing needs in the formal economy and have never been manipulated to meet the needs of household reproduction. The White Australia policy which restricted migrant intake throughout much of the first half of the 20th century to white Anglo Saxon immigrants and more recently to skilled migrants restricted the option for Australian households to turn to transnational domestic workers as cheaper alternatives for childcare and other domestic help.

DOMESTIC SERVANTS IN AUSTRALIA

Higman's excellent historical work has documented in detail the rise and fall of domestic service in Australia. As Figure 14.1 shows, the percentage of private domestic servants in Australia rose steadily from 1800 to 1860, thereafter declining steadily to virtually zero by 2000, with the exception of a small rise during the Depression years of the 1930s. According to Higman (2002:24), the rapid increase up until the mid-nineteenth century may be explained by the spread of British colonial society which was based heavily on a master/servant hierarchy. Convicts provided much of the labour for domestic service prior to 1850 with many convict women assigned to private households as servants. As convict transportation drew to a close, poor women from the British Isles were increasingly offered assisted migration packages to move to Australia as domestic servants. Domestic servants were one of the most common forms of assisted

FIGURE 14.1   Private domestic servants, Australia, 1800–2000

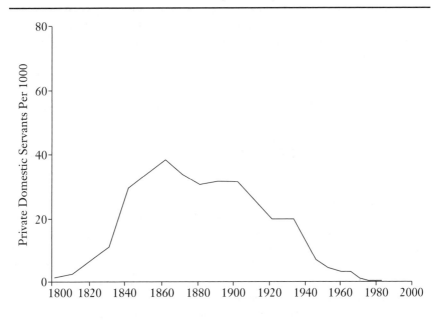

SOURCE: Higman, 2002:21.

migrants to Australia between 1837 and 1859 as they not only provided much needed labour in the colony, but also contributed to the broader aim of civilising the British outpost by increasing the female population (Higman, 2002).

At the same time, some households employed ethnic minority women as domestic servants, including some Chinese, Indians and Melanesians. As Higman (2002) reports though, the percentage of ethnic minorities employed in domestic service was always small as they lacked demographic weight in the Australian population. Moreover, the White Australia Policy actively deported any overseas worker who overstayed their indenture term (Higman, 2002:61). This policy, which was formulated by the Immigration Restriction Act of 1901, governed Australia's immigration intake until after the Second World War (Jupp, 1991; Burnley, 2001). Australians saw themselves as primarily an outpost of the British Empire and the emphasis was on maintaining strong links to British heritage and culture with a mainly British, Irish and Scottish migrant intake. The overwhelming priority of the Australian government was for British settlers who could help keep Australia white and predominantly Anglo Saxon, although it was quite prepared to use non-British indentured labour to meet the needs of certain industries or regions (Saunders, 1982; 1984).[2] A key requirement of the indentured system was that the labourers had to return to their home country at the end of their period of service. Keeping Australia white was also adopted as a key priority by the Australian Trade Union movement in order to protect Australians from the threat of cheap substitute labour from overseas.[3] At national trade union congresses in the early part of the 19th century, the maintenance of a white Australia was proclaimed as one of the central tenets of the trade union movement (Sutcliffe, 1967:53, 158, 182).

Some aboriginal women also worked as domestic servants in white households between about 1840 and 1930, although like the overseas born workers, the numbers were always small. For most of the aboriginal women, domestic service was forced upon them against their will. The Aborigines Protection and the Restriction of the Sale of Opium Act 1897 provided the means to rigorously control and subjugate the indigenous population (Huggins & Blake, 1992:45). "A major provision of the Act was the power to remove Aborigines forcibly to and from areas designated as reserves by the State" (Huggins & Blake, 1992:45). Many young girls were forcibly removed from their parents and sent to institutions where they were trained in domestic duties and the Christian faith (Tonkinson, 1988; Huggins & Blake, 1992; Higman, 2002). Invariably these young girls were subject to harsh treatment, ill-fed, ill-clothed and poorly educated (Huggins & Blake, 1992:47). "Male and female Aboriginal children reared in reserves and mission dormitories were purposefully schooled with an inferior educational syllabus which prepared them for lowly, gender-specific labour tasks (Huggins & Blake, 1992:50). There is also abundant evidence that aboriginal domestic servants were often poorly treated by their employers (Tonkinson, 1988; Huggins & Blake, 1992; Huggins, 1995; Walden, 1995).

By 1901, Kingston (1975) estimates that about half of the female working population in Australia was engaged in domestic service of some kind. The majority of these women were white, working class and Australian born (Higman, 2002). As Australia's industrial economy developed, women were steadily pulled away from domestic service into process work in factories and later from there to jobs in health, education and finance in the emerging service economy (Kingston, 1975:61; Higman, 2002). By 1947, the percentage of employed women in domestic service jobs had declined to about 18 per cent and at least half of these women were employed by boarding houses, hotels, hospitals and restaurants. Thus the opening up of new avenues of employment for women in the manufacturing sector and later the expanding service sector, offering employment with better conditions and rates of pay, contributed significantly to the decline of private domestic service in Australia.

In addition to the changes in Australia's economic base that drew women out of domestic service and into other forms of employment, cultural factors have also played a significant role in the decline of paid domestic help in the Australian home. Of particular importance is the fact that the domestic economy is no longer defined as an arena of work. Rather the work that takes place within households has been explicitly defined over the course of the 20th century as an integral component of women's proper role as mothers and wives. The ideology of family life in Australia and the dominant model of a male breadwinner state, that reached its peak in the 1950s and 1960s, encouraged, if not forced, wives to remain at home as full-time mothers and housewives. The idea that housework and childcare might be undertaken by someone other than the wife/mother flies in the face of policies that directly defined women's role within the home and work within the household as "non-work" (Baldock, 1983; Cass, 1983; Bryson, 1992).

THE MALE BREADWINNER STATE

One of the defining moments in the history of the gender division of labour in Australia was the setting of the first basic wage in 1907 by Justice Higgins of the High Court of Australia. The wage was intended to provide for a man and his wife and two or three children in frugal comfort (Summers, 1975:336; Bryson, 1992:168). Higgins claimed that whereas the normal needs of a man included domestic life and that he was legally obliged to support a family if he had one, the same was not usually true of women. He concluded that women were not therefore entitled to equal pay, but merely to a wage that would enable a single woman without dependents to find her own food, clothing and shelter. It was only in industries where women competed for male jobs that women should be paid the male rate in order to prevent men from being pushed out of those jobs. This legislation had far-reaching consequences. It effectively enshrined in law the view that women are dependents and that a family should consist of a full-time male breadwinner and stay-at-home wife.

Other pieces of legislation in the early 20th century also helped consolidate the gender division of labour and women's place within the home as full-time carers and dependents. Legislation around employment-protection policies and wages was based

383

on gendered assumptions about the male breadwinner and female unpaid homemaker. The 1911 report of the Royal Commission into the Hours and General Conditions of Employment of Female and Juvenile Labour in New South Wales stated six main objections to women working:

1. Women working encouraged the use of contraception. This was problematic in a time of "populate or perish".
2. Women working risked miscarriage.
3. Women who worked had to stop breastfeeding and this risked infant mortality.
4. Women working used up all their energy on making money and hence neglected the home.
5. Women working encouraged idle and extravagant men.
6. Married women working were a bad influence on single girls.

It was of course necessary for many working class women to earn a wage to supplement the family economy. For married women this usually entailed taking on work that could be carried out within the confines of the household such as sewing, laundry, childcare or taking in boarders. For unmarried working class women the dominant form of employment during the early part of the 20th century was domestic service.

Of course employment for women was only possible outside of marriage. Even women without children were actively discouraged from employment through policies such as the marriage bar which prohibited married women from employment in the public service right up until 1966. Women's employment was defined as an inferior substitute to marriage. Moreover the status of the working man was definitely improved if his wife was not employed (Kingston, 1975:138).

The development of industrial factories created a pull factor for young unmarried working women who were increasingly pulled from domestic service work into factory work. But there was also a push factor. Reiger (1985) has shown how an emerging class of reformers, technocrats and experts sought to reshape the family home and women's role within it. The domestic economy movement in Australia, at its peak in the late 19th century, sought to elevate housework to a new professional status with an emphasis on scientific training and the need to teach women, particularly middle class women, how to do the chores once performed by working class servants. Housework was promoted as a new profession, combining a range of managerial, scientific and creative skills. In addition, new tasks were invented, ostensibly to make housework more efficient, but actually resulting in an increase in the amount of time spent on housework (Reiger, 1985).

One of the distinctive features of Australian society is the high level of home ownership compared to other similar nations. Game and Pringle (1979) have argued that owning a home has developed as an integral feature of Australian family life. According to Game and Pringle (1979), marriage and home ownership became ingrained in Australia from the late 19th century. The "suburban dream" was made possible not just by economic conditions and the relative affluence of the working class, but also by a gendered division of labour in which men were full-time breadwinners and women were full-time homemakers and carers.

In the light of these historical underpinnings and specifically policies around male and female employment and social welfare, Bryson (1992), Baker (2001) and others have defined Australia as a male breadwinner state. Under this model, policy-makers assume that people live in heterosexual families in which men are the primary earners and women are wives, mothers and caregivers. Men are financially responsible for the women they live with and for their children. If a male earner is not present in the household, either because of death or desertion, the state will replace a portion of the breadwinner's wage through various income support programmes. For example the widows pension was paid to women on the basis of a perceived need for the state to provide support to women who had lost a male breadwinner. This policy was only replaced in 1973 when the Labour government introduced the supporting mother's benefit, later extended to fathers in 1977. As Roe (1983) points out this was a remarkable development as it redefined dependence in terms of motherhood rather than solely on the basis of marital status.

More recently and particularly since the 1970s, the state has begun to move away from this kind of model to a more egalitarian, individual approach to social support. A range of policies has been introduced that recognise and give some legitimacy to alternative family forms. These policies include sole parent pensions, equal pay legislation, divorce reform, enforcement of laws against domestic violence, anti-discrimination legislation, equal opportunity legislation, state support for childcare services and reproductive rights. These developments have coincided with a marked increase in the participation of married women in paid employment. For example, in 1954 less than one in three women in Australia aged 15–64 years old (29 per cent) were employed and only 31 per cent of these women were married. By 1998, 60 per cent of women were employed and 61 per cent were married (Australian Bureau of Statistics, 1998). Most strikingly, the labour force participation rate of married women has increased from 34 per cent in 1968 to 63 per cent in 1998 (Australian Bureau of Statistics, 1998). These changes have been brought about by a combination of changing labour market structures (such as the decline of the manufacturing sector and rise of the service sector), the removal of legal barriers (such as the marriage bar) and the passing of other forms of legislation that improved women's access to paid work, (such as equal pay for equal work legislation, the Equal Employment Opportunity Act and the Sex Discrimination Act), as well as changing social attitudes about gender roles.

Despite these massive increases in female labour force participation rates (and in particular, *married* women's labour force participation rates), women's employment patterns over the lifecourse still continue to look very different to men's employment patterns. Specifically, most women work part-time for a significant proportion of their working lives, particularly when there are young children in the household, while the majority of men work full-time for the duration of their working lives.

Australia has one of the highest concentrations of women in part-time employment, with women occupying just over 70 per cent of all part-time jobs in 2002 (Summers, 2003:161). Women's participation is closely tied to the age of their youngest child. In 1997, 46 per cent of married mothers with a child under four years old were employed, but most of these mothers were in part-time employment (Australian Bureau of Statistics, 1998).

While the participation of men in part-time employment has also increased slightly in recent years, the increase is associated with men's increased participation in higher education during the early years of the lifecourse, and at the other end of the lifecourse, a tendency to work part-time during the retirement years. The dominant pattern then is for men to enter full-time employment after they complete their education and to remain in full-time employment until retirement. For women, the dominant pattern is to enter full-time employment after education and to remain there until the birth of the first child. Employment then usually declines dramatically, although not completely, until the youngest child enters school (Evans, 2000). Women with teenage and older dependent children are more likely to work full-time than women with children in primary school.

It is not difficult to understand the reasons why women leave employment or move into part-time employment upon the birth of the first child. First, the Australian labour market is still largely structured around a male breadwinner model of employment with hours and conditions that leave little room for the flexibility needed to accommodate the needs and timetables of young children. Second, compared to countries such as Sweden and Norway that have specifically sought to develop policies that enable parents to combine paid and unpaid work (such as very generous maternity and paternity leave policies), there is little in the way of work and family policies in Australia that encourage women to maintain full-time employment when they have young children. Third, childcare is typically expensive and often difficult to access. Fourth, despite over three decades of equal pay for equal work legislation, the gender gap in earnings between men and women is still clearly evident and in recent years has widened due to the introduction of enterprise bargaining, thereby encouraging women rather than men to withdraw from paid work to take on caring responsibilities. Finally, much research has shown that the burden of childcare and housework duties fall disproportionately on women's shoulders, even when they are in full-time employment (Baxter, 2002). Hence when women do engage in full-time employment they are still typically responsible for a substantial proportion of unpaid labour and when they have young children, are the group with the least amount of leisure time (Bittman, 1998; Baxter, 2002).

Moreover, recent analyses have argued convincingly that current policies under the Howard Liberal government have actively discouraged women from combining employment with motherhood and have eroded some of the gains made by Australian feminists in the 1970s and 1980s (Summers, 2003). For example, rather than introducing paid maternity leave as advocated by the Sex Discrimination Minister in 2001, Prime

Minister Howard opted instead for a "Baby Bonus" that enables women to have a portion of their tax refunded from the year prior to having their first baby. But in order to receive it women must stay out of employment for five years (Summers, 2003:153–4). As many commentators have noted, if the baby bonus was designed to slow the fertility decline in Australia by encouraging women to have more children it would apply to the second child, or subsequent children, rather than to the first born. But as Summers (2003:154) notes, that is clearly not the intention: "The Baby Bonus is quite clearly designed to entice women from the workforce—and then to force them to stay home for as long as five years". After five years out of paid work, it is very difficult for women to re-enter the labour market, especially into any form of skilled or professional employment (Summers, 2003:155). This policy, in combination with punitive effective marginal tax rates on family assistance payments for two income families and increasingly expensive and difficult to access childcare places, has meant that the overall result has been to encourage women with children to stay out of the workforce.

PATTERNS OF DOMESTIC LABOUR IN AUSTRALIA

Feminist reformers in the 1960s and 1970s were optimistic that changes in the labour force participation rates for married women, in combination with increased awareness of the value of women's unpaid work in the home, would lead to an increased involvement of men in domestic labour and a more equal domestic division of labour between men and women. In addition, it was assumed that other social changes would alter the way men and women organise their household responsibilities. These include a much smaller but nevertheless significant decline in men's labour force participation rates, the decline in fertility levels, the delay in entering a marital relationship, increased rates of de facto cohabitation, and increasing divorce rates. In other words, the expectation has been that changes in patterns of family formation and dissolution, in conjunction with the changing gender distribution of paid work, would lead to changes in the distribution of work between men and women in the home. But to a large extent, this has not happened. It is largely undisputed that women in Australia, as in all other western nations do approximately three quarters of household work (Baxter, 1997; 2002).

Figure 14.2 shows time spent on domestic labour per week for men and women in Australia in 2001. The data come from the first wave of "The Household, Income and Labour Dynamics in Australia (HILDA) Survey", which is an Australian national panel survey comprising 7,692 households and 13,969 individuals (FaCS, 2002). The data show that women spend about 18 hours per week on housework tasks (defined in this survey as preparing meals, washing dishes, cleaning house, washing clothes, ironing and sewing) compared to men who spend just over six hours per week. Childcare (defined in this survey as playing with your children, helping them with personal care, teaching, coaching or actively supervising them, and taking them to childcare, school

FIGURE 14.2   Hours per week spent in domestic labour by gender

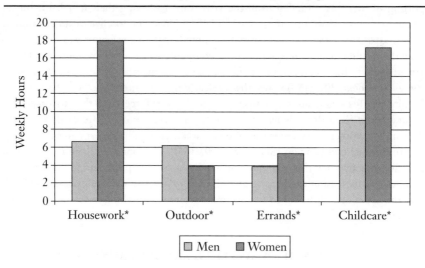

SOURCE: FaCS, 2002.

NOTES:

*   t-test indicates that differences between men and women are significant at p<0.5.

N for Housework, outdoor and errands is 11,735. N for Childcare is 5,579.

or other activities) is also primarily the responsibility of women, requiring about 17 hours per week compared to about nine hours per week for men. Men do more of the outdoor housework tasks (repairs, improvements, painting and car maintenance) than women, while the division of labour on errands (paying bills, driving children to school and activities, and shopping) is divided roughly equally.

These patterns change minimally when the sample is confined to dual earner households in which both husbands and wives are in full-time employment (defined as 35 or more hours per week), as shown in Figure 14.3. The most significant difference is that women in these households do much less housework. This suggests that women in full-time employment spend less time on housework than other women. This is consistent with other studies showing that women cope with the competing demands of paid and unpaid work by reducing the time they spend on domestic labour (Baxter, 2002). Interestingly though women in full-time employment spend a little more time on average on childcare tasks compared to the total sample of women, perhaps in an effort to compensate for time away from children while in employment. Men also appear to spend additional time on childcare in dual earner households, indicating that

FIGURE 14.3 Hours per week spent in domestic labour in dual-earner households (with both partners in full-time employment[a]) by gender

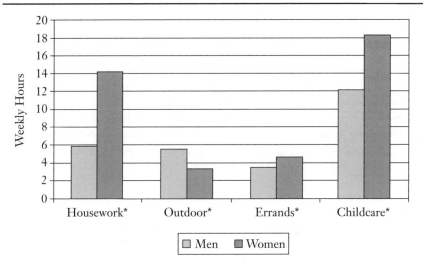

SOURCE: FaCS, 2002.

NOTES:

*   t-test indicates that differences between men and women are significant at p<0.5.

a   Full-time employment = Employed for 35 hours per week or more.

N for Housework, outdoor and errands is 419. N for Childcare is 234.

they participate more in these activities when their wives are in full-time employment. There is no evidence, however, that men take on extra housework tasks when wives are in full-time employment a pattern consistent with earlier research (Baxter, 2002).

Moreover, there is little evidence of a trend toward increased employment of paid help for domestic labour, and no evidence of a trend toward paid live-in help. A recent Australian survey in 2000 suggests that only about 18 per cent of households employ paid help for household tasks (Baxter et al., 2003). Meagher (2003) reports even lower figures. Using evidence from Household Expenditure surveys conducted by the Australian Bureau of Statistics in 1998, she found that only three per cent of households report spending money on help with housework. Part of the variation may be due to the fact that a significant proportion of paid domestic help in Australia may be part of the informal cash economy and respondents will be less likely to record this expenditure in government surveys. Either way it is apparent that the use of paid domestic labour is not widespread amongst Australian households.

There is some evidence, however, that the cleaning services industry forms a significant component of the Australian economy with 5,938 registered businesses in June 1999, employing 95,001 persons (Australian Bureau of Statistics, 1999). But the majority of these businesses are involved in the cleaning of commercial buildings and offices, with only 12 per cent cleaning domestic premises as their main activity (Australian Bureau of Statistics, 1999).

As shown in Figure 14.4, when asked why paid help was not used, 51 per cent of women in the Negotiating the Lifecourse survey indicated that they could not afford to pay for domestic help, 49 per cent felt that others did not do the job well enough, and 41 per cent indicated that they felt that they really should be doing this work themselves (note that these figures do not add to 100 per cent as respondents were able to indicate more than one response). There are also some interesting gender differences in these

FIGURE 14.4 Attitudes towards paying other people to do household work by gender

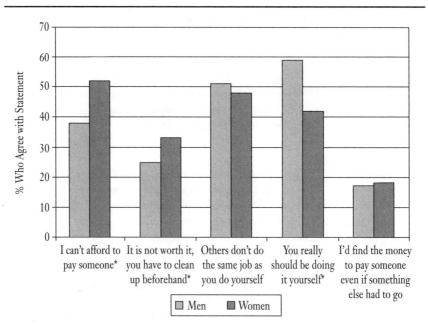

SOURCE: Baxter et al., 2003.
NOTES:
*   Chi-Square test indicates that differences between men and women are significant at p<0.5.
N = 1692.

patterns. Men were significantly more likely than women to feel that this is work that "really should be done yourself", an especially interesting result given that men do significantly less of it than women. Overall, the economic impediment to paying for domestic help is less significant for men than the cultural impediment of feeling that it is inappropriate to pay for domestic help. The reverse pattern was apparent for women with economic factors weighing more heavily than cultural factors.

CONCLUSION

Australia differs from other countries in our region by not employing transnational domestic workers to carry out routine household tasks. Although servants were quite common in middle-class Australian households at the turn of the 20th century, these workers were typically the daughters of working class families who were employed on a short-term basis prior to marriage and the establishment of their own households. The use of household servants declined rapidly after the First World War as the manufacturing sector grew and jobs with better conditions and pay became available for young single women. The most recent evidence on the use of paid help for domestic work indicates that less than 20 per cent of households pay for domestic labour. When they do, this help is usually casual labour rather than live-in help and is typically part of the informal economy.

The reasons for the absence of transnational domestic workers in Australia can be found in the immigration and employment policies. Until the middle of the twentieth century, Australia operated under a White Australia policy that discouraged non-British migrants. At the same time, the trade union movement and centralised wage fixation operated to prevent the influx of cheap foreign labour. After the end of the Second World War, the White Australia policy was dismantled, but the aim was then to encourage mainly skilled migrants to fulfil the labour shortages of an expanding manufacturing sector, and more recently the new industries developing within the service sector.

Moreover, work within the household was gradually defined from the early twentieth century onward as a natural part of women's role as mothers and wives, and increasingly as non-work. The family wage gave priority to men's labour over women's and effectively defined women as the unpaid dependents of the male breadwinner. As the manufacturing sector grew and domestic servants became increasingly scarce, the domestic labour movement with the support of the Australian government who were keen to increase the fertility rate and keep unemployment rates low, redefined housework and childcare as women's natural duty. Other policies such as the widow's pension and the marriage bar reinforced the view that women are dependents on a male breadwinner, or in their absence, on the state. Although some of these policies have changed in recent years, women's labour force participation patterns still look quite different to men's and reflect women's dual responsibilities for paid and unpaid labour. Women in Australia do at least 70 per cent of unpaid household work and mothering and they typically cope with this demand by working part-time or withdrawing from the labour force at certain periods of the childbearing and childrearing stage. Men on the other hand, tend to work full-time in paid labour throughout their lifecourse. At the same time, there is evidence that the current Australian government has actively pursued a policy of discouraging women from remaining in employment after childbirth.

Despite this, we have seen a reduction in the amount of time that women are spending on household work in recent years (Baxter, 2002). However, this is not due to increased employment of household help; instead, it may be the result of changes in patterns of consumption and food preparation styles. For example, time spent cooking may have been reduced as a result of the rapid expansion of take away food, and pre-prepared food. It is unlikely that paid household help will increase markedly in Australia in the future. What is more likely given the current trends is for changes in styles of housing and patterns of food preparation and consumption that reduce the amount of time spent by women on housework tasks.

To the extent that the state has developed policies to address the problems faced by women who are forced to combine paid work in the formal economic sphere with the demands of home and family, it has largely focused on policies that enable women to combine these responsibilities, rather than policies that would help to shift responsibility for domestic work to men or to outside agencies. For example, family-friendly policies do not challenge the gender division of labour within the home, nor do they confront the organisation of the labour market that operates predominantly on a male breadwinner model. Rather, policies such as flexible work hours, family leave, part-time permanent work and job sharing are designed to ease the burdens of women with family responsibilities, rather than challenge the current gender division of labour. The likely result is a further entrenchment of the gender division of labour in the home rather than a shift toward greater involvement by men or an increase in the percentage of households employing outside help.

NOTES

1   I would like to thank Belinda Hewitt and Kate Riseley for providing much valued research assistance for this chapter. The chapter also benefited considerably from the comments of the editors and the other participants in the Workshop on Contemporary Perspectives on Asian Transnational Domestic Workers, Asian MetaCentre for Population and Sustainable Development Analysis, National University of Singapore, 23–25 February 2004.

2   A system of indentured labour was common in some parts of Australia, such as the Queensland sugar industry from about 1834 though until about 1920. In this case, the labour was brought from the South Pacific, primarily Melanesia. Indentured labour was also recruited from China especially during the gold rush period between 1847 and 1900. The gold rush also saw the flow of Chinese free immigrants especially towards the end of the 19th century, many of whom established small businesses to support the expanding urban population generated by the gold rushes (Moore, 1992).

3   As early as 1873, there was a dispute in Victoria over working hours in which miners refused to work on Saturday afternoons. When management substituted the miners with Chinese

labour the unions successfully lobbied for legislation that would ban Chinese workers above certain numbers from the mines (Sutcliffe, 1967). Similar disputes occurred in other states at later dates. After the First World War, the threat of cheap substitutable labour was extended to include not only migrants, but also women. The trade union movement was active in promoting various pieces of protective legislation that restricted women from entering certain occupations (Damousi, 1992).

REFERENCES

Australian Bureau of Statistics. 1998. *Australian Social Trends*, Cat No. 4102.0, Australia: ABS.

―――. 1999. *Cleaning Services Industry Australia, 1998–99*, Cat No. 8672.0, Australia: ABS.

Baker, M. 2001. *Families, Labour and Love: Family Diversity in a Changing World*, Crows Nest, Australia: Allen and Unwin.

Baldock, C. 1983. Public policies and the paid work of women. In *Women, Social Welfare and the State*. Edited by C. Baldock & B. Cass. Sydney: Allen and Unwin, 20–53.

Baxter, J. 1997. Gender equality and participation in housework: A cross national perspective. *Journal of Comparative Family Studies*, 28(3), 220–47.

―――. 2002. Patterns of change and stability in the gender division of household labour in Australia, 1986–1997. *Journal of Sociology*, 38(4), 399–434.

Baxter, J., P. McDonald, D. Mitchell, A. Evans, E. Gray, & T. Breusch. 2003. *Negotiating the Lifecourse, Wave 2, 2000*, (computer file). Canberra: Australian Social Science Data Archive, The Australian National University.

Bittman, M. 1998. The land of the long lost weekend? Trends in free time among working age Australians, 1974–1992. *Loisir et Societe/Society and Leisure*, 21(2), 353–78.

Bryson, L. 1992. *Welfare and the State*, London: Macmillan.

Burnley, I. 2001. *The Impact of Immigration on Australia: A Demographic Approach*. Melbourne: Oxford University Press.

Cass, B. 1983. Redistribution to children and to mothers: A history of child endowment and family allowances. In *Women, Social Welfare and the State*. Edited by C. Baldock & B. Cass. Sydney: Allen and Unwin, 54–84.

Damousi, J. 1992. Marching to different drums: Women's mobilisations 1914–1939. In *Gender Relations in Australia: Domination and Negotiation*. K. Saunders & R. Evans. Sydney: Harcourt, Brace, Jovanovich, 350–75.

Evans, M. 2000. Women's participation in the labour force: Ideals and behaviour. *Australian Social Monitor*, 3(2), 49–57.

FaCS. 2002. *Households, Income and Labour Dynamics Australia (HILDA) Wave 1*. Confidentialised Unit Record File, Canberra: Commonwealth Department of Family and Community Services.

Game, A. & R. Pringle. 1979. Sexuality and the suburban dream. *Australian and New Zealand Journal of Sociology*, 15(2), 4–15.

Higman, B. 2002. *Domestic Service in Australia*. Melbourne: Melbourne University Press.

Huggins, J. 1995. White aprons, black hands: Aboriginal women domestic servants in Queensland. *Labour History*, 69(Nov), 188–95.

Huggins, J. & T. Blake. 1992 Protection or persecution? Gender relations in the era of racial segregation. In *Gender Relations in Australia: Domination and Negotiation*. Edited by K. Saunders & R. Evans. Sydney: Harcourt, Brace, Jovanovich, 42–58.

Jupp, J. 1991. *Immigration*. Sydney: University of Sydney Press.

Kingston, B. 1975. *My Wife, My Daughter, and Poor Mary Ann: Women and Work in Australia*. Melbourne: Nelson.

Meagher, G. 2003. *Friend or Flunkey? Paid Domestic Workers in the New Economy*. Sydney: University of New South Wales Press.

Moore, C. 1992. A precious few. Melanesian and Asian women in Northern Australia. In *Gender Relations in Australia: Domination and Negotiation*. Edited by K. Saunders & R. Evans. Sydney: Harcourt, Brace, Jovanovich, 59–81.

Reiger, K. 1985. *The Disenchantment of the Home: Modernizing the Australian Family, 1880–1940*. Melbourne: Oxford University Press.

Roe, J. 1983 Women and welfare since 1901. In *Women, Social Welfare and the State*. Edited by C. Baldock & B. Cass. Sydney: Allen and Unwin, 1–19.

Saunders, K. 1982. *Workers in Bondage: The Origins and Bases of Unfree Labour in Queensland 1824–1916*, St. Lucia: University of Queensland Press.

————, ed. 1984. *Indentured Labour in the British Empire 1834–1920*. Canberra: Croom Helm.

Sutcliffe, J. T. 1967. *A History of Trade Unionism in Australia*. Melbourne: Macmillan.

Summers, A. 1975. *Damned Whores and God's Police: The Colonization of Women in Australia*. Harmondsworth: Penguin.

————. 2003. *The End of Equality: Work, Babies and Women's Choices in 21st Century Australia*, Sydney: Random House.

Tonkinson, M. 1988. Sisterhood or Aboriginal servitude? Black women and white women on the Australian frontier. *Aboriginal History*, 12(1), 27–39.

Walden, I. 1995. "That was slavery days": Aboriginal domestic servants in New South Wales in the twentieth century. *Labour History*, 69(Nov), 196–209.

Appendices

Appendices

Appendix 1 Summary information about transnational domestic workers (TDWs) from sending countries

Sending country	Estimated population of TDWs currently overseas	Period when women first left as TDWs	Main destinations of TDWs	Main regulatory mechanisms	Signatory to international conventions on migrant workers			Level of NGO activities for migrant workers
					ILO No. 97[a]	ILO No. 143[b]	UN MWC[c]	
Philippines	1,000,000[d]	1970s	- Gulf countries (Saudi Arabia, UAE, Kuwait)[e] - Also Hong Kong, Singapore, Taiwan and Italy[f]	- Recruitment agencies regulated and monitored to prevent illegal recruitment. - Legal departing migrant workers must undergo Pre-departure Orientation Seminars run by NGOs rather than recruitment agencies. - Enactment of the Migrant Workers and Overseas Filipinos Act of 1995 (RA 8042) establishing mechanisms for protecting migrant workers at all stages of migration. - Enactment of the Anti-Trafficking Act of 2003 (RA 9208), which aims to eliminate trafficking of women and children.	No.	No	Yes	- Migrant NGOs provide support and services to migrant workers and their families (e.g. paralegal assistance, information programmes). - NGOs lobby the government for better and more responsive policies to address the needs of the migrant sector. - Link up with other NGOs in the region to protect and promote the rights of overseas Filipino workers.

Appendix 1 Summary information about transnational domestic workers (TDWs) from sending countries (cont'd)

Sending country	Estimated population of TDWs currently overseas	Period when women first left as TDWs	Main destinations of TDWs	Main regulatory mechanisms	Signatory to international conventions on migrant workers			Level of NGO activities for migrant workers
					ILO No. 97[a]	ILO No. 143[b]	UN MWC[c]	
Indonesia	1,000,000	1980s	- Saudi Arabia - Malaysia - Hong Kong - Taiwan - Singapore	- Recruitment agencies are required to be licensed and are regulated by the Ministry of Manpower and Transmigration. - Prospective migrants are subjected to mandatory medical examination. - Mandatory orientation and training at *Lembaga Uji Kompetensi* (LUK) to equip migrants with basic language skills, competency in performing designated work and knowledge on rights and responsibilities. - Mandatory purchase of basic insurance policy at US$15 via recruitment agencies to cover health and accidents.	No.	No	Yes	- A growing number of NGOs focusing on migrant workers in the Post-Suharto era (after 1998). - NGOs provide services such as education, training and legal aid. - KOPBUMI, a coalition of civil society groups concerned with migrant workers, plays an instrumental role in lobbying the government.

Appendix 1 Summary information about transnational domestic workers (TDWs) from sending countries (cont'd)

Sending country	Estimated population of TDWs currently overseas	Period when women first left as TDWs	Main destinations of TDWs	Main regulatory mechanisms	Signatory to international conventions on migrant workers			Level of NGO activities for migrant workers
					ILO No. 97[a]	ILO No. 143[b]	UN MWC[c]	
Sri Lanka	572,600	Early 1980s	- Saudi Arabia - Kuwait - UAE - Lebanon	- SLBFE licenses job agents, registers migrants, collects research data, provides minimal services for migrants' families. - Passport, training certificate, medical exam, contract, foreign visa, and insurance required for travel. - Two-year contracts. - Indifferently enforced agreements with host countries on conditions and wages. - Embassies and consular offices in main labour receiving countries handle complaints and repatriate stranded workers.	No.	No	Yes	- ILO and IOM present, working at policy and government level. - Local branch of American labour union AFL-CIO facilitates and funds organising efforts. - Two NGOs liaise with international migrants organisations, lobby policy makers, promote social awareness, organise local groups. - 30 grassroots migrant worker associations with about 50 members each. - Other NGOs sometimes deal with human rights and women's and migrants' issues. - Civil activism at nascent stage.

Appendix 1 Summary information about transnational domestic workers (tDWs) from sending countries (cont'd)

Sending country	Estimated population of TDWs currently overseas	Period when women first left as TDWs	Main destinations of TDWs	Main regulatory mechanisms	Signatory to international conventions on migrant workers			Level of NGO activities for migrant workers
					ILO No. 97[a]	ILO No. 143[b]	UN MWC[c]	
Bangladesh	15,000	1976	- Saudi Arabia - Kuwait - UAE - Bahrain - Oman - Qatar - Lebanon - South Korea - Hong Kong	- Migrants must be aged 35 years or more. - Must be married and accompanied by husband. - Must have a letter of appointment/work permit and valid visa. - Minimum wage is set at US$106 per month for employers. - Employers must provide migration cost to recruiting agency. - Maximum fee charged by recruiting agencies must not exceed US $70. - Recruiting agencies must have a permanent training centre in Dhaka and round the clock office at Saudi Arabia.	No.	No	Yes	- Civil activism at nascent stage.

Appendix 1 Summary information about transnational domestic workers (TDWs) from sending countries (cont'd)

Sending country	Estimated population of TDWs currently overseas	Period when women first left as TDWs	Main destinations of TDWs	Main regulatory mechanisms	Signatory to international conventions on migrant workers			Level of NGO activities for migrant workers
					ILO No. 97[a]	ILO No. 143[b]	UN MWC[c]	
Bangladesh (cont'd)				- Ministry of Expatriate Welfare and Overseas Employment together with Bureau of Manpower Employment and Training (BMET) implements regulatory activities and supervises a few welfare measures.				
India	No estimates available	- Evidence of migration from 1830s onwards. Recent movement since 1975.	- Saudi Arabia - UAE - Jordan - Hong Kong - Singapore - UK - USA	- Emigration clearance to be obtained from Protectorate of Emigrants for those moving to selected countries.	No.	No	No	- Variable. Specific NGO activities by and for Indian domestic workers are most developed in Hong Kong and the US.

[a] International Labour Organisation Convention No. 97 (Migration for Employment, Revised).
[b] International Labour Organisation Convention No. 143 (Migrations in Abusive Conditions and the Promotion of Equality of Opportunity and Treatment of Migrant Workers).

c The International Convention on The Protection of the Rights of All Migrant Workers and Members of their Families (MWC) adopted by the United Nations and which came into force on 1 July 2003.

d There are no stock estimates of Filipino women working abroad as domestic workers. According to the Survey of Overseas Filipinos of October 2002, there were 286,000 women workers in the "Sales and services elementary occupations" (which was under the major occupation group, "Labourers and unskilled workers"). Note that the figure is not limited to service workers and domestic workers in particular (www.census.gov.ph/data/sectordata/2003/of0204.htm, accessed 20 December 2004). This appears to be a very low estimate. Compare this, for example, with a media report which cites that there are 700,000 Filipino domestic workers in the Gulf countries alone (note that the source or basis of the estimate was not mentioned) ("No legal protection for Pinay maids in Gulf," in www.journal.com.ph/news.asp?sid=13&month=10&day=20&year=2004, accessed 20 December 2004). The estimate of one million is based on rough computations using the stock estimate of 4,681,735 (i.e., 3.17 million temporary migrants land-based workers and 1.51 million unauthorised migrants). According to data on deployment in 2002, some 30.8 per cent of all new hires among land-based workers comprised service workers (not just domestic workers alone) (www.poea.gov.ph/ DeployedNewHiresbySkillandSex. xls, accessed 20 December 2004). Assuming that 25 per cent of temporary migrants and unauthorised migrants are domestic workers, this will yield an estimate of 1,170,434. Although domestic workers are overwhelmingly women, in some countries, e.g., Italy, Greece and Spain, men also engage in domestic work for lack of other occupational options. Note also that caregivers/caretakers are not included in this estimate.

e The breakdown by country was not available in the report ("No legal protection for Pinay maids in Gulf," in www.journal.com.ph/ news.asp?sid=13&month=10&day=20&year=2004, accessed 20 December 2004); the countries were identified based on the data on stock estimate of overseas Filipinos as of December 2003 (www.census.gov.ph/data/sectordata/2003/of0204. htm, accessed 20 December 2004).

f Countries with at least an estimated 50,000 Filipino domestic workers.

Appendix 2 Summary information about transnational domestic workers (TDWs) in receiving countries

Receiving country	Estimated population of TDWs	Main countries of origin of TDWs	Period of first arrival of TDWs	Main regulatory mechanisms in receiving country	Signatory to international conventions on migrant workers			Level of NGO activities for migrant workers
					ILO No. 97[a]	ILO No. 143[b]	UN MWC[c]	
Hong Kong	216,000	- Philippines - Indonesia - Thailand - India - Nepal	1970	- The Employment Ordinance stipulates minimum wage, rest days, statutory holidays, annual leave, sickness allowance, maternity leave, wages in lieu of notice and worked holidays, long service payment and the right to join labour unions. - Employees' Compensation Ordinance requires all employers to have a valid insurance policy for their domestic workers to cover all their liabilities for compensation. - Monthly levy payable by employers. - Employers must have a minimum monthly household income of US$1,925.	Yes	No	No	- Welfare and humanitarian aid to migrant workers is provided mostly by religious organisations and NGOs. Temporary shelters for homeless migrants are almost entirely provided by NGOs. - Civil activism is fairly advanced with legally registered organisations, including migrant workers' unions and associations, NGOs, and employers' associations. Social education is provided to migrant workers largely by NGOs, with some official

Appendix 2 Summary information about transnational domestic workers (TDWs) in receiving countries (cont'd)

Receiving country	Estimated population of TDWs	Main countries of origin of TDWs	Period of first arrival of TDWs	Main regulatory mechanisms in receiving country	Signatory to international conventions on migrant workers			Level of NGO activities for migrant workers
					ILO No. 97[a]	ILO No. 143[b]	UN MWC[c]	
Hong Kong (cont'd)				- Foreign domestic workers are forbidden from changing jobs in the first two years of employment. If they break their initial contract, they cannot apply for a new job from within Hong Kong. - Foreign domestic workers cannot work for multiple employers or outside of the field of domestic work. - Foreign domestic workers do not qualify for permanent residency no matter how long they have been. - Under the "Two-Week Rule", those who are terminated must leave within two weeks of the expiration of their visas.				funding provided through the Hong Kong Home Affairs Bureau for research and public education. - A number of migrant workers' unions, NGOs, umbrella organisations of NGOs and labour unions lead in the advocacy of migrant workers' rights in Hong Kong.

Appendix 2 Summary information about transnational domestic workers (TDWs) in receiving countries (cont'd)

Receiving country	Estimated population of TDWs	Main countries of origin of TDWs	Period of first arrival of TDWs	Main regulatory mechanisms in receiving country	Signatory to international conventions on migrant workers			Level of NGO activities for migrant workers
					ILO No. 97[a]	ILO No. 143[b]	UN MWC[c]	
Hong Kong (cont'd)				- Rules for employing foreigners in China, including Hong Kong, apply equally to both expatriate professionals and foreign domestic workers.				
Taiwan	120,000	- Philippines - Indonesia - Vietnam	1992	- Three-year work permit; renewable twice only. - Employment permission regulated using a point system and quota control. - Medical checkup in the 6th, 18th and 30th months during a contract. - Monthly levy and compulsory security bond payable by employer. - Not covered by the Labor Standards Act (manufacturing and constructive migrants are covered).	No	No	No	- Most religious institutions provide direct service and advocate policy change. - Civil activism at expanding stage but the migrant sector remains marginal.

Appendix 2 Summary information about transnational domestic workers (TDWs) in receiving countries (cont'd)

Receiving country	Estimated population of TDWs	Main countries of origin of TDWs	Period of first arrival of TDWs	Main regulatory mechanisms in receiving country	Signatory to international conventions on migrant workers			Level of NGO activities for migrant workers
					ILO No. 97[a]	ILO No. 143[b]	UN MWC[c]	
Taiwan (cont'd)				- Not allowed to transfer employers in general. - Covered by the minimum wage.				
Singapore	150,000	- Indonesia - Philippines - Sri Lanka	Mid to late 1970s	- With effect from 1 January 2005, first-time foreign domestic workers must be between 23 and 50 years old and have a minimum of eight years of formal education. If the foreign domestic worker has previously worked in Singapore, she must be between 18 and 50 years old. - Employed on two-year renewable work permits. - Monthly levy payable by employer. - Bi-annual medical examination of foreign domestic worker for pregnancy and sexually transmitted diseases.	No	No	No	- Religious institutions main provider of social and welfare services. - Civil activism at nascent stage.

Appendix 2 Summary information about transnational domestic workers (TDWs) in receiving countries (cont'd)

Receiving country	Estimated population of TDWs	Main countries of origin of TDWs	Period of first arrival of TDWs	Main regulatory mechanisms in receiving country	Signatory to international conventions on migrant workers			Level of NGO activities for migrant workers
					ILO No. 97[a]	ILO No. 143[b]	UN MWC[c]	
Singapore (cont'd)				- Foreign domestic workers are not permitted to marry Singaporeans and Permanent Residents. - Employers have to pay a compulsory security bond. - First-time employers are required to attend an Employers' Orientation Programme. - First-time foreign domestic workers in Singapore are required to attend a compulsory Safety Awareness Course. - Foreign domestic workers are not covered by Workmen's Compensation Act. - Foreign domestic workers face immediate repatriation if any of the above is breached.				

Appendix 2 Summary information about transnational domestic workers (TDWs) in receiving countries (cont'd)

Receiving country	Estimated population of TDWs	Main countries of origin of TDWs	Period of first arrival of TDWs	Main regulatory mechanisms in receiving country	Signatory to international conventions on migrant workers			Level of NGO activities for migrant workers
					ILO No. 97[a]	ILO No. 143[b]	UN MWC[c]	
Singapore (cont'd)				- No standard work contract or minimum wage for all nationalities of foreign domestic workers.				
Malaysia	230,000	- Indonesia - Philippines - Sri Lanka - Thailand - Cambodia	Mid- to late 1980s	- Foreign domestic workers enter on renewable work permits of two years for an indefinite period. - Employer eligibility rules include minimum annual incomes (from US$9,474 to about US$19,000 depending on the nationality of the foreign domestic worker employed). - Minimum age requirement of foreign domestic. workers: 30 years old for Filipinas and 18 years old for Indonesians.	No (except for the state of Sabah in East Malaysia)	No	No	- Employment agencies allowed to form own national association for lobby purposes but the law prohibits foreign domestic workers from organising for their interests. - NGOs engaged in human rights, democracy, social justice, women's issues and workers' rights offer service delivery (including legal support) and advocacy efforts on behalf of transnational domestic workers.

Appendix 2 Summary information about transnational domestic workers (TDWs) in receiving countries (cont'd)

Receiving country	Estimated population of TDWs	Main countries of origin of TDWs	Period of first arrival of TDWs	Main regulatory mechanisms in receiving country	Signatory to international conventions on migrant workers			Level of NGO activities for migrant workers
					ILO No. 97[a]	ILO No. 143[b]	UN MWC[c]	
Malaysia (cont'd)				- Employment contracts are between employers and employment agencies rather than foreign domestic workers. - Annual levies and security bonds imposed on employer. - Annual medical examinations required of foreign domestic workers for pregnancy, sexually transmitted diseases and other major illnesses; immediate deportation within 24 hours if tested positive for any of the above. - Foreign domestic workers are not covered by Workmen's Compensation Act				

Appendix 2 Summary information about transnational domestic workers (TDWs) in receiving countries (cont'd)

Receiving country	Estimated population of TDWs	Main countries of origin of TDWs	Period of first arrival of TDWs	Main regulatory mechanisms in receiving country	Signatory to international conventions on migrant workers			Level of NGO activities for migrant workers
					ILO No. 97[a]	ILO No. 143[b]	UN MWC[c]	
Malaysia (cont'd)				- Foreign domestic workers are not permitted to marry citizens.				
Thailand	More than 200,000	- Burma	Late 1970s	- A registration fee of US$91 is required to be paid every six months. This includes a medical check-up, medical insurance and a work permit.	No	No	No	- Women's organisations, human rights and Burmese migrant advocacy groups have been targeting sex workers but little attention has been paid to domestic workers.
Canada	Best estimate is 4,000–5,000 under the LCP temporary work visa at any one timed	- Philippines - The Carribean - South America	Early 1980s	- Under the Live-in Caregiver Program (LCP), caregivers enter country with pre-immigrant status. - Federal government regulates the LCP while provincial governments regulate employment conditions of domestic workers.	No	No	No	- Mainly multi-ethnic NGOs who are concerned specifically with live-in caregivers. - Groups often combine advocacy work with service provision, and also lobby particular government offices and provide legal clinics.

Appendix 2 Summary information about transnational domestic workers (TDWs) in receiving countries (cont'd)

Receiving country	Estimated population of TDWs	Main countries of origin of TDWs	Period of first arrival of TDWs	Main regulatory mechanisms in receiving country	Signatory to international conventions on migrant workers			Level of NGO activities for migrant workers
					ILO No. 97[a]	ILO No. 143[b]	UN MWC[c]	
Canada (cont'd)				- Mandatory written contracts with prospective employers. Conditions include minimum wage, work week and employment standards. - Required to pass a medical examination by a doctor approved by Citizenship and Immigration Canada (CIC); no further medical surveillance is required once approved. - Required to complete 24 months of live-in work within 36 months of arrival before qualifying to apply for an open visa.				- Specific information programmes run by these agencies receive some funding from federal and provincial government. - NGOs not overtly political.

Appendix 2 Summary information about transnational domestic workers (TDWs) in receiving countries (cont'd)

Receiving country	Estimated population of TDWs	Main countries of origin of TDWs	Period of first arrival of TDWs	Main regulatory mechanisms in receiving country	Signatory to international conventions on migrant workers			Level of NGO activities for migrant workers
					ILO No. 97[a]	ILO No. 143[b]	UN MWC[c]	
Canada (cont'd)				- Required to be proficient in either English or French, have at least six months of full-time training in a field related to caregiving, and have a minimum qualification equivalent of a Canadian high school diploma.				

a International Labour Organisation Convention No. 97 (Migration for Employment, Revised).

b International Labour Organisation Convention No.143 (Migrations in Abusive Conditions and the Promotion of Equality of Opportunity and Treatment of Migrant Workers) and which came into force on 1 July 2003.

c The International Convention on the Protection of the Rights of All Migrant Workers and Members of their Families (MWC) adopted by the United Nations.

d As the exact number of entrants is not available, this figure is extrapolated based on those for landed immigrants, estimated at approximately 1,800 to 2,000 arrivals per year (based on proportions reported in Stasiulis & Bakan (1997:49) for the Foreign Domestic Movement Program and applied to most recent (2003) figures for landings for the Live-in Caregiver Program as reported by Citizenship and Immigration Canada (http://www.cic.gc.ca/english/pub/caregiver/caregiver-2.html#2, accessed 20 November 2003). While 2,000 migrants arriving per year is a conservative estimate, it concurs with government immigration targets (as reported in http://www.cic.gc.ca/english/pub/immigration2002.html#new1). Current estimates suggest that the figure is closer to 4,500.

REFERENCE:

Stasiulis, D. K. & A. B. Bakan. 1997. Regulation and resistance: Strategies of migrant domestic workers in Canada and internationally. *Asian and Pacific Migration Journal*, 6(1), 31-57.

Index

International Board of Advisors

Titles on Gender and Women Studies

Asian Women as Transnational Domestic Workers
edited by Shirlena Huang, Brenda S. A. Yeoh and
  Noor Abdul Rahman
ISBN 981-210-386-4

The Agency of Women in Asia
edited by Lyn Parker
ISBN 981-210-431-3

Chinese Women and Their Cultural and Network Capitals
edited by Kuah-Pearce Khun Eng
ISBN 981-210-293-0

The Mak Nyahs: Malaysian Male to Female Transsexuals
by Teh Yik Koon
ISBN 981-210-209-4

For information on pricing and availability, please log on to
www.marshallcavendish.com/academic